REPORTS

OF THE

UNITED STATES COMMISSIONERS

TO THE

PARIS UNIVERSAL EXPOSITION, 1867.

PUBLISHED

UNDER DIRECTION OF THE SECRETARY OF STATE BY AUTHORITY
OF THE SENATE OF THE UNITED STATES.

EDITED BY

WILLIAM P. BLAKE,
COMMISSIONER OF THE STATE OF CALIFORNIA.

VOLUME IV.

WASHINGTON:
GOVERNMENT PRINTING OFFICE.
1870.

CONTENTS.

PARIS UNIVERSAL EXPOSITION, 1867.
REPORTS OF THE UNITED STATES COMMISSIONERS.

EXAMINATION

OF THE

TELEGRAPHIC APPARATUS

AND THE

PROCESSES IN TELEGRAPHY

BY

SAMUEL F. B. MORSE, LL.D.,
UNITED STATES COMMISSIONER.

WASHINGTON:
GOVERNMENT PRINTING OFFICE.
1869.

INTRODUCTION.

An examination of the various objects in this department of the Exposition leads to the conclusion that since the former international exhibitions very little has been presented that is actually new. While displaying a great variety of beautiful modifications of instruments employed in the transmission of messages, showing the utmost mechanical skill and workmanship, deserving of the highest praise, it is found that most of them have already been exhibited in former international exhibitions, and have been noticed and described in the various reports of those exhibitions. Such instruments, for the most part, therefore, will require but a brief mention.

Some of the difficulties that were encountered in the pursuit of inquiries may as well be stated in the outset. The articles to be examined in the Exposition were not collected or arranged in one place as a class, but were widely dispersed under the products of the different countries, and had to be sought for in comparatively obscure parts of the vast area, surrounded by objects of a totally different character. Some of the instruments although named in the catalogue, could not be found; some named were actually not exhibited. Others had their complicated machinery carefully concealed under glass cases, or in their close frames of wood or brass, with the rather repulsive label "*ne touchez pas*, S. V. P.," to be met on the threshold, and which, though more politely expressed than our blunt Anglo-Saxon, "*hands off*," was quite as effective a barrier to free inquiry. To add to this inconvenience, there were, in most instances, no persons at hand, when the instruments were found, to explain the apparatus, and no printed or other description to be obtained. If, therefore, some of the instruments deserving of notice in this report are unnoticed, it will be seen that the neglect is one of necessity, and not of choice.

CONTENTS.

CHAPTER I.

TELEGRAPHS.

CHAPTER II.

SEMAPHORES.

CHAPTER III.

CODES.

CHAPTER IV.

BATTERIES, CONDUCTORS, AND INSULATORS.

CHAPTER V.

AUTOMATIC RECORDING, TRANSMITTING AND CONTROLLING.

CHAPTER VI.

INFORMATION CONCERNING TELEGRAPHS IN VARIOUS COUNTRIES.

APPENDICES.

TELEGRAPHIC APPARATUS, ETC.

CHAPTER I.

TELEGRAPHS.

DEFINITION OF TELEGRAPH AND SEMAPHORE, DISTINCTION BETWEEN THEM—ETYMOLOGY OF THE TWO WORDS—CHRONOGRAPH AND CHRONOSCOPE—NO EXAMPLE OF A TELEGRAPH UNTIL 1832—EXTENSION OF TELEGRAPHIC AND SEMAPHORIC SYSTEMS THROUGHOUT THE WORLD—RESULTS FLOWING FROM THE INVENTION OF THE GENERIC TELEGRAPH—SCIENCE ADVANCED BY THE TELEGRAPH—PRINCIPAL DISCOVERIES IN ELECTRICITY AND MAGNETISM PRIOR TO THE INVENTION OF THE TELEGRAPH—THE MORSE SYSTEM ADOPTED BY THE INTERNATIONAL CONVENTION AT PARIS—THE MORSE SYSTEM DESCRIBED—THE RELAY OR SECONDARY CIRCUIT—MODIFICATIONS OF THE MORSE APPARATUS—SIEMENS AND HALSKE'S AUSTRIAN MILITARY TELEGRAPH—HUGHES'S PRINTING TELEGRAPH, ITS CONSTRUCTION AND OPERATION—ARLINCOURT'S PRINTING APPARATUS—DUJARDIN'S PRINTING TELEGRAPH—PANTELEGRAPHS—BONELLI'S PANTELEGRAPHIC APPARATUS AS MODIFED BY COOK—ABBÉ CASELLI'S PANTELEGRAPH—LENOIR'S MODIFICATION, THE ELECTROGRAPH.

The telegraph, in the comprehensive sense in which it is usually but erroneously applied to all modes of communicating at a distance, is a very ancient invention, and in this expanded general sense cannot therefore be claimed by any modern inventor. But in the true sense of the word, as signifying imprinting or writing at a distance, the telegraph is a modern invention, and does not date further back than the year 1832.

It is, therefore, proposed to use the term telegraph in its strict etymological sense; thus distinguishing it from all other modes of communicating at a distance with which it has hitherto been confounded.

The terms *telegraph* and *semaphore* conveniently comprise, under two generic heads, all the modes of communicating intelligence from a distance not dependent upon actually sending it, either written, printed, or verbal, by some sort of couriers who travel over the interval between two or more points of intercommunication.

If the etymology of the two words telegraph and semaphore be examined, it will be perceived that the term telegraph from τηλε, at a distance, and γραφω, to write or imprint, and the term semaphore, from σημα, a signal, and ερω, to bear or convey, very accurately designate the difference between the two modes of communicating to a distance, to all which modes has hitherto been indiscriminately applied the appellative *telegraph*, but not accurately, for it cannot strictly be applied to the semaphore, since the semaphore neither writes nor prints its signals at a distance. Professor Wheatstone (in a note on page 89, Juror's Report of 1862) makes a very proper discrimination between two instruments which he describes, naming them the chronoscope and the chronograph. A similar discrimination may be very justly made between the telegraph and the semaphore. Professor Wheatstone defines "chronoscope as an instrument by which the interval of time is observed, and chronograph an instrument by which it could be recorded." This is precisely the difference between the semaphore, which shows a signal to be observed, and the telegraph, by which the signal is recorded.

No example of a telegraph, therefore, in the strict sense of the word, appears to have existed previous to the year 1832. All the systems of communication to and from a distance until that date were, without exception, semaphores. True, in most instances, they bear the general name of telegraphs, yet an examination of the end proposed, the modes employed, and the results obtained, will show that none of them had more than a figurative title to the name telegraph. All of them propose but the conveyance of an evanescent signal; none of them propose a written or printed record of their intelligence. None of them, therefore, were strictly telegraphs.

Within a period of about thirty years the telegraphic systems, as well as the semaphoric, by electricity have literally been extended throughout the world, not only covering the vast area of the two hemispheres each with a net-work of these intellectual railways, but the subtle telegraphic thread, through American and British enterprise, has been carried underneath the deep Atlantic, uniting together the two great networks of the two hemispheres.

This vast reticulation of electrical conductors is, for the most part, used for telegraphic purposes; some of the electrical systems for communicating at a distance are, indeed, still semaphoric, but even these are more or less modified by the electrical and mechanical means that have been so efficaciously applied in the modern telegraphs.

The birth and inauguration of the generic telegraph has not only opened a new field for the labors, and given direction to the ingenuity of the mechanician, suggesting numerous varieties of form and distribution of parts, but it has also given a fresh impulse to the researches of the philosopher into the mysteries of its most efficient agent, electricity. It has been the servant of the astronomer; it has assisted in the determination of longitudes;[1] it has promoted the science of meteorology, and been tributary in many ways to the advancement of our knowledge of terrestrial phenomena. It has also directly stimulated and influenced the various systems of electrical semaphores. The application of the

[1] "It was suggested by Professor Morse to the distinguished Arago, in 1839, that the electro-magnetic telegraph would be the means of determining the difference of longitude between places with an accuracy hitherto unattainable." The first experiment of the kind resulted in the fulfillment of the prediction. The difference of longitude between Battle Monument Square, Baltimore, and the Capitol at Washington, was accurately determined by Captain Wilkes, by means of the telegraph, June 12, 1844.—See Vail's "American Electro-Magnetic Telegraph," p. 60, 1845.

electro-magnet has produced a great variety of most ingenious semaphoric instruments. It has modified and perfected the needle systems and the dial or cadran systems, as well as the varieties of the letter-printing telegraphs. These all owe to this application their most effective results. These will be noticed in their place. While thus signalizing some of the more important results to science, and to the art of communicating intelligence to a distance, flowing from the invention of the electro-magnetic telegraph, the writer would not assume so much the position of a discoverer in science as the applier of the results of scientific investigators to the practical development of the telegraph. It is, therefore, eminently fitting that the more important and prominent of these discoveries and results should be briefly noticed.

The apparently insignificant and unimportant observation of Galvani rests at the foundation of the brilliant series of discoveries which have made electricity the servant of man in many ways. The first plans of semaphores by electricity were confined, till the year 1800, to machine or static electricity, but from the intractable nature of the agent employed all of them proved unavailable. Semaphores by electricity were at that period, fifty years from the reported first suggestion of the idea by Franklin,[1] abandoned as impracticable. In the year 1800 Volta contrived the pile known by his name. The chemical effects of this pile suggested the idea of electric communication, by the employment of the decomposing effects of Voltaic electricity, and a semaphore based upon this scientific fact received a definite form in the complicated and unavailable plan of Sœmmering in 1811. In the year 1819 Oersted discovered that the magnetic needle could be deflected by the Voltaic current. Schweigger improved upon the primary element of Oersted's discovery just as Volta had done upon his own primary element of a single pair, and demonstrated that the magnetic effect of the current was increased by repeating the primary element, and hence resulted his celebrated multiplier. Arago, and also Davy, in the year 1820, observed the attraction of iron filings by a conducting wire, and Arago subsequently magnetized steel wires by inclosing them in a straight helix of wire, through which the Voltaic current was passed. Ampère discovered that when the Voltaic current is passed in the same direction through two parallel wires they attract each other, and that when passed in opposite directions they repel each other. Upon this observation is founded his theory of magnetism and electro-magnetism, which led to the method of magnetizing adopted by Arago. As early as 1824 investigations had commenced upon the power of wires to conduct Voltaic electricity. Two laws, opposed to each other, bearing upon the conductibility of the current, were announced; the one by Barlow in 1824, the other by Ohm in 1827. Barlow's law was, "that the conductibility was inversely proportionate to the square root of the lengths, and directly as the diameters of the wires, or as the square roots of their sections." The

[1] For a note in regard to Franklin's suggestion, see appendix D.

other and the true law is, "the resistance by bodies to the conduction of electricity is directly as their lengths, and inversely as the areas of their cross-sections." This law, says Dr. Page, was proved many years since by Davy, Pouillet, Becquerel, Christie, Ohm, Fechner, and others. It is now known as Ohm's law.

In 1825 Mr. Sturgeon, of England, made the first electro-magnet in the horse-shoe form, by loosely winding a piece of iron wire with a spiral of copper wire. In the United States, as early as 1831, the experimental researches of Professor Joseph Henry were of great importance in advancing the science of electro-magnetism. He may be said to have carried the electro-magnet, in its lifting powers, to its greatest perfection. Reflecting upon the principle of Professor Schweigger's galvanometer, he constructed magnets in which great power could be developed by a very small galvanic element. His published paper in 1831 shows that he experimented with wires of different lengths, and he noted the amount of magnetism which could be induced through them at various lengths by means of batteries composed of a single element and also of many elements. He states that the magnetic action of "a current from a trough composed of many pairs is at least not sensibly diminished by passing through a long wire," and he incidentally noted the bearing of this fact upon the project of an electro-magnetic telegraph, (semaphore?)

In more recent papers, first published in 1857, it appears that Professor Henry demonstrated before his pupils the practicability of ringing a bell by means of electro-magnetism at a distance.

It is claimed for M. Pouillet that in 1830 he constructed very powerful magnets on the same principle of the electro-magnets of the present day; and about the same time Professor Moll, of Utrecht, experimented to produce great magnetic effects with a powerful galvanic battery.

The needle system or electric semaphore owes its origin to a suggestion of the renowned La Place, in 1820, expanded about the same date in more of detail by Ampère; it appears to have been first experimented upon by Schilling, of Cronstadt, but practically realized on a small scale by those distinguished German savans Messrs. Gaus and Weber, of Göttingen, in 1833. It was improved by Messrs. Cooke and Wheatstone in 1837, and extensively introduced into Great Britain, and, so far as European countries are concerned, first transformed by the genius of Steinheil, of Munich, in 1837, from an electric semaphore into an electric telegraph. In the mean time the first electro-magnetic telegraph was devised in the United States in 1832, and shown in practical operation in 1835.

If it be asked what telegraphic system is specifically announced as most developed and extended throughout the world, the answer would seem to be definitely and summarily given in the proceedings of the International Telegraphic Convention held in Paris in March, 1865, composed of the representatives of twenty of the principal nations of Europe, assembled for the special purpose of examining the various projects, in order to adopt a uniform system, and to regulate international telegraphy for their common benefit. They thus decree in their third article: "L'appareil Morse reste provisoirement adopté pour le service des fils internationaux." Concise as is this announcement, as the result of their deliberations, it proclaims that the Morse system—an American system—is preferred for special international service throughout Europe.

Russia, Norway and Sweden, Denmark, Hamburg, Hanover, Prussia, Holland, Belgium, France, Wurtemberg, Bavaria, Saxony, Austria, Spain, Portugal, Baden, Switzerland, Italy, Greece, and the Ottoman Empire, by their respective ambassadors, took part in this convention, and these, it will be seen, comprise all the nations of continental Europe.

Great Britain is the only nation in Europe not represented in this convention; but even in Great Britain the Morse system is the one almost exclusively used in all her colonial possessions, in India, Australia, and Canada, and to an increasing extent also in the United Kingdom, especially in connection with the continental telegraph lines.

In view of these facts, it would seem to be proper, if not indeed necessary, to inquire, as a preliminary step to any examination of the telegraphic and semaphoric instruments in the Exposition, what is this Morse system which has obtained such universal popularity?

THE MORSE SYSTEM.

The Morse system was the introduction and the addition of a new art to the means of communicating at a distance. It is the invention of that art which remained an undeveloped germ until 1832, shut up in the etymology of the word telegraph. It is the art of writing or printing at a distance in one or more places at the same time.

When the first practicable mode for demonstrating such a result was devised in 1832, it was the birth of a new art. It was emphatically the first realization of a telegraph.

An art proposes a result, and includes the means and processes for producing that result.

1. The new art proposes as its result the marking, writing, or printing at a distance.

The means and process consist of—

2. A system of signs, to wit, a conventional code or alphabet adapted to marking, writing, or printing.

3. Of clockwork machinery to regulate the movement of a strip of paper or other material, upon which the signs are to be marked, written, or printed.

4. Of a lever bearing a pencil, fountain pen, printing wheel, stylus, or other marking instrument, for marking, writing, or printing the code of signs upon the paper.

5. Of the application of an electro-magnet, the power of which mediately and mechanically actuates the marking lever, for writing or printing.

6. Of the application of a salt to paper, to prepare it for receiving marks by electro-chemical decomposition.

7. Of a manipulator to close and open an electric circuit at regulated times, to charge and discharge the electro-magnet, or to bring into action the decomposing effects of electricity. Directly connected with the process of writing or printing the signs of the code, the sounds of the lever in writing or printing the letters were found to address the ear, adding a semaphoric result, inherent in the peculiar code of signs devised for writing and printing.

Thus much is new and peculiar to the Morse system. It comprises part of the means for operating the new art, and is precedent to the modes of application of the power, (electricity,) the effective agent for accomplishing the result.

The art thus invented employs as its most effective agent dynamic electricity, generated in some of the well-known methods of generating electricity.

The application of this power is effected by a combination with the preceding means:

1. Of a main line or circuit of electric conductors, connected with the poles of a galvanic battery or other generator of electricity, and having the helices of the electro-magnet as part of the circuit.

2. The armature of this magnet affixed to a lever is operated by the electro-magnet and an adjustable reacting spring, when the magnet is charged and discharged by closing and opening the circuit.

3. The lever bearing a pen, or other marking instrument, is made to mark (as well as to sound) the signs of the code, or by the closing and opening of a second circuit, having within it a battery and electro-magnet, armature, and pen-lever; the pen-lever is made to mark the signs upon the paper, or to sound them at any desired distance, thus producing the final result. This, in brief, is the Morse system.

An instrument embodying these essential portions of the invention was constructed and seen in operation by many witnesses in the autumn of 1835, demonstrating the practicability of the art.

THE RELAY.

The relay or secondary circuit was devised to obviate a foreshadowed difficulty in the possible, not to say probable, weakening of the magnetic power in a long line.

This relay (or, as it was at first named, the receiving magnet, because it received its impulse from the distant station to be transmitted to the register) is simply an electro-magnet, whose only mechanical duty is to close and open another circuit. The accompanying figure explains its office.

M M is the electro-magnet with its coils of wire, the two extremities of which are connected with the main line circuit at L′ L″, thus constituting the coils of the magnet part of the main circuit. When, therefore, the main circuit is charged from the distant station, the electro-magnet M M is charged and becomes a magnet. To utilize the power thus created, a delicate upright lever of metal has at one end a cross-axis *b*, and at the other end it oscillates between the points of two adjusting screws *c* and *d*.

Fig. 1.

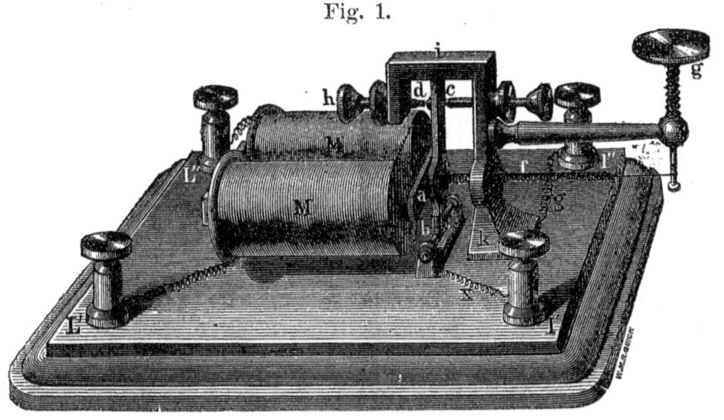

The Relay Magnet.

Erected before the face of the magnet poles, the lever has attached to it a soft iron armature, which is attracted to the point of the adjusting screw *h* at *d*, when the magnet is charged, and brought back to its rest by an adjustable spring *g*, when the magnet is discharged against the insulated point *c* of the other adjustable screw. The circuit called the local circuit, connected by a local battery with the magnet of the register, is connected by its extremities with the relay at the binding screws *l′ l″*.

The operation of the relay is as follows: The binding screw *l′*, holding one extremity of the local circuit, is connected with the metal of the lever, which oscillates between the points *d* and *c*, while the other binding screw, holding the other extremity of the local circuit, is connected with the metallic frame *k*. While the lever rests against the insulated point *c*, the local circuit is open, for the insulation prevents metallic contact; but when the relay magnet is charged, it attracts the armature *a*, thus causing the lever to make metallic contact at *d*, and so closing the circuit, as long as the magnet is charged; when it is discharged, the spring *g* brings back the lever against the insulated point *c*, and opens the circuit at *d*.

THE MORSE SYSTEM INTRODUCED IN EUROPE.

In the spring of 1838 this telegraph was introduced to the European world through the French Academy of Sciences, under the auspices of the distinguished Arago, and in the autumn of that year it was breveted in France.

This is the invention which has received the free, unsolicited suffrages of the International Telegraph Convention. It has features of individuality which distinguish it from all other systems of communicating intelligence at a distance, and its universality is undoubtedly mainly due to the result which it proposes and accomplishes, (to wit, a written or printed record,) and also to the simplicity of the mechanism by which that result is obtained.

Adopted in countries renowned for consummate skill in the manufacture of philosophical instruments and delicate instruments of precision, it is natural to expect that the telegraphic instruments constructed by the accomplished mechanicians of these countries, while preserving the essential principles of the original telegraph, would take many forms and display a great variety of mechanical adaptations to produce the result most effectively.

It ought to be here mentioned, however, to the credit of the mechanicians of the United States, to whom was intrusted the manufacture of the first Morse telegraphic instruments in use on the American lines, that most of the instruments, not only in form, but in point of efficiency, compactness, and finish of workmanship, in accuracy of mechanical adaptation and durability, were not inferior to most of those now manufactured and used in Europe. Many of the modifications in form, and the varied distribution of parts of the mechanism in the American instruments, take precedence in time of the European instruments. But the beauty and accuracy of mechanical finish in the great majority of the instruments, it is conceded, are for the most part in favor of the European mechanicians. Especially is this the case in the ingenious instruments used for imprinting the common or Roman letter, first attempted by Vail as early as 1837; afterwards effectively accomplished by House, but subsequently the instruments for which were so admirably perfected by Hughes, and are sent forth from the ateliers of Digney frères, Froment, and others, in France, and Siemens & Halske in Germany.

SIEMENS AND HALSKE'S MODIFICATION OF THE MORSE APPARATUS.

An example is given here of one of the modifications of the Morse apparatus by those distinguished savans and mechanicians, Messrs. Siemens & Halske, of Berlin.

The magnets, two in number, *m m′*, straight, but not united as in the ordinary horseshoe magnet, are placed horizontally instead of vertically, as in the original instruments. The poles *r* of the magnet *m′* have each a facing, outside the coil, of soft iron. The core of the other magnet *m* has a continuation from each pole of soft iron, acting as an armature, to be attracted by the facings of soft iron of the magnet *m′*.

A frame *p p*, from the center of which is the printing lever with its embossing point, is attached to the armature. The ends of the coils of the magnets *a* and *b* are carried to the terminals A and B.

By this arrangement of magnets the attraction of opposite polarities is efficaciously utilized. In all other respects the apparatus is not materially different from the original Morse. Notwithstanding the theoretic advantage of this modification, an experience of some time on the German, Danish, and Russian lines has led to its general abandonment for other modifications, or for the original Morse pattern.

Fig. 2.

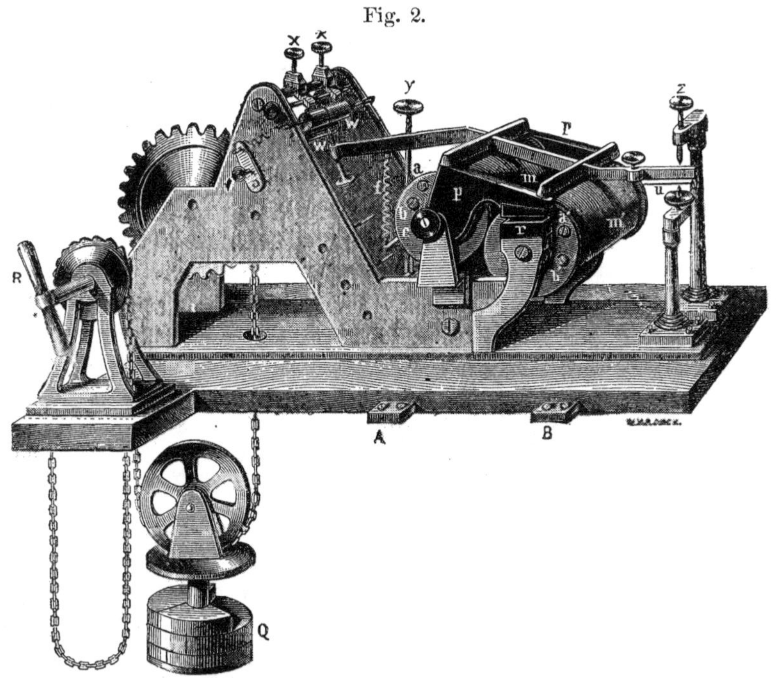

Siemens & Halske's modification of the Morse apparatus.

Another modification of the Morse by Messrs. Siemens & Halske is seen in Fig. 3. It consists in a mode of supplying the ink to the printing wheel.

An inverted bottle B B containing the ink is fixed, with a felt stopper, above and touching the printing wheel *c*. In all other respects it is essentially the original printing-wheel apparatus of one of the first Morse instruments, which was supplied with ink from a sponge. It has, however, in addition, the mode of bringing the paper to the wheel instead of the wheel to the paper, the device of Messrs. Baudouin and Digney frères, which is seen in the next diagram.

Fig. 3.

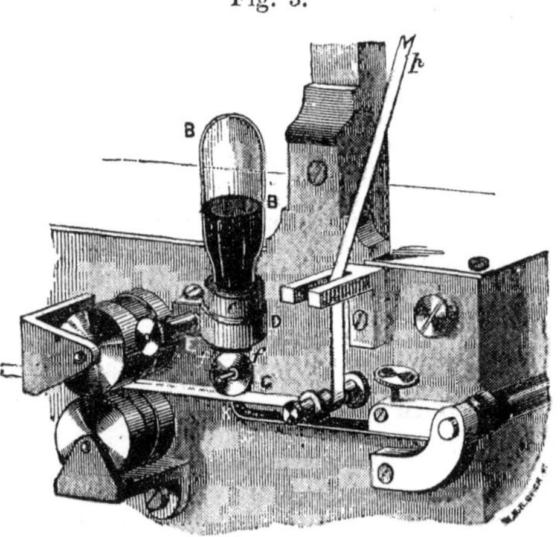

Siemens & Halske's Inking apparatus.

BAUDOUIN AND DIGNEY FRÈRES' MODIFICATION.

This ingenious modification is the invention of Messrs. Baudouin and Digney frères, of Paris, and is a real improvement. It consists in bringing the paper to the inking wheel, instead of the wheel to the paper. The rest of the apparatus is in all essential respects the Morse apparatus.

Fig. 4.

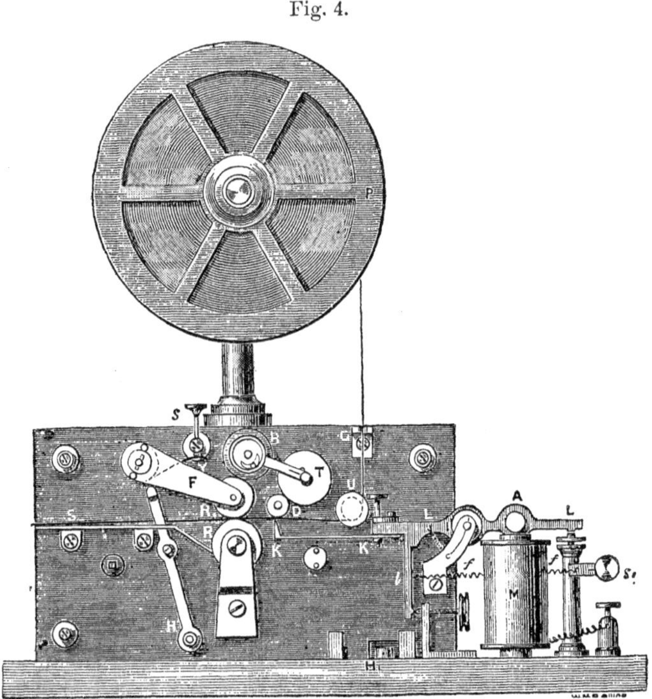

Baudouin and Digney Frères' Inking apparatus.

M is the electro-magnet. A is the armature upon the lever L L, hinged at I. The improvement consists in a prolonging of the lever by attaching to the writing extremity of it a thin metal slip K K, bent slightly upward toward the small printing wheel D. T is a felt ink roller, kept moistened with ink, against which the printing wheel D turns to receive the ink on its edge. The paper from the paper wheel P passes through a guide G down and around a pulley wheel U, and is drawn by the rollers R R' near but not touching the printing wheel D. So long as the magnet is not charged the paper passes beneath the printing wheel without a mark, but so soon as the magnet is charged the slip, or as it is termed in French, the "couteau," rises, and the edge of the couteau raises the paper against the inking wheel, and a mark longer or shorter, as the magnet continues charged, is made upon the paper. This mode of bringing the paper to the wheel requires so much less power than bringing the wheel to the paper, that for very considerable distances the relay necessary to furnish greater power in order to emboss the paper can be dispensed with. This, we have said, is a real improvement, and its simplicity has given it a wide popularity. It is the simplest of all the modes of recording. It is this instrument that goes by the name of the "ink writer."

Still another modification by Messrs. Siemens & Halske is seen in Fig. 5.

The peculiarity of this modification is in the manner of supplying ink to the printing wheel by a reservoir of ink A *a*, in which the printing wheel *c* revolves, half immersed in the fluid; but in this case the wheel is brought up to the paper.

The reservoir is hinged at *n*, and is raised or depressed by the screw *b* to regulate the flow of ink to the wheel.

Fig. 5.

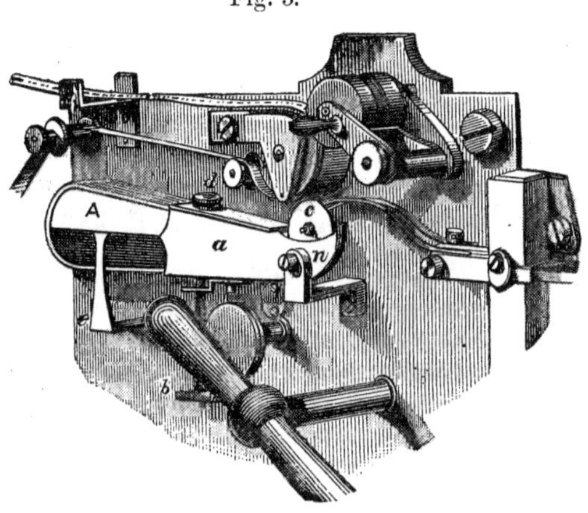

Siemens & Halske's modification of the Ink-writer.

Of all these modes of ink-writing that of Messrs. Baudouin and Digney frères is the simplest and best.

Did it not lead too far away from the special duty with which the writer is charged, it would be a most agreeable occupation to notice in detail many of the ingenious, if not always practical, modifications of the telegraph apparatus by the German, French, and English savans and mechanicians, such as the mode of sending dispatches both ways at the same time over the same wire, said to be originally devised by the Austrian savant, Dr. Gintl; and also the modifications of the same, by Herrn Frischen and Siemens & Halske; also the method devised by Stark, of Vienna, of transmitting two messages along a single line in the same direction, together with the modifications of this device by Kramer, Bosseda, Maron, Edlund, and others; also of Wheatstone's automatic printing apparatus, and of Stohrer's double style apparatus. But inquirers must be referred to the able works of many authors of telegraph treatises, especialy to Sabine's "History of the Telegraph," and to Blavier's "*Nouveau Traité de Télégraphie Électrique.*" To M. Sabine's courtesy the writer is indebted for leave to use many of his engravings of apparatus which are introduced into this report.

AUSTRIAN MILITARY TELEGRAPH.

Among other apparatus is the military telegraph apparatus of Austria, exhibited by the Imperial Royal Direction of Telegraphs in Vienna.

Baron Benedek says, according to the Paris Times of September 1,

1866, that a nation before entering upon a war should provide itself with *three* great elements, and "the Baron classes them in the order of their utiliy. First, *a good commander;* second, *iron roads*, (railroads;) third, *the electric telegraph.*"

The whole Austrian group, under the superintendence of the Baron d' Ebner, colonel of engineers, is remarkable for the completeness and beautiful workmanship, as well as scientific skill, of the various apparatus pertaining to electricity and its various uses in modern warfare, These uses, except so far as they include telegraphic service, are irrelevant to the present report, although to the military student in the highest degree instructive and interesting. Through the courtesy of the Baron all were explained, and a pamphlet given entitled "*Notice sur les objets formant l'exposition collective du ministère de la guerre I. R. d'Autriche à l'Exposition Universelle de Paris.*"

The Morse apparatus, compactly and beautifully made by J. Leopolder, of Vienna, is the principal telegraphic instrument used in the military telegraph. The Austrian pamphlet does not, however, give the details of the mode of constructing and regulating the military telegraph. These have been obtained from a very excellent and lucid pamphlet of about one hundred pages by E. Costa de Serda, *capitaine d'état major*, published in Paris.

A short extract from the introduction of this pamphlet supplies some of the desired details. The whole pamphlet is worthy of careful study. Under the head of different species of campaign telegraphs, Capitaine de Serda says:

"Two species of telegraphic apparatus are most usually employed in a campaign:

"I. The Morse apparatus, modified by Digney,[1] comprising—

"*a.* Wagons, with the materiel necessary to the construction of a line of over six miles English.

"*b.* Two wagon stations.

"II. Electro-magnetic dial apparatus, comprising the wagons with the necessary materiel for the construction of a line about six miles English, and the two telegraph apparatus."

Under the head of *Propriétés particulières et emploi de ces deux sortes du télégraphe*, he continues: "The Morse apparatus and its numerous modifications are found in use on the greatest number of permanent lines. This consideration, joined to the facility with which they can be connected with the existing lines, has caused this apparatus to be adopted for the campaign telegraph. The Digney apparatus, in particular, has the advantage of producing the signs printed in ink upon a band of paper, and that which is of greater importance it can be operated without the relay, but it requires experienced operators.

"The magneto-electric apparatus, on the contrary, is much more

[1] The *modification* here spoken of is Digney's mode of using the original *inking wheel*, elsewhere explained in this report.

simple. It is transported upon the wagons at the same time with the materiel, and can be operated by less able telegraphists, but it has the inconvenience of leaving no written record of the dispatch.

"At all times it is essential for military purposes to have both these kinds of apparatus."

NOTE BY MR. DE SERDA.—"These two kinds of telegraph apparatus are not the only ones which can be advantageously used in a campaign. Many models have been proposed or employed, and one is embarrassed to make a choice of them. The essential condition is, that they be strongly made, and easily transportable. Of the number of apparatus fulfilling these conditions, we cite the *Morse apparatus*, which is operated by the Daniel battery, (it is in use in many of the German armies,) and the military telegraph of M. Hipp, described in the Telegraphic Annals, (first year.) As to the two apparatus which we use, in accordance with our instructions, they have already been proved. The telegraph Digney [Morse] was operated in the Italian campaign in 1859. The dial electro-magnetic telegraph [semaphore] of Siemens is used upon the established lines of Bavaria, and has been adopted as the campaign apparatus of the Hanoverian army.

"The more immediate purpose of these telegraphic systems is their employment in the defense of coasts, of rivers, of mountain passes, to put an army in communication with its base of operations."

For more minute details of all that pertains to the construction and organization of the military telegraph, reference must be had to the pamphlet of M. Serda, transmitted with this report, which will amply repay the attention bestowed in its perusal.

From the statement in the pamphlet of the Austrian ministry of war, that "the application of the electric telegraph to military operations dates from the year 1854," it seems not to be known that the proposal for such an application was made to the French minister of war as early as the winter of 1838–'39. The circumstances are these: Morse, in September, 1838, exhibited his telegraphic invention to the French Academy of Sciences. The French minister of war, at that period, was General Bernard, a personal acquaintance and friend of the writer while the general was in the service of the United States, and on my visit to Paris, with my invention, he showed me many attentions. After dinner at the minister's one day, while some of the guests were amusing themselves in the billiard saloon, the writer was engaged in describing the nature of his invention to the general, and incidentally the manner (almost identical with the present plans in use) in which the invention could be used in military operations, stating his belief that the army which first made use of the telegraph in its operations must inevitably be the victor. The general listened with the deepest attention, and requesting reticence on the subject, said, "I will send an officer to you for further explanation." Accordingly, in a day or two afterwards, an officer—a marshal, an aged man—called to see the apparatus, to whom I imparted the plan.

The marshal was skeptical, opposing objections at every step, the principal one, however, being the fact that the telegraph wagon proposed, with the necessary apparatus, would add greatly to the materiel of the army, and so to its incumbrance. No reasoning that any such disadvantage would be more than counterbalanced by the obvious advantages availed to gain his favor to the project. He could not be moved from his position. He left me fully persuaded that it was a chimerical plan, and probably reported against it, for it was not again the subject of conversation with the minister. It should be borne in mind, as an apology for this feeling of the old marshal, that at that time the telegraph had nowhere been practically established, and that serious doubts were entertained, even in high scientific quarters, whether the telegraph could ever be made a practicable, or, at least, a practical enterprise. The skepticism of the marshal, therefore, had a plausible basis. It was not till the telegraphic lines had been extended on the continent, and successfully tested, that the ingenuity of the skillful was turned to the obvious advantage to be derived from a military telegraph. Modern warfare has been materially modified by its means. The Crimean campaign, the campaign in Italy, the civil war in America, and the later campaign in Austria, have all demonstrated that the telegraph is a potent engine, and has become an indispensable agent in military operations.

PRINTING TELEGRAPHS.

HUGHES'S PRINTING TELEGRAPH.

It was the original intention to give full descriptions of the telegraphic apparatus displayed in the Exposition, and in pursuance of this intention much labor and time were expended in examining and describing many of the instruments—labor and time which might have been spared had the fact been earlier recognized that most of the apparatus had been exhibited in previous international exhibitions, and had been fully and much better described in the Juror's Reports of these exhibitions by learned and competent savans. The labors of this report, therefore, are reduced mainly to noticing those which appear to possess some novelty; to giving references to descriptions in former reports and in other published works of the most important apparatus, and to examining and discussing any professed improvements.

A modification of the telegraph, by D. E. Hughes, from the ateliers of E. Hardy, of P. Dumoulin Froment, and Digney frères, Paris, Nos. 4, 10, and 13, of the catalogue, will now be noticed.

Among the many modifications of the telegraph displayed in the Exposition, the adapting of it to the imprinting of the ordinary alphabetic characters is one that early engaged the attention of the ingenious. None, however, have so just a title to pre-eminence as the ingenious printing instrument of Mr. D. E. Hughes. After the operation of the first instrument of Morse, in 1835, demonstrating the practicability of recording intelligence at a distance, the success of the original instrument, in producing this new result, naturally suggested the idea that the ordinary letters of the alphabet might be also recorded or imprinted as successfully as the Morse code of signs, and hence originated the earliest device of Alfred Vail, esq., for printing the Roman letters. Mr. Vail, in 1837, was associated with Morse, and after studying the operation of this first Morse instrument, proposed and draughted his plan of a printing instrument, a description of which he has given in full, with diagrams, in his work entitled the "American Electro-Magnetic Telegraph," published in 1845. The complicated machinery necessary to produce the result, which seemed more curious than useful, and its slowness of operation, compared with the Morse instrument, were obstacles to its practical application. It was never practically tested. The result, however, which was proposed, to wit, the actual printing of the Roman letter, possessed a fascination which took strong possession of the minds of ingenious men, and one of them, R. E. House, esq., devoted his genius and rare mechanical skill to the construction of an instrument of great beauty and effectiveness, which, to a limited extent, is still in operation.

Fig. 6.

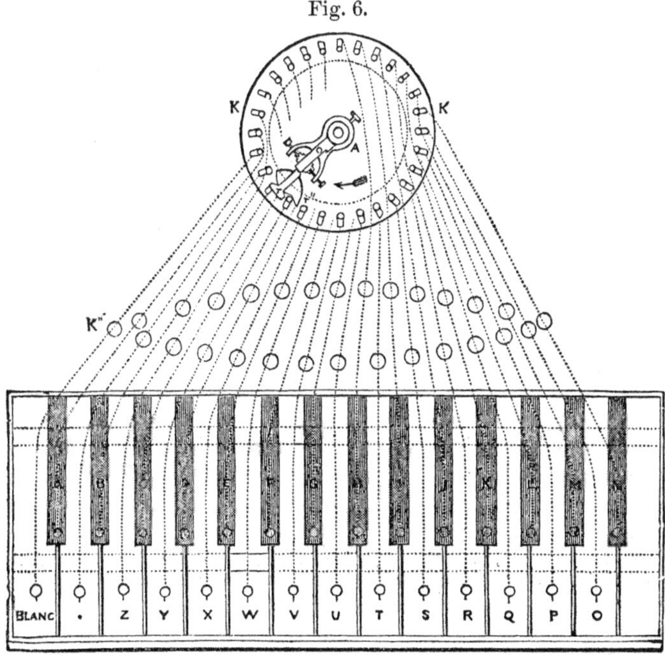

Key-board of the Hughes apparatus.

The Hughes apparatus is of too much importance to pass undescribed, or to be dismissed with merely a reference to a description in books. Not being able to obtain from the accomplished inventor (owing to his absence in the East) a description from his own pen, which would have been preferred, the writer of this report avails himself of the lucid description and illustrations of Robert Sabine, esq., who has courteously permitted duplicate illustrations to be made for this report from his valuable work, "The Electric Telegraph," published in London by Virtue Brothers, in 1867:

"The essential principle of this highly ingenious system is the synchronous movements of the type-wheels at two or more stations, and of the power to press a strip of paper at each of the stations simultaneously against the types on the corresponding parts of the wheels, by the action of a single electric wave or impulse.

"A clockwork at each station turns, with a continuous and uniform motion, an axle, at the extremity of which the type-wheel is supported. The synchronism is attained by the aid of a vibrating spring and anchor escapement. The rotation of the type-wheel is transmitted to a vertical arbor, furnished at its lower extremity with a horizontal arm traveling over a circular disk, in which is arranged a series of contact pins, in number corresponding to the types. Each pin, therefore, represents a letter, and is raised when it is wished to telegraph this letter along the line. The horizontal arm, which travels around the disk with a motion uniform with that of the type-wheel, comes in contact with the pin just at the moment when the corresponding type is at the lowest point and closes an electric circuit, by which the paper is lifted up against the type-wheel and the letter printed.

"The key-board used to elevate the contact pins is shown in Fig. 6. It consists of twenty-eight keys, alternately white and black, marked with the twenty-six letters of the alphabet, a full stop, and a blank, corresponding to an empty space on the type-wheel. Below each of the keys is a movable lever whose fulcrum is at K″, and which terminates at the bottom of one of the contact pins K K, arranged in a circle in the metal box A, in the top and bottom of which are holes for the ends to protrude—the upper holes being long to allow of a radial motion. Each pin is held down by the pressure of a small spring, but may be elevated by pressing down the corresponding key of the piano board.

"Fig. 9 gives a vertical section of the printing instrument and key-board. The section shows a white key hinged at K″, connected to its lever K′, a contact pin *k*, on the right, and also to a black key, whose lever reaches to a contact pin on the left of the box A. The contact pins are provided with shoulders to limit their movements in each direction.

"The horizontal arm, which travels over the circle of contact points, is attached to the bottom of the vertical arbor Q, to which motion is imparted by the beveled wheel G on the shaft G_2. It is made up of three principal parts: the arm *r*, jointed at *a*; the resting piece, or earth contact, *r′*; and the shovel *r″*. The vertical shaft of Q is of brass, and is divided electrically into two parts by an insulating ring of ivory *q*. The lower part is supported by the central pedestal, which is insulated from the box A by a non-conducting ring.

"The continuation of the jointed arm *r*, which is held by the portion of the shaft above the insulating ring *q*, is pressed down by a spring, which keeps a small screw in the middle of the continuation in metallic contact with second piece *r'*, supported by the portion of the shaft below the ring. The shovel *r''* is of steel.

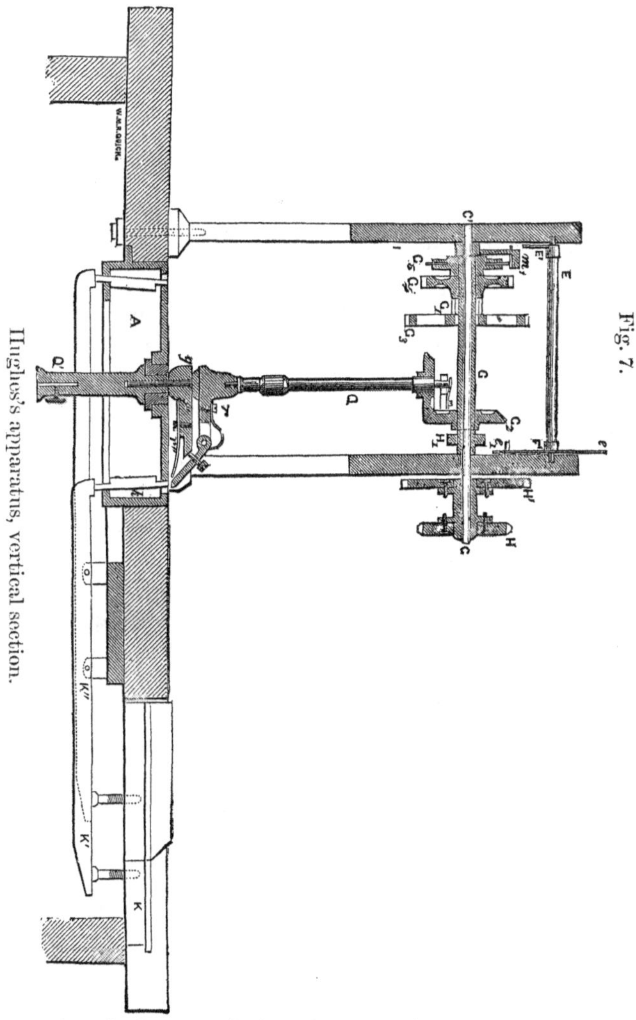

Fig. 7.

Hughes's apparatus, vertical section.

"When a key is depressed the corresponding contact pin is elevated, and if the arbor Q is in motion, the extremity of the arm *r* mounts upon the elevated pin, by which contact between *r* and *r'* is interrupted and that of *r* with *k* established. The arm *r* having made contact with the shovel *r''*, which immediately follows it, pushes the pin *k* in its slot outside the circumference swept over by *r*; so that if the latter made another revolution while the finger is kept down on the key, no second contact is made, and the same letter is not repeated. The operator feels a vibration of the key as the shovel passes by the pin, and is thus made aware that the letter has been printed.

"The type-wheel H contains on its circumference, in twenty-eight equal spaces, twenty-six letters of the alphabet, a dot, and a blank space; it is fixed to the extremity of the axis C C′, which is put in motion by means of the hollow axis G enveloping it in the greater part of its length. The connection between C C′ and G is made by the mediation of a fine ratchet-wheel G_5 attached to the axis G, the click m_1 being on the axis C C′. On the latter are supported, besides the type-wheel and the click, a corrector H′, or wheel with long narrow teeth, equal in number to the types, serving to establish precision between the movements of the horizontal arm r and the type-wheel. On the same axis is a wheel H_1, having a notch at one part of its circumference for stopping the type-wheel when the blank space is opposite the printing press, in case it should spring forward.

"The hollow axis G is turned by clock-work moved by a weight, a wheel of which engages with the pinion G_1, and supports besides the ratchet G_5 and beveled wheel G_2, already mentioned, the escape wheel G_4, and a tooth wheel G_3, which locks into the pinion I′, Fig. 8, of the printing shaft I.

"The printing-shaft turns seven times as fast as the type-wheel, and carries a fly-wheel I″ at one extremity, in order to overcome the inertia of a small shaft, whose duty is to lift the paper up to the type-wheel at the other extremity. This is shown partly in section in Fig. 8. The printing-shaft I, and its continuation i, are locked together by means of a ratchet-wheel I_1 and click i'.

Fig. 8.

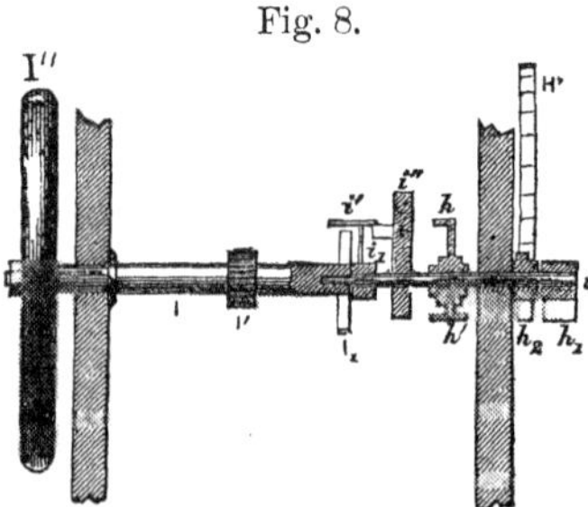

"At the end of the continuation shaft i is a cam h_1, for lifting the press and the paper against the type-wheel.

Fig. 9.

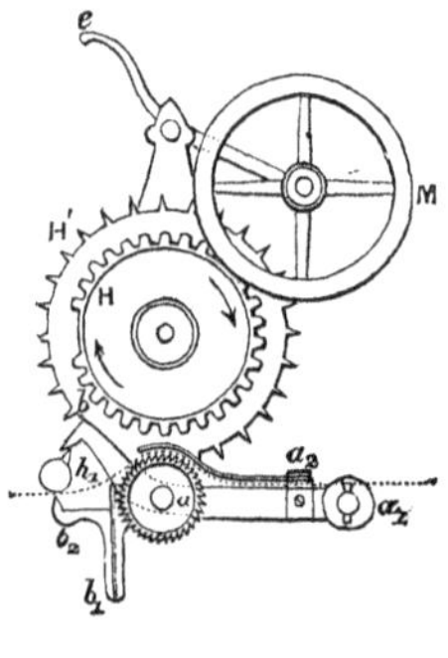

"The printing press is shown in Fig. 9. Underneath the type-wheel is a small cylinder a, over which the paper is led, its axis being in the middle of a bent lever b, turning at a_1; attached to it is a ratchet-wheel in the teeth of which catches a click affixed to a movable piece b_1, terminating in the rectangular arm b_2, which is forced upward by a spring attached to the frame of the apparatus, but is stopped against the axis i. When i makes one revolution, the cam lifts the arm b of the lever, together with the cylinder a and paper strip up to the lowest tooth of the type-wheel, by which the paper strip is impressed with the print of the type, kept inked by an inking-roller M. The cam being very sharp, the movements of ascent and descent are proportionally rapid, and the paper touches the type during only an infinitely short space of time. The axis continuing to turn, the cam meets the arm *b*, and depresses it, causing the click to draw round the cylinder and advance the paper a certain distance.

"By the side of the ratchet-wheel I′, the printing-shaft carries an escapement *h h′*, arrested by a continuation of the lever L L′, moving with the armature of the electro-magnet. The armature is of soft iron, supported at the extremity of a lever D, over the poles of the electro-magnet, Fig. 10. The lever turns between supports on the axis, and

Fig. 10.

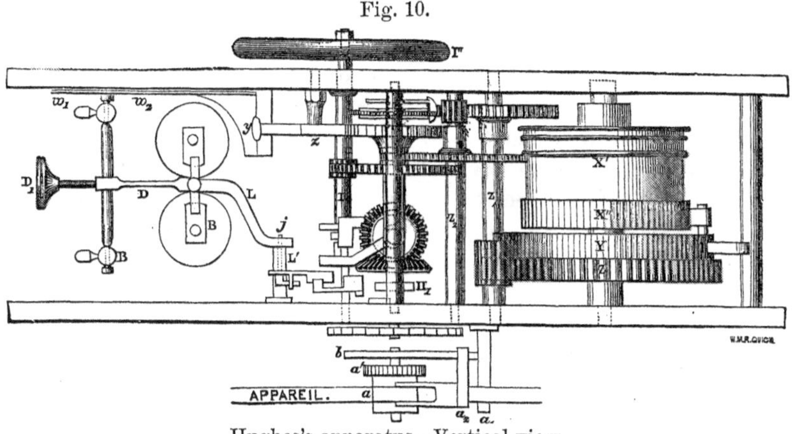

Hughes's apparatus—Vertical view.

tends to rise by the force of a spring regulated by the adjusting-screw D′.

"The screw *d′*, Fig. 11, on the end of the lever L L′, turning on the axis *j*, sits over the armature; the other end of the lever engages with one of the pallets of the escapement *h h′*, and governs the motion of the axis *i*. When a current traverses the coils of the electro-magnet, the armature and lever are depressed, the click is put in gear, and the pallet *h* of the escapement, released, turns with the axis *i*. At the moment when the pallet *h′* passes under the lever, it relifts it, and depresses the screw *d′*, returning thereby the armature to the poles of the electro-magnet, and at the same time throwing the click out of gear.

Fig. 11.

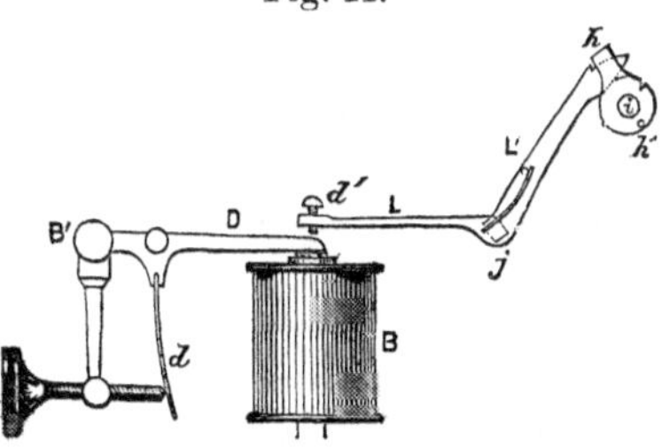

"The magnet B is of novel construction. It consists of a permanent horseshoe magnet, with soft iron cylindrical continuations on the poles. These continuations are each encircled by a coil of wire. When no current passes through the coils, the armature is attracted to the poles by the magnetism distributed in the iron. This force is opposed by the adjusting spring, which is so regulated that, the armature being in contact, a very weak current is able to neutralize the attraction.

"The printing-shaft has also the duty of correcting the movement of the type-wheel, and of insuring always that, at the moment of printing a letter, the type is in its proper position. This is effected by means of a curved cam h_2 on the axis i. The instant the cam h' lifts the arm b of the frame carrying the printing roller, the projection h_2 locks into the teeth of the wheel H′, and adjusts, if it be necessary, its position. If, on entering the teeth of H′, the cam has to push the wheel forward, or to accelerate the motion of the axis C C′, the click m is pushed onward, passing over one or more of the teeth of the ratchet-wheel G_5. If, on the contrary, the cam has to retard the motion, the click pulls the ratchet-wheel backward, for which purpose the latter is not made rigid on the axis, but is formed of a disk held between leather washers, supported by two plates of metal fixed on the hollow shaft G.

"The electric circuits of the apparatus are very simple. The bottom of the vertical shaft Q is connected to earth, and the upper part to one end of the coils of the electro-magnet, the other end being to line. One pole of a battery is connected to the levers k of the contact pins; the other pole to earth. At two corresponding stations the plates of the batteries must always be looking the same way, because the home apparatus is intended always to work as well as that of the distant stations, and the armature of its magnet is only liberated by currents in one direction.

"When a current arrives, therefore, from the line, it passes first through the coil B of the magnet, then through the vertical shaft Q, which it descends and goes over from the screw in the jointed arm v to the resting-piece r', and from this to earth. When a current is to be transmitted, the operation consists principally in interrupting the earth circuit, and inserting the battery into the break. This is done by the contact-pins and jointed arm of r. A key being depressed, the arm r, in its journey, rides over the pin, and its screw is lifted up from contact with r', which breaks the direct earth circuit; at the same time the contact of r' with the pin k, which is in communication with a pole of the battery through the lever K, sends a current from the battery (K k r Q) through the coils of the magnet into the line, &c.

"Suppose two such apparatus, properly adjusted, at the extremities of a line of telegraph, the clock-work wound up, the electrical connections properly established, and the type-wheels locked; the employé who desires to transmit presses down the key of his instrument; this pushes up the corresponding contact peg in the circle K, and when the chariot arrives over the pin, the extremity of the piece r rides over it, separating the earth contact and introducing the battery into the line circuit. The current passes through the vertical shaft, the coils of the magnet, and line wire to the other station, where it circulates in the coils of the magnet, the vertical shaft, &c., and goes to earth.

"In traversing the coils of the magnets of both instruments, the current weakens the attractions of the armatures to the poles of the electro-magnets; the former are forced off by the spring, the screws d' are raised and the levers L at the same time depressed. The pallets *h* of the escapements *h h′* are thereupon released, the axis *i* put into gear with I, and the type-wheels released. During the revolution made by the axis *i*, the cylinders *a* are raised by the cams, and lift the paper up to the printing-wheels at the moment when the latter are unlocked. No letter is printed, because the blank space in the type-wheel occurs just there. The paper strips and cylinders descend again, the former advancing a step. The clicks are then disengaged from the ratchets, and the pallets *h* recaught by the levers L′, which were lifted up, causing the armatures to be pushed down again to the poles of the magnets.

"If a key answering to any letter be now pressed down, the current is repeated the moment the chariot passes over the raised contact pin; the printing axis is put in motion, the letter printed, and the paper pushed on as before, and so on, until the message is completed.

"It sometimes happens that the apparatus do not agree when one of the stations sends its message. In this case the employé at the receiving station advises his correspondent of it by giving him a signal; both then arrest their type-wheels, and the transmission is recommenced, beginning always with the blank.

"To avoid the inconvenience of irregular working, which might arise from changes in the battery power, Professor Hughes has adopted a method of short circuiting the coils of the electro-magnet the instant after the armature is released, that the current, whatever may be its intensity, comes into play only long enough to effect the required weakening of the magnetic attraction. This is done by connecting one end of the electro-magnet coils with D, and the other end with L, in addition to the other connections, and by adjusting the screw *d′*, so that, when at rest, the armature reposing on the poles does not touch it; but as soon as the neutralization occurs it is lifted up by the force of the spring, and the coils short circuited by contact of D with *d′*.

"The speed of transmission attained by this apparatus is very great. The chariot and type-wheel revolve about one hundred and twenty times in a minute, and an expert manipulator can transmit on the average two letters during a single revolution of the shaft.

"The word '*telegraph*,' for example, is completed in six turns, as follows:

First turn	*blank* and *t*.
Second turn..........................	*e l*.
Third turn...........................	*e*.
Fourth turn..........................	*g r*.
Fifth turn	*a p*.
Sixth turn...........................	*h*.

"The French word '*bonté*' is done in four turns—

First turn..........................	Blank.
Second turn..........	*b o*.
Third turn	*n t*.
Fourth turn.......................	*é*.

"Another example is the word '*dintz*,' more fortunate than either, being transmitted during a single revolution."

In summing up the advantages and disadvantages of the Hughes apparatus, Mr. E. E. Blavier, vol. II, pp. 268, 269, says:

"The dispatches by the Hughes apparatus received upon the strip of paper are directly transmitted to those for whom they are destined without any transcribing. The strip of paper is cut off and pasted in lines upon a leaf of ordinary paper. * * *

"The strip upon which is the impression at the place of departure is preserved for the control. The errors and the delays which attend the copying of the dispatches, and the expense of clerk-hire, are thus diminished.

"Errors can also be *revised* during the transmission made by incorrect manipulation, or erroneous reading of the text to be transmitted. But there occurs no confusion in the signs received, as may happen in the Morse system when certain letters resemble each other, or in the apparatus for fugitive signals where all depends upon the attention of the operator.

"These advantages are common to all the printing apparatus, but that which distinguishes the apparatus of M. Hughes is the great speed of transmission that he gives, which is due to this, that each letter requires but a single passage of the current, and to this that there is no stopping of the apparatus during the transmission.

"This speed surpasses greatly that attained by all the other systems.

"Upon the lines of four hundred or five hundred kilometers, (thirty-one miles English,) for example, fifty-five to sixty dispatches of twenty words in an hour can be easily transmitted with the Hughes apparatus on condition that the labor is continuous and the order of transmission is not often changed. Under the same conditions from thirty-five to forty dispatches can with difficulty be obtained by the Morse apparatus,[1] and from twenty to twenty-five with the dial apparatus or escapement printing instruments.

"On the other hand, the manipulation of the Hughes instrument requires expert and intelligent operators; for the want of skill cannot be remedied by a slower transmission, as with the dial or Morse instruments. It is very complicated, and in consequence is liable to frequent derangement. It cannot, therefore, be used for ordinary stations, *(postes secondaires,)* where the Morse instruments will always be preferred because of their great simplicity. For the important offices connected directly by the wires, it is eminently practical, and it has already rendered great services; its use is daily extending."

It is to be remarked, in regard to this extremely ingenious instrument, that it is not the special result, to wit, the printing of the ordinary letter of the alphabet, that gives to it its prominence and its great excellence; these are due rather to the greater quantity of intelligence it pro-

[1] For correction of these erroneous figures, see *Statement of comparative speed*, &c., Chap. v.

fesses to transmit in a given time. It must be admitted that aside from the simplicity of the apparatus by which the Morse characters are transmitted, one of the chief merits of the Morse apparatus has hitherto been that a greater amount of intelligence in a given time, and by simpler means, can be transmitted and recorded by it than by any other system. It is now asserted that the Hughes apparatus transmits more than the Morse, as the latter is now usually operated. If, however, it shall be ascertained that the Morse has been underestimated in its speed of transmission, or if, by some modification or improvement in manipulation, or skill in the operator, it should be demonstrated that the Morse transmits as rapidly as the Hughes, or even if it should be with somewhat less rapidity, the improvement of whatever nature would in all probability cause the Hughes apparatus to give place to the improvement, provided it was not encumbered with great complication. For, be it remarked, the public as well as the telegraph administrations are most interested in having the greatest quantity in the shortest time, and will care very little whether the telegraph clerk who receives a dispatch has come to the knowledge, for example, of the letter E by the simple dot [.] of the Morse code, or by the usual E of the Roman alphabet. It is the same letter in either case, and that process which can with due economy and least complication send the greatest number of them in a given time will be preferred to all others[1].

ARLINCOURT'S PRINTING APPARATUS.

For a clear description of this very ingenious Roman-letter printing apparatus, (which was also exhibited at the great exhibition of 1862, and is briefly noticed in the record in the Practical Mechanics' Journal,) the inquirer is referred to the excellent work of Blavier, vol. II, pp. 226 to 233. Mr. Blavier, however, after describing it, says: "This apparatus, notwithstanding its apparent complication, gives good results, and has been employed with success upon some lines. It, nevertheless, has the inconvenience common to the dial apparatus of requiring a great number of emissions of the current for each letter, and cannot be used but upon short lines."

Many of the instruments in the Exposition bear only the name of the mechanician in whose ateliers they have been constructed, but in the apparatus mentioned in the catalogue under the following numbers, as well as in some of the apparatus of Messrs. Digney frères, there is a distinct recognition of the original inventor. These instruments differ very little from each other, and not at all in the essential features of the original Morse apparatus. They are, without exception, well made and practically effective.

---

[1] The above remarks were made in the autumn of 1867, just after the close of the Exposition. Since that time, as will be seen by reference to experiments on rapidity of transmission with the Morse apparatus in the United States, the rapidity of the manual operation of the Morse apparatus is shown to far exceed the rapidity of Mr. Hughes's apparatus.

"No. 64. Longoni & Dell Acqua, of Milan—The Morse Telegraph, modified by Moroni.

"No. 61. Joseph Pik, Warsaw—Telegraph, Morse system.

"No. 66. Joseph Poggioli, Florence—The Morse apparatus complete.

"No. 7. T. A. M. Sortirs—The Morse apparatus.

"No. 49. Leon de Hamar, Pesth, Hungary—Telegraph apparatus of Morse.

"No. 50. Jean Leopolder, Vienna—Typographic telegraph, with the Morse characters."

DUJARDIN'S PRINTING TELEGRAPH.

This apparatus is composed of a manipulator (Fig. 12.) and a register (Fig. 13.)

Fig 12.

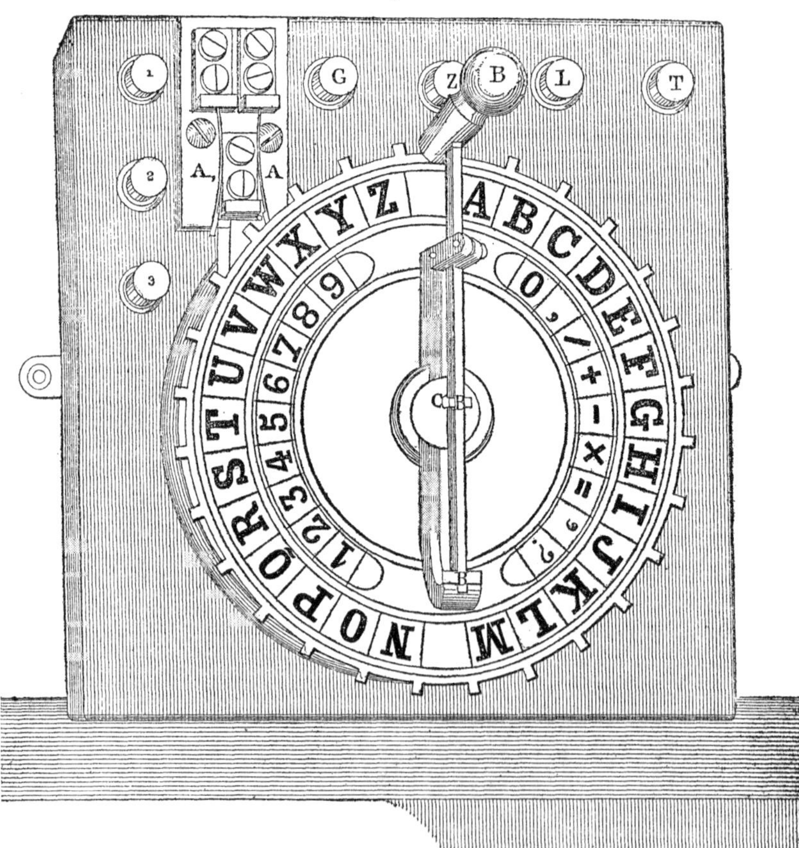

Printing Telegraph of Dr. Dujardin, of Lille—Manipulator.

The manipulator consists of a wheel (*à gorge sinueuse*) of fourteen undulations, making the commutator A oscillate, which sends over the line at each turn of the wheel twenty-eight currents, alternately positive and negative, succeeding each other without any appreciable interval.

The axis of this wheel bears a crank B, which moves above a divided dial, upon which are engraved, upon two concentric circles, the let-

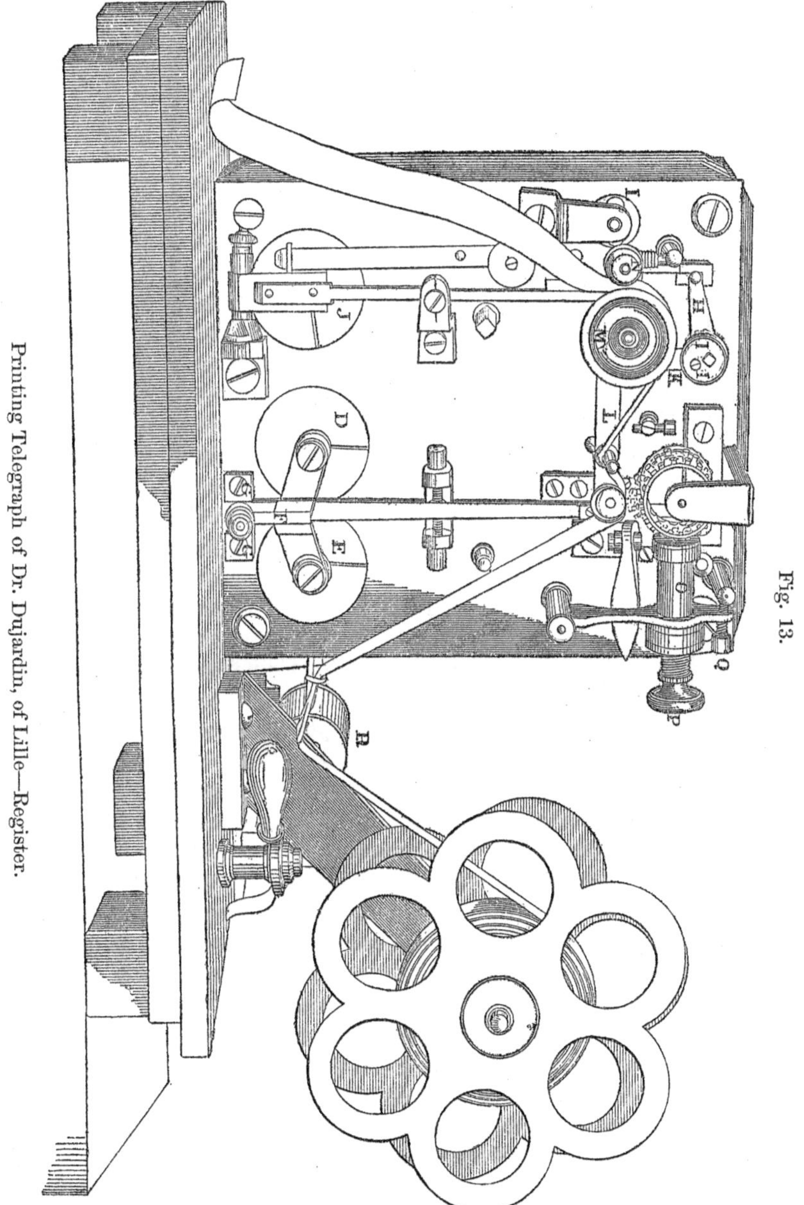

Fig. 13.

Printing Telegraph of Dr. Dujardin, of Lille—Register.

ters, the numerals, and other conventional signs. When the crank is stopped before any letter, and is sunk in the corresponding notch, the shaft C, which is articulated with this crank and traverses the axis of the dial, is pressed down, and causes to move under the manipulator a double commutator, which produces an impression of the letter by means indicated presently. During the reception, the crank of the manipulator ought to be constantly kept down.

The receptor or register is composed of two trains of wheels serving the one to turn the type-wheels, the other to produce the impression, and (*déclanchés*) each by a special electro-magnet. The last movable wheel of the first train of wheels carries an escapement wheel of fourteen teeth, and two type-wheels—the one for letters, the other for numerals—acting alternately. These wheels are cut out in the form of rings and fitted into one another, so that they resemble an ×, whence their name of cross-wheels. The electro-magnet D E oscillates the pallet F, polarized by the piece of iron G, which is itself polarized by the magnets placed under the register. The last movable wheel of the second train of wheels carries the stop H and the eccentric I. The halting magnet (*aimant boiteux*) J, by the intervention of a fork with two prongs, serves to release the stop H, and allows it to make a complete revolution. During this revolution the eccentric I, by means of a crank K, raised above the lever L, is made to strike the paper against the types. The axis of the second movable wheel of the impression wheel carries the cylinder (*entraineur*) M and the roller N, which moves forward the paper during the revolution of the stop. The plug or ink-stopper O presents a particular arrangement; it is a brass tube, in which is moved a piston by a screw P, and which contains an oleaginous ink. A disk of velvet, which gives passage to the ink, shuts the tube, and is found constantly in contact with the types of the wheel which does the work. The screw of the regulator Q allows to the velvet to press more or less upon the types. The electro-magnet shut up in the box R serves to cause the local current in the printing electro-magnet to pass at the proper time.

When it is desired to transmit, the crank of the dial is turned, and, from this movement of rotation, a series of currents, alternately positive and negative, result, which, in a biforked manner in the electro-magnets D, E, and R, produce on the one part the rotation of the type-wheels, and on the other the permanent attraction of the pallet of the electro-magnet R, which carries the current by which the printing is done. When the crank is pressed into the notch corresponding to the letter which it is desired to print, the double commutator under the manipulator is brought into action. This double commutator serves on the one part to break the current of the line and to put into a position of reception the apparatus of the operator who transmits, and on the other part to transfer the battery current of the line to the local circuit which is employed, it may be altogether or only in part. Upon the divided dial and at the extremities of the same diameter are found two empty divisions, which serve to make the spaces between the words, and work the change of the type-wheels. When the crank is pressed into the division between Z and A the wheel for the letters is brought into action, and when the crank is pressed into the division between M and N it is the other wheel which is brought into action.

The apparatus which is here described permits the transmission of twenty-three words per minute, and has operated actually between Paris and Lille in a very satisfactory manner. The speed of transmission amounts to from thirty to thirty-five words, by substituting for the dial manipulator a key manipulator, and employing a little different register from that described. The apparatus thus modified can operate at very great distances. It has operated thus very regularly during six months between London and Edinburgh, and if it has not been definitely adopted in England by the Electric Telegraph Company, it is that at the present time it does not print the numerals.

PANTELEGRAPHS.

One of the two modes by which writing or printing was to be effected at a distance was the mode of recording by the chemical decomposition of a metallic salt by means of the electric or galvanic current. Although the earliest experiments successfully proved the practicability of this mode of recording, yet the simplicity aimed at by the writer of this report in devising his process, turned his attention more engrossingly to the second or mechanical mode of recording by means of the electro-magnet. Subsequent to these results, obtained as early as 1835, Davy, in England, devised and patented, in 1839, a plan of marking by chemical decomposition which, however, has never been in practical use. Bain, still later, in 1846, proposed his method of marking the Morse alphabet by the successful application of a more sensitive salt than had been employed. Bakewell, in England, in 1851, further developed the electro-chemical mode of marking, by devising and accomplishing an interesting result, which has since been expanded and improved by Bonelli,[1] of Florence, and more recently by Caselli and Lenoir. By the genius and skill of these distinguished men, the electro-chemical process has been successfully applied to the production at a distance of perfect fac similes of writing and drawing.

BONELLI'S APPARATUS MODIFIED BY COOK.

Just at the moment of transmitting this report to Washington, an interesting article from the Anglo-American Times, London, February 27, gives the latest information respecting this ingenious modification by

[1] The lamented death of the gifted Italian, Bonelli, has retarded the perfecting of his autographic system. It is, nevertheless, advancing to perfection through the genius, perseverance, and energy of his friend, Henry Cook, esq., who showed in Paris the instrument in a progressive state. It gave great promise of taking a high position among the telegraphic instrumentalities of the day.

Henry Cook, esq., of Bonelli's automatic instrument. The article is given entire:

"We translate the following from a French paper:

"'NEW SYSTEM OF TELEGRAPHY.

"'This morning the Emperor Napoleon III condescended to examine at the Tuileries the new telegraphic system invented by the late Mr. Bonelli and Mr. Cook, partner of the American banking house of Messrs. Norton & Co. After a practical and complete examination of the new apparatus, his Majesty expressed his satisfaction on all points, and invited the inventor to come the following day at noon to show the Empress the rapidity and accuracy of the instruments, which far surpass all yet seen in telegraphy. The advantage of Mr. Cook's system consists in the absolute exactness of the messages transmitted, and we need not point out this value to men of business who are aware what errors are committed with the instruments in use, occasioning inconvenience and pecuniary loss. Mr. Cook's system also enables three messages to be transmitted in the time now taken for one. In short, his Majesty considered the benefits of the new system so important that he has authorized M. the Count de Vougy, director general of telegraphs, to give the inventor every facility necessary to bring his telegraphic apparatus into general use.

"'Mr. Cook, in connection with the celebrated Italian telegrapher, M. Bonelli, has devoted many years and very large sums of money to the perfection of Bonelli's system. Since the decease of the latter, the improvements made by Mr. Cook have been so satisfactory as to attract much attention to the system, not only in Europe, but in the United States, where plans are being arranged for its general introduction. For Great Britain it has been most favorably considered by Lord Clarendon, who has had an opportunity for a careful examination of its merits. At the second interview, both the Empress and Prince Imperial were present. The printing and autographic instruments were tested with great success. The special objects of the improvements of Mr. Cook are perfect accuracy and great rapidity in all seasons. No action of temperature or climate have any detrimental effect on these instruments, which so far have worked better in bad weather than in fair. The special importance of positive accuracy cannot be denied, and with these instruments it is insured. Mr. Cook's system is grounded on Chevalier Gaetano Bonelli's patent, which he purchased in 1860, and by years of labor and outlay improved into the instrument just submitted to the Emperor. The original instrument constructed from this patent was automatic, and required fifty wires, working simultaneously yet independently, while the present needs but one. The first improvement was the production of a telegraphic machine reducing the number to eleven wires, then to five, though even this number barred its general adoption, notwithstanding its power to print forty messages per hour, insuring accuracy, and being independent of synchronism. The present instruments were further modified by Messrs. Bonelli and Hipp, but to Mr. Cook is due the final improvements which now make them so nearly perfect. The machinery is simple and strong, the parts delicate in substance, are of steel, and there is nothing which with ordinary wear should get out of order. The instruments are said to be capable of transmitting one hundred and sixty messages per hour, but in reality they can accomplish from eighty to one hundred, the maximum of other instruments being forty. The system also permits greater speed in delivery. The address is first printed, and the envelope can be addressed while the rest of the dispatch is printing off. When finished, the paper is passed between rollers of blotting paper, and dispatched—no need to read it, its accuracy is sure. The simplicity of the plan enables the authors of the system to engage to send messages cheaply—children, boys, or girls being soon able to set up the type. Experiments prove that fourteen and a half words per person per minute ean easily be attained; thus machines, at the rate of eighty messages per hour, would transmit one thousand six hundred words per hour; two type-setters would compose one thousand seven hundred and forty; one machine clerk and two type-setters can, therefore, keep the instrument at the maximum pace of work. During the interruption of a line, the time by existing systems is now lost; by Mr. Cook's apparatus the messages are set up as they arrive. The moment a line is reported good the messages are sent through at the utmost speed, and lost time may thus to a great extent be retrieved.'"

It may be remarked that, properly to estimate the value of this modification, the actual result must be considered, assuming that, other things being equal, that system which can transmit the greatest quantity of dispatches in a given time is the best.

In this, as in the other automatic devices, the time required to prepare the dispatches for transmission is an essential element in the calculation. Whether this time of preparation can be economically lessened by dividing the labor of preparation among several persons is a matter mainly of finance. Whether it is economy to employ one person for a particular work, or whether several persons can accomplish it sooner, is outside the merits of the transmitting machine. The preparation is a work to be accomplished precedent to the duties of the machine. The ability of the instrument to transmit that which has been prepared is the main point to which attention will be directed.

The instruments are said to be "capable of transmitting one hundred and sixty messages per hour," but this, we presume, is the maximum under the most favorable circumstances, for it is immediately added, "that in reality they can accomplish from eighty to one hundred."

In the preparation for transmission it is stated that "experiments prove that fourteen and a half words can be set up by one person in a minute;" that is to say, if one person is employed to prepare a dispatch for transmission of sixteen hundred words, then twenty words (or one dispatch) would require five and a half words more than could be prepared in one minute. But allowing that even eighty dispatches, equaling sixteen hundred words, could thus be prepared in one hour, it will be perceived by reference to the speed tests of the Morse, given in the table, Chapter V, that Morse operators have far exceeded that rate, having in fact transmitted the entire eighty in the time that the Bonelli instrument was ready to commence transmission.

Nevertheless, the beauty and (compared with the automatic methods of other modifiers of the system) the simplicity of Mr. Cook's modification and improvement of Bonelli's method were greatly admired. Experience alone will determine whether it can be economically and advantageously used.

It is to be heartily and sincerely hoped that its ingenious improver may realize his most sanguine expectations, and the objections we have hinted at find a successful solution.

From the well-known liberality of the French administration, under the able guidance of its distinguished chief director, it is sure to have a fair trial.

APPARATUS OF THE ABBÉ CASELLI.

The apparatus of the Abbé Caselli is somewhat complicated, and is very expensive, but it is a beautiful and efficient apparatus, producing its results with perfect success.

It is easy to imagine many cases in the affairs of a government, as well as in common life, where the result accomplished by such an apparatus would be of immense advantage, and, although too expensive for general or ordinary use, it is destined to become a necessity to governments as an adjunct to other systems, furnishing, in many exigencies, a verification of official orders and other acts, demanding a more immediate conveyance than by the mail.

For a complete description of this exceedingly beautiful apparatus, the inquirer is referred to the lucid and accurate description of it in Blavier, vol. ii, from page 274 to 301.

LENOIR'S MODIFICATION—THE ELECTROGRAPH.

No. 13 of the catalogue is an apparatus for producing a similar result, by M. E. Lenoir, which he calls an "electrographe." It is much less complicated in appearance than the Abbé Caselli's, occupying scarcely more space than an ordinary Morse apparatus. A specimen of its results in fac-simile drawing is transmitted to the department.[1] The specimen was produced in the Exposition on a short circuit, and no opportunity was afforded of proving its efficacy at a distance, or to ascertain at what distance it was capable of operating. It is regretted that a description promised has not been received, as the apparatus, from its simplicity, prepossessed one strongly in its favor. Specimens by Lenoir's process are also transmitted.[1]

[1] Deposited in the library of the Department of State.

CHAPTER II.

SEMAPHORES.

THE DIAL OR CADRAN SYSTEMS—THEIR ADAPTATION TO SPECIAL SERVICE—PERFECTION OF WORKMANSHIP IN THE INSTRUMENTS EXHIBITED—SOUNDERS OR ACOUSTIC SEMAPHORES—CATON'S SOUNDER FOR USE IN THE FIELD—ORIGIN AND NATURE OF THE ACOUSTIC SEMAPHORE—THE MORSE CODE ADAPTED TO RECOGNITION BY EACH OF THE FOUR SENSES—PROFESSOR STEINHEIL'S BELL SOUNDER—BRIGHT'S BELL SOUNDER—MORSE'S ORGAN-PIPE SOUNDER—SIGNAL SEMAPHORES—NIGHT SIGNALS BY MADAME COSTON—COSTON FIRE SIGNALS—AUSTRIAN FIELD SIGNAL APPARATUS.

DIAL OR CADRAN SYSTEMS.

In the semaphoric class of instruments, for communicating at a distance, a great variety of forms adapted to various service were displayed in the Exposition. The most common form was that of the dial or cadran, containing around the circumference of a disk the letters of the ordinary alphabet and the numerals. This kind of instrument is operated by a handle, which moves an indicator to the desired letter upon the disk. This movement causes, by a "step by step" action, an index upon a dial at a distance to move and stop at the same letter. The interior machinery of these various instruments is as various as in ordinary clock movements for the indication of time. All of this class of semaphores have long been invented and in use in the United States, and are well adapted to special service, usually on more limited circuits, and for private use, between places of business in or near cities, between private residences, and between railway stations. The indication of the common letter on the dial dispenses with the necessity, in the ordinary operator, of becoming familiar with a conventional code; but the operation is necessarily slow, and, therefore, not so well adapted to administrative or commercial purposes as the telegraphic apparatus, which has the paramount advantage of leaving its record, a convenience which the simple dial or cadran apparatus does not possess. Many of these dial semaphores in use in Europe are admirably constructed in the ateliers of those accomplished mechanicians Digney frères, Bréguet and Froment, in Paris, Siemens & Halske, in Berlin, Hipp, in Neufchatel, and many in England and in other countries, displaying the greatest beauty and perfection of workmanship.

SOUNDERS, OR ACOUSTIC SEMAPHORES.

CATON'S FIELD SOUNDER.

No. 75 is designated in the catalogue as "Pocket field telegraph apparatus," and is exhibited by J. D. Caton, esq., of Ottawa, Illinois. It is what is called a sounder in some of the treatises on the telegraph. It is a direct offspring of the semaphoric quality of the Morse recording in-instrument. The sound of the pen lever in recording with the Morse apparatus indicates also to the *ear* the signs of the Morse code that are at the same time being indicated to the *eye* upon the moving strip of paper. The sounds of these letters hold the same relation to the written telegraphic letters that speech does to written or printed language.

As some misapprehension exists as to the origin and nature of the acoustic semaphore, a few words of explanation and correction will not be considered out of place.

There is a peculiarity inherent in the nature of the original Morse code, which adapts it for recognition by each of four at least of the senses. It addresses not merely the sight by its written character, but the hearing, the taste, and the touch. It allows therefore, of course, recognition by sound. This quality of the Morse code, of being recognized by more than one of the senses, does not belong to ordinary alphabetic characters, and arises from its novel construction. The principle of the Morse code is this: it is formed from broken or unequal parts of a continuous line. It is composed of shorter and longer lines, or, as they are usually styled, dots and dashes, the shorter line being a dot, and the longer a dash. Each letter therefore is a line, or group of lines of different lengths, each group being a combination of these elementary parts, differing from all the other groups. For example, A is represented by a short and a long line, thus, - —; B, by a long line and three short ones, thus, — - - -; N, by a long line and a short one, thus, — -, and so on. These differences are at once recognized by the eye when written, but in the process of writing them by the Morse apparatus each group or letter is also indicated to the ear by its sound. The rationale of this peculiarity is this: in writing or printing either the dot or the dash in these groups the pen-lever produces two sounds, as well in making a dot as in making a dash. One of the two sounds is caused by the stroke of the pen-lever against the stop, which limits its motion in one direction, and the other of the two sounds is caused by the stroke against the stop, which limits its motion in the other direction. These sounds are the natural and ordinary accompaniment of the process of writing or printing the letters.

It might seem, at first blush, that, as each dot and each dash has equally two sounds, the one would be confounded with the other; but the difference by which a dot and a dash is distinguished the one from the other is, not by the number of the sounds, but by the difference of the interval, in the respective cases, between the first and second sound. In the one case, that of the dot, the two sounds which indicate it are separated by a short interval of time; in the other case, that of a dash, the two sounds have a *longer* interval between them. This difference of interval very soon becomes familiar to the ear, and enables the operator to hear as well as to see the transmitted dispatch. This acoustic effect is, in fact, the half-way result of a process arrested before its entire completion; completed, indeed, to the ear, but not, as yet, to the eye. Or the whole process may perhaps be better described as producing two results, either of which suffices, and therefore either may be dispensed with at pleasure, or both used together. This choice of results is exemplified in the various instruments using the Morse code. This sounder, for example, dispenses with the writing apparatus, and thus becomes a semaphore; on the other hand, the various inking instruments dispense with the sound, and are wholly dependent upon the written record, while the embossing instruments using the dry point have the double advantage of both results: they have the aid of the ear as well as of the eye. The inking process, therefore, it will be perceived, while gaining an advantage in one direction, loses an advantage in another. It is noiseless, and in consequence has the disadvantage of the electro-chemical process. On this point Mr. Sabine hints at this disadvantage of noiselessness as a probable cause that the electro-chemical process has not been popular. He says (p. 180) "the noiseless operation of the electro-chemical telegraphs may have assisted in keeping this method of recording out of more general use. It is always indispensably necessary to combine an alarm with the system, to call the attention of the manipulator—not so necessary with the Morse, which is, in working, always accompanied by the rattle of the beam and armature." Another disadvantage of the electro-chemical process is hinted at—that it lacks an economic arrangement for translation; that is, as a relay or means of repetition, which is an inherent, natural advantage in the Morse embossing system.

The first acoustic semaphore using the Morse code was the original recording instrument shown by the writer in 1835, at which time this acoustic peculiarity was not only noticed, but was then made known to others, and was considered of sufficient importance to be secured by letters patent drawn up in 1837. The claim therein is for a mode of communicating intelligence "by signs and sounds, or either."

The pen-lever in all the earlier instruments, as at this day, had this acoustic character, and whether recording or not upon the moving strip of paper, distinctly indicated the letter by its sound. It should be remarked that this acoustic quality rendered any other alarm unnecessary.

The sounder exhibited in the American section is the Morse pen lever, without the pen, thus separating from the register the acoustic portion, which is neatly compacted in a box no larger than a snuff-box. The following description of the instrument is taken from the report upon the United States section: "This instrument consists of a pair of helices, each two inches long and three-fourths inch in diameter, encased in a thin cylinder of hard rubber. They are wound with No. 36 insulated copper wire. The armature is one and five-eighths inch long, one-twentieth of an inch thick, and one-quarter of an inch wide. The sounding lever, of brass, is one and a half inch long, is placed horizontally, from the center of which drops a perpendicular arm, to which the armature is attached. The free end of the sounding lever plays between the milled heads of two set screws, the upper of which is inserted in the lower. This connects with a branched anvil, the two legs of which rest upon a brass sounding board, one and three-eighths inch in diameter, which is concave beneath, and is attached with three screws to the bottom of the case, a diminutive adjusting spring, actuated by a milled head, adjusting post with milled headed connecting screws. At the opposite end of the magnet is a key of very thin tempered brass, one-quarter of an inch wide and one and three-quarters inch long, with ivory finger-piece, connecting points of platinum, and a current breaker with ivory handle. This completes the mechanical contrivances, and the whole is inclosed in a hard rubber case, with a cover like a snuff-box.

"The external dimensions, when shut, are, length, five inches; breadth, two and a quarter inches; height, one and a quarter inch. The ends of the box are semi-circular. The case stands upon four brass legs, three-eighths of an inch diameter and three-eighths of an inch long. Entire weight, ten and a quarter ounces.

"Here are all the instruments necessary for a complete telegraph office, where the operator receives by sound. No local circuit is required, but it is operated on the main circuit. The report is as clear, distinct, and audible as that of an ordinary sounder actuated by a local circuit. It is designed for use in the field or out of doors. A telegrapher will attach it to the main line anywhere in the country in five minutes, when he can send and receive messages with the same facility and accuracy that he can in a regular telegraph office. Mr. Caton states that during the war he supplied the government with a large number of these instruments, but was unable to fill all of the orders of General Stager, who had charge of the government telegraph department. Nearly all telegraph superintendents are supplied with them, as well as very many operators, who never travel without them. Their invaluable services in case of railroad accidents may be readily appreciated, and at the west they are in constant use. An account of their services thus rendered each year would fill a volume, and, really, no train should ever move without one, in the hands of a competent operator."

It was beautifully finished, and was sent to the Exposition by Judge J. D. Caton, of Ottawa, Illinois, and manufactured in Ottawa by Mr. Robert Heming, whose telegraphic instruments are among the best inthe country.

Various modifications of the acoustic apparatus have subsequently been made in Europe.

PROFESSOR STEINHEIL'S SOUNDER.

Professor Steinheil was the first in Europe, who attempted an acoustic method by causing the magnetic needle, by which he also recorded signs, to strike upon two bells of different tone, according as positive or negative currents were made to pass through the conductor.

SIR CHARLES BRIGHT'S SOUNDER.

Sir Charles Bright, in England, introduced, at a still more recentdate, an efficient modification of the acoustic apparatus upon the lines of the

British and Irish Magnetic Telegraph Company. The modification consisted in substituting two bells of different tones to indicate the Morse code in place of the stops used in the original Morse instrument, by which a louder as well as a varied sound was given, and utilizing the negative and positive currents to operate the bells. Experience would seem to have proved that of the two modes originally indicating the Morse code, to wit: by writing and by sound, the acoustic mode is becoming more extended and is even preferred in large districts for ordinary communication. The reports from various parts of the United States, from Great Britain, and from the East Indies show that it has some advantages over the writing mode; but when used as an instrument separated from the writing apparatus, it has the disadvantage common to all semaphores of having no record for justification or control. The bell apparatus is also said to be complained of in the larger offices, on account of the greater noise they produce creating confusion, but this defect is easily obviated by deadening the sound to any desired degree of loudness.

The substantial improvement, however, in Sir Charles Bright's modification of the sounder consists in applying the Morse adaptation of the electro-magnet to Steinheil's plan of using two bells of different tones, and operating them by the alternations of the positive and negative currents of electricity. In a recent letter of Sir Charles Bright to Professor Morse he says: "The sound instrument which I adopted for the magnetic company consists of two bells, dull in sound and differing in note, placed on each side of the operator about on a level with his ear. These are worked by a relay sending currents through one or the other, according to the signals required. Two keys are used for sending, one for the right hand, or positive current, the other for the left, or negative current. One wire is, of course, used. There is no difference in the duration of either signal, and in this is the saving of time, compared with the sounders (the Morse) used here, (in the United States,) where, in employing dots and dashes, the latter (I take it) require three times the duration of a dot. In the other the signals are all dots, but a Morse operator can use it by considering one key as a dot, the other as a dash, but sending dots on both. It is the quickest instrument of a non-mechanical kind."

On this it may be remarked that, theoretically at least, this modification of Sir Charles Bright's is the perfection of the sounder. In view, however, of the skill and ability displayed by the American operators in their results in speedy transmission with the Morse sounder, it is difficult to conceive that, practically, any improvement of it could be made. Yet, as there is theoretically an economy of time in Sir Charles Bright's modification, it may prove to be practically as well as theoretically better.

MORSE'S ORGAN-PIPE SOUNDER.

One of the modifications by Morse himself, experimented upon by him as early as 1845, gives the sound of each letter of the Morse code more accurately than any yet devised; and although not practically adopted, because of the greater advantages of the written mode in simplicity of apparatus, is yet, perhaps, worthy (at a time when the acoustic method is received with favor) to be revised and made practical, at least so far as to satisfy curiosity. The method devised by him was by an organ pipe so connected with a small bellows as to be opened and closed by the pen-lever, in the act of writing a dot or a dash. It is at once obvious that in indicating a dot, the pipe would give a short, sharp sound, but in indicating a dash the sound would be correspondingly prolonged. The short and long intervals, therefore, by which the dot and the dash are now distinguished, in the ordinary acoustic instruments, are, by this method, more completely expressed, reducing the code to *musical expression*, to crotchets, and semibreves. The disadvantage which suggets itself is the necessity of a bellows apparatus for a constant supply of air to the pipe, adding materially to the complication of the machinery; and it has also the inconvenience just alluded to, by its loudness, (which indeed might easily be moderated,) of confusing the ear where many instruments are within hearing of each other.

SIGNAL SEMAPHORES.

NIGHT SIGNALS, BY MADAME MARTHA J. COSTON.

This is a very ingenious and effective semaphore, which commends itself from its simplicity. Three lights of different colors, white, red, and green, are so flashed or burned in combinations representing the numerals 1, 2, 3, 4, 5, 6, 7, 8, 9, 0, and also two letters A and P—in all twelve combinations. The light is produced by the combustion of a peculiar pyrotechnic composition for each of the desired colors.

A handle or holder is all that is necessary, ordinarily, to hold the selected color:

A flash of white indicates the numeral	1
A flash of white followed by red	2
A flash of white followed by green	3
A flash of red	4
A flash of red followed by white	5
A flash of red followed by green	6
A flash of green	7
A flash of green followed by white	8
A flash of green followed by red	9
A flash of white, red, and green	0
A flash of white, red, and white	P
A flash of red, white, and red	A

When a communication is to be made, the white, red, and white are quickly and successively flashed, indicating the letter P, (prepare,) and when answered by red, white, and red, indicating the letter A; the correspondence commences by flashing the respective colors of the numbers desired to be sent.

Experience has demonstrated the usefulness of the "Coston fire signals," and they have passed the practical test with success. They have been approved and recommended, not only by our own accomplished naval officers, and our marine department, but also by the French ministry of the marine, and distinguished French officers. They have been definitively introduced into our own service, and also into that of France.

The accomplished inventor has more recently improved her system, by the use of what she calls parachute rockets discharged from a pistol or gun; but on the same principle of colored lights.

AUSTRIAN FIELD SIGNAL APPARATUS.

The semaphoric apparatus No. 52, "Austrian field apparatus," is an example of the adaptability of the Morse code not merely to the telegraph, but to almost every kind of semaphore, whether they be signals on land, or through the Atlantic cable, or by flags in the marine. Various semaphores have adopted this convenient code, by some modification of it on the same principles.

This field apparatus consists of a pole some fifteen feet in height, having at its top three disks of thin metal, each turning upon a horizontal axis within a circular frame, so as to present, at will, its full orb, or the thin diameter. These three disks are thus arranged ○ ○○. The upper disk represents, when shown singly, the dot of the Morse code; the two lower disks, shown together, represent the dash or line of the Morse code. The mode of its action may be illustrated by describing the process in conveying to a different station the word *fire*. This word in the Morse code would be thus written, [– – — – – – – — – –.] The disks in their normal state are supposed to present to the spectator their thin edge, and so are invisible at a distance. The first movement, therefore, in conveying to a distance the word fire, is to darken the upper disk, by turning it so as to show its full orb thus, ⊙ ○○; when this is recognized at the distant station, by a similar movement there, the disk resumes its normal condition, having indicated a dot. This movement is repeated, conveying a second dot, and then the two lower disks are darkened ○ ⊙⊙, indicating a line, after which the upper disk is once more darkened, adding another dot to complete the letter F, its completion being indicated to the distant station by the darkening of all the disks at once. In this manner all the letters, numerals or signs of the Morse code can be indicated, and correspondence to any extent may be carried on semaphorically by this simple arrangement. This mode is slow, but other circumstances being favorable, it is efficient.

CHAPTER III.

CODES.

ETYMOLOGY OF THE WORD CODE—THE ORIGINAL MORSE CODE AND THE MODERN MODIFICATIONS—ITS UNIVERSAL ADOPTION—THE ALPHABET, CYPHERS, PUNCTUATION MARKS, AND OFFICIAL SIGNS—SPACE-LETTERS—INVESTIGATION OF THE FREQUENCY OF OCCURRENCE OF THE VARIOUS LETTERS IN THE LANGUAGE—INCONVENIENCE OF CONFOUNDING THE SPACE-LETTERS WITH OTHERS—THE EUROPEAN MORSE CODE CONTAINS FIVE ADDITIONAL SIGNS—DIFFICULTIES ATTENDING A CHANGE IN THE ESTABLISHED CODE—PROPOSED IMPROVEMENT OF PUNCTUATION AND OFFICIAL SIGNS—THE MORSE CODE AS MODIFIED AND ADOPTED IN EUROPE SHOULD BE ADOPTED IN THE WESTERN CONTINENT.

THE MORSE CODE.

Without occupying time in discussing the etymology of the word *code*, (which strictly means a digest or collection of laws reduced to order,) or the propriety of its use in the present connection, it is found to be applied in the various reports on telegraphy, and it is therefore adopted as a concise term to designate the system of signs, or signals, employed in the telegraphic and semaphoric instrumentalities of the present day.

As pertinent directly to these instrumentalities the codes adopted and proposed come to be treated of.

Given the first idea of a telegraph in its strict etymological sense, or the possibility of writing or printing at a distance, the most natural first thought would be to devise some mode of expressing, by writing or printing, at a distance, the letters or numerals of the inventor's native language.

The complication of machinery required for this purpose was then the first serious difficulty to be overcome. To express numerals by dots seemed to be the simplest mode of obviating this difficulty, for when this simplicity was left out of view, the complication of machinery to produce the ordinary letters or numerals seemed an insurmountable obstacle.

Therefore, in considering the mechanical means at command for producing at a distance any permanent mark, it was perceived that by means of the electro-magnet the motion of a lever, up and down, could be easily and surely commanded; and if a pencil at one extremity of it were made to strike upon a piece of paper a dot would be made whenever the magnet was charged and quickly discharged. This action, however, without a further device, would be unavailing to produce variety, since the lever motion is limited to the simple movement of up and down. Hence the idea of moving the paper at a regular rate beneath the pencil. Thus a dot could be made on the moving ribbon of paper, which, passing onward, the paper was ready to receive (after an interval more or less extended) another dot or series of dots. Thus the ability

The original Morse code and its modern modifications.

ORIGINAL MORSE CODE.	Units. 1 2 3 4 5 6 7 8 9 10 11 12	MODERN MODIFICATIONS.	Units. 1 2 3 4 5 6 7 8 9 10 11 12	
Letters—				
A	· —			
B	— · · ·			
C	· · ·	C	— · — ·	
D	— · ·			
E	·			
F	· — ·	F	· · — ·	the original Q.
G	— — ·			
H	· · · ·			
I	· ·			
J	— · —	J	· — — —	
K	— · —			
L	———	L	· — · ·	the original X.
M	— —			
N	— ·			
O	· ·	O	— — —	
P	· · · · ·	P	· — — ·	the original 1, numeral.
Q	· · — ·	Q	— — · —	
R	· · ·	R	· — ·	the original F.
S	· · ·			
T	—			
U	· · —			
V	· · · —			
W	· — —			
X	· — · ·	X	— · · —	the original 9, numeral.
Y	· · · ·	Y	— · — —	
Z	· · · ·	Z	— — · ·	
&	· · · ·			
Numerals—				
1	· — — ·	1	· — — — —	
2	· · — · ·	2	· · — — ·	
3	· · · — ·	3	· · · — —	
4	· · · · —	4	· · · · —	
5	— — —	5	· · ·	
6	· · · · · ·	6	— · · · ·	
7	— — · ·	7	— — · · ·	
8	— · · · ·	8	— — — · ·	
9	— · · —	9	— — — — ·	
0	———	0	— — — — —	
Punctuation signs—				
Period .	· · — — · ·	.	· · · · · ·	Period.
Comma ,	· — · —	;	— · — · — ·	Semicolon.
Interrog. ?	— · · — ·	,	· — · — · —	Comma.
Exclam. !	— — — ·	:	— — — · · ·	Colon.
Quota. " "	· — · — · — — —	?	· · — — · ·	Interrogation.
Parenth. ( )	· — · · —	" "	· — · · — ·	Quotation.
		!	— — · · — —	Exclamation.
		-	— · · · · —	Hyphen.
		'	· — — — — ·	Apostrophe.
		/	— — — — — —	Sign of fraction.
		( )	— · — — · —	Parenthesis.
			· · — — · —	Underscore.

to produce dots in groups at pleasure was demonstrated, and, consequently, groups of dots expressive of the various numerals were devised. In pursuing the experiments with the numerals whose elements were a simple dot and space, it was perceived that, by means of the moving paper, not merely a dot could be produced at pleasure, but if the magnet was kept charged while the paper was in movement, the pencil produced a line long in proportion to the time in which the magnet was charged. This fact introduced a third element for combination, to produce variety in the groups, indicating letters as well as numerals, to wit: the line or dash, so that dots, spaces, and lines, in any variety of combination, were at command for forming a code of signs. Hence originated what is now universally recognized as the Morse code.

ORIGINAL MORSE CODE.

To enable the inquirer to understand the modifications of that code which has become the universal telegraphic means of correspondence, the original code is given, (see diagram) together with the slight modern changes which experience has suggested as improvements.

THE MODIFIED MORSE CODE.

The following is the modified Morse code, adopted throughout the world, as used in France, Belgium, Holland, Prussia, Austria, Italy, Spain, Portugal, Switzerland, Russia, Sweden, Denmark, Norway, Turkey, Greece, Syria, Persia, Egypt, India, Africa, Great Britain, and also in Australia, and in other countries:

1. *Alphabet.*

Letter.	Sign.	Letter.	Sign.	Letter.	Sign.
A	· —	J	· — — —	T	—
Ä	· — · —	K	— · —	U	· · —
B	— · · ·	L	· — · ·	Ü	· · — —
C	· — ·	M	— —	V	· · · —
D	— · ·	N	— ·	W	· — —
E	·	O	— — —	X	— · · —
É	· · — · ·	Ö	— — — ·	Y	— · — —
F	· · — ·	P	· — — ·	Z	— — · ·
G	— — ·	Q	— — · —	Ch	— — — —
H	· · · ·	R	· — ·		
I	· ·	S	· · ·		

2. *Ciphers.*

Cipher.	Sign.	Cipher.	Sign.
1	· — — — —	6	— · · · ·
2	· · — — —	7	— — · · ·
3	· · · — —	8	— — — · ·
4	· · · · —	9	— — — — ·
5	· · · · ·	0	— — — — —

3. *Punctuation, &c.*

		Sign.			Sign.
Full stop	.	· · · · · ·	Sign of exclamation	!	— — · · — —
Semicolon	;	— · — · — ·	Hyphen	-	— · · · · —
Comma	,	· — · — · —	Apostrophe	'	· — — — — ·
Colon	:	— — — · · ·	Line of fraction	$\frac{3}{8}$	— — — — — —
Sign of interrogation	?	· · — — · ·	Parenthesis	( )	— · — — · —
*Inverted commas	" "	· — · · — ·	*Sign for underscoring,	John	· · — — · —

* To be placed before and after the respective signs.

4. *Official signs.*

	Sign.		Sign.
Public message	· · ·	Interruption	· · · · · · · · ·
Official telegraph message	· —	Conclusion	· — · — · — ·
Private message	· — — ·	Wait	· — · · ·
Call signal	— · — · — · —	Receipt	· — · · — · · — ·
Understood	· · · — ·		

The length of a dot being taken as a unit, the lengths of the different signs will be as follows:

A dash =3 dots.
The space between the signs of a letter=1 dot.
The space between the signs of 2 letters=3 dots.
The space between the signs of 2 words=6 dots.

On examining these codes with their modifications it will be seen that there are six letters or signs in the original Morse code, to wit, *C, O, R, Y, Z, &*, called *space letters*, because they are distinguished by spaces in the body of the letter. These letters were devised on the basis of simplicity, or economy of space, the inventor being anxious that no letter should exceed the extent of five units or dots in length, and it will be perceived that, with the single exception of the letter J, none of them exceed that number.

Another principle in constructing the code was also specially observed, the frequency of occurrence of the various letters in the language was studied, and for this purpose the arrangement of the type boxes in the cases of a printing office was examined in order to ascertain the relative frequency of the letters by the size of the type boxes. Those found to be most used were E, I, T, A, N, O, S, the letter E being the most copious of all; then followed the letters C, D, F, H, L, M, R, U. These letters occurring most frequently in the language were, therefore, constructed of the fewest and shortest elements. The letter E is represented by a single dot [-]; the I and T within the space of two dots or units; and so on, none of the rest (with the single exception mentioned above of the letter J) exceeding five dots or units.

All the numerals, the more readily to distinguish them from the letters, were each comprised within the value of six dots or units.

The space letters were very early found in practice to have the inconvenience of being confounded with other letters. For example, the C, [- - -] was apt to be mistaken for I, [- -], E, [-], or, if not well rendered, for S, [- - -], &c. But after the introduction of the alphabet into practical use, it became next to impossible to make the desired change, which was attempted by the inventor, even on the first public line; so it was reluctantly suffered to exist. Notwithstanding the defect has always been acknowledged by the inventor, and the substitution of other combinations for the space letters often proposed, yet so soon as the first operators had acquired the practical use of the original code, the change seemed hopeless.

The construction of this code originally on the basis of simplicity and economy of space, resulting in economy of time, furnishes an example of a good general principle, the principle of simplicity, carried to excess.

This defect in the code through the ingenuity of European savans, who have given it their attention, has been remedied in conformity with the general principles of the original code, but it still required more than ingenuity to accomplish the remedy. Governmental power was necessary to command the change, and thus to overcome the difficulty of change so early encountered in the United States in attempts to improve the original code.

The remedy consists in the substitution of other combinations of the short and long lines, in place of the space letters. This has been done, indeed, by some sacrifice of simplicity, and an increase of the aggregate amount of units in the entire code, but the inconvenience of the space letters has thus been remedied, and the modification is a substantial improvement.

The substituted groups for the space letters, however, were but five in number. In five other instances, indeed, the combination of dots and dashes in the original code representing a particular letter is changed to represent another. The original Q [. . — .] now represents F; the original X [. — . .] represents L; the original numeral 1 [. — — .] represents P; the original F [. — .] represents R; and the original numeral 9 [— . . —] represents X. These latter changes appear to be arbitrary, and no improvement. On the contrary the change adds a unit in extent to each of four of the letters, while the fifth alone (the R) remains the same in length as before.

The original F is..........	4 units.	The new F is............	5 units.
The original L is..........	4 units.	The new L is............	5 units.
The original P is..........	5 units.	The new P is............	6 units.
The original R is..........	4 units.	The new R is............	4 units.
The original X is..........	5 units.	The new X is............	6 units.
	22 units.		26 units.

It will be noticed that the established European Morse code contains five additional signs constructed on the same general principles, to represent peculiar accented letters not in the English alphabet, but necessary in the alphabets of the continent; these are:

A	[· — · —]	= 6 units.
É	[· · — · ·]	= 6 units.
Ö	[— — — ·]	= 7 units.
Ü	[· · — —]	= 6 units.
CH	[— — — —]	= 8 units.

Each of the numerals in the original Morse code is of the value of six units. The ten characters, therefore, for numerals amount, in aggregate value, to sixty units, while the aggregate value of the new signs for numerals is seventy-five units. Notwithstanding this addition, there is a substantial improvement in the construction of the new signs for numerals. Although the first four numerals, 1, 2, 3, 4, of the original code were as readily recognized as in the new arrangement by the number of dots commencing the sign, yet the last six numerals were not so ingeniously arranged for recognition as in the new arrangement, which is perfect. The first five numerals are readily recognized by the number of dots, while the last five, by counting each line of the sign as two, and adding the number of dots which end the sign, the cypher intended is unerringly given.

As a rule, it is not well hastily to insist on changes in the established code, to the disturbance and discomfort of so large and skillful a body as are the telegraph operators, for by every change they are compelled not merely to learn a new sign, but to *forget* an old one; and it is a question for international settlement whether it is not better to suffer a little inconvenience from an acknowleded imperfection than to attempt a remedy which must necessarily give annoyance to thousands.

IMPROVEMENT OF PUNCTUATION AND OFFICIAL SIGNS.

This remark is not intended to deter from the attempt to improve the defective punctuation signs and official signs which appear cumbersome and wasteful of space, and therefore of time. The inventor suggests the following substitute for these signs:

Proposed punctuation signs.

		Letters.	No. of units.	No. of units in adopted code.
Period	.	E ·	1	6
Semicolon	;	S · · ·	3	9
Colon	:	SS · · · · · ·	7	9
Comma	,	M — —	4	9
Interrogation	?	T —	2	8
Quotation	" "	U · · —	4	8
Exclamation	!	X — · · —	6	10
Hyphen	-	N — ·	3	8
Apostrophe	'	A · —	3	10
Sign of fraction	\	R · — ·	4	12
Parenthesis	( )	I.I. · · · ·	5	10
Underscore, or italics	——	I · ·	2	9
			44	108

This proposed improvement condenses this part of the code by reducing the aggregate value of the eleven punctuation signs to forty-four units of space; the original punctuation signs, only six in number, being of the aggregate value of forty-seven units of space, and the punctuation signs of the present adopted code being of the aggregate value of one hundred and eight units of space.

In this proposed change in the punctuation signs, two of the official signs are appropriated which can be transferred to the punctuation signs, and their places supplied in the official signs by other letters, to wit: The S [. . .] now used to signify "Public message," and proposed by the inventor to be transferred to signify "semicolon," may be supplied by I [. .], K [— . —]; and the A [. —] now used to signify "Official telegraph message," and proposed by the inventor to be transferred to signify "apostrophe," may be supplied by F [. . — .]. This adds, indeed, seven units of space to the aggregate length of the sum of official signs, but the "call signal" might easily be reduced to C [— . — .], which at once subtracts five units from the seven, and "conclusion" might be represented by D [— . .], which subtracts six units more; and "receipt" would bear reduction to R T [. — . —], which subtracts five units more from the aggregate, resulting in an aggregate gain of nine units.

The comparison between the present and the proposed "official signs" gives the following result.

The present official signs contain in the aggregate sixty-six units of space.

The proposed official signs contain in the aggregate fifty-seven units of space, thus:

Official signs.

		Units of Space.
Public message	· · — · —	8
Official message	· · — ·	5
Private report	· — — ·	6
Call signal	— · — ·	6
Understood	· · · — ·	6
Interruption	· · · · · · · · ·	9
Conclusion	— · ·	4
Wait	· — · · ·	6
Receipt	· — · —	7

Since the Morse code as modified prevails throughout the eastern continent, it is very desirable that in the United States—and, indeed, throughout the whole western continent—also, the slight changes adopted and proposed should be practically carried out by the telegraph companies, thus producing a *uniformity* in one great element of international intercourse, the *telegraphic alphabet of language*, and furnishing one realized example of that uniformity which so many of the master minds of the world at this day aspire to create in other world-wide interests.

For some further remarks on the principles of the code, see the article in this report on the *acoustic* character of the code, in treating of *semaphores* and the *sounder*.

CHAPTER IV.

BATTERIES, CONDUCTORS, AND INSULATORS.

FAILURE OF ALL ATTEMPTS TO EMPLOY FRICTIONAL ELECTRICITY FOR COMMUNICATING AT A DISTANCE—USE OF VARIOUS FORMS OF BATTERIES FOR GENERATING DYNAMIC ELECTRICITY—USE OF MAGNETO ELECTRICITY—FARMER'S THERMO-ELECTRIC BATTERY—LECLANCHÉ'S BATTERY—THE MAGNETO-ELECTRIC BATTERY OF S. HJORTH, OF COPENHAGEN—LADD'S DYNAMO-ELECTRIC APPARATUS—LETTER FROM DR. WERNER SIEMENS—OBSERVATIONS UPON THE CONVERSION OF MECHANICAL EFFECT INTO ELECTRIC CURRENTS WITHOUT THE EMPLOYMENT OF PERMANENT MAGNETS, BY DR. WERNER SIEMENS—SULPHATE OF MAGNESIA BATTERY—SUBMARINE TELEGRAPH CABLES—FARMER'S COMPOUND TELEGRAPH WIRE—THE MORSE BATHOMETER—PROPOSED NEW MODE OF LAYING AND RAISING SUBMARINE TELEGRAPH CABLES—INSULATORS AND INSULATION—BROOKS'S PARAFFINE INSULATOR—INSULATION TEST OF THE BROOKS AND OTHER INSULATORS—DAY'S KERITE INSULATOR—MEMOIR BY PROFESSOR SILLIMAN UPON INSULATION AND PROTECTION OF ELECTRICAL CONDUCTORS—ACTION OF OZONE UPON TELEGRAPHIC INSULATION—LETTERS UPON THE VALUE OF KERITE AS AN INSULATOR.

BATTERIES OR GENERATORS OF ELECTRICITY.

Static or frictional electricity has long since been discarded as an agent in the electrical instrumentalities for communicating at a distance. All attempts hitherto to make it practicable have failed, and all the devices for that purpose, however ingenious, as most of them were, must be consigned to the category of failures. The principal form of electricity, which has been effective, either in the semaphore or in the telegraph, is dynamic electricity, usually generated by the chemical action of acids upon metals, or the decomposition of metallic salts. The earliest form of Voltaic battery, even the first column of Volta, is available to produce the actual result required either of showing a signal, as in the semaphore, or making a record, as in the telegraph. The earliest form employed by Morse in 1835, and with success so far as to show the practicability of recording, was the well-known Cruikshanks battery. Since this early period many modifications and substantial improvements in the battery have been made, and the constant batteries of Daniel, of Grove, and of Smee, in England, and others on the European continent, have given greater facility in operating the instruments both of the telegraph and semaphore. But the introduction of magneto-electricity, one of the grand results of the generic discovery of Oersted, and of the more recent discoveries of Faraday, have furnished the means of constructing a new generator of electricity, which takes its place intermediately between the frictional and the Voltaic, having less quantity than the Voltaic and less uncontrolable intensity than the frictional instruments. The Voltaic, however, has the quality of giving more readily a continuous current, and is therefore better adapted to recording in all the instruments using the Morse code.

FARMER'S THERMO-ELECTRIC BATTERY.

The batteries exhibited have little of originality. With one or two exceptions, they generally show unimportant modifications of those long known.

The thermo-electric battery of Farmer, of Boston, (No. 74,) is one of novel construction, and deserving of special notice.

Fig. 15.

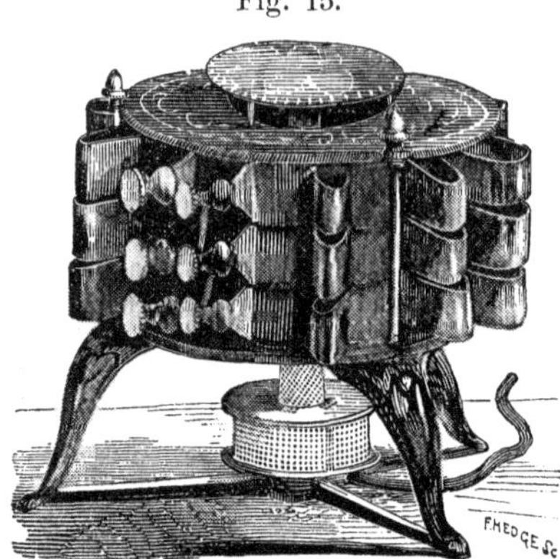

Farmer's Thermo-electric Battery.

The engraving (Fig. 15) represents this battery. It consists of three rings of nine pairs each. A common rubber tube conveys ordinary street gas to a gas burner or gas stove under the center of the battery. A deflector is placed at the top to keep the heat down in the center. All that is required to put the battery in operation is to turn on the gas and light at the burner. The battery acquires its maximum activity in a few moments, when it works continuously and constantly as long as it receives heat.

These batteries are made of various sizes, weighing from a few pounds to half a ton. One of this larger class is now in operation, and is capable of depositing about one pound of copper per hour, at an expense of five or six pounds of coal in the same time.

The smaller batteries are more conveniently operated by gas or lamp. These latter are very convenient for medical use or for telegraph local batteries. The somewhat larger battery gives all the effects of a series of cells, (of the acid batteries in common use.)

These batteries are admirably suited to the wants of the exact experimenter, and render the most useful assistance in their investigations where an absolutely constant current is required, being capable of working for an indefinite period without a perceptible variation in the strength of current which they deliver. Their utility is very apparent to the electrotyper who desires a uniform current, and to the electro-gilder and silver-plater they are especially commended, because they require no acids, mercury, or liquids of any kind in their operation.

The saving which they effect in time, attention, waste, their cleanliness, the readiness with which they can be put into operation, the small expense of working them, and their durability, commend them to all.

Where an establishment is doing sufficient work to require the use of one of such size as can be operated by coal as a fuel, the economical production of electricity by their use is very obvious, five or six pounds of coal being capable of evolving as much electricity as one and a half pound of zinc, five or six pounds of sulphuric acid, and one ounce of mercury.

These batteries, like any series of cells, can be coupled to suit the work they have to perform. As compared with the acid batteries, these batteries have been worked with Boston gas as follows: ten pairs equal to one Smee cell in power; twenty-four pairs equal to one Daniels cell in power; forty-four pairs equal to one Grove cell in power. But in calculating for a battery to perform work for an indefinite period, an addition of 50 per cent. upon the above list is recommended, as the heating power of gas differs very materially in different places. Naphtha has been used with perfect success, and found very economical.

The principal objects kept in view in this invention are, first, to make a battery of sufficient power to be available for industrial uses; second, that it should be reasonably durable; third, that it should be convenient to use; fourth, that it should not be too costly.

With regard to the first object, one has been constructed and used which has deposited 12 pounds of copper, from a sulphate of copper solution, in twenty-four hours, by the consumption of less than 110 pounds of anthracite coal. Smaller ones have been constructed that are most conveniently operated by a gas flame, and which will evolve 50,000 feet-pounds of electricity by the consumption of one pound of common coal gas.

These latter are made of various sizes, and capable of evolving from 20 to 300 feet-pounds of electricity per minute. A common pint-cup Grove cell will evolve 80 feet-pounds of electricity per minute. The current from this (gas-consuming) thermo battery is the most constant and uniform of any that I have ever used, and is admirably adapted to the requirements of exact research.

With regard to the second head, the durability of the thermo battery depends much on the temperature at which it is worked. At all temperatures there appears to be a gradual increase in the specific resistance of the alloys which enter into its composition, but the more slowly the lower the temperature of the heated junction. One of about 150 feet pounds per minute power has been in nightly use for nearly a year. Its power has not been recently measured, but it is still in working order. Some have been in almost daily use by physicians for nearly two years.

Third. The gas-consuming batteries are as convenient as need be, requiring only to be attached by a flexible or other pipe to a gas-burner. The large battery fired with coal needed attention every three or four hours.

Fourth. The thermo battery is much more costly than an acid battery of equivalent power, in the first instance; but the cost of daily maintenance is less. A thermo battery, equivalent in power to four or five Grove cells, costs about ninety dollars.

A thermo battery, to be heated by waste steam, could be operated at trifling cost, and would be very durable, but the amount required to do a given amount of work with only 120 degrees difference of temperature between the junctions, might be of inconvenient size and first cost.

In this battery the two elements used are, German silver for the negative pole, and an alloy of zinc and antimony for the positive pole. The proportions of the zinc and antimony used are, about ninety-six parts antimony and fifty-three parts zinc, as mixed in the melting pot. The pairs are arranged around a central source of heat; and the outer junctions are cooled by radiation and connection.

LECLANCHÉ'S BATTERY.

This battery is much in use in the French telegraph administration. It consists of a prism of carbon for its positive pole, which is surrounded by a mixture of peroxide of manganese and carbon pulverized, filling the porous jar. This jar is put into the glass jar containing a solution of sal ammoniac; within the same glass jar and solution is a prism of amalgamated zinc, forming the negative pole. Its action is thus: On closing the circuit, the sal ammoniac is decomposed, the chlorine of the solution is absorbed by the zinc, the negative pole; while the hydrogen and the ammoniac pass to the positive pole, reducing the peroxide of manganese. According to the inventor's explanation, "the peroxide of manganese mixed with carbon being a good conductor of electricity, the system may be considered as a single fluid element, in which the positive pole is formed of an artificial metal having a great affinity for hydrogen."

MAGNETO-ELECTRIC BATTERY OF S. HJORTH.

This invention by S. Hjorth, of Copenhagen, relates to improvements introduced into the construction of magneto-electric batteries, with a view to obtaining by a slow motion of the armatures any required quantity or intensity of electric fluid.

The improved battery may be constructed of different circles of bar magnets, set partly around and partly above each other, with corresponding intermediate armatures mounted on wooden or other suitable disks on a central shaft, made to rotate by suitable mechanism.[1]

When quantity of the electric fluid is required, the currents are collected by rings, and from thence pass by conductors to a commutator mounted at the upper end of the central shaft. When intensity is desired, the conductors may be connected in one length according to circumstances.

The armatures are provided with false poles, the dimensions of which correspond with those of a certain number of magnets of similar polarity; say for instance eight or nine bars. The changes of polarity in the armatures at each revolution will consequently be equal to the number of these armatures multiplied by the respective series of magnets of similar polarity.

The power developed being in ratio with the number of changes of

[1] Drawings of this apparatus, submitted with the report, are deposited in the library of the Department of State.—EDITOR.

polarity produced at each revolution, an advantage may be obtained by the application of equal numbers of armatures and magnets. This arrangement is composed of three disks, each provided with ninety-six armatures, corresponding with the same number of magnetic bars, so that each revolution gives rise to changes of polarity equal to

$$96 \times 96 = 9{,}216 \times 3 = 27{,}648.$$

The armatures are coiled with wire internally and externally. The two intermediate circles of permanent magnets are fixed to brass rings.

The armature wheel or disk is formed of hard wood or other suitable material, and is provided with two rings, composed of vertical bars overlapping each other, in which the armatures are geared.

It is evident that the concentric series of magnets and armatures, as also the number of these elements, may be increased or decreased according to the effect to be produced. In all cases, the armature disks should be arranged "step-ways," so that when the armatures of the first series have completely passed between the magnets, those of the following series reach but half way, and those of the third series only commence to be drawn in between the magnets. The force of attraction being thus added to the power applied to the central shaft, the motion of the latter is necessarily facilitated by increase in the power of the magnets.

The form, dimensions, and general details of construction of the apparatus above described may be varied according to its intended application.

LADD'S DYNAMO-ELECTRIC APPARATUS.

This apparatus is not in the catalogue, but was exhibited in the English department.

A French journalist thus enthusiastically speaks of it:

"In the judgment of all competent persons, the most astonishing object in the galleries of the Champ de Mars is the machine of Mr. Ladd, constructor of physical instruments, of London, exhibited under the name of Dynamo-Electric Apparatus. Very extraordinary in its principle, in its construction, and in its action, it is composed essentially of two plates of soft iron about two feet long, one foot wide, and four inches thick, kept at a distance of a few inches from each other. They are both of them attached by their ends to two kinds of cylindrical surfaces, also of soft iron, in the bosom or hollow of which turn two armatures of Siemen's cylinders, of soft iron, grooved upon their two faces and covered according to their length by insulated copper wire. An insulated copper wire sufficiently large surrounds also the two plates in compacted spirals perpendicular to their length, and going from one plate to the other, so as to form a closed circuit. The current pervades it through a commutator designed to maintain it always in the same direction. The second armature, on the contrary, is entirely out of the circuit of the first armature and of the plates of soft iron. It turns simply opposite the second poles of the plates, and becomes the seat of an induction current always in the same direction, which, conducted by the wires soldered to the two poles, goes to produce outside the effects of light, of heat, of motion, of affinity, or of chemical decomposition, as may be desired.

"It is perceived that in itself this whole mass of soft iron, of copper wires, without steel, without magnets, is absolutely inert. How can life and activity be given to it? By providing it with a small quantity of magnetism, by priming it magnetically. It is sufficient for this strictly to place properly the plates by putting them in the magnetic meridian, so that the terrestrial magnetism may communicate to it a slight magnetism. But it is better to make to pass once, and once for all, through the wire which surrounds the plates, the current from a Daniels's, Smee's, or Bunsen's battery, which, after having made them temporarily electro-magnets, leaves them, the circuit being broken, with a little of residual magnetism, which magnetism for the future (and if they are not left too long to themselves) renders them always ready for action, or to create torrents of electricity of which they become the source. We have thus passed from absolute inertia to static or powerful activity. Motion completes all the rest. It is sufficient, in fact, to turn at the same time the two armatures, so that in returning constantly upon itself, the inductive current engendered at first by the residual magnetism incessantly increases the polarity or the activity of the plates, which have become powerful electro-magnets, and so that the second armature becomes the point of departure of an electric current of quantity and intensity proportional to the rapidity of rotation of the armatures, or to the force expended by the operator. With the machine exhibited, of which we have given the dimension so small, the exterior current is equivalent to that of twenty-five or thirty Bunsen elements.

"It supplies a Foucault regulator of medium size, and maintains at a white heat a platinum wire of more than a yard in length and half a millimeter in diameter. Here then is the immediate transformation, from the only condition, a small quantity of residual magnetism, by means of mechanical motion, first of power, next of electrical effects, then luminous, calorific, and chemical, &c. Nothing in fact is more simple, more effective. Nothing also is more grand, more unexpected, more mysterious. Mr. Ladd has borrowed from Mr. Wyld his plates, leaving out the magneto-electrical apparatus, substituting for it simply the residual magnetism and adding a second armature, which is the new element of his invention. He has taken from Messrs. Wheatstone and Siemens their return of the current upon itself, forcing it thus to increase itself, constantly multiplying itself, and like them rejecting the battery, for which there is no necessity."

If others do not go quite so far as this earnest French writer in designating the apparatus of Mr. Ladd as the "most astonishing object" in the whole Exposition, they will certainly agree with him in his admiration of the *effects* of this beautiful instrument, and in his designation of them as "grand, unexpected, and mysterious." Mr. Ladd is stated to have borrowed from Messrs. Wheatstone and Siemens their method of causing the current to return upon itself.

An account is given of this discovery from the pen of the discoverer, the eminent Dr. Werner Siemens, of Berlin, who seems to have observed this effect and utilized it, apparently concurrently with Professor Wheatstone, but in reality a little before him, as will be seen by the following letter addressed to Professor Morse:

"BERLIN, *December* 30, 1867.

"Herewith I send you the translation of my communication to the Academy of Sciences in Berlin. I have had it done in London, for we are very weak in English here. As you see by the date of the communication, the publication took place about one and a half month sooner than my brother's and Mr. Wheatstone's speech in London. Already, in November of last year, my first machine was in working and made known to the scientific men here. Wheatstone added something new to it. Ladd has the merit of having shown a larger machine than that in operation in Paris. I had not enough machine power in the Prussian department, and on that account did not take a very large machine with two cylinders, like Ladd's. If you should visit Berlin on your return journey, (which I hope,) I can show you this machine, which gives a brilliant electric light and produces ten cubic centimeters of oxygen and hydrogen gas per second. I could also show you other interesting apparatus. A new mechanical tachygrapher for Morse writing, and an electric distance measurer. This would be especially useful to steamships, as with them we can measure the exact distance of steamers, light-houses, coasts, &c., while in motion."

"ON THE CONVERSION OF MECHANICAL EFFECT INTO ELECTRIC CURRENT WITHOUT THE EMPLOYMENT OF PERMANENT MAGNETS.—When two parallel wires forming part of the circuit of a galvanic battery are approached to or separated from each other, a diminution or augmentation of the strength of current in the whole circuit is observed, according as the movement is in the direct or the inverse direction of the forces which the currents in two wires exercise reciprocally upon each other.

"The same phenomenon is observable still more remarkably when the poles of two electro-magnets, whose wires form parts of the same galvanic circuit, are made to approach or recede from each other. If the direction of the current in one of the wires is changed at the moment of their greatest or least distance, as is the case in all electro-dynamic rotating apparatus, a lasting diminution of the current occurs as soon as the apparatus is put into motion. This diminution of the current of the battery by opposite induction current it is which renders it impossible to employ galvanic electricity successfully as a motive for the production of mechanical effects. Suppose such a machine to be turned backward by some foreign force, it is evident that these induction currents must add themselves to that of the battery, which they proportionally strengthen; and since an increase of this circuit current is necessarily followed by an increase of magnetism in the soft-iron cores, and then again by a further corresponding increase of currents, and so on, the accumulation very soon reaches a point at which the galvanic battery may be removed from the circuit without occasioning any perceptible diminution in the resulting current. The moment the rotation is interrupted, however, the current ceases and the magnetism vanishes. Sufficient magnetism remains, nevertheless, in the iron to cause the process of accumulation to recommence from the moment that the rotation is renewed. It is only necessary, therefore, to magnetize the iron once by a galvanic current of short duration in order to render it forever afterwards capable of being recalled into action by simple rotation.

"The direction of the current depends upon the polarization of the residuary magnetism; and it can only be changed when, by means of a galvanic current, the residuary magnetism of the iron is changed.

"The effects here described take place also with every electro-magnetic machine whose movements depend upon the attraction and repulsion of electro-magnets whose wires form a single circuit. Nevertheless, in order to provide apparatus especially for showing powerfully the phenomena of the dynamo element, a particular construction is found to give the best results. The wire of the stationary electro magnet must have a sufficient magnetic inertia, so that the strength of the attained magnetism does not diminish during the reversing of the current in the wire of the rotating armature. It is also essential that the armature should be so constructed that during its rotation the opposite polar faces of the electro-magnet should be always magnetically closed. These conditions are best fulfilled by the employment of the band form of armature proposed by me some years ago, and which has since then come very generally into use. The armature in question consists of a cylinder of soft iron rotating upon its axis. It carries an insulated wire wound in two deep longitudinal grooves, one in each side. The poles of a battery of permanent magnets, or, in this case, those of the stationary electro-magnet, are cut out so as to let the armature rotate with the least possible space between them.

"By means of a machine constructed upon this principle, if the proportions of the various component parts are justly determined and the commutator properly placed, and a sufficient velocity of rotation given to the barrel armature, a current may be produced in the wire which is so intense that it develops heat enough to burn the covering with which the wire is insulated. This accident, however, can be avoided, when the machine is required to be kept in constant action, by the introduction of resistances or by moderating the velocity of rotation.

"Magneto-electro inductors do not increase in power proportionally with an increase of dimension, whereas with the machine in question the reverse is the case. The reason of this is that in permanent magnets the magnetism increases in a very small ratio to the weight of metal of which they are made, and that with a battery of permanent magnets it is impossible to concentrate their action upon a limited surface without their mutually diminishing their strength to a very material extent. On this account steel magnets are not well adapted for employment in magnet inductors which are required to produce very strong currents. It is true that such machines have been made with permanent magnets, which have given an intense electric light, but, in order to attain this, they were required to be of colossal dimensions, and were correspondingly expensive. In addition to this, the magnets lost very soon the major part of their magnetism, and the machine therefore its force.

"Mr. Wyld, of Birmingham, has lately constructed a machine for the production of powerful magneto-electric currents, whose capability he has increased by the employment of two barrel inductors of my construction, as described above. In the larger of the two he has substituted an electro-magnet for the battery of permanent magnets, setting it in action by the current of the smaller one, and as the electro-magnet becomes more strongly magnetic than permanent magnets could, the resulting current is correspondingly stronger.

"It is easily seen that Wyld has, by this construction, considerably obviated the difficulties found in employing steel magnets. But independently of the inconvenience attending the use of two inductors, his apparatus has still the disadvantage that it is directly dependent upon the steel magnets of the first inductor for the efficiency of its operations."

SULPHATE OF MAGNESIA BATTERY.

A new battery is described by Mr. McGowan, general superintendent of telegraphs in Victoria, Australia, as producing an economy over the sulphate of copper battery, used for the local battery to work the register.

This form is known as the sulphate of magnesia battery, and has been patented. "The containing cell is of more than ordinary large dimensions; the negative and positive elements are copper and zinc, cylindrical in form, and the exciting fluids are, 1, sulphate of magnesia, in the form of a nearly saturated solution; 2, sulphate of copper in broken crystals. The former surrounding the metals in the containing vessel; the latter, in partial solution, admitted through a perforation at the extremity of a conical glass receiver placed within the interior cylinder."

CONDUCTORS, CABLES, ETC.

SUBMARINE TELEGRAPH CABLES.

In consequence of the success which has attended the use of submarine telegraph cables, and especially the great success of the Atlantic cable enterprise, the attention of the skillful has of late been turned to the importance of improving and perfecting them.

There were many electrical experiments made with submarine conductors for various scientific purposes previous to their application to telegraphy.

It is believed that the first submarine telegraph line was laid and operated in New York harbor by Morse, in October, 1842. Although destroyed early after its submersion, by the anchor of a vessel getting under way, it was not destroyed until the fact of its ability to transmit dispatches was fully demonstrated. The gold medal of the American Institute was bestowed for this success.

Since that date the skill of European, especially of English, French, and Prussian savans, has succeeded not only in improving the construction of submarine cables, but in extending them in various directions from the United Kingdom across rivers, straits, and channels, and through seas, until the islands and continents of the eastern hemisphere are to a great extent telegraphically united, and the great enterprise of the day, the Atlantic telegraph, through the skill and perseverance and capital of English and Americans, has been the overcoming of the apparently insurmountable obstacle of an ocean deemed until recently unfathomable. It is unnecessary here more than to allude to this well-known enterprise, since the exhaustive history of it is familiar to all who have read the history of the Atlantic telegraph in the graphic pages of Doctor Russell and the Reverend Henry Field.

COMPOUND TELEGRAPH WIRE.

As directly connected with the improvement of submarine cables, attention is drawn to the "compound telegraph wire," the invention of Moses G. Farmer, esq., of Boston, who exhibited the thermo electric battery, already described, page 52.

Mr. Farmer, in a letter to Professor Morse, dated Boston, July 29, 1868, thus describes this valuable improvement, and the tests to which it has been subjected:

"I sent to you, a little time since, a pamphlet relating to our new compound telegraph wire, composed of a steel core and a copper covering, the whole coated with an alloy, principally tin, for preservative purposes. You will take in at a glance the numerous advantages of this wire.

"As has been most fully shown by Thomson's researches, and amply demonstrated by the working of the Atlantic cable, the speed at which a line can be worked is directly as its conductivity, and inversely as its electro-static capacity. The distance, also, which can be reached is directly as the conductivity, and as the degree of insulation. Anything, therefore, which improves the conductivity, or diminishes the static capacity, or increases the insulation, is a benefit.

"Let us look for a moment at the comparative conductivity, strength, and specific weight of iron, steel, and copper. I have carefully measured and recorded one or all of these elements for more than fifty samples in common use. I find upon an average that from two and three-quarters to three miles of common telegraph iron wire would break of its own weight if suspended vertically; about one mile and three-quarters of copper, and about seven and a half miles of the steel which we use. I copy my coefficients:

Steel, 7.47
Galvanized iron, 2.91
Copper, 1.72 $\left(\frac{Tl}{w}\right)$

"Now, for weight per mile, take the diameter of the wire in inches, and multiply its square by—

For steel, 13373.
For iron, 13800.
For copper, 15400. $\left(\frac{w}{ld^2}\right)$

"The result will be the weight per mile, 5280 feet.

"Now, for conductivity, assume as unity a round wire of chemically pure copper, one-twentieth of an inch in diameter; it would weigh thirty-nine and one-ninth pounds per mile. I will copy my latest coefficients, which, if multiplied by the weight per mile, will give the actual conductivity in terms of the unit above assumed, viz:

$$\left(\frac{cl}{w}\right)$$

For steel,	.00262.
For copper,	.02045.
For galvanized iron,	.00355.

"The coefficient for copper, .02045, is one for commercial copper, which I used in making up the tables in the pamphlet referred to. We now use a copper, for which the proper coefficient is .02301, or ninety per cent. of pure copper, (which would be .02556.)

"The resistance of 5280 feet of pure copper wire, weighing 39.11 pounds, would be about 21.3 B. A. units.

"Now, with the help of these coefficients, let us examine two or three wires. No. 8 iron wire weighs three hundred and seventy-five pounds per mile. (*Vide* Shaffner, L. Clark, M. G. Farmer.) Hence its tensile strength, or the weight which would break a short length of it, would be $T=2.9\times375=1087$ pounds, and its conductivity would be $C=.00355\times375=1.331$—Farmer's latest; ($C=1.298$, L. Clark.) This refers to ordinary galvanized iron wire, at about ten or ten and a half cents per pound, and not Washburn's best at fourteen cents.

"Now, take fifty-six pounds per mile of steel:

Its $T=7.47\times56=418.$
Its $C=.00262\times56=.1467.$

"Take, now, fifty-six pounds of copper per mile, and we have:

Its $T=1.72\times56=96.$
Its $C=.02045\times56=1.145.$
Or its $C=.02301\times56=1.288.$

"Now the combined strength of the two would be—

T steel + T copper = T compound.
$418+96=514$ pounds.

"And the combined conductivity would be—

C. steel + C. copper = C. compound.

.146+1.145=1.291.

"Or, as we now make it—

.146+1.288=1.434.

"Thus we have a compound wire weighing one hundred and twelve pounds per mile, having a conductivity of from 1.291 to 1.434, according to the copper used, fully equal, if not superior, to that of average No. 8 galvanized iron wire, (1.298 to 1.331,) which compound wire will require $\frac{514}{112}$=4.58, or four and a half miles, to be suspended vertically to break of its own weight, being more than fifty per cent. stronger than iron wire in proportion to the weight which it has to sustain. Hence it can probably be put up with fewer poles per mile, thus increasing the degree of insulation.

"I will here insert two tables:

Galvanized iron wire.

Posts.	Sag.	$T\ i$	C	T	$\frac{w}{l}$	$\frac{Ti}{T}$
38	1	144.3	1.136	928	320	.155
38	2	72.2	1.136	928	320	.077
38	3	48.1	1.136	928	320	.052

Compound wire.

Posts.	Sag.	$T\ i$	C	T	$\frac{w}{l}$	$\frac{Ti}{T}$
23	1	140	1.331	514	112	.272
23	2	70	1.331	514	112	.136
22	3	47	1.331	514	112	.091

"So that with twenty-three posts per mile, instead of thirty-eight, the insulation would be 33—23÷23=$\frac{65}{100}$= sixty-five per cent. better, and with a sag of two feet, the strain on the wire at the insulator would be only about one-seventh of that required to break a short length of the wire; and with a sag of only one foot, the strain would be less than one-third of its ultimate strength. The uniformity and homogeneity of the steel render it less likely to break from flaws, (and the short experience which we have had with it shows this.) The saving of cost per transportation is evident at a glance.

"Now let us look at a larger wire. Suppose 187 pounds per mile of steel and 188 pounds per mile of copper equal 375 pounds per mile, (same weight as a No. 8 galvanized iron, which has a tensile strength of 1087,) and a conductivity of 1.331 (at best average:)

	$\frac{w}{l}$	T	C	$\frac{Tl}{w}$
Steel	187	1397	.490	7.47
Copper	188	329	4.324	1.72
Summary	375	1720	4.814	4.59

"Here we have an increase over No. 8 of $1720-1087 \div 1087 = \frac{58}{100}$, or fifty-eight per cent. in tensile strength, an increase of $4.814-1.331 \div 1.331 = 261$ per cent.; or, in other words, we could reach three and a half times as far with the compound wire as with the iron of equal weight per mile, while the insulation could be improved by the use of fewer poles per mile, this wire being nearly sixty per cent. the stronger."

Table showing the relative weight, strength, and conductivity of the compound and other wires.

	$\frac{w}{l}$	T	C	$\frac{C}{C\ fe.}$
Table No. 1	375	1091	1.331	1
Table No. 2:				
Steel	187	1397	.490	......
Copper	188	325	4.324	......
Compound	375	1722	4.814	3.61
Table No. 3:				
Steel	119	889	.311	......
Copper	119	205	2.737	......
Compound	238	1094	3.048	2.29
Table No. 4:				
Steel	52	388	.136	......
Copper	52	89	1.196	......
Compound	104	477	1.332	1
Table No. 5:				
Steel	78	583	.204	......
Copper	297	511	6.831	......
Compound	375	1094	7.035	5.28
Table No. 6:				
Steel	357	2768	.935	......
Copper	18	31	.414	......
Compound	375	2799	1.349	1
Table No. 7:				
Steel	136	1016	.356	......
Copper	43	74	.989	......
Compound	179	1090	1.345	1
Table No. 8:				
Steel	56	418	.147	......
Copper	56	96	1.288	......
Compound	112	514	1.435	1.07

Explanation of Columns.—1st, $\left(\frac{w}{l}\right)$ weight per mile; 2d, (T) tensile strength; 3d, (C) conductivity; 4th, $\left(\frac{C}{C\ fe.}\right)$ conductivity compared with common No. 8 galvanized wire.

Table No. 1 contains the elements for the average of No. 8 galvanized iron telegraph wire; table No. 2, compound wire of equal weight; table No. 3, compound wire of equal tensile strength; table No. 4, compound wire of equal conductivity; table No. 5, compound wire of equal weight and tensile strength; table No. 6, compound wire of equal weight and conductivity; table No. 7, compound wire of equal tensile strength and conductivity; table No. 8, compound wire, our ordinary equivalent of No. 8 galvanized iron wire, such as costs ten to eleven cents per mile at present.

The improvement of Mr. Farmer in the construction of telegraph wire is considered of so much importance as to warrant the insertion here of a more detailed specification of its advantages; and in view of the obstacles encountered in the construction of lines in the Ottoman Empire, to which the energetic director of Turkish telegraphs alludes in his letter to the United States minister resident in Constantinople, inserted in Chapter VI, (obstacles occasioned by the accumulation of ice upon the wires in certain localities,) we specially commend the fact that the compound wire seems specially adapted to obviate these difficulties:

"There is a growing tendency in this and other countries to employ larger wire for telegraph purposes, in order to obtain a greater conducting capacity.

"Notwithstanding the many disadvantages attending the use of large telegraph wire, No. 4 has been adopted on important lines and for long circuits, in England, Russia, and other countries, solely for its superior conductivity; and it is well understood by telegraphers in general, that for the rapid and successful operations of the circuits, much depends upon this element. Especially is this the case in wet weather and upon long lines.

"Under certain conditions of the lines, consequent upon wet weather, *superior conductivity* will accomplish that which increased battery power utterly fails to do; and repeaters at intermediate offices, with their necessary main batteries, accomplish but imperfectly and unsatisfactorily, as a general rule, and in many cases fail to do altogether.

"Pure copper wire, having a conducting capacity of nearly seven times that of galvanized iron wire, has, of course, a great advantage in this respect for telegraph purposes. Its use, however, has been prevented in consequence of lack of sufficient strength to sustain itself.

"In the American compound telegraph wire this vital objection to the employment of copper alone for this purpose is obviated, and a conductivity and relative strength, superior to that of galvanized iron, are combined in a lighter wire.

"The composite parts of this wire are steel and copper, the steel forming the core, and serving mainly for strength, while the copper serves more especially as a superior conductor.

"In regard to relative strength it is well known that the breaks in ordinary galvanized telegraph wire, occasioned by accumulations of ice and snow, and from other causes, occur at weak points, or at imperfections which are caused by flaws existing in the iron before galvanizing, as well as from the effects of that process.

"We therefore claim that our compound wire, even with a relative strength no greater, theoretically, than that of a galvanized iron wire, will be much less liable to breakage from these causes, in consequence of the uniformity of strength in the steel core, while, in fact, the relative strength itself, of the compound wire, is very much the better of the two. (See table beyond.)

"Steel wires, of sizes varying from No. 12 to No. 16, stretched from pole to pole, across streams from one-quarter to three-quarters of a mile in width, in the United States, which have withstood the accumulations of ice and sleet for years, are good illustrations in this connection. One special instance may be cited of a No. 16 steel wire, between fourteen hundred and fifteen hundred feet in length, which has been in operation across the Kennebec River, in Maine, for the past eight years; and which, we are informed by the superintendent of the line, has parted twice only during that period—in each case having been untwisted at a joint by the great strain upon it caused by an immense accumulation of ice, the wire itself remaining intact.

"The advantages of increased conductivity and strength having been briefly set forth, there are other practical advantages to be gained in the use of the American compound telegraph wire, to which we would respectfully call the attention of contractors and telegraph companies.

"Large wire is used only because of its superior conductivity; and it is obvious that a light wire is preferable in handling and stringing, which can be done with less labor.

"Also, maintaining a superior conductivity and relative strength, the lightness of this wire will admit of an average of at least ten poles to the mile less than would be otherwise necessary.

"This reduction in the number of poles per mile will not only conduce to economy in construction, but it will effect a decrease of twenty-five per cent. or more in escape of the electric current.

"In stringing over the tops of buildings, stretches may be safely made double the length of those taken with the ordinary telegraph wire, and yet with less strain upon the insulators.

"Another point in its favor is the imperishable nature of copper, which, in this wire, is the exposed metal; the zinc coating of the galvanized iron being deteriorated near the sea, and from the effect of gases, &c., from chimneys, while copper will remain, under such conditions, unimpaired. In fact, under all circumstances, the durability of the com pound wire is greatly superior to that of the galvanized wire in general use.

"In the construction of lines there are many cases in which the expense of transportation of telegraph wire from the manufactory to its destination is an item of considerable magnitude. By reference to the accompanying table it will be readily seen that with the same or a much greater conductivity, as compared with galvanized iron, the compound wire weighs very materially less, with no disadvantage whatever arising from its lightness.

"Referring again to 'conductivity,' which has been the chief objective point in the production of this wire, it will be observed that this element may be largely increased without sacrificing strength, and without recourse to an unwieldy and cumbersome medium for conduction.

"Increased conductivity admits of a reduction in battery power, with a consequent decrease in the escape of electricity. Long circuits are worked with greater facility, and the rains and the fogs lose their time-honored power to prevent the passage of the electric current where it should properly flow.

No. I.—Commercial table showing the absolute and relative strength and conductivity of the compound wires.

GALVANIZED IRON WIRE.				COMPOUND STEEL AND COPPER WIRE.				
Size.	Weight per mile.	Relative strength.	Conductivity.	Conductivity.	Relative strength.	Weight per mile.	Sizes of steel.	Size of compound.
12	161	2.9	.53	.53	5.5	62	17	16+
11	208	2.9	.69	.69	5.1	70	17	15—
10	263	2.9	.87	.87	4.7	79	17	15+
9	313	2.9	1.03	1.03	4.9	99	16	14
8	375	2.9	1.29	1.29	4.6	112	16	14+
7	449	2.9	1.48	1.48	4.4	121	16	13—
6	525	2.9	1.73	1.73	4.5	147	15	12—
5	610	2.9	2.02	2.02	4.3	161	15	12
4	720	2.9	2.38	2.38	4.0	179	15	12+
3	835	2.9	2.76	2.76	4.2	216	14	11—
2	969	2.9	3.20	3.20	3.9	238	14	11+
1	1121	2.9	3.71	3.71	3.8	263	14	10—

Special table No. II.

GALVANIZED IRON WIRE.				COMPOUND WIRE.			
Size.	Relative strength.	Weight per mi	Conductivity.	Conductivity.	Weight per mile.	Relative strength.	Size.
4	2.9	720	2.38	2.65	198	4	11—
6	2.9	525	1.73	1.86	139	4	13+
8	2.9	375	1.29	1.35	101	4	14
9	2.9	313	1.03	1.12	83	4	15
10	2.9	262	.87	.95	71	4	15—

Special table No. III.

GALVANIZED IRON WIRE.				COMPOUND WIRE.			
Size.	Relative strength.	Weight per mile.	Conductivity.	Conductivity.	Weight per mile.	Relative strength.	Size.
4	2.9	720	2.38	2.65	257	5	10—
6	2.9	525	1.73	1.86	181	5	12+
8	2.9	375	1.29	1.35	131	5	13+
9	2.9	313	1.03	1.12	108	5	14+
10	2.9	262	.87	.95	95	5	14—
12	2.9	161	.53	.60	58	5	16

Special table No. IV.

GALVANIZED IRON WIRE.				COMPOUND WIRE.			
Size.	Relative strength.	Weight per mile.	Conductivity.	Conductivity.	Weight per mile.	Relative strength.	Size.
4	2.9	720	2.38	2.65	160	3	12
6	2.9	525	1.73	1.86	112	3	14+
8	2.9	375	1.29	1.35	81	3	15
9	2.9	313	1.03	1.12	67	3	16+

"The term relative strength, used in the preceding tables, denotes the quotient obtained by dividing the strain which would break the wire by its weight per mile.

"The gauge here used is that employed by Washburn and other telegraph-wire makers.

"Table I compares several sizes of galvanized iron wire with the American compound telegraph wire of equal conductivity and a relative strength from thirty to ninety per cent. greater, showing that the compound wire need have only about one-third the weight of galvanized iron wire to be relatively stronger, and at the same time to possess equal or greater conductivity.

"It is evident why this should be so, since the best commercial copper possesses more than six times the average conducting capacity of galvanized iron wire; and the steel which enters into the compound wire has nearly three times the tensile strength of galvanized iron wire of equal size.

"The relative strength of the steel which is used in the American compound telegraph wire averages 7.47; that of the copper, 1.72; while the average relative strength of galvanized iron wire, as found by testing various samples of the best in the market, is only 2.9.

"Hence it is clearly evident that, by varying the proportions of steel and copper in the compound wire, any desired relative strength can be given between the limits of 1.72 and 7.47; and, at the same time, any desired conductivity can be had along with it.

"It will be seen, however, that a high relative strength is more costly than a low one, for the reason that steel possesses a less specific conductivity than copper, and this difference of conductivity is greater than the difference of cost.

"But, in the construction of lines of telegraph, while an increased relative strength adds to the cost of the wire used, it, on the other hand, effects a saving in the number of poles and insulators required, thus reducing the total cost of material and its transportation, which is often of great importance; therefore increased relative strength is, on the whole, more economical.

"Table II shows wires of different conductivities, all possessing a relative strength of four.

"In table III the wires all show a relative strength of five, while

"Table IV shows wires with a relative strength of only three, which is at least three per cent. better than the average of telegraph wire, and the strength of the larger sizes is certainly ample. From this table it appears that we can get the conductivity of a No. 8 galvanized iron wire by using a compound wire weighing only eighty pounds per mile. Such a wire would be handled with the greatest ease, as a man could readily carry a mile or more upon his back.

"By using either of the two larger sizes sho wn in this table, all the advantages of a heavy iron wire, which would weigh from five hundred to seven hundred pounds per mile, can be secured by a compound wire weighing less than one hundred and seventy-five pounds per mile.

"Other sizes than these in the above tables can be made possessing intermediate or greater relative strength and of any desirable conductivity.

"The foregoing tables are based on the employment of a copper which shall possess seventy-eight one-hundred ths of the conductivity of a chemically pure copper wire.

"The standard unit of conductivity here employed is that of a round copper wire one-twentieth of an inch in diame ter, chemically pure, and one foot in length.

"In making up the coefficients of tensile strength, conductivity, and weight per mile of galvaniz ed iron wire, for comparison with the compound, as per tables, careful tests were made and an average taken from several samples, including some of the best qualities found in the market."

At the risk of some repetition the following observations upon conductors and insulation are extracted from a more recent publication by the American Compound Telegraph Wire Company, of which Mr. Moses G. Farmer is the consulting electrician:

"The method most commonly in use now, and always likely to be, for the construction of lines of telegraph, is to stretch a line of wire in the air from one pole to another, attaching it to the pole by the intervention of an insulator, connecting each end of the circuit with the ground. The reason we use an insulator is that we wish to transmit as much as possible of the current to the far end of the line before it enters the ground.

"Now, as a current of electricity divides itself into as many branches as there are paths open for it to travel in, and since the proportion of the whole current flowing in any particular path depends on the conductivity of that particular path, in comparison with the sum of the conductivities of all the paths, we wish to diminish the number and value of the paths of escape down the several posts which support the line.

"To maintain a current of electricity in a line of telegraph we employ some form of galvanic battery. Those most generally used are the Grove nitric acid and the Daniel's sulphate of copper battery. About five of the latter are equivalent to three of the former in ability to work a long line.

"Since, however good the insulator may be, some small portion of the current escapes from the line, over it, down the post to the ground, it is manifest that if the line be long, the posts many, and the insulators very poor, a small portion only of the entering current may reach the far end of the line.

"The law which governs this may be thus enunciated. If the current upon the line near the battery be called the entering current, and that upon the distant end near where it enters the ground be called the arriving current, then the distance to which any stated fraction of the entering current will reach is proportioned directly to the square root of the conductivity of the wires, to the square root of the insulating power of the insulator, and inversely to the square root of the number of poles per mile used. It is customary, of late, to compare the resistance of different wires with one another, by referring them to the standard adopted by the British Association for the Advancement of Science.

"This unit is sometimes called an ohm, or an ohmad, a name given in honor of Dr. G. S. Ohm, who so fully developed the laws which govern the distribution and action of a galvanic current; an unit a million times larger than this, and called a megohm, is used to compare the resistance of insulators.

"A round wire of pure copper, one-twentieth of an inch in diameter and about two hundred and fifty feet in length, nearly represents this unit of resistance; a nearer representation of it is a round wire one foot in length, and one hundred and forty-eight one-thousandths of an inch in diameter, made from an alloy composed of two parts of silver and one part of platinum.

Since a pure copper wire is from six to eight times as good a conductor as an average iron wire of the same size, and since the distance to which we can work a line of telegraph depends, among other things, upon the conductivity of the line, it is plain that it would be desirable to use copper if it answered as well in other respects as it does for conductivity; and the first lines in this country were actually constructed of copper, but it was soon found that its ductility and inferior tenacity rendered it inapplicable to the purpose. So iron wires soon came to be substituted for copper, and size No. 9, weighing about three hundred and twenty pounds per mile, was selected, as it seemed to generally possess about the same conductivity as did the No. 16 copper wire, which had been hitherto used.

"Since 1847 iron wire has been almost wholly used in this country, until within the past year, when the American compound telegraph wire made its appearance. This wire is the result of almost numberless attempts which have been made to utilize the well-known conducting power of copper; and it is at last accomplished by uniting copper, the best conductor, with steel, the strongest known material; thus at once securing lightness and strength with great conductivity in the same wire, copper being six or eight times as good a conductor as iron, and steel being twice or thrice as strong.

"The American compound telegraph wire has a core of carefully-selected and well-manipulated steel, which core is first tinned, and then has drawn upon it a strip or ribbon of the very best Lake Superior copper, which is selected with the greatest care.

"In the course of its manufacture it goes through a great number and variety of processes, such as annealing, tempering, drawing, &c., and the completed wire is finished by passing it through a bath of melted tin, by which the copper and steel are welded into and made one complete whole.

"The smaller sizes are generally drawn into lengths of one thousand to fifteen hundred feet, and are put up in mile bundles, three or more pieces being carefully joined together at the factory.

"A wire of ordinary iron, weighing about three hundred and twenty pounds per mile, and known to the trade as No. 9, will offer from seventeen to twenty-two units of resistance or ohms to the mile. A compound wire composed half of steel and half of copper, offering the same mileage resistance, will weigh only about one hundred pounds per mile; an iron wire of average quality, weighing three hundred and seventy-five pounds per mile, and known as No. 8, will offer the same mileage resistance as a compound wire of less than one-third that weight.

"None is suffered to go out from the factory as first-class wire, in which the conductivity of the copper is less than ninety per cent. that of chemically pure copper.

"It is manifestly a great advantage to use a light wire, if it presents the required ability to sustain itself, since it produces less strain upon the insulators, which are always brittle, and requires posts of less strength to sustain it. The cost of transportation is also less, as also is the cost of handling in stringing, &c.

"The compound wire possesses another advantage, based on the fact that steel, even at a low temper, possesses a great degree of elasticity, so much so that it can be stretched or elongated one two hundred and fiftieth part of its length without taking a permanent set; but will, upon removal of the strain, return to its original length; and it is a fact that when a tree falls upon a line of the compound wire and does not break it, when the tree is removed the wire returns nearly or quite to its original position, instead of remaining stretched as does an iron wire.

"From this cause a line of compound wire keeps up to its original height, and does not sag more and more year after year, as an iron wire does.

"In order to show clearly the advantages which the compound wire offers in the construction of lines of telegraph, it may be well to compare the relative conditions as to strength and ability to work lines built of iron wire, with equally efficient lines constructed with compound wire.

"A very common mode of construction has been to use No. 9 iron wire, weighing three hundred and twenty pounds, and putting it up on thirty-five poles per mile, with glass insulators on wooden pins, which insulators, in a long-continued rain-storm, would not offer more than two or three megohms of resistance. We will suppose one wire used, the posts to be twenty-five feet above ground. If the wire be of very good quality it will offer eighteen ohms per mile of resistance, and if it be soft it will generally break at a strain of about one thousand pounds; but there being always more or less of flaws in a mile of the wire, if it be put up very taut it will break a few times the first year. We will suppose the posts one hundred and fifty feet apart, and the sag of the wire midway between the posts to be nine inches; this would be called pulled up pretty straight. The strain on the wire near the insulator would be two hundred and fifty pounds, or twenty-five per cent. of the ultimate strength of the iron; and it would be more than that, as the strength of a wire is that of its weakest cross-section, and there being occasional flaws, two hundred and fifty pounds would sometimes be as much as one-third of the real strength of the wire.

"With a mileage resistance of eighteen ohms, and with thirty-five insulators per mile, which offer three megohms resistance each in a very rainy day, the fraction of the entering current which would reach the end of the line, two hundred and fifty miles distant, would be about five and one-third per cent. The apparent resistance of the line, measured from one end, would be only about two hundred and thirty-eight ohms, instead of four thousand five hundred, which it would be if the line were insulated to absolute perfection. Suppose now that ordinarily thirty Grove cups are used at one end only, the total electro-motive force of the thirty cups will be about forty-eight volts, and the internal resistance of the thirty cups should not exceed twelve ohms; then the total resistance of the circuit, with all the relays cut out, would be $238 + 12 = 250$ ohms, and the strength of the entering current would be one hundred and ninety-two thousandths of a megafarad, or one hundred and ninety-two thousand farads.

"This is from ten to fifteen times as much strength of current as is ordinarily required to work a relay; and, indeed, the five and one-third per cent. of it, or ten thousand one hundred and seventy-six farads is amply sufficient to work the relay at the distant end of the line.

"We will now suppose that we employ a compound wire weighing two hundred pounds per mile, ninety pounds of this wire being steel and one hundred and ten pounds of it being copper—its breaking strain will be about one thousand and forty pounds; one-fourth of this will be two hundred and sixty pounds, and if it be put up on nineteen posts per mile, with a sag of sixteen inches midway between the poles, the ratio of the span to the sag will be the same as in the former case. The tension on the wire will be the same fraction of its ultimate strength, as in the case of the iron wire on thirty-five poles per mile; and from its superior homogeneity it will be less likely to break.

"Now, on a line thus constructed, the conducting resistance being 7.72 ohms per mile, and there being only nineteen insulators of three megohms each per mile, we shall find that *thirty-four per cent.* of the entering current arrives at the terminal station, two hundred and fifty miles distant, instead of five and one-third, as with the No. 9 iron wire; and we shall find that twelve cups of Grove's battery will cause as strong a current to arrive at the distant end as did the thirty cups on the previous iron wire.

"Some of the best constructed lines in the United States use a wire of extra quality, weighing three hundred and eighty pounds per mile, with as low a mileage resistance as thirteen ohms.

"These lines are built on thirty-eight to forty posts per mile, with glass insulators that in a hard rain do not show more than nine megohms resistance each.

"A line so constructed would be capable of transmitting ninety per cent. of the entering current to a terminal station seventy miles distant, and ten per cent. of the current to a terminal station four hundred and eighty-four miles distant.

"But if a compound wire, half of steel and half of copper, weighing one hundred and forty pounds per mile, and having a mileage resistance of twelve ohms, be put on twelve posts instead of thirty-eight, with the same kind of insulators, we should find that ninety per cent. of the entering current could be transmitted over a line one hundred and thirty-one miles long, and ten per cent. over a line seven hundred and fifty miles in length.

"If, instead of the compound wire, weighing one hundred and forty pounds—only about three-eighths the weight per mile of the iron—we make it weigh the same, namely, three hundred and eight pounds per mile, its mileage resistance would be only four and five-tenths ohms; and if it be put up, as in the last example, we should find that ninety per cent. of the current would be received at a terminal station two hundred and thirteen miles distant, and similarly ten per cent. at a station twelve hundred and twenty-five miles away.

"It is clear that the principle involved in the foregoing examples, namely, transmitting an increased percentage of the current by means of superior conductivity, or insulation, or both, is applicable to the double transmission and other intricate systems, as well as to the working of long circuits, and general operations in humid weather.

"*Increased conductivity* becomes of special importance to those systems which strive for greatly increased rapidity of transmission, particularly on long lines, as *this feature alone* aids us to overcome the retardation due to lateral induction.

"Its special advantages are also manifest on lines which may be liable to contact with trees, as the percentage of a current which will pass beyond a given local fault will be greater as the conductivity of the wire is increased. In other words, the greater the conductivity of the wire the less the escape from it.

"We have thus endeavored briefly to set forth a few of the advantages which this wire offers to enterprising contractors and companies which desire to remove the odium that has hitherto been the standing reproach of American lines."

THE MORSE BATHOMETER.

This is an instrument designed to aid submarine telegraphy exhibited by Sidney E. Morse and G. Livingston Morse, of New York. In regard to this bathometer the pertinent remarks of C. W. Siemens upon the apparatus in the Exhibition, in England, of 1862, may be quoted. He says: "New discoveries and inventions, represented most likely by some ill-executed model, will naturally occupy only a modest position among the great crowd of brilliant objects surrounding us at a great exhibition, and are overlooked, or only half appreciated, until their real worth becomes gradually apparent, in the course of years, through the results they are destined to produce." This it is believed very aptly applies in the present case. The instrument referred to attracted little attention, from its unpretending size and appearance, and the jurors who examined it evidently misapprehended or overlooked its peculiarities. Its main principle was supposed to be the compression of air, which experience has long since proved cannot be successfully used as a means of ascertaining the depth of very deep water, and this erroneous impression probably turned away the attention of the jurors from the novel contrivances in this curious instrument.

The Morse bathometer is a double bathometer, by which the depth of the water in the deepest parts of the ocean may be ascertained, at one sounding, by two entirely distinct and independent methods. Messrs. Morse, in the course of their experiments, made the remarkable and, in its applications to investigations of the bottom of the sea, inestimably important discovery that small hollow glass spheres can be constructed which will retain their buoyancy in the deepest parts of the ocean, being neither crushed nor permeated by water under the enormous pressure at those great depths. They have made hollow glass spheres so light that they would float in water with more than half of their bulk above the surface, the spheres being between three and four inches in diameter, and the glass less than a tenth of an inch thick, and they subjected these light and fragile bodies, in the cistern of an hydraulic press, to a pressure of seven tons on the square inch, which is the pressure at the depth of about thirty thousand feet, or nearly six miles in the ocean. The spheres came out from this severe trial of their strength and impermeability whole, and empty of everything but air. In the construction of their bathometer Messrs. Morse deposit these spheres, in any required number, in a tube of tin, wood, or other suitable material, the tube being commonly of four inches interior diameter, several feet long, ballasted at its lower end so that it will stand and float upright in the water, and surmounted at the upper end by a conical or parabaloidal cap, having a socket on the top, in which a very light straight rod of any desired length may be securely fastened. When a sounding is to be made an elongated weight, sufficiently heavy to carry the whole instrument rapidly down, is attached to the lower end of this upright, ballasted tube, and so attached that the moment a small weight, which moves in advance, strikes the bottom of the sea, the large weight will be infallibly detached and allow the tube, by its own buoyancy, to ascend with the rest of the apparatus to the surface. As this instrument is not encumbered with a line, or with anything causing irregularity of motion, it moves through the water with uniform velocity, both in its descent and ascent, and the time of its disappearance below the surface may, therefore, be taken as a correct measure of the depth of the water. If, for example, it should be found to occupy just ten minutes in descending to and ascending from a depth of one thousand fathoms, its disappearance for just twenty minutes would indicate that the depth was two thousand fathoms. The rapidity of the descent and of the ascent of each instrument will be regulated, of course, by the amount of weight suspended from, and of buoyancy inclosed in, the tube. It can easily be made to go down and return in very deep water in less than a tenth part of the time required when a line is used.

But this bathometer, as has already been remarked, is double. In determining the depth of the water at any point, Messrs. Morse do not confine themselves to calculations based on the interval of time elapsing between the disappearance and reappearance of their instrument at the surface. They inclose in any convenient part of their tube, to be carried down and brought back with it, another instrument, which enables them, on its return to the surface, to mark, with the greatest precision, the true depth of the sea at the place of the sounding. This instrument, which is based on the principle of the compression of water, and is the proper Morse bathometer, is thus constructed. A glass bottle (it may be of the capacity of a pint, more or less) is completely filled with freshly distilled water, and closed at its neck with an India-rubber stopper. Through the center of this stopper passes, longitudinally, a short glass tube of very small bore, open at both ends, and extending beyond the stopper in both directions, namely, an inch or more within the bottle and two or three inches on the outside. One end of an India-rubber tube three or four inches long, open at both ends, and, when open, of about an inch in diameter, is then passed over the neck of the bottle and made tight there by winding around it fine wire or cord, which presses it close to the glass. The bottle is then sunk in a vessel of distilled water till the water rises above the mouth of the India-rubber tube, which is held up and open to receive it. Mercury, sufficient to fill the tube to the extent of one-half or more of its capacity, is then poured in, the mouth of the tube closed, and a cord or wire wound tightly around at the end, under water, thus converting the India-rubber tube into a bag filled in nearly equal portions with mercury and distilled water. On inverting the bottle, the mercury, from its specific gravity, occupies the lower half of the India-rubber bag, and keeps the water from access to the lower orifice of the glass tube, which passes now from the bottom of the bag through the stopper into the bottle. When this bottle of water, thus prepared, is placed at the bottom of the sea, the pressure of the external sea water, acting through the India-rubber bag, and through the mercury in the bag and in the glass tube, compresses the fresh water in the bottle, and the mercury is forced from the bag into the bottle to fill the void caused by the compression. The quantity of the mercury forced into the bottle is a perfect measure of the extent of the compression of the water, and this compression is always exactly proportioned to the height of the compressing column—that is, of the depth of the sea. It is only necessary, therefore, to measure the mercury forced from the bag into the bottle to know with the greatest precision the depth of the sea at the lowest point of descent of the bottle. To facilitate the measuring of the mercury, Messrs. Morse, in constructing their bottle, cause a glass tube several inches long, of even bore and closed at the outer end, to be inserted in the end of the bottle opposite to the neck, so that on inverting the bottle the mercury, which at first rests in the neck on the stopper, falls into this meter tube, which is graduated, and thus shows the depth of the sea by the height of the mercury, as in the barometer and thermometer the height of the mercury indicates the weight and heat of the air.

As the bulk of all liquids is greatly affected by temperature, as well as by pressure, the indications of any bathometer based on the principle of the compression of water, in the construction of which this consideration has been overlooked, will be wholly unreliable. Messrs. Morse have guarded effectually against all error from this source, as the bottle containing the water which they compress is kept during the whole period of every sounding in a small wooden case surrounded by ice, and the temperature of its contents, therefore, is always precisely thirty-two degrees of Fahrenheit. It is, of course, not necessary to send down a deep-sea thermometer with their instrument.

The following are among the advantages of the Morse bathometer:

1. *The rapidity with which it does its work.*—Six hours and more, it is said, are commonly consumed in paying out and hauling in a line with a sinker attached to it in water two thousand fathoms deep. The Morse bathometer, it is estimated, can be made to go down to this depth and return in less than thirty minutes.

2. *The certainty of its operation.*—When properly constructed, it it can never fail. The various contrivances for sounding the sea by sinking weights or instruments, which are raised again with a line from the bottom, fail so frequently in very deep water that explorers have now abandoned the tral of them there, and it seems to be generally admitted by scientific men that in the greatest depths of the ocean no reliable sounding has ever yet been made. In the Morse bathometer the weight always carries the instrument to the bottom; the detachment

of the weight at the bottom is made by their device perfectly certain, and when the weight is detached the rest of the apparatus can never fail to rise to the surface.

3. *The Morse bathometer is automatic.*—The momentary attention of a single operator is all that is necessary to effect a sounding in the greatest depths of the ocean. He puts ice into the case with the bottle, marks the latitude and longitude on the tube, screws the long, straight rod into the socket at the upper end of the tube, hangs the weight on the hook at the lower end, and drops the instrument into the sea. It then takes care of itself. By its own power it moves, rapidly and uniformly, from the surface to the bottom, deposits its load there, and returning as rapidly, or (if desired) more rapidly, to the surface. The operator need not even wait to pick it up. The tube, with the bottle which it incloses and the rod which rises from it into the air, will live and ride triumphantly above the surface, amid the lashings of the waves and winds of all the storms it may encounter, and whoever picks it up, at any time or at any place, however distant, may know, merely by examining the bottle, the true depth of the sea at the point marked on the tube, and may publish the information to the world. If he chooses he may then mark on the tube the time when, and the latitude and longitude of the place where, the instrument was picked up, adjust the bathometer by dropping the mercury into the bag, and re-inserting the stopper in the neck of the bottle, put ice in the case, hang a new weight on the hook of the detaching apparatus, and cast the whole instrument again into the sea, to be again picked up by another person at another place; and thus one instrument, in process of time, may be used to make scores or hundreds of soundings, at the cost for each sounding of only the bag of sand required to sink the instrument, the few ounces of ice that surround the bottle, and the few minutes of time occupied in readjusting.

4. *The mathematical accuracy of its marks of depths.*—The Morse bathometer in its indications of depth is not affected by currents. A line, during the long time consumed in its descent, may be so swayed by currents and counter-currents that a length of twice, and more than twice, the perpendicular depth of the water may be required to reach the bottom. The measure of the depth of the sea by a line is therefore eminently unreliable; but this instrument, constructed on the principle of the compression of water, which is always precisely as the perpendicular height of the compressing column—that is, as the depth of the sea, without regard to currents—must mark this depth with scientific precision.

5. *The cheapness of the instrument.*—A tin tube a few feet long and three or four inches in diameter; four or five hollow glass spheres of a size adapted to the tube; a small glass bottle in a wooden case; three or four ounces of mercury; a light fishing rod, ten or twelve feet long, with any glittering substance at the end that will attract attention

at a distance; and a twenty-pound weight, which can be made for a dime by casting plaster of Paris into the form of a long narrow bucket, and filling the bucket with sand or stones — these are the items in the cost of an instrument with which the greatest depths of the ocean can be sounded, quickly, certainly, automatically, and with perfect scientific exactness.

Is it too much to expect that, with the facilities afforded by this instrument, we shall soon have at least one sounding on every square mile accessible by ships of the three-fourths of the surface of the earth covered by water, and that with these soundings artists will construct a perfect model of the bottom of the sea, in which all its depressions below the level of the surface will be minutely and accurately represented? How long will it be before we can have an equally accurate map-in-relief of the one-fourth of the earth's surface that rises above the water? Not until man has visited every square mile of Central Africa, of Central Australia, and of every empire, and every island from which he is now excluded by inhospitable climates and inhospitable men.

Strange! that the bottom of the sea—the widest field of the geographer, three-fourths of his entire field, hitherto covered with a thick veil, defying all attempts to penetrate it—should at last, by such simple means, be opened everywhere for the investigation of everybody, so that the true shape of its whole vast expanse can now be more readily, accurately, and minutely dotted down on paper, and represented in sculpture, than the true shape of any large district of the dry land inhabited by man and revealed daily in the light of the sun!

PROPOSED NEW MODE OF LAYING AND RAISING SUBMARINE TELEGRAPH CABLES.

Messrs. Sidney E. Morse and G. Livingston Morse, of New York, propose a new method of laying submarine telegraph cables. Submarine telegraph cables have hitherto been laid, as nearly as possible, in one continuous straight line on the bottom of the sea. It is obvious that when a cable has been thus laid, it cannot be raised from the bottom to the surface in the deep sea without breaking it, and then raising successively each of the two parts, and that it cannot be repaired there and relaid without splicing to the two broken ends new cable of a length equal to at least twice the depth of the sea at that point. Messrs. Morse propose to lay the cable on the whole line, in the first instance, in such a way that it can be raised at any time for repair, or for any other purpose, at any assigned station or stations on the line, and then relaid, without breaking it.

In laying a submarine cable entirely across the ocean, Messrs. Morse propose to employ two vessels. The first and larger vessel is to carry the telegraph cable in any required length, either enough for the whole line, or for one or more sections of the line, as may be desired, together with the ordinary apparatus for laying this cable on the bottom of the sea. The second and smaller vessel is to carry, first, a lifting cable, long enough at least to reach the bottom of the sea at the deepest point on the line, and strong enough to support a weight equal to the weight in water of ten miles of the telegraph cable, if the depth of the sea on any part of the line should be as much as two miles, and proportionally stronger if the water should be deeper, this lifting cable having firmly attached to its lower end a strong, heavy iron ring, seven or eight inches or more in diameter; and, secondly, as many properly-constructed iron hooks as there are stations on the line, at which provision is to be made for raising the telegraph cable; each hook to be strong enough to support the ten miles or more of telegraph cable; the shank of each hook to be provided at short intervals with five, six, or more barbs, all pointing downwards, but in various directions, each barb being as stout and strong as the hook itself, and the shank terminating in an eye, in which is firmly fastened the end of a galvanized-iron wire rope; it may be five or ten miles long, or more, and between one-eighth and one-fourth of an inch in diameter; the strands of this wire rope to be untwisted at suitable intervals to embrace wooden cases in the form of cylinders, about four inches in diameter and of indefinite length, but with tapering, conical ends; the cylindrical part of each wooden case to contain a sufficient number of three-and a-half-inch hollow glass spheres to give the wire rope any required buoyancy at any required intervals.

Thus freighted the two vessels leave a terminus, let us suppose, in France, to proceed along the arc of a great circle, nearly due west, to Newfoundland, a distance of about two thousand miles, to lay the telegraph cable so that it may be raised at any future time without breaking it, at any one of nineteen stations one hundred miles apart. The smaller vessel goes ahead on a nearly due west course, and is followed by the larger vessel, from which the telegraph cable is payed out and laid on the bottom of the sea in the usual way. After the smaller vessel has proceeded one hundred miles it stops, turns with its bow to the north, and, one of the hooks having been suspended from its stern, with the ring at the end of the lifting cable under one of the barbs on the shank of the hook, waits for the larger vessel, which, as it passes on its westerly course, deposits its cable in the hook and proceeds until the telegraph cable rests again on the bottom, leaving a certain length suspended from the stern of the smaller vessel in the form of two catenarian curves, extending each from the hook to the bottom of the sea, one in an easterly and the other in a westerly direction. If the depth of the sea at that point should be two miles, the speed of the larger vessel in laying the cable could be so regulated that the span between the two points at which the cable would touch the bottom would be eight miles, and in that case the length of cable included in the two catenarian curves would be about nine miles, and the hook and lifting-cable would support nine miles of telegraph cable at the stern of the smaller vessel. The smaller vessel should then proceed due north for two miles, the lifting-cable meanwhile being allowed to sink and unwind itself from a reel till the whole of the nine miles of telegraph cable included in the catenarian curves is deposited on the bottom of the sea, as nearly as possible at right angles to the general course of the rest of the line. The lifting-cable should then be made, by the weight of the ring at its end, to detach itself from the hook, and should be drawn up and wound again around its reel in the smaller vessel, which should all the while be continuing on its course due north paying out the iron-wire rope and its inclosed glass-sphere buoys to any desired distance—five miles, or ten miles, or more if deemed expedient. The galvanized-iron wire rope should be made to terminate in an anchor, and when this anchor is dropped in the sea the rope may be made, by a previous proper disposition of the glass-sphere buoys, to assume any desired form, either that of one long arch or of a succession of arches, rising in the water from the bottom, and as near the bottom or as far from it as may be deemed best. The deposit of the anchor at the end of the galvanized-iron wire rope completes the laying of the first section of the line, and the other sections may be laid by repeating the whole process.

The process of raising again to the surface a telegraph cable thus laid is very simple. The latitude and longitude, both of the hook and of the anchor of the wire rope, it should have been remarked, must be accurately taken when they are deposited on the bottom of the sea. When the telegraph cable is to be raised, the smaller vessel, with the lifting-cable on board, and a small line, long enough to reach nearly to the bottom of the sea, and having a small hook or grapple of proper construction at its lower end, must be sent to any point of latitude between the latitude of the hook and the latitude of the anchor of the wire rope, and to any meridian within a few miles either east or west of that on which the wire rope is floating below, supported by the encased glass-sphere buoys. With the small line depending from its stern, and extending, with its sinker and hook, nearly to the bottom of the sea, the vessel must then be moved to the east or to the west, till this line shall cross the wire rope and bring it to the surface. When brought to the surface the wire rope must be parted, and the part connected with the anchor temporarily buoyed, while the end of the other part is taken on board the vessel, and, after passing the heavy iron ring of the lifting-cable over it, must be held on board until the ring carries the lifting-cable down to the bottom, the wire rope guiding it till the ring passes the barbs on the shank of the hook which holds the telegraph cable in its grasp. Then, by drawing up the lifting-cable the ring will catch under one of the barbs of the hook, and by continuing to draw up, while the smaller vessel is moved two miles on a southerly course, or on a course directly opposite to that pursued in laying it, the part of the telegraph cable included originally in the two catenarian curves will be raised again to the surface without being broken.

Among the advantages of this mode of laying submarine telegraph cables are the following:

1st. All risk of losing the cable while laying it is avoided. More than three hundred miles of the Atlantic telegraph cable of 1857 were finally lost, and more than half of the Atlantic telegraph cable of 1865 was temporarily lost, while the operators were in the act of laying them. These losses would not have occurred if those cables had been laid on the plan here proposed and described. After the parting of the telegraph cable in each case the vessels would have returned to the last raising-station with a lifting-cable, and after raising the telegraph cable from the bottom to the surface at that point, the operators would have underrun the raised part till they had come to the broken end, spliced this end to the broken end of the cable in the ship, and proceeded with the work of laying the cable on the bottom.

2d. The risk of losing the cable after it has been laid is divided by the number of raising-stations on the line. The Atlantic telegraph cable of 1858, although successfully laid through its whole line, after a few days of feeble life was totally and finally lost. No one knows where or what was its malady. It may have been confined to a few feet or to a single point on the line. If it had been laid on the plan herein proposed the place of the fault might soon have been found, the defective part might possibly have been easily removed, and the whole cable restored to permanent and efficient life.

3d. The danger of encountering storms and fogs while laying the cable is avoided. On the plan proposed by Messrs. Morse the cable is laid by sections, and after one section is laid the work may be left for weeks, or for any length of time, and then resumed. The sections may be of such length that a single section can be laid in a single day; and, if the day is judiciously selected, embarrassment from the weather will rarely occur, and, when it does occur, will be of comparatively little importance; but when the cable is laid in one continuous line for two thousand miles without stopping during the fourteen days neccessary to lay such a length of line, experience proves that it will be very difficult to avoid serious embarrassment from the weather, even in the most favorable season of the year.

4th. Less length of cable will be required to connect the termini of the line. The length of cable actually used to connect the termini in Ireland and Newfoundland of the Atlantic telegraph cable of 1858 was about fifteen per cent. greater than the distance of the two points from each other, measured on the arc of the great circle between them, and, in the cable of 1866, it was about twelve per cent. greater. As this distance in each case is nearly two thousand miles, it is clear that more than two hundred miles of telegraph cable were lost by *unnecessary slack* in attempting to lay the cable across the Atlantic Ocean in one continuous straight line under circumstances uncommonly favorable to economy in the length of cable used; for, in 1866, the weather was so favorable that the ships deviated very little from the true line in their course. The loss of these two hundred miles is not merely the loss of the cost of so much cable, but, as more words could be transmitted through the cable in any given time if it were two hundred miles shorter, the loss will continue to be felt through the whole life of the cable in the diminution of its capacity to earn income. If the cable had been laid in sections, on the plan proposed by Messrs. Morse, and had been carefully and deliberately laid upon that plan, after soundings at very short intervals along the line with the aid of the bathometer of Messrs. Morse, it could have been made to conform so accurately to the arc of the great circle, and to all the swells and hollows of the bottom of the sea, that the slack might have been almost confined to the stations at which it would have been purposely made, in order to furnish at those stations the necessary means for raising the cable from the bottom to the surface without breaking it. The loss of cable by slack at one of these stations, a loss by which an advantage so desirable is gained, need be only one mile, even when the water is two miles deep, as has been already stated in the account of the Morse process of laying the cable. The loss at twenty stations need, of course, be only twenty miles, or less than one-tenth part of the length superfluously expended in the method hitherto pursued in laying submarine telegraph cables.

Instead of a lifting-cable, Messrs. Morse propose, in some cases, to send down, to be attached to one of the barbs on the shank of the hook, a buoy, composed of very large hollow glass spheres, inclosed in a tube, the spheres being sufficient in number and buoyancy to support and raise through the water to the surface the whole of that part of the telegraph cable included originally in the catenarian curves. They would put the heavy iron ring over the end of the galvanized-iron wire rope held on board of the vessel, and then attach the buoy to the upper side of the ring, while to the lower side they would attach a weight sufficiently heavy to draw the buoy slowly to the bottom. After the ring, guided by the wire rope, has passed the barbs on the shank of the hook at its end, (the hook which holds the telegraph cable in its grasp,) Messrs. Morse would cause the weight, by a simple device, to detach itself from the ring, and the ring would then be drawn under one of the barbs by the buoy, which, at first very rapidly and afterwards slowly, would rise and draw the telegraph cable to the surface. The weight may be made at little cost by inclosing sand and stone in a bag, or in any suitable cheap material. By this mode of raising the telegraph cable the time and labor of men at a windlass would be dispensed with. The whole work would be performed automatically by the buoy and the weight, and at the expense only of the sand necessary to sink the buoy from the surface to the bottom, and the cable would be raised far more speedily and satisfactorily by this process than it could be by human labor.

Messrs. Morse also propose to apply their above-described method of laying and raising a long galvanized-iron wire rope, suspended by inclosed glass-sphere buoys in the form of an arch or arches near the bottom of the sea, to the end of a submarine telegraph cable laid in one continuous straight line from a station on shore to any assigned point of latitude and longitude in mid-ocean, which point would thus be constituted a telegraph station on the bottom of the sea, accessible for use by the master of any ship who should have a telegraph instrument on board, and a small line long enough to reach the bottom at that point, and who might be acquainted with the latitude and longitude of the mid-ocean terminus of this telegraph cable, and also with the latitude and longitude of the anchor at the outer end of the galvanized-iron wire rope. Knowing these points, and allowing the small line with a sinker and hook at its outer end to run out from the stern of his ship till the hook approached the bottom, this ship-master would cross the galvanized-iron wire rope with his small line, bring the rope on board, and, without breaking it, underrun it towards the telegraph cable till he came to the light insulated copper wire in which the telegraph cable, for a distance equal to the depth of the sea at that point, should be made to terminate, and then, by connecting this insulated copper wire with his telegraph instrument, he could send and receive communications to and from the shore. After doing this he might drop the iron wire rope and the light insulated copper wire into the sea, and they would automatically assume the position from which they were raised, and be ready to render their services to any other ship-master traversing that part of the ocean.

EXHIBITORS OF CABLES.

Specimens of cables were also exhibited by J. L. A. Machabée, 46 Rue de Veuves, Paris; by Rattier & Co., 4 Rue des Fosses, Montmartre; by A. Holtzman, of Amsterdam; by W. T. Henly, 27 Leadenhall street, London; by William Hooper, 7 Pall Mall, London; and by D. Nicoll, Oakland's Hall, Kilburn, London.

INSULATORS AND INSULATION.

THE BROOKS PARAFFINE INSULATOR.

This insulator was exhibited, but is not in the catalogue. The Brooks insulator has a wide popularity. The tests of its efficiency, in comparison with many other insulators, show it to be deserving of the popularity it has acquired. It is extensively sought after on European lines. The only plausible drawback is the apprehension that the paraffine may deteriorate in the course of time. Hitherto, however, it has stood the test of years. Whether the objection is a substantial one time alone can determine. In conversation with some of the jurors at the Exhibition, this insulator was spoken of as the best that had been submitted to them. There is an insulator in use in India called the "Brooke Insulator," which must not be confounded with the Brooks insulator. In alluding to the former, the director general of telegraphs in India, in his return to

Parliament, says: "I attribute the bad working of the better Indian lines to the department being inflicted with the Brooke bracket and insulator, both of which are most thoroughly unfit for the purpose for which they were designed." The American Brooks insulator is a totally different nvention.

Fig. 16.

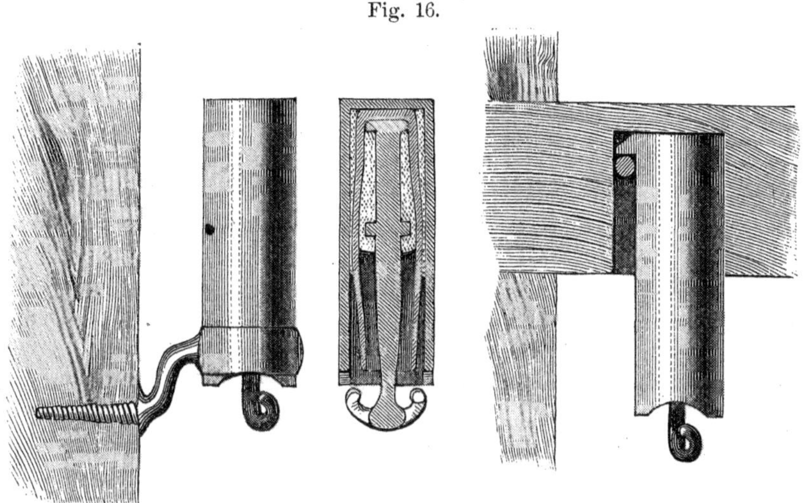

The Brooks Paraffine Insulator.

It is constructed as follows: An iron stem or wire holder is cemented into a glass bottle or vessel; the bottle is again cemented into a cylindrical iron shield. The cement is composed of sand and sulphur. The cement and cast iron are saturated with paraffine, and the whole surface of the insulator covered with paraffine.

Sulphur of itself is a great dialectric, or insulating material when dry, but upon crystallizing, it checks and becomes porous, admitting moisture when exposed to the air, which is prevented by the use of paraffine, as herein stated. Paraffine is repellant of moisture, and prevents it settling in continuous surface upon the insulator. In form the insulator has great length and small sectional area in order to obtain greatest current resistance.

Either point of the hook is nearer the iron shield than any other part of the hook, consequently surcharges of atmospheric electricity pass outside the glass and prevent fracture or injury to the insulator.

Insulation test of Brooks's and other insulators.

Description of insulator.	Date	March 1, 1868	March 9, 1868	March 20, 1868	March 26, 1868	March 31, 1868.
	Temperature	47° Fahr.	49° Fahr.	52° Fahr.	48° Fahr.	43° Fahr.
	State of weather	Very dull	During and after rain	Atmosphere damp	During and after much fine rain.	During a thick fog and frost.
	Constant of inst	334	336	335	333	327
	Number of cells	500	100	500	500	500
	Number of insulators tested.	Deflection (conductivity) in degrees on Thomson's astatic galvanometer per insulator.	Deflection (conductivity) in degrees on Thomson's astatic galvanometer per insulator.	Deflection (conductivity) in degrees on Thomson's astatic galvanometer per insulator.	Deflection (conductivity) in degrees on Thomson's astatic galvanometer per insulator.	Deflection (conductivity) in degrees on Thomson's astatic galvanometer per insulator.
United Kingdom Telegraph Company's large porcelain	4	3,500	330	20,000	10,600	40,600
Varley's double porcelain cup	4	4,500	450	37,500	25,000	50,000
British and Irish Magnetic Telegraph Company's porcelain	4	30,000	1,600	35,000	18,500	60,000
United Kingdom Telegraph Company's small porcelain	4	800	150	11,850	14,500	50,060
Brooks's patent insulator, with 6-inch screw shank and iron cap	5	2	0	2	1	4
Do.....do.....do	6	3	0	11	6	4
Do.....do.....do	6	7	0	4	6	1
Brooks's patent insulator, with 6-inch screw shank and iron cap lug for cross-arms	1	200	80	194	80	3

Constant of galvanometer. 1. Daniel Cell. Through 1,000,000 ohmads.

DAY'S KERITE INSULATOR.

The kerite compounds of Austin Goodyear Day, mentioned in the following memoir, were honored by two medals and an honorable mention by the jury of the Exposition Universelle, to whom the subject was referred. These awards covered other products than the electrical cables and insulators which are the special object of the descriptive memoir.

NOTE UPON INSULATION AND KERITE, BY PROFESSOR SILLIMAN.

The exhibition of the kerite, this product of the persevering labors and experiments of Mr. Day for so many years, furnishes an example of the not infrequent inappreciation, or rather overlooking, of an invaluable discovery, when modestly presented, as in this case, among the more showy articles by which it was surrounded.

True, it received honorable mention as "artificial India-rubber," and a bronze medal for its very limited application to "India-rubber cases;" but its superlative value as a substitute in insulation for India-rubber and gutta-percha was not, for it could scarcely be, appreciated, presented as it was simply in one of its more ordinary applications; so that heedless neglect is not charged upon the jury, but it is mentioned rather as an example of the existence of an unnoticed quality in an apparently trifling discovery, necessarily latent to superficial inquiry; a quality which is destined in this case to have a most important bearing upon submarine and subterranean telegraphy.

The kerite, in its condition simply as artificial rubber, is classed under Group V, Class 44; but in its application to telegraph wires as an insulator, is properly treated of in the present Group VI, Class 64.

The following memoir upon insulation and protection of electrical conductors for telegraphic purposes, describing the new insulating covering for telegraphic conductors known as kerite, of Austin G. Day, has been supplied for this report by B. Silliman, professor of general and applied chemistry in Yale College:

"Among the American products exhibited at the Exposition at Paris in 1867 was a series of specimens produced from a new artificial caoutchouc, prepared by Mr. Austin G. Day, of Seymour, Connecticut.

"Among these specimens was a new telegraphic covering and insulator, which constituted one of the applications of Mr. Day's invention. The product in this and many other forms is termed by the inventor 'kerite,' and at the Exposition it was presented as it existed in 1867. Since that date, however, some important improvements have been made in the preparation of this insulator, which render it yet more completely indestructible by natural and other agencies than any other material which has yet been discovered, leaving, in fact, nothing more to be desired in this direction. By means of these improvements the use of a considerable proportion of the sulphur previously employed in the vulcanization is dispensed with, a much less quantity of that agent sufficing to effect vulcanization on bodies thus oxidized, while at the same time new and highly useful properties are developed, in virtue of the less liability of the kerite produced to attack by oxidizing agents, like ozone. In this manner a body has been produced which resists in the most remarkable manner the solvent and destructive action of the most powerful chemical reagents, including ozone, while preserving all the required physical qualities of perfect insulation, resistance to extremes of heat and cold, and flexibility with firmness.

"ACTION OF OZONE UPON TELEGRAPHIC INSULATORS.—In the course of the investigation connected with this subject I have discovered that the most destructive of all agents upon these insulators is an ozonized atmosphere. Exposed for a short time to such an atmosphere, electrical conductors, covered with the most carefully prepared English gutta-percha or vulcanized caoutchouc, begin even in a few hours to show signs of disintegration, and shortly the covering breaks up and cleaves off, leaving the conducting wire exposed. The rapidity of this action is proportioned to the activity of the ozonized atmosphere. With the slow oxidation of phosphorus as the source of the ozone at temperatures below 12° C, the action is slow, requiring one or two days' time to manifest itself with gutta-percha, but with the same means at a temperature of 20° or 25° C, the action of the ozone becomes much more rapid, and will sometimes develop itself even in an hour or less.

"This is especially true if the covered conductor is coiled in a close spiral of short radius—*e. g.*, of two or three centimeters; the state of tension thus produced is peculiarly favorable to the rapid action of the destructive agency of the ozone.

"This important observation I have confirmed by many experiments variously modified, and upon every description of insulating material which I have been able to procure. The results explain why it is that no covering for aerial lines has yet been discovered which will withstand for any reasonable period the action of the atmosphere without soon cleaving off and hanging in shreds from the conductor. The atmosphere is never without this allotropic modification of oxygen, and its action upon the insulation is not the less certain because it is somewhat slow.

"The fact of greatest practical importance in this connection is that certain specimens of Day's kerite have withstood perfectly, in my experiments, this powerful agent of destruction, even where exposed to an atmosphere so highly charged with ozone as to destroy in thirty minutes other electrical insulators usually esteemed the best. I have continued such trials on the kerite in question for thirty consecutive days in such an atmosphere, without developing the slightest fault in the covering. By the use of this test I have been able to declare to the inventor, from time to time, which of his numerous products were worthless or imperfect, and thus to eliminate the valuable results of his synthetic experiments, until at last he has obtained a product which fully meets the requirements of the problem, leaving nothing more to be desired in this direction. For aerial and underground electrical cables this invention offers the solution of the great obstacle which has hitherto obstructed the progress of telegraphy; while for submarine cables the kerite offers a far more economical insulation than any which has yet been obtained, and one fully equal if not greatly superior to any other in its insulating power against electrical leakage. On this latter point I appeal to the electrical tests of Mr. Farmer, the well known electrician of Boston, which are appended:

"Of the value of this new insulator, as tested by the actual experience of telegraphic lines, we are fully assured by the experience of well known telegraphic constructors who have employed it. To this point is the testimony of Messrs. Chester, of New York, and of Mr. Callahan, whose opinions, founded upon their own experience, are given in their letters, which are also appended.

"ACTION OF OTHER CHEMICAL AGENTS UPON KERITE.—As respects the action of other chemical reagents upon the kerite covering, I have to add very briefly that I have submitted it to the test of numerous powerful bodies in contrast with other insulators or coverings, and always with the most marked advantage in favor of the kerite. The most important of these agents are carbonic disulphide, ($C\,S_2$), nitric acid, ($H_2\,N\,O_4$), sulphuric acid, ($H_2\,S\,O_4$), sulphuric dioxide, ($S\,O_2$), nitric per oxide, ($N_2\,O_3$), chlorine gas and alkaline hydrates, *e. g.*, sodic hydrate ($H\,Na\,O$) and potassic hydrate, ($H\,K\,O$). Such reagents are useful in guiding the inventor in perfecting his synthetic experiments; but it is hardly necessary to say, that in the actual experience of telegraphy, cables are never exposed to these powerful reagents which the chemist resorts to in his laboratory. We may safely conclude, also, that a product which can withstand the continued attacks of atmospheric ozone must be regarded as safe from all other causes of destruction which may be encountered in nature.

"This last remark is open to only one important qualification. It remains to be seen whether the marine borers of tropical seas and the ravages of the white ants of tropical regions, which are known to destroy gutta-percha coverings, may not also attack with effect the kerite. I have caused cables to be prepared to test this question in the waters of the Bay of Aspinwall, and also to be buried in situations where they are fully exposed to the ravages of the white ant. These specimens of kerite have been prepared with carbolic acid, (phenol,) compounds of which, as applied to ship timber, I have found in certain investigations undertaken some years since for the naval department of the United States government, to offer the only effectual cure to the attacks of the marine animals.

"The trials now in progress in Aspinwall and upon the Isthmus of Panama will soon decide this question for the kerite cable.

"In conclusion, we are led as the result of this investigation to express the opinion, that in the present state of our knowledge the 'kerite' of Day is the best material yet found for telegraphic use, offering at once the greatest resistance to electrical leakage and to all the causes of destruction, whether chemical, atmospheric, or vital, to which electrical cables are liable, whether in air, earth, or water."[1]

LETTERS UPON THE VALUE OF KERITE AS AN INSULATOR.

The following is the letter referred to from Mr. Moses G. Farmer, dated at Boston, February 12, 1869, and addressed to Mr. Day:

"I have made numerous tests of the insulating power of your 'kerite' covering for telegraph wires.

"It is well known that in cables which have the same relation subsisting between the diameters of the core and of the contained strand, the relative insulating power is in proportion to the time which it takes for the cable to lose half of a given charge.

"The Atlantic cables fall to half charge in about one and one tenth hours, while a sample of your kerite-covered wire, which I operated upon, was thirteen hours in falling to half charge, showing it to be a most wonderful insulator.

"Wishing for you the utmost success in introducing this truly valuable invention, I remain."

The letter of Messrs. Charles T. & J. N. Chester, dated New York, November 13, 1868, is as follows:

"In reply to your inquiries as to our experience in the compound known as kerite wire, we would say that we have been familiar with your experiments and have examined your products during the last two or three years, and have been so well satisfied that this kerite-covered wire fulfilled many requirements not hitherto found in insulated wire, that we have induced many of our friends to purchase and test the wire, and the result of these tests has been to establish the excellence of the fabric as superseding any other for the purpose of insulation. These tests have been made in at least two hundred exposed places in the prominent cities of the Union and Canada, in connection with fire-alarm telegraphs. They have also been made with underground wires, as at Vassar College and Dartmouth College. Some of these wires have been laid two years; they have given excellent satisfaction. In the course of our experience we have had occasion to test many insulated wires under water, and find it rare to obtain a piece of much length without an escape, even with delicate instruments. A few days since we were about to ship one thousand feet of small size office kerite wire, not intended for subaqueous use. A test of this with a battery of fifty cells and a delicate acting apparatus, gave no deflection whatever. We believe its insulating properties very extraordinary."

Edward A. Callahan, esq., the superintendent of the Gold and Stock

[1] Dated at New Haven, Connecticut, January, 1869.

Telegraph Company, makes the following statement in his letter to Mr. Day, dated at No. 18 New street, New York, November 10, 1868:

"In reply to your inquiries with reference to your kerite insulated wire, I take great pleasure in making you the following statement:

"It has, under all circumstances, given us the fullest satisfaction. The peculiar nature of our business renders it necessary for us to use the most perfectly insulated wire. I have tried several and various kinds of insulated wire before using yours, but have been obliged to take it all down, and have now substituted your kerite insulated wire in its stead.

"Your wire, which I strung in December, 1867, is, so far as we are able to judge, as good as the first day we put it up. We have tested it after three days constant rain, and could not find one degree of escape. We use it in gas-pipes, where we twist six wires together. We hold this to be as severe a test of its insulating properties as it can be put to, and have never been obliged to look at one of these gas-pipes for crasses, grounds, or escapes. We now use it for office wire, where it is sometimes placed near furnaces, subjected to a very high temperature, and again where it is exposed to the most intense cold, and I have not been able to detect the slightest change from its original condition.

"I am very favorably impressed with it, and can see no reason why it will not last for an indefinite number of years.

"You ask my opinion for underground purposes. We have exposed it to the extreme cold and heat of the past year; strung over the roofs of buildings, which we consider the best test of its indestructible and insulating qualities that it can be submitted to, while placing it under ground would be favorable as a protection."

CHAPTER V.

AUTOMATIC RECORDING, TRANSMITTING, AND CONTROLLING.

AUTOMATIC RECORDING—IMPROVEMENT AND MODIFICATION NOT THE SAME—THE GENERIC TELEGRAPH—THE ELECTRO-CHEMICAL PROCESS—THE ELECTRO-MAGNETIC MODE OF RECORDING—THE PENCIL POINT—INKING PROCESSES—TRIPLE PEN—STEEL POINT—AUTOMATIC TRANSMISSION—EMBOSSED PAPER PROCESS—AUTOMATIC APPARATUS OF SIEMENS AND HALSKE—SPEED OF TRANSMISSION—BLAVIER ON SPEED OF TRANSMISSION—COMPARATIVE SPEED BY DIFFERENT INSTRUMENTS—RECENT RESULT IN FRANCE IN SPEED OF TRANSMISSION—AUTOMATIC TRANSMISSION IN PRUSSIA AND SPEED OF TRANSMISSION—COMPARATIVE SPEED OF TRANSMISSION—CRITICAL REVIEW OF THE RESULTS—AUTOMATIC CONTROL—MORSE'S METHOD—SORTAIS APPARATUS—MORSE STOPPING APPARATUS.

AUTOMATIC RECORDING.

At the very earliest conception of the art of writing or imprinting at a distance, in one or more distant places at the same time, the best modes of practically demonstrating it were, as a matter of course, the subject of absorbing attention in the mind of the inventor. No sooner, therefore, did the idea of the possibility of making an automatic record of intelligence from a distance occur to its originator, than it became his main purpose to demonstrate by some means, and by the simplest means he could then devise, that it was not merely possible, but that it must be realized in some way, and made an accomplished fact. Indeed, the production in some way of this automatic record was the key-note of his whole theme.

It cannot, therefore, be thought strange, that a great variety of possible modes suggested themselves to him; nor is it more strange that, after he had demonstrated one mode as practicable, subsequent inventors, in following the original track which led to the demonstration of that mode, should find that many of the devices occurring to them in their speculations, which seemed to them new, had been anticipated by the original discoverer of the new road. It could scarcely be otherwise, nor does this consideration by any means involve a charge of plagiarism against claimants to these same devices; a more charitable position is that while pursuing the new route opened to them, the same objects would independently attract their notice. Such, however, would be ready to allow that the objects which to them are novelties may not be novelties to him who opened and first explored the new path.

The original proposition of writing or printing at a distance must not be considered as merely a brilliant but crude idea, sent forth by its originator to be developed and equipped by others; it was from the moment of its conception the hourly occupation of his thoughts for days and months, long before it was deemed by others to be more than the chimera of an ill-regulated imagination. These modes in their embryo state were conceived, indeed, in comparative seclusion, without even the opportunity or the means to put them except in part into tangible shape, other than in drawings, until months and even years had elapsed; for the first apparatus, although conceived in its essential characteristics as early as 1832, and mainly existing in drawings, (partly embodied, indeed, at that date,) was not in a shape to give a substantial practical demonstration of the successful result until 1835. This is not the date given by the inventor but by numerous witnesses, who are in agreement in testifying to seeing it in operation at that time.

That the earliest instrumentalities should be crude and capable of more or less improvement, every one experienced in invention will readily allow. But what is improvement? An improvement, or, as the French style it, *perfectionnement*, has a different meaning from improvement in the strict sense of that word. As often loosely used at the present day, the word modification would more accurately express the change or changes made in the instrumentalities of an invention. An improvement is a modification, but the reverse is not always true; a modification is not, of course, an improvement, but it would be technically styled so at the Patent Office. Even a change in an apparatus, for the purpose of gaining some presumed advantage, may accomplish its immediate purpose, while, at the same time, it may involve countervailing disadvantages in complication and expensiveness which may more than neutralize the advantage, and so the result of modification may be on the whole a loss and not a gain.

It is not uncommon to misapprehend the true nature and extent of a modification. While ignorant of the nature of that invention upon which a modification is based, it is not so easy to know if the modification is an unimportant change, or is, indeed, an improvement. A casual observer, without a thorough knowledge of an original invention is very apt to confound the new and the old, and in noticing a new arrangement is often led to consider the whole as new. Proper discrimination is necessary, that no injustice be done to any of the laborers in the same field of invention.

It will not be deemed egotistical on the part of an inventor, if in the attempts of others to improve his invention he should now and then recognize the familiar features of his own offspring, and claim their paternity. The attempts at improvement in the telegraph have been mainly directed to modes of recording, to wit: to modifications of the original inking apparatus; to modes of imprinting the ordinary alphabetic character; to automatic transmission of dispatches; to autographic transmission of dispatches and designs, and to automatic control of a distant apparatus. There have also been attempted improvements in batteries or generators of electricity.

In order, therefore, to demonstrate and elucidate any professed improvement upon an art in any of its processes, it becomes not a matter of choice but of necessity in the very outset, first, to set forth clearly the original processes or instrumentalities professed to be improved. This necessity must be an apology (if any apology is required) for so often recurring to the original invention of the Morse telegraph.

THE GENERIC TELEGRAPH.

The more thoroughly its early history becomes known the more clearly will it be erceived and acknowledged to be the generic telegraph. The means and processes of this first telegraph have been adopted, and have become not only the efficient instrumentalities of all the modern telegraphs, but the modern semaphores have also derived from the instrumentalities applied in the telegraph some of their most efficient means of accomplishing their more limited results; for example, the adoption of the electro-magnet, giving to the telegraph its semaphoric or acoustic quality.

Fig. 17.

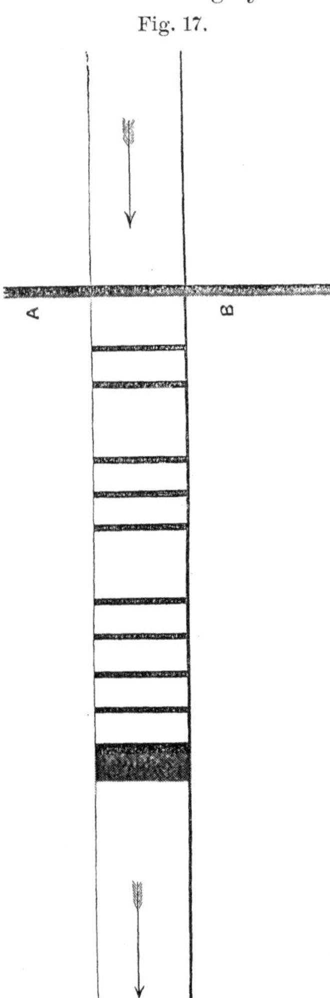

In illustration, therefore, of the earlier processes of the telegraph, diagrams of some of the modes of recording first tried by the inventor are given—modes used by him with more or less of success in the first constructed instruments.

THE ELECTRO-CHEMICAL PROCESS.

The earliest mode devised for producing a record was an electro-chemical process.

The inventor had the idea before landing from the ship in 1832 that his purpose of recording might be accomplished by the use of some salt, so easily decomposable, or so sensibly influenced by electricity in its passage through a conductor that a mark upon paper impregnated with such a salt might be the result, by simple contact with the conductor at the moment of an electrical charge. A magnetic effect was known to exist. Was there any other effect available to produce a mark? This was the problem to be solved.

With no means on board the ship for any experiment, this suggested mode was reserved to be tried at the close of the voyage. Coincident with the electro-chemical mode the electro-magnetic or mechanical mode of marking was elaborated, and the various devices for using the power of the electro-magnet reduced to drawings.

On testing the first electro-chemical mode by simple contact with a conductor in an electric state with the hope to produce the result in the diagram, the experiment failed with the salt that had been suggested, and with several other salts that were experimented upon in that manner. The paper impregnated with the salt in this case was made simply to pass beneath and in contact with the conducting wire. If no current was passing in the wire the paper would show no mark, but when a current was sent through the wire the paper should show marks across the strip like those in the diagram. The thinner lines represent the dots, the thicker lines the dashes of the conventional code, This was the theory. Submitted to experiment, as has been stated, it failed in practice. But by passing the electric current through the paper impregnated with various salts the marking was produced more or less perfectly, yet attended with so many inconveniences that the electro-chemical mode was temporarily reserved for future experimenting, in order to perfect the electro-magnetic mode, which promised a surer and better result. Perceiving that by the electro-magnet he had command of a power capable at will to make a line of any length upon a moving strip or ribbon of paper, the inventor found that the dots and spaces and eventually the dashes of the code he had already devised were readily made by any convenient marking instrument, such as a pencil or pen or printing wheel. The object, then, of the inventor was to adopt the best of the several devices which had suggested themselves to him.

THE ELECTRO-MAGNETIC MODE.

The first and most obvious was that of a pencil at one extremity of the lever, as in Fig. 18.

Fig. 18.

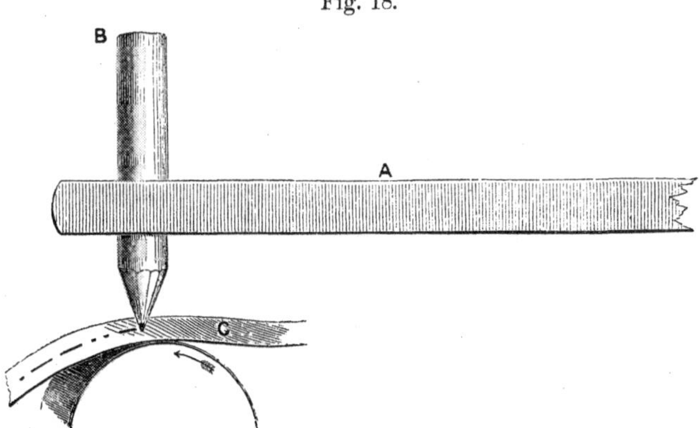

The Pencil Point.

The marking with the pencil B gave a successful result, but the blow in striking the paper often broke the point of the pencil and required constant attention, and produced many interruptions, so that the use in the manner seen in the diagram was early abandoned; but the pencil was immediately used in the manner shown in the first constructed instrument of 1835, as seen in Fig. 18, by which the damage to the point of the pencil was avoided, yet still the constant wearing away of the pencil presented a difficulty to be removed.

Fig. 19.

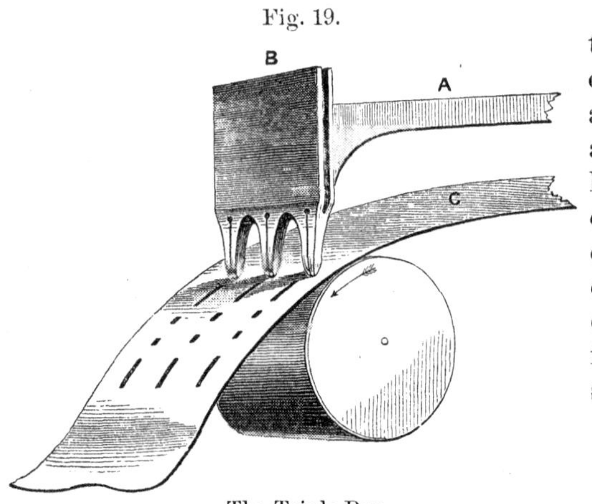

The Triple Pen.

This was attempted by the use of fountain pens of various construction; at first a single pen formed a capillary tube, which had the inconvenience of outnot giving out its ink if of action for any length of time. To remedy this defect the form of the fountain pen was like that shown in Fig. 19.

THE TRIPLE PEN.

This gave the dispatch by a three-fold line, so that in case one pen should be clogged and fail to record, one or both of the other pen secured the record. This method for some time produced good results. It was the mode exhibited to the Congress at Washington in the session of 1837–'38, and to the Academy of Sciences in Paris in 1838, described by M. Arago from its appearance as "*un petit rateau*," or little rake.

THE PRINTING WHEEL.

There was also another mode successfully used in the early experiments, seen in Fig. 20, by a printing wheel, as in the modern ink-writers,

Fig. 20.

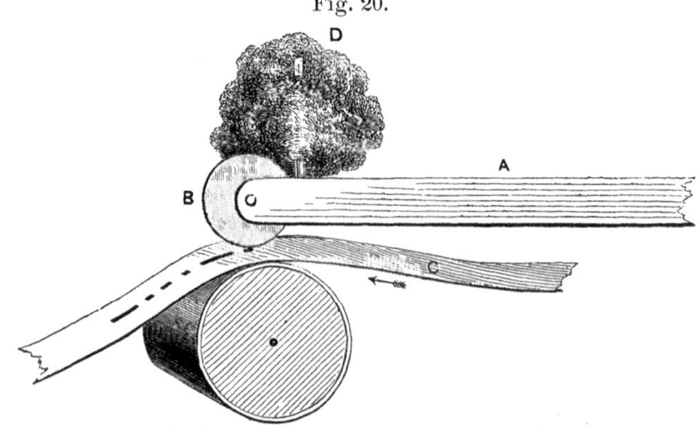

The Printing Wheel.

the only difference between this original mode and the present ink-writers being the supply of ink to the wheel originally by a sponge instead of the modern felt wheel. All these modes are distinctly specified in Morse's caveat of 1837, in the Patent Office at Washington. Why was not the last mode, so identical with the modern ink-writers, which are so popular, at once adopted in practice? The inventor was desirous of avoiding several inconveniences attendant on all the modes of using ink. The drying of the ink upon the ink-wheel, especially in dry climates and in warm weather, would often render the inking process unreliable. Again, unless care were specially taken there was constant danger of an over-charge of ink, soiling the paper and producing grave interruptions.

THE STEEL POINT.

To avoid these inconveniences a steel point *(point sèche)* was devised and used, which marked the paper strip, by the interposition of a blackened or colored paper between the point and the paper strip, as in the ordinary manifold copying process. This also was successful, but did not remove every inconvenience. It was then that the idea of embossing the paper directly with the same stylus, in the mode now known as the dry point or embosser, (the *point sèche,*) was conceived and adopted. Fig. 21 shows this mode.

Fig. 21.

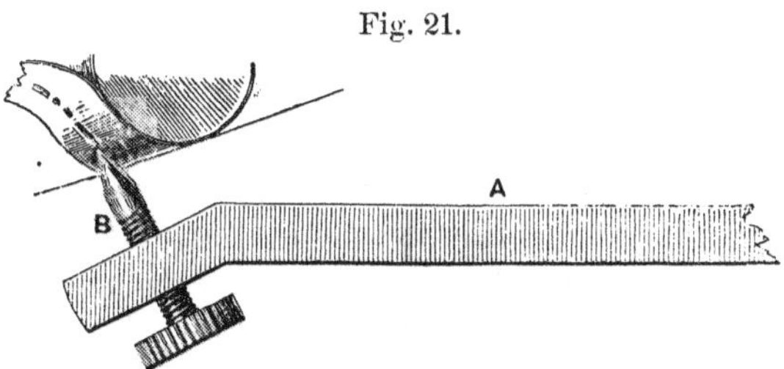

The Steel Point.

This was considered by him a substantial improvement, since the simple stylus at the extremity of the lever was always in order, requiring no attention. It dispensed with ink and all its inconveniences and complication, and reduced the apparatus to its minimum of simplicity.

MODES OF MARKING OR RECORDING.

It is customary, in treating of this part of the telegraphic apparatus, by many historians of the telegraph, to consider this steel point or embossing mode as the primary mode devised by the inventor, and the inking or printing wheel as a modern improvement upon it by others. This is a mistake. The inventor considered the dry point or embosser as an improvement on his original inking apparatus devised and used as early as 1845, and was patented in April, 1846, and in the employment of his inking wheel by modern mechanicians, he thinks that some of the advantages of the dry point have been overlooked, while some of its disadvantages have been unduly exaggerated. These latter are stated to be—first, the disadvantage of being obliged to read the letters by a particular light and shadow fatiguing to the eye. A simple remedy to this is the application of a light ink roller to the top of the embossed letter as it issues from the stylus, in such a way that the ink touches the top only of the raised letter. This has been successfully done, and is a mechanical arrangement easily made, and it obviates this disadvantage, and at the same time obviates the second disadvantage, which is, that an embossed message, when the paper is rolled up, loses its raised character, and leaves the paper blank, so that the record is obliterated. If inked in the way just suggested this difficulty disappears. The third disadvantage is, that it requires a relay in order to furnish the requisite power to emboss the characters. This is the most plausible of all, and so far as it is desirable to dispense with the relay, the mode of inking the characters devised by the Messrs. Digney frères, to wit: by bringing the paper up in contact with the ink wheel, instead of the ink wheel down upon the paper, as in the original mode, is a successful and valuable improvement. It must be said, however, on the other side that the dispensing with the relay, is, under some aspects, of doubtful economy, especially in view of the acoustic effect of the pen lever in the act of embossing; this effect is destroyed in the silent operation of the inking process, but with the relay and steel point is retained, and is of so important a character as to have modified to a considerable extent the whole process of telegraphic or rather semaphoric communication by the Morse apparatus.

To offset these disadvantages charged against the dry point there is one manifest advantage in its employment which seems so obvious that it is a matter of some surprise that no one of the ingenious mechanicians, who have been intent on improvements, should not have long since discovered and applied it. This advantage is the special applicability of the dry point process to automatic transmission.

AUTOMATIC TRANSMISSION.

The automatic process was the original mode devised for the first demonstration of a strictly telegraphic result. As special attention in the present day is being given to this mode, in the hope so to perfect it as to supersede other processes, it may not be amiss to dwell a moment upon its character.

The original automatic process of the first instrument in 1835 was accomplished by metallic type, set up in composing sticks or rules, and carried beneath the lever by an apparatus called the "port rule," which bore forward the prepared rules in proper succession. This mode required several distinct operations: First. The preparation of an indefinite quantity of the metallic type to be furnished to each office. Second. The setting up of these type in the rules or composing sticks. Third. The placing of these rules in their order in the transmitting apparatus. Fourth. The mechanical operating of the port rule. Fifth. The distribution of the type after the whole operation of transmission has been completed.

The automatic type process of Siemens, which we shall presently examine, requires the same several operations as the original automatic type process.

An automatic process by Wheatstone, not in the catalogue, requires, first, a peculiar apparatus, called the perforator, for punching holes in a strip of paper; second, another apparatus, called a transmitter, by which the paper thus prepared is carried forward to operate the levers of contact; third, another apparatus, called the receiver, which gives the recording result upon a strip of paper at a distance.

These last two—transmitter and receiver—are modifications of the original Morse manipulator or key, and the Morse register, in order to increase the speed of the mechanical movements of each instrumentality.

In Wheatstone's process the perforator is a different instrument from the Morse manipulating key, and much more complicated, and requires a different mode of operating it, a new manipulating process is to be learned by the operator in addition to his usual acquirements. The punched paper requires more time in its preparation than the usual embossing or writing process of the Morse system. When once prepared, however, it has the advantage over the type setting mode that no distribution of type is necessary after the transmission has been completed.

The transmission and reception of the message in all these modes differ very little from each other.

EMBOSSED PAPER PROCESS.

The general advantage proposed to be obtained by automatic transmission is that a greater quantity of intelligence can be transmitted in a given time by this mechanical mode than by the ordinary or hand manipulation with the Morse key, or manipulator, and that this may be accomplished by having the dispatch, if of great length, set up or prepared by dividing it into what are called by printers "takes" or convenient portions, and employing several operators who, at the same time, prepare their several takes, by setting up the type, or preparing the punched paper to be used in the transmission. The mode proposed by the writer of this report has the advantage of greater simplicity as a result of the embossing process with the *point sèche.* For this mode requires no type setting, no new instrument for preparing the paper; no new process of punching paper to be learned by the operators. The operator prepares his dispatch in the usual way, by embossing the paper, as if sending a dispatch. It is then at once ready for transmission; needing no perforations nor other preparation. The paper strip with the embossed characters is simply passed beneath a delicate lever like that of the relay magnet. As every embossed part passes under the lever, contact is made longer or shorter according to the length of the embossed line.

The result is the same as by the type process and the punched paper process.

The only variation which may possibly be required in the present Morse apparatus is a more perfect mechanical embossing point, a small wheel, for example, instead of a blunt point, by which the embossed characters shall receive a stronger and bolder relief, and paper more capable of this stronger embossing.

These are within the ordinary mechanical capabilities of good workmanship.

AUTOMATIC APPARATUS OF SIEMENS AND HALSKÉ.

No. 39 of the catalogue comprises the telegraphic and semaphoric instruments of those accomplished mechanicians and savans, the Messrs. Siemens and Halské, of Berlin, so profound in scientific research and prolific in every variety of ingenious and novel philosophical instruments. Among the most noteworthy in the Exposition is their automatic apparatus, which, it appears, has been operated with successful results upon the German lines. Those who are familiar with the early history of the generic telegraph will recognize the fact that the automatic mode of recording was embodied in the first telegraphic instrument devised by the writer in 1832, and it was the first mode by which the new art was demonstrated in 1835. At that early period the automatic was deemed to be the only practical, if not practicable, mode of insuring a perfect record. The details of this process are to be found in the earliest specifications and descriptions and models of the Morse invention in the Patent Office at Washington, and the instrumentalities are very fully described and illustrated by diagrams in Vail's earliest work on the telegraph, published in 1845.

The general features of this first Morse automatic process may be briefly stated to consist of—

First. The embodiment in a species of cogged type of the numerals to be recorded, consisting of lines, dots, and spaces—the elements of the Morse code. This was accomplished in November and December of 1832. Subsequently the inventor extended the principles of his code to the letters of the alphabet, which were added to the numerals, and, with some special signs for punctuation and office signals, completed his original code.

Second. Of rules or composing sticks, in which the desired type were set up.

Third. Of the port rule or instrument, by which the rules when prepared with their type were carried forward to operate.

Fourth. A lever to close and open the electric circuit at the regulated times.

In this part of the automatic process of the new art, the inventor early made many modifications, some of which are also fully described by Vail.

Experience soon suggested that however desirable on account of accuracy was this automatic mode, manipulation by the hand with a simple rocking lever possessed many advantages, among which was the dispensing with the complicated machinery of types, composing sticks, and port rules, and the consumption of time in preparation, and this simple manipulator was found to be sufficiently accurate for the ordinary requirements of the telegraph. This manipulator holds its place in the telegraph instruments at this day.

SPEED OF TRANSMISSION.

To ascertain the quantity of intelligence that could be recorded in a given time was not in the early period of the history of the telegraph so much a desideratum as to know that any could be recorded; and the comparatively little that was accomplished by the new art, in its first essays, was in such vastly greater quantity than could possibly be transmitted by any of the semaphoric modes previously in use, that for some time the public were content with the success already achieved.

In process of time, however, stimulated chiefly by the enterprising spirit of the conductors of the American Associated Press, the lightning was invoked to send what it sent more rapidly, or rather to send more in a specified time, and hence the minds of the ingenious were concentrated on modes of manipulating a greater quantity in a given time.

In estimating the speed of transmission, it is obvious that other circumstances than the time occupied in manipulation, whether by the hand key, (the circuit closer,) or by automatic machinery, must be considered in making a fair estimate.

Precedent to transmission there must be taken into the account, first, the cost and nature of the apparatus; second, the number of employés necessary to prepare the copy for transmission; third, the number of employés necessary to receive and prepare it for delivery at the distant station; fourth, the comparative time required to prepare the copy for transmission; and then follows, fifth, the time occupied in transmission; and, sixth, the distance to which it can be transmitted.

To illustrate the necessity for taking into the account these propositions, let a given quantity of intelligence, and the same intelligence, be presented at the same moment to be sent by the several apparatus respectively. That system which first delivers the intelligence complete at the distant station will (other things being equal) bear away the palm. I say other things being equal, for in an economic point of view, the first, second, and third propositions must be insisted on. For it is easy to conceive twenty wires with an apparatus and operators furnished to each, and the copy divided into twenty parts or "takes," (to use the nomenclature of the printing office,) and each operator sending his allotted portion or "take" at the same time, and thus the whole could be transmitted in a twentieth part of the time required to send the whole by a single wire, apparatus, and operator. It is at once perceived that, although this might be successfully accomplished, it could not be accomplished with economy. Hence the economic means enter materially into the estimate of the final result.

Again, in the test of the Morse apparatus, its semaphoric quality, by means of the simple acoustic arrangement, has shown, in mere rapidity of transmission, at least, its superiority over the proper telegraphic quality of the same apparatus. The telegraphic quality, however, is that which is considered in most of the European administrations as a necessity, because it furnishes, by its permanent recorded result, that control which the system of government surveillance makes absolutely necessary, and which does not belong to any mere semaphoric mode. This fact is to be taken into the account in estimating speed of transmission. All the automatic processes are telegraphic. There is a limit to the quantity that can be transmitted and recorded in a given time, for the most part quite inside of the result of the acoustic or semaphoric mode.

Experience alone can decide on the comparative advantages of these two modes.

The Morse process of recording by electro-chemical decomposition attracted early attention, and occupied the time and employed the skill of several ingenious men in Europe, but especially of Bain, who gave it greater efficiency by the application of a more sensitive salt than had been previously applied. This process is attended with great inconveniences, but these have not prevented its use to some limited extent. In theory, however capable of producing greater speed, (sometimes obtained in exceptional cases,) there are practical as well as theoretical difficulties which have hitherto disappointed the flattering expectations of its friends, and interposed serious obstacles to its general adoption.

The immense rapidity of the passage of the electric current suggests that there is scarcely a limit to the quantity of intelligence that might be transmitted in a given time. Theoretically, indeed, any speed yet attained could be increased almost indefinitely; but this speed is limited not by the speed of electricity, but by the action of the necessary intervening mechanical instrumentalities. Were the speed of electricity the sole element to be taken into consideration, the amount of intelligence that could be transmitted can scarcely be computed; but the mechanical agencies of a more sluggish nature which mingle in the process foreshadow a limit, and it is precisely here that the ingenious savant and mechanician find a profitable employment for their research and skill in modifying and improving the automatic process.

BLAVIER ON SPEED OF TRANSMISSION.

As pertinent to this subject, a quotation is made from the excellent work of M. Blavier, volume i, page 188, of his calculations of the possible speed of transmission:

"The speed of transmission which can be obtained with an instrument depends not only on the rapidity of manipulation that can be increased, by mechanical means, almost indefinitely, but also on the nature and length of the line. It depends, in fact, on the register itself, and it is well to ascertain for each instrument the maximum number of signs that it can give—that in which its power of transmission consists.

"For the Morse apparatus, the question reduces itself to know how many dots (or points) the register can receive in a minute.

"A movable armature over against an electro-magnet can, under the influence of interrupted currents, effect at least from five thousand to six thousand oscillations in a minute, but on condition that their extent shall be extremely small, and it would be insufficient to produce signs upon a band of paper, even admitting that the speed of unrolling the paper can be definitely increased. For, in order that the lever shall be lifted and mark a sign, there must be a determinate time which varies with the form of the apparatus, and above all with the mass of the lever.

"When in the Morse apparatus the *(point sèche)* dry point is used, the lever is always very massive; it allows also the addition of a relay, and even with a very rapid unrolling of the paper not more than 300 or 400 dots per minute can be obtained. An apparatus *(à molette)* with printing wheel, operating by the intervention of a relay, can give from 800 to 900 dots. In fact, a Morse apparatus *(à molette)* with printing wheel, without a relay, constituted in the best possible manner, that is to say, in which the armature, the lever, and the knife are as light as possible, a condition which may be obtained by reducing their dimensions, and even their densities, by the employment of aluminum, can give even 2,000 dots per minute.

"When the number of dots that can be transmitted is known, it is easy to estimate the corresponding number of words.

"In considering the duration or extent of a dot as unity, and in designating it by 1, the duration or extent of a line is 3; the separation (or space) between the signs in the same letter is 1; that of two letters, 3; that of words, 6 units. In taking at hazard a great number of words, (one or two pages of a book for example,) and in writing in the signs, every dot and line and space can be counted for the number of corresponding units, to calculate the total number of units necessary to express the aggregate of the words; and then, if the sum is divided by the number of words, we have the mean number of units which correspond to a word.

"Thus it is found that each word, including the blank space between the words, is represented by the average of 48 units.

"If, then, the apparatus can receive 2,000 dots in one minute, which with their blanks (or spaces) represent 4,000 units, the number of words which can be transmitted will be $\frac{4000}{48}$, or eighty-four words per minute. Besides, it is necessary that the signs be made distinct upon the paper band. In order to read them easily, the separation of the signs and the length of the dots ought to be at least three-quarters of a millimeter.[1]

"If the paper is unrolled at the speed of $1^m.20$ per minute, the

[1] A millimeter is .0394 of an inch, *i. e.*, about one twenty-fifth of an inch.

greatest number of units equal to three-quarters of the millimeter, .02955 of an inch, is 1,600, which corresponds to thirty-five words per minute. If this speed is to be surpassed, the speed of unrolling the paper must be increased either by employing a more powerful spring or by contracting the wings of the fly.

"The speed of unrolling the paper at the rate of $1^{m}.20$ is more than sufficient; for twenty-five words per minute can never be in practice surpassed, only in exceptional cases, and the space that each dot occupies must be above three-quarters of a millimeter to render the reading more easy."

"Manipulation by the hand, by means of the manipulator previously described, presents many inconveniences. It cannot be absolutely regular; it varies according to the skill and even to the character of the operator. Besides, it is forcibly limited, since the greater part of the operators attain with difficulty to fifteen or eighteen words per minute and the most skillful do not exceed twenty-five."

From this calculation of M. Blavier, therefore, it would seem to be demonstrated that twenty-five words in one minute, or fifteen hundred in one hour, is the greatest number that can be given by hand manipulation, yet this can only apply to the distinct recording of the signs upon the band of paper. The hand manipulation upon the sounder, which involves the use of the Morse manipulator in the same manner as if recording, gives a greater number of words in a minute than any automatic recording process yet practically employed, as will be presently shown.

COMPARATIVE SPEED BY DIFFERENT INSTRUMENTS.

The comparative speed of transmission, or the quantity of words in a given time, by different instruments is stated in the official documents of two national administrations as follows:

The single dispatch is calculated at *twenty words*, and the number of dispatches at so many in *one hour*.

Of such dispatches—

[1] In France the Morse is rated at twenty in one hour; the Hughes, at fifty in one hour; the dial system, at fifteen in one hour; the Caselli, (hesitatingly,) at forty in one hour.

In Prussia the Morse is rated at twenty to thirty in one hour; the Hughes, at forty to fifty in one hour; the Siemens, at sixty in one hour.

The distance or the length of the conductors, or their equivalent, in resistance, is an important element in the calculation. This element is not given in the French calculation.

In the Prussian experiments the distance measured by resistance coils is stated in one instance at 2,700 English miles, and in another at 540 English miles.

Not satisfied that justice had been done to the Morse system in this comparative statement by rating it at twenty telegrams in an hour, a

[1] See Chapter V, questions to, and answers of, Viscount de Vougy.

request was made to the president of the Western Union Telegraph Company to have the speed of transmission fairly tried upon the American lines. Accordingly, an executive circular was issued, and in conformity with its requirements the results were duly sworn to and attested by notaries public.

The following table embodies these results:

Table of results of the trial of speed by the Morse apparatus.

Name of operator sending.	Name of operator receiving.	Date of trial.	Number of telegrams of twenty words each in one hour.	Number of words in one hour.	Number of words in one minute.	Distance in English miles.
John H. French	John H. Dwight	Jan. 18, 1868	80	1, 600	26⅔	310
Charles F. Stumm	L. A. Somers	Jan. 28, 1868	96	1, 920	32	135
Thomas L. A. Valiquet and F. S. Kent.	A. B. Hilliker	Feb. —, 1868	99	1, 980	33	1, 650
Thomas L. A. Valiquet and F. S. Kent.	A. B. Hilliker	Feb. —, 1868	102	2, 040	34 2-7	1, 650
Thomas L. A. Valiquet and F. S. Kent.	A. B. Hilliker	Feb. —, 1868	111	2, 220	37 1-9	1, 650
G. M. Shape	E. Curry	Feb. 8, 1868	131½	2, 631	43 5-6	450
R. J. Hutchinson	L. A. Somers	Jan. 29, 1868	126½	2, 530	42 1-6	631
William S. Kettles	Reese and W. Sherman.	Jan. 19, 1868	94	1, 880	31⅓	1, 300
M. Mareau	William Wallace	Jan. 19, 1868	110	2, 202	36 1-7	700
M. Marks and J. Bagley, first trial.	N. J. Snyder	Jan. 21, 1868	125	*2, 500	41⅔	90
M. Marks and J. Bagley, second trial.	N. J. Snyder	Jan. 21, 1868	126	2, 520	42	450
James Fisher	James Leonard	Autumn, 1860	156	3, 120	52	
James Fisher	James Leonard	Autumn, 1860	165	3, 300	55	
R. J. Hutchinson	N. J. Snyder	Feb. 19, 1860	135	2, 704	45	100
Edward C. Stewart	N. J. Snyder	Feb. 20, 1860	127	2, 540	42⅓	100
M. Marian	William Wallace	Jan. 19, 1860	111¼	2, 224	37	663
P. H. Burns, Boston	Walter Phillips, Providence.	May 8, 1868	136½	†2, 731	45½	40

* By the repeating of a line, the number of words was actually 2, 510 in one hour.

FIRST TRIAL, (divided into six parts of ten minutes each.)

First 10 minutes, M. Marks,	410 words.
Next 10 minutes, Charles Bagley	404 words.
Next 10 minutes, Charles Bagley	369 words.
Next 10 minutes, Charles Bagley	454 words.
Next 10 minutes, Charles Bagley	434 words.
Next 10 minutes, Charles Bagley	429 words.
60 minutes	2, 500 words.

SECOND TRIAL—

First 9 minutes, M. Marks	373 words.
Next 11 minutes, Charles Bagley	450 words.
Next 10 minutes, Charles Bagley	374 words.
Next 10 minutes, Charles Bagley	460 words.
Next 10 minutes, Charles Bagley	430 words.
Next 10 minutes, Charles Bagley	433 words.
60 minutes	2, 520 words.

† This recording of 2, 731 words in one hour, by Walter Phillips, of Providence, Rhode Island, and the recording of 2, 520 words in the same time, by N. J. Snyder, at Philadelphia, are the greatest feats in telegraphic transmission that have yet been accomplished by the Morse apparatus in any country. The instrumentalities were the Morse sounder, or acoustic instrument, (the cost of which is about eight dollars,) a battery, and two operators, one at each terminus of a line. In these seventeen trials the average is 119½ dispatches, of twenty words each, in one hour, or two dispatches in one minute.

Speed of the Hughes apparatus and of Siemen's automatic type-presses.

	Number of telegrams of twenty words each in one hour.	Number of words in one hour.	Number of words in one minute.
The Hughes apparatus—In France	50	1,000	$16\frac{2}{3}$
In Prussia	40 to 50	800 to 1,000	$13\frac{1}{3}$ to $16\frac{2}{3}$
The Siemen's process—In Prussia	60	1,200	20

RECENT RESULT IN FRANCE IN SPEED OF TRANSMISSION.

At the late opening of the Legislative Assembly in Paris, (1869,) the speech of the Emperor on the occasion was transmitted from Paris to various capitals. It will be seen that extraordinary efforts were made to transmit it by telegraph with the utmost speed. We copy from the French journals the following account of the result:

"Nothing could be more curious and interesting than the aspect which was presented yesterday after the speech of the Emperor, in the central telegraph station.

"The day before, orders had been given that the lines and apparatus should be inspected with care and put in order. At half past 12 o'clock the entire body of officials were at their posts waiting the word of command.

"Scarcely had the first copies been distributed to them than *two hundred employés* were put to work, and the transmission was made with a dizzy rapidity, of which the following figures will give some idea:

"The imperial speech contains about 1,200 words.

"London received it in fourteen minutes; Berlin, in one hour and nine minutes; Florence, in one hour and forty minutes; Brussels, in forty-five minutes; Vienna, in one hour and fifty minutes.

"The difference in time to the advantage of London is explained by this fact: that four wires (or circuits) were used for the transmission of the speech to that capital, while only one was used for the others."

This feat of transmission by telegraph, scrutinized, gives the following comparative result. The speech containing 1,200 words was sent entire to London in fourteen minutes; but four wires (with, of course, as many instruments) were needed to accomplish the result, so that, divided between the four, each wire or instrument transmitted 300 words in fourteen minutes, equivalent to fifty-six minutes by one wire, to send the whole 1,200 words. By referring to the table of results in the trial of speed of the Morse apparatus, (in 1868,) it will be perceived that the minimum of the results, by the American operators, amounted to 1,600 words in one hour, which is in excess of the estimated number per hour of the greatest speed attained in this late European feat.

The time in which the speech was transmitted to Brussels upon one wire, to wit, forty-five minutes, is the greatest speed in this case; but this is equivalent to 1,500 words only per hour.

From these results it will be seen, in comparing them with the results of other modifications of the apparatus, that the original simple Morse apparatus maintains its superiority in the telegraphic field. Its simplicity of construction, its cheapness, its efficiency, its requirement of so few employés in its management, are the qualities which have given it its world-wide popularity, and have caused its universal adoption.

Notwithstanding this simple apparatus has proved its ability to accomplish so much, the desire for more has turned the minds of the ingenious upon devising many modifications of the apparatus.

The *automatic type telegraph* (No. 39) exhibited by Messrs. Siemens and Halské of Berlin is an apparatus of the same general character as the original Morse apparatus, but, it is scarcely necessary to add, of superior beauty of mechanical execution, like everything that comes from their extensive ateliers.

AUTOMATIC TRANSMISSION IN PRUSSIA.

Being in Berlin in February, 1868, the writer called on the courteous and obliging directors and superintendent of the Prussian telegraph, the Colonel Herr von Chauvin, and Herr von Frischen. By the latter officer he was shown into the apartment in which was arranged the automatic modification of Messrs. Siemens and Halské, a duplicate of their apparatus in the Exposition, (No. 39.) Besides the instruments for transmission, there were cases of type, (giving to the apartment the appearance of a printing office,) and a corps of some ten or twelve employés.

The following written questions were put to Herr von Frischen, to which he gave their annexed answers:

"1. Question. What instruments are necessary in this automatic process?

"Answer. Two instruments, a transmitter and receptor.

"2. Question. What is their respective cost?

"Answer. *Transmitter*, with 150 *long* rules and 35 *short* ones, and 15,000 types, cost 700 Prussian thalers, (or about $525 in gold.) *Receptor* costs 105 thalers, (or about $78 75 gold.)

"3. Question. What time does it take to prepare the message in type, for transmission?

"Answer. *Three minutes* to prepare a message of twenty words, together with eight words for the direction, or address, in all twenty-eight words; and half a minute to revise and see that all is right.

"4. Question. What is the practical speed of transmission and reception by the type process?

"Answer. *Forty-five* single messages in one hour by the present sized wire for 120 German miles, or 540 English miles. We can send at the same time in four different directions to Königsberg, Frankfort-on-the-Main, Cologne, and Brussels.

"5. Question. What is the practical speed of preparation, transmitting, and reception by the punched-paper process?

"Answer. Experiments in the room with 600 German miles (or 2,700 English miles) resistance, a single message of twenty words can be sent in half a minute with the magneto-electric current; and with double battery (galvanic) current, one minute. With better apparatus the same speed can be attained in both cases. The preparation of the paper by hand for a single message of twenty words takes three minutes; prepared by the key-board, like Hughes's key-board, a single message is prepared in one minute.

"6. Question. What distance is the magneto-electric current available practically in telegraphing?

"Answer. The same distance as the galvanic current.

"7. Question. What difficulties do you experience in the present mode of automatic transmission?

"Answer. The great number of employés necessary.

"8. Question. How many employés are necessary in preparing and transmitting a certain amount by one instrument?

"Answer. *Ten* (10) persons to prepare; *two* (2) to transmit; and *two* (2) to revise; in all fourteen (14)."

For the purpose of corroborating these statements, the following letter was addressed by the writer in February, 1868, to Messrs. Siemens and Halské, the mechanicians of the automatic type process, which was examined in the Prussian office, the counterpart of No. 39 in the Exposition:

"Will you oblige me with answers to the following questions, which I shall be happy to insert in my report?

"1. What kind of instruments, and how many, for one apparatus complete, are required in your automatic processes? How many in the *type process?* How many in the *punched-paper process?*

"2. What is the cost of each separate instrument in a single set, and what the cost of all together?

"3. How much time is required to prepare a message of twenty words for transmission by the type mode? How much by the punched paper mode?

"4. What is the regular practical speed of transmission and of reception by the type process, and what by the punched paper process?

"5. What are the difficulties you encounter in your automatic processes?

"6. How many employés are required to prepare, to transmit, and to receive messages?"

To the above questions the following replies were courteously accorded:

"We beg you to excuse the lateness of the answer to your favor of the 17th February. The delay was caused by the condition of the punched-paper apparatus, not so far finished as to be able to give you the desired information.

"1. The complete electro-magnetical type transmitter, sufficient for transmitting seventy messages in one hour, consists of—

	Thalers.
1 transmitting instrument	150 00
1 receiving instrument, inkwriter, with variable speed of its clock-work	110 00
150 letter rods (type rules) in which to set up the type, at 5 thalers	750 00
15,000 types, at 20 thalers per 1,000	300 00
6 letter cases, at $5\frac{2}{3}$ thalers	34 00
15 cases for the rods, (type rules,) at $1\frac{1}{2}$ thalers	22 15
The complete instrument, (about $1,024 in gold)	1,366 15

"The time for composing one dispatch of twenty words, five minutes; for distributing, four minutes; so that all preparations of every message require nine minutes.

"For the above-named speed of transmission there will be necessary, twelve men for setting up and distributing; two men for transmitting; and two men for receiving and writing down the messages.

"2. For transmission by the punched-paper arrrangement there will be required the following instruments:

	Thalers.
1 key-board puncher	250 00
1 handle puncher	80 00
1 magneto-electrical transmitter	125 00
One complete instrument	455 00

"The speed of transmission by this arrangement is one hundred and twenty messages in one hour. By the key-board puncher, one letter is completely finished as soon as the corresponding key is touched; therefore one man will be able to prepare the same number of messages as the transmitter gives away.

"However, we add the hand puncher for reserve or corrections. Instead of the magneto-electrical transmitter, we employ likewise a transmitter for reversed battery currents. The cost of such instruments is 120 thalers.

"This manner of transmission requires paper furnished with holes to drive it regularly.

"We manufacture also machines especially constructed for this perforation, at the price of 90 thalers each.

"For the service of this instrument are sufficient: one man for punching; one man for transmitting; two men for receiving and writing down the messages.

"This number of officers is necessary only if the automatic transmitter is continually in use, and it is only in this case the employing of the instrument seems lucrative.

"If there are always two lines at disposal, one for transmitting and the other for receiving, there is no difficulty in this automatic arrangement.

"Inclosed is a sample of a message prepared by the hand puncher, and transmitted by the magneto-electrical instrument. We have written on it the time occupied in preparation and transmission. The dispatch was worked through a resistance of 500 German miles, or 30,000 Siemens units of resistance," (equivalent to about 2,000 English miles.) * * *

Table of the comparative speed of transmission, by the different instrumentalities, on the basis of one dispatch of twenty words.

Kind of apparatus.	Time of preparation for transmission of one dispatch.	Time in transmitting one dispatch.	Number of employés.	Cost of the instruments, in gold.	Estimated average number of dispatches in one hour, taking into account time of preparation.	Stated average number in one hour.
	Minutes.	*Minutes.*				
Siemens & Halské's type process:						
According to Siemens & Halske, in their ateliers	9	½	16	$1,024 00	6⅔	70
According to Herr von Frischen, in the central office .	3½	½	14	603 75	20 to 60	40 to 45
Punched-paper process:						
According to Siemens & Halské..................	2½	½	4	431 25	*36	120
According to von Frischen...	1 to 3	½ to 1½	......	....	†20 to 60	....
Hughes	No time...	....	2	350 00	40 to 50	....
Morse..........................	No time...	....	2	14 00	119½	....

Remarks.—The discrepancy between the estimated average and the stated average arises doubtless from not taking into account, in the stated average, the time of "preparation for transmission."

* The sample referred to of the punched-paper process contains one hundred and fifty letters, occupying in the preparation and transmission two and a half minutes, equivalent to three hundred letters in five minutes, or sixty words, or three dispatches of twenty words each in five minutes, that is, at the rate of thirty-six dispatches in one hour.

† If it takes three minutes to prepare a single message of twenty words, it would take two hundred and ten minutes to prepare seventy dispatches for transmission, equivalent to three and a half hours. If one minute is required for preparing one dispatch, then one hour and ten minutes are required to prepare seventy dispatches previous to transmission.

CRITICAL REVIEW OF THESE RESULTS.

In presenting this table of results, it ought in fairness to be stated that, in all these automatic processes, the number of dispatches in an hour is estimated from a recorded dispatch made by the instrument itself, while the number by the Morse apparatus is the result of the acoustic method, recorded, indeed, but by an employé or clerk. The difference is in the efficiency of the two kinds of record for control. In the one case it is dependent on the automatic mechanism, which records upon the paper ribbon; in the other, it is dependent on the skill and faithfulness of the clerk transcribing as he hears it from the sounder. Sir Charles Wheatstone has recently devised an automatic punched-paper process, somewhat similar to the process of Messrs. Siemens and Halské, for a description of which we must refer to the jurors' reports of the London International Exhibition of 1862, Class XIII, pp. 69, 70. It is stated in that report that one hundred and sixty-six letters per minute were transmitted by it on a line of three hundred and twenty-four miles, equivalent to about one hundred dispatches in one hour. But in this case, as in the other automatic processes, the essential element of the time necessary to prepare the message previous to its transmission does not enter into the calculation. It is also stated in the same report that 1,476 words, equivalent to seventy-three dispatches per hour, are the greatest number that can be transmitted by the most expert clerk in the English telegraphic service. This rate, it will be seen, is greatly exceeded by the American operators in the late test of speed of transmission.

In making a comparison of the relative speed of transmission from the moment it is presented for that purpose until received at the distant station, it is necessary to take into the account—

1. The time required to prepare the dispatch for transmission.
2. The time of actual transmission.
3. The time for imbodying the received dispatch.
4. The number of employés necessary to accomplish the whole process.
5. The comparative cost of the apparatus.
6. The cost of maintenance of the employés, and the expense of repairs to the instruments.

For our purpose it is necessary at present only to consider the first and second of these points. On the supposition that a dispatch, say of 1,600 words, is presented at the office, at the same moment, for transmission, to be sent by the respective instruments, to wit, the Siemens and Halské automatic type telegraph, the Siemens and Halské punched-paper process, the Wheatstone punched-paper process, the Hughes apparatus, and the Morse apparatus, what would be the result of each?

The Siemens and Halské type-process takes three and a half minutes to prepare each dispatch of twenty-eight words for transmission; 1,600 words contain fifty-seven such dispatches, consuming, therefore, in the preparation, three hours and thirty minutes before transmission. Forty-five of these messages can then be transmitted in one hour, or the fifty-seven in one hour thirteen and a half minutes, which, added to the time of preparation, gives four hours forty-three and a half minutes as the time consumed in transmitting 1,600 words.

If the punched-paper process of Siemens and Halské be tested, the preparation of a dispatch of twenty words takes three minutes by hand, or one minute by a key-board instrument or perforator. Taking the lowest estimate, of one minute, then eighty messages, or 1,600 words, are prepared for transmission in one hour and twenty minutes, and in their transmission forty minutes more are consumed, making the time for completing the dispatch of 1,600 words two hours.

If from the data given of the capacity of the automatic punched-paper process of Sir Charles Wheatstone we make a comparative test, (the time of preparation not being stated,) we must assume that the time of preparation of a dispatch of 1,600 words previous to transmission can scarcely be less, by his perforator, than by the perforator of Messrs. Siemens and Halské. One hour and twenty minutes are therefore consumed in this preparation. If now the transmission of these eighty dispatches is accomplished at the rate given of one hundred dispatches in one hour, we must add forty-eight minutes, making the whole process two hours eight minutes.

The Hughes consumes no time in preparation, but commences transmitting at once, and the 1,600 words are, therefore, transmitted in one hour and thirty-six minutes.

The Morse consumes no time in preparation, but commences transmitting at once, and the 1,600 words are, therefore, transmitted in one hour.

This examination gives the following result:

	Hours.	Min.
The Siemens & Halské type-process, 80 dispatches..........	4	43½
The Siemens & Halské punched-paper process, 80 dispatches..	2	00
Wheatstone's punched-paper process, 80 dispatches...........	2	08
Hughes apparatus, 80 dispatches	1	36
Morse apparatus, 80 dispatches............................	1	00

It is urged in favor of the automatic type-process, as well as the punched-paper process, that the preparation of the dispatches by type or punched paper can be expedited by multiplying the number of perforators and employés, and thus the difficulty of the time consumed in preparation (which is stated to be an objection) is obviated; for if 1,600 words, or eighty dispatches, be divided, for example, into eight "takes," or sections, and eight perforators be used by eight employés, each preparing his own "take" at the same time, then the whole eighty dispatches are prepared in one-eighth of the time, and the time by the—

Type process, 4*h.* 43½*m.*, is reduced to .... 35*m.*
Punched-paper process, 1*h.* 20*m.*, is reduced to .... 10*m.*

To this time of preparation add time of transmission, respectively, and we have—

Type process, 40*m.*—altogether to .... 1*h.* 15*m.*
Punched-paper process, 48*m.*—altogether to .... 58*m.*

So that we have this result: The punched-paper process requires eight perforators and eight employés to accomplish what the Morse, with but one operator, accomplishes in the same time, (less only by two minutes.) Where wages are very low, and the employment, therefore, of an increased operative force is comparatively of little importance, there may be an advantage in employing the punched-paper process; but in an economic point of view, where the wages of employés are high, there would be no advantage in its adoption, except in exceptional cases.

AUTOMATIC CONTROL.

SORTAIS'S APPARATUS.

T. A. M. Sortais, of Lisieux, exhibited a mode of automatic control of a distant apparatus, (No. 7,) devised about the year 1861 or 1862.

It was early considered to be a great desideratum, so to have a distant apparatus under the control of a corresponding office, that even in case of the absence of the operator of that apparatus, a dispatch might still be recorded by the instrument, and so be independent of the presence of any attendant. One of Morse's earliest devices, for this purpose, patented in France in 1838, as well as in the United States, consisted of the union of two operations: 1st, of a means of setting in motion the distant recording apparatus; and, 2d, of a means of arresting the motion of the apparatus at any desired time. Both these operations being successfully accomplished, it is plain that a dispatch could be recorded, whether the attendant was present or not.

These means were based, first, on the sudden release of the fly that regulates the speed of the clock-work, by the first movement of the pen lever, in recording a dispatch. This part of the operation was simple enough. The detent that arrested the fly, being a small lever in contact with a friction wheel upon the axis of the fly, was easily removed by this first movement, and the clock-work set in motion, and the strip of paper was then ready to receive any amount of written characters. The second operation, that of arresting the apparatus, after the desired characters were completed, was based upon a replacement of the detent of the fly, or the small friction lever, upon the friction wheel, after the completion of the dispatch. This was accomplished in the very first instance successfully by an apparatus not now necessary to describe, in which there was the addition of a second electro-magnet, so adding complication to the instrumentalities. This was almost immediately modified by the improvement which Morse has described and specified in his French letters patent of August 18, 1838, as well as in his American patents. This improvement, in brief, consisted in slightly attaching, but not fixing, the detent or small lever by one extremity to the axis of one of the slower wheels of the clock-work in such a manner as to slip upon the axis when the friction lever was raised, but not so easily as not to hold its position when raised by the action of the pen lever. The other extremity of the small lever acted as a detent, by its friction, upon a friction wheel upon the fly axis, when brought in contact with it, and thus arrested the movement of the apparatus. The arm of the small friction lever was connected, by a thread or wire, with the pen lever above the friction lever, in such a manner, that when the pen lever rose it lifted the friction lever from the friction-wheel, and allowed the movement of the apparatus; but when the pen lever fell, it did not by that act abase the friction lever, which remained in its raised position, and was kept raised slipping on the axis of the slower wheel of the apparatus at every movement upward of the pen lever, and could only return to its position on the friction-wheel by the slower movement of the axis to which it was attached after the pen lever had for a given time ceased to act.

Another and an earlier mode, and the one fully described and illustrated by diagrams in Vail's work, of 1845, as well as in the specifications of Morse's patents, and which may also be found copied into the work of the Count du Moncel, is on the same principle. This earlier mode for automatic control is herein described with a diagram, following the description of M. Sortais's method.

The method of M. Sortais seems to have been devised without a consciousness that the same result had been already achieved by a mode similar in principle to his ingenious device.

The reasons so well given by M. Sortais for making this improvement upon the recording instrument, it will be seen by reference to Morse's patents, were those that suggested to him his original device for the purpose.

M. Sortais says: "The Morse apparatus, such as are in use at the present day, present a grave inconvenience. They can neither be put in motion, nor be arrested by themselves after being put in motion; in other words, they are not automatic. *Consequently, during the absence of the employé from the receiving office, no dispatch can be transmitted; it would be the same if this employé is absorbed in some urgent labor. As to the control of the service, no signal indicative of delay, is indicated either in the receptions or the expeditions.*

"An automatic system, on the contrary, will allow of the transmission and the recording of correspondence in the absence of the employés, and besides it offers to the administration the means of vigorously controlling the vigilance of the employés."

M. Sortais, in these remarks, was undoubtedly unaware that against the "grave inconveniences" he enumerates, Morse had already devised and applied a complete remedy more than twenty years before Mr. Sortais's modification of it.

M. Sortais has politely furnished a diagram, which illustrates his method of accomplishing this automatic control. It is an improvement on the Morse mode of automatic control, since it requires less power to put it in action, and it can be affixed to those Morse instruments of Messrs. Digney and Siemens's improvement, which dispense with the relays.

There has been a question of *utility* raised in regard to the advantage of this automatic control. Experience alone can determine the occasions when it may be of use.

The fact that the telegraphic service requires for the most part the constant presence of an operator would seem to indicate that this automatic control was considered more curious than useful; but upon lines established for infrequent or only occasional use, (for example such as may be established between the residence of a manufacturer and his distant workshops or offices,) there can be nó doubt of its utility, since it enables him to dispense with the constant attendance of an operator. In such cases M. Sortais's ingenious and beautiful improvement is recommended as specially valuable.

The following is the description of M. Sortais's method of control:

The apparatus of M. Sortais consists of a ratchet-wheel G, bearing a lever *(d'embrayage) h*, and above which reacts one of the movable parts of the clock-work of the telegraph apparatus, and in a detent E, put in action by the aid of the printing lever of the electo-magnet, by the pin *d'*.

Fig. 22.

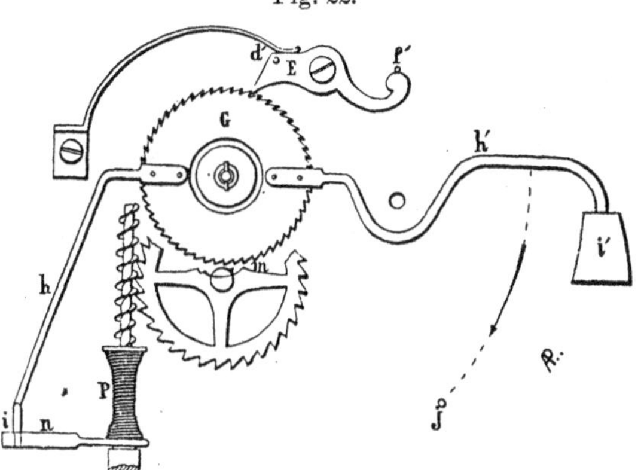

Sortais's Controlling Apparatus.

The lever *(embrayeur) h* is balanced by a counter-weight *i'*, which has a tendency to disengage it from the fly-wheel upon which it should react to stop the mechanism. But in its normal state it cannot yield to this movement because of the catch of the detent which maintains the ratchet-wheel in a determinate position. At that time it strikes against the detent *n* fixed to the axis of the last but one wheel, which at each revolution of itself makes the rachet-wheel advance one notch.

When the apparatus is put in action by the electro-magnet the catch of the ratchet-wheel is disengaged, and as this is no longer sustained, the lever *h* which is upon it is disengaged by its counter-weight *i'*, and the *(déclanchment)* is in action. If this action is instantaneous, the catch of the ratchet-wheel moves with it, and at each turn of the last but one wheel in the clock train, the ratchet-wheel advances one tooth, the lever *(d'embrayage)* falls, to encounter, after a certain number of impulses of the ratchet-wheel, the finger *n* of the axis which commands the fly-wheel and stops the movement of the apparatus. If the play of the electro-magnet occurs in the slighter intervals corresponding to the signals, the ratchet-wheel will keep itself separated from the catch, consequently it will only be after interruptions of a sufficient length of time that the stopping will be produced.

MORSE'S STOPPING APPARATUS.

This was invented in 1837, and is here illustrated with the diagram from Vail's book of 1845.

Fig. 23.

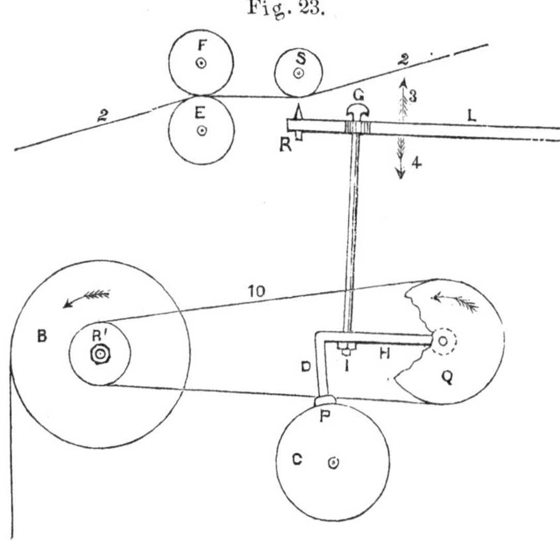

Morse's Stopping Apparatus.

B is the slowest wheel in the train. Upon its axle R′, prolonged outside the walls of the clock-work, is fixed a pulley wheel R′, of small diameter, and another pulley wheel Q, of much larger diameter, on the prolonged axle of another of the slow wheels of the train. An endless band 10 unites these two wheels. A bent arm H D fixed upon the axle of Q, under and parallel to the pen lever L, rests at P upon a friction wheel C, fixed upon the axle of the fly. The pen lever L having the stylus for marking, R, has a light rod or small wire A loosely hinged at I in the bent arm, and playing loosely through an aperture in the lever L, and held by its head G. The paper 2 2 passes under the groove cylinder S, drawn between the two rolling cylinders E and F.

When the pen lever L is brought into action in striking the stylus R against the paper at S, the rod A lifts the bent lever D H from the friction wheel C upon the fly shaft, and allows the movement of the clock-work. The endless band 10 is thus made to slip upon the smaller pulley wheel. But the pen lever in descending does not carry down the bent lever D H, because the rod A has free play, and rises in the lever at G; so that the lever L in descending does not replace P upon the friction wheel C. This can be accomplished only by the slower action of R′ gradually acting by the band 10 to replace P upon the friction-wheel. So long as the pen lever is in action, the rod A repeats its action upon the bent lever D H, and keeps the point P raised from the friction-wheel. But so soon as the pen lever ceases to act, the slow movement of the band 10 moving in the direction of the arrows, gradually replaces P upon the friction-wheel and stops the machinery.

This was one of the first modes devised and used by Morse to control the distant apparatus. By comparing this with the mode by which M. Sortais accomplishes the same result, it is perceived that although the original mode called the stopping apparatus, and early patented by

Morse, accomplished its result well, the more recent one of M. Sortais accomplishes it better.

The following appears in the New York Express of May 19, 1863, showing that the same result substantially was obtained by the ingenious Professor Wheatstone, apparently unconscious that it had been accomplished some twenty-five years previous in the United States:

"AUTOMATIC CONTROL OF THE TELEGRAPH.—Professor Wheatstone has just perfected a most extraordinary and valuable improvement in telegraphs—a private letter-printing apparatus working by itself, so that no clerk or attendant is required. A merchant can now lock up his counting-house, and on his return find every message faithfully recorded in legible type during his absence by this beautiful little machine. (So tells us the Boston Transcript.)"

The only novelty in this "improvement" is the adapting to machinery for printing the ordinary letters the automatic controlling apparatus invented by Professor Morse in 1837, and which he patented in France in 1838, and in Washington in April, 1846, and by which "no clerk or attendant is necessary at the distant terminus, and by means of which a merchant can now lock up his counting-house, and on his return find every message recorded during his absence." All this is substantially announced in the Report of the Committee of Commerce of the House of Representatives, December 30, 1842. In detailing the superior advantages of Professor Morse's invention, the chairman says: "Possessing an advantage over electric telegraphs heretofore in use, inasmuch as it records in permanently legible characters on paper any communication which may be made by it, *without the aid of any agent at the place of recording, except the apparatus*, which is *put in motion at the point of communication.* Thus the recording apparatus, called the register, *may be left in a closed chamber, where it will give notice of its commencing to write by a bell, and the communication may be found on opening the apartment.*"

CHAPTER VI.

INFORMATION CONCERNING TELEGRAPHS IN VARIOUS COUNTRIES.

THE UNITED KINGDOM OF GREAT BRITAIN AND IRELAND, STATISTICS OF ELECTRIC TELEGRAPHS IN—LETTER OF SIR CHARLES BRIGHT—INDIA—FRANCE, QUESTIONS TO AND ANSWERS FROM VISCOUNT DE VOUGY—HOLLAND—PRUSSIA—AUSTRIA—DENMARK—LETTER OF DIRECTOR GENERAL FABER—SWEDEN—LETTER OF DIRECTOR GENERAL BRÄNDSTRÖM—SPAIN—ITALY—EGYPT—TURKEY—AUSTRALIA—PERU.

GREAT BRITAIN.

The following questions were addressed by Professor Morse to the eminent secretary of the Submarine Telegraph Company, Sir James Carmichael, Baronet, London, directing the telegraphic correspondence between the United Kingdom and the Continent. Sir James has courteously sent the subjoined answers:

"1. What telegraphic systems are used in the British dominions?

"Answer. The system used by the Submarine Telegraph Company for correspondence between Great Britain and the continent of Europe is the Morse exclusively. The systems used by the United Kingdom Telegraph Company are the Morse and the Hughes type-printing instrument. The systems in use by the Magnetic Telegraph Company are[1] Bright's patent bells for the most important circuits, *i. e.*, for lines on which rapidity of working is essential, and on which there is a large amount of business. For other circuits (railway lines, &c.) Highton's single-needle instrument is used. The system used by the London District Telegraph Company is one brought out by Mr. Tyers, and is a single-needle instrument which is worked with the Morse code. The Electric and International Telegraph Company use the Morse system for international work, and also for large circuits; Dujardin's type-printing instrument, and the double-needle instrument, (Cooke and Wheatstone.)

"2. How many of each system?

"Answer. The number of instruments in use by each company is given in the accompanying table, extracted from the volume of miscellaneous statistics issued in March, 1867. A later volume, to the end of 1867, is now in course of publication. The number of instruments of submarine company is fifty-one, as per last return.

"3. What are the advantages and disadvantages of each system, in

[1] The "patent bells" instrument of Sir Charles Bright is an improvement, as well as a modification of the original Morse sounder. The improvement consists in utilizing the positive and negative currents, to vary the sound, creating an economy of time in transmission.—S. F. B. M.

cost of instruments and repairs, in rate of speed or quantity of intelligence in a given time?

"Answer. Highton's single-needle instrument is said to be the cheapest, costing only about 50*s.* or £3. The type-printing instruments are the most costly, but transmit with great rapidity. The instrument known as 'Bright's patent bells,' transmits an average of forty words a minute. The Submarine Telegraph Company working direct between London and Paris can transmit forty messages an hour, taking long and short together, by one Morse circuit.

"4. How many miles of conductors are constructed?

"Answer. This question is answered by the annexed extract. (See table.)

"5. What are the expenses and receipts per annum, and the net revenue to the state or to the companies?

Answer. Copies of the reports of the various companies, for the year 1867, are annexed and will show these particulars."

ELECTRIC TELEGRAPHS IN THE UNITED KINGDOM.

Statistics of electric telegraphs for the use of the public, in the United Kingdom, in each of the years 1863, 1864, *and* 1865.

Telegraph companies.	Length in miles of telegraph lines.			Length in miles of wires used.			Number of stations open for the public.		
	1863.	1864.	1865.	1863.	1864.	1865.	1863.	1864.	1865.
Electric and International	8, 282	8, 658	9, 306	39, 756	41, 691	45, 044	1, 022	1, 022	1, 022
British and Irish Magnetic	4, 196¾	4, 329½	4, 401	17, 257½	18, 554	18, 668	464	479	491
Southeastern Railway*	316	318	323½	2, 642½	2, 996½	3, 064½	94	102	104
London, Brighton, and South Coast Railway	212	217½	240¾	541½	583¼	688	46	48	57
London district†	107	115	123	430	454	470	81	80	83
The United Kingdom	‡831	1, 343	1, 672	‡5, 099	8, 096	9, 506	‡48	100	125
Total	13, 944¾	14, 981	16, 066¼	65, 726½	72, 374¾	77, 440½	1, 755	1, 831	1, 882
Submarine, (telegraph to Calais, 24 miles; to Boulogne, 25 miles; to Dieppe, 78 miles; to Jersey, 30 miles; to Ostend, 70 miles; to Hanover, 80 miles; and to Denmark, 380 miles.)	887	(§)	(§)	2, 683	(§)	(§)	(‖)	(§)	(§)

* The Southeastern Railway Company has no working arrangements with either of the electric telegraph companies.

† Exclusive of private telegraphs provided by this company for firms and persons having two places of business, and for the London fire brigade and general post office.

‡ This additional mileage and stations was only completed and opened in November, 1863.

§ No return.

‖ Upwards of 3,000 in foreign countries.

Statistics of electric telegraphs—Continued.

Telegraph companies.	Number of instruments.			Number of public messages.		
	1863.	1864.	1865.	1863.	1864.	1865.
Electric and International	4, 489	5, 136	5, 778	(*)	(*)	(*)
British and Irish Magnetic †	1, 042	(‡)	(‡)	827, 424	1, 030, 142	1, 251, 265
Southeastern Railway	142	158	159	62, 968	69, 623	88, 711
London, Brighton, and South Coast Railway	69	74	92	43, 208	52, 942	66, 523
London district	192	191	195	247, 606	308, 032	316, 272
The United Kingdom	172	285	358	226, 729	518, 651	743, 870
	....	....	6, 582	....	....	....
Submarine	§51	(‡)	(‡)	‖345, 784	(‡)	(‡)

* Not ascertained.

† The number of messages to and from the Continent transmitted jointly by this company and the Submarine Telegraph Company, and the number of messages for railway companies, newspapers, and news rooms, are not included with the messages for the public.

‡ No return.

§ Exclusively for continental traffic.

‖ To and from foreign countries.

LETTER OF SIR CHARLES BRIGHT.

From a letter received from Sir Charles Bright in August, 1868, at the moment of his leaving New York for Liverpool, the following extracts are made. Sir Charles says:

"Generally, as regards the instruments in the United Kingdom, the Electric Telegraph Company use the Morse instruments on the principal commercial circuits, and the needle instrument on small and unimportant circuits, and also for the railway stations and signaling.

"The magnetic company use my sound instrument since 1854, for nearly all the circuits, (some railway stations excepted, where a single needle system is used.) The railway companies seem to prefer the needle instrument; so we supply them.

"The Submarine Company use the Morse instrument only, their wires being all in circuit with the continental system.

"The United Kingdom Company, (a small company, started since you were in England in 1857,) use the Morse instruments, and also several Hughes type-printing instruments.

"The only modification in the Morse instrument is the use of ink instead of the point in registering the marks. The needle instrument is much the same as of old, except that a single wire and single needle is used.

"The sound instrument, which I adopted for the Magnetic Company, consists of two bells, dull in sound, and differing in note, placed on each side of the operator about on a line with his ear. These are worked by a relay sending currents through one or the other, according to the signals required. Two keys are used for sending; one for the right or positive (+) current; the other for the left or negative (—) current. One wire is, of course, used. There is no difference in the duration of either signal, and this is the saving of time, compared with one of the sounders used here, (in the United States,) where, in employing dots and dashes, the latter, (I take it,) require three times the duration of a dot. In the other the signals are all dots; but a Morse operator can use it by considering one key as a *dot*, the other as a *dash*, but sending dots on both. It is the quickest instrument of a non-mechanical kind."

INDIA.

The total number of miles of telegraph lines in India, in 1866, was 13,390⅛ miles, and of offices 174. At the rate of three instruments to two offices, there would be 261 instruments.

FRANCE.

QUESTIONS TO, AND ANSWERS FROM, VISCOUNT DE VOUGY.

In January, 1867, the following questions were addressed to the administrator of the French telegraphs, the Count de Vougy, at the request of the Western Union Telegraph Company:

"Can you oblige me by furnishing me with—

"1. A copy of the tariff of charges on telegrams in France, and, so far as practicable, in other European countries?

"2. The number and names of the telegraph systems in use in France; how many of each system are employed, and their adaptedness or fitness for particular service?

"3. The average number of messages or telegrams, of a certain length, sent daily?

"4. The comparative number capable of being sent by each system?

"5. The proportion between those for the government service and for private or commercial service?

"6. Where can be obtained telegraphic maps of lines in France and in other countries?

"7. Is the English needle system anywhere in use in France?"

The following is the answer of Count de Vougy, dated Paris, February 20, 1867:

"I have collected the different documents that you had the goodness to request from me, and I have the pleasure of sending them to you:

"I. [1]The first is the general tariff of telegraphic dispatches of the French empire. It comprises two distinct parts—the one relating to the interior correspondence, the other to the international correspondence. There is, besides, as complementary, the Moniteur Télégraphique

[1]The documents here mentioned were sent to the company in New York three months before my appointment as United States Commissioner.—S. F. B. M.

of December, 1865, remaining in use, to determine the taxes of the offices (not numerous) elsewhere, which have not yet adhered to the rules of the international convention, concluded at Paris the 17th of May, 1865.

"I have also added to the tariff the text of their convention, and the regulations made in consequence.

"A note, in which is collected the information that the administration in France possesses on the interior tariffs of different states of Europe, in short, completes this first series of documents.

"II. Four systems of apparatus are employed by the French administration: 1. The Morse apparatus. 2. The dial apparatus. 3. The Hughes apparatus. 4. The Caselli apparatus. There are counted in the service of the Morse system, 1,600; dial system, 1,180; Hughes system, 135; Caselli system, 6.

"The inherent merits of the Morse system, and of which the principal ones are its marvelous simplicity, and great reliability in its action, maintain its use on the greatest number of the net-work of lines.

"The Hughes apparatus replaces it, however, with advantage upon the conductors of great length, when the quantity of dispatches to be transmitted is in abundance.

"The apparatus *à cadran*, or dial apparatus, is employed in a certain number of city and semaphoric offices, the agents of communes and of the marine, who manage these posts, not being always in a condition to acquire the knowledge necessary to work an apparatus less elementary.

"As to the pantelegraph of Caselli, the public has not been permitted to make use of it but upon two or three principal lines, and besides has not shown much eagerness to profit by the advantages it presents. A printing dial apparatus, invented by M. d'Arlincourt, has been tried with success upon some lines of small extent, but it has not yet been admitted into definite practice.

"III. Statistics, drawn up in 1860, have permitted us to ascertain that the number of telegrams of twenty words, transmitted during this same year, amount to sixty-three per cent. of the telegrams of all lengths sent in the same period. There has not been kept an account since then, in a precise manner, of the comparative number and extent of these dispatches. I am inclined to think, nevertheless, that the proportion of these telegrams which do not exceed twenty words, the minimum limit of the tax, is augmented during the last years in the same proportion as telegraphic correspondence has been popularized.

"The pamphlet bearing the title '*Tableau des produits des bureaux de l'état en* 1865,' will furnish you with many interesting indications upon the extent of the French net-work of wires, and upon the results of its working. It is in place to remark, at all times, that these results do not include the state correspondence, free from tax, and of which the receipts, estimated by order, have amounted for the year 1865 to the sum of 1,800,631 francs 18 centimes. The French administration publishes this document every year. I will hasten to send to you that which relates to the year 1866 as soon as it shall appear.

"IV. The productive power of the different apparatus used in the service is represented in practice by the following means, determined (upon the interval in the space of an hour) for telegrams composed uniformly of twenty words:

The Hughes apparatus	50
The Morse apparatus	20
The dial apparatus	15
The Caselli apparatus	40

The mean attributed to this last cannot, however, be considered as precise, the surface of the paper, which serves as the basis of the tax, bearing a number of words, more or less large, according to the form of the writing of the sender.

"V. In 1864 the total number of private dispatches has been 1,967,748; that of the official dispatches, 526,613; 1865 has furnished for the one 2,473,747, and for the other 568,647. The approximative proportion between the transmissions of the state and those of private persons is then about one-fourth.

"VI. The map or chart of the telegraphic net-work in France is not in the market. It is published by the administration, but the works executed in the last year have rendered it incomplete and inexact upon so many points that it cannot at the present time give a just idea of the state of our telegraphic communications. A new edition is going to be put to press, and you may be sure, my dear sir, that you shall receive one of the first proofs.

"I send you, to supply in some degree, in the absence of this document, and also to inform you upon the telegraphic net-work of the different European states, a copy of a chart published about a year ago by the Prussian government. But I expect, likewise, to transmit to you soon a more detailed document on the international net-work of our continent.

"VII. The English needle system is not in use in a single office in France.

"I add to the different pamphlets, which answer the questions contained in your letter, a late document which includes the complete collection of the laws, decrees, rules, and instructions which regulate the French telegraphy. It bears the title of "*Recueil Administratif*," and comprises five volumes bound, and a bundle destined to form the sixth volume, to the end of 1867.

"If these different publications, and the indications contained in this letter, do not entirely meet the wishes of the Western Union Company, I remain, my dear Mr. Morse, with pleasure, at your disposal to complete them as far as possible.

"I avail myself of your obliging offer to furnish, on the part of the company, all the information that may appear interesting to my administration to obtain upon American telegraphy. For this purpose I am preparing a series of questions, and I will have the honor of soon sending them to you.

"In conclusion, I take advantage of this communication to give you, as a mark of my personal respect, a volume, in which is collected the diplomatic documents of the international conference of Paris." * *

HOLLAND.

The following is a letter of M. Faring, the referendary charged with the direction of the state telegraphs in Holland, to Hon. Hugh Ewing, United States minister to Holland, dated the Hague, April 27, 1868:

"In answer to the letter of Professor Morse, of the 22d instant, which I have received through you, I have the honor to communicate to you that the telegraphic system known by the name of the English needle system is not employed anywhere by us, neither on the lines of the state, nor on those of private companies.

"I propose to send you soon an answer to the other questions of Professor Morse, which were addressed to me in your letter of the 22d instant." * * *

As proposed in the preceding, the following letter of the referendary Faring to the minister resident of the United States at the Hague, the Hon. Mr. Ewing, dated the Hague, May 7, 1867, was written as a further answer to the questions proposed by Professor Morse:

"In accordance with the promise of my letter of the 27th April last, No. 3,188, I have the honor to address you the inclosed information respecting the Netherland telegraphs, requested by Professor Morse, in your letter of 22d April last.

"In that which follows, the order of the questions proposed has been observed:

"I. There are two telegraphic systems now established upon the telegraphic state lines, the Morse system, (*à molette*,) with the inking wheel, after the construction of Messrs. Digney, and the Hughes system. This last has been but lately introduced, and is not used but upon the most frequented lines.

"On the 1st of January, 1868, there were in use, of the Morse apparatus, 216; of the Hughes, 3.

"The railroads which are operated by private companies, (and of which I cannot give more precise information,) employ about 150 instruments, of which the greater part are constructed after the Morse system, with or without a constant current. Upon some of these railroads the dial instruments are still used, but these instruments are rapidly disappearing.

"II. On the 1st of January last the net-work of telegraph lines of the state had an extension of 2,328.3 kilometers, with a total length of wire of 6,863.2 kilometers.

"III. From the preceding, it results that the telegraph service of the state, as well as of the railroad, is almost exclusively performed by instruments constructed after the Morse system, the Hughes instrument doing service only on the most frequented lines, and the dial instruments disappearing more and more. It is not, therefore, necessary to discuss the question of the relative value of the different systems for greater or lesser distances, nor for the railroad service.

"The use of the telegraph for domestic life or for cities scarcely exists with us.

"IV. The receipts of the state telegraphs amounted in 1867 to about 500,000 florins of Holland; the expenses to 750,000 florins. The expense of the maintenance of the lines during the same year was about 175,000 florins; the expense of new constructions, 240,000 florins.

The price of a Morse apparatus (*à molette*) constructed by Digney frères, Paris, is	180 florins.
Of a relay magnet	80 florins.
Of a key or manipulator	14 florins.
Of a commutator	10 florins.
Of a galvanometer	15 florins.
Total Morse apparatus	299 florins.
Total cost of a Hughes instrument constructed by P. Dumoulin Froment	800 florins.

"V. The number of persons attached to the state telegraphs are found in a circular to the different European telegraph administrations, a copy of which I have the honor to inclose herewith. I also inclose a copy of the report to the King upon the condition of the Netherland telegraphs in 1866, and a copy of the new map of our telegraph lines."

* * * * * *

The circular alluded to in the foregoing letter is here given. It is signed by Faring, charged with the direction of the telegraphs, and dated the Hague, February 11, 1868:

"Conformably to the article 57 of the convention of Paris, I have the honor to send to you below some statistical information upon the personnel and the offices on the 1st January, 1868, the extent of lines and telegraphic wires, as well as the number of dispatches over the net-work of the Netherlands during the year 1867:

"DIRECTION.—The referendary, charged with the direction of the telegraphs of the state; the controller, charged with the working and responsibilities of the lines; three principal clerks; the engineer, charged with the technical service; two assistant engineers.

"EMPLOYÉS OF THE OFFICES.—Nine inspectors of the lines, directors of the offices; 44 directors of offices; 23 sub-directors; 225 telegraphists, (operators;) 49 clerks; 142 manufacturers of instruments.

"PERSONNEL OF TECHNICAL SERVICE.—Ten conductors; 10 inspectors.

"NET-WORK OF THE STATE.—Length of lines, 2,328.3 kilometers, (about 447 English miles;) length of wires, 6,863.2 kilometres, (about 1,340 English miles.)

"NUMBER OF OFFICES.—Of the state, including four auxiliary, 87; of private companies, 107. (Among those last offices, there are 38 which, being established, [*dans des localités de service*,] by the bureaus of the state, are not inserted in this list.)

"NUMBER OF APPARATUS.—Morse system, 216. Some steps have been taken to introduce the Hughes apparatus upon some of the lines of the Netherlands net-work.

"WORK OF 1867.—	
Number of internal dispatches	492,733
Number of international dispatches...	370,340
Number of *in transitu* dispatches	249,964
Number of dispatches (*de service*) in service of the line....................	7,188
Total	1,120,225

"Receipts, 495,800.40 florins Holland.

"The uniform tax for the telegraphic correspondence between two Netherland offices, whether they pertain to the state or to some private company, has been reduced since the 1st of January, 1868, from 0.50 to 0.30 florins of Holland for one simple dispatch." * * *

PRUSSIA.

In a letter from Professor Morse, dated February 15, 1868, to Herr von Chauvin, director general of the Prussian telegraphs, he requested answers to the following questions:

"1. Can you oblige me by furnishing me with a copy of the tariff of charges on telegrams in Prussia, and, as far as practicable, in other countries?

"2. The number and names of the telegraph systems in use in Prussia; how many of each system are employed, and their adaptedness or fitness for particular service?

"3. The average number of messages or telegrams of a certain length sent daily?

"4. The comparative number capable of being sent by each system?

"5. The proportion between those of government service, and for private or commercial service?

"6. Where can telegraphic maps be obtained?

"7. Is the English needle system anywhere in use on the Prussian lines?"

To these questions the obliging director general made the following answers, in a letter dated March 6, 1868:

"1. The tariff applicable to the telegraphic correspondence of North Germany is determined as follows:

"*a.* For dispatches exchanged between the bureaus of the North German Confederation: First zone, (distance of 14 German miles,) 5 silver groschen; second zone, (distance of 50 German miles,) 10 silver groschen; third zone, (distance over 50 German miles,) 15 silver groschen.

"*b.* For dispatches exchanged between North Germany and the other states belonging to the South German Telegraphic Union, (Austria, Bavaria, Wurtemberg, and Baden:) First zone, (distance of 10 miles,) 8 silver groschen; second zone, (distance of 45 miles,) 16 silver groschen; third zone, (over 45 miles,) 24 silver groschen.

"*c.* Dispatches destined for other European states are taxed in conformity with the tariff prescribed by the convention of Paris. * * * (This tariff fixes the terminal or final tax, which reverts to each state for the correspondence, (*en provénance,*) or at the destination of its offices, and that of transit, which reverts to each state for the correspondence which passes through its territory.) The taxes mentioned above apply to the simple dispatch of twenty words.

"2. The telegraphic systems adopted by my administration are the Morse apparatus, the Hughes apparatus, and the Siemens type apparatus.

"The Hughes apparatus is principally fitted to operate upon the direct lines which are freed from the labor of the intermediate offices, and upon which the correspondence is very active and continuous. It operates between Berlin on the one side, and Paris, Vienna, Warsaw, Frankfort-on-the-Main, Breslau, Koenigsberg, Hamburg, Cologne, on the other side.

"The type apparatus of Siemens is employed in the exchange of correspondence between the large cities of Prussia.

"In the North German offices, (not including those of the railways,) there are in actual use of the apparatus Morse, 2,692; apparatus Hughes, 24; apparatus Siemens, 6.

"3. The mean number of dispatches daily transmitted by the North German offices (not including the dispatches in transit) is 7,075.

"4. The comparative number of dispatches which can be transmitted by the different systems in the space of one hour is, [1] 20 to 30 for the Morse apparatus; 40 to 50 for the Hughes apparatus; 60 for the Siemens apparatus.

"5. The dispatches indicated above are in the following ratio: 2.6 per cent. dispatches of the state; 2.2 per cent. dispatches of the service; 95.2 per cent. private dispatches.

"6. The English needle apparatus has never been in use in Prussia."

Two Morse instruments cost 111 florins each, or 222 florins. The

---

[1] See Chapter V for a correction of this estimate.

two together cost less than one-third of the cost of one of the Hughes apparatus. If, then, two Morse instruments are employed, with one operator to each instrument, which is equivalent to the manning of one Hughes, we have the means of doubling the number of dispatches, in the comparison of the two apparatus, (the Morse and the Hughes.) But the recent tests of the capacity of the Morse show that a single Morse instrument can transmit even as high as 130 dispatches, of twenty words each, in one hour, while a single Hughes instrument can transmit at the utmost from fifty to sixty per hour.

We have, therefore, this result: Two Morse: two operators; cost, 222 florins; 260 dispatches. One Hughes: two operators; cost, 700 florins; 60 dispatches.

REMARK.—If two Morse apparatus are employed at the same time, each requires a circuit, that is, two circuits, while the Hughes requires but one. This makes an important difference in the calculation; but still the result is one hundred and forty in favor of the work of the two Morse apparatus against the work of one Hughes apparatus.

DENMARK.

LETTER OF DIRECTOR GENERAL FABER.

In answer to questions similar to those addressed to the telegraphic administrations of other countries, the following information has been furnished by the director general of Danish telegraphs in a letter to the Hon. George H. Yeaman, United States minister to Denmark, dated May 2, 1868:

"1. Throughout this kingdom the Morse telegraphic system is the only one used on the government lines as well as on private and railway lines, the instruments being partially of an older construction with relays, partially newer ones without relays, and writing with ink. The fire telegraph in this city has magnetic-induction dial instruments of the manufacture of Messrs. Siemens and Halske, in Berlin. The English needle system is nowhere in public use in Denmark. On the lines of the government we have 124 Morse instruments; on private lines, 21 Morse instruments; on railway lines, 58 Morse instruments; on the fire telegraph line in Copenhagen, 22 induction dial instruments.

"2. The government lines have an extension of 950 miles English, containing 2,298 miles of single wire; the private lines have an extension of 324 miles, with 338 miles of single wire; the railway lines have an extension of 265 miles, with 275 miles of single wire; the fire telegraph in this city contains 11 miles of line by 20 miles of single wire.

"3. According to the experience made in this country, I should prefer:

"For long distances and for short ones, the Morse system with a line current; for railway service, the same with constant current; for city or domestic use, the magnetic-induction dial apparatus of Messrs. Siemens and Halske.

"4. The account of the last year, as we take it here from April 1 to March 31, having not yet been quite finished, an exact indication of the aggregate receipts and expenses cannot be given. Approximately the receipts of the government telegraph have amounted to 151,500 rigsdaler, and the expenses to 142,330 rigsdaler, of which latter 24,650 rigsdaler are costs of maintenance. One hundred and fifty functionaries are engaged in the telegraph service of the government. The number of those in private and railway telegraph service I cannot state exactly, but calculate it to be about eighty.

"5. According to the desires expressed by Professor Morse, I append to this a map of the telegraph lines and stations in Denmark, a statistical survey of the traffic on the Danish lines in the year 1867, and a representation of the extension of the government, from their first establishment to the expiration of the year 1866."

SWEDEN.

LETTER OF DIRECTOR GENERAL BRÄNDSTRÖM.

The following is a letter from the director general of Swedish telegraphs to his excellency General Bartlett, United States minister resident at the court of Sweden, dated Stockholm, April 19, 1868:

"I have the honor to acknowledge the receipt of your letter of the 14th instant accompanied with that of Professor Morse, addressed to you of the date of March 18 last, and I hasten to answer the questions of the professor respecting Sweden.

"As to Norway, whose offices and telegraph lines are under the jurisdiction of a special administration, I am persuaded that you will obtain all necessary explanations by addressing the chief of this administration, M. le Directeur Nielson, whose address is Christiania.

"It is the system Morse, which is exclusively adopted for all the offices of the administration of telegraphs in Sweden. This system is also employed for all the telegraph offices of the railways, except in some small offices where the dial apparatus is used.

"The English needle system has not been used in any part of Sweden.

"It is probable that sooner or later the administration of the telegraphs will adopt, for some of the principal lines, the Hughes system, but at the present time we have none of this apparatus.

"In regard to the organization of the Swedish telegraphs, the extension of the lines belonging to the administration of the telegraphs, the expenses for repairs of these lines, the internal taxes of the country, &c., I hope that Mr. Morse will find sufficient explanations in consulting the accompanying printed papers, to wit: First, notices of the organization of the Swedish telegraphs, and statistical table of the action *(du mouvement)* of the dispatches during the year 1866; and, second, international notification of the Swedish administration of the telegraphs, to the date of April 27, 1868, containing statistical information for the year 1867.

"The accompanying map indicates all the telegraph offices of the country. The lines marked as being in construction are already completed." * * * *

The following is the information alluded to in the foregoing letter, issued as a circular by Director General Brändström, and dated April 27, 1868:

"Conformably to article 57 of the convention of Paris, we have already had the honor to send to you, on February 27 last, the map of our telegraphic net-work prepared to the end of the year 1867.

"Here is some statistical information upon the personnel, the offices in service, and the extent of the lines and the telegraph wires at the same epoch, as well as a table of the action of the dispatches upon the Swedish net-work during the said year.

PERSONNEL.

a. Central administration.—One director general, 2 inspectors general, 2 assistant inspectors general, 1 professor of physics, (*physicien,*) 1 intendant general of economy and accounts, 1 secretary-in-chief, 1 keeper of the records, 1 keeper of the books, 1 cashier, 1 intendant of the materials, 2 examiners, 5 other employés—total, 19 persons.

"*b. Employés in the electric offices.*—Thirteen directors, chiefs of the principal offices; 86 commissaries, chiefs of offices of the second and third classes, or placed in an office of the first class, either as assistants of the chief or as cashiers; 169 assistants, chiefs of the smaller offices, (of whom 21 are women,) or employed in the others—in all, 268 persons.

"*c. Employés in the optical offices.*—Eighteen chiefs of offices; 22 employés, subalterns—in all, 40 persons.

"TELEGRAPHIC OFFICES.—Offices belonging to the telegraphic administration—

(*a.*) Electric	96
(*b.*) Optical	18
	114
Offices of state railways, (of which 21 are open for international correspondence)	91
Offices of private companies, (of which 23 are open for international correspondence)	70
Total	275

"The number of apparatus, (Morse system,) employed in the offices of the telegraph administration is 277.

"*Lines of the telegraph administration.*

	Length of lines.	Length of wire conductors.
	Kilometers.	*Kilometers.*
Lines established on the railways	1, 033	3, 420
Lines established on the great roads	4, 525	8, 273
Submarine cable between Sweden and the Isle of Gotland	103	103
Submarine cable between Sweden and the Isle of Oland	3	3
	5, 664	11, 799

	Kilometers.
Lines with one wire	2, 089
Lines with two wires	1, 903
Lines with three wires	1, 172
Lines with four wires	312
Lines with five wires	82
Lines with six wires	45
Lines with seven wires	30
Lines with eight wires	31
Total length of the wires	5, 664

"The submarine cable between Sweden and Prussia, which is seventy-three kilometers in length, and contains three wire conductors, belongs in common to the two countries.

"At the same time Sweden possesses, in conjunction with Denmark, the cable laid in the Sound. This cable is fifteen kilometers long, and contains four wire conductors, of which, however, only two are in use.

"*International correspondence in* 1867.

Names of the states.	Number of dispatches from the state, and private dispatches sent from Sweden for Norway and foreign countries.	Number of dispatches from the state, and private dispatches received in Sweden from Norway and from foreign countries.	Total.
Norway	14, 802	11, 532	26, 334
Algiers and Tunis	85	61	146
North America	4	8	12
Austria	112	141	253
Baden	37	46	83
Bavaria	58	42	100
Belgium	704	711	1, 415
Bremen	345	254	599
Denmark	14, 705	16, 698	31, 403

"*International correspondence in* 1867—Continued.

Names of the states.	Number of dispatches from the state, and private dispatches sent from Sweden for Norway and foreign countries.	Number of dispatches from the state, and private dispatches received in Sweden from Norway and from foreign countries.	Total.
Egypt	2	3	5
Spain	354	351	705
Finland	1,989	2,057	4,046
France	3,295	3,256	6,551
Great Britain and Ireland	9,702	10,598	20,300
Hamburg	4,587	4,911	9,498
Italy	234	252	486
Lubec	1,201	988	2,189
Malta	1	8	9
Mecklenburg	344	407	751
Moldavia, Wallachia	5	2	7
Holland	1,053	1,010	2,063
Portugal	124	140	264
Prussia	4,004	3,743	7,747
Russia, European, (except Finland)	2,144	1,967	4,111
Saxony	144	98	242
Switzerland	131	126	257
Turkey, European	5	19	24
Tnrkey, Asiatic	1	1	2
Wurtemberg	21	16	37
Other German states	84	94	178
	60,277	59,540	119,817

"*Comparative table of the transmission of dispatches, and their receipt in* 1866, 1867.

	1866.			1867.			Increase in 1867.			
	Number of dispatches.	Proportional number.	Receipts.	Number of dispatches.	Proportional number.	Receipts.	Dispatches.		Receipts.	
		P'r ct.	*Francs.*		*P'r ct.*	*Francs.*	*Number.*	*P'r ct.*	*Francs.*	*P'r ct.*
Service, interior	272,834	64.2	402,645	314,025	63.3	528,894	41,191	15.1	66,249	14.3
Service, international	94,974	22.3	} 440,909	120,943	24.4	} 441,991	25,969	27.3	} 1,082	0.25
Transit	57,098	13.5		61,137	12.3		4,039	7.1		
Total	424,906	100	903,554	496,105	100	970,885	71,199	16.8	57,774	7.45

"*Revenues and receipts for the year* 1867.

"For the electric lines:

	Francs.
1. Revenues:	
a. Receipt proceeding from the correspondence........	961,328
b. Contribution from certain communes for the rents of the offices, &c....................................	9,556
c. Subsidy accorded by the government for the construction of new lines, and the multiplication of wire conductors..	263,320
Total......................................	1,234,204
2. Expenses:	
a. Salaries of the officers, repair of the old lines, &c....	905,150
b. Construction of new lines, and multiplication of wires.	248,504

"For the optical lines, (semaphores:)

1. Revenues:	
a. Receipts proceeding from correspondence............	3,332
b. Subsidy accorded by government....................	40,781
Total......................................	44,113
2. Expenses:	
Salaries of officers, and repairs of the telegraph, &c....	42,066

SPAIN.

LETTER FROM DIRECTOR GENERAL SANZ.

The following is a letter from the director general of Spanish telegraphs to the minister of the United States, John P. Hale, dated Madrid, April 27, 1868:

"In reply to your valued favor of the 21st instant, I, to-day, have the pleasure of giving you the following information, which you have requested of me:

"The system of telegraphs used in the government lines in Spain is solely and exclusively that of Morse. As an auxiliary to this apparatus, there is also used an English needle for the purpose of observing the calls at one end of the line when the Morse apparatus is being used at the other.

"The extent of the lines is 10,735 kilometers, and of the wires 24,134 kilometers.

"As the Morse system is the only one used, there is, of course, no means of comparing it with others.

"The railway companies use for their purposes Breguet's dial apparatus.

"The receipts for charges on dispatches amount to 8,424,510 reals, (equal to $42,122 55 gold.)

"The personal expenses (pay of officers, operators, &c.) amount to 9,044,500 reals, ($45,222 50 gold,) and the expenses for working materials (wires, chemicals, &c.) to 3,704,020 reals, ($18,520 10 gold.)

"I inclose a telegraphic map and other documents, which may serve to give a detailed knowledge of the organization of the telegraphic system in Spain, and also the letter which was put into my hands at the central office."

ITALY.

From Italy, in addition to answers to questions, there have been received, through the prompt attention of the United States minister to Italy, his excellency George P. Marsh, a large number of valuable public documents, relating to the telegraph, which have been sent to the department at Washington.

The following are the statistical data of Italian telegraphs furnished by the director general, in answer to the same questions which had been addressed to other telegraph administrations:

"I. On January 1, 1868, there were in operation—

Morse apparatus	1,017
Hughes apparatus	14
Total	1,031

"II. Miles of line, 9,496 English miles; miles of wire, 22,211 English miles.

"III. Apparatus best adapted for long distances and for short ones: The Hughes, if the lines are in the best condition, and with much difficulty, otherwise the Morse. For railway service: The Morse. For city or domestic use: This service has not yet in Italy had any great development. What there is now in the city is done by the Morse apparatus. If this service becomes more active the Hughes may be better, or better the tubular system adopted in Paris and Berlin.

"Effective revenues for private dispatches of 1867, 4,278,925 francs; ordinary expenses, 4,100,000 francs; extraordinary expenses, 180,000 francs; cost of apparatus and other material, (see allegato *o*;) personal expenses for maintenance of the apparatus of 1867, 24,168.50 francs, adding a small sum for the purchase of small materials for repairs. Total number of employés, 2,374. (For distinction of grades and classes see table marked *a*, and the manuscript of the allegato *a*.)

"IV. No English system is in use in any part whatever of Italy.

"V. For fuller information on the condition of the telegraph in Italy see the accompanying documents."[1]

[1] The documents alluded to have been forwarded to the department, and are as follows:

(*a*.) Organico dell' Amministrazione dei Telegrafi Italiani, del 18 Settembre, 1865, e successive variazioni, 17 Ottobre, 1866, e 8 Dicembre, 1867.

(*b*.) Regolamento pel servizio dei telegrafi, del 4 Marzo, 1866.

EGYPT.

The telegraph administration in Egypt was addressed through the United States consul general, Hon. Charles Hale, in Alexandria, and, through his prompt attention, the following information, supplied by Hartley J. Gibson, esq., director of Egyptian telegraphs, was received in reply to questions proposed:

"Question 1. Please give the names of the telegraph systems employed in the Egyptian dominions, and the number of each system.

"Answer. The Egyptian government telegraphs under my direction are confined to those in the Soudan country, the whole of which are worked on the 'Morse' system.

"Question 2. How many miles (English) of telegraph connection, and how many miles of telegraph wires?

"Answer. They commence at Assouan, and are all in construction. The whole lines are constructed with two wires, (No. 8, not galvanized,) thus affording two lines.

Telegraph lines in Egypt.

	Miles line.	Miles wire.
Assouan to Wady Halfa	215	430
Wady Halfa to Ourdeh	260	520
Ourdeh to Ambaked	120	240
Ambaked to Berber	170	340
Berber to Metammeh	110	220
Metammeh to Khartum	112	224
Berber to Kassala	240	480
Kassala to Souakim	270	540
Massouah to Kassala	250	500
	1,747	3,494

(*c.*) Regolamento per la correspondenza telegrafica nell' interno dello stato, del 10 Dicembre, 1865.

(*d.*) Servizio dei vaglia telegrafici.

(*e.*) Servizio dei vaglia semaforico.

(*f.*) Servizio dei nell' interno delli cittá.

(*g.*) Tariffa generale dei despacci.

(*h.*) Guida indice dei circuiti e uffici del regno.

(*i.*) Casta delle linea telegrafiche di correspondenza generale ed internazionale, 1 Giugnio, 1867.

(*k.*) Casta delle linea telegrafiche di tutti i fili, 1 Giugnio, 1867.

(*l.*) Casta delle linea telegrafiche delle distanze del 1865.

(*m.*) Tavola delle commùnicazione pel systema "Morse."

(*n.*) Modelli degli isolatori in uso.

(*o.*) Nomenclatura e prezzi del materiale.

(*p.*) Relazione statistica pel biennio 1865'-66.

(*q.*) Bullettino telegrafico. Publicazione mensile continente disposizioni ufficiali, e una parte non ufficiale di studi, invenzioni e notizie diversa si unisce quello, di Marzo, 1868.

"The line between Assouan and Berber is completed, with the exception of the section between Wady Halfa and Ourdeh. This part of the country is so infested with white ants that iron posts are a necessity. These have accordingly been procured and sent to their destination, and before the end of November, (1868,) this section will be completed.

"The section between Massouah and Kassala has not yet been commenced. That between Berber and Kassala is under construction, and on its completion in November next, that between Berber, Metammeh, and Khartum will be undertaken.

"Independently of the towns mentioned, there are others on the route where stations exist, and many intermediate ones will be hereafter organized.

"Of the delta telegraph lines I refrain now from speaking; but I believe there are about 820 miles of line, a considerable portion of which comprise two or more wires.

"Between Alexandria and Cairo (135 miles) they have one wire, worked on the 'Morse' system. The line also from Cairo to Gaza (300 miles) is worked by that system; on all the rest, including about 600 miles from Cairo to Assouan, the double needle is used.

"Question 3. Which system has experience shown to be best adapted to the following purposes, to wit: A, for long distances; B, for short distances; C, for railway service; D, for city or domestic use?

"Answer. With regard to your question 3, my experience goes to prove the following: A, the 'Morse;' B, the 'needle;' C, the 'needle;' D, the 'Morse.'

"Question 4. What are the aggregate expenses and receipts, cost of instruments, of maintenance, and number of employés?

"Answer. Quite unanswerable.

"As a postscript to my note, I add, that the telegraph lines owned by foreign nations in Egypt are three, to wit: 1st. The Mediterranean and Malta Company's line, Alexandria to Suez, 220 miles of line, 440 miles of wire. 'Morse system.' 2d. The Suez Canal Company, from Zagazig to the Isthmus, (distance unknown.) 'Morse system.' 3d. The Alexandria and Ramleh Railway Company's line, (five miles,) ten miles wire. 'Needle.'

"A line is proposed by the Egyptian government from Zagazig to Wady."

TURKEY.

LETTER FROM HON. J. P. BROWN.

The following letter, of the date of June 1, 1868, has been received from Hon. John P. Brown, secretary of legation to the Ottoman Porte, in answer to one addressed to him in relation to Turkish telegraphs:

"Many thanks for your interesting pamphlets on the subject of your invention of the telegraph. Dr. Staniatades, of this city, was a pupil at the college, (New York City university,) when your discovery was originally made known, and can vouch for what you have stated therein. He remembers clearly that you were the sole inventor. I feel much interest in all that concerns yourself and the telegraph, from the fact that I first spoke of it personally to his late Majesty Sultan Abdul Mejid, and with Dr. J. L. Smith, of Louisville, Kentucky, and Dr. C. Hamlin, exhibited the wonderful invention to his Majesty and all of his ministers and others at the palace of Beyler Bey on the Bosphorus.

"His Majesty wished them to have it put up between his capital and Smyrna, and I told him that I feared the people would cut the wires. Since then 'Morse's telegraph' is spread over the whole of the empire.

"The minister resident has sent me your two letters of inquiry, and I will in a day or two report to him on the same. In the mean time I have been able to report to him that the 'English needle system' is *not* used in any part of this empire. The present minister of public works, telegraphs, &c., is H. G. Daûd Pacha, a Catholic Christian, (late governor general of the Lebanon,) and a very learned and intelligent man.

"A Mr. Hughes (an American) was here some time since, at the request of the Porte, to instruct pupils in his system, (I believe one which prints the letters;) and I suppose the report which I am promised from the director will show this. At all times ready to be of any service to you."

The following is a letter to his excellency E. Joy Morris, United States minister to the Ottoman Porte, from James Millingen, esq., director of telegraphs, dated Pera, June 4, 1868:

"I have the honor to communicate, according to your request, the information respecting the Ottoman telegraph administration, accompanied with a map of the telegraphic net-work.

"In 1863 our net-work comprised 6,490 kilometers of lines, and 13,821 kilometers of wires, and 52 stations.

"To-day we possess 27,500 kilometers of lines, 56,230 kilometers of wires, and 310 stations, divided into stations of international service, and stations of interior service. Consequently, in the space of five years, our net-work has more than quadrupled.

"We are connected directly with Austria by three routes, Mostar-Melkovich, Scodra-Castellastua, and Gradiska; Italy, by Valona, Otrente; the principalities Moldo-Valques, by three routes, Tultcha-Ismail, Tultcha-Galatz, and Rustchuk-Giurgevo; Serbia, by two routes, Nissa-Alexinatz and Widdin-Negotin; Persia, by Hannokin (haggi Cara) Kirmanohah; Egypt, by Gaza-Elarich; Greece, by Polo-Lamia; and, finally, with the Indian telegraphic net-work, by the cable ending at Fao.

"The cables which put the Ottoman empire in communication with the Archipelago, and which belong to an English company, are nearly all interrupted; but, according to advices we have recently received, we hope they will shortly be re-established.

"We have but a few small cables in the Bosphorus, to the Dardanelles, and in the Danube: four in the Bosphorus, of 1,500 meters each, of which two are for the Indian transit; two to the Dardanelles, of 3,000 meters each; five in the Danube, of which two above Ismail, of 1,000 meters each; one above Galatz, of 1,500 meters; one above Soulina, of 1,500 meters; and one above Rustchuk, of 1,500 meters.

"All our great lines are constructed with two wires of galvanized iron of four millimeters in diameter. Some small branch lines, or for interior service, are constructed with wire of three millimeters diameter.

"The great Asiatic line from Constantinople to Fao has been constructed with two wires of six millimeters, because of the great distances of the stations. In fact, the mean distance of these stations is 102 kilometers; but from Kerhuk to Bagdad it is calculated at little less than 350 kilometers; and, in short, Moussoul works with Bagdad, a distance of 520 kilometers, without intermediate relays.

"Upon the line from Asia, Pera works sometimes direct with Sivas, a distance of 910 kilometers, without intermediate relays. All these wires of the first quality are annealed with charcoal.

"The insulators employed are, of the Siemens model, in castings of metal; the French model, in porcelain, furnished by the house of Brequet. For some time we commenced to employ the Belgian collar-model.

"In consequence of the difficulties of the ground, the want of railroads, and of carriage ways, the lines followed tracts for the most part arbitrary. But the present direction is turning its attention to rectifying these, as far as possible, by taking advantage of new routes, which are being constructed in different parts of the empire.

"Our posts are of oak, and some of them of pine, (spruce.) They are neither injected nor carbonized at their base.

"The administration thinks seriously of the improvement of construction, which owes its delay only to some local difficulties.

"The apparatus employed are all of the Morse system, furnished by the manufacturers, Bréguet, Siemens & Mouilleron, to the number of 1,020. We employ, also, the apparatus Hughes, upon the great line of transit from Pera to Valona, and also between Pera and Semlin; soon it will be put between Pera and Bagdad to facilitate the Indian correspondence. This apparatus is better for a long line, while for shorter distances the apparatus Morse is more convenient.

"The dial apparatus are no longer employed upon our lines. They require to operate all these apparatus about 16,000 Daniel elements, French model.

"Towards Bagdad we have some posts *(en fonte)* of cast iron, which have not given the results that we expected, as the administration has given them up to be employed on other lines. During the winter we have had to contend against violent winds, tempests, and inundations, which have raised and prostrated the posts, for our lines traverse forests, precipices, raviñes, and some abrupt mountains, where the superintendence and the repairs were difficult to be executed, but with the actual repairs of the tracks these inconveniences have nearly completely disappeared. In certain countries some turbulent hordes often interrupt the communication from malevolence or from simple curiosity, believing that they can by this means discover the mysteries of the telegraph. Accustomed to-day to this new mode of correspondence and influenced by such measures that they are interested in the good repair of the line, we have no longer any fear on that score.

"Upon certain parts of our lines the wires are covered every winter with a layer of frost which attains sometimes a prodigious thickness, so as to render the wires ten times heavier than in their normal state, producing numerous breaks.

"This fact, which occurs always in the same places, and the results of which are so difficult to avoid, is not known to be explained but by a special meteorological tendency of the places.

"The direction seeks to avoid these places in removing the lines every time that repairs are necessary. In spite of these inconveniences without number, thanks to an inspection well organized, the interruptions are of less duration, and for nearly five months the Indian transit has not been interrupted a single instant. In fact, Constantinople is in direct communication every night with Vienna on the one side, and Fao upon the Persian Gulf on the other. Vienna has worked many times with Diarbekir, Alexinatz, and Semlin with Fao. Pera, at the same time, communicates with Bushire, in the south of Persia, and with Kurachée, the first Indian station, a distance of about five thousand kilometers.

"Notwithstanding the above-mentioned obstacles, results like these make comment unnecessary, for they suffice to give an exact idea of the actual Ottoman telegraph.

"These ameliorations are due to measures taken nearly two years ago at the creation of responsible inspectors, and, in short, to the complete reorganization of the direction.

"Before closing it will not be amiss to notice the existence of two services, distinct and very different—the international service in the European languages, and the interior service in the Turkish language, services which cannot be confounded, seeing the impossibility of assimilating the letters of the two alphabets, that which requires a double personnel and involves a multitude of other difficulties that cannot be overcome, but by practice the experience of many years, and some recent improvements.

"The Indian dispatches reach us ordinarily on the same day, and are transmitted immediately to Valona, Belgrade, or Vienna; but the English public has raised many complaints on the subject of the delay experienced in these dispatches. We ought to remark on this subject, that the said dispatches do not come all the way in our territory, and that we often even receive them from the foreign post offices with an ancient date, and that, in short, the person to whom they are addressed seldom knows by what way his dispatch is to come to him.

"Dispatches for India can go three different ways: 1. The way through Turkey to Fao, and the cable in the Persian Gulf. 2. The way through Turkey as far as Hannékin, and from there the Persian route by Bushire. 3. Finally, the Russo-Persian way, without passing through Turkey.

"After a special convention the dispatches we receive from Europe for the Indies ought to be transmitted by us in equal parts by the way of Fao and by the way of Hannékin. We receive them ordinarily from Europe by the way of Valona or Belgrade.

"There are also some errors which render the dispatches sometimes undecipherable. The Turks, to remedy these inconveniences, have placed upon all the lines of the great Asiatic line special employés, for the most part English, and who are charged with the control of these dispatches. Further, it is a recognized fact that nearly all our employés are more or less linguists, a fact which necessarily facilitates the exchange of international correspondence." * * *

AUSTRALIA.

Samuel W. McGowan, esq., general superintendent of electric telegraph in Victoria, (Australia,) has politely furnished two reports of the advancement and condition of his department for 1867 and 1868, which have been forwarded to the State Department at Washington. They contain maps of telegraph lines in a portion of Australia, and tables of the financial condition of the department under his charge.

In his report of 1867 he alludes to orders for two of "Messrs. Siemens & Halske's patent rapid writing type instruments," and also for "one of Professor Wheatstone's patent rapid writing instruments," which it was thought would afford greater facilities for speedy transmission. Respecting these, Mr. McGowan remarks: "In working either apparatus it is essentially necessary that the line should be in the best possible state of electric conductivity and insulation. Atmospheric disturbances or other existing cause would militate much more against successful transmission than under ordinary circumstances. It must also be borne in mind that in using the rapid writing instruments, the *staff of operators* at each terminal of the line will require to be largely augmented—the one for preparing the type or other transmitting material, the other for effecting the task of transcribing the matter as received from the recording instrument."

This necessity for the augmentation of the number of employés is a disadvantage complained of at Berlin as one of the great difficulties in the automatic type-printing apparatus of Messrs. Siemens & Halske.

By reference to Mr. McGowan's report for 1868, this remark will be found: "The order for a supply of the rapid writing automatic instruments mentioned in my last report has been canceled, owing to the enhanced cost of manufacture, and the probable gain in the working of the lines being overborne by the large expenditure involved."

The following questions were addressed to Samuel Walker McGowan, esq., superintendent general of telegraphs in Victoria, Australia, and the answers annexed returned under date of November 9, 1868:

"1. What systems of electro-telegraphic communication are in use in Australia?

"2. How many instruments of each system?

"3. Which system has your experience shown to be the best adapted to the various services required?

"4. Is the English needle system in use in Australia; and if so, to what extent?"

"Answer 1. The system known as Morse's electro-magnetic recording telegraph, and (to a small extent for local purposes,) Wheatstone's visual alphabetical magneto-induction telegraph.

"Answer 2. Of the Morse system there are—

In Victoria	87
In New South Wales	62
In Queensland	33
In South Australia	66
In New Zealand	25
In Tasmania	7
Total	280

"I do not take into account any other system, as none other is employed on the lines throughout the country. Professor Wheatstone's instruments are employed for local lines between the government offices, &c., and are not, so far as I am aware, used on any of the ordinary lines.

"Answer 3. I have no hesitation in giving my opinion in favor of the Morse system for all purposes requiring the transmission of large correspondence, where simplicity, accuracy, and the retention of a record of all messages, as actually transmitted, are matters of importance. During an experience of nearly twenty-two years solely devoted to my present profession, I have seen many other systems in practical operation, but none with which I am acquainted appears to me to fulfill so thoroughly all the requirements of a really efficient telegraph as the particular system now under mention.

"Answer 4. The English single and double needle system (Henley's magneto-induction instruments) was in use on some short railway lines in South Australia for a few years, but it has since been replaced by Morse instruments."

The expansion of the telegraph in Australia, in the three years 1863, 1864, 1865, is indicated in the following table:

Telegraph lines in Australia.

Year.	No. of stations.	No. of miles wire.	No. of telegrams.	Receipts.
1863	66	2,585½	234,520	£24,733
1864	70	2,626½	256,380	29,122
1865	79	3,110½	279,741	*34,770

* In 1867 there were in the colony of Victoria 86 stations, 2,526½ miles of line, and 3,119½ miles of wire.

In the Australian Return to Parliament for 1867, in the Appendix B, at p. 26, there is a column headed "Average number of words per hour." The minimum is 800 words=40 dispatches; the maximum is 1,500 words =75 dispatches per hour. It is worthy of notice that these dispatches are sent by the Morse apparatus, and that, therefore, the skill of the Australian operators is far greater than that of their European brethren, their minimum being double the number of dispatches sent by the same apparatus in Europe, and nearly equal to the number ordinarily transmitted by the operators in the United States, while their maximum number is triple the number of the European operators in the same time.

PERU.

Through the courtesy of his excellency Signor Bareda, the Peruvian minister to the United States, the following information has been obtained in answer to questions proposed to the Telegraph Administration of Peru:

"Question 1. What systems of telegraphy are in use in Peru, and the number of instruments under each system?"

"Answer. In the first line established in Peru (from Lima to Callao) the French system of Bréguet (the dial system) was used. This was changed on the formation of the 'National Telegraph Company,' which substituted that of Morse with closed circuit, *(circuito cerrado.)* There is a double line between those places, and four apparatus are employed. Since the years 1865, 1866, two lines were built by the government, one between Tacua and Arica, (44 miles,) and another between Arequipa and Islay, (90 miles,) and both of these lines employ the Morse system. Each line is simple, and consequently only four apparatus are in use, (one for each station.")

"Question 2. How many English miles of telegraph *connection*,[1] and how many miles of wire?

"Answer. By supreme decree of July 26, 1867, permission was given

[1] From some cause this question was misapprehended, and is answered as if it had been "telegraphic concession," instead of "telegraph connection."

to Don Carloz Paz Soldan, without guarantee or subsidy, to organize a 'National Telegraph Company,' which should build a line between Callao and Lima, and as far as Lambayeque, (500 miles,) with stations in Chancay, Huacho, Casma, Santa Trujillo, San Pedro, Chiclayo, and Lambayeque, and permission to extend lines to intermediate points.

"The government, by way of protection, and as compensation for a discount of fifty per cent. from the tariff in its favor, on messages, gave (as a loan at six per cent., payable in twenty years,) $50,000 worth of materials and telegraphic articles, which it had in the custom-house, at the cost of the whole at Callao.

"The company has already in operation the line between Callao and Lima, and to Huacho, (90 miles,) and is constructing between Huacho and Casma, (60 miles of this finished, and the work goes on.) Also it has a line to Chorillos, which is being extended to Pisco and Ica, and the completion of this line, already built as far as Mala, (60 miles from Lima,) is expected by the end of September, (160 miles to Ica.)

"The company has also commenced work on the line from Lima to Cerro de Pasco, (180 miles,) and this will be extended to Iarma, Jauja, Huancayo, Ayaeucho.

"At the time of giving the concession named to Paz Soldan, the government conceded permission to build the line between Lima and Ica, to one Morse, an American, with concession also of $25,000 in materials. This individual did not do anything, and has since died, and the concession now remains void, as the National Telegraph Company is finishing this line.

"The government of the dictator, Colonel Prado, offered $46,000 subsidy to an American company, which proposed to place a cable from Panama to Chiloe.

"As the acts of the dictatorship have been annulled, that concession also remains void.

"Recapitulating, there is no other pending concession than the one granted to the 'National Telegraph Company' for the line to Lambayeque, (500 miles.)

Lines already built:

Arequipa to Islay, on account of government	90 miles.
Tacua to Arica, on account of government	44 miles.
Lines of National Company:	
Lima to Callao	6 miles.
Lima to Huacho	90 miles.
Lima to Mala	60 miles.
Line completed in Casana and Huamey	60 miles.
Total already built	350 miles.

In construction:

Mala to Yca	100 miles.

Huamey to Huacho .... 66 miles.
Lima to Cerro de Pasco ....180 miles.

Total ....346 miles.

"It can be stated that at the end of this year (1868) we will have in operation 700 miles of telegraph.

"Question 3. Which system has experience shown to be best adapted to the following purposes, to wit: A, for long distances; B, for short distances; C, for railway service; D, for city or domestic use?

"Answer. To this question we cannot give particulars, on account of our short experience.

"Question 4. What are the aggregate expenses and receipts, cost of instruments, and maintenance, and number of employés?

"Answer. The expenses have not as yet been very large. You can state them now at $200 per mile. The receipts are calculated to give nine per cent. now, but when all the lines are in operation, will be twenty-five per cent. on capital. The cost of instruments is the same in all the markets from which we ask them, adding exchange. The number of employés which the government has on the two lines, between Arequipa and Islay, and Arica and Tacua, is twelve, and four directors, which is more than necessary. The National Company has now in five stations already opened, and three about to be opened, (also one at the palace for the use of the government,) say nine stations altogether, nineteen employés and ten conductors, and four horses, for the use of these; altogether twenty-nine employés.

"All its service is American. It has a building in Lima, with its various departments separate; another in Callao, and is about to buy in Huacho and Chancay—twelve instruments altogether.

"Question 5. Have you maps, documents, or other works illustrative of the extent and condition of the telegraph in any part of South America?

"Answer. We have no maps. By next steamer I will send more particulars, regulations, &c., and a letter I have written for the instruction of telegraphers.

"Question 6. Is the English needle system employed on any of the lines in South America?

"Answer. No."

APPENDICES.

A.—NUMBER OF THE MORSE APPARATUS USED IN EUROPE.

The following is the number of the Morse apparatus employed in the various European and Australian telegraph administrations in the year 1867:

France	1,600
Holland	216
Italy	1,017
Denmark	203
Austria	1,300
Switzerland	478
Belgium	590
Prussia	2,692
Ottoman Empire	1,020
Sweden	277
Australia	280
	9,673

In England, in one company, (the Electric and International Telegraph Company,) it is stated that there are 7,245 instruments. From this statement, taken in connection with another by the chairman of the company, that "the needle system first used had been superseded by the Morse," and "the ink-writer," which is also a Morse instrument, it may be inferred that the greater part of the 7,245 instruments are the Morse. Mr. Sabine, however, states that—

This company has in use of the Morse instruments	662
The United Kingdom Company	300
British and Irish London District Company	100
Total	1,062

From Russia, Spain, and Norway no official statement of the number of Morse instruments has been obtained; but an estimate made from a comparison of the proportion between the number of stations and instruments in other countries, renders it safe to estimate at a minimum—

Russia	624
Spain	262
Norway	110
	996

Exclusive, therefore, of the number of Morse instruments employed in the entire western continent, and Greece and Egypt, on the eastern continent, the numbers amount to 11,731 Morse instruments in use on the eastern continent. No direct statement of the number of Morse instruments in India has been obtained, but from the "return" to the House of Commons on the East India telegraphs, made June 22, 1868, sufficient information is gathered to give an estimate of the probable number. In casual conversation with one of the firm of a house which furnishes a good proportion of the telegraph apparatus for the United States, and mentioning the estimate of the number of Morse apparatus in use exclusive of America, (placing it at nearly 12,000,) he was asked for an estimate of the number in America. He replied that that number might be safely doubled for America alone, stating at the same time that every office had at least two instruments, and that in the last two months alone he had filled orders for 500 of the Morse sounder.

In the appendix of the "Return," D, p. 52, under "Tests upon which a signaller" (operator) "is to be promoted," one of the tests is "proficiency in transmitting and reading Morse signals." If, therefore, the Morse is employed in the same proportion to the number of offices as in other countries, the number of offices in 1866 is found to be 172, which makes the number of instruments 258. This number, added to the aggregate of 11,731, gives a total of 11,989 Morse instruments. Most offices or stations have two Morse instruments, sometimes more; hence in estimating the number of instruments, it has been assumed that the proportion between offices and instruments may safely be estimated at one and a half instruments to an office, or three instruments to two offices. On this basis the number of instruments in countries where the number is not definitely given has been estimated.

B—INVENTION OF THE TELEGRAPH.

TWO LETTERS ON THE QUESTION: "IS THE WORLD INDEBTED TO THE UNITED STATES FOR THE INVENTION OF THE TELEGRAPH?"

PARIS, *July* 18, 1868.

DEAR SIR: Being in company with some English friends a few evenings ago, there was a sharp controversy (conducted, however, with general good feeling) on the subject of the telegraph, and the question was raised: "To whom is the world indebted for the invention of the modern telegraph?" I contended that it was to the United States, while my English friends insisted that it was to England. On asking their authority for such a dictum, one of the gentlemen referred me to an article in the London Times, published in March or April, in which it was distinctly claimed that the world was indebted to England for the telegraph. He also seemed well posted in other documents, which he took from his library. I asked the favor of a loan of them for a few days. Let me quote from them:

1. In presenting the Albert Gold Medal of the Society of Arts in London, in November of last year, (1867,) to William Fothergill Cooke, esq., the chairman of the society claimed that it was conferred for the "practical introduction of the electric telegraph, not only to this country, (England,) but to every country in the world."

2. In a note also (p. 6) of editor's preface of a pamphlet by Rev. T. F. Cooke, (brother of the distinguished introducer of the electric semaphore into England,) he thus writes in commenting on the award of the society: "The award says, speaking of Mr. Cooke, 'To whom this country (England) is indebted.' Mr. Varley extends this claim, 'To whom *Europe* is indebted;' and another writer makes the claim absolute, 'To whom the *world* is indebted,' including *America*."

3. Then follows a note, which requires some explanation. He says: "This country (Great Britain) was the only country in which practical telegraphy was introduced at the date of the award, (April 27, 1841.) And on Dr. Hamel's authority we learn that Mr. Samuel Morse, of America, dates back his idea of an electric telegraph to 1832, and seems not to have known that the idea had existed for a century before. His signal apparatus, original, simple, and highly meritorious, was worked out gradually and very much later. It was not till 1844 that the first telegraph line from Washington to Baltimore was completed; when, on the 24th March, the first short telegram of four words (dictated by a Miss Ellsworth, and still preserved in the Historical Museum at Hartford, Connecticut, as the *first*,) announced the existence of a practical telegraph on the American continent. This was just five years after the Great Western Railway Telegraph was at work daily between London and Drayton, and after the varied experience of England was known and studied, both in Europe and America; and three years after the Brunel award was made publicly known."

4. In the very able pamphlet, "Government and the Telegraphs," presented to Parliament in opposition to the bill for the government purchase of the telegraphs, (attributed to the distinguished chairman of the Electric and International Telegraph Company, (Mr. Grimston,) the same claim is made to having given the telegraph to the world. It is in these words, at page 19: "The system they (the company) introduced has become, within a period of about twenty years, the basis from which has sprung not only all the systems of the United Kingdom, but the entire net-work of telegraphs throughout the globe."

5. As pertinent in this connection, I quote from page 11 of the same pamphlet the following passage relating to the instruments used by the company. After stating that "everything that has ever been proved to be practically useful had been adopted," he says: "This has been specially the case with regard to instruments. The earlier needle

instruments used in the principal circuits were soon superseded by Bain's printer. That again was superseded by the Morse instruments, which are now gradually giving way to the *ink writer*, an improved instrument on the same system."

These are a few of the extracts made from the journals and pamphlets which my English friend thought substantiated the English claim to the position, "that to England the world was indebted for the electric telegraph." I called at your hotel yesterday to show them to you, but to my grief you had left the country. I feel an interest, in common with some others of our countrymen, to know the truth in this matter, and I am sure I cannot apply to a more competent person than yourself for the facts. Will you not spare a little time to give them to me? I know some English women of high intellectual position who are quite as enthusiastic in espousing my side of the question as any American can be. Please direct care of C. B. Norton & Co., 16 Rue Auber.

I remain, with friendly regard, yours,

C.

Prof. S. F. B. MORSE, *New York, U. S. A.*

POUGHKEEPSIE, *September* 25, 1868.

MY DEAR SIR: Although absorbed just now in the labors of arranging my materials for my commissioners' report on the telegraph apparatus of the Paris Exposition, I snatch a few moments to answer your letter of the 18th July, and to remark on the extracts which you have quoted from publications, some of which I had already seen. Although the position taken by the English writers, from whose works you have made your extracts, is certainly untenable in the sense of having given the modern instrumental system of telegraphs to the world, yet the boast, regarded in the sense of extending the telegraph wires, cables, and land lines throughout the world, has some plausibility, since this extension, particularly in submarine lines, is greatly due to English capital, energy, and skill. But even in these qualities, the palm must be divided with the United States, France, Prussia, and Russia, to say nothing of the local assistance of other states through which the wires are carried.

If we look more closely into the composition of the telegraph as a whole, it will be seen that it is divided into two very distinct, yet correlative parts, to wit: The wire conductors or electrical thoroughfare, and the terminal instruments using this thoroughfare. A good illustration of these correlative parts is found in the railway system; there is the iron roadway and the locomotive. So, in the telegraph system, there is the iron roadway (the electrical conductors) and the instrumental system, for transmission over the way. The two parts, both in the railway and the telegraph, separated, would be inoperative for any useful purpose. The locomotive without the rail, and equally the rail without the locomotive, are inoperative. So the recording or signal instruments, without the conductors and the conductors without terminal instruments, are equally inoperative for any useful purpose.

There may be a difference of opinion regarding the relative importance of these two correlated parts, as there once was between the organist and the bellows-blower, (excuse the badinage,) the latter contending that in the production of the music the organist must use the copulative pronoun "*we*," when boasting of his performance, since without the labors of the blower the organ would be dumb.

Yet, to revert to the railroad illustration, the inventor of the locomotive, or its improver, works in a distinct department, and the builder of the road would not be entitled to claim for himself the merit of an improved locomotive, or the whole railroad, because he had extended the latter to a greater distance.

Since you have numbered your extracts, I will allude to them by their numbers.

Nos. 1, 2, and 4. On these extracts I observe that they furnish good examples of history made erroneous, by confounding things wholly unlike, by not regarding proper distinctions. Many errors proceeding from this source made it necessary for me to draw attention to the important distinction between the *semaphore* and the *telegraph*. I say important, because the proper definition of these terms removes from conflict the *meum* and *tuum* of two modes of communicating at a distance, differing in essential particulars in process and means from each other, yet treated of as conjoined under the name "telegraph" by most writers. The general use of the word, as applied to all modes of communicating at a distance, ought not to be cited as an objection to strict definition, when the progress and accuracy of history render such a definition a necessity. The improvement of the semaphore—indeed, the invention of the *electric needle semaphore*, so far, at least, as the making it a *practical instrumentality*—belongs to William Fothergill Cooke; but the telegraph, in its strict definition as a means of recording at a distance, belongs to Morse. The philological or etymological distinction, therefore, is not a fanciful, or captious, or capricious quibble.

3. In the note here quoted the telegraph and semaphore, as you perceive, are assumed to be the same invention, whereas the invention of Morse is a telegraph, and the invention of Cooke is a semaphore. Hence the events and dates set forth in this note are inapposite to prove priority. The question, which of the two systems was first practically introduced to public use, is discussed by the writer as if the date of the introduction settled the date of the invention.

The invention is one thing; its practical introduction quite another. They are referable each to different times. The time of the invention is one time, the time of its practical introduction is another; they may or may not be coincident. The invention, strictly speaking, must be precedent to its practical introduction. The agencies for the latter may be indefinitely delayed, without affecting the fact of the previous existence of that which is to be practically introduced.

There was no necessity for the writer's citation of Hamel as an authority that Morse dates back his idea of an electric telegraph to 1832. (Hamel, I may say in passing, is no authority for any statement affecting me.) This citation is accompanied by a reflection upon my supposed ignorance of the fact that the "idea" had existed "a century before." What idea? The idea of the possibility of using electricity as a means of communicating at a distance may have been a century old, but that was not my idea of 1832. The idea of 1832 was the possibility of *producing an automatic record at a distance by means of electricity*—the idea of a true telegraph—and this original idea was immediately followed by devising the process and means for carrying the idea into effect. This was the new idea of 1832, now realized in the adoption of the Morse telegraphic system throughout the world.

If it was necessary for the writer to cite an authority to prove that I dated back my idea of an electric telegraph to 1832, there was better authority at hand than that of the prejudiced Dr. Hamel to show what that idea was. The Chief Justice of the United States, in delivering the decision of the Supreme Court, says: "The evidence is full and clear that when he (Morse) was returning from Europe in 1832, he was deeply engaged upon this subject during the voyage, and that *the process and means were so far developed and arranged* in his own mind that he was confident of ultimate success."

Now, "process and means, developed and arranged," pertain to something more than a barren idea.

The note further says: "It was not till 1844 that the first telegraph line from Washington to Baltimore was completed, when the first short telegram announced the existence of a practical telegraph on the American continent." In other words, 1844 was the date of the practical introduction of the invention of 1832; and the "first telegram of four words" was, indeed, the first on this first public line, but not the first produced by the invention.

The electric semaphore of Mr. Cooke was demonstrated and practically introduced on a short line on the 25th of July, 1837. This is the date of its practical introduction, but not the date of his invention.

His invention goes back to an earlier date, at least to 1836.

The electric telegraph of Morse was demonstrated in 1835, before many witnesses; it was practically introduced for public use in 1844; but neither of these dates is the date of the invention, to wit: the date when "the process and means were developed and arranged." This was in 1832.

5. From the statement in this extract, it appears that on the lines of the company in Great Britain, which has the greatest extent in the United Kingdom, (the Electric and International Telegraph Company,) the electric needle semaphore was originally practically introduced through

the genius, skill, and energy of Mr. Cooke. But the writer, the chairman of the company, says, "this system was superseded by what is called the Bain printer;" and that was in turn "superseded by the Morse instruments," (that is, by the American telegraph.) But this again, it seems, was superseded by an instrument, which has received the name of "Ink-writer," a new name only for the original Morse instrument—one of his earliest modes of recording.

On the general subject of your letter I would say, if England's claims are sound, and the world is indebted to England for the telegraph, there should be the evidence of it in every country. The English needle system ought to be seen in use everywhere, not merely in Europe, but in America also, since America is included, by the writer you quote, in the class of debtors to England for the telegraph. It may be well, therefore, to inquire in what countries of the world the English needle system is in use. In reply to this question, I have the means of correct information from the highest sources, elicited in the answers from the various national administrations to the direct question I proposed to them, when engaged in my labors at the Exposition in 1867, "Is the English needle system in use in your country?"

The several administrations have given the following answers:

FRANCE.—"Not in a single office."—*Count de Vougy, Administrator of French Telegraphs.*

HOLLAND.—"It is not employed anywhere with us, neither on the lines of the state, nor of private companies."—*Referendary's letter.*

ITALY.—"The English needle system is no longer in public use in any part of Italy."—*United States Legation, Florence.*

DENMARK.—"The English needle system is not in use anywhere in Denmark."—*United States Minister, Copenhagen.* "Throughout the kingdom the Morse system is the only one in use, whether on government, private, or railroad lines. The English needle system is nowhere in public use in Denmark."—*Director General Faber.*

AUSTRIA.—"The English needle system is nowhere in use in this empire."—*United States Chargé d'Affaires in Vienna.*

SWITZERLAND.—"There is no use made in Switzerland of the English needle system; in fact, none other than the Morse system."—*Superintendent Telegraph Bureau, Berne.* "The only telegraph system employed in Switzerland is that of Morse. We do not hesitate to express our conviction that no known system at this day better fulfills the required conditions than that which we have in use, and of which M. Professor Morse is the inventor."—*Director General of Telegraphs.*

BELGIUM.—"It is long since the Belgian telegraphs have used the English needle apparatus."—*Farsia.*

EGYPT.—"The Egyptian government lines are confined to those in the Soudan country, the whole of which are worked on the Morse system."—*Director of Telegraphs.*

SPAIN.—"In Spain the telegraph system employed on the government lines is solely and exclusively that of Morse."—*Director General of Spanish Telegraphs.*

PRUSSIA.—"The systems of Prussia are Morse, Siemens, and Hughes. The English needle system has never been in use in Prussia."—*Director General De Chauvin.*

SWEDEN.—"It is the Morse system which is exclusively adopted for all the offices of the telegraph administration of Sweden. The English needle system has not been employed in any part of Sweden."—*Director General Brandstrom.*

OTTOMAN EMPIRE.—"The English needle system is not used in any part of this empire."—*United States Secretary of Legation, J. P. Brown.* "The English needle system is not in use in any part of the Ottoman Empire."—*United States Minister E. J. Morris.*

Indirectly I learn it is not used in Russia. It is nowhere used in North or South America, not even in the British possessions.

To these facts, from so many of the telegraph administrations of the world, add the significant additional facts, stated by Mr. Grimston in your extract No. 5, which shows that the English needle system, at first so widely extended and used in the United Kingdom, is now for the most part abandoned in Great Britain, as it has been universally on the continent, and its place supplied by other systems, the Hughes and the Morse, but chiefly the latter, (both American systems.) If, therefore, in every nation where the telegraph has been established, it is the original Morse system, or in part the Hughes, which is adopted, and that even in the United Kingdom itself the English system has been abandoned for the American, it appears to me you have the facts you have desired to sustain your position that the world is indebted to the United States rather than to Great Britain for the modern telegraph. If these facts are not in accord with the preconceived opinions of your English friends, I wish I had the time, and indeed the ability, to do anything like justice to the multitude of Britain's master-minds in science and inventions, for whom I have the highest admiration. My list of these honored names would swell this already prolix letter to too great a bulk. At the risk, nevertheless, of making an invidious selection, I cannot forbear mentioning the names of Professor Faraday, of William Fothergill Cooke, esq., of Sir William Thompson, of Dr. Whitehouse, of Sir Charles Bright, and of Cromwell F. Varley. The labors of the last four savans in giving effect and practicality to the Atlantic telegraph ought to be held in lasting remembrance.

But I must close with the assurance of my sincere respect.

Your friend and servant,

SAMUEL F. B. MORSE.

C. ———,

Care of C. B. Norton & Co., 16 Rue Auber, Paris.

C.—TELEGRAPH STATISTICS.

[Compiled by George Sauer, Esq.]

Through the courtesy of George Sauer, esq., who has bestowed much labor and statistical talent in collating and arranging telegraph statistics, and who has prepared for publication a valuable work on the telegraph, interesting tables have been furnished in proof-sheets, which he has kindly transmitted in advance of the publication of his work. And in this connection, the opportunity is improved to acknowledge obligations not only to him, but also to very many distinguished men in various countries. General acknowledgments are made to the United States diplomatic agents at the various courts of the Eastern Continent, and also to the chiefs of the telegraph administrations of the various countries, for their prompt, courteous, and satisfactory replies to the inquiries addressed to them. An indebtedness is also felt to many individual friends in the United Kingdom for valuable information; among these are Sir James Carmichael, Bart., Sir Charles Bright, M. P., and Robert Sabine, esq., the latter the author of a valuable treatise on the telegraph. From Australia also statistics have been received from the energetic and experienced general superintendent of telegraphs in Victoria, S. W. McGowan, esq., the first introducer of the telegraph into Australia.

Statement showing the average number of messages per mile and per station in Europe.

Years.	MESSAGES PER MILE OF TELEGRAPHIC LINE.							MESSAGES PER MILE OF TELEGRAPHIC WIRE.							MESSAGES PER STATION.						
	France.	Belgium.	Switzerland.	Prussia.	Russia.	Norway.	Great Britain.	France.	Belgium.	Switzerland.	Prussia.	Russia.	Norway.	Great Britain.	France.	Belgium.	Switzerland.	Prussia.	Russia.	Norway.	Great Britain.
1851	6	54	......	......	......	......	......	......	22	......	......	......	......	......	530	......	......	......	......	......	......
1852	22	65	......	23	......	......	......	......	27	......	11	......	......	......	1, 002	927	......	1, 016	......	......	......
1853	32	119	......	24	......	......	......	......	40	......	14	......	......	......	1, 561	1, 239	1, 169	1, 109	......	......	......
1854	51	111	105	45	......	......	......	......	39	......	24	......	......	......	1, 844	1, 342	1, 439	2, 280	......	......	......
1855	39	125	120	54	......	49	127	......	32	......	24	......	44	22	1, 709	1, 284	1, 679	2, 282	......	1, 041	1, 501
1856	51	158	152	67	......	122	123	......	59	......	28	......	94	25	2, 157	1, 985	2, 162	2, 323	......	2, 557	1, 553
1857	58	219	170	67	27	89	131	......	63	......	26	20	56	27	2, 419	1, 920	2, 098	2, 464	1, 690	1, 888	1, 580
1858	57	220	150	57	26	62	130	......	70	114	22	20	49	27	2, 399	1, 043	1, 946	2, 268	1, 964	1, 552	1, 386
1859	60	221	261	77	26	74	156	......	81	120	28	21	60	33	2, 496	2, 308	2, 113	3, 181	2, 057	2, 255	1, 762
1860	53	246	167	80	37	85	171	......	88	119	28	24	67	22	1, 880	1, 568	2, 096	3, 202	2, 509	2, 412	1, 806
1861	56	250	168	87	43	76	184	......	96	126	30	26	61	38	2, 023	1, 630	2, 114	3, 381	3, 194	2, 134	1, 527
1862	89	250	194	109	43	81	211	......	97	132	37	27	66	46	2, 988	1, 489	2, 161	3, 353	3, 318	2, 571	1, 656
1863	100	263	230	122	42	92	228	3[illegible]	107	138	40	24	75	48	3, 268	1, 726	2, 296	2, 985	2, 626	2, 937	1, 818
1864	107	293	250	125	40	103	262	33	123	153	50	2[illegible]	84	54	3, 209	1, 960	2, 309	3, 247	2, 723	2, 112	1, 034
1865	125	335	277	182	......	114	290	40	124	159	57	......	94	60	2, 596	2, 195	2, 346	3, 287	......	3, 690	2, 287
1866	134	513	277	209	......	122	......	42	187	163	63	......	99	......	2, 351	3, 168	2, 355	3, 650	......	......	......
1867	139	533	297	193	......	......	......	42	174	154	51	......	......	......	2, 163	3, 460	......	3, 013	......	......	......

Telegraph statistics of France.

Years.	NUMBER OF STATIONS, LENGTHS OF LINES, ETC.					NUMBER OF MESSAGES.			PRODUCE OF MESSAGES.			PROFIT AND LOSS.			
	Lengths of lines.	Lengths of wires.	Number of stations.	Number of instruments.	Number of persons employed.	Inland.	International.	Total.	Inland.	International.	Total.	Gross receipts.	Expenditure.	Profit.	Loss.
	Miles.	*Miles.*							*Francs.*	*Francs.*	*Francs.*	*Francs.*	*Francs.*	*Francs.*	*Francs.*
1851	1, 325	....	17	....	....	....	....	9, 014	....	....	76, 722	99, 582	1, 194, 467	....	1, 094, 884
1852	2, 149	....	43	....	....	....	....	48, 105	....	....	542, 891	565, 751	1, 299, 739	....	733, 988
1853	4, 440	....	91	....	....	....	....	142, 061	....	....	1, 511, 909	1, 617, 166	1, 794, 090	....	176, 923
1854	5, 745	....	128	....	....	....	....	236, 018	....	....	2, 064, 983	2, 284, 274	2, 393, 769	....	109, 495
1855	6, 540	....	149	....	....	....	....	254, 532	....	....	2, 487, 159	2, 860, 919	3, 066, 149	....	205, 229
1856	7, 000	....	167	....	....	....	....	360, 299	....	....	3, 191, 102	3, 494, 719	3, 364, 479	130, 239	....
1857	7, 100	....	171	....	....	....	....	413, 616	....	....	3, 333, 695	3, 690, 939	3, 759, 526	....	68, 587
1858	8, 098	....	193	....	....	349, 887	114, 086	463, 973	1, 794, 918	1, 721, 715	3, 516, 633	3, 902, 078	4, 398, 627	....	496, 549
1859	10, 000	....	240	....	....	453, 998	144, 703	598, 701	2, 072, 314	1, 950, 485	4, 022, 799	4, 450, 270	4, 659, 106	....	208, 835
1860	13, 620	....	383	....	....	568, 365	151, 885	720, 250	2, 358, 525	1, 829, 540	4, 188, 065	4, 770, 240	5, 570, 064	....	799, 824
1861	16, 468	....	455	....	....	734, 252	186, 357	920, 357	2, 840, 445	2, 079, 292	4, 919, 737	5, 676, 864	6, 594, 407	....	917, 542
1862	17, 113	....	508	....	....	1, 291, 774	226, 270	1, 518, 044	2, 984, 490	2, 317, 950	5, 302, 440	6, 265, 683	7, 301, 046	....	1, 035, 363
1863	17, 518	57, 455	537	....	....	1, 490, 023	264, 844	1, 754, 867	*3, 305, 993	2, 631, 911	5, 937, 904	6, 987, 521	8, 163, 423	....	1, 175, 900
1864	18, 222	60, 458	610	....	....	1, 654, 406	313, 342	1, 967, 748	3, 565, 933	2, 557, 338	6, 123, 272	7, 315, 922	8, 373, 098	....	1, 057, 175
1865	19, 763	63, 591	953	....	....	2, 098, 640	375, 102	2, 473, 747	4, 159, 445	2, 892, 694	7, 052, 139	8, 161, 218	8, 983, 460	....	822, 241
1866	21, 264	70, 351	1, 209	....	....	2, 379, 681	462, 873	2, 842, 554	4, 513, 095	3, 194, 495	7, 707, 590	8, 810, 283	8, 983, 460	....	73, 157
1867	23, 090	70, 330	1, 486	....	....	2, 682, 810	531, 185	3, 213, 995	4, 969, 618	3, 690, 226	8, 659, 845	....	....	....	....

* The receipts are exclusive of government business, amounting in the aggregate to about 1,000,000 francs annually, which, if added, would show an increase in lieu of a deficiency.

Telegraph statistics of Belgium.

Years.	NUMBER OF STATIONS, LENGTHS OF LINES, ETC.					NUMBER OF MESSAGES.			PRODUCE OF MESSAGES.			PROFIT AND LOSS.			
	Lengths of lines.	Lengths of wires.	Number of stations.	Number of instruments.	Number of persons employed.	Inland.	International.	Total.	Inland.	International.	Total.	Gross receipts.	Expenditure.	Loss.	Profit.
	Miles.	*Miles.*							*Francs.*	*Francs.*	*Francs.*	*Francs.*	*Francs.*	*Francs.*	*Francs.*
1851	257	626	10	20	32	6, 652	7, 373	14, 025	....	....	88, 674	88, 674	309, 116	220, 441	....
1852	420	998	28	60	40	9, 807	17, 410	27, 217	....	....	165, 973	165, 973	102, 947	....	63, 025
1853	437	1, 312½	42	74	57	14, 159	38, 195	52, 050	....	....	265, 536	265, 939	170, 735	....	94, 800
1854	454	1, 550	45	87	71	16, 719	43, 696	60, 415	....	....	280, 845	280, 845	139, 795	....	141, 050
1855	490	1, 596	50	97	75	17, 279	44, 154	61, 433	....	....	265, 939	265, 379	161, 500	....	104, 439
1856	501	1, 676	50	113	90	32, 862	66, 411	99, 273	....	....	359, 979	395, 579	202, 599	....	156, 980
1857	543	1, 835	62	138	113	41, 434	77, 616	119, 050	....	....	407, 011	407, 011	283, 171	....	123, 840
1858	661	2, 077½	75	155	126	47, 673	98, 053	145, 726	....	....	413, 926	413, 926	293, 891	....	120, 035
1859	887	2, 402	85	178	144	65, 465	130, 775	196, 240	....	....	506, 006	506, 006	375, 343	....	130, 662
1860	916	2, 569	144	234	158	80, 216	145, 603	225, 819	142, 344	382, 846	527, 743	527, 743	403, 500	....	124, 243
1861	1, 079	2, 808	165	265	155	97, 945	171, 023	268, 968	171, 225	396, 306	588, 532	588, 532	408, 261	....	180, 271
1862	1, 174	3, 002	196	271	167	105, 274	186, 513	291, 787	176, 643	428, 401	605, 044	605, 044	515, 800	....	89, 244
1863	1, 655	3, 875	241	365	185	188, 825	227, 288	416, 113	211, 063	401, 299	612, 363	612, 363	653, 780	41, 417	....
1864	1, 867	4, 421	279	421	217	252, 301	294, 196	546, 497	282, 591	506, 806	789, 399	789, 399	670, 424	....	118, 974
1865	2, 012	5, 433	307	481	267	332, 721	341, 316	674, 037	345, 289	520, 350	865, 640	865, 640	948, 516	82, 876	....
1866	2, 200	6, 243	356	556	309	692, 536	435, 469	1, 128, 005	407, 532	553, 580	962, 213	962, 213	1, 217, 496	255, 282	....
1867	2, 424	7, 444	374	603	336	819, 668	474, 202	1, 293, 870	471, 279	602, 935	1, 074, 214	....	....	....	....

Telegraph statistics of Switzerland.

Years.	NUMBER OF STATIONS, LENGTHS OF LINES, ETC.					NUMBER OF MESSAGES.			PRODUCE OF MESSAGES.			PROFIT AND LOSS.			
	Lengths of lines.	Lengths of wires.	Number of stations.	Number of instruments.	Number of persons employed.	Inland.	International.	Total.	Inland.	International.	Total.	Gross receipts.	Expenditure.	Loss.	Profit.
	Miles.	*Miles.*							*Francs.*	*Francs.*	*Francs.*	*Francs.*	*Francs.*	*Francs.*	*Francs.*
1852	....	....	34	....	....	2, 876	....	2, 876	3, 541	....	3, 541	6, 507	424, 081	417, 573	....
1853	....	....	70	....	....	74, 095	8, 491	82, 586	77, 388	50, 481	127, 870	144, 645	289, 120	144, 475	....
1854	1, 228	....	90	....	....	109, 599	18, 568	129, 167	109, 927	98, 959	208, 887	235, 688	218, 718	....	16, 970
1855	1, 354	....	97	....	....	133, 936	28, 915	162, 851	133, 563	117, 828	251, 391	305, 821	324, 520	18, 698	....
1856	1, 494	....	105	....	....	169, 376	57, 696	227, 072	178, 896	141, 050	319, 947	393, 441	367, 312	....	26, 129
1857	1, 535	....	124	....	....	192, 664	67, 500	260, 164	206, 130	163, 095	369, 226	450, 529	406, 045	....	44, 484
1858	1, 649	2, 161	127	200	....	180, 489	66, 613	247, 102	191, 109	152, 487	343, 597	462, 279	428, 892	....	33, 386
1859	1, 774	2, 380	131	215	....	196, 425	90, 451	286, 876	213, 072	212, 515	425, 587	631, 327	504, 963	....	126, 364
1860	1, 857	2, 549	145	246	249	208, 311	95, 619	303, 930	224, 484	183, 944	408, 429	488, 286	439, 856	....	48, 329
1861	1, 970	2, 623	157	249	265	217, 700	114, 233	331, 933	233, 631	214, 424	448, 056	502, 429	421, 039	....	81, 389
1862	1, 970	2, 901	177	280	294	241, 814	140, 638	382, 452	259, 308	271, 109	530, 418	583, 915	502, 002	....	81, 913
1863	1, 982	3, 080	199	308	322	298, 778	158, 093	456, 871	318, 495	312, 253	630, 749	676, 885	570, 846	....	101, 03
1864	2, 062	3, 360	223	....	346	325, 165	189, 787	514, 952	344, 829	270, 488	615, 318	657, 583	572, 083	....	85, 499
1865	2, 132	3, 720	252	410	373	364, 118	227, 096	591, 214	381, 376	345, 186	726, 564	768, 582	657, 533	....	111, 048
1866	2, 410	4, 098	284	441	417	383, 158	285, 758	668, 916	400, 152	284, 319	684, 471	727, 615	687, 390	....	40, 225
1867	2, 395	4, 612	333	463	....	397, 289	311, 685	708, 974	412, 019	363, 004	775, 024	....	....	....	....

Telegraph statistics of Norway.

Years.	NUMBER OF STATIONS, LENGTHS OF LINES, ETC.					NUMBER OF MESSAGES.			PRODUCE OF MESSAGES.			PROFIT AND LOSS.			
	Lengths of lines.	Lengths of wires.	Number of stations.	Number of instruments.	Number of persons employed.	Inland.	International.	Total.	Inland.	International.	Total.	Gross receipts.	Expenditure.	Loss.	Profit.
	Miles.	*Miles.*									*Rixdolls.*	*Rixdolls.*	*Rixdolls.*	*Rixdolls.*	
1855	471	532	22	...	44	19, 253	3, 663	22, 916	...	...	29, 422				
1856	481	625	23	...	55	47, 943	10, 839	58, 812	...	...	78, 925				
1857	824	1, 310	39	...	98	57, 273	16, 402	73, 675	...	...	110, 544				
1858	1, 468	1, 847	52	...	125	73, 848	16, 860	90, 708	...	...	136, 021				
1859	1, 571	1, 955	52	...	129	95, 505	21, 745	117, 250	...	...	171, 894				
1860	1, 571	1, 955	52	...	129	106, 665	26, 629	133, 294	...	...	217, 490	2,061,173 (1855–1865)	2, 610, 854	459, 681	...
1861	1, 690	2, 087	53	...	130	98, 165	29, 662	127, 827	...	...	229, 976				
1862	1, 700	2, 115	65	...	130	106, 060	32, 650	138, 710	...	...	247, 041				
1863	1, 808	2, 234	65	...	131	130, 218	36, 918	167, 136	...	...	251, 228				
1864	1, 931	2, 358	68	...	138	159, 968	39, 766	199, 734	...	...	280, 810				
1865	1, 931	2, 358	71	...	138	169, 386	51, 608	220, 994	...	...	307, 822				
1866	2, 205	2, 710	73	...	152	191, 563	77, 812	269, 375	...	...	343, 645	343, 645	345, 776	2, 131	...
1867	...	...	...	...	...	...	...	...	...	...	...	...	...	...	...

Telegraph statistics of Prussia.

Years.	NUMBER OF STATIONS, LENGTHS OF LINES, ETC.					NUMBER OF MESSAGES.			PRODUCE OF MESSAGES.			PROFIT AND LOSS.			
	Lengths of lines.	Lengths of wires.	Number of stations.	Number of instruments.	Number of persons employed.	Inland.	International and transit.	Total.	Inland.	International and transit.	Total.	Gross receipts.	Expenditure.	Loss.	Profit.
	Miles.	*Miles.*							*Thalers.*	*Thalers.*	*Thalers.*	*Thalers.*	*Thalers.*	*Thalers.*	*Thalers.*
1852	2, 070	4, 232	48	....	306	....	....	48, 751	....	....	114, 539	114, 539	173, 993	59, 454	....
1853	2, 328	3, 927	50	....	266	....	....	55, 161	....	....	209, 944	209, 944	266, 689	56, 745	....
1854	2, 595	4, 803	51	....	298	....	....	116, 313	....	....	328, 506	328, 506	374, 062	45, 556	....
1855	2, 821	6, 492	67	....	409	83, 737	68, 983	152, 820	168, 725	265, 397	434, 122	434, 122	265, 038	....	169, 084
1856	3, 314	7, 837	91	....	540	159, 975	61, 436	221, 411	283, 785	307, 253	591, 038	591, 038	388, 571	....	202, 467
1857	3, 580	9, 128	98	....	568	179, 340	62, 205	241, 545	313, 383	413, 134	726, 517	726, 517	431, 175	....	295, 342
1858	4, 384	10, 981	109	....	596	159, 685	87, 517	247, 202	210, 900	519, 644	730, 584	730, 584	551, 317	....	158, 693
1859	4, 513	12, 493	110	....	659	284, 812	65, 185	349, 997	257, 601	550, 920	808, 521	808, 521	571, 791	....	257, 204
1860	4, 785	13, 774	120	....	722	239, 781	144, 554	384, 335	214, 476	576, 625	791, 101	791, 101	587, 769	....	203, 332
1861	5, 269	15, 609	136	....	780	289, 381	169, 621	459, 002	244, 236	631, 547	875, 783	875, 783	588, 998	....	286, 785
1862	6, 034	17, 946	197	....	936	462, 996	197, 505	660, 501	258, 386	696, 164	954, 550	954, 550	690, 066	....	264, 484
1863	7, 150	21, 851	294	....	1, 169	639, 486	238, 102	877, 583	313, 362	726, 499	1, 039, 961	1, 039, 961	787, 710	....	252, 251
1864	8, 086	25, 230	388	....	1, 508	1, 012, 040	247, 550	1, 259, 590	340, 165	809, 848	1, 150, 008	1, 150, 008	951, 312	....	198, 696
1865	8, 787	28, 254	486	....	1, 758	1, 133, 624	383, 831	1, 527, 455	402, 832	839, 657	1, 242, 489	1, 242, 489	1, 068, 337	....	174, 152
1866	9, 386	30, 970	538	....	1, 976	1, 483, 415	480, 615	1, 964, 030	487, 758	788, 027	1, 275, 785	1, 275, 785	1, 149, 527	....	126, 258
1867	13, 364	43, 072	857	....	2, 816	1, 885, 452	697, 948	2, 582, 400	624, 912	790, 178	1, 418, 090	1, 418, 090	1, 216, 285	....	201, 805

Telegraph statistics of Russia.

Years.	NUMBER OF STATIONS, LENGTHS OF LINES, ETC.					NUMBER OF MESSAGES.			PRODUCE OF MESSAGES.			PROFIT AND LOSS.			
	Lengths of lines.	Lengths of wires.	Number of stations.	Number of instruments.	Number of persons employed.	Inland.	International.	Total.	Inland.	International.	Total.	Gross receipts.	Expenditure.	Loss.	Profit.
	Miles.	*Miles.*							*Roubles.*	*Roubles.*	*Roubles.*	*Roubles.*	*Roubles.*		*Roubles.*
1857	4, 840	6, 715	79	....	....	78, 047	55, 509	133, 556	248, 500	208, 492	456, 992	412, 250	322, 955	....	89, 295
1858	6, 175	8, 042	90	....	....	98, 256	58, 538	156, 794	276, 711	245, 141	521, 852	457, 569	359, 980	....	97, 589
1859	9, 417	11, 343	118	....	....	164, 293	78, 456	242, 749	411, 497	329, 129	740, 626	656, 045	556, 688	....	99, 357
1860	10, 904	16, 745	160	....	....	303, 008	98, 471	401, 479	735, 427	296, 794	1, 032, 221	940, 009	828, 861	....	111, 148
1861	12, 926	21, 402	175	....	....	433, 110	125, 919	559, 029	965, 473	333, 831	1, 299, 304	1, 176, 762	1, 020, 616	....	156, 146
1862	15, 070	24, 086	195	....	....	512, 685	134, 557	647, 242	1, 155, 989	346, 035	1, 502, 024	1, 368, 953	1, 268, 071	....	100, 882
1863	17, 445	30, 364	281	....	....	589, 554	148, 299	737, 853	1, 341, 271	362, 183	1, 703, 454	1, 534, 830	1, 497, 125	....	37, 705
1864	21, 119	37, 330	308	....	....	677, 911	160, 742	838, 653	1, 464, 750	407, 909	1, 872, 659	1, 724, 118	1, 674, 236	....	49, 882
1865	....	....	....	....	....	....	....	....	....	....	....	....	....	....	....
1866	....	....	....	....	....	....	....	....	....	....	....	....	....	....	....
1867	....	....	....	....	....	....	....	....	....	....	....	....	....	....	....

Statement showing the progress of telegraphy in France, Belgium, Switzerland, and Austria.

Years.	FRANCE.			BELGIUM.			SWITZERLAND.			AUSTRIA.		
	Number of messages.	Gross receipts.	Average cost per mess'ge.	Number of messages.	Gross receipts.	Average cost per mess'ge.	Number of messages.	Gross receipts.	Average cost per mess'ge.	Number of messages.	Gross receipts.	Average cost per mess'ge.
		Francs.	*Francs.*		*Francs.*	*Francs.*		*Francs.*	*Francs.*		*Florins.*	*Florins.*
1851	9, 014	76, 722	7. 84	14, 025	88, 674	6. 32	....	....	....	44, 911	128, 736	2. 86
1852	48, 105	542, 891	11. 28	27, 217	165, 973	6. 10	2, 876	3, 541	....	62, 716	209, 547	3. 34
1853	142, 061	1, 511, 909	10. 64	52, 050	265, 536	5. 07	82, 586	127, 870	1. 55	109, 347	308, 158	2. 82
1854	236, 018	2, 064, 982	8. 14	60, 415	280, 845	4. 65	129, 167	208, 887	1. 62	190, 552	549, 697	2. 88
1855	254, 532	2, 487, 159	9. 77	61, 433	265, 939	4. 33	162, 851	251, 391	1. 53	204, 221	607, 745	2. 97
1856	360, 299	3, 191, 102	8. 68	99, 273	359, 579	3. 62	227, 072	319, 947	1. 41	251, 948	778, 294	3. 08
1857	413, 616	3, 333, 695	8. 06	119, 050	407, 011	3. 42	260, 164	369, 226	1. 42	381, 720	888, 905	2. 33
1858	463, 973	3, 516, 633	7. 60	145, 726	413, 926	2. 84	247, 102	343, 597	1. 37	419, 449	760, 811	1. 81
1859	598, 701	4, 022, 799	6. 72	196, 240	506, 066	2. 57	286, 876	425, 587	1. 48	692, 379	951, 240	1. 37
1860	720, 250	4, 188, 065	5. 81	225, 819	527, 743	2. 34	303, 930	408, 429	1. 34	700, 795	991, 275	1. 41
1861	920, 357	4, 919, 737	5. 34	268, 968	588, 532	2. 19	331, 933	448, 056	1. 35	846, 953	1, 226, 404	1. 44
1862	1, 518, 044	5, 302, 440	3. 49	291, 787	605, 044	2. 07	382, 452	530, 418	1. 42	946, 675	1, 267, 966	1. 34
1863	1, 754, 867	5, 937, 904	3. 38	416, 113	612, 363	1. 47	456, 871	630, 749	1. 38	1, 130, 625	1, 290, 447	1. 14
1864	1, 967, 748	6, 123, 272	3. 11	546, 497	789, 399	1. 44	514, 952	615, 318	1. 20	1, 610, 663	1, 322, 948	0. 82
1865	2, 473, 747	7, 052, 139	2. 85	674. 037	865, 640	1. 28	591, 214	726, 564	1. 23	1, 786, 955	1, 435, 478	0. 80
1866	2, 842, 554	7, 707, 590	2. 71	1, 128, 005	962, 213	0. 85	668, 916	684, 471	1. 03	2, 507, 472	1, 644, 742	0. 66
1867	3, 213, 965	8, 659, 845	2. 69	1, 293, 870	1, 074, 214	0. 83	708, 974	775, 024	1. 00	....	....	....

Statement showing the progress of telegraphy in Prussia, Spain, Russia, and Norway.

Years.	PRUSSIA.			SPAIN.			RUSSIA.			NORWAY.		
	Number of messages.	Gross receipts.	Average cost per mess'ge.	Number of messages.	Gross receipts.	Average cost per mess'ge.	Number of messages.	Gross receipts.	Average cost per mess'ge.	Number of messages.	Gross receipts.	Average cost per mess'ge.
		Thalers.	*Thalers.*		*Dollars.*	*Dollars.*		*Roubles.*	*Roubles.*		*Rixdollars.*	*Rixdolls.*
1851												
1852	48, 751	114, 539	2. 35									
1853	85, 161	209, 944	2. 46									
1854	116, 343	328, 506	2. 82									
1855	152, 820	434, 122	2. 84	2, 085	38, 042	18. 290				22, 916	8, 414	0. 36
1856	221, 411	591, 038	2. 67	4, 346	76, 084	17. 530				58, 812	22, 572	0. 38
1857	241, 545	726, 517	3. 01	26, 772	146, 911	5. 480	133, 556	456, 992	3. 42	73, 675	31, 615	0. 42
1858	247, 202	730, 584	2. 95	113, 171	303, 665	2. 686	156, 794	521, 852	3. 33	90, 708	38, 902	0. 43
1859	349, 997	808, 521	2. 31	210, 426	523, 807	2. 450	242, 749	740, 626	3. 05	117, 250	49, 161	0. 42
1860	384, 335	791, 101	2. 06	230, 108	558, 227	2. 420	401, 479	1, 032, 221	2. 57	133, 294	62, 256	0. 46
1861	459, 002	875, 783	1. 90	236, 089	620, 678	2. 650	559, 029	1, 299, 304	2. 32	127, 827	65, 773	0. 51
1862	660, 501	954, 550	1. 45	282, 098	526, 079	1. 850	647, 242	1, 502, 024	2. 32	138, 710	70, 653	0. 52
1863	877, 583	1, 039, 961	1. 18	433, 110	587, 218	1. 350	737, 853	1, 703, 454	2. 31	167, 136	71, 851	0. 42
1864	1, 259, 590	1, 150, 008	0. 91	613, 265	611, 644	0. 980	838, 653	1, 885, 355	2. 25	199, 734	80, 331	0. 40
1865	1, 527, 455	1, 242, 489	0. 81	767, 909	631, 682	0. 810				220, 994	88, 037	0. 40
1866	1, 964, 030	1, 275, 785	0. 65	666, 462	533, 558	0. 800				269, 375	98, 282	0. 36
1867	2, 582, 400	1, 656, 419	0. 64	533, 376	554, 476	1. 030						

D.—FRANKLIN AND ELECTRICAL SEMAPHORES.

It has frequently been asserted (on what authority I know not) that the first idea of an electric semaphore originated with Franklin. I have sought in vain in the publications of Franklin's experiments and works for anything confirmatory of this assertion. On mentioning the subject to my friend, Professor Blake, he kindly proposed examining the writings of Franklin in order to elicit the truth. From him I have received the following:

"I have consulted several works for the purpose of ascertaining, if possible, the foundation for the statement that Franklin suggested the idea of semaphores by static electricity. I have not yet found any such suggestion, but I have noted that following the experiments by Dr. Watson, and others, in England, to determine the *velocity* of the electric discharge, and the time supposed to be required for the electrical discharges across the Thames, by which spirits were kindled, &c., (in 1747,) Dr. Franklin, in 1748, made some similar experiments upon the banks of the Schuylkill, and amused his friends by sending a spark 'from side to side through the river without any other conductor than the water.'[1] (This was in 1748, at the end of the year.) In 1756, 'J. A. esq.,' of New York, (James Alexander,) presented to the Royal Society a proposition 'to measure the time taken by the electric spark in moving through any given space' by sending the discharge or spark down the Susquehanna or Potomac, and around by way of the Mississippi and Ohio rivers, so that the 'electric fire' would have a circuit of some thousands of miles to go. All this was upon the supposition or assumption that the electric fire would choose a continuous water conductor rather than to return or pass through the earth. Franklin presented a paper in reply, in which he says, 'the proposed experiment (though well-imagined and very ingenious) of sending the spark round through a vast length of space, &c., &c., would not afford the satisfaction desired, though we could be sure that the motion of the electric fluid would be in that tract, and not underground in the wet earth by the shortest way.'[2]

"Can it be possible that Franklin's experiment of firing spirits and showing the spark and other effects of the electric discharge across the river originated, or forms the foundation for, the statement that he suggested the semaphoric use of electricity?"

---

[1] Vide Priestley's History of Electricity.

[2] Franklin's Experiments on Electricity, and Letters and Papers on Philosophical Subjects. 4to. London, MDCCLXIX, pages 282, 283.

E.—CATALOGUE OF WORKS ON TELEGRAPHY.

The following are the titles of a few of the constantly increasing number of treatises on the telegraph:

Title of works.	Names of authors.	Place of publication and date.
Telegraphie	Prof. Steinheil	Munich, 1838.
The American Electro-magnetic Telegraph	Alfred Vail	New York, 1845.
Traité de télégraphie électrique	L'Abbé Moigno	Paris, 1849.
Elektrische Telegraphie	F. Kohl	———. 1850
Electric Telegraph Manipulator	C. V. Walker	London, 1850.
Manuel de telegrafia electrica	Matteuci	Pisa, 1850.
Kurze Darstellung, &c	W. Siemens	Berlin, 1851.
Mémoire, &c	W. Siemens	Berlin, 1851.
Die elektromagnetische Telegraphie	T. Bauerbaum	Berlin, 1851.
Recherches sur la télégraphie électrique	Gloesner	Liége, 1851.
Traité général des applications	Gloesner	
Ueber elektrische Telegraphie	Pelchrzun	Potsdam, 1853.
Katechismus der elektrischen Telegraphie	J. A. Forsach	Leipzig, 1853.
The Electric Telegraph	Dr. Lardner	London, 1855.
Exposé, &c	Du Moncel	Paris, 1855.
Revue des applications, &c	Du Moncel	Paris, 1857.
Télégraphie électrique	Du Moncel	Paris, 1861.
Traité d'électricité	De la Rive	Paris, 1858.
L'électricité et les chemins de fer	De Castro	Paris, 1858.
Cours théorique, 2 vols	E. E. Blavier	Paris, 1859.
Telegraph Manual	T. P. Schaffner	New York, 1859.
Electric Telegraph	Highton	London, 1862.
Handbuch der Telegraphie	Kuhn	Leipzig, 1866.
Die electromagnetische Telegraphie	Schellen	Brunswick, 1866.
Manuel de la télégraphie	Breguet	Paris.
Anwendung des Electromagnetismus, &c	Dub	
Electromagnetismus	Dub	
Telegraph History	A. Jones	New York.
Telegraph History	——Turnbull	Philadelphia.
Telegraph History	George Prescott	Boston, 1860.
The Electric Telegraph	Robert Sabine	London, 1867.
The Electric Telegraph	Lardner & Bright	London, 1867.
Télégraphie électrique	J. Gavarret	Paris, 1861.
Telegraph Manual	R. S. Culley	London.
Manual of Telegraphy*	Prof. J. L. Smith	New York
Modern Practice of the Electric Telegraph, a handbook for electricians and operators	Frank L. Pope	New York.

* An excellent compendium, brief but lucid.

F.—MATERIALS AND APPARATUS EXHIBITED.

The following catalogue of the apparatus and articles exhibited in Class 64, Group VI, is from the French catalogue of the Exposition, arranged under the various countries exhibiting them, but renumbered for the greater convenience of reference.

For reasons given in the introduction, many of these are unnoticed in the report.

FRANCE.

1. MINISTRY OF THE INTERIOR.—Exhibit by the administration of the telegraph lines, the various instruments employed on their lines.
2. A. JOLY, 29 rue Saint Sulpice, Paris.—A printing telegraph apparatus.
3. J. L. A. MACHABÉE, 46 rue de Veuves, Paris.—Telegraphic cables.
4. E. HARDY, 21 rue de Sèvres, Paris.—The telegraphic apparatus of M. M. Vavin, of Fribourg, the autographic apparatus of M. David, and the printing apparatus of M. Hughes.
5. A. CAUMONT, 79 boulevard Malesherbes, Paris.—Telegraphic apparatus, &c.
6. CH. CROS, 14 rue Royale, Paris.—Telegraphic apparatus.
7. T. A. M. SORTAIS, of Lisieux, (Calvados.)—The Morse apparatus.
8. LECLANCHÉ, 22 rue Fontaine St. Georges, Paris.—Galvanic battery.
9. E. GRENET, 14 rue Castiglione, Paris.—Galvanic battery.
10. P. DUMOULIN FROMENT, 85 rue Notre Dame des Champs, Paris.—Telegraph apparatus, Hughes & Caselli.
11. P. A. J. DUJARDIN, of Lille.—Telegraph apparatus and battery.
12. ZALINSKI MIKORSKI, 103 rue d'Enfer, Paris.—Galvanic battery.
13. E. LENOIR, 109 boulevard du Prince Eugène, Paris.—Autographic telegraph.
14. H. LÉGER, 24 rue des Bourdonnais, Paris.—Acoustic apparatus.
15. P. GUILLOT, 29 route de Choisy, Paris, and J. GATGET, 90 boulevard Mazas, Paris.—Magneto-electric telegraph apparatus.
16. L. BRÉGUET, 39 quai de l'Horloge, Paris.—Telegraphic apparatus, paratonneres, &c.
17. G. A. TABOURIN, of Lyons.—Telegraph, called hydro-dynamic.
18. DIGNEY FRÈRES & Co., 8 rue de Poitevins, Paris.—Telegraph apparatus.
19. THE ABBÉ J. CASELLI, 20 rue de l'Ouest, Paris.—The pantelegraph.
20. RATTIER & Co., 4 rue des Fossés Montmartre, Paris.—Telegraph cables.
21. L. GUYOT D'ARLINCOURT, 3 bis rue de la Bruyère, Paris.—Printing telegraph.
22. A. F. CACHELEUX, 103 rue de Grenelle St. Germain, Paris.—Telegraph apparatus.
23. E. E. BLAVIER, of Nancy, (Meurthe.)—Treatise on the telegraph, 2 vols.
24. P. D. PRUD'HOMME, 4 bis rue St. Martin, Paris.—Telegraph apparatus.

HOLLAND.

25. A. HOLTZMAN, of Amsterdam.—Telegraphic cable.

BELGIUM.

26. LÉON DELPERDANGE, 15 rue Zérézo, Brussels.—Work respecting subterranean telegraph lines.

27. CH. DEVOS, 8 rue des Croisades, St. Josse-ten-Noode, Brussels.—A commutator for 40 lines for the bureau central of the telegraphs.
28. ANT. J. GÉRARD, 5 Place St. Lambert, Liège.—Autographic telegraph.
29. MICHAEL GLOESENER, 55 rue des Augustins, Liège.—Telegraphs, electric, ordinary, and submarine; printing telegraph; autographic telegraph; needle telegraph; dial telegraph; model of electric bells; paratonneres, or lightning arresters.
30. LESAGE & CO., 8 rue du Gazomètre, Brussels.—Telegraph apparatus.
31. JEAN MICHAEL J. NAPLE, of Farciennes, (Namur.)—Telegraph apparatus, comprising two systems, that of the dial and letters, and that called artistic. They can be alternately used. Another apparatus with keys. The clock-work serves alternately for sending or receiving.

ENGLAND.

32. JOSEPH BOURNE & SON, Denby Potteries, Derbyshire.—Vitrified stone-ware insulators.
33. W. E. HENLEY, 27 Leadenhall street, London.—Submarine telegraph cables.
34. WILLIAM HOOPER, 7 Pall Mall east, London.—Telegraph cables.
35. D. NICOLL, Oakland's hall, Kilburn, London.—Wire and telegraph cables.
36. SIEMENS BROTHERS, 3 Great George street, Westminster, London.—Telegraphic apparatus.

CANADA.

37. ERNEST CHANTELOUP, of Montreal.—Telegraph apparatus.

PRUSSIA, AND STATES OF NORTHERN GERMANY.

38. ROYAL DIRECTION OF THE PRUSSIAN TELEGRAPH, Berlin.—Insulators complete.
39. WERNER SIEMENS AND J. G. HALSKE, Berlin, and CHARLES H. SIEMENS of St. Petersburg, &c.—Apparatus for distributing type dispatches; machine for composing; machine for distributing; apparatus for rapid writing; three apparatus for writing in color; apparatus for writing in relief; apparatus of wheels, *(appareils à roues;)* magnet indicators; two small magnet indicators for a private telegraph; an electric indicator of the height of water; small bridge in portable boxes for measuring resistance, &c.
40. GUILLAUME HORN, 45 Brandenburgstrasse, Berlin.—Polarized telegraph for writing in blue, with its accessories.
41. W. GURLT, 61 Krausenstrasse, Berlin.—Telegraph complete of Morse.
42. LEVIN & CO., Berlin.—Two telegraph apparatus.

43. BERNARD BEHREND, Coeslin.—Specimens of paper for the telegraph.
44. CHARLES JULES VOGEL AND A. HABERSTOLTZ, 39 Ritterstrasse, Berlin.—Specimens of copper wire, and (*de maillechort recouverts de soie et de coton*) for telegraph and offices.
45. RICH. BELLÉ, Aix-la-Chapelle.—Electric bells.

GRAND DUCHY OF BADEN.

46. H. MEIDINGER, of Carlsruhe.—Electric battery.

BAVARIA.

47. THE SOCIETY OF PASIGRAPHY, of Munich.—Pasigraphic books, in eighteen sheets, for the use of international telegraphy.

AUSTRIA.

48. THE CHEVALIER CH. ADOLPHE DE BERGMÜLLER, 8 Augustinerstrasse, Vienna.—Telegraph for the service of the police and fire-department.
49. LÉON DE HAMAR, Pesth, Hungary.—Telegraph apparatus of Morse, with key.
50. JEAN LEOPOLDER, 3 Theresianumgasse, Vienna.—Station telegraphs typographic telegraph, with the Morse characters; portable telegraph.
51. JEAN MÖERÄTH, 25 Alsengrund, Vienna.—Plan and process for laying submarine cables.
52. IMPERIAL ROYAL DIRECTION OF TELEGRAPHS, Vienna.—Telegraphic materials adopted for war service; carbon battery.

SWITZERLAND.

53. THE FEDERAL MANUFACTORY OF TELEGRAPHS, HASTER & ESCHER, Berne.—Telegraph apparatus.
54. M. HIPP, Neufchatel. Apparatus for the telegraph, clocks, and chronographs.

SPAIN.

55. THE DIRECTION GENERAL OF TELEGRAPHS, MOREUIL & BONET, Madrid.—Printing telegraphs, and material for telegraph stations.

PORTUGAL.

56. MAXIMILIAN HERMANN, Lisbon.—Electric telegraph apparatus.

DENMARK.

57. S. HJORTH, of Copenhagen.—Magneto-electric battery.
58. JULES THOMPSEN, of Copenhagen.—Battery of polarization.

RUSSIA.

59. RUSSIAN COMPANY FOR THE MANUFACTURE OF CAOUTCHOUC, at St. Petersburg.—Telegraph wire and insulators.
60. GALVANIC ESTABLISHMENT OF ENGINEERS, at St. Petersburg.—Electric telegraph apparatus.
61. JOSEPH PIK, Warsaw.—Telegraph, Morse system.

ITALY.

62. THOMAS PICCO, Alexandria.—A lightning arrester.
63. GASPARD SACCO, Turin.—Telegraph apparatus.
64. THE LONGONI & DELL'ACQUA, Milan.—Morse Telegraph, modified by Moroni, with accessories.
65. GAETAN BONELLI, Florence.—A type telegraph called "Telegraph with a shuttle," by Bonelli & Hipp; the simple autographic apparatus; the accessories for the use of this last.
66. JOSEPH POGGIALI, Florence.—The Morse apparatus complete.
67. JOSEPH AND IGNACE TREVISANI, and FRANÇOIS ERNEST HALLIE, of Ascoli Piceno.—A submarine cable.
68. BÉLISAIRE DETTI & SON, Naples.—A submarine cable; pen proper to substitute for the pencil for writing telegraphic dispatches.
69. ALBERT BALESTRINE, Paris.—Electric plummet with its line, called the sounding line; model of submarine stations, for the telegraph; model of a machine for laying the cable; plan of a transatlantic line; profile of five stations.

TURKEY.

70. HARISCHE OGLOU, of Eyalet and city of Sivas.—Electric batteries for the telegraph.

EGYPT.

71. Porous cups of the earth of Keneh, for the electric batteries.

UNITED STATES OF AMERICA.

72. S. E. AND G. L. MORSE, of Harrison, New Jersey.—Model of a new mode of laying and raising submarine cables, and a bathometer for deep-sea soundings.
73. Mrs. M. J. COSTON, Washington, D. C.—Telegraphic night-signals.
74. M. G. FARMER, Boston, Massachusetts.—Thermo-electric battery.
75. J. D. CATON, Ottawa, Illinois.—Pocket field-telegraph apparatus; the Morse sounder.

PARIS UNIVERSAL EXPOSITION, 1867.

REPORTS OF THE UNITED STATES COMMISSIONERS.

REPORT

UPON

STEAM ENGINEERING,

AS ILLUSTRATED BY THE

PARIS UNIVERSAL EXPOSITION, 1867,

BY

WILLIAM S. AUCHINCLOSS,

HONORARY COMMISSIONER.

WASHINGTON:

GOVERNMENT PRINTING OFFICE.

1869.

PREFACE.

"HARTREE HOUSE," BIGGAR, SCOTLAND,
August, 1867.

GENTLEMEN: The scope of these remarks embraces the general subject of steam engineering, as illustrated by the Paris Exposition Universelle. Our instructions limit the field of research to "those products which are *most* advanced" in the various departments of engineering science. Although they thus direct special inquiry towards the inventions of rare merit and novelty developed since the International Exhibition of 1862, their spirit is understood to include those which have endured the test of long service in foreign countries, and have yet to receive an appropriate recognition in our own land. The analysis is necessarily brief, and on most subjects must be regarded as indicative rather than exhaustive.

Points of novelty and difficulty have as far as possible been simplified by illustrations, and the addresses of inventors and owners procured with care for the assistance of those who may desire more detailed information. It is hoped that the effort may assist in diffusing some of the practical lessons flowing from this remarkable achievement of French genius, system, and refinement.

Very sincerely yours,

WM. S. AUCHINCLOSS,
Civil Engineer.

The COMMISSIONERS OF THE UNITED STATES.

CONTENTS.

CHAPTER I.

RAILWAY ENGINEERING.

CHAPTER II.

PORTABLE ENGINES, CRANES, AND FORGINGS.

LIST OF PLATES.

STEAM ENGINEERING.

CHAPTER I.

RAILWAY ENGINEERING.

LOCOMOTIVES—TABULAR STATEMENT OF THE RELATIVE DIMENSIONS OF LOCOMOTIVES OF DIFFERENT COUNTRIES—THE LOCOMOTIVE "AMERICA"—THE TANK ENGINE "TITAN"—SMOKE BURNING ENGINES—AUSTRIAN LOCOMOTIVES—THE MAHOVOS—FAIRLIE'S DOUBLE ENGINE—MYER'S LOCOMOTIVE—CAST-STEEL CYLINDERS—"BRIQUETTE" FUEL—SLEEPERS, TIES, AND CLIPS—SIGNALS—ERHARDT'S PORTABLE SCALE—RAILWAY DYNAMOMETER—RAILWAY CARRIAGES—CAR INTERCOMMUNICATION—RAILWAY CARRIAGE SPRINGS AND WHEELS.

I.—LOCOMOTIVES.

Among the 33 locomotives on exhibition may be studied almost every phase of modern practice. Of these, fourteen are furnished by France, five each by England and Belgium, four by Prussia, two by Austria, and one each from the United States, Russia, and Bavaria. They vary in magnitude between the two French extremes, as found in the colliery engine of 2′.9½″ gauge, weighing 6½ tons, and the immense four-cylinder freight engine of Messrs. Ernest Gouin & Co., whose weight, loaded, equals 59 tons.

The physical geography of each country indelibly impresses itself on the character of the engines required for its traffic service. With the necessity of surmounting great elevations and following sharp curves, imperative in Alpine passes, has appeared a new class of engine specially designed for the purpose. Where railways traverse level country, increased powers of traction and greater economy of fuel are the essential desiderata. The belief that an intelligent idea of the relative dimensions and proportions obtaining in these different countries can most concisely be formed by placing side by side the practice of prominent makers, has led to the preparation of the following table, in which the dimensions have all been converted to the United States standards. It should here be remarked that the most liberal minded manufacturers attached a carefully prepared card to their engines and greatly facilitated such a comparison.

Tabular statement of the relative dimensions and proportions of locomotives in different countries.

Builders of locomotives.	Class of engine.	Constructed for—	Number of cylinders.	Position of cylinders.	Diameter of cylinders.	Stroke of piston.	Style of link motion.	Cubic contents of cylinders.	Ratio of contents to heating surface.	BOILER. Diameter of shell.	BOILER. Height of axis above rails.	BOILER. Length of grate.	BOILER. Width of grate.
					Inches.	*Inches.*		*Cubic feet.*		*Ft. In.*	*Ft. In.*	*Ft. In.*	*Ft. In.*
Grant Locomotive Works	Passenger	Exposition	2	Outside	16	22	Shifting	5. 12	1:175	4 0	6 4	5 7½	2 9¼
Robert Stephenson & Co	....do	Egyptian government	2	Inside	16	22	....do	5. 12	1:202	4 1	6 8	4 0	3 6
Kitson & Company	Freight	Exposition	2	....do	16	22	....do	5. 12	1:170	3 10	6 1¼	4 2	3 5
Lilleshall Company	Passenger	......do	2	....do	16	21	Allan's	4. 88	1:239	4 3	....	5 5	3 5
Ernest Gouin & Company	Freight	Northern railway of France	4	Outside	17⅓	17⅛	Shifting	9. 47	1:174	4 9	7 2	6 2	5 3
Graffenstaden Company	....do	Eastern railway of France	2	Inside	16 9-16	23 11-16	....do	5. 9 & 3. 39	1:153	4 11⅛	6 10⅛	7 5¾	3 6
J. F. Cail & Company	Passenger	Northern railway of France	2	....do	16 9-16	22 1-16	....do	5. 49	1:208	4 2¼	6 11	5 3	3 4⅛
J. F. Cail & Company	Freight	......do	2	Outside	19 11-16	25 9-16	....do	9.	1:206	4 11⅛	6 9	7 5	3 3⅜
Ivry shop	Passenger	Paris and Orleans Railway Company	2	....do	16½	25 9-16	Stationary	6. 31	1:233	4 0 13-16	6 8½	4 6⅝	3 4
Belgian Society	Freight	Grand Duchy of Luxemburg railway	2	Inside	17 11-16	25 9-16	Allan's	7. 23	1:185	4 4	....	5 10⅞	3 7⅜
M. Mesmer	....do	Central Belgian railway	2	Outside	15¾	22	Shifting	4. 96	1:224	4 0	6 1¼	4 1	3 3
Krauss & Company	....do	Grand Duchy of Oldenburg	2	....do	14	22 1-16	Allan's	3. 93	1:205	3 11	....	3 6	3 1¼
Commentary	Colliery	3 foot 3⅜-inch gauge	2	....do	12 9-16	15¾	Shifting	2. 26	1:175	2 11	....	3 6¾	1 11
Schneider & Company	....do	2 foot 9½-inch gauge	2	....do	8	14 3-16	....do	0. 82	1:234	2 6	3 9⅜	2 0¼	1 7

Tabular statement of the relative dimensions and proportions of locomotives in different countries—Continued.

Builders of locomotives.	Class of engine.	Constructed for—	BOILER. Top plate of fire-box above front of grate.	Top plate of fire-box above back of grate.	Number of tubes.	Diameter of tubes. (Outside.)	Length of tubes.	Pressure of steam per square inch.	Area of heating surface.	Area of grate surface.	Ratio of grate to heating surface.	WHEELS. Total number of wheels.	Total number of coupled wheels.	Diameter of driving wheels.
			Ft. In.	*Ft. In.*		*Inches.*	*Ft. In.*	*Lbs.*		*Sq. Ft.*				*Ft. In.*
Grant Locomotive Works.	Passenger..	Exposition	4 9½	4 9½	*142	2	10 11	150	84 & 812	15.75	1:57	8	4	5 7
Robert Stephenson & Co..	....do......	Egyptian government	4 11	4 11	161	2	11 4	160	83 & 955	14.	1:74	6	0	6 6
Kitson & Company	Freight...	Exposition	4 10¾	4 1¾	140	2	10 9½	150	82 & 790	14.2	1:61	6	4	5 6
Lilleshall Company	Passenger.	......do	....	....	186	1⅞	11 2	120	112 & 1,009	18.5	1:61	6	0	7 0
Ernest Gouin & Company.	Freight...	Northern railway of France	4 3	3 7	275	†2	8 2⅝	115	‡1,271, 215, & 162	32.3	1:51	12	6 & 6	3 5 15-16
Graffenstaden Company..	....do......	Eastern railway of France	6 0⅞	4 3⅛	276	2	9 10⅛	130	160 & 1,265	26.3	1:54	6	6	4 3⅛
J. F. Cail & Company	Passenger..	Northern railway of France	4 7⅛	4 1¼	164	2	12 5¾	115	79 & 1,066	17,6	1:65	6	4	5 10⅞
J. F. Cail & Company	Freight....	......do	4 2¾	3 3¾	249	2	13 5⅝	115	97 & 1,780	24.3	1:77	8	8	4 3⅛
Ivry shop	Passenger..	Paris and Orleans Railway Company.	....	....	179	1 15-16	16 4⅞	133	88 & 1,387	15.1	1:97	6	4	6 8½
Belgian Society	Freight....	Grand Duchy of Luxemburg railway..	....	....	200	2	11 10	115	104 & 1,238	21.3	1:63	6	6	4 9
M. Mesmer	....do......	Central Belgian railway	4 11	4 11	150	2	13 2	110	79 & 1,034	13.3	1:83	6	4	4 11
Krauss & Company	....do......	Grand Duchy of Oldenburg	....	....	160	1⅞	10 0	150	808	10.8	1:75	4	4	4 11⅛
Commentary	Colliery....	3 foot 3⅜-inch gauge	3 10	3 10	98	1⅝	8 6⅝	115	52 & 345	6.8	1:58	6	6	3 4⅝
Schneider & Company	....do......	2 foot 9½-inch gauge	....	....	72	1½	5 10	110	25 & 167	3.2	1:60	4	4	2 6

* Copper. † Inside. ‡ The superheater contains 162 square feet of heating surface, and the water-heater 215 square feet.

Tabular statement of the relative dimensions and proportions of locomotives in different countries—Continued.

Builders of locomotives.	Class of engine.	Constructed for—	WHEELS. Diameter of carrying wheels.	WHEELS. Wheel base.	WHEELS. Extreme centers of coupled wheels.	WEIGHTS. Weight of engine empty.	WEIGHTS. Weight in working order.	WEIGHTS. Weight on 1st and 2d drivers.	WEIGHTS. Weight on 3d and 4th drivers.	WEIGHTS. Weight on 5th and 6th drivers.	WEIGHTS. Weight on carrying wheels.
			Ft. In.	*Ft. In.*	*Ft. In.*						
Grant Locomotive Works	Passenger	Exposition	4 of 0 30	22 3½	8 6	......	61, 600	22, 400 & 22, 400	......	......	16, 800
Robert Stephenson & Co.	do	Egyptian government	3 9 & 3 9	15 8	......	60, 480	67, 200	36, 960	......	......	21, 280 & 15, 680
Kitson & Company	Freight	Exposition	4 0	15 6	7 9	57, 400	62, 720	21, 280 & 21, 280	......	......	20, 160
Lilleshall Company	Passenger	do	4 3 & 4 3	16 6	......	61, 710	70, 560	28, 336	......	......	23, 520 & 18, 704
Ernest Gouin & Company	Freight	Northern railway of France	......	19 8¼	7 5¾	109, 340	131, 780	22, 000 & 23, 320	18, 920 & 21, 120	21, 120 & 25, 300	......
Graffenstaden Company	do	Eastern railway of France	......	11 7¾	11 7¾	67, 120	77, 270	26, 490 & 26, 510	24, 270	......	......
J. F. Cail & Company	Passenger	Northern railway of France	3 11 15-16	14 5 5-16	7 0 11-16	60, 500	67, 760	25, 300 & 24, 860	......	......	17, 600
J. F. Cail & Company	Freight	do	......	13 11 5-16	13 11 5-16	84, 700	95, 440	26, 400 & 24, 160	25, 520 & 19, 360	......	......
Ivry shop	Passenger	Paris and Orleans Railway Company	3 10½	13 1½	6 11	66, 000	74, 800	......	......	......	......
Belgian Society	Freight	Grand Duchy of Luxemburg railway	......	13 5½	13 5½	70, 560	79, 520	26, 880 & 26, 880	25, 760	......	......
M. Mesnier	do	Central Belgian railway	3 7⅝	10 10	5 5	49, 500	56, 670	19, 820 & 19, 820	......	......	17, 030
Krauss & Company	do	Grand Duchy of Oldenburg	......	8 0½	8 0½	......	39, 600	19, 800 & 19, 800	......	......	......
Commentary	Colliery	3 feet 3⅜-inch gauge	......	10 0⅛	10 0⅛	33, 220	43, 300	14, 170 & 14, 170	14, 960	......	......
Schneider & Company	do	2 foot 9½-inch gauge	......	4 1¼	4 1¼	11, 420	14, 560	7, 280 & 7, 280	......	......	......

Tabular statement of the relative dimensions and proportions of locomotives in different countries—Continued.

Builders of locomotives.	Class of engine.	Constructed for—	Number of wagons.	Up a grade of—	Speed between stations. (Miles per hour.)	TENDER. Diameter of wheels.	Distance between centre wheels.	Capacity of tank.	Capacity for coal.	Total weight, *per se*.	Total weight loaded.
						Ft. In.	*Ft. In.*	*U.S.gals*	*Pounds.*	*Pounds.*	*Pounds.*
Grant Locomotive Works	Passenger	Exposition				8 of 30	4 4	2,018			40,320
Robert Stephenson & Company	do	Egyptian government					(*)	(*)	(*)	(*)	(*)
Kitson & Company	Freight	Exposition					(*)	(*)	(*)	(*)	(*)
Lilleshall Company	Passenger	do					(*)	(*)	(*)	(*)	(*)
Ernest Gouin & Company	Freight	Northern railway of France	45	1 in 200	16			(†)	(†)		
Graffenstaden Company	do	Eastern railway of France				‡3 11⅝	5 3 & 4 11	2,073	6,700	38,020	61,970
J. F. Cail & Company	Passenger	Northern railway of France	18=317,000 lbs.	1 in 200	38	3 11 15-16	9 10⅛	1,850	4,600	21,560	42,000
J. F. Cail & Company	Freight	do	45	1 in 200	16	3 5¾	8 2⅜	2,115	4,840	21,120	44,220
Ivry shop	Passenger	Paris and Orleans Railway Company			44		(*)	(*)	(*)	(*)	(*)
Belgian Society	Freight	Grand Duchy of Luxemburg railway					(*)	(*)	(*)	(*)	(*)
M. Mesmer	do	Central Belgian railway				4 of 3 8	6 11	1,188	3,360	16,460	30,100
Krauss & Company	do	Grand Duchy of Oldenburg	Equal 160 tons.	1 in 200	25			(†)	(†)	(†)	(†)
Commentary	Colliery	3 foot 3⅜-inch gauge	40 (Empty.)	1 in 84	16			†636	†1,760	(†)	(†)
Schneider & Company	do	2 foot 9½-inch gauge						(†)	(†)	(†)	(†)

* Not stated. † Tank engine. ‡ Steam tender. Cylinder 15 inches and 16 9-16 inch stroke. 6 coupled.

THE LOCOMOTIVE "AMERICA."

Our own country was most creditably represented in the engine "America," furnished by the Grant Locomotive Works, of Paterson, New Jersey. The class of engine and workmanship produced by this company and its predecessor, (the New Jersey Locomotive and Machine Company,) are too favorably known to admit of extended remark. As presented in this engine they were a source of conscious pride to those who had crossed the Atlantic, as well as surprise to continental minds, the majority of whom are imbued with exceedingly plain ideas on the subject of locomotive ornamentation. Some go so far as to consider any attempt at the latter a grave misdemeanor, and paint their entire engines a solemn lead color or funereal black, without a single pencilling of gay colors to relieve the dull monotony. Of course, the contrast was very marked between such and the "America," with her bright German silver jacketing on boiler, cylinders, chimney, and head-light, her cab beautifully inlaid with ash, maple, black-walnut, mahogany, and cherry; with the tender, shaded, striped, and ornamented in a manner common to American practice. The cast-iron tender truck wheels and hollow-spoked driving wheel centers gave rise to many speculations among those who have not yet learned their value. Much skill is evinced in the arrangement of the parts, and the reduction of their weight to a minimum consistent with strength. The link motion is well schemed and counter weighted by volute springs, instead of the clumsy weights so general on foreign engines. A fitting acknowledgment of the high order of workmanship displayed was made in the award of a gold medal to the builders.

STEPHENSON & CO.'S LOCOMOTIVES.

The locomotives of Messrs. Robert Stephenson & Co., Newcastle-on-Tyne, and the Lilleshall Company, of Shropshire, are similar to each other in proportion and design. The boiler of the first engine is made with Alton's patent thick edged plates, the longitudinal joints being lap-welded, and the transverse butt under a welded covering strip, to which they are double riveted. Both longitudinal and transverse sections of such boilers are exhibited by the Low Moor Iron Company, who own the exclusive right of manufacture. The plates are rolled with a uniform thickness of three-eighths of an inch, to within about eight inches of each transverse butting edge, where they gradually increase to a thickness of five-eighths of an inch, through which portion the holes are drilled or punched for the rivets. A section of the covering strip measures eight by five-eighths of an inch. The ordinary shifting link motion (without rocker) operates the valves. Its reversal can be accomplished either with the regular hand lever, or by a hand wheel operating a horizontal screw, into the groove of whose thread the latch of the lever catches. To accommodate itself to the arc described by the latch in the motion of the lever, the screw is swollen at its center, being turned to the same radius of curvature as the arc. The hand wheel performs its duty rapidly, and furnishes a very simple and efficient means for reversal. A general employment of the screw-reversing motion is observable on foreign locomotives, in fact almost sufficiently so for the practice to be regarded as universal. Another feature, and one that is common in Prussia and other continental countries, consists in the use of sliding double furnace doors. Horizontal slides are bolted to the furnace front, and receive the plate doors which are operated by two plain levers and a connecting link. The arrangement serves a good purpose in event of a tube collapsing, as it more effectually protects the fireman. This engine is one of great excellence, and a model of good workmanship. That of the Lilleshall Company differs principally in the construction of the boiler, the arrangement of the link motion, which is of the Allan variety—giving virtually constant lead and equal opening of the ports in front and back stroke, for every notch of the reversing lever—and by the addition of a comfortable wrought iron cab.

The engine of Messrs. Kitson & Co., of Leeds, is remarkable for the same excellence of workmanship displayed on the Stephenson locomotive.

THE TANK ENGINE "TITAN."

"Titan" is the name of an immense tank engine built by Messrs. Gouin & Co. for the Northern Railway of France. It was designed specially for heavy freight service, and completes an order for ten, the balance of which are now actively employed. Its novelty lies principally in the arrangement of the boiler; the main shell and fire box are the same as used in ordinary practice, but instead of the products of combustion passing away through a vertical stack after leaving the tubes, they enter a front connection, return through two horizontal dome shells on the back of the boiler, and then into a horizontal escape pipe which conducts them far enough away to prevent interference with the duties of the engineer. They pass through wrought-iron tubes in the first of these horizontal domes, which are surrounded by the live steam, thus insuring a perfectly dry supply for the cylinders, and in a measure superheating the steam. Feed water fills the second dome and is heated by the main escape pipe through its center.

The grate bars (cast in accordance with the system of Mr. Belpaire) are only three-eighths of an inch wide on the head and spaced five-sixteenths of an inch apart. Of these there are three sets running longitudinally, and terminated by a transverse one at the tube end of the fire-box. The vast volume of steam generated by this boiler supplies four cylinders, each pair of which connects with six coupled wheels. Although capable of drawing great loads, these engines are said to have an undue oscillation when moving at high velocities, and, as might be supposed, are peculiarly severe on the road-bed. For a drawing of this engine with dimensions, see Plate I, Fig. 1.

The Graffenstaden engine is the only one exhibited having a steam tender. The arrangement of the parts is clearly shown by the outline sketch, Plate I, Fig. 2, in which the dimensions are given in metres and decimal parts of the same. The internal diameter of the connecting inflexible steam pipe is $3\frac{3}{16}$ inches. A screw reversing gear throws the link into forward or back motion. Its workmanship is of the first order and much skill is evinced in the counterbalancing of the out and inside cranks with their connecting rods.

SMOKE-BURNING ENGINES.

The Paris and Orleans Company send an engine built at their Ivry shop for express passenger service, and furnished with the smoke-consuming apparatus of Mr. Tenbrinck. Since its first appearance on the road in 1864, it has travelled 91,000 miles, or on an average 3,500 per month. The mean consumption of fuel during that time was twenty-one pounds per mile, and expenses for repairs amounted to $532, a little in excess of one-half cent per mile.

Twelve engines of the same type were subsequently constructed by the company and have given equally as satisfactory results. The Krupp tyres on the carrying wheels of this engine were replaced after having travelled over 43,000 miles, but the drivers have neither required turning down nor renewal. A word about the smoke-consumers so much in favor on this railway. The object of the invention is to prevent the direct passage of the products of combustion from the fire to the tubes of the boiler, thus concentrating a more intense heat in the fire box. It is accomplished by an inclined bridge wall extending across the fire box, which springs from a point immediately below the tubes, and has an inclination of about 30° with a horizontal line. From the tube sheet the wall projects over a distance of about two-thirds the length of the fire box. A similar inclination is given to the grate, which causes it to run nearly parallel with the wall. This wall is merely a copper box having a 3½-inch water space, it is hung inside the furnace by suitable angle iron cleats and maintains a circulation by four pipe connections with the water legs of the boiler, while a little cement closes the fissure between its edges and the sides of the furnace. Copper plate five-eighths of an inch in thickness is used for such bridge walls, and the circulating tubes are made with internal diameters of three inches. The system was first applied to engine No. 91, of the Eastern railway of France, in the month of November, 1859, where it continued to work with perfect satisfaction until the date of removal, viz: February, 1867, during which time the engine had travelled 162,000 miles. On examination the copper box was found to be in nearly as perfect condition externally as when first adjusted. For the purposes of firing three doors are considered necessary. That nearest the grate is made 33 inches wide by 6½ high, and immediately over this two circular ones, each 9½ inches in diameter. Steel is extensively used by this company in the construction of their engines, the boiler shell of the locomotive in question is made of plates five-sixteenths of an inch in thickness.

The Paris and Lyons Railway Company are represented by a well designed and neatly executed locomotive, to which the system of Mr. Thierry is applied for introducing fine jets of steam over the fire. This device will be mentioned at greater length in connection with the subject of steam boilers. It has already been applied to over 500 locomotives belonging to this company.

Mr. Walschaërt's system of operating the valves may be seen on several locomotives in the Belgian department. The parts are so arranged that the desired motion results from the combined action of a single eccentric and the cross head of the piston rod, through the medium of a rocking link and lever connections. From the amount of space required in the location of the details it can more readily be adapted to outside than to inside cylinder engines. The motion developed is analogous to that of a stationary link, but cannot be ranked its superior, when sufficient care is bestowed in proportioning the latter; besides this, the effort expended in reversing the engine is no less arduous. The locomotive built by Messrs. Krauss & Co., of Munich, is the first one produced by their new establishment. A glance at the dimensions, weights, and power given in the table, furnishes satisfactory evidence of its success. Mr. K. is convinced, after seventeen years experience on Swiss and German railways, that the greatest strength with the least material can be gained by so incorporating the water tank with the main frame of the engine that it will form a deep box girder of the structure, while the rigidity is secured by frequent staying. On this principle the tank plates are sufficiently strong if made only one-fourth of an inch in thickness, but with a depth of three feet. The boiler is formed of steel, as well as the reciprocating parts of the machinery, its fire box plates are corrugated and the grate bars widely separated for the purpose of burning peat. The details of the connecting rods, injector, lubricators, &c., are well studied and possess several ingenious features.

The most perfect specimens of workmanship in the French department are supplied by the widely-known firm of Messrs. Schneider & Co., of Creuzot. They are three in number; the first has 16×24 inch cylinders, and was built from drawings prepared in England. The second, named the "St. Laurent," is a six-coupled tank engine designed for service on the railways in the neighborhood of Creuzot, and the third engine for the collieries of the same place. The latter is exceedingly compact, simple, and represents a type which may to advantage be extensively copied.

AUSTRIAN LOCOMOTIVES.

In the Austrian department may be seen a ten-wheeled coupled locomotive, built by the State Railway Society for service on a short road in Hungary, on which there are ascents of one in fifty and curves of

360 feet radius. Six of the wheels are coupled together and connected with two cylinders eighteen and one-third inches diameter by twenty-four and seven-eighths inches stroke. The other four support a truck, between whose axles the fire box of the boiler is situated; its front is pivoted to the frame of the six wheels. A crank-shaft over the forward wheels of the truck, with connecting rods to their crank-pins, and the pins of the drivers serves for transmitting motion from the drivers to the wheels of the latter. This engine, with its tender, (loaded,) weighs fifty-seven and one-half tons, is exceedingly complicated, and under no circumstances likely to be reproduced in the United States.

THE MAHOVOS.

A curious invention has recently been produced by Mr. C. Schoubers-zky, of 15 Wosnesenscaja, St. Petersburg. Its object is to dispense with steep gradients on railways by the addition of a carriage to each train, which shall act the part of a storehouse for momentum developed during a descent, whence it may be reproduced at will and assist the locomotive on the opposite ascent. He has given the title of "Mahovos" to this new motor and introduced a working model in the Russian department of the Exposition. The track for the same is 110 feet in length, having a rise of four feet in this distance. Near its lowest point is located a turn-table for reversing the "Mahovos" and a tank to receive the water contained in its train of five cars. The model weighs 275 pounds. The machine itself will readily be understood from the accompanying drawings on Plate I, where an end view and section, a side view and a vertical view are given. The ponderous fly-wheels a, a, are seen, in the end view, resting by the rollers b, upon the central pair of wheels d, d, which run upon the track between two larger truck wheels c, c. The five cars filled with water weigh in the aggregate 1,390 pounds, and are coupled in front of the "Mahovos" at the top of the grade. When ready for starting the two large fly-wheels are lowered until their axle rests on the four friction rollers and these in turn on the six carrying wheels of the truck through the medium of four rolls on their shafts. Under the impulse of gravity the train commences its slow descent, during which a high velocity is ultimately imparted to the fly-wheels. It reaches the turn-table after a lapse of two minutes. At this point the cars, being detached, continue their journey until the tank is reached, into which having discharged about 800 pounds of water, they are then led back to the turn-table. In the mean time the fly-wheels with their shaft are raised out of gear, the Mahovos turned end for end, and made ready to reascend after the coupling of the cars takes place. This being accomplished, the fly-wheels are lowered a second time, when the cars rise quickly to the starting point. The principle would have been more intelligibly illustrated by a track of double the length, having both a descending and an ascending grade. Although claimed by the inventor, that it is peculiarly adapted to conducting the loaded cars of a colliery down a steep hill and reascending with the empty ones, it is difficult to discover what advantage such an expensive substitute would have over the ordinary method of rope and pulleys. In the practical application of this method Mr. Schouberszky designs making the fly-wheels of cast-steel and so proportioning them that each will contain twelve tons of metal, and resist the centrifugal force due to a velocity of 800 revolutions per minute. He estimates the work developed by a velocity of 500 revolutions at 500 horse-power, and that such machines are available on grades of one in twenty-five. The benefits to be derived seem most apparent when considered as an assistant of railway motors in thinly settled hilly countries, where the traffic will not warrant heavy outlay in tunnels, grades, viaducts, &c. The principal restriction to its application one would naturally suspect will be found in the necessity of constructing entirely free of curves that portion of the line where its assistance is demanded.

FAIRLIE'S DOUBLE ENGINE.

But this method of overcoming grades tends to increase an element of evil already too prevalent on railways, viz: the transportation of unremunerative weight. In connection with this subject the models submitted by Mr. R. F. Fairlie, of 56 Gracechurch street, London, in the English department, are worthy of the closest examination. This gentleman has, as it were, condensed the old idea of placing an engine and tender in front and another in the rear of a train destined to ascend a steep grade. He, having first discarded the two tenders as useless in whatever light they may be considered, has joined the fire boxes of the engines, thus forming *one*, and so arranged each of the frames with its wheels, cylinders, &c., that it is free to vibrate around a central pivot in conformity with any curvature given to the rails. By this arrangement the furnace must be fired from either side, along which also are the tanks, bunkers, &c., as clearly shown on Plate I, Fig. 5. The advantages accruing are numerous. What was previously unremunerative weight immediately becomes effective; not by overburdening a certain set of wheels, but by assigning a uniform amount to each. The engine may be run in either direction, and is consequently independent of turntables. At the same time, and on account of the position held by the two pivots, it is able to pass any curve that was possible with the single engine, and by the increase of its tractive force to surmount grades otherwise impassable. Mr. Fairlie, however, has advanced further than models, and already has engines built on his principle and running on the Neath and Brecon railway, a line which passes through the mountainous district of South Wales. They have worked with admirable success on grades of one in fifty. It should not be overlooked in estimating the value of this system that the parts of such engines are readily interchangeable, not only admitting of greater facility in the repairs, but also diminishing the number of engines large roads are usually compelled to keep in stock. Mr. Fairlie's agents in the United States are John Cooke, esq., of the firm of Danforth, Cooke & Co., Paterson, New Jersey, and George E. Gray, esq., consulting engineer to the Central Pacific railroad.

MEYER'S LOCOMOTIVE.

The system of Messrs. J. J. & Adolphe Meyer, of Mulhouse, France, is analogous to that just mentioned, but makes use of the ordinary locomotive boiler, and places one of the frame pivots under the centre of the fire grate, the other under that of the smoke box. These gentlemen furnish their engines with the Stradel coupling link, of which Messrs. J. F. Cail & Co., of Lille, are the agents. The parts of this link are so disposed that the strain exerted by the train acts as if applied at the centre of gravity of the locomotive, even during its passage around the sharpest curves. Pl. I, Fig. 6.

Ere the publication of these remarks a new era will have been inaugurated in the history of railway engineering. The rails spanning Mount Cenis from St. Michel, in France, to Susa, in Italy, a distance of forty-nine miles, are now laid and the ballasting nearly accomplished. So that within a few months the toilsome ride of ten hours, by diligence, will be reduced to one of six, besides saving the frequent changes of baggage now inevitable. Mr. J. B. Fell, the patentee of the adopted system, exhibits drawings of his locomotives and a model passenger car. The former are being built by Messrs. Gouin & Co., of Paris, the latter is from the manufactory of Messrs. Chavelier, Cheilus, Jr., & Co., of 61 Quai de Grenelle. As this very ingenious system will then have appeared and been discussed in the light of actual experience, any further remark at this time seems unnecessary.

CAST-STEEL CYLINDERS.

Before passing from the subject of locomotives it should be mentioned that the Society of Mines and Steel Works of Bochum, Prussia, exhibit a remarkable cylinder formed of cast steel. It has been bored, and the valve seat faced off, and although many of the cores used in the moulding were quite intricate, in no portion can the slightest imperfection be discovered. Again, in the French department are immense copper plates rolled by the firms of Messrs. Estivant Brothers, and L. L. Etrange & Co., of the following dimensions: $16' 5'' \times 7' 1'' \times \frac{31}{64}''$; $17' 4\frac{3}{4} \times 5' 2\frac{3}{4}'' \times 1\frac{5}{16}''$; $24' 5\frac{3}{4}'' \times 5' 7'' \times \frac{1}{4}''$; $24' 7\frac{1}{2}'' \times 6' 7\frac{1}{2}'' \times \frac{1}{4}.''$

Their unusual size suggests the propriety of using them for the two sides and roof of copper fire boxes now so much in vogue, thereby saving two unnecessary seams.

"BRIQUETTE FUEL."

The general use on the continent of "briquettes," as fuel for locomotives is a matter of deep interest to our railway companies, both as respects economy of consumption and room required for storage. They are composed of finely-powdered, washed coals, cemented with a material which forms the refuse of starch factories, or with coal tar. The mixture is subjected to the pressure of a piston in a cylindrical or polygonal case, and then exposed to a current of hot air in a kiln for about three hours. The resulting blocks weigh on an average eight pounds, and burn with a residue of from four to seven per cent. of ashes. The experience of the Austrian railways is, that they evaporate 7.2 pounds of water per pound of coal. Their introduction has been most rapid on the prominent roads of France and Belgium.

II.—RAILWAY PLANT.

SLEEPERS, TIES, AND CLIPS.

The rapid extension of railway interests in tropical countries, as Egypt, India, Algeria, and South America, with the increased scarcity of timber for ties in more civilized portions of the world, have concentrated the efforts of inventive talent towards the production of what may justly be termed a permanent road-bed. The present Exposition contains some interesting signs of progress in this direction; a few only will be selected as types, uniting simplicity of construction with practical utility.

The cast-iron pot sleeper introduced on the Alexandria, Cairo and Suez railway, by Mr. R. Stephenson, in the year 1851, receives the unqualified approbation of the local engineers, as best adapted to the compact sands of the Suez isthmus and the loose alluvial soil of the Nile delta. Even heavy engines running at high speeds over the Egyptian rails (which weigh 65 pounds per yard) have no serious effect on these sleepers. As to the rigidity of the road-bed compared with the wooden-sleeper system, we are sure that those who have travelled the length of this route must have discovered no cause for complaint; but, on the contrary, have admired the smooth running of the trains. This sleeper is exhibited in the English department, together with two of similar principle, but different in design. That known as Griffen's patent is an oval casting, (26 inches by 17 inches) having a channel along the dome-like surface for the reception of the rail; distance bars are let into cored sockets and maintain the uniformity of the gauge. The Economic Permanent Way Company, of London, manufacture a hollow chair whose upper surface forms portion of a cylinder 30 inches long, the chord of the arc 13 inches and vers-sine five inches. A channel cored in the back of the casting receives the rail, which is held in place by two bolts passing through four lugs, two fixed and two movable. Distance bars regulate the gauge, and the chairs are placed 44 inches between centres. The system of Mr. J. Vantherim, of Fraisans, is adopted on portions of the Northern railway of France and the railway of Lyons. He substitutes a rolled iron sleeper for wood, and retains the rail with gibs and keys passing through wrought-iron clamps and the sleeper. The latter has a base of 10 inches, height of 2⅝ inches; is 5 inches in width at the top and ¼ inch in thickness. A curvature with a vers-sine of 3 inches is impressed on all the sleepers, thus carrying their centres below the ballast, and by the arched form imparting greater rigidity to the beam. See figures on Plate I.

The Marcinelle Couillet Company, of Charleroi, Belgium, exhibit a section of railway with its wrought-iron ties attached, which has been in actual service during four and a half years, and gives evidence of great durability. It is worthy the attention of parties opposed to wrought-iron ties, (from their want of the elasticity peculiar to wooden ones,) since it forms a compromise between the two; in which wood acts as the mere cushion; iron the solid foundation. The rails are 4⅞ inches deep, with 2¾-inch head and 4⅛-inch base, the gauge 4 feet 8½ inches; all the joints are formed on the "fished principle," and secured with 4¾-inch bolts. The sleepers are simply rolled I-beams 8 feet 5 inches long, (7 inches deep, $\frac{5}{16}$-inch web and 2½-inch heads,) placed 36 inches between centres. Instead of resting directly on these, a painted oak block is interposed between them and the rail. Such blocks are 10 inches long, by 6¼ inches wide, by 2½ inches thick, and have a channel 4⅛ inches wide by ¼ inch deep, in which the base of the rail rests. Two ¾-inch bolts (with 1⅝-inch round washers) secure the rail to the I-beam; the latter, it should be observed, lies with its web in a horizontal position. The bolt holes are bored close to the flanges of the rails, to allow of the washers clamping the latter, and the points of the bolts are slightly burred to prevent the loosening of the nut. An increase in the diameter of the washer might be made with evident advantage.

The Hartwich system, introduced on the Rhénan and Cologne railway dispenses with sleepers altogether, by using very deep rails having broad bases. Their rails are rolled 9⅜ inches deep, (with 2⅜-inch head, 4¾-inch base, ⅜-inch web,) and the gauge regulated by 1-inch rods placed six feet three inches apart, having threads on their ends and a nut on each side of the rail webs. To preserve the upper parts of these deep rails from variation, the rods pass through holes only three inches below the head, and every fourth space between rods has an intermediate one near the lower flanges of the rails. Fish-joints give the rails the rigidity possessed by continuous beams, while the ballasting covers all except their heads. Steel rails, and iron rails with steel heads, are well represented in all the departments and produce the impression that the plain iron rail, for roads of very extensive traffic, will soon be a relic of the past. Several manufacturers show specimens of steel reversible crossings, while Austria and Holland are creditably represented by those of chilled iron.

Mr. G. E. Dering, of Lochleys, Welwyn Herts, England, exhibits samples of a tempered steel spring clip for rail joints, which appeared in the Exhibition in 1862, and has since performed good service on lines like the Great Northern, also Great Southern and Western railways.

Fig. 1.

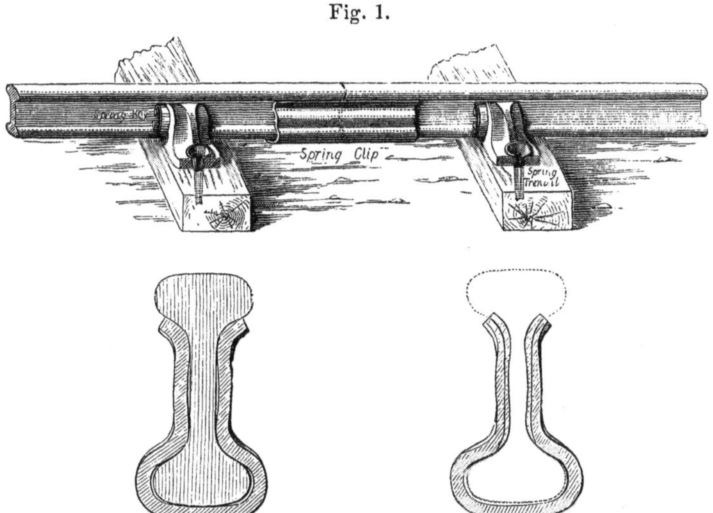

Dering's tempered steel Clip.

This clip forms a steel case enveloping the extremities of the rail, and binds the same with increased tenacity under the pressure of heavy loads. A joint constructed on this principle was carefully tested by D. Kirkaldy, esq., and found to have a deflection of 1.31 inch under a load of 26,000 pounds, with supports 36 inches apart. When the load was removed the clip assumed its normal condition free of permanent set. He also tested under the same conditions two rails united by the ordinary fish-joint. Seventeen thousand pounds served to produce a deflection of 2.78 inch, from which the joint failed to recover after the removal of the load. This clip is entirely free of bolts, nuts, &c., which are liable to become loose even under the closest inspection.

The subject of railway plant should not be concluded without first alluding to a new spike thimble. One serious objection to soft, cheap timber for railway ties has hitherto been the liability of the spikes holding down the rails to become loosened. This results in part from the tendency of the rails to spread under the action of heavy trains running at high speed, thus crowding the spike laterally into the soft fibre. Mr. Desbrière, 68 Rue de Provence, Paris, has patented a cast-iron thimble for surrounding the spike and bringing a greater number of the fibres to bear in resisting its crushing effect. These thimbles are two inches in diameter, one and one-quarter inch thick, having a three-quarter-inch square or round hole cored in the centre, and are slightly dished on the under side. A recess one-quarter inch deep is left on the upper side in which the rail rests, and prevents any tendency to its rotation. Either spikes or galvanized wood screws (three-fourths inch by four and a half inches) are used for retaining the rails. Specimens of ties laid with these thimbles in April, 1862, on the Algerian railway, near Blidah, well illustrate the benefits to be derived. They are in use on the Northern railway of France, at Charentes and at Mount Cenis. This principle might render important service in parts of our own country where ties of durable close-grained woods are difficult to procure.

SIGNALS.

A stranger travelling on Austrian railways during the night cannot fail to observe that all the switch targets are illuminated, and present the same red and white signal at night as in the day. The engineer is thus obliged to remember but one system of signals; lights cannot be misplaced, and a fruitful source of accident is avoided. Previous to the year 1851 it was customary on the same railways to hang a red lantern on one extremity of the target, and a white on the other. As this practice constantly gave rise to accidents by the misplacement of the lanterns, it attracted the attention of Mr. Wolf Bender, engineer of the Austrian State Railway Society, who invented and applied to all the switch staves in the empire a circular metallic target thick enough to receive a lamp. The faces of this target were concave, and in front of the lamp on both sides were placed conical screens, which reflected the direct horizontal rays of light back on the colored faces of the target. Mr. Bender also entered into an elaborate mathematical discussion of the proper angle for the face of the screen and radii of curvature for that of the target, which he published in Vienna. His latest improvement consists in forming the target like a short *thick* arrow, painted red and white, and the use of glass reflectors, which has a decided advantage over the former arrangement.

Fig. 2.

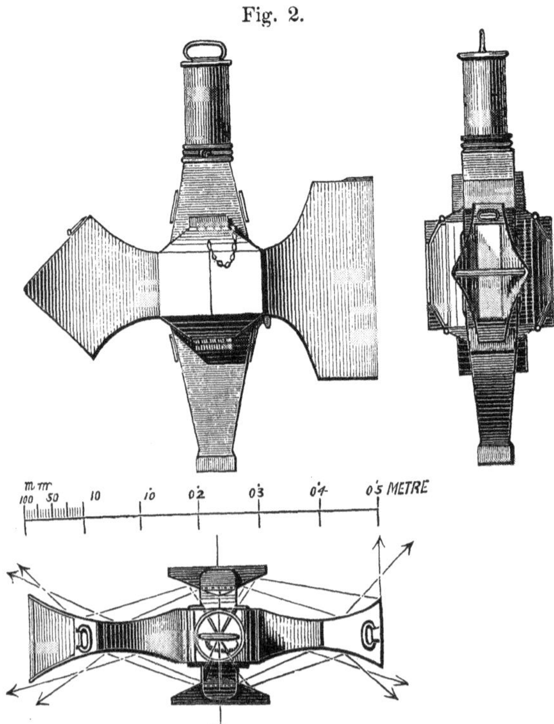

Bender's Railway Signals.

The idea is one which might advantageously be adopted by all companies using targeted switches. The Austrians not only illuminate their switch targets, but, on the arrival of a train at any station where supper is served, they place a triangular-shaped lantern on the side of one car, the glasses of which are inscribed with the train's destination. This is a great convenience, where stations are large, trains numerous, and a sudden departure imperative.

The other railway lanterns and lamps, such as those exhibited by Mr. E. Masson, 7 Rue Laguée, and Messrs. Leon Luchaire & Co., 25 Rue Erard, Paris, are specially adapted to continental railway coaches, and for the most part of little interest in connection with our system of construction.

The well-digested system of railway points and signals invented by Messrs. Saxby & Farmer, of London, and extensively applied on English railways, is too generally known and appreciated to require a lengthy description of the illustrated model they have placed on exhibition.

III.—SCALES—DYNAMOMETER.

ERHARDT'S PORTABLE SCALE.

Locomotive and car builders often experience the want of suitable scales by which they can determine the total weight of different classes of rolling stock, as well as the distribution of that weight upon the springs. Platform scales for weighing loads between five and fifty tons are necessarily large, complex, and very costly. On railways generally, the scale is erected at a prominent station, and the rolling stock sent thither for inspection, instead of the more economical method of sending a set of scales to the stock. Mr. Richard Hartmann, of Chemnitz, Saxony, exhibits in the Prussian department a form of scale recently patented by Mr. Erhardt. The construction is shown by a figure upon Plate I. The apparatus combines two levers of the first and third kinds on a light iron frame. One extremity of this frame is drawn down in the form of a lip, and rests on the outer flange of the rail upon which the engine to be weighed stands. The other arm of the frame is maintained in a vertical position by a stand plate. The fulcrum of the lever of the first kind is near the lip of the frame. This lever has a lip turned on its short arm designed to catch under the tread of the wheel close to its point of contact with the rail. The long arm of the lever extends behind the vertical arm of the frame, and there forms its connection with a lever of the third kind, g, which performs the functions of a steelyard. For properly ascertaining the weight of an engine, as many of these scales are required as there are wheels to the engine, or as there are wheels having springs united by equalizers. The engine should be placed on a level, well-ballasted track; during the process of weighing it will be raised about one-sixteenth of an inch from the rails. The stand plate attached to the scale frame can be adjusted by the screw at e, to meet the inequalities of the ground and preserve its vertical position. Each scale weighs 107 pounds, exclusive of the weights, which are 42 pounds. Its capacity ranges between 1,600 pounds and 16,000 pounds. A very marked contrast was observable between these compact portable apparatuses of Mr. Erhardt (which are generally adopted on the continent) and the five scale platforms in the French department, on which stood a ten-wheeled engine. The latter were very cumbrous fixtures, and mounted in an elaborate manner, quite regardless of expense.

RAILWAY DYNAMOMETER.

The only apparatus designed to indicate the force and speed of railway trains is that contributed by the director of the Eastern railway of Prussia, and was invented by Mr. E. Holzt, of Bromberg, (Plate II, Figs. 1, 2, 3.)

The idea of this device is to cause the coupling link between the draw-hooks of any two cars to act through a compound lever and spring, registering the tension exerted, by means of a pencil on a piece of paper moved by clock-work. The model represents the end sills of the cars with their regular attachments of plunger buffers and draw-hooks; the hooks are intended to connect rigidly by a draw-bar with their mates on the opposite extremities of the cars. The coupling link is composed of two shackles united by a right and left-threaded bolt, which is turned by an attached handle and ball. The only difference between it and the ordinary attachment is that instead of both shackles looping over the draw-hooks only one is thus fastened, while the other connects with the short arm of a lever (of the first kind) whose long arm hangs down towards the ground. This lever is in turn attached to the draw-hook by two triangular plates, which pass each side of it and are secured by a pin forming its fulcrum. The long arm is connected by a horizontal link with a second lever whose fulcrum occupies the remaining angle of the triangle, and is restrained at its opposite extremity by means of a spring. At this point a pencil is fastened, which, during the motion of the train, traces an irregular line on a paper passing over drums and caused to rotate at a definite speed by clock-work. The tin box containing this mechanism—the drums, paper, &c.—is readily detached, so that any adjustment can be effected without a stoppage of the train.

Mr. Holzt publishes a neat lithograph of this apparatus, (a portion of which is reproduced, Plate II, Figs. 1 to 5;) among other points of interest it gives a sectional view (Fig. 5) of 79 miles of the Eastern railway, between the cities of Bromberg and Dirschall; immediately over this (Fig. 5, *a*,) is drawn a card taken by the dynamometer while attached to a train passing over that route. The apparatus seems well adapted to accurately test the merits of different car bearings, the resistances developed at varying speeds, and kindred subjects of inquiry.

IV.—RAILWAY CARRIAGES.

TWO-STORY RAILWAY CARRIAGES.

The inspector of plant and rolling stock on the Western rai'way of France exhibits two carriages, combining in a clever manner the continental and American systems of construction. This gentleman, Mr. J. B. Vidard, also the patentee of the system, has his office at 49 Rue de Londres, Paris. The object aimed at in his invention is to carry the greatest number of passengers (comfortably) with the minimum of dead weight in the rolling stock. It is accomplished by building upon the

Fig. 3.

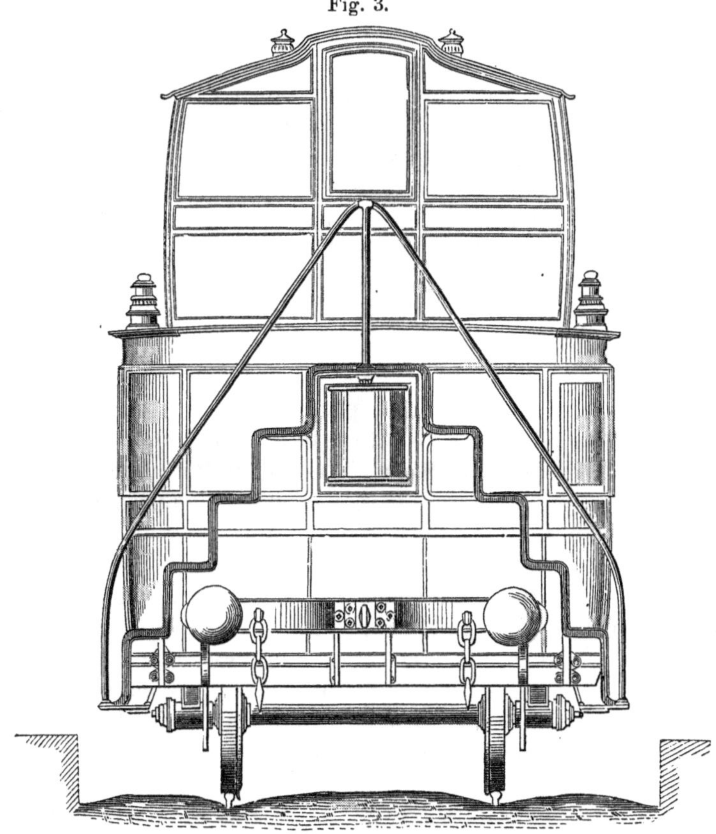

Vidard's Two-story Railway Carriage.

roof of a carriage, constructed on the European principle of compartments, a second narrower carriage, having seats and a central passage, as common in the emigrant cars of the United States. This second story communicates by end doors with four flights of wrought-iron stairs passing down the ends of the car from platforms in front of each door, and terminated by the main foot-boards which run along the sides in front of the compartment-doors. The impression first produced by such a combination is that in practice it would be found top-heavy. This difficulty is obviated by reducing the height of the two stories to a minimum; the second-story roof is arched over the passage way in a manner similar to that adopted on our street cars, and the main body is framed low, so that the wheels pass up through the floor and under the seats, as practised by the same car-builders. This of course places the main sills below the height of buffers common on continental roads. In order to make the new system conform to the old, it is necessary to bend up the sills, like sleigh runners, to the height requisite for the central stroke of buffers. On those American roads where the standard of buffer height is 30 inches, this additional expense would not be incurred. The Eastern railway of France has 26 of these carriages in constant service, and has yet to discover any lack of stability. The main body of the carriage is 24 feet 4 inches by 9 feet 2 inches wide. The sills are made of I-beams, the posts of wood, the first roof-beams of T-iron, and the second of trough iron. The outside panelling of the entire carriage, as well as that of the doors, is of galvanized sheet iron; inside sheathing of wood, which in the first-class compartments is covered with cloth, in the second with leather. The upholstering conforms to the requirements of the different classes. The lamps are inserted from the side instead of the roof. The body is mounted on two hammered axles 4⅛ inches in diameter, with collarless journals 8⅝ by 3½ inches in diameter. The wheel centres are of wrought iron, and to them tires of 36 inches diameter are bolted. The pedestals are of the same material, formed after the continental pattern. In these fit axle boxes possessing many remarkable features They are of a cylindrical form, 6½ inches in diameter and bored 4⅛ inches on the wheel side, (the same as the axle diameter.) From that end to the front of the box they are recessed as follows:

First, a suitable cavity, in which are sprung leather packing gaskets; second, the recess into which are placed a series of steel rollers, (4⅜ inches long by $\frac{11}{16}$ inch diameter,) completely enveloping the journal and bearing against the smooth interior of the box. Longitudinally these are confined by two brass journal rings 1½ inch wide, bored the same diameter as the journal. The rollers are united at their extremities by a succession of small-link plates. All of these articles are entered to their place from the front of the box, over which a brass cap is secured on threads cut in the cast iron. The cap is locked by a pawl-catch, which prevents its rotation. The thrust of the axle is received on a steel pin (1¼ inch diameter by 3 inches long) screwed in the centre of the brass cap, being held to its work by a lock-nut, and bearing on a corresponding pin inserted in the end of the axle journal, thus greatly reducing the thrust friction. The journal friction is converted into rolling friction by means of the steel rollers. Below the box is cast a cellar, from which the rollers lap up oil continuously. The links prevent them from wearing ridges in the soft parts of the box. It will merely be remarked, in passing, that this system of employing rolling friction on a car journal possesses many advantages over another exhibited in the same department. In the latter a series of balls are confined between two grooved circular plates; the top plate is fastened rigidly to the main spring, the lower travels on a ring turned on the axle journal as well as on the balls. The axle is transversely guided by a small loosely-fitting box entered in the pedestal. The axle boxes of Mr. Vidard's car are surmounted by four semi-elliptic springs. Each spring is composed of seven leaves 3 inches wide, two $\frac{5}{8}$ inch thick, and five of $\frac{1}{2}$ inch thickness; span of spring equal to six feet. The brake is applied from the interior of the upper compartment, while its staff passes down outside of the car. The highest point of the roof equals thirteen feet six inches from the rails; the main foot boards, along which the guard travels, are two feet from the same. The coupling links are composed of two shackles united by a right and left-threaded bolt, after the plan universally adopted on continental railways, and which contributes sensibly to the passengers' comfort by always keeping the buffers in contact, preventing thereby sudden shocks while the train is in motion. The following comparative table, extracted from a pamphlet issued by Mr. Vidard, clearly sets forth most of the economic results to be derived from this system:

Comparative table of railway carriages.

Composition of trains.	Weight, empty.		Seats furnished.		Estimated cost, (gold.)		Dead weight per passenger.
	Per carriage	Total.	Carr'ge.	Total.	Carriage.	Train.	
Continental carriages—Train of 15 carriages, like those on the Western railway of France:	*Pounds.*	*Pounds.*					*Pounds.*
Four carriages, first class	12,790	51,160	24	96	$1,800	$7,200	....
Four carriages, second class	13,450	53,800	40	160	1,320	5,280	....
Seven carriages, third class	12,790	89,530	50	350	1,060	7,420	....
Total	....	194,490	....	606	....	19,900	320
Vidard's carriages—Train of eight carriages:							
Coupés, first class	....	....	5	40	....	....	....
Coupés, second class	....	....	24	192	....	....	....
Coupés, third class	....	....	46	368	....	....	....
Total	15,000	120,000	....	600	$1,800	$14,400	200

Whence it appears, that with eight carriages weighing 120,000 pounds, he is able to transport as many passengers as would formerly require a train of fifteen. Besides a saving in the first cost of the rolling stock, he effects the transportation with a dead weight of only 200 pounds per passenger against 320. If our American system is scrutinized, we believe it will appear that few roads effect their transportation with less than 500 pounds dead weight per passenger. Of course sleeping coaches are not considered, for with them the weight frequently reaches twice this amount. It is problematic whether or not this system could be generallly adopted in the United States, where passengers are accustomed to so great latitude in their movements. But on lines converging towards large cities, as New York, Philadelphia, St. Louis, &c., where the laboring classes reside within a radius of five or ten miles, it could be made to them a great boon, as well as source of profit to the railway companies. For instance, where the companies now transport 120 passengers in two cars weighing 60,000 pounds, they could carry 240 passengers in three cars weighing 45,000 pounds, thus keeping the *actual* rolling weight at about the same figure, also the cost of transportation. But they could diminish the rate of fare to them fully 25 per cent. and still receive 50 per cent. in excess of their gross profits from the 120 passengers. Cheaper travel would be attended by its legitimate results—an increase of those who would make the suburban districts their homes—and greatly extend the business of roads adopting so liberal a policy.

IRON FRAMES FOR RAILWAY CARRIAGES.

As at home, so on the continent, the advantages possessed by iron frames for railway carriages and cars over those of wood have of late been universally conceded. The superior rigidity thereby imparted maintains the integrity of the whole fabric and throws the function of elasticity entirely upon the springs, instead of sharing that attribute between the main sills or girders and the springs. Practice seems divided between the use of trough and I-beams. The I-beam is convenient for attaching the cross-framing of the floor, and the trough beam for a secure fastening of the pedestals. The end sill or buffer is usually of hard wood, posts of the same, and roof beams of T-iron. Freight cars with deep sides are furnished with small trough beams in lieu of stakes. The I-beams of carriages 30 feet long are usually rolled to a depth of 9 inches, with heads of 3½ inches width.

It may be of interest here, to note the progress of the French in the general manufacture of I-beams. The celebrated house of Petin H. Gaudet & Co., Rive de Gier, Loire, furnish most remarkable samples. Each beam weighs between 4,900 and 5,500 pounds, and shows signs of good rolling. Their dimensions are given in the subjoined table:

Gaudet & Co.'s rolled I-beams.

Class of beams.	Height of beam.	Length of beam.
	Inches.	*Ft. In.*
I section	39⅜	31 10
I section	27⅝	41 8
I section	23⅝	50 3
I section	19⅝	61 7
I section	15¾	71 3
I section	14¾	85 9
I section	11¼	104 7
I section	11	103 5

BESSEMER STEEL PANELS.

There is one other use of iron which seems to promise signal diminution in the weight of structure as well as increased durability. It consists in forming all the panels of a railway carriage from large sheets of galvanized iron, attaching the same by screws to the wooden posts, and covering the joints with a neat moulding. A still greater refinement is the employment of Bessemer steel, as shown on a first-class carriage in the French annex. These plates of $\frac{1}{32}$ of an inch in thickness are of large area, very smooth, and susceptible of a good finish in the hands of the painter. The general effect of this piece of workmanship would be difficult to surpass.

AMERICAN HOSPITAL CAR.

The well-known firm of Wm. Cummings and Son, of Jersey City, New Jersey, exhibit a beautifully executed model of an American hospital car, complete in all its appointments, and built to the scale of one-quarter. The system adopted for hanging the litters is clearly shown, the details of the trucks perfect. The patent brake of Wm. G. Creamer, affixed to the platform, is too generally appreciated to require comment. It must be confessed that the system of axle-boxes and pedestals regarded with most favor on our railways seems unnecessarily bulky and heavy when compared with many sanctioned by foreign practice. That of Mr. Delannoy, engineer of the Sceaux & Orsay railway, France, may be cited among others as combining great simplicity and compactness, with a judicious arrangement of the parts respecting lubrication and the effect of strains.

STREET CARS.

Mr. John Stephenson, of New York, has sent a car built for the India Street Railway Company. The furnishings are made with special reference to the requirements of the climate, and the roof fitted with two longitudinal seats, to which the ascent is made by ladders at the extremities of the car. The careful selection of material for resisting the various strains, the shaping of the same for securing the greatest strength with the minimum quantity, and the total absence of braces, ties, &c., save at points subject to severe strains, are characteristic features in the cars produced by this maker, and present a valid claim to the highest regard as models of their class.

FREIGHT CARS.

The employment of short cars mounted on four wheels for the transportation of freight is well-nigh universal in England and France. In parts of Germany the freight cars are mounted on two four-wheeled trucks similar to the American pattern. The practical limit of wheel-base to a car having four wheels has hitherto been regarded as small, on account of the parallelism of its axles, which causes serious wear of the rails on sharp curves. An invention of Messrs. Bournique & Vidard, exhibited in the French annex, obviates this difficulty by allowing each axle to assume a radial position with reference to the curve. The principle of construction is clearly shown in the sketches on Plate III, Figs. 1, 2, and 3. The car was built by Messrs. Gargan & Co., in 1866. Since then it has traveled continuously on the Western railway of France (between Paris and Havre) with an average load of 14 tons. It has also made journeys with loads of 16 tons on curves of 380 feet radius, working with perfect regularity. Its general dimensions are: 26 feet by 8 feet 6 inches wide; 13 feet 6 inches between centres of axles. The wheels are of wrought iron, and 39 inches in diameter; total weight equals 14,500 pounds. The inventors make the following comparison between their system and that in general practice:

	Old system.	New system.
Gross weight of a train........tons..	400	400
Number of wagons necessary for the train........	50	27
Weight of wagons........tons..	225	178
Weight of their load........tons..	175	222
Mean weight of loaded wagon........tons..	8	14. 8
Average cost of wagons........	$600	$740
Average cost of train........	$30, 000	$20, 0C0

From which it appears that this system effects the passage of 27 per cent. more goods, with a corresponding diminution of dead weight in rolling stock, and a reduction in first cost of the train of about 33 per cent.

CAR INTERCOMMUNICATION.

It is curious to note how the various principles of philosophy are being marshaled into the service of those who may have occasion to communicate with the guards of railway trains, in such a moderately exciting event as the coupé taking fire or the attack of an assassin. *Direct* application to the engineer under such circumstances, by means of a bell rope properly protected, is apparently esteemed a dangerous liberty. Hence the use of galvanic batteries, lights, pneumatically struck bells, &c. In the English department, Mr. W. H. Preece, of Southampton, exhibits a system of electric signals, which, so far as concerns the traveler, is illustrated by the model showing the interior of a coupé, near the roof of which is placed a circular glass plate about 7 inches diameter covering a small ring; surrounding this are inscribed the following directions: "To warn the guard, break glass and pull the ring." The French department contains three specimens of electrical apparatus contributed respectively by Messrs. Prudhomme, of Paris; A. Archad & Co., of the same city, and the Eastern Railway of France; also, a pneumatic system. The latter is the invention of Mr. Jolly, 61 Quai de Grenelle, Paris, and is shown applied to two highly finished cars manufactured by Messrs. Chevalier Cheilus, jr., & Co. Upon his system there is placed in the roof of each coupé a small brass cylinder, from one end of which communication is maintained by lead pipes along the sides and under the cars, (rubber tubes between cars,) with a corresponding cylinder in the guard van. The cylinders in the coupés are fitted with pistons having handles on the ends of the piston-rods; a spiral spring keeps the piston at the *pipe* end of the cylinder. In the guard van the spring tends to keep the piston *away* from that end, and the piston-rod supports an escapement of clock-work arranged for imparting motion to a bell-hammer. The operation is simple: the passenger pulls the handle of the coupé cylinder; rarefaction of the air within takes place, which being propagated to the guard-van cylinder, its piston yields and brings the clock-work immediately into action.

In Prussia and Austria the cause of difficulty is in great measure removed by carrying the partitions between coupés no higher than the backs of the seats, except for smoking carriages. The backs being high, one feels as great a degree of seclusion as in a box coupé, yet with the privilege, if necessary, of calling in assistance from the adjoining compartment. In cases of fire, the guard's running-board affords a means of escape, as in most cases the door fastening on one side or the other is not secured. The use of such running-boards and hand-rails is justly made compulsory in many countries.

RAILWAY CARRIAGE SPRINGS.

It is an interesting fact, in regard to steel springs for railway carriages and wagons, that Prussia, Austria, and Belgium combine the leaves in a manner not yet practised in France. Only a single spring prepared on this principle can be found in the English department, among the specimens of Messrs. J. Brown and Co., (limited,) of Sheffield. The leaves of elliptic and semi-elliptic springs are usually bound together by means of a central strap or buckle of wrought iron, held in place with a rivet, or by indentations in the buckle. To prevent a transverse motion of the ends of the leaves, it has been customary to forge near the extremities of each leaf two "slots" and projecting pins, arranging them in such a manner that the slots and pins will match those on the adjacent leaves. The new system consists in rolling the spring steel with a single central corrugation, thus forming on the one side a groove $\frac{5}{16}$ inch wide by $\frac{1}{8}$ inch deep, and on the other a corresponding rib. When these plates are cut up and built into springs they are bound by a buckle as well as a $\frac{3}{16}$-inch central rivet. It is evident that the action of the leaves is not impeded in a longitudinal direction while perfectly guided in a transverse, and one would naturally conclude that their thickness (on account of increased depth) might in a measure be reduced. The corrugations in no way interfere with the spring bolts or hangers, but are caused to fade away near the extremities of those leaves to which the attachments are made. Nearly all the railway carriages sent by the countries mentioned are furnished with springs of this character.

CAR WHEELS.

The practice of nations seems much divided on the subject of the proper material for car wheels. The wrought-iron wheel is almost exclusively adhered to in England, France, and Prussia; while Holland and Austria discover features worthy of attention in the cast iron. The general properties of the wrought-iron spoke wheel are familiar to all. The Society of Providence, (limited,) whose office is at 208 Quai Jemmapes, Paris, display specimens of rolled wrought-iron wheel centers, without weld, whose radial section is similar to an I-beam. Upon such centers the tire is held with four $\frac{7}{8}$-inch rivets.

The Society of Mines and Steel Works, Bochum, Prussia, exhibits a remarkable cast of wheels. It was formed by stacking the flasks 22 wheels high, with the hubs in contact, and then pouring in crucible steel through a side runner. Although this cast was made more as a matter of curiosity, it is quite customary with this company to arrange them in tiers of six wheels each, and thus save the numerous side runners required when cast singly. One swinging of the set in the lathe answers for facing up all the treads and flanges. These wheels have a single plate and are 40 inches in diameter.

Mr. Krupp, of Essen, Rhenish Prussia, is also extensively engaged in the manufacture of cast-steel wheels.

Messrs. De Dietrich & Co., of Niederbronn, Bas-Rhin, send two samples of their cast-iron double-plate chilled wheels, from the Utrecht Foundry, Holland, of which Messrs. Kreuseman & Vanden Wall Bake are the proprietors. There are four wheels: one cast-iron double-plate wheel 38 inches diameter, and three of various diameters, having each six ribbed spokes.

The Austrian contributions are by A. Ganz, of Ofen, Hungary, and Mr. Dernö, of the same section of country. The former gentleman is the most extensive manufacturer in Austria, and makes a double plated wheel similar in design to that known in America as the "Snow patent." He exhibits a wheel (No. 2,410) 38 inches diameter cast in 1856, which has served under a 10-ton four-wheeled wagon for the last 11 years. The tread of this wheel appears in excellent condition, the metal close grained without signs of honey-combing. The director general of the Austrian I. R. P. State Railway Society certifies to the fact of this wheel having run 50,000 miles. The road on which these wheels are used is 419 miles in length, and pursues a southeasterly course from Vienna through Hungary. In respect to climate the trial is most severe. Its merits are certainly appreciated or the shop number would not extend as high as 84,981, which was noticed on a wheel cast during the present year. The wheels, as usual, have three core holes in the back. The only peculiarity about these holes is a V groove cast near the opening, into which, when the core is removed, an eighth of an inch sheet-iron disk is sprung. This method is employed on wheels designed specially for passenger coaches, and prevents the entrance of stones, which, rattling within a wheel of so large diameter, become a source of much annoyance.

CHAPTER II.

PORTABLE AND TRACTION ENGINES—CRANES AND FORGINGS.

ENGINES—CRANES—SINGLE PIVOT CRANES—CHRÉTIEN'S PORTABLE CRANES—BRITISH CRANES—BOILER FOR THOMPSON'S CRANE—HYDRAULIC HOIST—STEAM HAMMERS—PRESSED FORGINGS—UNIVERSAL STRIKERS—STEAM OLIVER—ENDLESS SAW.

I.—ENGINES.

A growing preference for steam over manual power for agricultural purposes, is clearly shown by the number and variety of traction and portable engines exhibited in the English, French, and Belgian departments. No very marked novelties are noticeable upon inspecting the same, but rather the evidence of careful study on the part of the designers to effect economic use of fuel by means of steam jacketing, heated feed water, expansion valves, and a correct balancing of the parts. In England the manufacturers have been stimulated by competitive trials, instituted under the auspices of the Royal Agricultural and other societies, to a healthy emulation, resulting in a marked elevation of the standard of excellence. Her principal manufacturers are Messrs. Aveling & Porter, 72 Cannon street, London; Ransomes & Sims, of Ipswich; John Fowler & Co., of Leeds; Clayton Shuttleworth & Co., of Lincoln; and Messrs. Ruston Proctor & Co., also of the same town. The traction engine of Messrs. Aveling & Porter achieved in the park the feat of drawing five loaded wagons (weighing thirty-five tons) up a gentle ascent. Its workmanship is of the first order, and superior to that of its rivals.

Messrs. Ransomes & Sims exhibit self-moving as well as portable engines. One of the latter drives a section of the British machinery department, but receives its steam from the supply boilers without the main building. Under ordinary circumstances a pressure of 100 pounds per square inch is carried in the boiler; the cylinders are 9 inches diameter by 12 inches stroke, the engine speed 125 revolutions per minute, thereby developing (under a full load) from 25 to 30 horse-power, at an expense of 2½ pounds of coal per indicated horse-power. Most of this engine's working parts are made of case-hardened iron or forged from steel, a copper heater is placed in the chimney, and independent expansion valves on the back of the main valves. The forward axle of their self-moving engine is mounted with hemispherically concave and convex king-bolt plates, enabling the wheels to adapt themselves to the inequalities of a road without causing an inclination of the engine.

Messrs. John Fowler & Co., the celebrated manufacturers of steam-ploughing machinery, have introduced an important improvement in the gearing of their engines. By casting all the driving gears of steel, they do away with exaggerated proportions and save the difficulties experienced through frequent breakage.

A differential-motion device is the main feature in the engine of Messrs. Clayton, Shuttleworth & Co. It enables the driving wheels to accommodate themselves free of strain to sharp curves, at the same time they remain in gear and receive the full power of the engine.

Among the French houses of note may be mentioned: Messrs. J. F. Cail & Co., of Paris; F. Calla, 54 Rue Philippe de Girard, Paris; and Hermann Lachapelle, 144 Rue du Faubourg Poissonnière. Their engines are mounted on solid bedplates and these in turn bolted to the boilers, in place of the direct attachment so much in favor among British manufacturers. Expansion valves and other refinements are quite common.

A very neat road engine of three horse-power, the invention of Mr. Larmanjat, is exhibited by A. M. Ed. Vianne, of 18 Rue Dauphine, Paris. The boiler is constructed on the locomotive principle and mounted on three wheels, the pilot sits in front of the smoke box, while the engineer performs his duties from a foot board behind the fire box. The design of the machinery is also like that of a locomotive, with the exception that the crank shaft carries on its opposite extremities pinion and spur wheels, gearing with corresponding ones on the main wheel shaft. Accordingly as one or the other of the clutches (which transmits the motion of these gears) is thrown into action, the speed of the engine is increased or diminished. Two parallel levers with boxes on the wheel shaft, extend beyond the back seat of the platform; they carry near the main a counter axle, having small driving wheels, and to these motion is imparted by an endless chain over pulleys on both shafts. It follows, that when the extremities of the levers are forced down (by a screw on the end of the carriage) the small drivers rest upon the ground and the large ones become elevated. Four degrees of velocity result from this combination, so that a proper speed for ascending grades may be readily selected. On an ordinary road from 6 to 10 miles per hour is considered the engine's average speed, (when loaded,) but where the incline equals 1 in 150 the small wheels must be thrown into action and the speed is reduced to about two and a half miles. The quality of the workmanship is best judged by the fact that this engine has already run over 1,000 miles without the slightest repair. It is valued at $1,600, (gold.) The ease with which it is manipulated, both as respects speed and direction, combined with the comfort and security afforded, strongly recommend the system to public favor.

II.—CRANES.

England, France, Belgium, and Prussia are the only countries contributing cranes to the Exposition. Of these, there are six stationary, eight portable, and four self-propelling. They have all seen service previous to the public opening of the building, during which time the latter class proved themselves of special benefit by carrying heavy machinery and locating it upon prepared foundations. They will also assist in removing the same at the close of the Exposition. The principal feature worthy of note in the stationary cranes is the invention of Mr. C. Neustadt, 71 Rue de Chabrol, Paris. He makes use of a plate link chain, which, instead of winding on a drum until two or three successive layers are formed, merely passes three quarters of the distance around a pinion having teeth entering between the links, and is then discharged into a box on the crane post. The diameter of a pinion for a crane of six tons capacity will not exceed 4 inches, and since there is no possibility of the chain coiling successively on the pinion, the leverage will continue the *same* when the weight reaches the point of the jib, as it was on leaving the ground. Mr. Neustadt also counterbalances the handles of his crane with a suitable casting. He exhibits two cranes, one for lifting six and the other 10 tons. This system will prove of benefit in the construction of hand cranes for heavy weights, also in positions where it may be difficult to place a drum capable of carrying a long chain.

SINGLE PIVOT CRANES

Messrs. Haute Viveaux & Co., of Dammarie-sur-Saulx, France, send four single pivot cranes composed of cast and wrought iron, one limited to six tons and the others 10 tons each. By them the principle of Mr. Neustadt is followed, but with the use of straight instead of plate link chains. Their jibs are elliptical in section and formed by riveting together boiler plates bent with the proper curvature. The "Society Hauts Fourneaux de Maubeuge" exhibit a self counterpoising portable crane. The track carrying the weighted box rises at its extremity with a curve resembling a semi-cycloid and overhangs the crane car to the same extent as the jib. The "fall," although double, has not its extremity fastened at the end of the jib, but returns over a second sheave to a third at the extremity of the counterpoise track arms, over which it passes and is secured to the counterpoise weight. By this arrangement the counterpoise is made to travel out on its track arms far enough to equalize the action of the weight raised by the crane. It should be observed in this disposition, that the chain is continuous over all the sheaves, one extremity being fastened to the counter-weight box while the other is secured to the hoisting drum. In like manner, when the time arrives for landing the load, the counterpoise returns to a position near the pivot of the crane, thus removing at the same time all weights tending to destroy the equilibrium.

CHRÉTIEN'S PORTABLE CRANE.

The most novel portable crane in the Exposition is the invention of Mr. J. Chrétien, 150 Boulevard Richard Lenoir, Paris, Plate III, Figs. 4, 5, and 6. In place of double cylinders acting on gearing with link valve motions, &c., the lower extremity of his crane jib is a steam cylinder about 14 inches bore by nine feet stroke. The cross-head of the piston rod works on guides attached to the inner surfaces of the two I-beams forming the remaining portion of the jib. Where the connecting rod would properly be attached is introduced a sheave over which the hoisting chain passes. One end of this chain is fastened to the extremity of the jib, the other, having taken one-half a turn around this sheave, runs over another at the end of the jib and so down to the load. The combination, therefore, is that of a single movable pulley, in which the weight is attached to the fall, and the power to the movable pulley. If the weight must be raised 30 or 40 feet, as, for instance, the dumb-waiter of a public building, the length of cylinder need not be altered, but the cross-head should have three or four sheaves instead of one, which is also true of the fixed pulley. Mr. C exhibits a specimen of this character in constant service at the restaurant of the "International Circle building." On the side of the pivot opposite the jib is a trough girder, at whose extremity the boiler is attached. Within this girder the operator stands, for firing, giving steam to the jib cylinder, and rotating the crane. Its sides carry tanks for water and fuel. Rotation on the axis is produced by means of a spur wheel fixed on the car and a pinion, whose shaft runs up the side of the girder to a handwheel connection above. A pawl attachment is made at the end of the jib to the sheave, for arresting its motion, and an automatic device secured to the valve for reversing the same if by accident the piston should approach too near either head of the cylinder. This style of crane is rapid and perfectly noiseless in its action, is cheaply fitted, and acts directly on the load, without gearing or clutches between power and weight.

BRITISH CRANES.

The cranes of Messrs. Geo. Russell & Co. and Alexander Shanks & Son, of Scotland, similar in design, are limited to burdens of five and six tons in weight. Their average pressure of steam is 60 pounds per square inch, and consumption of coal about 56 pounds per hour.

On the crane of Messrs. Geo. Russell & Co. the rotation gear is actuated by an endless chain from the main shaft, tightened with an idler pulley, which yields in the event of the jib meeting an obstruction, thus suspending the rotation.

BOILER FOR THOMPSON'S CRANE.

Mr. R. W. Thompson, of Edinburgh, Scotland, exhibits a portable two-tons crane equipped with a boiler and winding engine of his own invention. The boiler belongs to the upright tubular class constructed with a high fire-box. Its tube sheet is first pierced by a circle of tubes near the fire-box walls, then by the flanged opening of a spherical vessel, depending from the sheet within the upper portion of the fire-box. The water of the boiler freely circulates within this vessel, which is designed to be the main steam generator, and deflects with its surface all the flames arising from the fire, against the sides of the fire-box. The engine is called a "differential rotary." It has but one cylinder, parallel to whose axis lies a shaft with two fixed elliptic spur wheels, separated by a distance greater than exists between the heads of the cylinder and keyed as shown in the sketch. The cylinder contains four closely fitting sector blocks whose combined cubic contents equals nearly three-quarters that of the cylinder. Two of these blocks are rigidly attached in a diametral line to a short shaft passing through only one head of the steam cylinder, the other two similarly with a shaft passing out through the opposite head. Both of these short shafts carry elliptic spur wheels which gear with those on the main parallel shaft. The effect produced by these elliptic spurs (if the fly wheel is turned by hand) is that of causing two diametral sides of the sectors on the one shaft to approach two on the other, when having almost reached their line of contact a retrograde motion begins. While rotation of the sectors goes on within the steam cylinder, they continue the independent motions of oscillating to and fro. In regulating the steam supply these sector blocks act as valves for the two steam and two exhaust ports in the cylinder. In other respects Mr. Thompson's crane does not differ materially from other portable articles of the same class.

Fig. 4.

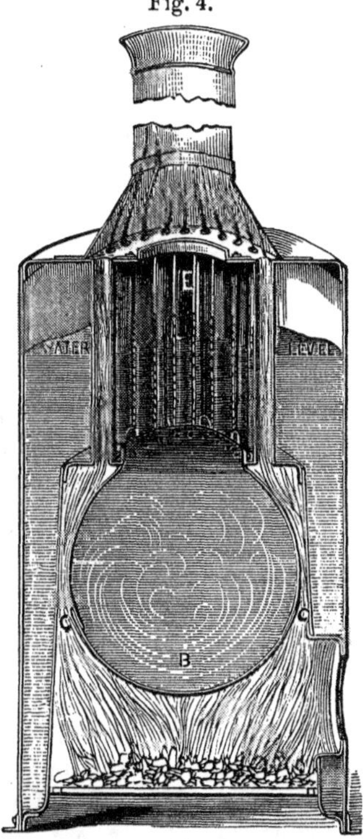

Boiler for Thompson's Crane.

The four self-propelling cranes are the workmanship of Messrs. Stothert & Pitt, Bath; Appleby Bros., London; James Taylor & Co., Birkenhead; and the Belgian Manufacturing Co. Their hoisting powers range between five and six tons. Two of them are arranged for raising and lowering their jibs by power, a useful feature in the accurate location of massive articles. Double cylinders and link motions are common to all, while friction clutches take the place of those having teeth. The crane of Messrs. Stothert & Pitt is specially worthy of note from the simplicity of its gearing combination, in which respect it greatly excels the one contributed by the Belgian Manufacturing Company. The chain of the latter company's crane is arranged upon the system of Mr. Neustadt.

HYDRAULIC HOIST.

In addition to the applications of manual and steam power for raising weights, hydraulic force has its representatives in two platform elevators, designed by Mr. Leon Édoux, of Paris, for carrying visitors from the floor to the roof of the main building. Each platform is inclosed by a wire cage and furnished with seats for twelve passengers. They are guided in their ascent by eight hollow cast-iron columns and counterbalanced by as many weights within, to which they are attached by chains. The two rams (each 9⅞ inches external diameter) are made in joints of cast iron screwed together; they each fit cylinders 98 feet in length, which are sunk in the ground. When the platform reaches the landing stage near the roof 69 feet of the ram tube has left the forcing cylinder; its surplus length steadies the amount then in the air. The motive power is said to be that of the city of Paris water pressure, or 45 pounds per square inch. If allowed to act with full force it accomplishes the ascent of the platform in 75 seconds, its descent in 55. Although these two elevators are the only working illustrations of the principle, its adaptability to iron smelting furnaces, railway freight stations, &c., is clearly shown by drawings adorning the neighboring walls.

III.—FORGING.

STEAM HAMMERS.

The complete revolution which has taken place in the manufacture of steel has developed tools capable of working large ingots into shafts, plates, &c. Hammers suitable for drawing down iron are found totally inadequate to the demands of steel, which must be worked at much lower temperature and with increased rapidity. For large steam hammers of the ordinary construction, a solid firm foundation nearly equals the first cost of the tool, and even when laid is of doubtful permanence. Messrs. Thwaites & Carbutt, of Bradford, England, exhibit a most interesting set of models, drawings, and photographs of hammers, designed by Mr. Ramsbottom for overcoming these difficulties. Their analysis, however, lies in the province of another committee. Messrs. Thwaites & Carbutt have greatly improved their own steam hammers by the substitution of wrought for cast iron in the standards. Their workmanship is of the finest character; all holes are drilled and reamed to fit exactly the rivets they receive and the edges of the plates are carefully planed. They exhibit the drawings of a hammer just patented which gives fair promise of success. On opposite sides of its anvil block are sunk two vertical cylinders whose covers are flush with the forge floor; their piston trunks rise to a point higher than the face of the anvil where they are rigidly fastened to a heavy horizontal cross-head carrying the hammer head proper on its under side, yet virtually the cross-head, trunks, and this head combined, form the hammer. The valve motion is so arranged that both cylinders receive and exhaust steam at the same instants. It will be observed that the piston areas for the down stroke are reduced by the areas of the trunks. The patterns for a hammer of this description are preparing; its merits, therefore, will be discovered before many months.

In the Belgian department Mr. Auguste Detombay, of Marcinelle, exhibits a ten-tons steam hammer with cast-iron forked standards bolted on a large oblong bed plate. Each standard bifurcates at the bend, (where breakage usually occurs,) and by its improved proportions increases the strength of that weak point as well as adding materially to the stability of the machine; the standards are cored, forming box beams. This arrangement, however, reduces the room available around the anvil for the manipulation of large forgings, and in this respect is not as desirable as the wrought-iron system adopted by English manufacturers.

Near the hammer just mentioned stands one built by Lucien & Co., of Braine le Comte, which is double-action in the distribution of the steam, and has an automatic hand motion. The cast-iron standards have the same section as an I-beam and bolt to a bed plate independent of the anvil block. It is rated at three-tons hammer and recommended for shafts under twelve inches in diameter.

The steam hammer of Messrs. Varrall, Elwell & Poulot, 9 Avenue Trudaine, Paris, has a single box-beam standard bolted to the same bed plate as the anvil block. It is automatic, also double-acting when required. The valve is operated by bell cranks connected with levers and wedge-shaped "dogs" against which a roller on a short stud in the hammer head presses, when the head reaches either extremity of its stroke. The arrangement scarcely admits of an explanation without complete drawings.

PRESSED FORGINGS.

For the many intricate shapes into which it is necessary to forge wrought iron the hydraulic press is becoming an indispensable apparatus to the large shops of Great Britain and the continent. At the London exhibition of 1862 there was introduced by the Austrian Society of State Railways a powerful machine of this character designed for the rapid forging of piston spiders, cross-heads, wheel centers, &c. The machine was invented by Mr. T. Haswell, manager of the company's Vienna machine shops. Its pressure capacity was 840 tons, and performed its work with perfect satisfaction. The details of the press are clearly shown by the accompanying illustrations, (Plate IV, Figs. 1, 2, and 3.) To the present Exposition the company have only sent samples of the work performed by their machine. Among these are a box-shaped locomotive cross-head, two driving axle boxes, one piston spider, and a crank axle. The cross-head has a socket punched in it, (for receiving the end of the connecting rod,) which is 8 inches long by 3 inches wide by 11 inches deep, also a boss for the piston rod and its key; the dies have successfully formed the other inequalities on the block as grooves for guides, &c.

Mr. F. A. Egells, of Berlin, exhibits a large press (built from these drawings of Mr. Haswell) which has seen service during the nine months previous to its departure. He values this press at $4,400, (gold.) The cylinder has a steam jacket with mahogany lagging, the castings are well proportioned, their finish workmanlike.

By far the finest display of pressed wheel forgings are those of Messrs. L. Arbel Deflassieux Bros. & Peillon, of Rive de Gier, Loire. Their wheels are nine in number, varying in size from 26 inches to 6 feet 6 inches diameter. Those designed for locomotive use have the dead weights and bosses pressed on during their manufacture. Through lack of actual contact between the dies "fins" are always formed on the forgings, but these seldom exceed in thickness one-eighth of an inch for wheels of moderate diameter.

The economy of press forgings is strikingly apparent in the manufacture of drawhooks for cars, buffer plates on the ends of stems, fixtures for brakes, &c. Samples of such articles are exhibited by Mr. Delletrez, senior, 51 Avenue d'Eylau, Paris, and Messrs. Constant Bros., of Ivry, Seine.

The Messrs. Russery & Larcombe, of Rive de Gier, Loire, employ the hydraulic press in the manufacture of locomotive crank axles. They illustrate the method by which the pressure is applied with two sample axles. One of these shows the effect of pressure exerted on three points of a straight shaft, by which means a rough-shaped crank is crushed down; the other, the transforming effect of powerful dies in moulding the rough crank to the ordinary form. The Eastern and Western railways of France are among the largest customers of this firm.

DAVIES'S UNIVERSAL STRIKER.

For general smithy purposes no tool will be found so acceptable as the universal striker exhibited by Mr. D. Davies, of Crumlin, near Newport, England, (Figs. 5, 6, and 7.) It possesses rare novelty and has but recently been reduced to a *perfectly* simple practical form. One of these machines gives employment to eight fires, dispenses with a gang of helpers, and produces the forgings for one-third the ordinary cost; at the same

Fig. 5.

Davies's Universal Striker.

time it occupies but one-quarter of the area usually required. The hammer is worked directly by steam, and with its cylinder, steam chest, &c., is mounted in a horizontal cylindrical casing on top of a hydraulic column. This column has a range of four feet, through which it can raise the hammer to suit the work. The horizontal cylindrical casing is cast with teeth around its edge into which a pinion meshes and is operated with a hand-wheel. By this means the inclination of the blow is accommodated to the forging of oblique surfaces, as in Fig. 5. A foot lever in front of the anvil, see Fig. 6, connects with the throttle and places the admission of the steam entirely under the control of the smith.

Fig. 6.

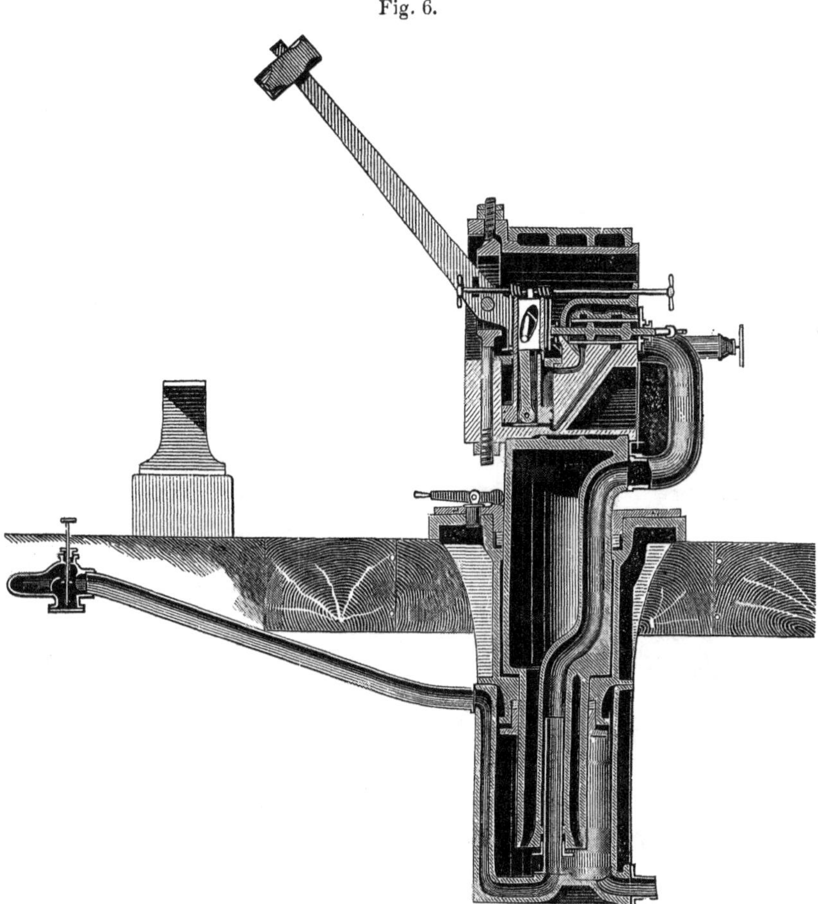

Davies's Universal Striker—section.

The steam and exhaust passages of this apparatus are all *central* pipes with stuffing boxes, and in no way interfere with either the rotation of the horizontal cylinder or that of the column. Hence, around it may be located four swage blocks or anvils on any of which work can be arranged while the others are in service, see Fig. 7, thus saving the time ordinarily consumed in the change of swages and fastening of the work. On account of its quick, rapid motion it is more efficient than hand labor in welding together plates, which when forged by it require no scarfing. It can hardly fail to become an inensdispable tool in all shops.

Fig. 7.

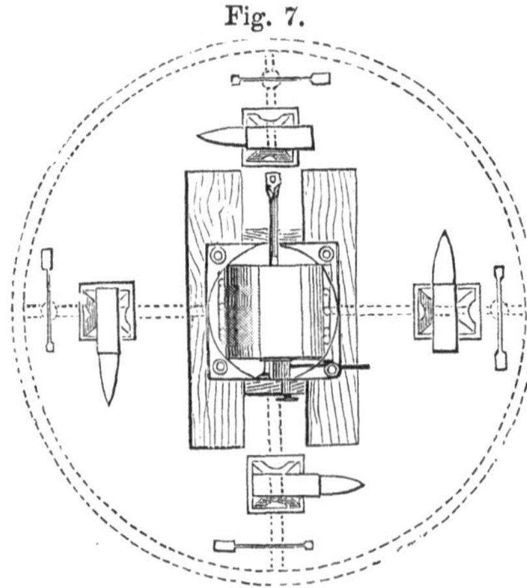

Davies's Universal Striker—plan.

STEAM OLIVER.

B. & S. Massey, of Manchester, exhibit a steam oliver, with specimens of its work. The hammer handle has a fixed fulcrum on the opposite extremity of the machine to the anvil, and is grasped midway by the forked piston rod of an oscillating cylinder. This cylinder has a simple slide valve operated by a foot lever extending to the front of the machine, and so counterweighted that the hammer will always rise from the anvil when there is no pressure on the lever. The working parts are suitably protected from iron scales and arranged for renewal when worn out. The machine occupies an area of only three feet seven inches by two feet, and is specially adapted to the wants of bolt manufacturers and car builders. Its construction is indicated in Fig. 8.

Fig. 8.

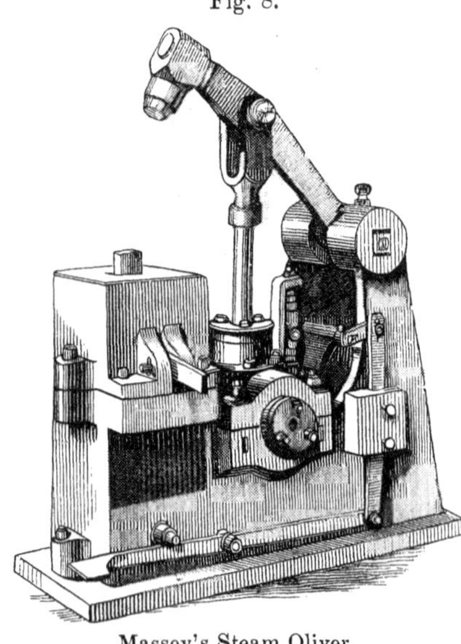

Massey's Steam Oliver.

The forging of threads on wood screws has been practised in France with much success. Messrs. Auguste Jubert Brothers, of Charleville, Ardennes, exhibit in their case of "general furnishing" three bolts for armor plates. The machine with which they perform this work (being analogous to the Ryder forging machine) is fitted with top and bottom swages to match the desired thread. The point of the heated bolt is inserted between these swages, which rapidly form the threads; it is then fed along with a constant motion of rotation, being guided by the lower swage until the thread is perfected the proper distance. The quality of the bolts thus produced is so much superior to those cut cold with dies, that these gentlemen receive twenty per cent. more for their work than others are able to command.

ENDLESS BAND SAW FOR IRON.

Since the invention of the endless band saw by Mr. I. L. Perin, of 97 Faubourg St. Antoine, Paris, and its entry in the Exposition of 1855, the circular plate saw has been rapidly loosing ground in public estimation, so that at present every country in Europe is represented by finely finished samples of these wood-cutting tools. In France it has been applied to ivory, and in Great Britain to iron. The latter adaptation was first made by Colonel Clerk, at Woolwich. In the war department annex are specimens proving his great success. The first one is an Archimedean spiral (of three turns) cut from a block 9 inches square by 6 inches in thickness. The second is mounted in a glass case on a red velvet background and is composed of a crown on either side of which are the letters "W. D." below the words "Royal Carriage Department, 1867." These were sawed from a plate of iron one inch in thickness. The letters are quite artistically executed, and the sawed surfaces smooth. The experience of the department leads them to recommend a speed of 250 feet per minute for a band saw cutting 1-inch iron plates. The teeth of their saws are set and filed straight, having 10 to the inch, the width is $\frac{5}{16}$ of an inch. They use the hardest saw steel that can be obtained and with soap and water as a lubricant run the saw for four or five hours without sharpening; the latter operation requires half an hour for its completion. Any curved line can be cut in plates of the above thickness with a feed of 1½ inch per minute. By this system very little waste of material is incurred and the sawed surfaces are so smooth that they require but slight after-finishing. It may not be inappropriate to note that previous to Colonel Clerk's experiments with the band saw, Mr. Krupp used the circular saw for cutting out his steel crank axles, lubricated with soap and water, and found the expedient so much more economical than reduction by a slotting machine that he has continued the practice.

CHAPTER III.

STEAM GENERATORS.

NEW BOILERS—HOWARD'S AND BELLEVILLE'S BOILER—BOILER OF MESSRS. EDWARD GREEN & SON—IMBERT & CO.'S HORIZONTAL AND TUBULAR BOILER—THE EXPOSITION SUPPLY—BOILER FIXTURES—THIERRY'S FUEL ECONOMIZER—BERENDORF'S BOILER TUBES—GREEN'S FUEL ECONOMIZER.

I.—NEW BOILERS.

It is quite evident from an examination of the boilers recently invented that the aim of their constructors has been greater security against explosion and ability to carry steam at a higher than ordinary pressure. They are naturally divided into two classes by the materials which predominate in their construction, viz: wrought or cast iron. In all, the primary object is to subdivide the mass of the water acted upon by the flame, thus rendering an explosion local, and not such as would shatter the whole fabric. The ones claiming particular attention are: First, those composed of a series of lap-welded tubes, as exhibited by Messrs. J. & F. Howard, Bedford, England, and I. Belleville & Co., No. 6 Avenue Trudaine, Paris; second, the cast-iron boiler of Messrs. Ed. Green & Son, 14 St. Ann Square, Manchester; and third, the rivetless boiler of Messrs. Eugene Imbert & Co., of St. Charmond, France.

HOWARD'S AND BELLEVILLE'S BOILER.

The boiler of the first makers combines fifty-four vertical tubes and assists in supplying steam to the British machinery department. The tubes with their connections stand in a chamber of brick work immediately beyond the furnace, which is built of fire bricks and shaped as shown in Plate V, Figs. 1 and 2.

The products of combustion freely circulate among the tubes, and having passed through a return flue below the chamber, where the lower extremities of the tubes reduce the remaining heat to a temperature of about 250° Fahrenheit, they escape into the stack. The tubes are cut from wrought iron pipes 7 inches diameter, $\frac{1}{4}$ of an inch in thickness, with a length of 5 feet. One end of each is closed by welding on a wrought-iron disk. Six or eight of these tubes are then placed in row and have their open ends stepped in as many grooves cast around the openings in the horizontal pipe, the latter, it will be seen, forms a means of intercommunication for the tubes in a row. When thus placed a gland ring and rubber gasket are slipped over each tube and drawn firmly down to the cast-iron pipe by two bolts whose heads are let into sockets cast on the sides of the pipe. It will be observed that these pipes unite at diagonally opposite corners and lie in the same horizontal plane with the union plates which rest on flanges cast along their sides. These plates form the division between the combustion chamber and the lower flue, exposing the upper portion of the cast-iron tubes to the products of combustion in the chamber, their lower half to those in the flue. Into the head of each wrought-iron tube is screwed an inch nipple six inches in length, a transverse tube carries the steam received through these nipples to a long cast-iron pipe which serves the purpose of a steam dome. From the top of the chamber (which rests immediately on the tops of the tubes) hang transverse curtain plates for compelling the products of combustion to circulate near the lower extremities of the tubes that otherwise would course near the roof of the chamber and too highly superheat the steam. The rows of tubes also are so arranged that the currents of heated gas are constantly caused to impinge against the tubes and pursue a sinuous pathway to the flue. There remains but one essential feature of the boiler to be described, viz: the maintenance of the circulation. This is accomplished by standing a short tube of small diameter within each wrought-iron tube having its lower extremity serrated for the free passage of the water and its upper extending to a point below the proper water level. The effect of these tubes is to secure the particles of water within from the action of the heat on those without their surface, thereby establishing water columns of different densities whose efforts to equalize each other develope constant currents. In the event of an accident to any of the tubes the removal is readily accomplished through the top of the chamber without affecting the others. Their vertical position facilitates the rapid escape of the steam particles, while their comparatively thin shells offer a ready passage to the caloric for the speedy generation of the steam. In firing these boilers a pressure of 75 pounds per square inch is usually produced in twenty minutes with 220 pounds of fuel. The manner in which the heated chamber incloses the steam portions of the tubes is favorable for the production of slightly superheated steam. Messrs. J. & F. Howard give the following as the results of experiments conducted with a "Cornish" and "safety boiler" placed side by side, of the same nominal horse-power under the same conditions.

Results of experiments with the Cornish and safety boiler.

Class of boiler.	Time.	Coal consumed.	Water evaporated.	Escaping gases by Gauntlett's pyrometer.
	Hours.	*Cwt.*	*Gals.*	° *Fah.*
Cornish boiler	4	15½	654	500
Safety boiler	4	9⅝	682	250

A pressure of 1,200 pounds has been put on one of these boilers without any indications of leakage or rupture; the bursting pressure of the tubes is about 2,000 pounds per square inch, but they are only subjected to a hydraulic test of 500 pounds per square inch. One important consideration in boilers of like construction is the fact that the water level has with safety a wide range; instead of being limited to a few inches it may recede more than a foot without danger. It is natural to suppose that a system of scrapers with these tubes would be found beneficial; even if made to travel slower than those of Messrs. Ed. Green & Son, they would still be conducive of more perfect heat absorption and leave less for radiation from the brick work of a long flue. Engineers who have had the pleasure of transporting (within the last few years) any of the immense boilers that have crossed the plains for Colorado and Montana Territories cannot fail to recognize, among other advantages, the extreme portability possessed by this boiler.

Fig. 9.

Belleville's Return-tube Boiler.

The boiler of Messrs. I. Belleville & Co., like the foregoing, is composed of wrought-iron lap-welded tubes, but of much smaller diameter, and arranged in a horizontal stack over the furnace. Mr. B. has studied the subject of non-explosive steam generators since the year 1850 and is now being rewarded with the general adoption of his boilers by the largest manufacturing companies of France, as well as the imperial marine. His combination comprises a number of tubes, having an external diameter of two and three-fourths to three and one-fourth inches, cut to a certain length, and with threads chased on each of their ends. These tubes are united in a series of horizontal layers by a species of "return bend," but differing from the commercial article by having, in the back of each, two small hand-hole plates for access to the interior of the tubes. The layers of tubes thus united over each other form a series of folds, the first and last layer of which terminate on the same side. They enter two wrought-iron boxes, small in section but in length equal to the width of a fold. The boxes are called "collectors;" the lower receives the feed-water, while the upper one contains the T-headed extremity of the steam pipe, which is perforated with small holes to prevent priming. This combination of piping is inclosed within suitable walls, as shown in Fig. 9. The water space compared to the steam room bears about the ratio of one to two; the object of this is to subject as little water as possible at one time to the action of the flames; the quantity being small renders an automatic feed essential. Mr. B. accomplishes this by suspending a drum outside of the boiler near the water line and placing a float in the same which acts on the valve of the feed pump. A top and bottom pipe connection between this drum and the boiler maintains a uniform pressure within the drum. The steam, after leaving the collector, enters a dome on top of the boiler, where it is obliged to pass under a diaphragm plate and deposit any grit or impurity it may contain before it enters the engine cylinder. As the French law of 1856 is very stringent in the event of an accident from an explosion, it is not surprising that such a boiler whose security is guaranteed should meet with popular favor. On the transport La Vienne and dispatch boat Argus the usual evaporation of these boilers is eight pounds of water per pound of coal. Their compact compass and exceeding lightness strongly recommend them for "steam launch" boats.

BOILER OF ED. GREEN & SON.

Messrs. Ed. Green & Son's boiler is made entirely of cast iron. It is composed of a series of hollow foruses or rings, whose shortest diameter is three feet, and diameter of a right section about ten inches. Flanges for pipe connections are cast at the quadrant points, on the outer circumference of each forus; a cap is bolted on those flanges that will stand vertically in the combination, while the other two are bolted to pipes. The lower one of these pipes is supported by saddles which give it an inclination like the keel of a vessel on the stocks. Upon openings in the same, one flange of each forus is bolted until they form a row standing on the pipe like the ribs of a vessel on its keel. The second parallel pipe is bolted to the remaining top flanges. Looking at the combination in the direction of the pipes a cylindrical opening three feet in diameter is left, their full length, at one end of which grate bars are supported. The whole is arched in with fire-brick; the radius of this arch being three inches greater than that of a forus, permits a free circulation of the products of combustion. A cast-iron front closes the furnace extremity, the opposite connects with the chimney. The lower cast iron pipe receives the feed-water; it is also used for the blow-off. The upper connects with a third, forming the steam dome. Each forus stands so perfectly distinct that the products of combustion are at liberty to circulate around them and rise to the under side of the arch. No provision seems to have been contemplated for preventing their passage *solely* along the arch and consequently their too rapid escape. It is claimed in addition to the great strength of this combination that the expansion and contraction of the foruses will tend to keep them free of scale. The existence of four openings in each forus adds greatly to the probability of these castings being uniform in their thickness by preventing the possibility of the core floating in the molten metal, and admits of a semi-revolution of the piece after a long exposure to the flames.

IMBERT & CO.'S HORIZONTAL TUBULAR BOILER.

The boiler of Messrs. Eugene Imbert & Co. is of the horizontal tubular class, having a cylindrical furnace introduced through one head; its novelty lies in the total absence of rivets. The dimensions of the shell are three feet one and one-fourth inch in diameter by nine feet six inches long; of the fire-box, twenty-three inches diameter by four feet three inches long, both of which parts are welded and form one piece; the steam dome twenty inches diameter by two feet high is also a single piece, flanged and fastened to the shell with tap bolts. Total heating surface is 162 square feet, and government pressure stamp 150 pounds per square inch. The grate bars, bearers, bridge-wall, and furnace door are arranged for withdrawal *en masse.* In welding the heads to the cylindrical portion of the boiler, there appears first to have been formed a small rib on the inner surface a short distance from the edges; after the heads were entered against these ribs the lips were worked down until a perfect weld was produced. As a piece of workmanship this boiler is very remarkable, and dispels all doubt in the mind of an observer as to the possibility of working iron to any required shape.

The only process exhibited for burning the vapors of petroleum mixed with air in the tubes of a boiler, is the invention of Mr. A. Lévêque, 6 Rue St. Foy, Paris, and is located in one of the annexes.

THE EXPOSITION SUPPLY.

All boilers that render active service are excluded from the grand building and have had suitable places assigned them in the park. The

English department draws its main supply of steam from three boilers manufactured by Messrs. W. & J. Galloway & Son, of Manchester. They were built from the same drawings and are collectively rated at 138 nominal horse-power. The type is that of the Cornish tubular, with a cylindrical shell two-thirds of whose surface is encased by brick-work. Each boiler is six feet and six inches in diameter by twenty-four feet in length and furnished with the patent conical flue tubes of the firm. The boilers are covered with Spencer's "non-conducting composition," (a mixture of vegetable and mineral substances with the residue of refined cod-liver oil,) which is claimed to be more durable than felt and to be non-combustible.

The American department draws its supply from a boiler exhibited by Mr. Jules Lecherf, of 38 Rue du Grand Balcon, Paris; it is built on what is commonly known as the French principle.

The departments of France and Belgium are furnished with steam from the boilers of Messrs. Tenbrinck & Bonnet, 13 Rue Servandon, Paris; Meunier & Co., Lille; and L. Vassivière, of Lyons. The boilers of the first makers consist of three shells arranged on the French principle, with the single difference that the lower shells are only co-extensive with the length of the grate. The products of combustion having passed under and over the upper shell, escape from a side opening into a brick chamber enclosing three heater tubes, and away by a flue near the ground into the chimney. Their heating surface equals 580 and grate surface 38 square feet. Messrs. Meunier & Co. furnish plain cylindrical boilers whose fire-boxes are of cast steel; the products of combustion, after crossing a bridge wall, travel through the tubes to a back connection, afterwards by two return passages under the boiler to the chimney. The two boiler of Mr. Vassivière are respectively 40 and 50 nominal horse-power. They are guaranteed to evaporate between eight and a half and nine pounds of water per pound of coal; their heating surfaces are 650 and 710 square feet, working pressure 60 pounds per square inch.

II.—BOILER FIXTURES.

In the department of boiler attachments and fixtures it is observable that nearly all safety-valves are made double; on long boilers one is placed near each end of the same. Besides glass water-gauges metallic floats are used; their stems trip the valves of small whistles when the water reaches too low a level. There are two generally approved ways for indicating the actual level by the stems. That of the celebrated mechanician, Mr. E. Bourdon, is to move a lever attached to the stem, whose extremity records the height over a graduated scale, while Mr. Pinel, of Rouen, secures to the float stem an L-shaped bar magnet, see Plate III, Fig. 7. The attraction of the magnet point, exerted through the dial plate upon a piece of soft iron wire, causes the same to roll up and down the face of the dial as the volume of water is increased or diminished. The advantage of this system lies in the freedom of motion allowed the stem of the float; having no packings, it is impossible for it to rust fast in its bearings. The French exhibit several automatic boiler feeders in their annex, but none as well worthy of attention as that of Mr. G. A. Riedel, of Philadelphia, which preserves the water level at a uniform height, and vastly increases the security of boilers against explosion. Pipe connections, such as T-joints, crosses, elbows, &c., are made of wrought instead of malleable iron, and present a neat finished appearance. Among the prominent exhibitors are Messrs. Lloyd & Lloyd, of Birmingham, and Gandillot & Company, 22 Rue Clausel, Paris.

THIERRY'S FUEL ECONOMIZER.

The subject of successful fuel combustion as obtained by a limited escape of steam within the furnace of a boiler has met a practical solution by the invention of Mr. Thierry, of 146 Faubourg St. Denis. He places within a boiler furnace and over the door a horizontal pipe having connections with the steam dome. Several holes one-sixteenth of an inch in diameter are drilled in this pipe, and so located that the escaping steam will be projected into the furnace, to which a sufficient quantity of air is admitted through a damper in the furnace door. Mr. Thierry has introduced his "economizer" in England, Austria, Spain, Portugal, Turkey, Italy, Belgium, and in all instances guarantees a saving of from eight to twelve per cent. Mr. Grandperrin, of 141 Rue de Charenton, aims at the same result with his invention; he dispenses with the horizontal pipe, and screws in through the plates of the water space an appratus shaped like a conical shell. This is formed with two inner cases which divide the interior into three compartments, the central one of which opens to the atmosphere on one extremity, while small pipes piercing the other spaces form channels

Fig. 10.

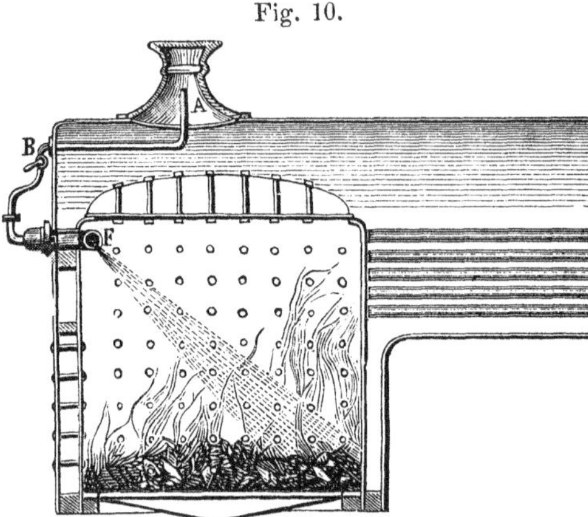

Thierry's Fuel Economizer.

Fig. 11.

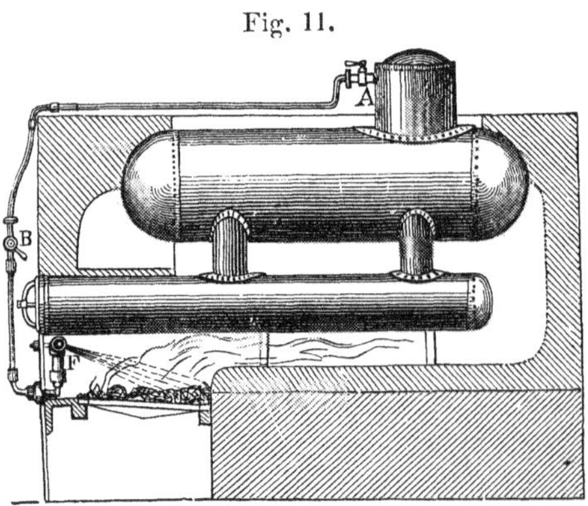

Thierry's Fuel Economizer—section.

for the air to the furnace. The first annular space surrounding this inner shell has a pipe connection with the steam dome and by small tubes with the furnace. Through the second annular space the hot water freely circulates. A shell for a boiler of 100 horse-power is about five inches in diameter, with 16 ($\frac{1}{16}$-inch) steam jets and 14 ($\frac{1}{4}$-inch) air jets intermingled on the upper surface of the shell. Such a disposition of the holes fills the upper part of the fire-box with heated air and steam, instead of projecting the same directly over the fire.

BERENDORF'S BOILER TUBES.

Mr. Berendorf, of 294 Rue Mouffetard, exhibits a system for entering and removing the tubes of boilers. He brazes a conical thimble on the extremities of each tube, and draws them into the holes of the tube sheets by means of a nutted bar and two steel caps; one cap presses only on the tube, the other on the opposite tube sheet. Their removal

Fig. 12.

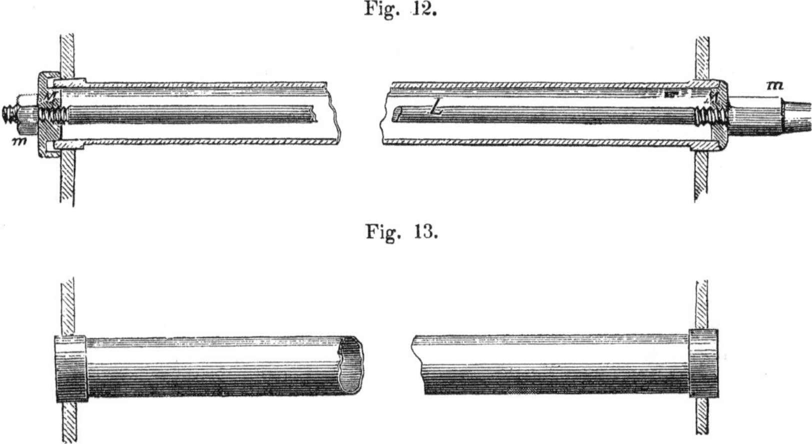

Fig. 13.

Berendorf's Boiler Tubes.

is effected with equal facility by simply reversing the caps before applying the pressure. Messrs. Farcott & Sons bolt the heads of their cylindrical boilers to the shells, and are able at any time to remove the entire furnace tubes and heads with but little difficulty. In the French department is exhibited by E. Bourdon, Esq., 74 Faubourg du Temple, Paris, a steam gauge designed for registering pressure (during all hours of the day) with a pencil upon a pasteboard card caused to rotate by clockwork. Radial lines on the card represent the hours and their fractional parts, while concentric circles show the varying degrees of pressure. An apparatus of this description can render very valuable service in experimental trials of engines and boilers. If priority of invention formed an element in the classification, it could readily be proved that a transfer of the above to the American department would be appropriate. Among the manometers of Messrs. Schäffer & Budenburg, of

Magdeburg, Prussia, is an apparatus for registering pressures of less than 600 atmospheres. This is accomplished with a Richard's indicator, having a small piston and powerful spring. A motion of rotation is imparted by internal clock-work to the card-paper drum; on the paper a pencil traces a pressure line during the continuance of the force and the action of the clock-work. From this card the mean daily pressure is deduced and the times when the greatest pressure was exerted.

GREEN'S FUEL ECONOMIZER.

The boilers supplying steam to the British department are furnished with Green's patent "fuel economizer." Plate V, Fig. 3. This simple and efficacious apparatus for supplying boilers with feed-water of a high temperature is now reported as applied to 823,000 horse-power in Great Britain, Russia, France and Prussia. The title of the firm is Messrs. Edward Green & Son, 14 St. Ann square, Manchester. It is many years since Mr. Green first conceived the idea of keeping constantly clear, by means of ascending and descending external scrapers, a series of feed water pipes placed vertically in the flue between boilers and their chimney. Previous experimenters had failed to extract in any marked degree the heat from the products of combustion, simply because they ignored the fact that the soot constantly deposited on feed-water pipes forms a most perfect non-conductor. Since the discovery he has developed improved apparatus for operating the scrapers and superior methods of mechanical detail in fitting the pipes. At the present time he possesses a well-nigh perfected invention which, upon the concurrent testimony of the principal manufacturers in Great Britain, effects a positive saving in fuel consumption of 20 per cent. and delivers feed-water with a temperature varying from 240° to 270° Fahrenheit. In the British annex Mr. Green exhibits a combination of 36 pipes (occupying a space six feet long by two feet three inches wide by seven feet ten inches in height.) By means of these dimensions and the accompanying figure on Pl. V. the details of the construction may be most readily understood.

The cast-iron pipes are four and one-half inches external diameter, and arranged in four rows of nine each; the distance between those in row is three and one-half inches and that between rows is two and three-fourth inches. The pipes in row have all their upper extremities, united by horizontal pipes, their lower by pipes parallel to the same. The horizontal pipes are closed on two of their diagonal extremities, and open on the other two for the reception and delivery pipes of the feed-water. Before uniting the system of piping the fitting portions are all turned and bored with a slight taper and finally forced together by powerful machinery expressly designed for the purpose. Two vertical scrapers of cast-iron bear against the opposite sides of each pipe, in the same manner that a pawl rests against a ratchet-wheel. One extremity of each scraper expands into a semi-circular blade and embraces one-half the circumference of the pipe; the other extremity has its axis on a cast-iron T-bar. This bar is hung horizontally between the rows of pipes and extends the length of the row. Attached to its upper surface and at right angles to its direction are as many pins, (one inch diameter by twelve inches long,) plus one, as there are tubes in the row. These pins form the axes on which the scrapers freely vibrate during the ascent and descent of the bar. It should be observed that the scrapers, on account of their position on the upper side of the bar and inclination towards the pipes, have a tendency to bear more firmly against them during the ascent of the bar than in the reverse motion. Each T-bar thus arranged carries the scrapers for the two rows of pipes at its sides, and a sufficient bearing against the pipes is given to the bar for the preservation of its horizontal position during motion. Each set of two bars is connected by a chain passing over a chain pulley mounted outside and above the "economizer." This chain is of such a length, that when one bar with its scrapers is at the foot of two rows of pipes, its mate is at the upper extremities of the other rows. A number of these drums with worm-wheels on their sides are driven by a horizontal shaft belted from a main line. This shaft is arranged with an automatic reversing gear, which imparts to the bars and their scrapers a uniform reciprocating motion. Of course the number of pipes composing any system depends upon the number and capacity of the boilers, but the foregoing dimensions give an idea of how closely the tubes can be arranged.

As a general rule, however, the heating surface of the "economizer" is made equal to that of the boilers. The apparatus as a whole is remarkable unique, in no way liable to become disordered, neither is it constructed in a way that impairs the draught of the chimney. Its economic results are beyond question.

CHAPTER IV.

STATIONARY ENGINES.

ENGINES FROM THE UNITED STATES—CORLISS'S ENGINE—ALLEN'S ENGINE—HICK'S ENGINE—BEHRENS'S ENGINE—SHAW'S ENGINE—GREAT BRITAIN AND EUROPE—VANDENKERCHOVE'S ENGINE—SCRIBE'S ENGINE—ROTARY AND GAS-ENGINES—LEATHER BELTING—TRANSMISSION OF POWER TO GREAT DISTANCES—HIRN'S TELODYNAMIC CABLE—CALLES'S HYDRO-AERO-DYNAMIC WHEEL.

I.—ENGINES FROM THE UNITED STATES.

To the American engineering public but few striking novelties are presented amid the large collection of stationary steam-engines on exhibition. For the most part, these comprise special and ingenious adaptations of well-known mechanical devices to the old varieties of the beam and horizontal engines, but seldom evincing the development of new principles. In the latter field it is a matter of congratulation that our own country has made most rapid progress; as represented by the inventions of Messrs. Corliss, Allen, Hicks, Behrens, Ericsson, and Shaw, it contributes the typical engines in the Exposition of 1867. Although the majority of these builders are widely known and well represented throughout the Union, it may not be amiss to briefly describe their several contributions.

CORLISS'S ENGINE.

The Corliss Steam-engine Company, of Providence, Rhode Island, have sent a 30 horse-power horizontal engine, finished with all the mechanical refinement for which their works are justly celebrated. This engine has a large fly wheel which serves as a pulley for the broad driving belt; the frame is light and directly connects the main pillow-block with the head of the cylinder. No massive bed-plate is required for its support, but merely a solid foundation, on which may rest the cast-iron legs bolted to the pillow-block and the cylinder. There are four valves, two steam and two exhaust, placed at the extreme ends and directly upon the bore of the cylinder; being made independently adjustable, it follows that the time of commencement, extent, and rapidity of the movement of each may be arranged accurately to correspond with the theoretical requirements. Motion is imparted to them by a single eccentric acting through the medium of a vibrating disk, sometimes called a "wrist-plate," from which radiate the valve connections. Apart from the simplicity of the device, an important advantage is gained in the utilization of the crank motion's known irregularity, to give the valves a rapid motion at the instant of opening or closing. The closing movement of the liberated steam-valves is effected by straight steel springs, coiled upon an arm of gentle curvature, whereby undue tension is avoided and a fulcrum always furnished for the action of the springs. Air "dash-pots" arrest the motion of these springs when released. In the mechanism pertaining to the steam-valves is embodied a provision whereby in the course of its ordinary reciprocative movement (and at *any* point of the same) the parts directly and permanently connected with the valve may be detached from the control of the "wrist-plate" and surrendered to the action of the steel spring. This detachment is effected by the impinging of a certain movable arm, or "latch," (forming part of the opening mechanism of the valve,) against a "stop" connected with and held in position by the governor. By this contact a slight deflection of the moveable arm is caused, resulting in such a disengagement of the apparatus, that while the parts impelled by the "wrist-plate" continue their movement unimpeded, the valve, on the contrary, becomes subject to the tension of the bent spring, which instantly draws it over the port. The detachment and consequent closing of the steam-valves is thus made dependent upon the position of the governor, while the latter, having no labor to perform, remains sensitive to the changes in speed. This engine, on account of its perfectly noiseless automatic motion; the extreme sensitiveness of its cut-off; its graceful and carefully studied proportions, as well as its highly polished surfaces, has attracted marked and appreciative attention. In a comparison of the different classes exhibited, it is significant to observe how minutely its features have been copied by noted builders of other nations, as indicative of the esteem with which they regard its novelties.

ALLEN'S ENGINE.

The engine invented by Mr. J. F. Allen, of New York, has been greatly modified in the hands of Mr. Charles T. Porter, of the same city, and made a special branch of manufacture by the Whitworth Company, Manchester, England. The latter have placed three representative engines on exhibition in the British department, one for driving a portion of the line shafting in the main building, and two of smaller proportions arranged with excellent forethought for illustrating the principle and detail of the parts. The former has a cylinder 12 inches diameter and 24 inches stroke of piston; 200 revolutions per minute is the average velocity, giving, consequently, a piston speed of 800 feet per minute. While one of the latter has certain sections removed, revealing thereby the valves, steam passages, piston, &c., a slow speed imparted through a belt to the fly-wheel clearly demonstrates the manner in which the governor and valves perform their respective functions. Its consort is operated by steam, and astonishes engineers who have been accustomed to speeds varying between 200 or 300 feet per minute, by its wonderful rapidity. The maximum number of revolutions attained has been as high as 700, corresponding to a piston speed of 1,400 feet per minute, and yet this remarkable feat was accomplished without jar or noise, so perfectly are the parts fitted and balanced. The large engine is furnished with a jet condenser, which is simply a modification of the approved form used in marine engines. It is placed on a separate foundation, immediately back of the steam cylinder, and has for a displacement piece a single-acting cast-iron plunger, operated by the prolonged piston-rod. To adapt this to the requirements of the high speed incident to its connection, the point of the plunger is turned with the same radius of curvature that Mr. Whitworth has found most efficient on his celebrated projectiles, also its weight exactly equals that of the amount of water displaced. Besides these precautions, small diaphragm plates are attached inside of the condenser, to prevent the generation of waves which would result from the sudden impact of the plunger against the water. The rubber disk-valves have but a short motion, and are self-closing, by means of spiral springs. The main bed-plate of the engine extends from the cylinder-head, to which it is bolted, to a point sufficiently beyond the crank-shaft for receiving the large pillow-block of the same. This bearing is made unusually long, and thus insures absolute rigidity of the shaft. The connecting-rod, formed of steel, has a length equal to thrice the stroke. Since Mr. Allen's engine is based on the principle that work should be performed by the development of high velocity in a small mass, the fly-wheel is consequently of much less magnitude than used on engines of equal indicated power. The cylinder is duplex, that carrying the piston forms a sleeve-like casting, which is bored and turned, then forced into the outer cylinder where, being supported only by fitting strips at the extremities, it is effectually guarded by a complete envelope of steam from irregular expansion. With reference to the proper piston for a high-speed engine, Mr. Porter has found the most satisfactory results to accompany the use of one without packing, but with a wide face carefully turned to the same diameter as the bore of the cylinder, and having the same channeled by small V-grooves. These lodge the water condensed from the first steam that enters the cylinder, and thus create a packing of sufficient resistance for the steam. There are two valve-chests on the side of the cylinder, one for the valves regulating the steam, the other for those controlling the exhaust. The former valves are rectangular and work between scraped surfaces; they are balanced by the pressure of the steam on their opposite sides, while the latter are of the same construction as the ordinary flat slide-valves. These valves being placed near the extremities of the cylinder, the cubic contents of their passages is reduced to a minimum, a condition of economy too often overlooked in high-speed engines, especially locomotives. All the valves are actuated by one stationary link. Motion is transmitted to those regulating the exhaust through a "rocker" having opposite arms; the connecting stem being pinned rigidly to the top of the link imparts an invariable action to the valves. The steam-valves have their stems attached to two other rockers, and these in turn have connecting stems pinned to the sliding-block of the link. To this block the "Porter patent governor" is connected, which, acting under an increased or diminished velocity, causes the block to traverse the link, and effects an earlier or later cut-off of the steam. The combination is very sensitive, and when running with a light load cuts off almost simultaneously with the commencement of the stroke. An invariable "lead" results from the employment of the stationary link, which latter is a curious modification of the ordinary form; for instead of receiving its motion from two eccentrics, having each a connecting-rod, the link-block is cast *on* the strap of the eccentric. Its position is maintained by the ordinary mode of suspension, and the distance from its centre to that of the main shaft is made thrice that of the eccentric's throw; the latter is placed in the radial plane of the crank-pin axis, and on the same side of the main shaft as the pin. As already intimated, the Allen engine, by using velocity instead of mass for the development of "work," has been brought to an exceedingly compact compass. It is perfectly under the control of its steady, yet keenly sensitive governor, while the rapid expansion of high-pressure steam in its jacketed cylinder is accomplished free of condensation, and attended with well-known economic results. It has worked with remarkable smoothness and regularity during the Exposition, and daily furnished indicator cards, clearly illustrating the perfection of its parts. (See Plate V, Fig. 4.)

HICK'S ENGINE.

Of all the direct-acting engines (with a fixed cut-off) in the Exposition, that furnished by the Hick's Engine Company, of Newcastle, Delaware, is the most simple, compact, and ingenious. Its working parts consist of four trunk pistons with their connecting rods strapped to the pins of a double crank-shaft. They operate in one casting forming the four cylinders, while the direction of rotation imparted to the shaft is governed by a slide-valve moved with a simple hand-lever. Each of these trunks is single-acting, and so cored within as to form three chambers. At proper intervals, passages open from these chambers which, in the course of the trunk's stroke, communicate with corresponding ones leading to the steam-supply, as well as the channels for the exhaust. But one of the three chambers opens into the vacant cylinder; this serves as an inlet for the steam in the commencement of the effective stroke, and as outlet for the same during the latter part of the return. It is not used in the first part of the return stroke, because when the trunk piston has nearly completed its effective stroke, it uncovers an exhaust passage through which the steam can escape. This channel is immediately closed on the passage of the crank over its dead center; hence the necessity of opening an escape for the remaining vapor, which would otherwise be greatly compressed and offer serious resistance. The steam for each cylinder enters its trunk through that of the adjoining, while its own trunk effects the cut-off of the same; as this occurs in the most rapid portion of the trunk's travel, the cut-off is necessarily sharp and decisive. Its extent is regulated by the length assigned to the longitudinal passage in the construction of the engine. From the nature of the passage uncovered by the trunk the exhaust anticipates the completion of the stroke, and thus always exhibits a free line on an indicator card quite independently of the direction in which the engine is running. Hence, from this engine a much better theoretical card can be procured than is possibly the case with an ordinary slide-valve actuated by a single eccentric. Leakage of the steam between the trunks and their cylinders is prevented by a key in each trunk which is able to expand the same in a circumferential direction. Compared with two double-acting locomotive cylinders of the same stroke, it will be observed that three or four times the length of cylinder is required by this arrangement to accomplish the same work. The simplicity of the parts strongly recommend its use in places where skilled engineering assistance is difficult to procure. An indicator of this engine is given on Plate V, Fig. 5.

BEHRENS'S ENGINE.

Mr. Behrens, of New York, exhibits a rotary engine and pump combined similar to that invented by Mr. Repsold, of Hamburg, in 1862.

Fig. 14.

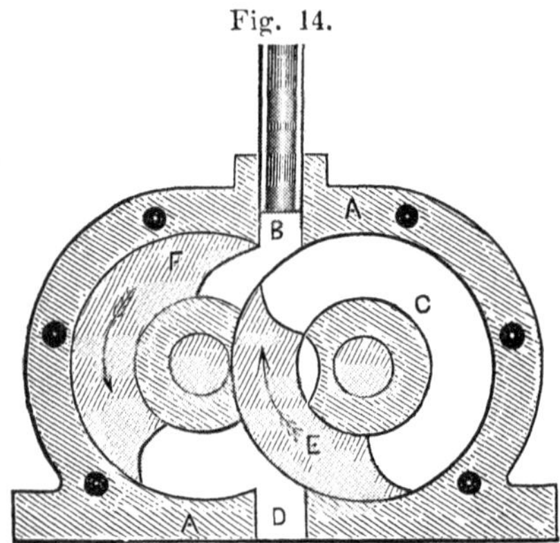

Behrens's Rotary Engine—section.

It consists of two double cylinders mounted horizontally on a bed-plate; through their axes run two parallel shafts, whose motions are rendered synchronous by spur gears keyed on firmly in the intervening space. Within these double cylinders and attached to their shafts are four segmental piston blocks, whose curved ends match each other in the progress of their rotation. Top and bottom passages to one of these cylinders admit and release the steam, and corresponding ones on the other perform the same functions for the liquid to be raised. All four cylinders are bored to the same diameter, but the length of the steam double cylinder is proportioned to the power required for forcing the liquid. Whatever may be the defects of the steam cylinder with reference to its packing, the design for a pump is well worthy of attention, as it possesses remarkable qualities for both suction and forcing combined with admirable simplicity. The last two engines are furnished with governors patented by Mr. Pickering, of New York. This gentleman exhibits samples of the various sizes he manufactures, from those adapted to engines of a few horse-power to others suitable for marine engines of several hundred. His governor balls are riveted in the centers of three laminated straight steel springs. Each spring is composed of five leaves, which are riveted at their upper and lower extremities to collars upon the governor spindle. The valve operated is of the piston variety and perfectly balanced, so that little labor is required of the balls. This peculiar combination and riveting of the springs renders the governor highly sensitive to the least variation in speed. Its simplicity is very prominent in a comparison with the specimens in the French department.

SHAW'S ENGINE.

Mr. Philander Shaw, of Boston, exhibits a roughly constructed hot-air engine in the American section of the park, but one which, by its originality of design, has attracted much attention. The engine is constructed with two vertical cylinders, having single-acting trunk pistons hung from the opposite extremities of an overhead working-beam. The beam center is prolonged on the side towards the furnace sufficiently for receiving a fixed arm, from which the connecting rod runs to the crank of the main shaft. The furnace is hermetically closed; from it the heated air and products of combustion pass over to the cylinders, with an average pressure of fourteen pounds per square inch, to which they are admitted by suitable valves. While one piston is making the upward stroke its annular face acts as an air-pump for forcing cold air into a heater, whence it flows under the grate, to sustain combustion. This is succeeded by the down stroke, which draws cold air into the annular space and expels the gases just used, through the tubes of the heater to the stack. By a neat arrangement of the parts the fine cinders are prevented from cutting the cylinders, and the same are kept sufficiently cool. A diagram of the working will be found on Plate V, Fig. 6.

II.—GREAT BRITAIN AND EUROPE.

The three most notable copies of the Corliss engine principle are by Messrs. Hick, Hargraves & Co., of Bolton, England, Messrs. Gebrüder Sulzer, of Winterthur, Switzerland, and Mr. A. Duvergier, Lyons, France. The leading difference in the engine of the first manufacturers is in the release of the cut-off valves; the finger clips are double; it, however, substantially corresponds in other details. The Swiss engine is the same in respect to the frame, speed, functions of valves, &c. It has four puppet instead of as many circular slide-valves, and these are operated by cams on a shaft running parallel to the axis of the engine. The governor varies the point of cut-off by merely altering the radial lines of contact between the valve connections and their cams, but leaves the exhaust motion invariable. The French engine is characteristic more for the imitation of principle than details. Its bed-plate and overhanging cylinder are like those of the Allen engine. The governor acts on the cut-off valves through the block of a rocking link to which their stems are secured, and whose oscillating motion is derived from the same eccentric that actuates the exhaust valves.

The Woolf system of working steam of high pressure in one cylinder, and expanding the same in a second of greater diameter, has many exponents contributed from the different countries of Europe. A large double beam engine (built by Mr. T. Powell of Rouen) having four cylinders, drives the machinery in a section of the French department. Its two high-pressure cylinders occupy the relative position to those in which the expansion takes place, that the air-pump of an ordinary beam-engine does to its cylinder. Cam shafts geared from the main shaft regulate the operation of the puppet-valves. The workmanship of this engine is of the first order, yet, like many of its contemporaries in the same department, it furnishes but meager material for a report on novel forms of stationaries.

VANDENKERCHOVE'S ENGINE.

Mr. Prosper Vandenkerchove, of Gand, Belgium, has labored earnestly towards reducing to a minimum the cubic contents of the numerous steam passages incident to a double-cylinder expansion engine. His system is embodied in a large horizontal engine having two opposite cranks on the main shaft, double guides, cross-heads, connecting-rods, &c. The two cylinders receive the live steam in jackets surrounding each, whence having passed through puppet-valves to the high-pressure cylinder and performed a portion of its duty, it is allowed to escape and expand in the large cylinder by the opening of the intermediate slide-valves.

Its final escape is effected through separate exhaust-valves in the large cylinder. For these various duties *six* valves are required, thus attaining the object at a sacrifice of simplicity, yet the engine in other respects gives promise of the most economical results. The drawings, Plate V, Figs. 7 and 8, are self-explanatory of the system.

SCRIBE'S ENGINE.

The engine of Mr. Gustave Scribe differs from the foregoing in the

Fig. 15.

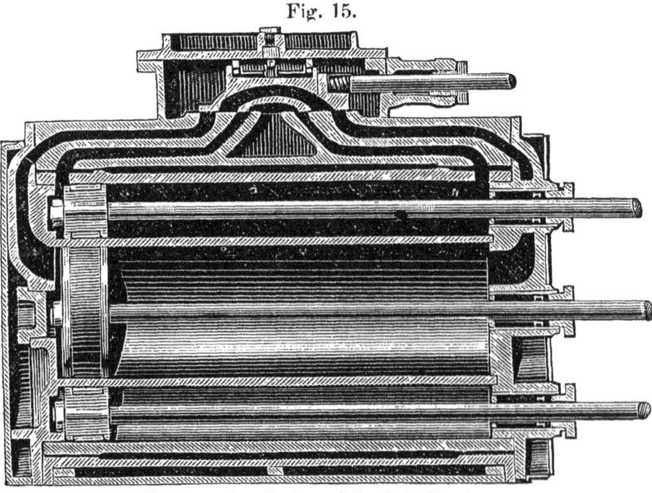

Section of cylinder of Scribe's Engine.

position of the cylinders and valve motion. He places the axis of the high-pressure cylinder coincident with that of the low and immediately ahead of the same, towards the crank shaft. The two piston-rods of the low-pressure cylinder run parallel to the sides of the high and are attached to the same cross-head that holds its single piston rod; thus one connecting rod, crank, cross-head, &c., satisfy the requirements of the engine. The main objection to this arrangement is that the port carrying the exhaust high-pressure steam from the front end of the small cylinder to the back end of the large is necessarily of great length; in the 50 horse-power engine on exhibition this distance equals eight feet.

An engine in the Swedish department constructed by the Bergsund Company of Stockholm displays a ready means of obviating this difficulty. They (so to speak) slide the high-pressure cylinder of Mr. Scribe's engine into the low-pressure, after the manner of a telescope; thereby producing a central high-pressure cylinder surrounded by a low-pressure one having an annular piston. The three piston-rods as before are connected with the same cross-head and transmit motion to one crank arm. This system is highly esteemed in Sweden and appears destined, by the ingenious distribution of the steam, coupled with a compact arrangement of parts, to attract the careful study of marine engineers.

ROTARY AND GAS-ENGINES.

Among the varieties of foreign rotary engines the most prominent are from the works of Messrs. Pillner & Hill, Newport, England, and R. W. Thompson, of Edinburgh, Scotland. In the engine of the former firm, the steam acts upon two spur-wheel pistons; the prolonged main shaft is designed to drive directly a wire rolling-mill, and revolve at 500 turns per minute. That of the latter is termed a "differential rotary," and has already been noticed in connection with the subject of steam cranes.

The "disk engine" of Mr. A. Molard, Luneville, France, stands in the annex, but so closely resembles in detail those constructed for screw steamers by Messrs. J. & G. Rennie, London, that it claims no special attention.

There are three forms of illuminating gas-engines on exhibition. The two first differ principally in the method of ignition; Mr. Lenoir employing a galvanic battery, while Mr. Hugon employs a simple flame introduced and cut off by an ordinary slide-valve. The third form is the invention of Mr. N. A. Otto, of Cologne, Prussia; in it the Hugon flame is used; the gas, having been ignited, propels the piston freely up the vertical cylinder, until the partial vacuum produced by the explosion causes its less rapid return; during which the rod acts on the driving shaft by means of gearing, and imparts the desired rotation. Beside gas-engines, are several others actuated by water pressure and electro-magnetism. The latter seem interesting when regarded as mere skirmishing efforts with a power whose future influence can scarcely be estimated. It is understood that another committee have prepared papers on those varieties of motive power whose adaptation is more modern than that of steam, and to this fact must be attributed the cursory character of the foregoing remarks.

After having glanced at the different novelties for the development of power, the next subject of interest will be the transmission of the same for the performance of work; and first, with reference to one of the oldest means, viz: leather belting.

III.—TRANSMISSION OF POWER.

LEATHER BELTING.

An examination of the different leather departments, and the varieties of belting in actual use, reveal a tendency on the part of manufacturers to improve the quality of wide belts by securing 2-inch strips along their edges. Specimens of this character are exhibited by Messrs. Webb & Son, Stowmarket, England; Mr. William Ruland, of Bonn, Prussia; H. Lemaistre & Co., Brussels, Belgium; Placide Peltereau, 32 Rue d'Hauteville, Paris; Poullain Brothers, 99 Rue de Flandre, Paris; and others of less note. The material forming these strips is (with a single exception) leather of the same quality as the belt. The methods of attachment are variable, as laces, threads, rivets, eyelets, and brass screws. The English use the threads, Prussians the laces, and the French all the varieties enumerated. Mr. P. Peltereau, proprietor of one of the largest houses in France, makes a remarkable display, not only of belts and their mountings, but of different kinds of leather; such as tanned elephant hide, varying in thickness from one-fourth to one-half an inch, and hippopotamus hide, from one inch to one and a half inches in thickness. His 8-inch and 10-inch belts have leather facings two inches wide on their edges. Each of these facings is attached by two leather laces, whose stitches have three-fourths of an inch span, and run in parallel lines, separated by one and one-fourth inch.

The "inextensible belt," for which, at a previous exposition, he received a gold medal, has steel instead of leather edging strips. These strips, for a 10-inch belt, are two inches wide by one-sixty-fourth of an inch in thickness, and attached by two riveted rows of copper tacks. These tacks are one-eighth of an inch in diameter, and placed three and one-half inches between centres.

Messrs. Poullain Brothers join their single and compound their double belts with headless one-eighth of an inch brass screws. This is accomplished with a very ingenious machine, of which there are several types in the French department. It carries a coil of plain brass wire, which, while being fed to the work, passes through a die of twenty-eight threads to the inch. The screw thus formed enters the belt at a point closely clamped by a foot-lever, and having passed through is cut off. Finally, the belt being placed on a surface plate, the points of all the screws are slightly riveted. The most compact and expeditious of these machines is the invention of Mr. Cabourg, 74 Rue St. Honoré, Paris.

Mr. E. Scellos, of 74 Boulevard du Prince Eugène, exhibits what he terms a "homogeneous belt," for 150 horse-power. This belt is nineteen and one-half inches wide by three-fourths of an inch in thickness. It is composed of 104 leather strips three-fourths of an inch in width, laid longitudinally with reference to the belt, and laced transversely; the distance between laces is one and one-fourth inch, and diameter of lace equals three-sixteenths of an inch. The advantage of edge-bound wide belts, where frequent shipping is an essential, we think will be readily conceded; and to what extent they can supplant double belts is a subject worthy of experimental inquiry. The use of very wide belts is seldom resorted to in the machinery department. One of the stationaries has two central ribbed pulley rims bolted to the arms of its fly-wheel; on these run four belts six inches in width; another has two 12-inch edged belts, and so on—the inclination was always to increase the number rather than the width of the belts.

TRANSMISSION OF POWER TO GREAT DISTANCES.

For the transmission of power to great distances, leather and rubber belts are rendered useless by their extreme elasticity, and the expensive character of their intermediate supports; while shafting with bevel gears consumes the applied power in excessive friction, elasticity, &c. These difficulties were studiously met and successfully solved by Mr. C. F. Hirn, of Colmar, Haut Rhin, in the year 1860; the practical working of his invention was partially displayed at the exhibition of 1862. In the park of the present Exposition, his system is clearly shown by the operation of a centrifugal pump, deriving its power from a stationary engine, working on the opposite side of the artificial lake, and distant some 500 feet from the pump. This so-called "telodynamic" system is based on the substitution of a high velocity developed in a small mass, for its converse, viz: large mass moving with small velocity. The power-conductor is simply a light wire rope, passing over pulleys of large diameter, and upheld at intervals of about four hundred feet by support-pulleys. The construction of these pulleys, and their supports, is shown by the accompanying figures, 16 and 17, giving a side view and end view, and a section of the rim of the pulley. The two extreme pulleys, or those which receive and distribute the power, are rotated at speeds having a circumferential velocity of 1,800 to 4,800 feet per minute. It has been the practice to make these of cast iron, but steel is recommended where higher veloci-

Fig. 16.

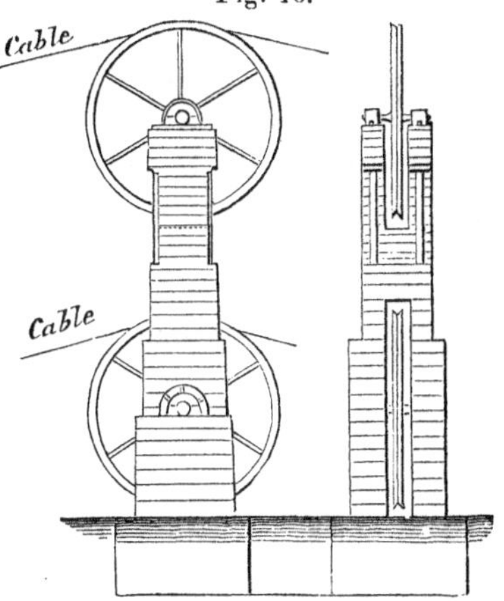

Supports for Hirn's Telodynamic Cable.

ties are necessary. The face of the pulley is channeled by a deep V-groove, while the bottom of the latter has a filling of gutta-percha which adapts itself more and more perfectly to the rope, and entirely prevents slip and wear. Fig. 17 is a section of the rim of the support-pulley, showing the cable A, resting upon the gutta-percha cushion B. Herein lies the secret of its practical success; a result only attained after most discouraging experiments upon pulleys constructed successively of copper, wood, cast iron, &c., with facings of leather, India-rubber, horn, lignumvitæ, and box-wood. Experience has proved that the loss of power by the telodynamic system is quite trifling, and arises mainly from the resistance of the air to the arms of the pulleys, the friction of their axles, as well as the rigidity of the rope in its passage over the pulleys. It has been found that two pulleys, twelve feet in diameter, making 100 revolutions per minute, with a cable of seven-sixteenths of an inch diameter, can by means of a circumferential velocity of 4,000 feet per minute, transmit 120 horse-power (to distances less than 400 feet) without sustaining a loss of more than two and one-half per cent. If this limit is exceeded, it will become necessary to introduce support-pulleys of seven feet diameter, and for these there should be estimated a mechanical loss of about one per cent. per 3,300 feet of distance traveled. The pecuniary expense, independent of the ground-rent, amounted to $1,000 (gold) per 3,300 feet, plus $600 for the receiving and distributing pulleys, with their respective shafts and supports. It is evident that this system cannot be limited in its application by rectilinear transmission, but is susceptible of all the changes in direction which inclined pulleys can command. There are already between 400 and 500 instances of its employment in connection with the manufacturing interests of the continent. Its advantages in respect to our own country can hardly be over-estimated.

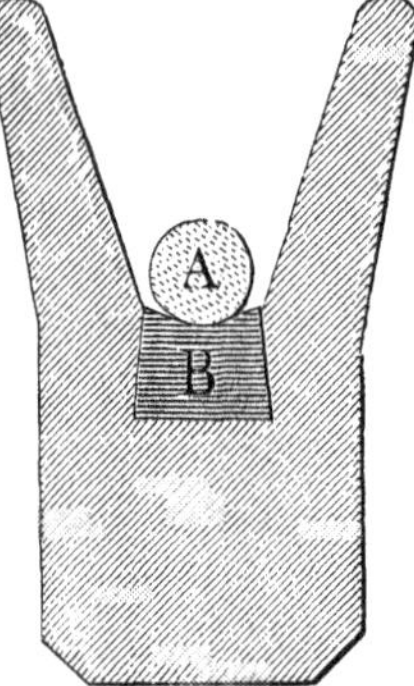

Fig. 17.

CALLES'S HYDRO-AERO-DYNAMIC WHEEL.

Another form of transmission may be seen in the Belgian department, which is the invention of Mr. A. Calles, mechanical engineer resident in Brussels. Its special object is the distribution of motive power throughout large cities with the same facility that now obtains in the cases of water and gas. Besides perfect freedom from the dangers incident to the use of steam-boilers, this power can be furnished on more economical terms than steam and when not wanted can be instantly shut off. It requires no lofty stack or chimney on the premises, but, in addition to its work, purifies the atmosphere of the manufactory by the fresh oxygen constantly introduced; it also occupies but little space, and needs only casual attention. The motive power is compressed air, which after traversing iron pipes is finally allowed to escape under a submerged water-wheel (having curved buckets) where the excess of water displaced on one side of the wheel over that on the other, causes that side to rise, and with a constant flow of the air the rotation is rendered uniform. Spur gearing applies the power. The action of this so-called "hydro-aero-dynamic" wheel is analogous to that of an undershot water-wheel, but developes more useful effect in virtue of its submergence, the friction thereby being greatly reduced and the possibility of leakage guarded against. The water surrounding the wheel is contained by a tank and only requires replenishing as evaporation takes place. The wheel on exhibition is located in the rotunda of the Belgian annex, distance, 600 feet from its double-acting air-compressor pump, which is belted from the shafting in the main building. Fourteen elbows are introduced in the supply pipe for the purpose of increasing the resistance offered the air. The diameter of the pipe is 3¾ inches, through it the air flows with a velocity of 104 feet per second under a pressure of 3⅜ pounds per square inch. The piston of the pump is $23\frac{11}{16}$ inches diameter, and makes 40 double strokes per minute of 27⅝ inches travel. The hydro-aero-dynamic wheel is 9 feet 10 inches in diameter, and of its 30 buckets, 13 are continually performing service. Its speed is six revolutions per minute, or three buckets per second, each of which receive in passing the supply pipe 1.78 cubic foot of air. The inventor estimates the power expended (under these conditions) in compressing the air at 9½ horse-power, and that given out by the wheel at 9 horse-power, or at a loss of about five per cent. It is considered that under increased pressure this machine is capable of transmitting and redeveloping a power of 15 horses. The system offers peculiar advantages in connection with powder mills and pyrotechnic establishments.

CHAPTER V.

MARINE ENGINES.

Great Britain—Engines for the Sappho—France—Engines for the iron-clad L'Océan—Engines for the iron-clad Le Cerbère—Engines for the Friedland—Dimensions of the engines for the Friedland.

In the comparatively short time that has elapsed since the London exhibition, but slight advance can be expected in a department like that of marine engineering, where the structures are erected at immense cost, and in the event of failure attended with such disastrous financial results. Yet the present exposition is not wanting in signs of progress. The principal contributions are from Great Britain, Switzerland, and France, that of the latter is remarkably extensive. Switzerland is represented by a large paddle-wheel engine built by Messrs. Escher, Wyss & Co., of Zurich, for the Rhine navigation service. It has two inclined direct-acting parallel cylinders, constructed on the Woolf principle; the pillow-block frames for the crank shaft rest on eight wrought-iron rod supports. A third intermediate crank operates the air pumps, which are bolted to the main horizontal bedplate. The workmanship is fair, but the design of no special interest.

I.—GREAT BRITAIN.

ENGINES FOR THE SAPPHO.

One surprising feature in the present exposition has been the introduction and performance of marine engines rated at several thousand horse-power. In the English department are a pair of direct acting trunk engines, a superb piece of workmanship, by Messrs. John Penn & Son, of Greenwich. These were built for her Majesty's ship Sappho and will develop over 2,000 horse-power when cutting off at one-third the stroke. The diameter of each cylinder is 70 inches; as the cranks are designed to make 90 revolutions per minute, the piston speed will be 540 feet. The condensers have a tube surface of 5,600 square feet, and receive their circulating water from two centrifugal pumps driven by independent engines. A shifting link motion operates the main slide-valves, besides these there are two starting valves actuated by independent eccentrics. The cranks and link motion are accurately balanced, the castings beautifully finished, cylinders lagged with mahogany held by brass bands; in fact each piece tells the same story, viz: careful study, good taste, and surpassing skill. The same firm exhibit a neat engine for a twin screw-launch as well as sundry models of marine engines. A fine collection of the latter in the same department represents the practice of the following makers: Messrs. Maudslay Sons & Field, London; Wm. Denny & Brothers, Dumbarton; J. & G. Rennie, London; Humphreys & Tennant; and Messrs. Havenhill, Hodgson & Co., of London. In addition to these a history of the changes which have taken place in the royal navy since the introduction of the screw as a means of propulsion, is illustrated by an interesting collection of 105 models. These include ships of two and three decks, frigates, corvettes, gun-boats, tugs, paddle dispatch, yachts, troop-ships, and first, second, and third class iron-clads.

There are two engines for twin screw-launches besides the one exhibited by Messrs. Penn. The first, by Messrs. Maudslay, has a regular locomotive boiler, whose furnace-door faces the bow of the boat. On each side of the fire-box are bolted two inverted cylinders acting directly on the crank-shafts. These are capable of yielding 40 horse-power when the cranks are running at 330 revolutions per minute. The total weight added to a launch by the use of these engines is about 7,000 pounds. The second, by Messrs. Rennie, has the additional advantage of two furface condensers supplied with water by small centrifugal pumps belted from the main shaft. The necessity of carrying tanks filled with fresh water is thus avoided, at very slight sacrifice of space, but with economy in point of weight.

II.—FRANCE.

In respect to novelty the most interesting features are found in the French department. Their typical form is that of three horizontal back-action engines placed side by side, which exert their force on the same crank-shaft, receiving first the steam in the central cylinder, and afterwards expanding it in those adjacent. This principle was first introduced in the imperial navy by M. Dupuy de Lôme, the director of *matériel* under the minister of marine. It has altogether eight illustrations in the Exposition; three consist of engines of great magnitude, the fourth of only the reciprocating parts sustained in like manner to the bones of a skeleton for showing their relative position when in service, and the remainder a collection of neatly executed models.

Before discussing more fully this representative type of engine, brief allusion will be made to the general display of the department.

In the main building are thirteen elaborately finished models, ten of which were contributed by the company of the Mediterranean Forges and Shipyards, office 28 Rue Notre Dame des Victoires, Paris; the balance by the government works at Indret. Messrs. Schneider & Co., of Creuzot, have at much expense erected two complete engines in their building within the park. The largest, of 950 nominal horse-power, is identical in principle, though differing slightly in detail, with the imperial engine to be described. It has three cylinders of 82$\frac{5}{8}$ inches diameter and 4 feet 3$\frac{1}{4}$ inches stroke. The average number of revolutions is fixed at 55, and anticipated actual power at 3,800 horses. After removal from the Exposition it will be re-erected on the iron-clad frigate L'Océan. The second, designed for the iron-clad ram Le Cerbère, is a double-cylinder back-action engine of 265 nominal horse-power, one of a pair for twin propellers, yielding in the aggregate 530 horse-power. Each cylinder is 47¼ inches in diameter, with a stroke of 2 feet 3½ inches. The engine will be worked at a speed of 88 revolutions per minute. It is next in point of workmanship to that of Messrs. Penn, but more complicated in the details.

For the purpose of exhaust, injection, or delivery pipes the French are commencing to use seamless rolled copper tubes, which may be bent to almost any desired curve. The most complete assortment is that of Messrs. Estivant Bros., 71 Rue du Temple, Paris, varying in size from pipes of only a few inches diameter to those of 16⅝ inches outside diameter, $\frac{7}{32}$ of an inch in thickness and 17 feet in length. Another was observed 12⅜ inches diameter, weighing 484 pounds, and bent to a right angle upon a radius of curvature of about 30 inches. The process of bending was ascertained to be the same as that in ordinary practice with pipes of smaller diameter.

Near the imperial engine is one of 450 nominal horse-power, erected by Messrs. Mazeline, of Havre, of fine workmanship, but with no essential difference demanding a separate description.

ENGINES OF THE FRIEDLAND.

The representative engine was built for the steamer Friedland, belonging to the imperial navy, at the government works of Indret. It has been erected complete in all its parts (save reduced boiler power) within one of the buildings bordering the river Seine, from which the supply of water for the condenser is drawn. All the parts occupy the same relative position to each other that they will when located on shipboard. The main shaft, fitted with its thrust-bearing universal joints, clutch, brake, and pillow-blocks, transmits motion to a brass 4-bladed propeller of 19 feet 8¼ inches diameter and 28 feet 4⅝ inches pitch. Its blades are not cast solid on the hub, but secured to the same by means of large pivots entering sockets, and arranged to admit of adjustment. Steam is raised in the boilers every morning and let on between the hours of 12 and 3 p. m., furnishing thereby one of the most instructive public entertainments in the whole Exposition. From a careful examination of the accompanying drawings it is evident that this engine is virtually formed by bolting together three horizontal back-action engines of uniform dimensions. In describing the action of the steam and the relation of the parts, it will be convenient to consider the engine as working in the forward motion, and to designate its cylinders as middle, first, and second, calling that nearest the bow of the ship the first. The ends of the cylinders nearest the crank-shaft the fronts. The steam enters through pipes on the outer sides of the first and second cylinders to the steam cases surrounding the same, and being slightly superheated it yields up a portion of its heat to these bodies. Having circulated around them, it is admitted through two throttle valves to the central part of the middle cylinder's valve. It will be observed that each cylinder has a large D slide-valve, (Figs. 18 and 19,)

Fig. 18.

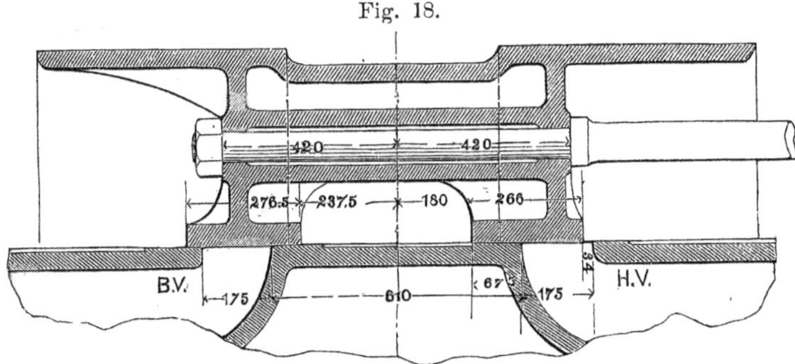

Valve for the first and second cylinders.

Fig. 19.

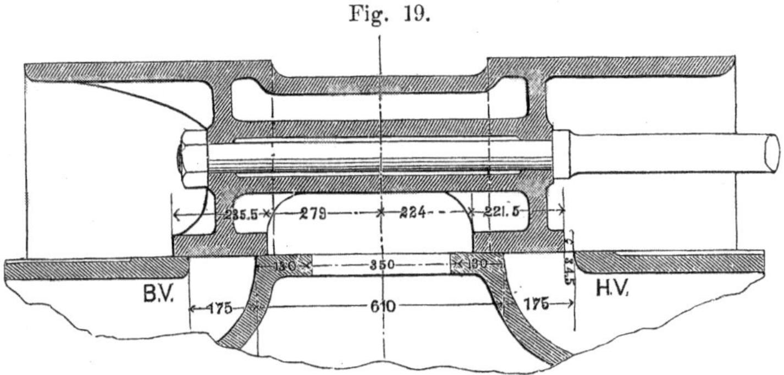

Valve of the middle cylinder.

whose central portion *always* performs the office of admitting and cutting off the steam; hence the lap occurs on the inside of the valve; its outer edges regulating the exhaust are line and line with the edges of the ports. From this receptacle it enters the middle cylinder, from which it is cut off after the piston has completed $\frac{9}{10}$ of its stroke. When the piston attains to within $\frac{1}{20}$ of a complete stroke, this steam is released and continues to exhaust throughout almost the entire return stroke. Instead of exhausting to the condenser it first enters cylinder No. 1, (when backing, No. 2,) where it continues expanding until the valve of No. 1 cuts off at the $\frac{3}{4}$ stroke mark. But previous to this occurrence the valve of cylinder No. 2 opens, and the expansion goes on simultaneously in both cylinders. This single exhaust is not permitted to complete the $\frac{3}{4}$ stroke of No. 2, but receives aid at its $\frac{5}{8}$ point on as far as the three-quarters point, from the steam, which then begins to exhaust from the opposite side of the middle cylinder. Finally, the steam effects its escape from Nos. 1 and 2 to the jet condensers placed opposite these cylinders; by having only two of these, ample intermediate space is left for attending to the cross-heads and their connections. For a clear understanding of how these changes are effected, the dimensions of the valves must be examined, the means by which they are moved, as well as the inherent peculiarities which arise from the irregularities of the crank's motion. On the first point the following table will be found of assistance:

Table of dimensions of parts of the engines of the Friedland.

Parts.	Extreme cylinders.	Middle cylinder.
	Inches.	*Inches.*
Diameter of cylinder	82 11-16	82 11-16
Stroke of piston	51⅛ also 51¼	51¼
Cut off of steam, front end	42⅛ also 42¼	47⅝
Cut off of steam, back end	37½ also 37⅝	44⅞
Average cut off	78-100	9-10
Travel of valve	19 11-16 also 19 23-32	19 11-16
Distance between ports	24 3-32	24 3-32
Width of ports	6 15-16	6 15-16
Inside lap, front end	3 9-16	1 13-16
Inside lap, back end	4	2⅜
Outside lap	0	0

60 revolutions, 512 feet piston speed.

The main shaft is forged with three cranks, to which the connecting-rods from the cross-heads are respectively attached; immediately over it lies the valve stem shaft with its three cranks, which receives motion

Fig. 20.

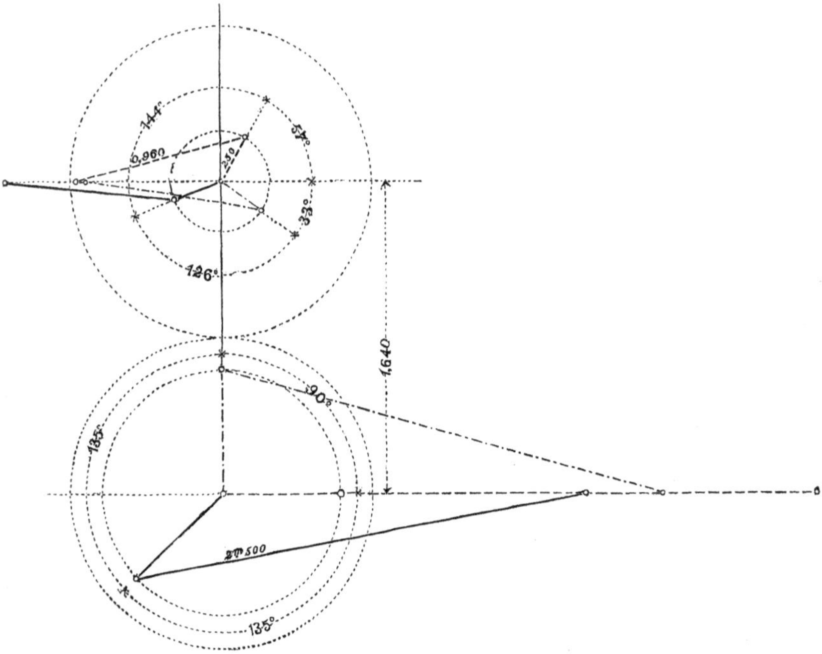

Diagram of positions of main and valve cranks.

from the former through two spur-wheels, whose pitch circles are each $64\frac{9}{16}$ inches diameter. The main cranks are not arranged for dividing the circle into parts of 120° each, but rather into portions of 135°, 90°, and 135°, (see Fig. 20,) in which 90° represents the arc between the cranks of cylinders 1 and 2, and 135° (equal to three-fourths of a semicircle) the arc between the crank of the middle cylinder and each of the adjoining ones. This is also true of the valve-cranks, whose divisions are 144°, 90°, and 126°; the latter arc includes the space between the middle cylinder and No. 1; 144° between the same and No. 2. If it were simply necessary for the engine to run in one direction, the valve stem shaft might be keyed to the spur-gear at its extremity, with a certain amount of angular advance. For running the engine in an opposite direction, this advance must be reversed. This is accomplished by allowing the spur-wheel to run loosely on the valve-shaft, making its action on the same subservient to that of a crank-pin, whose crank arm bears against the side of the wheel and is keyed firmly to the shaft. The range in arc of the pin equals 114°; its motion is regulated by thirteen teeth secured to the inner side of the slotted arc, which mesh with a pinion on the crank-pin. A small spur-wheel is cast on one side of the pinion, which works with a second pinion on the overhanging end of the valve stem shaft, gearing with it in the ratio of $2\frac{86}{100}$ to 1. It only requires $3\frac{3}{8}$ revolutions of the latter pinion for producing a traverse in arc of 114° by the crank-pin. The pinion is fastened to a hand-wheel $78\frac{3}{4}$ inches diameter; by rotating this $1\frac{11}{16}$ times, the engine is thrown from working full-gear forward into mid-gear, and by double the number of revolutions from full gear forward to full gear back. A small locking hand-wheel prevents any accidental rotation of the large one.

The following method is observed in adjusting the starting-crank arm: first bring the main and valve-crank arms of cylinder No. 2 to their front or back dead centers, then enter the large spur-gear in such a manner on the valve-shaft that the central radius of the slotted arc will also be on the same dead center; finally, having brought the starting-arm of the valve shaft to the same center, key it firmly to the shaft. The use of a crank motion for operating the valves occasions several irregularities in their action, which are in a measure mitigated by adjustments in lap and angularity. For instance, the motion of the valves being quicker over the back ports of the cylinder than over the front, their inside lap for the back end is made to exceed that for the latter by an amount given in the table. Also the cut-off, for like reason, finds the piston farther advanced on its backward stroke than it does on the forward. Again, the arc included between the valve-crank of the middle cylinder and that of No. 1, is increased from 135° (the amount between the cranks of their main-shaft) to 144°, a difference of 9°, for the purpose of bringing the lead, point of cut-off, and exhaust sufficiently late in the stroke to meet the requirements of the other cylinders. When running in full gear, the pistons have but little cushioning, so that any attempt to effect an earlier cut-off must be attended with an increase of the same. The accompanying analytical sketch of the valve motion (Fig. 20) will assist a closer examination of this system. In conclusion, it will be observed that the immediate advantages arising from its adoption are a perfectly uniform rotary motion of the propeller shaft, (without the introduction of counter weights,) an effective expansion in cylinders surrounded by superheated steam, great simplicity and interchangeability of the parts, as well as an immense strength due to the cellular character of their arrangement. It has already met with much favor in France, which fact, considered in the light of its many novelties, fairly entitles the subject to a most thoughtful consideration.[1]

[[1] Elaborate drawings of the engines of the Friedland were submitted by Commissioner Auchincloss, with his report, and are deposited in the library of the State Department.—EDITOR.]

PARIS UNIVERSAL EXPOSITION, 1867.

REPORTS OF THE UNITED STATES COMMISSIONERS.

CIVIL ENGINEERING

AND

PUBLIC WORKS.

BY

WILLIAM P. BLAKE,

COMMISSIONER OF THE STATE OF CALIFORNIA.

WASHINGTON:

GOVERNMENT PRINTING OFFICE.

1870.

CONTENTS.

EXTENT OF THE EXHIBITION IN CLASS SIXTY-FIVE.

MATERIALS FOR CONSTRUCTION.

NOTICE OF THE LAKE-WATER TUNNEL, CHICAGO.

THE SUEZ MARITIME CANAL.

MISCELLANEOUS NOTICES.

WITH TWO LITHOGRAPHIC PLATES SHOWING THE CONSTRUCTION OF THE CHICAGO LAKE-WATER TUNNEL.

CIVIL ENGINEERING AND PUBLIC WORKS.

I.—EXTENT OF THE EXHIBITION IN CLASS SIXTY-FIVE.

Class 65 of the Exposition included "Civil Engineering, Public Works, and Architecture." It is not proposed to give in these pages a full and comprehensive report upon this class. The design has been especially to notice the exhibition, by the Board of Public Works of Chicago, of the plans and details of the Chicago lake-water tunnel, of which no adequate description appears to have been given in the reports upon the Exposition. In addition, a few of the notes upon some of the other important and striking exhibitions in the same class have been written out and amplified by the aid of publications received since the close of the Exposition. Some departments of the subject have already been noticed in more or less of detail in the other reports of this series. For example, the increasing use of Coignet's agglomerated béton in construction, and the methods of paving in Paris with asphalt and with bitumen, have been carefully described in the reports made by Messrs. Leonard and Arthur Beckwith. Some observations upon the railways of France will be found in the general report, and some of the building materials are noticed in the report by Commissioner Bowen. An adequate notice of the extremely rich and varied display of materials used in the construction of great public works would alone form a volume far exceeding the limits allowed for this memorandum. Such materials include not only all varieties of stone, from granite to the ornamental marbles, but mortars, cements, artificial stones, bricks, and tiles, cast and wrought iron in various forms, zinc and other metals, wood, &c.

Very interesting and valuable reports have been made by the French and British commissions upon all these materials. One by Prof. Delesse will be found in Tome X of the Reports of the International Jury; one by Captain Ponsonby Cox, R. E., upon "Civil Engineering," in Vol. IV of the British Reports; and upon "Limes and Hydraulic Cements," by Lieutenant Colonel Scott, R. E., in the same volume. Roads and bridges, and internal navigation, foundations, and various special engineering operations have been elaborately reported upon by Baron E. Baude, of the International Jury.

EXHIBITION OF MODELS AND DRAWINGS BY FRANCE.

The most complete and comprehensive exhibition in this class was made by the minister of public works of France. It was unrivaled for its extent, interest, and value, and included models, on a large scale, of bridges, canals, forts, docks, light-houses, &c., and was accompanied by complete drawings and explanations. Some of the most striking of these objects were the model of the great arched bridge at St. Sauveur, the Napoleon bridge in the High Pyrenees, (scale $\frac{1}{25}$,) the foundations of Fort Chavagnac at Cherbourg, and the light-house de la Banche, with sections showing in detail the arrangement of the interior.

In regard to the excellence of the representations of civil engineering in the French section, and the general inadequacy of the exhibition from other countries, Captain Ponsonby Cox, R. E., observes as follows:

"Although there is no science which has given to the world such important practical results within the last few years as that of civil engineering, and though there is probably none which has made more real scientific progress, its recent progress and later results are far from being adequately represented in the Exposition of 1867.

"In the French section only is there a satisfactory exhibition in engineering proper; the other European nations, as well as the United States of America, are but slightly represented; our own country can hardly be said to be represented at all. This is much to be regretted, for undoubtedly a well-assorted collection of models or drawings of the most important engineering works scattered all over the world, which are due to the energy and skill displayed by English engineers within the last few years, would, if placed side by side with the magnificent collection of models and plans in the French section, have formed an exhibition most interesting and instructive, and would have added much to the available knowledge of the civil engineering of the world, and saved much of the labor thrown away in re-inventing. From this point of view the Paris Exposition cannot but be looked upon as a great opportunity lost. The public works of London alone might have supplied admirable examples in the great railway stations and river bridges recently constructed, as well as the works connected with the main drainage and the Thames embankment. The materials for a good display exist, no doubt, in the works of Great Britain and her colonies, but we do not possess, (nor does any other nation possess,) for tabulating these materials, such a machinery as France has in her establishment 'des Ponts et Chaussées,' her 'École des Mines,' 'des Arts et Métiers,' &c."

PROGRESS SINCE 1855.

Baron Baude, member of the committee of admission of Class 65, who prepared the introduction to the class catalogue, points out among the principal technical improvements realized since 1855: 1. The progress made in the trades of hydraulic lime, cements, artificial stones, potteries, slate, and asphalts, and in that of hammered metal applied to the preservation and decoration of roofs. 2. The increase in the use of metal structures, which are more and more appreciated every day. 3. The increase in the number of machines employed in working wood for joiners and other work. 4. The constantly increasing application of compressed air in places deep and difficult of access. 5. The ingenious methods of lifting heavy bridges, viaducts, and other metallic works. 6. The new system of movable dams. 7. The recently invented and powerful dredging apparatus. 8. The application of electricity to light-houses, and the new combinations made with a view to assist navigation, among which may be reckoned the creation of a system of coast semaphores.

PUBLIC WORKS OF SPAIN.

A very interesting exhibition of models of the principal public works of Spain was made by the Board of Direction of Public Works, and was accompanied by a memoir giving a short notice of each model and a general notice of the condition of the public works in Spain, and of the special laws and regulations under which they are executed[1]. The collection contained numerous models of light-houses, models of machines and wagons used in the construction of the port of Grao de Valencia; models of the port of Tarragona; of the jetties of the port of Corogne; of the Sima aqueduct upon the canal of Isabel II; and of various bridges, reservoirs, aqueducts, and machines used in the execution of extensive public works. It was also accompanied by six volumes of photographs of the most remarkable of the public works of Spain.

II.—MATERIALS FOR CONSTRUCTION.

GRANITES, PORPHYRIES, JASPERS, AND MARBLES.

Among the hard stones worked in France are the syenites, granites, and porphyries of the Vosges, the green melaphyre of Tournay, the granites and protogines of Mont Blanc. The jaspers of St. Gervais, near Mont Blanc, are attracting much attention for their beauty and novelty. The quantity is supposed to be inexhaustible, and blocks of large size are obtained. The rock is believed to result from the metamorphism of a bed of sandstone of the Triassic period.

It is banded and brecciform in structure, and presents a great variety of colors most capriciously mingled, the most conspicuous being blood-red, rose, and green. It is traversed by veins of white quartz. These beautiful jaspers were represented at the Exposition by two splendid columns at the entrance of the glass-house for the equatorial plants. Similar columns have been placed in the new opera house. The cost of the stone is 1,500 francs the cubic metre at the quarry, and 2,000 francs delivered in Paris, but it is supposed that when the quarry is fully opened the price will be reduced.

---

[1] Notice sur l'état des travaux publics en Espagne et sur la législation spéciale qui les régit. Traduit de l'Espagnol, Madrid, 1867.

Of marbles, France has a bountiful supply. They are obtained chiefly in the Vosges, the Alps, and Pyrenees, and from Boulogne and the Jura. Quarries at the last-named locality are regularly worked on a large scale and blocks are furnished at low prices.

The French section contained a great many beautiful marble columns designed for the new opera house. The marbles came from the quarries of Sarrancolin, (Hautes-Pyrenees,) St. Beat, (Haute-Garonne,) Félines, (Hérault,) St. Antonin, (Bouches-du Rhone,) Porcieux, (Var,) Jeumont, (Nord.)

According to the French customs returns, the exportation of French marble, which was valued at only 350,405 francs in 1855, constantly increased until the value had reached 1,140,279 francs in 1866. The importation of marble has also increased regularly during the same time, being valued at 1,038,271 francs in 1855, and at 2,357,115 francs in 1866. The disposition to use marble in construction is increasing in France.

The following figures show the prices in francs per cubic metre of the marbles most in use in France during 1867. These figures and the preceding relating to the marble industry of France are compiled from the report of Prof. Delesse:

Sarrancolin	1,012
Campan mélangé and Campan vert	1,232
Rosé clair	792
Griotte d'Italie	1,012
Griotte œil de perdrix	1,117
Languedoc	792
Brèche impériale	682
Vert de Maurin, (serpentine)	1,122
Brocatelle jaune, violette ou jaune fleurie	847
Sarrancolin de l'ouest	572
Henriette	627
Noir française	374

The display of marbles from Italy was peculiarly fine, remarkable alike for the beauty of the material and for the liberality and taste displayed in the selection of the specimens. They were in blocks a foot square and beautifully polished. The Institute Technico de Firenze also sent a splendid series of specimens of all varieties of the Italian building stones, among them a series of sixty polished blocks of serpentine of as many different shades and colors.

From Algeria there was a fine collection of some four hundred specimens, in cubes measuring six inches on a side, of the building stones of that country. These were collected by the "Service du genie militaire: des ponts et chaussées." The series contained a great variety of marbles, among them the beautiful light-colored "onyx marble," so-called, now much prized and used for interior decoration in France.

Belgium is extremely rich in marble of various colors, particularly the much esteemed black marbles. They are obtained in the provinces of Namur, Liege, and of Hainaut. Of the black marbles those of Denée and of Furnaux are much exported to France, Germany, and Italy. The fine black marble of Golzinnes is nearly all sent to Paris. The black marble from the quarries of Peruwelz and of Basècles (Hainaut) is very solid, and is exported in considerable quantities to all parts of Europe and to America.

There are ninety marble quarries in the province of Namur; they employ nearly eight hundred and six men, and the value of the annual production is estimated at eight hundred and sixty thousand francs. The quarries of Wellin yield nearly four hundred cubic metres of marble annually, of a value of forty thousand francs. It is estimated that not less than three million francs of capital is invested in the marble industry of the province of Namur alone.

But Belgium is rich in quarries of all kinds of building stones, not only marbles, but granite, paving stones, sandstone, slates, &c., as will be seen from the annexed tabular statement of the number of quarries and value of their products in the year 1864.[1]

Production of stone for the purposes of construction in Belgium, in 1864.

Provinces.	No. of quarries.	No. of workmen.	Value of the products.
			Francs.
Hainaut	463	10, 419	13, 445, 940
Namur	763	4, 020	4, 424, 897
Liege	280	2, 248	1, 868, 670
Brabant	139	1, 893	1, 933, 200
Luxembourg	106	1, 328	1, 085, 897
Limbourg	13	51	11, 875
Totals	1, 764	19, 959	22, 770, 479

The marbles of Algeria were well represented at the Exposition, particularly the "marble onyx" from quarries worked formerly by the Romans. It is beautifully veined in parallel layers like onyx, and appears to be of stalagmitic origin. It resembles the Mexican stalagmitic marble. Fine specimens of onyx marble were shown also in the Russian section.

From Scotland and from Cornwall there were several very finely wrought specimens of granite, and from Sweden a fine display of the porphyry of Elfdalen. In the Bavarian section there were two fine vases of a green dioritic porphyry.

The following table shows the weight per cubic metre of some of the various stones employed in the construction of the new Grand Opera House of Paris, and the pressure per square centimetre which each will sustain before crushing.

[1] From the Catalogue des produits industriels et des œuvres d'art, section Belgique.

Weight and strength of some of the varieties of stones used in the construction of the Grand Opera House.

Description of stone and locality.	Weight.	Crushing Weight.
Jasper of Mont Blanc, St. Gervais	2, 716	1, 839
Brown granitoid porphyry, Bazoches	2, 585	1, 487
Green porphyry, (melaphyre)	2, 855	1, 111
Red granitoid prophyry, Autun	2, 585	1, 080
Porphyroidal granite, St. Martin du Puy	2, 567	1, 077
Micaceous granite, Lormes	2, 694	1, 077
Red syenite, Servance	2, 654	901
Syenite, ("feuille-morte,") Servance	2, 683	867
Porphyroidal granite, Servance	2, 643	715
Marble, ("sanguin,") Sampans, Jura	2, 637	1, 076
Marble, (violacé)	2, 663	994
Pierre de Damparis, Jura	2, 683	898
Pierre de l'Echaillon, Commune de Rivière	2, 726	852
White Echaillon, St. Quentin	2, 529	781
Yellow Echaillon, Lignet	2, 686	777
Rose-colored Echaillon	2, 472	606
Pierre de Anstrude, Yonne	2, 261	365
Soft stone, Yonne	2, 161	369
Pierre de Ravières	2, 157	377
Grès bizarré, Lutzelbourg	2, 130	215

CEMENTS AND ARTIFICIAL STONES.

Cements were exhibited in great variety from France and Belgium, not only in the crude and commercial state, but worked up into various objects and molded into blocks of a form suited for testing by pressure and weighting.

One of the most interesting displays was made by the French Cement Company of Boulogne-sur-Mer, which received a gold medal. An apparatus for testing the strength of cements was included in their exhibition. Blocks of the hardened cement, about eight inches long and shaped like a stout letter **I**, were placed between strong iron clamps, and made to form a link in the chain by which a heavy platform was suspended. Upon this platform below, heavy weights were piled nearly to the limit of the strength of the slender neck of the cement block. One of these blocks, formed of four volumes of sand and one of cement, and one and a half inch square, sustained a strain of nine hundred kilogrammes. Another one, four inches square, composed of two volumes of sand and one volume of cement, sustained a weight of twelve hundred kilogrammes. The sand used in these experimental blocks was very coarse, nearly as large as beans or peas. Another method of showing the strength of their cement was by building a column of brick-work about six feet long, extended horizontally like an arm, and supported at one end only.

This cement is artificially prepared by mixing intimately and with great care 79½ per cent. of carbonate of lime, in powder, with 20½ of clay, and then burning at a high temperature. There are now many establishments in France, Prussia, Germany, Austria, and Russia, where enormous quantities of excellent cement are manufactured. In one of the establishments recently started in France, at Pouilly, the method consists in crushing together two kinds of argillaceous limestone from the Lias; one containing 43.5 per cent. of lime, the other a belemnitic limestone, which contains 48 per cent. of lime. The first gives the cement known as the Pouilly, and the intimate mixture of the two gives a cement with the composition of the Portland cement. An analysis of this cement gives the following result:

Lime	62. 00
Silica	23. 00
Alumina	8. 50
Oxide of iron	5. 50
Water and carbonic acid	1. 00
Sulphate of lime	traces.

M. Delesse gives the results of some recent analyses of Portland cement by Dr. Zuirek, of Berlin, as follows; three samples came from the principal works for the manufacture in England, and the fourth from the establishment of the Brothers Menkow, at Schwerin:

Analyses of four samples of Portland cement.

	Robins.		White Bros.		Knight, Bevans & Sturge.		Menkow.	
Silica	22. 74		22. 59		22. 30		24. 01	
Alumina	7. 74		6. 43		3. 31		5. 73	
Oxide of iron	3. 70		4. 03		9. 75		2. 39	
Lime	56. 68	92. 08	57. 87	92. 56	58. 17	95. 02	63. 77	97. 68
Magnesia	0. 57		0. 55		0. 91		0. 96	
Potash	0. 46		0. 74		0. 41		0. 49	
Soda	0. 19		0. 35		0. 17		0. 33	
Sulphate of lime	1. 66		2. 67		1. 17		0. 24	
Carbonate of lime	3. 50	7. 59	0. 84	6. 51	1. 34	5. 02	0. 67	2. 11
Insoluble residue	0. 50		0. 77		1. 06		0. 93	
Hygrometric moisture	1. 90		2. 23		1. 47		0. 27	

The Vicat cement is much more used in France now than formerly. It is manufactured on a large scale by Mr. Joseph Vicat, a graduate of the École Polytechnique, and the son of the celebrated engineer. He forms a paste with clay and slaked lime in powder. This is made into loaves, which soon set and harden so that they are not injured by the weather, and do not require housing or artificial drying, as is the case when unburned materials are used. These loaves are then burned. This is substantially the process invented by his father. M. Delesse observes of the qualities of this cement, that it is homogeneous, the elements being in perfect combination; the clay is changed into silicate, which is completely decomposed without residue in a dilute acid. The setting is slow and does not commence for several hours after the mixing as mortar. The weight of this cement pulverized, but not compacted by ramming, varies from thirteen to fourteen hundred kilogrammes to the cubic metre.

Some interesting applications of this cement were shown. It is used for making artificial breccias by mixing it with fragments of marble of various colors, molding it into the desired form, and then by grinding and polishing the surface a beautiful mosaic is produced. Blocks so made may be sawed into slabs and polished like marble. They are hard and non-absorbent of moisture, and are said to be suitable for exterior decoration.

Among the hydraulic limes, that of Theil, Ardèche, continues to hold its high rank. The limestone beds from which it is obtained are highly fossiliferous, and are over three hundred feet thick. Simple burning is all that is required to produce the cement. An establishment for its manufacture at Lafarge has thirty-four furnaces and produces three hundred and forty tons of sifted lime daily. The price is fifteen francs per ton, and it weighs seven hundred kilogrammes per cubic metre. It is particularly valuable for marine constructions, and can be wetted with either fresh or salt water. It was used for the formation of the artificial blocks sunk to form the breakwater piers at Port Said.

The agglomerated béton of Mr. Coignet was most fully represented at the Exposition, and was used in the construction of the reservoirs and for the foundations of the outer gallery. For a full description of this material, its preparation and uses, reference is made to the special report by Mr. Leonard F. Beckwith. Reference may also be made to the publication by M. Coignet[1] and by M. Claudel.[2]

OXYCHLORIDE OF MAGNESIUM CEMENT.

By mixing magnesia with oxychloride of magnesium a cement is formed analogous to that made with zinc oxide and the oxychloride of zinc. Both of these cements are the invention of Mr. Sorel. The hardness of the cement varies with the density of the chloride solution. An increased hardness is given by saturating the chloride of magnesium with chloride of barium or with sulphate of magnesia. The addition of one part of quicklime, or two parts of carbonate of magnesia, in one hundred of the chloride at 25° Baume, augments the hydraulic properties.

FERRUGINOUS CEMENT.

M. Alfred Chenot proposes to form a ferruginous cement by mixing iron in a state of extreme subdivision with sand. A cement so formed has long been known and used to a certain extent in the United States. M. Chenot proposes to manufacture the iron in a state of sponge and upon a large scale, by reducing iron ore, mixed with carbon, in a close furnace.

---

[1] Emploi des bétons agglomérés, etc., par François Coignet, Paris, 1862.

[2] Pratique de l'art de construire, Paris, 1863.

RANSOME ARTIFICIAL STONE.

This remarkable compound is adapted not only to interior, but, to exterior construction, and rivals the natural sandstones in hardness and durability.

It is formed by mixing sand with soluble silicate of soda, and, when molded into the desired form, treating the mass with a solution of chloride of calcium. A double decomposition takes place, hydro-silicate of lime is formed, and binds the grains of sand strongly together. For a full description of this artificial stone and its applications, reference is made to the report by Commissioner Barnard upon the Industrial Arts.

ZINC FOR CONSTRUCTION.

Zinc in its various forms of sheets, wire, nails, and stamped ornaments appears to be much more used in construction in Europe than in the United States. The display by the Vieille-Montagne Company, and the Silesian Zinc Company of Breslau, was very extensive. Some of the advantages claimed for this material over other materials for roofing are its lightness, tenacity, and cheapness compared with lead, slates, or tiles. The Vieille-Montagne Company claim that the inclination of zinc roofs need not exceed $0^m.1$ per metre, while slate requires $0^m.3$, and tile $0^m.45$.

For a building $12^m.50$ long by $6^m.80$, covered with No. 14 zinc, at 80 francs the 100 kilogrammes, the cost would be:

	Francs.
With zinc, 1,075.09 francs, or per square metre................	13.45
With slates, 1,245.97 francs, or per square metre..............	15.60
With tiles, 1,745.96 francs, or per square metre...............	21.80

For a shed $63^m.00$ long, $18^m.00$ wide, with an iron frame, and covered with No. 14 corrugated zinc, at 80 francs per 100 kilogrammes, the cost would be:

	Francs.
With zinc, 18,749 francs, or per square metre..................	16.50
With tiles, 22,767 francs, or per square metre.................	20.10

For temporary constructions they advertise sheets Nos. 10 and 11, which weigh $3^k.45$ to $4^k.15$ per square metre. It does not require painting, and the old sheets may be sold for thirty-five to forty per cent. of the cost of new.

The Silesian Zinc Company manufacture zinc sheets of all sizes and thicknesses, from two ounces per square foot upward. The large plate exhibited is seventeen feet long by fifty-four inches wide, and three-quarters of an inch thick. It could have been made twice as long as this, and with a total weight of forty-two hundred pounds, if room could have been procured for its installation. The corrugated sheets of large curve when laid lengthwise are made nine feet long and up to forty-one inches in breadth. These sheets are used chiefly for roofing large railway stations or other large buildings. The new exchange at Berlin is covered with zinc from this establishment. Annexed is a table of the sizes and weight of zinc sheets, in avoirdupois pounds and fractions, which may be serviceable to constructors and engineers.

Table of the weights of sheets of Silesian sheet zinc.

Gauge.	Weight per English square foot, about—			32″ × 84″				36″ × 84″				36″ × 96″				42″ × 96″				48″ × 96″			
				Weight per sheet, about—			Sheets per cwt., toll weight, or about 110¼ lbs. English.	Weight per sheet, about—			Sheets per cwt., toll weight, or about 110¼ lbs. English.	Weight per sheet, about—			Sheets per cwt., toll weight, or about 110¼ lbs. English.	Weight per sheet, about—			Sheets per cwt., toll weight, or about 110¼ lbs. English.	Weight per sheet, about—			Sheets per cwt., toll weight, or about 110¼ lbs. English.
	Pounds.	Ounces.	Drams.	Pounds.	Ounces.	Drams.		Pounds.	Ounces.	Drams.		Pounds.	Ounces.	Drams.		Pounds.	Ounces.	Drams.		Pounds.	Ounces.	Drams.	
3	......	3	15	4	9	8	24	5	2	13	21.3	......	......	......	......	......	......	......	......	......	......	......	......
4	......	4	13	5	10	......	19.6	6	4	13	17.5	7	3	4	15.3	......	......	......	......	......	......	......	......
5	......	5	12	6	11	9	16.4	7	8	13	14.6	8	9	13	12.8	......	......	......	......	......	......	......	......
6	......	6	11	7	13	1	14.1	8	12	......	12.6	10	......	6	11	11	11	10	9.4	13	7	2	8.2
7	......	7	12	9	......	9	12.2	10	3	5	10.8	11	9	11	9.5	13	9	12	8.1	15	8	7	7.1
8	......	8	14	10	6	6	10.6	11	9	11	9.5	13	4	8	8.3	15	8	7	7.1	17	12	8	6.2
9	......	10	5	11	15	11	9.9	13	9	12	8.1	15	8	7	7.1	18	1	2	6.1	20	12	13	5.3
10	......	11	14	13	12	8	8	15	8	7	7.1	17	12	8	6.2	20	12	13	5.3	23	15	7	4.6
11	......	13	9	15	12	......	7	17	12	8	6.2	20	6	10	5.4	23	15	7	4.6	26	14	3	4.1
12	......	15	8	18	1	2	6.1	20	6	10	5.4	23	7	4	4.7	26	14	3	4.1	30	9	15	3.6
13	1	1	12	20	12	13	5.3	23	7	4	4.7	26	14	3	4.1	31	7	15	3.5	35	8	15	3.1
14	1	4	5	23	7	4	4.7	26	14	3	4.1	30	9	15	3.6	35	8	15	3.1	40	13	4	2.7
15	1	7	1	26	14	3	4.1	30	9	15	3.6	34	7	3	3.2	40	13	4	2.7	45	14	15	2.4
16	1	10	11	31	7	15	3.5	35	8	15	3.1	39	5	15	2.8	45	14	15	2.4	52	7	14	2.1
17	1	14	8	35	8	15	3.1	39	5	15	2.8	45	14	15	2.4	52	7	14	2.1	61	3	14	1.8
18	2	2	2	39	5	15	2.8	44	1	8	2.5	50	1	12	2.2	61	3	14	1.8	68	14	6	1.6
19	2	6	13	45	14	15	2.4	50	1	12	2.2	58	......	5	1.9	68	14	6	1.6	78	11	14	1.4
20	2	10	11	50	1	12	2.2	55	1	14	2	64	13	9	1.7	73	7	14	1.5	84	12	12	1.3

MR. HEWITT ON THE USE OF STEEL FOR RAILS.

The manufacture of steel rails for railways has been discussed by Commissioner Hewitt in his report upon iron and steel, and some observations upon the form of rails will be found in the report by Commissioner Auchincloss. Since the publication of the report of Mr. Hewitt the writer has received from him the following letter, dated New York, October 20, 1869, giving the result of later investigations abroad:

"Having made a visit to Europe during the past summer, with Mr. John Fritz, manager of the Bethlehem Iron Works, at Bethlehem, Pennsylvania, for the purpose, mainly, of acquiring information in regard to the use of steel for rails, I do not think that I can render a more acceptable service to the railroad interests of the United States than by adding to my report a brief statement of the conclusions at which we arrived.

"First. It appears to be certain that on all roads doing a large business, and especially where heavy engines are run at a high speed, *steel* must be substituted for *iron*, on the *wearing surface* of the track. The steel may be either puddled, or made by the Siemens-Martin, Bessemer, or crucible process; but, whatever kind of steel may be employed, care must be taken that the steel be of good quality, and adapted to the purpose. This demands skill in the *manufacture* and care in the *inspection*. Unless the skill is used, and care exercised, there will soon be the same complaint in regard to the quality of steel as has existed in regard to the qual ty of iron.

"Second. For roads having a small traffic, iron rails are, as yet, more economical, provided light engines and moderate speed are employed. If proper care is used in the manufacture and inspection, and a price paid sufficient to cover the cost of good materials and workmanship, there is no more difficulty now than there was in former years in procuring iron rails of good quality. The real cause of the inferiority of modern rails appears to be due solely to the unwillingness of railroad managers to pay a price adequate to meet the actual cost of good iron and skillful work.

"Third. The question as to whether all steel rails, or iron rails with steel heads, should be used, is mainly one of first cost. There have been slight objections to steel-topped rails, when cast steel is used for the head, arising out of the liability of the steel to separate from the iron; but this objection is now removed, both in Europe and in this country, by the experience which has been gained at Dowlais, in Wales, and at Trenton, in New Jersey, and it is safe to affirm that steel and iron can be certainly united so as not to separate in the weld. The experience with the Booth rail, on the New York Central railroad, also goes to show that it is not necessary to weld the steel and the iron at all, leaving it merely a question of prime cost as to whether the heads shall be welded or not. As to all steel rails, whether made from Bessemer, Siemens-Martin, or crucible steel, the only objection appears to be in their liability to break in very cold weather, but the percentage of such accidents is very small; and, all things considered, it is difficult to decide whether this objection is of more weight than the possibility of a separation of the steel from the iron in the steel-topped rails. On the whole, we came to the conclusion that we would take either the *all-steel* or the *steel-topped* rails, properly made, giving the preference to the one which could be supplied at the lowest price per ton. In other words, we believe that the question of first cost should alone decide whether to use steel-topped rails or rails made entirely from steel, provided the quality of the materials used and the workmanship are equally good in both cases.

"The Siemens-Martin process has solved the only difficulty which existed in regard to steel rails when worn out, by working them over as the raw material for new rails. This process is now in operation at most of the leading works in Europe, and can be seen at work at Trenton, New Jersey, producing steel which welds perfectly to iron, and therefore admirably adapted for steel tops."

III.—LAKE TUNNEL AND WATER-WORKS, CHICAGO.

THE SUPPLY OF WATER TO CHICAGO.

The Board of Public Works of the city of Chicago sent elaborate drawings, upon a large scale, of the tunnel and accessory constructions which were then nearly completed, for the supply of the city with pure water.

The source of the supply is Lake Michigan, from which the water is pumped by steam-engines and distributed in pipes in the usual manner. During the year ending March 31, 1867, the quantity pumped was 3,168,760,609 gallons, being an increase of nearly 391,000,000 gallons over the quantity pumped during the previous year. This gives a daily average of 8,681,536 gallons. The quantity of coal consumed in pumping was 3,761$\frac{710}{2000}$ tons, and the expenses, including salaries and repairs, amounted to $44,452 14, or $14 03 per million of gallons.

Before the construction of the lake tunnel about to be described, this water was drawn from an inlet-basin, upon the margin of the lake. During the severity of winter quantities of ice accumulate across the entrance of this inlet-basin, forming a ridge or barrier, so as to cut off effectually the supply of water from the lake, and thus necessitating the exertions of gangs of men day and night to keep a passage open to the pump-well. This difficulty, and the constantly increasing numbers of small fish, and the fouling of the water along the shores by the sewage of the city, and deposits of small streams, led the citizens to the project of obtaining the water from a point so far out in the lake as to be beyond these local annoyances. But before the final adoption of the plan of a tunnel, to extend two miles under the bed of the lake, some five or more different methods of securing the pure water were more or less considered. These were—

1. The extension of the old inlet pipe a mile out into the lake, at an estimated cost of from $66,000 to $125,000 for the iron pipe alone.

2. A brick tunnel, six feet in diameter, and extending a mile out into the lake.

3. Removal of the pumping works to Winetka, about sixteen miles north of the city, and conducting the water to the city in pipes from a reservoir placed upon the high ground at Winetka.

4. Filter beds, at an estimated cost of $107,500.

5. A subsiding reservoir, at an estimated cost of $107,775.

THE LAKE TUNNEL.

The plan of tunneling two miles under the bed of the lake was proposed by E. S. Chesbrough, esq., the city engineer, and was executed under his superintendence. It is one of the most novel, successful, and economically executed engineering enterprises of the present time, and justifies a notice in considerable detail.

The notice which follows has been freely compiled from the information given in the annual reports of the Board of Public Works of the city of Chicago to the common council, and from the manuscript notes and explanations supplied by Mr. Chesbrough, at the request of the writer. The two lithographic plates, also, which illustrate the description, are engraved from photographic reductions of the large drawings which were displayed at the Exposition.

The plan of tunneling was adopted by the board of public works as early as 1863. During that summer examinations were made along the whole line of the contemplated work by boring, at short intervals, to the depth proposed for the tunnel, to ascertain the character of the material through which it would pass, and various observations were made to test the quality of the water at the proposed outer end and inlet for the tunnel, and to ascertain also the distance from the shore to which the water of the river reached after certain most marked discharges of the river into the lake. From the borings it was found that the material through which the tunnel would be built was uniformly clay, and apparently of a firm and even character; and the observations concerning the effect of the river on the lake showed that, even when most marked, no trace of its influence could be detected much more than a mile and a quarter from the shore. The information obtained on these and various other points satisfied the board that the tunnel would accomplish the results sought for, and that the work was entirely practicable. The necessary drawings and specifications were prepared as speedily as practicable, and advertisements were issued in New York and Boston, as well as in Chicago, inviting proposals for the doing of the work. The bids were received and opened September 9, 1863, most of the parties submitting proposals being present at the opening.

The following record describes particularly the bids received for constructing the tunnel complete:

Bids received for the lake tunnel September 9, 1863.

Name of bidder.	Lake tunnel complete.	Lake tunnel and land shaft alone, in case there should be two lake shafts.	Lake tunnel and land shaft alone, in case there should be three lake shafts.	Lake tunnel and land shaft alone, in case there should be four lake shafts.
James Andrews, Pittsburg, Pennsylvania	$239, 548	$151, 987	$148, 000	$144, 000
James J. Dull and James Gowen, Harrisburg, Pennsylvania	315, 139	....	....	....
Stephen C. Walker, Asa D. Wood, and F. W. Robinson, New York	*315, 000	....	....	....
Thomas Williams, John McBean, A. S. Brown, and George Neilson, Chicago	†490, 000	....	....	....
Hervey Nash, Chicago	‡40	....	....	....
D. L. DeGolyer, Chicago	§620, 000	410, 000	400, 000	¶380, 000
William Baldwin, New York	‖1, 056, 000	....	....	....

* "Meaning to include but one intermediate lake shaft. This proposal is based upon the supposition that the material to be excavated is firm, and such that the tunnel can be made and the masonry built without the use of permanent bracing. But if in the prosecution of the work, to secure its safety, permanent bracing should be required, the attendant increased expenses shall be paid by the city. The chief engineer to decide the amount."

† "For all the work except the iron cylinders for shafts. In case sand or gravel veins occur, to be paid for extra. This sum includes four cribs."

‡ Per lineal foot.

§ "I run the risk of all loose earth, sand, or gravel."

‖ "$100 per lineal foot, if material is 'stiff blue clay soil.' If otherwise, extra pay and extra time will be required."

¶ "360,000?"

The bid of Messrs. Dull and Gowen, of Harrisburg, Pennsylvania, being unconditional, and for the whole work, it was accepted as the lowest and best bid, and the contract, which will be found embodied in this notice beyond, was drawn up. Subsequently to the execution of the contract the board decided to change the manner of constructing the land shaft, which was originally designed to be wholly of brick. This change consisted in substituting three cast-iron cylinders, each ten feet long, essentially like the iron cylinders proposed for the outer lake shaft, in place of the brick-work of the upper thirty feet of the shaft. This was done to facilitate the sinking of the shaft through the bed of quicksand overlying the clay, the distance through the quicksand to the clay being about twenty-four feet.

In place of a description in detail of the construction of the tunnel, the contract and specifications are given in full, particularly as the work is minutely described, and as the contract shows not only what was at first required of the contractors, but, together with the notes and explanations, shows also the changes which it was found desirable to make during the progress of the work.

LAKE TUNNEL CONTRACT.

LOCATION AND GENERAL DESCRIPTION.—The tunnel is to commence at such point as may be selected by the board of public works, on the lot now occupied by the pumping works of the city of Chicago, at the east end of Chicago avenue, and on the shore of Lake Michigan; and to extend two miles out under the lake, in a straight line, at right angles to the general direction of the shore.

The bottom of the inside surface of the east end of the tunnel shall be sixty-six feet below the ordinary level of the lake, or sixty-four feet below what is usually known as "City Datum;" and the bottom surface shall descend uniformly at the rate of two feet per mile to the west end of the tunnel.

There are to be one land and two to four lake shafts; the land shaft at the west end, one lake shaft at the east end, and the remaining lake shaft or shafts at such intermediate points as shall be determined upon by said board, when the proper time for locating them shall arrive. The lake shafts are to consist of cast iron cylinders, and to be protected by hollow pentagonal cribs.[1]

The tunnel is to be very nearly circular in form, and to have an interior width of five feet, and height of five feet and two inches.

CRIBS.—It has been proposed to construct four cribs, on the supposition that this number might be required to complete the tunnel in two years, but if, after commencing the work, it shall be found in time that one or more of them may be omitted, such omission shall be made; and for this reason but two cribs[2] shall be commenced before the probable rate of progress in the tunnel, from the land shaft, shall have been satisfactorily ascertained.

DESCRIPTION.—The cribs are to be five-sided, each outer side to be fifty-eight feet long. There is to be a central space in each crib, in form similar to the outside, leaving the thickness between the central space and outside of the crib twenty-five feet. The interior and exterior sides of the cribs are to be perpendicular from their bottoms to their tops, which are to be five feet above the ordinary surface of the lake; hence the outermost crib is to be forty feet high. The height of the others will depend upon their location, which will be determined during the progress of the work.

The outer crib is to have three openings through its sides, one opening through each of the western and southern sides; each opening to be five feet high and four feet wide, and to be connected with the top of the crib by a well four feet square. The most northern opening is to have its bottom five feet above the bottom of the crib, the middle one eleven feet higher, and the southern one eleven feet higher than the middle. Each opening is to be furnished with an iron paddle gate, to be worked by means of an iron rod, from the top of the crib, as shown on plans.

[1] Only one lake shaft and one crib were constructed.

[2] Only one crib, the outer one, was found necessary.

Each crib is to be provided with two gates,[1] each two feet high, and one and a half foot wide, placed five feet above the bottom of the crib, and against the wall of the inside space. These gates to be used for regulating the sinking of the cribs to their places, and worked by rods from the top of the crib, as shown on plans. Wrought-iron gratings to protect these gates must be provided, as shown on these plans.

MODE OF CONSTRUCTION.—The bottom of each crib shall be formed by an outer, inner, and middle line of twelve-inch square white pine timber, which shall be connected with cross-timbers of the same size, and with twelve-by-three-inch joists placed two feet apart from center to center, and the under side of the whole, except the central space of the crib, sheathed over with two-inch pine plank, fastened on by six-inch spikes, driven through each plank in every timber and joist, as shown on plan.[2] All the timbers and cross-timbers are to be connected by dovetail joints the full width of each timber, and of equal depth in each, the dovetail being one inch deeper at its end than at its shoulder. On the outer, inner, and middle lines of timber, and on the angle pieces of the outer and middle lines, solid walls of twelve-inch square timber are to be built up to a height of forty feet above the bottom for the outer crib, and to a height of five feet above ordinary water-mark for the other cribs. The middle wall extends solid from outside to outside of the crib; the inner wall only around the inner space. The angle timbers are eleven and a half feet long from tip to tip. Between the outer and middle walls there are two lines of cross-timbers on each side of the crib, and between the middle and inner walls three lines.[3] The cross-timbers are twelve inches square, placed twelve inches apart above each other, and extend through each wall. All of the timber and lumber, except the upper twelve feet in each outside wall, is to be of sound white pine. The upper twelve feet of the outer wall to be of sound white oak, free from sap, or any imperfections tending to hasten decay. All of the joints of the timbers at the angles of the outer and inner walls, at the ends of the middle walls, and at the ends of the cross-timbers, are to be dovetailed like those described for the bottom course of timbers in the crib, [at the corners.] Where the timbers of the middle wall cross each other, they are to be notched half and half. Whenever the ends of timbers butt against each other in the outer and inner walls, they must do so at the center of the end of some cross-timber, where the dovetailed end can be made to lap over the butt joint. On the bottoms and sides of the three openings through the outer crib, twelve-inch square timbers touching each other are to be run entirely through the ends; and across the

---

[1] This was afterward changed, and eight smaller and circular gates were constructed so as to regulate the flow of the water into eight water-tight compartments, which occupy the interior of the crib.

[2] Changed in construction to twelve-inch timbers.

[3] In construction, these timbers were placed so that each piece extended from the outer through the middle to the inner wall.

top of the openings six-inch planks are to be spiked, fitting close to each other. The walls from each opening to the top of the crib are to be formed of six-inch planks placed horizontally, and notched into the crib timbers wherever they can be.

The timbers in the outer and middle walls of each crib are to be fastened to each other by $1\frac{5}{16}$-inch square wrought-iron bolts thirty inches long, with ragged edges, and driven into the timber at an angle twelve degrees from a perpendicular, and inclining alternately toward each other. [The ragging was omitted.] The timbers of the inner wall are to be fastened in a similar manner to those of the outer and middle, except that the bolts are to be but one inch square.

Each outer angle of the crib is to be protected by a covering of wrought iron one inch thick, extending two feet each way from the corner, and from the top of the crib downward ten feet. These angle irons are to be fastened on by round wrought-iron one-and-a-half-inch bolts, one through every timber, on each side of the corner. The bolts are to be alternately long and short, the long being fastened through the middle timbers of the crib, and the short through the outer timbers, as shown on plans. The long bolts are to be used also in the lower part of the crib, from the bottom to the angle iron, in every other timber.[1]

The spaces between the joists at the bottom of the crib are to be filled with gravel or broken stone flush with the tops of the joists. The joists are to be planked over with two-inch pine, fastened down with six-inch spikes.[2]

There are to be twenty-five pair of one-inch round wrought-iron rods to connect saddles placed under bottom timbers and over top ones, as shown on plans. The forms and mode of placing the saddles and connecting the rods with them and with each other are shown on plans. [These were not put in.]

The whole of the joints on the bottom of the crib, around the outside and central space of the crib from its bottom to within four feet of the top, and the joints around the inside of the three openings and their wells, are to be thoroughly calked with oakum and paid with tar.[3]

Each crib shall, immediately after being towed to its proper position, be secured by one-and-a-half-inch iron cables to five Mitchell's mooring screws, forced ten feet into the clay at the bottom of the lake. The dimensions and form of these screws can be seen on plans.

Each crib is to be filled with sound rubble stone, from its bottom to its top, as soon after being moored as practicable.

---

[1] On each side of each angle, from the bottom to the top of the crib, and in place of the sheeting, a piece of oak twelve by fourteen inches was put in the line of the long bolts. It was cut down to three inches under the angle irons. A corresponding piece of oak, three inches wide all the way, was put at the other ends of the bolts on the middle wall.

[2] This was all made of twelve-inch timber.

[3] Every space from the bottom to the top of the crib, including the middle wall, was calked.

The angles of each crib shall be placed exactly in such positions as the board of public works may direct.

THE LAND SHAFT.—This will be located near and in the rear of the present pumping works of this city. From the surface of the ground to a depth of fifteen feet below the level of the lake, the shaft is to be twelve feet in diameter; and then it is to be contracted by a sloping offset of three feet all around to six feet diameter, to five feet below the bottom of the invert of the tunnel, a distance of sixty feet.[1]

The whole of the shaft is to be lined with brick masonry twelve inches thick, where the shaft is twelve feet in diameter, and eight inches thick, where it is six feet in diameter, and on the invert at its bottom. The masonry of the offset is to be twelve inches thick.

The masonry is to be formed of hard-burned, clear-ringing, and well-formed bricks, entirely free from lime, not less than eight inches long, two and a quarter inches thick, and four inches wide, to be laid upright in cement mortar, and in rings or shells four inches thick. The courses must be horizontal, the inside surface of the shaft must be true and cylindrical, and the joints between the bricks not over a quarter of an inch on the inside of each ring.

The cement mortar is to be equal to the best of Clark's La Salle, and mixed with one measure of clean sharp sand to one of cement, and used as soon as possible after being mixed.

The joints between the rings must be not less than half an inch, and all the joints in the masonry must be perfectly filled with mortar at the time the masonry is laid.

Where the natural soil around the shaft is sand or loose material, there is to be not less than twelve inches of thoroughly puddled clay on the outside of the masonry.[2]

Whatever timber and lumber may be necessary to support the earth around the shaft, before the masonry can be built, must be furnished and put in by the contractor.

The pumping, and all labor and machinery connected therewith, must be done and furnished by the contractor.

INLET CYLINDER FOR OUTER LAKE SHAFT.—To be nine feet in diameter inside, and two and a quarter inches thick. To be made in sections of about nine feet in length, so that seven sections will make up the total length of the cylinder, or sixty-four feet. The flanges to be five and five-eighths inches wide by two and a quarter inches thick, and to be faced in the lathe true and at right angles to the center line of the cylinder. Each flange to have a small annular groove turned into the face, to receive the putty to be used in making the joint, as shown on the drawing. Flanges to be drilled for bolts one and a half inch

---

1 The shaft was not executed in this way. Iron cylinders, three in number, and extending to a depth of thirty feet, were substituted. These were nine feet in diameter and one and a half inch thick. The shaft below was made eight feet clear diameter and twelve inches thick.

2 All spaces were filled with either concrete or brick work in cement.

in diameter and about seven inches between centers. The lower section to be turned a taper of one-sixteenth of an inch, in nine inches from the end on the outside. The balance of the section to be accurately and truly turned parallel the entire length above the taper.

The second and third sections, and, if required, the fourth section, from the bottom to be accurately and smoothly turned,[1] each section of a diameter slightly in excess of the one next below it, say the sixty-fourth part of an inch, and should there be any difference in the diameter of opposite ends of the same section, then the largest end to be connected uppermost.

The section next below the top one is to be provided with openings for inlet gates, plans and specifications for which will be given to the contractor whenever necessary after one month from the letting of the work, and all additional expense to the contractor in making such opening will be paid for as extra.

INTERMEDIATE CYLINDERS FOR LAKE SHAFTS.—To be one to three in number, to be nine feet in diameter inside, and one and five-eighths inch thick. To be made in sections of about nine feet in length, so that seven sections will make up the total length of cylinder, whether sixty-five, sixty-six, or sixty-seven feet. The flanges to be five inches wide by one and three-quarter inch thick, and faced as specified for the "inlet cylinder." Flanges to be drilled for bolts one and a half inch in diameter, and about seven inches between centers. Three or four of the lower sections to be turned on the outside as may be required, and as specified for the "inlet cylinder." The sections to be stiffened by two intermediate internal flanges two and three-eighths inches wide by one and three-quarter inch thick. At the top of the third or fourth section from the bottom, as may be required, the flange to have a double width to receive a bonnet or head for closing and disconnecting the cylinder at that joint, as delineated on the drawing.

The iron employed in the construction of the cylinders to be of good quality. The castings to be sound and free from sand holes or other defects.

Bolts for connecting the cylinders to be made of the best wrought iron, one and a half inch in diameter, with hexagonal heads and nuts.

Joints between cylinder section flanges to be made air-tight with thin red lead putty. All necessary work, materials, machinery, and tools for completing and putting in place the cribs and cylinders to be done and furnished by the contractor.[2]

THE TUNNEL PROPER.—The clear width of the tunnel is to be five feet, and the clear height five feet and two inches, the top and bottom arches to be semi-circles. The tunnel is to be lined with brick masonry

---

[1] Only the lowest section was turned, the castings proving sufficiently smooth for the others without turning.

[2] The intermediate cylinders and shafts thus provided for were not found necessary and were not put in.

eight inches thick, in two rings or shells, the bricks to be laid lengthwise of the tunnel with toothing joints. The mortar, character of materials, and workmanship are to be like those described for the land shaft.

The excavation for the tunnel, when through sufficiently firm clay, shall conform exactly to the outside of the masonry on the bottom and sides. On top, just enough of excavation above the masonry will be allowed, to give room to turn and key the upper arch properly.[1] Sections of not over two feet of the upper arch are to be built at a time, and immediately after each section is keyed, the space above it shall be filled with earth, which shall be put into the space in small quantities at a time, and thoroughly rammed until it becomes as solid as the natural soil above.

Should a soil be met with in any part of the tunnel requiring the sides, bottom, and top to be planked and braced before the masonry can be built, filling in, carefully and thoroughly done, shall be put in between the masonry and the boarding, in or between the masonry and sides of the excavation, as is specified for the upper arch in a firm soil. The material for this filling may be dry sand or puddled clay.[2]

All timber and lumber necessary for bracing and supporting the sides of the tunnel and shafts, previous to the completion of the masonry, must be furnished and put in place by the contractor.

The contractor must furnish and put in place all necessary air-pipes and apparatus for ventilating the tunnel, all pumps, steam-engines, hoisting apparatus and fixtures for the same, all sheds and shelters for the protection of workmen and materials on the cribs, and all necessary tracks, trucks, and other necessary implements for machinery for removing excavated material out of, and building materials into, the tunnel.

The contractor must also remove all excavated material taken out of each shaft to such points as shall be designated by the board of public works, provided said points shall not exceed three hundred feet from any shaft, and must provide all necessary tug-boats, scows, and other means of transportation, and implements required for such removal.

GENERAL SPECIFICATIONS.—The contractor shall furnish and maintain such lights as may be necessary to avoid danger to navigation; and in case of failure to do so, shall be liable for all damages the city may have to pay on account of such failure.

All materials, of whatever kind, to be used in the work, are to be inspected by the board of public works; and all unsuitable materials are to be immediately removed from the work by the contractor.

The contractor shall discharge from his employment, when directed by the board of public works, all unfaithful and incompetent workmen.

The board of public works must be permitted to remove such por-

---

1 In executing this part of the work, the masons soon learned to put in the masonry in clay ground without removing any more earth than was necessary for the regular arch.

2 All the filling about the masonry of the tunnel was made with brick and cement.

tions of the work as they may, from time to time, think necessary for the discovery of improper materials or workmanship; and the contractor shall restore such work at his own expense, in case it shall have been done improperly; and at the expense of said board if done in a proper manner.

Any work, materials, machinery, or tools necessary for the completion of the tunnel, cribs or shafts, omitted in the plan and specifications, shall be done or furnished by the contractor, and paid for as extra work, at such valuation as the board of public works may make. This section is not to apply to the completion of the work as specified, but only to extra work, and no tools and machinery to be paid for unless ordered by the board for extra work.

The contractor shall furnish men and stakes sufficient to enable the engineer in charge of the work to give the necessary lines and levels to construct the work by.

The contractor must deliver to the board of public works, on or before the first day of each month, a written statement of the amount of extra work done and extra materials furnished during the previous month.

The contractor will be required to keep the work in perfect repair for twelve months after the same shall have been faithfully completed to the satisfaction of the board of public works.

Monthly estimates will be made by the board of public works of the value of work actually done and in its permanent place; and on or about the sixth day of each month seventy-five per cent. of the estimated value of the work done the previous month will be paid the contractor; the remaining twenty-five per cent. being reserved as security for the faithful completion of the whole work.[1]

STATEMENT OF QUANTITIES OF MATERIAL IN THE OUTERMOST CRIB.[2]—38,814 cubic feet of white pine timber; 3,500 cubic feet of white oak timber; 20,251 feet, board measure, of white pine two-inch plank; 1,700 wrought-iron $1\frac{5}{16}$-inch square bolts, 30 inches long; 120 wrought-iron 1-inch square bolts, 30 inches long; 200 wrought-iron $1\frac{1}{2}$-inch round bolts, $13\frac{1}{2}$ feet long; 50 wrought-iron $1\frac{1}{2}$-inch round bolts, 18 inches long; 200 square feet of 1-inch angle iron; 6,025 cubic yards of stone filling; besides 6-inch spikes, and paddle and other gates.

EXTRACT FROM THE AGREEMENT TO CONSTRUCT TUNNEL.

The agreement for the construction of the tunnel was executed on the 20th of October, 1863, the contractors undertaking to perform all of the work under the immediate direction and superintendence of the board

---

[1] During the progress of the work this provision was changed by vote of the city council, and eighty-five per cent. was paid upon monthly estimates for all work done, including the crib before it was launched.

[2] The quantities of these materials were considerably increased in consequence of the changes made during the progress of the work.

of public works of the city of Chicago, and to their entire satisfaction, approval, and acceptance.

The city of Chicago covenanted and agreed, "in consideration of the covenants and agreements in this contract specified to be kept and performed by the said party of the first part, to pay to said party of the first part, when this contract shall be wholly carried out and completed, the sum of three hundred and fifteen thousand one hundred and thirty-nine dollars, ($315,139,) and for each foot of height that any one of the cribs for the protection of the lake shafts shall be built above the height stated in said plans and specifications, the sum of eight hundred and fifty dollars, ($850,) and for each pound of addition made to the cast-iron cylinders for the like shafts above that stated in the plans and specifications, the sum of twelve (12) cents. It is also agreed, that during the progress of the work monthly estimates will be made by the board of public works of the value of the work done and in its permanent place, and that seventy-five (75) per cent. [changed, as already noted, by vote of city council from seventy-five to eighty-five per cent.] of the amount of such estimates will be paid to the said contractors as they shall be issued, and that the remaining twenty-five (25) per cent. shall be reserved as security for the faithful completion of the whole work, and shall be paid when this contract is completed, and the work accepted by the said board. It is further mutually agreed by the parties hereto, that nothing hereinbefore contained shall be so construed as to hold the said parties of the first part responsible for any accident or injury that may happen to either of the cribs or lake shafts mentioned in said specifications, after the same shall have been duly fixed and secured in their place, in consequence of any defect or insufficiency inherent in the original plan or design for the same, and not attributable in any degree to any defect or imperfection in the execution of said work by the said parties of the first part."

THE PROGRESS OF THE WORK.

Ground was first broken for the work on the 17th of March, 1864, when the construction formally commenced. The iron cylinders, which had been ordered to protect the land shaft against the influx of the very wet sand and gravel known to overlie the clay for about twenty feet, did not arrive till after two months of detention. The progress at first was much slower than was anticipated, owing to the troublesome nature of the sand and gravel; but the hard clay was reached about the first of April, and the iron cylinders had been sunk through the sand. No serious difficulty afterward arose in the prosecution of the land shaft and shore end of the work. At the end of the year the tunnel had been finished from the land shaft out under the lake 2,139 feet, and July 10, 1865, it had reached 3,023 feet, and was extending outward at the rate of about twelve feet per day. August 25 it had reached a distance of 3,505 feet, and the masonry was about twenty-five feet behind the face.

In some places an average rate of progress of fourteen feet per day was made for a week at a time, but for the whole period this average was considerably less, owing to occasional interruptions from the breakage of machinery, strikes among the workmen, the meeting with and occasional explosion of gas, and other causes. The average for the year ending April 1, 1865, was thereby reduced to nine and one-tenth feet per day. The character of the ground was nearly uniform.

The back filling between the regular brick-work and the irregular surface of the excavation of the tunnel, which was originally intended to be of well packed earth, was made of masonry, because it was found very difficult to get the puddled clay used faithfully packed into the spaces. The ground generally was so uniform and favorable for excavation that the tunnel was cut with great precision, and an average of one inch thickness of cement mortar between the bricks and the clay walls was all that was required.

A tendency in the clay to swell was found at an early stage of the work, but the masonry resisted it perfectly. It, however, gave some trouble in the grading, for one portion would swell more than another. In order to facilitate the work, chambers and turn-tables were placed at intervals of one thousand feet. These were used for the storage of materials and for mixing cement, and for turn-out tracks for the cars. As the work progressed iron rails were substituted for wood in the tramways, and small mules were used to draw the cars instead of men. By all these facilities the economy and rapidity of execution of the work were increased.

VENTILATION.

The ventilation of the first half mile of the tunnel was effected by drawing the vitiated air out through a pipe connected with the chimney of the boiler furnace, but toward the last this method was found to be so ineffectual and unreliable that it was abandoned, and one of Alden's blowers was used with complete success.

PLACING THE CRIB.

The crib through which access was to be obtained to the bed of the lake for the excavation of the tunnel from that point shoreward, simultaneously with the progress of the shore end, was not placed in position before the 25th of July, 1865, when it was launched and towed out to its place in the lake. The work of sinking was delayed somewhat in consequence of defective arrangement of and accidents to the anchors. Just as it reached the bottom a storm came on, and as the crib was not sufficiently loaded to rest firmly upon the bottom, it was filled with water by means of a wrecking pump. After the storm had subsided, it was found that the crib had moved thirteen feet north of its true position, and that it had become firmly imbedded in the clay of the bottom of the lake. It was therefore deemed best not to disturb it, as the variation from the exact position was of no practical importance, and it was immediately filled with stone. It was afterward built up three feet higher, so as to be secure from the wash of the waves, and it was covered in by a building to serve for the protection of the workmen, the materials, and machinery. The seven iron cylinders making the iron part of the shaft, and sixty-three feet of it in height, were connected together, one by one, and lowered inside of the crib to the bottom of the lake, within the thirty feet wide open space in the center of the crib. The gates or valves, by which the water of the lake is admitted to these cylinders, are placed near to their upper end.

After the cylinders had been placed in the right position, they were forced downward into the clay some twenty-five feet, the water being wholly excluded. The masonry was then commenced. In the mean time the engine for hoisting and the necessary machinery were made ready, and the bricks, cement, and other materials and supplies were collected and stored in the building upon the top of the crib. For all these preparations a much longer time was consumed than was anticipated, and the work upon the tunnel at that end did not commence before the 1st of January, 1866, after which the work steadily progressed.

The material, through which this outer portion of the tunnel was excavated, was found to be similar to that at the in-shore end—a stiff, hard clay.

By August 15, 1866, the in-shore part of the tunnel had progressed 7,160 feet, and the outer or lake end 1,725 feet, leaving of the two miles, or 10,560 feet, only 1,675 feet to be excavated. This shows a progress at the land-shaft end of 5,135 feet since April 1, 1865, which, for a period of 427 working days, gives an average of twelve feet per day, including all stoppages of whatever nature. Frequently the rate was fifteen feet a day for a week at a time.

In commencing the lake-shaft end of the tunnel, it was excavated for about sixty feet to the eastward, in order to facilitate the alignment. The ground at the lake end was found to be very similar to that at the other, but more liable to cave in, and consequently rather more difficult and expensive to work.

COMPLETION OF THE TUNNEL.

On the 24th of November, 1866, the two parties which had been slowly nearing each other in their work of drifting and lining the tunnel, the one working from the shore shaft outward and the other from the lake shaft inward, were separated from each other by a thin wall of clay about two feet thick, 8,277 feet from the shore shaft and 2,290 feet from the lake shaft. On the 30th this barrier was removed, and the engineers passed through from one end of the tunnel to the other. When the work of the two parties was brought together, the two portions of the tunnel were found to coincide almost exactly both in line and level, the alignment varying but seven and three-fourths inches and the levels agreeing.

The masonry uniting the two parts of the tunnel was formally closed up December 6, 1866, by his honor Mayor Rice, and the citizens were permitted to inspect the work. There then remained the side chambers to be filled up and the entire tunnel to be cleaned out. This was all carefully done, and the water was first let into the tunnel from the lake on the 8th day of March, 1867, and on the 11th it was filled to the level of the lake. The water was then pumped out sufficiently to allow a boat to pass upward of half way from the crib to the land shaft. Not a brick was found to be displaced, and it could not be perceived that the slightest fracture had anywhere taken place by the pressure to which the masonry had been subjected. As it was very desirable to use the tunnel as soon as possible it was thought unnecessary to pump out the whole of the water, and the tunnel was again filled. The formal and public opening took place on the 25th of the month, and since that time Chicago has been free from the annoyances of impure and fetid water.

It is an interesting fact that this tunnel, like the Croton and Cochituate aqueducts, is found to deliver more water under a given head than the formula in common use calls for.

The following summary shows the number of days occupied in constructing the tunnel, the amount of excavation, and the quantity of materials, used:

Time and materials required in the construction.

Description.	Days occupied.	Excavation.	Brick work	Bricks.	Cement.
		L. feet.	*L. feet.*	*No.*	*Barrels.*
Extension west	37	144	144	43, 193	259¼
Land shaft	31	....	....	32, 000	114
Lake tunnel (center to center of shafts)	955	10, 567	10, 567	2, 393, 224	9, 582¼
Lake shaft	17	....	....	10, 207	31
Extension east	19	65	65	20, 880	106
Eight chambers	35	....	....	51, 250	246½
Grand totals	1, 094	10, 776	10, 776	2, 550, 754	10, 339

The total cost of the lake tunnel at the time of its completion amounted to $457,844 95.

This amount is made up of the following items:

Engineering and superintendence	$28, 744 02
Printing and advertising	375 13
Miscellaneous	6, 250 03
Labor	2, 096 20
Lumber	1, 142 72
Piles	1, 258 29
Hardware	53 85
Castings	597 55

Lake shaft gates and chambers	$12, 629 86
Dredging for crib	1, 500 00
Tugs for board and employés	6, 718 17
Discount on bonds	14, 685 35
Opening celebration	979 18
Dull and Gowen, (contractors)	380, 784 60
Total	457, 844 95

It appears from the statements and books of the contractors that the actual cost of their work, deducting profits, was not more than $330,500. The crib and outer shaft cost $117,500; the land shaft cost $12,000; the west extension and connection with the gate-chamber, no part of the original contract, cost $6,000, leaving $195,000 as the cost of the tunnel proper. This being 10,567 feet long made the cost to the contractors $18 45 per lineal foot. The usual prices paid for labor were, for laborers, $2; masons, $5; engine men, $3 per day; for brick, $14 per thousand; for cement, $2 75 per cask of 300 pounds.

ENGINE HOUSE AND PUMPING ENGINES.

Upon Plate I, which is somewhat crowded with figures, will be found plans, sections, and elevations of the tunnel, and particularly of the pumping works and engines. The upper figure shows, upon a small scale, a general plan of the whole line of the tunnel, with a plan of the pumping works and the old inlet-basin from which the water was formerly pumped at one end, and the crib or lake shaft at the other end.

In the right-hand lower corner of the plate will be found a section of the shore end of the tunnel, with the connecting shafts, pump well, pumping engine, the water tower, and connecting pipes. This section is along the line C D of the plan above it, which shows the general arrangement of the works and buildings, the direction of the shore inlet and of the end of the tunnel. An enlarged plan (scale $\frac{1}{370}$) of the engine house is given in the center of the lithographic plate, with a front elevation of the building and of the water tower upon the same scale in the left-hand lower corner.

The buildings for the pumping engines and water column are unusually commodious and beautiful, and are constructed of stone in the castellated style, from designs by W. W. Boyington, architect. They are shown in elevation and in plan upon a scale of $\frac{1}{370}$ upon Plate I. The building has a frontage of 148 feet in length and a depth of 144 feet 9 inches. Only one end is yet occupied by the pumping engines, space being reserved for others, which it is expected will be required before the year 1875. The site reserved is shown in the plan as also the places which were occupied by the engines erected in 1855 and in 1857.

One of the pair of pumping engines now in use is shown in section upon a scale of $\frac{1}{182}$. It is a double-acting pump twenty-eight inches in diameter and eight-foot stroke. The cylinders are forty-four inches in diameter and the stroke is the same as in the pumps. They take the water from a sump, or well, lined with brick and communicating by means of a curved tunnel with the main lake tunnel through the shore-end shaft, as shown upon the plan.

Upon Plate II will be found plans and sections of the crib and lake shaft, and its connections with the tunnel below, also details of the construction of the inlet gates and bulk-head. These plans and sections of the crib show the method of framing and bracing, and the filling with stone. The combined vertical section of the crib and shaft is upon a scale of $\frac{1}{184}$. The details of the tunnel inlet gates and the bulk-head are upon a scale of $\frac{1}{75}$. The details of construction of the chamber gates at the shore end are given upon Plate I.

IV.—THE SUEZ MARITIME CANAL.

HISTORICAL NOTICE.

The project of establishing water communication between the Mediterranean and the Red Sea is not a modern idea. Sesostris, who reigned in Egypt about 1700 B. C., is believed to have cut the first canal leading from the Nile to the Red Sea. This canal was reopened by Necho and Psammiticus about 650 B. C., and was repaired by Darius seventy-five years later. The Roman emperors Trajan and Adrian caused a branch to be dug to the main body of the Nile, and continued the canal to Suez. In the year 780, or about that time, the canal was partly filled up, and since the conquest of Egypt in 1380 the canal has been wholly abandoned. In 1799 Napoleon had a line of surveys extended across the isthmus, to ascertain the difference of level, if any, between the two seas. His engineer, who worked hurriedly and without proper instruments, reported a difference of nearly thirty-three feet. In 1847 M. Bourdaloue, a French engineer, ascertained that the difference of mean tide in the two seas amounted to only six and a half inches.

In 1854 Mr. Ferdinand Lesseps was authorized by Mohammed Said, for the Egyptian government, to form a company for the purpose of digging a ship canal from sea to sea, with the exclusive right of transit for ninety-nine years from the day of completion. The canal was begun in 1859 by Mr. Ferdinand Lesseps, and, at the date of this publication, is open to the commerce of the world.

The nature of the region over which the canal passes, the topography, the geology, the machines used in excavating, and the details of the construction were most fully shown at the Exposition by means of models, plans in relief, maps, photographic views, and descriptive publications. It is from the latter that the following descriptive notices have been chiefly compiled.

THE ROUTE OF THE CANAL.

But before proceeding to give some details of the construction and working of the various apparatus, a bird's-eye view of the great work is desirable.

The canal is one hundred miles long, and extends nearly north and south from Port Said, on the Mediterranean, to Suez, on the Red Sea. The isthmus at this place is low, and the canal follows a marked depression or valley, and for a great part of the distance is dug in the beds of shallow lakes, and traverses the dried-up basins of former lakes so far below the level of the adjoining seas that little or no excavation is required. The highest ridge or plateau is El Guisr, some ten miles wide, and rising to a height of about sixty-one feet above the sea level. Here a cutting some eighty-seven feet deep was required.

There is abundant evidence that at a comparatively modern geological epoch the two seas, if they did not unite through these remarkable depressions, at least approached so nearly that the isthmus was contracted to the plain of El Guisr, while the Mediterranean, filling the basin of the shallow lakes, washed the dunes of El Ferdane; and the Red Sea, by the Bitter Lakes, reached the opposite side of this narrow plateau. Numerous shells, similar to existing species, found fossil in the interior, and abundantly distributed over the surface, confirm the accuracy of this view. Mr. Lesseps thinks that this was the place crossed by the children of Israel, led by Moses and Aaron.

The greatest length of the basin of the Bitter Lakes is about twenty-two miles, and it varies in width from two and a half to five miles. The depth below the sea level ranges from eight to nine metres, about thirty feet. This vast depression has been filled through the canal by the waters of the adjoining seas. It is computed that this basin contains nine hundred millions of cubic metres of water, and it now forms a vast interior lake, where the navies of the world may float in safety. It has been a dry and parched desert from time immemorial, and its bottom was covered with salt and crusts of gypsum, in fantastic forms. It now serves not only as a convenient waiting place for vessels, but equalizes the flow of the waters caused by the tides and the prevalence of northwest winds, and thus renders locks or gates in the canal unnecessary.

MATERIALS THROUGH WHICH THE CANAL IS EXCAVATED.

The materials through which the excavation of the canal has been made are generally soft and unconsolidated, being the sands and finer sediments of the delta of the Nile, overlaid by the accumulation of sand thrown up by the action of the Mediterranean. At Port Said a littoral cordon of fine sand separates the Mediterranean from Lake Menzaleh, a shallow expanse of water, dotted with low sandy islands, which appear to be remnants of ancient sandy beaches, and to rest upon lacustrine clays. Passing the Ballah Lakes (often without water) to El Ferdane, the surface becomes undulating, and the formations consist of sand, interstratified with beds of clay. In some places the sand is cemented so as to form true sandstone. Upon the plateau of El Guisr is the city of the same name, built by the company. From this place the view to the east and south comprises the deserts and mountains of Syria in the distance. The plateau des Hyènes, the Djebel-Mariam, and certain parts of the plain on the east of Lake Timsah, afford limestone suitable not only for burning but for construction.

As there was no port or protection for shipping upon the Mediterranean side, it became necessary to make one. This has been done by throwing out two piers or breakwaters, one two and a half miles long, the other one and a half mile long; one projecting beyond the other, but giving a clear passage into the harbor a quarter of a mile wide. The shore ends of these piers are about fifteen hundred yards apart; a triangular space is thus secured, land-locked, and gives a safe and commodious harbor, the best of any upon the eastern shore of the Mediterranean.

EXTENT OF THE EXHIBITION MADE BY THE COMPANY.

The exhibition made by the Isthmus of Suez Canal Company occupied a separate building in the park of the Exposition, and comprised: First. Plans in relief, photographs, drawings, models, machines, and charts, giving a general representation of the scene of operations, the means employed to carry them into execution, and the system of traction for the transport of merchandise from one sea to the other. Second. Various collections illustrating the natural history and geology of the Isthmus of Suez. Third. A diorama, showing that part of the isthmus crossed by the canals of the company.

FIRST PART.—No. 1. A relief plan of the isthmus, and a part of Lower Egypt, with the system of canalization of the delta of the Nile; the line of the railway from Cairo to Suez; the development of the fresh-water canal, and the cutting of the maritime canal across the Isthmus of Suez. No. 2. Plan in relief of the port and town of Port Said, erected by the company; entrance of the canal in the Mediterranean, with representation of the works. No. 3. Plan in relief of the town of Ismailia, located and built up by the company in the center of the isthmus, on the margin of Lake Timsah, at the point of junction of the maritime canal with the canal of fresh water derived from the Nile—the administrative center of the works. No. 4. Plan in relief of the port and town of Suez, and entrance in the Red Sea of the fresh and salt water canals, with representation of the works. No. 5. Plan in relief of the plateau of El Guisr, which is the most elevated point of the isthmus on the line of the maritime canal. This plan represents in detail the works in course of execution, and shows the cutting by means of which the company fills Lake Timsah from the Mediterranean. There are also shown the establishment of sheds for the excavators, the system of digging by manual labor, and the earthworks and trucks. No. 6. The general plan of an establishment at Ismailia, containing the machinery for raising and distributing fresh water along the whole line of works from Ismailia to Port Said, by means of three steam engines and two conduits, executed by Mr. Lasseron, contractor for the company. No. 7. A large model of the canal, on the scale of three in one hundred, on which were placed models of the principal machines employed in the excavation of the maritime canal, in their proper positions; that is to say, A, a dredging machine, excavating, and at the same time throwing up the earth to a considerable distance, (designed by Messrs. Borel and Levalley, contractors under the company, and constructed by the Society of the Forges and Works of the Mediterranean;) B, an apparatus connected with the dredging machines for throwing the earth over the banks when the latter are too high for the action of the dredges themselves, (plan by Messrs. Borel and Levalley, and executed by the same company;) C, a great lighter, intended to transport cases full of the excavated earth from the dredging machines to the elevating apparatus, (planned by Messrs. Borel and Levalley, and executed by Messrs. Gouin & Co.;) D, vessel employed to convey to the open sea, or to the middle of the lakes in the interior, the earth excavated by the dredging machines in those parts of the canal which are near the lake or the sea, (executed by Messrs. Henderson, Coulhorn & Co., and Mr. Thomas Bollin Seath, of Glasgow;) E, a lighter with side clap-valves, used for the same purpose as the previous vessel, with this difference, that the lighter being especially intended to carry the earth in the lagoons or basins in the interior of the country, is discharged by the side, (designed by Messrs. Borel and Levalley, and executed by Messrs. Gouin & Co.;) F, a dry excavator or dredging machine, employed at El Guisr. This apparatus is backed against the part upon which it operates, and throws the earth into trucks, brought to it by a locomotive, (planned by Mr. Couvren, contractor under the company, and executed by Mr. Galbert, of Lyons; the trucks by Messrs. Maize, Voisine, and Touchard, and the locomotives at Creuzot;) G, a tug intended to tow the daily trains carrying merchandise from Port Said to Suez, and *vice versa*, by the company's canals, (planned by Mr. Bouguié, and executed by Messrs. Claparede & Co., of St. Denis.) No. 8. A series of photographs, drawings, and charts, used in the preparation of the plans, in relief, and also the diorama representing the various works on the isthmus.

SECOND PART.—No. 1. A geological collection of the various soils found along the whole line of the salt-water canal, from one sea to another, (collected by Mr. Laurent Degousée, after the indications of M. Elié de Beaumont, senator.) No. 2. A collection of objects in natural history, and other things collected in Egypt, namely, medals and ancient coins, statuettes, pottery, mineralogy, shells, fossils, madrepores, petrifactions, reptiles, and butterflies. This collection, which belongs to the museum of Perphignan, and which the municipal council of that town kindly lent to the company, was collected in Egypt, and presented to his native town by Dr. Companys, jr., physician to the Suez Canal Company. No. 3. A collection of objects of natural history, plants, crustacea, mineralogy, insects, madrepores, fishes, and birds. This collection was made on the isthmus, and also in the waters of the Mediterranean, at Port Said, and in the waters of the Red Sea, at Suez, and at various interior lakes, by Captain Baudouin.

THIRD PART.—The diorama, executed by Roubé, decorator of the opera, under the direction of Mr. Alfred Chapon, architect to the company, after a complete and numerous series of photographs, shows from one end to the other the whole of that part of the isthmus which is traversed by the company's canal, as it exists at the present day, with the towns, the workshops, the machines, and the entrance-ports of the canal on the Mediterranean and Red Sea, Port Said and Suez.

THE DIMENSIONS OF THE CANAL.

The canal is 8^{m}.00 deep below the water-line. The breadth of the bottom ("plafond") is everywhere 22^{m}.00, but at the water-level it is 58^{m}.00, in that portion traversing El Guisr, Sérapéum, and Chalouf, a distance of about 33 kilometres in all. In other portions the breadth is 100^{m}.00.

The slope of the talus is determined in each region traversed by the canal by the nature of the earth and materials thrown out. The inclination is never less than two of base to one in height.

In those portions where the breadth is only 58^{m}.00 there is on each side, one metre below the surface of the water, a bench or causeway 2^{m}.00 wide, and where the breadth of the canal is 100^{m}.00 the breadth of the bench varies with the natural slope of the talus. The form of the section varies with the height of the banks and the nature of the materials. The annexed figures show the form at the ridge of El Guisr and

Fig. 1.

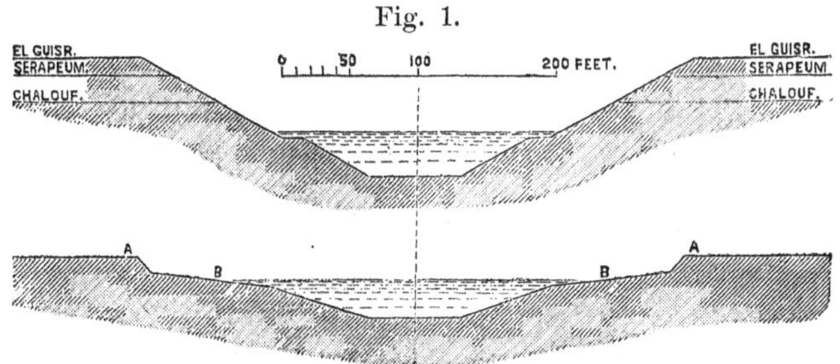

Fig. 2.

at the shallow lakes and low ground. Fig. 1 is the section across the canal at the high ground, and it indicates also the levels of Serapeum and Chalouf. Fig. 2 shows the form of the banks adopted to prevent washing down by the waves. The banks A A are 394 feet apart, thus leaving a low shelving bank B B. In order to deposit the dredgings at such a great distance as the banks A A, on each side, it was found necessary to resort to the use of dredges with long chutes.

THE GREAT DREDGES.

The following are the dimensions and general arrangement of the great dredges made for the company: Length of hull, $30^{m}.00$; breadth, $8^{m}.00$; depth, $3^{m}.00$; draught of water, $1^{m}.60$. The hull is of iron. The engine of each dredge is vertical, direct-acting, condensing, with two cylinders, and nominally 35 horse-power. The total heating surface of the boilers is 81 square metres. A single line of dredge buckets is supported in the center, the upper roller being $8^{m}.50$ above the water level. This line of buckets is $19^{m}.50$ long, and in some of the dredges the buckets have a capacity of 350 litres and in others 300 litres. The lower roller or bearing, over which the buckets pass, can be elevated and thrown forward of the boat so that an excavation may be made in advance where the banks are above the bottom of the hull.

These twenty dredges were supplied with ordinary chutes for the delivery of the earth into barges at the side, but afterward longer chutes were constructed so as to deliver the materials at a distance of $25^{m}.00$ from the dredge. Even these long chutes were found insufficient, and forty other dredges were ordered, four of them made with chutes $60^{m}.00$ long, eighteen with chutes $70^{m}.00$ long, and the others with the ordinary chutes. These dredges resembled in their general construction the first twenty, but the length of the hull was increased to $33^{m}.00$; the breadth to $8^{m}.30$; the depth to $3^{m}.16$, and the draught reduced to $1^{m}.50$. The engine had the same nominal power, exerting easily upon the pistons a force of 7,875 kilogram-metres. The boiler had a heating surface of 108 square metres. The dredge buckets had a capacity of 400 litres in some, and 300 in others. The dimensions of the transverse section of the links which united these buckets into an endless chain were $0^{m}.18$ by $0^{m}.058$. The bolts were of tempered steel, and the eyes were bushed with steel, also tempered; the holes being $0^{m}.07$ in diameter. The dredges with the ordinary delivery chutes had the upper roller placed $11^{m}.50$ above the water; and those with the chutes $60^{m}.00$ long had theirs at the same height, but those made with chutes $70^{m}.00$ long were raised higher, to $14^{m}.80$ above the water level.

The construction and general arrangement of these dredges with long chutes is shown by the accompanying figures. Fig. 3 is a vertical section and Fig. 4 a plan. The chutes are sustained by lattice girders, and they are supported upon a barge moored parallel to the side of the dredge, and in such a manner upon telescopic supports that they may be raised or lowered at pleasure by means of a hydraulic hoist, and thus be inclined at different angles.

The attachment of the chute to the dredge is not rigid but permits of much movement, and is formed by a horizontal hinge which permits the change of inclination when the chute is raised or lowered upon the barge. The supports on the barge are so made that the chute can be turned horizontally and thus be placed parallel with the canal in order that with one end resting upon another barge it can be moved from one place to another with ease.

The section of the chutes has the figure of a half ellipse $0^m.60$ deep and $1^m.50$ wide.

Two rotary pumps placed upon the dredge, and driven by the engine, throw a stream of water into the upper end of the chute, so as to wash the dredging down the slope. In case these pumps do not supply sufficient water to effect this washing out with some kinds of earth, the barge which sustains the chute also carries a portable engine working a pump capable of giving 150 cubic metres of water an hour. The water from this pump is delivered into the chute along its entire length by means of a pipe pierced with holes. In addition to this, an endless chain furnished with scrapers is made to move along the bottom of the chute whenever the materials are too stiff to be freely discharged by the aid of the water. Fine sand descends rapidly with an inclination of from $0^m.04$ to $0^m.05$ to the metre, when washed with a quantity of water equal to half of the material dredged. For clays, a slope of at least from $0^m.06$ to $0^m.08$ to the metre is required, but less water is necessary.

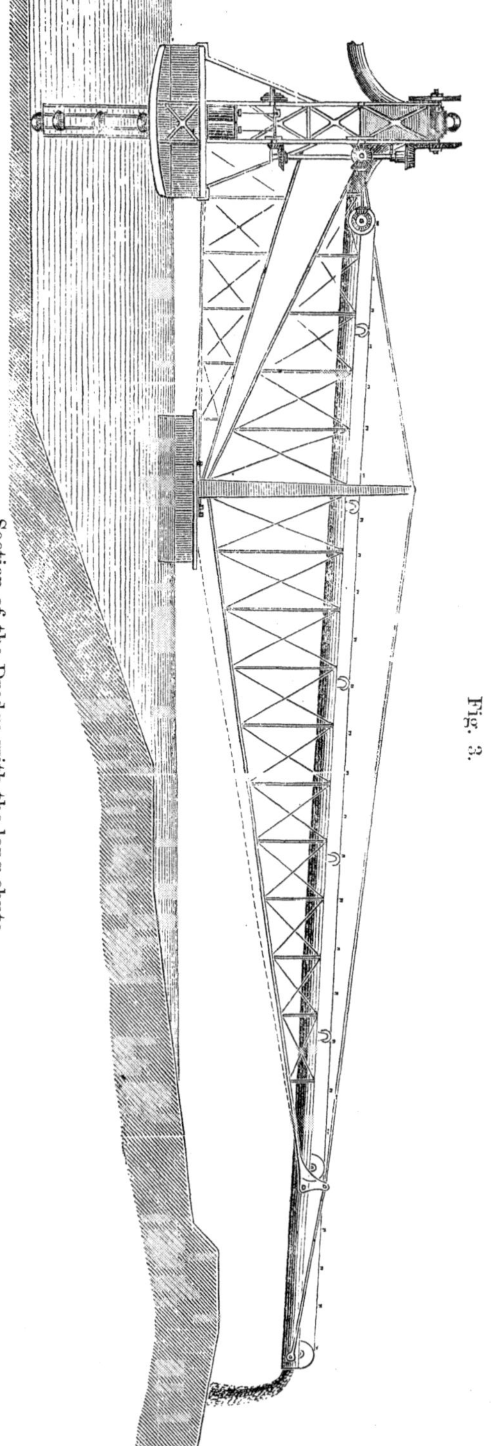
Fig. 3.
Section of the Dredge with the long chute.

The annual delivery of silt, sand, &c., by the dredges

Fig. 4.

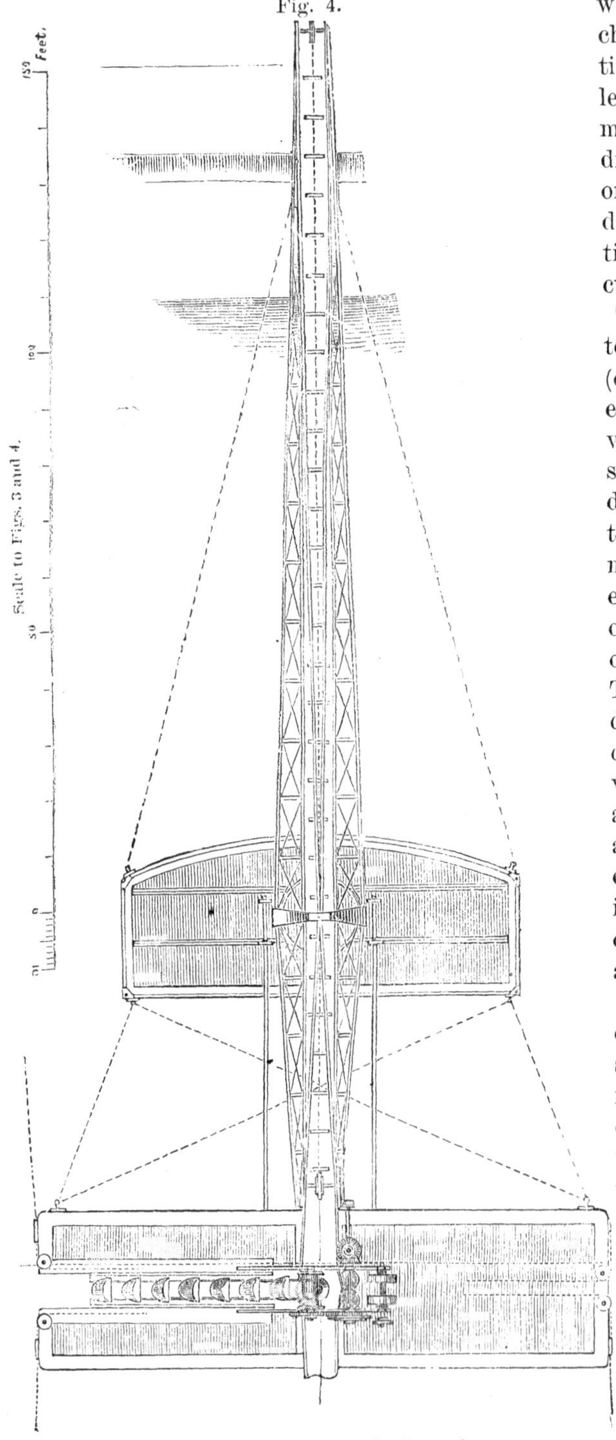

Plan of the Dredge with the long chute.

with the long chutes may be estimated to be at the least 350,000 cubic metres; that of the dredges, with the ordinary system of delivery, may be estimated at 300,000 cubic metres.

The slope of the exterior of the banks (*cavaliers*) deposited by the long chute varies from four to seven in one hundred according to the nature of the materials delivered, whether sandy or clayey and more or less compact. This great slope is due to the velocity of the water by which the materials are discharged, and it allows a great quantity of dredging to be disposed of without making a high bank.

These long-chute dredges are very simple and economical. They can be employed wherever the ground is not too high, and they do not cease to deliver the dredgings until the accumulation becomes too high for the lower end of the chute. They were used for nearly all that portion of the canal which traverses Lake Menzaleh, and for portions which traverse the plain of Suez, and the margins of the great lakes.

ELEVATING APPARATUS.

In those portions of the canal where the ground was too high to permit the long-chute dredges to be used, the elevating apparatus about to be described was substituted.

The attempt was first made to work with cranes placed upon the banks and having thirty-three feet radius of swing, by the aid of which boxes filled with the dredgings were lifted and swung out to the banks and dumped or emptied into a train of wagons on a tramway.

The elevating apparatus may be described as a portable inclined railway, extending from the dredger or barge loaded with dredgings, upward over the banks, and upon which trucks or "trollies" carrying the boxes filled with the dredgings were made to ascend, and finally to dump the contents at the further end. The contrivance is but another form of the long chute, the difference being that the slope is reversed and the track and trollies take the place of

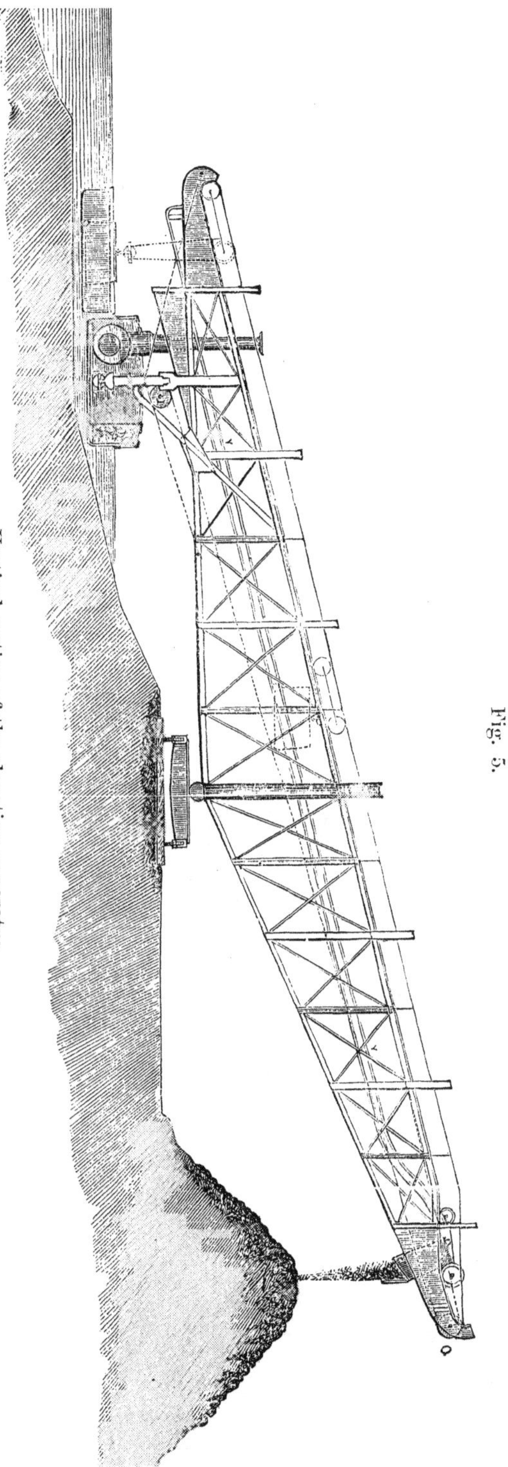

Fig. 5.

Vertical section of the elevating apparatus.

the chute along which, where the banks are low, the dredgings descend by gravity. Like the long chutes, the inclined tramway is supported about midway, not upon a floating barge, but upon a strong truck running upon a railway laid upon the bank and parallel with the course of the canal.

Fig. 6.

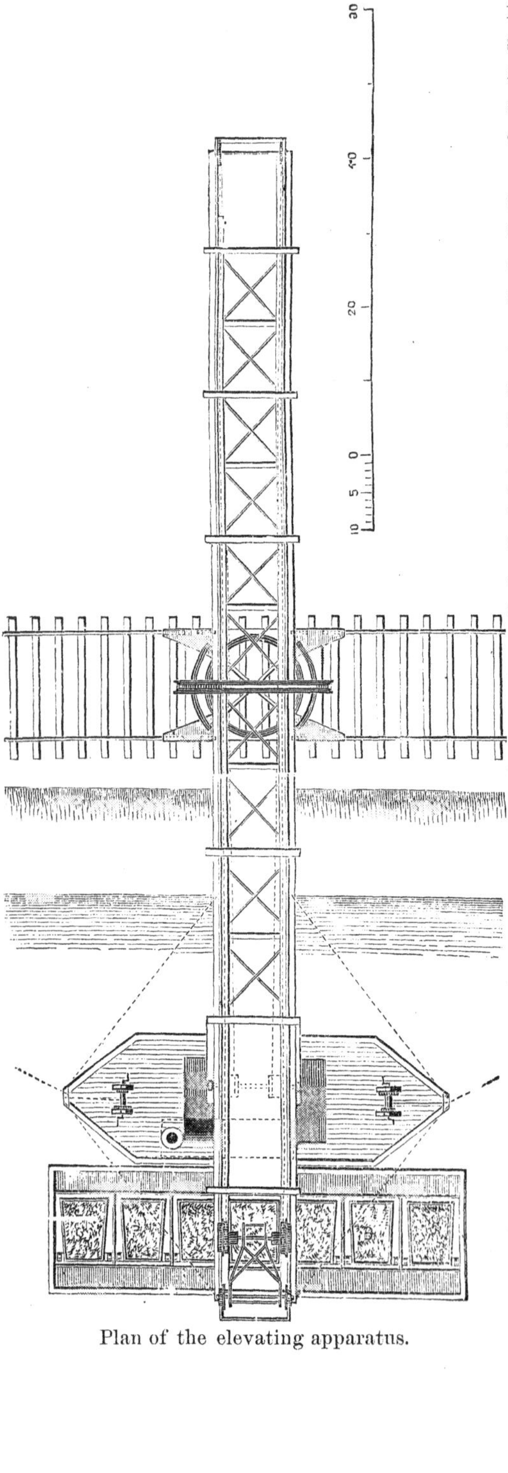

Plan of the elevating apparatus.

The two figures, Fig. 5, a vertical section, and Fig. 6, a plan, will give an idea of the construction of the apparatus.

The tramway is supported by two parallel lattice girders tied together by vertical struts and united above the track by arched ties. The length is about 150 feet, and the inclination is about $0^{m}.22$ per metre. The lower end is about $3^{m}.00$ above the surface of the water and the upper end over the bank is about $14^{m}.00$. The bank upon which the track carrying the truck is laid is raised about $2^{m}.00$ above the water. The lower end of the tramway rests upon a barge; the upper end is quite free and is at such a height above the bank that there is plenty of room for the accumulation of the dredgings.

When the apparatus is put into operation a float carrying the boxes of dredgings is floated under the lower and projecting end of the apparatus, and a box is hooked on to the trolly which is at the bottom of the track. A steam-engine upon the barge supplies the power for drawing the trolly and box up the incline and for tipping the box at the upper end.

The construction of the trolly is shown in Fig. 7, a side view, and Fig. 8, an end view. N N are the rails of the tramway, R the frame of the trolly, and U U the boxes of dredgings. The wheels are external, and the lower two are fixed upon the axle while the upper are loose, and the axle carries two larger wheels T T and drums S S. Upon these small drums S S the chain is coiled by which the boxes are supported, while on the larger drums T T iron cables are coiled in the opposite direction. These cables pass over a pulley O at the upper end of the elevator, and then return to the winding drum of the engine. When this cable is wound upon the engine drum it uncoils from the drum T, and by means of the chain winding upon S S raises the box vertically from the float until a stopper or guard V V comes in contact with the drum S, when the coiling upon S ceases and the trolly begins to travel up the incline as the cables unwind from T T. When the trolly and suspended box reach

Fig. 7. Fig. 8.

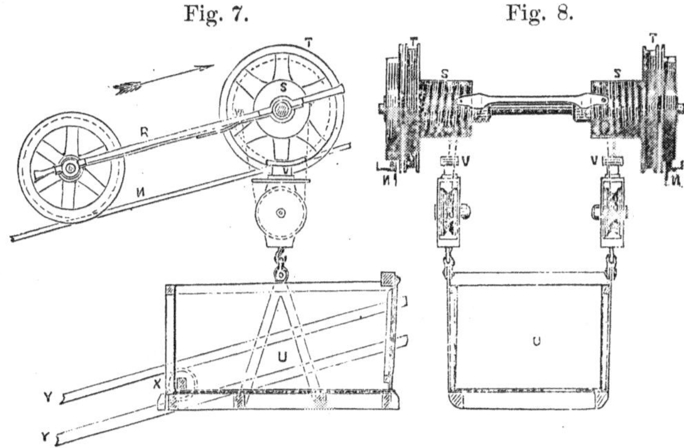

the upper end of the incline the box is tipped automatically, by means of rollers X running between guide rails Y Y, and which curve suddenly upward and thus raise the back end. The same guides serve to keep the box horizontal during the ascent.

RAFT BARGES.

For carrying the boxes filled with the earth, delivered by the ordinary dredges, rafts were used. These were made of two long water-tight boxes of sheet iron, $17^{m}.50$ long, $1^{m}.10$ wide, and $1^{m}.25$ high, kept at a distance of $3^{m}.00$ apart by means of eight open-work partitions, between which the boxes for the reception of the dredgings were placed. These boxes when filled were nearly submerged in the water. This arrangement has several advantages, not the least of which is that by being so low the chutes may be more inclined and the height of the dredge may be less. Ninety of these rafts were made use of.

VESSELS FOR TRANSPORTING THE SAND.

In the vicinity of the sea, and in the deep portion of the lakes, where the dredgings could not be deposited in *cavaliers* upon the sides of the canal, they were taken and emptied in the sea or the lakes by means of screw-propeller vessels called *bataux porteurs*. Of thirty-six of these boats ten were built in England and twenty-six in France. Those made in England are similar to those which are used upon the Clyde and the Tyne, and have, in general, the following dimensions: Length of hull, $41^{m}.15$; breadth, $7^{m}.01$; depth, $2^{m}.97$; length of the hold or pit, $15^{m}.24$; breadth of the hold at the level of the bridge, $5^{m}.79$; breadth at the bottom, $2^{m}.51$.

The pit or hold for the reception of the dredgings is central, and its capacity is about 180 cubic metres. It is closed at the bottom by six pair of trap-doors opening downward, held by chains which are wound around pulleys placed in a frame above the doors. The engine is nominally 50 horse-power, condensing, and works a screw $2^{m}.438$ in diameter. The speed of these vessels is from six to seven knots an hour. The boats made in France have a capacity of 200 cubic metres. Twelve of these have the hold central; the others have it double, a pit in each side.

For those portions of the work where the dredgings could not be de posited in banks *en cavalier*, and where the water was shallow, lighters with doors or valves at the side were used instead of the vessels with valves at the bottom. These lighters, called *gabares à clapets latéraux*, are built entirely of iron, and are $32^{m}.50$ long and $6^{m}.00$ wide. The hold for the dredgings, divided into six compartments, is $20^{m}.00$ long. It is divided along the center by an air-tight compartment of triangular cross-section, of which the bottom of the lighter forms one side. The length of the side clap-valves is the same as each compartment. They are $1^{m}.20$ high and are hinged at the top. These lighters are provided with double-cylinder, horizontal, high-pressure engines, and they carry from 80 to 90 cubic metres of dredgings and draw $1^{m}.20$ of water.

DRY EXCAVATORS.

This apparatus upon dry and elevated soils takes the place of the dredgers used for wet ground. It excavates the earth and delivers it into wagons placed upon a tramway. It was used at the ridge or plateau of El Guisr to enlarge the trench cut by the Egyptian laborers. The apparatus consists of a horizontal framework, a staging, supported by nine wheels upon a railway or tramroad of three rails, running parallel to the bench to be enlarged. This framework or carriage is $6^{m}.00$ long and sustains a boiler and two engines. One of these engines is used to put in motion a chain of excavating buckets, and the other to move the apparatus.

There are eight buckets, and they discharge the earth into a chute, which projects $3^{m}.00$ beyond the exterior rail and delivers into the wagons placed on a second and parallel tramway.

The weight of the apparatus is nearly 22,000 kilogrammes. The engine is fifteen horse-power. The amount excavated and delivered reaches 750 cubic metres in ten hours, in sandy soil, of little resistance. When, by means of these dry excavators, the cut was carried to the water level, the remainder of the excavation was cut by the dredges.

ARTIFICIAL STONE PIERS AT PORT SAID.

For the construction of the piers at Port Said stone blocks from quarries near Alexandria were at first employed. It was found, however, that the cost was too great, and it was decided to manufacture blocks of stone out of the beach sand and lime. The contract was given to Messrs. Dussaud frères, who were the constructors of similar work at Marseilles, Cherbourg, and Alger. The sand as it is dredged out of the harbor is made into a concrete or mortar with the hydraulic lime from Theil, Ardeche, in France. The materials are ground together with the addition of a small quantity of sea water from time to time, and when the mixture has about the consistency of thick mortar it is rammed into box molds made of plank. In about a week the blocks so made were set sufficiently to allow the planks to be removed, and the blocks were then permitted to remain exposed to the sun and air for three months before being taken to the line of the piers and submerged. The proportions of lime and sand used were 325 kilogrammes of lime, in dry powder, to one cubic metre of sand. The dimensions of the blocks are $3^{m}.40$ long, $2^{m}.00$ broad, and $1^{m}.50$ high; thus containing about ten cubic metres. A portion of the foundation of the piers was made with blocks of four cubic metres, but the casing was formed entirely of blocks of ten cubic metres, or about 370 cubic feet, and weighing about twenty-two tons. According to the calculations made in 1867, at the Exposition, the cubic contents of the piers would be 250,000 cubic metres. About thirty of these blocks were made daily in 1867, at a contract cost of 400 francs each, or about $8 50 per cubic yard. It was estimated that 30,000 would be required.

WORKS FOR THE SUPPLY OF FRESH WATER.

One of the most interesting of the accessory undertakings necessary to the construction of the canal is the aqueduct for the supply of fresh water for the workmen and boilers, and also for the irrigation of the soil. The great work, it should be remembered, was to be executed in a desert region, where no potable water could be procured by ordinary means, and a very large supply was required for the population at Port Said, at Ismailia, and at the various encampments along the route. This supply was obtained from the Nile. A canal was dug from the end of the ancient canal at Gassassine to a point on the route of the ship canal at Ismailia, nearly half-way between the two extremes. This work was executed under the direction of Mr. Cazeau, and cost 700,000 francs. Its length is thirty miles, its width sixty-six feet, and depth six feet, with a fall of two inches per mile. It was completed in 1861. From its termination at Ismailia the water was for some time distributed to the camps upon the backs of camels and donkeys, but a cast-iron pipe was afterward laid to Port Said and the water was forced through it by pumps a distance of fifty miles. A second pipe was afterward laid, and through these two pipes the whole line of the canal from Ismailia to Port Said is supplied.

The first pipe was six inches in diameter, and the second ten inches. Through these two pipes nearly 55,000 cubic feet of water are supplied daily.

The pumping engines are placed at Ismailia. They were constructed and placed under the direction of Mr. Lasseron. There are three steam-engines, two of fifteen horse-power each, and the third of twenty-five horse-power. The first two were erected in 1863, and the third in 1865. The two pipes connect by means of twenty joints furnished with gates. Upon the line of these pipes three great reservoirs are established, one of 500 cubic metres at El Guisr, upon the summit of the isthmus, the second, of like capacity, half-way between Ismailia and Port Said, and the third of 700 cubic metres capacity at Port Said. The pressure in the pipes reaches six atmospheres, and the highest reservoir has an elevation of only twenty metres.

SUMMARY OF THE EXTENT OF THE WORK.

At the date of the Exposition the total power of the steam-engines employed upon the isthmus was equal to 17,768 horse-power, and the monthly consumption of coal amounted to 12,219 tons. A population of 25,000 persons had been created in the midst of the desert, 13,000 of which were laborers, 6,388 of whom were Syrians, and 6,990 Europeans. The total amount of earth to be excavated, according to the plans and estimates, was 74,112,130 cubic metres, and on the first of January, 1869, less than 17,000,000 cubic metres remained to be taken out.

Among the greatest dredging works which have been executed in Europe the following are cited for comparison with the magnitude of the work upon the Suez canal.

Principal dredging works executed in Europe.

			Cubic metres.
Roadstead of Toulon	1848–'57,	9 years	7.400,000
Glasgow	1844–'65,	21 years	6,696,000
Newcastle	1862–'65,	3 years	6,999,000

It is also interesting to compare the extent of the work upon the piers at Port Said with similar undertakings in Europe. The length of the western jetty is about 3,100 metres, and of the eastern about 1,600 metres; the combined length being about 4,700 metres, and the total contents about 250,000 cubic metres.

The following table, for which I am indebted to the report by M. Ch. Marin upon the marine constructions represented at the Exposition,[1] shows the magnitude and cost of the principal jetties of France and England. The dimensions are stated in metres, and the cost in millions of francs. In order, however, to make a just comparison of the cost of these works, account should be taken of the differences between the bulk of the walls above and below the low-water line.

Principal marine jetties of France and England.

	Length.	Mean depth below low tide.	Total cost.	Cost per metre.	Period.
FRANCE.					
Cherbourg	3, 750	12. 00	67	18, 600	1784—1853
Alger	1, 900	18. 00	30	16, 000	1842—1860
Dikes and quays of Joliette	3, 000	11. 50	15	5, 500	1845—1852
Dikes of the Napoleon basin	2, 000	17. 00	19	10, 100	1859—1865
Fort Bayard	100 × 60	4. 50	7	....	1804—1866
Fort Chavagnac, Cherbourg	150 × 120	10. 00	5	....	1854—1864
ENGLAND.					
Plymouth	1, 600	10. 00	40	25, 000	1817—1851
Portland	2, 410	17. 00	34	14, 000	1850—1860
Holyhead	2, 250	15. 00	37	16, 500	1854—1865
Aurigny	1, 000	15. 00	16	16, 000	1847—1859
Jersey	1, 050	10. 00	8	7, 500	1846—1856

EXTRACTS FROM THE RULES FOR THE NAVIGATION OF THE SUEZ UNIVERSAL SHIP CANAL.

Article 1 provides that the navigation of the canal shall be opened to all vessels without distinction of nationality, provided they do not draw more than $7^{m}.50$, equal to 24 feet 7 inches English; the canal being $8^{m}.00$ in depth, equal to $26\frac{1}{4}$ feet English.

Steam vessels will be allowed to navigate through the canal, using their own propellers; sailing vessels, above fifty tons, will have to be towed with the service established by the company.

The maximum speed for vessels in the canal is provisionally fixed at ten kilometres per hour, equal to 5.4 English knots.

The tolls for the right of transit are calculated on the measurement tonnage of the ship. This tonnage is determined for the present by the official papers on board. The toll for passage from one sea to the other is ten francs per ton measurement, and ten francs each passenger, payable on entering, either at Port Said or Suez. The charge for berthing or anchoring either at Port Said, Ismailia, or opposite the new embankment near Suez, (after a stay of twenty-four hours,) and limited to twenty days at the utmost, is five centimes per ton per day, at the place assigned by the harbor-master.

[1] Rapports du jury international, t. x, p. 316. Travaux maritimes.

V.—MISCELLANEOUS NOTICES.

THE HYDRAULIC SERVICE AND THE VENTILATION OF THE EXPOSITION BUILDING.[1]

From data collected respecting the requirements of the numerous services which employ water as a basis of action, (production and condensation of steam, cleansing, watering, canals, cascades, &c.,) the committee of this Class estimated the quantity required for the use of the Exposition at ten thousand cubic metres per day. At the rate of one hundred litres per day, per person, this supply would be enough for a town of one hundred thousand souls. This large consumption does not all require, however, to be supplied under the same pressure; about one-half requires a charge of from twenty to twenty-five metres, while for the remainder a few metres suffice. The committee felt that it would be inconvenient to ask such a supply from the municipal authorities who have so many demands to meet, and who have not yet at their disposal the quantity of water which has been fixed as the desideratum; it was, therefore, determined to establish an independent supply for the Exposition, which might, upon an emergency, be supplemented or corrected by an appeal to the city reservoirs. This service has been arranged on the same basis, and after the same principles as the mechanical power; and divided, according to the required pressure, into two services of five thousand cubic metres each, with distinct channels; but which can be placed in communication with each other in case of necessity. The high service includes a reservoir of four thousand metres capacity, established at the summit of the Trocadero, on the side of the Avenue Malakoff, at the height of thirty-two metres above the level of the soil of the Exposition building; and a hydraulic establishment by the side of the river, immediately below the bridge of Jena. The low service is fed by the pumps of the great marine engine of Indret, of one thousand horse-power, set in motion by its own boilers in the shed by the side of the river, above the same bridge; these pumps are capable of lifting twelve hundred cubic metres per hour, and they will be supplemented, in case of necessity, by those belonging to the Company of the Forges and Construction Works in the same shed. In case these two powerful engines should stop at the same time, the service will be assured by another combination confined to five exhibitors—one of whom will take the water directly from the Seine, for the piece of water in the park; while the others will pump the required quantity through the conduits from this basin, in which the water will be maintained at a constant level. The pressure on the apparatus of the four last-mentioned constructors is regulated by a sheet-iron reservoir, the upper level of which is above that of the soil of the Exposition building. The high service supplies the irrigation of the park, the fountains, the hydrants,

[1] Extract from the statement by the committee of the Imperial Commission.—Translation.

&c.; and the low service, the condensers, the boilers, the cascades, and the canals.

The Imperial Commission caused to be constructed beneath the soil of the building a system of circular and radial galleries destined to conduct the air from without into the interior of the Exposition building, and there replace that which has been vitiated and heated by the mass of visitors. In order to insure more completely the effectiveness of the service, so necessary for the comfort of the public, the commission decided that the natural ventilation should be aided by artificial means; that is to say, by blowing machines based on the system of Messrs. Piaron de Mondesir, engineer of roads and bridges, and Tehaitre and Julienne, civil engineers. This arrangement is divided into four groups placed around the bu'ld-ing, and includes a force of about one hundred horse-power; the whole is intrusted to exhibitors on the principles above mentioned. These four centers will feed sixteen jets, corresponding with the sixteen radial passages of the building; and will cause to circulate therein, by means of ventilating gratings in the floor, a volume of seven hundred thousand metres of air per hour; so that the entire atmosphere of the Exposition building will be changed every two hours.

PORT OF TARRAGONA.

In the collection of models exhibited by Spain, already noticed, there were two of the great work of the port of Tarragona. One was a plan in relief of the port and the vicinity, showing the position of the quays and the quarries; the second is upon a larger scale and is a transverse section of the jetties, showing the position of the sunken rocks and of all the work in masonry.

This great work reaches back in time to the year 1790, and has been in great part executed by convicts. The length of the principal jetty is 1,300 metres, and the quantity of submerged blocks of stone is estimated at 1,085,900 cubic metres. They have succeeded in placing blocks of stone weighing 210,000 kilogrammes, representing a volume of 88 cubic metres.' These enormous blocks are quarried by means of powder, the blasting holes being $0^{m}.10$ in diameter, and $5^{m}.00$ deep, and 12 kilogrammes of powder for a charge. The interspaces of this mass of large rocks are filled with small fragments, and above all a layer of concrete is laid, and this forms the foundation for the pier.

EASING AND STRIKING CENTERING OF ARCHES.

A method, the invention of Mr. Beaudemoulin, of easing the centering of arches, by means of sand, was shown by a full-sized model in the park. Sheet-iron cylinders, about a foot in diameter and a foot high, are filled with fine dry sand and placed under the principals of the centering. These principals rest upon the sand by means of props which fit piston-like in the cylinders. Holes near the bottom of the cylinders permit the sand to flow out when cork stoppers are removed. As the sand runs out the pistons descend, and the rapidity and extent of the movement can be very easily controlled by regulating the flow of the sand.

PIVOT BRIDGE, BY CHAPIN & WELLS.

Messrs. Chapin & Wells, bridge builders, of Chicago, Illinois, exhibited a model of a pivot or swing bridge, which attracted considerable attention, and was honored by a silver medal.

The model was of the style of bridge known as "Howe's Patent Truss," with arched upper chords, and it represented a railroad pivot bridge of two hundred feet in length, the scale being half an inch to one foot. The bridge rests upon a turn-table twenty-four feet square, made of white oak, thoroughly trussed with wrought-iron bolts two inches in diameter, and so adjusted that the entire weight of the bridge can be made to rest upon the center pivot, which is made of cast steel. It is designed, however, that only two-thirds of the weight should rest upon the center pivot, and the remaining one-third to rest upon twenty-four cast-iron bearing wheels, sixteen inches in diameter, kept equi-distant from the center, and from each other, by wrought-iron radial arms, two inches in diameter. The wheels rest and travel upon a track of railroad iron, planed upon the top, and bent to the proper circle, twenty-two feet in diameter. The trusses of the bridge are twenty-eight feet high at the center, and ten feet high at the ends, and fourteen feet apart. The truss is divided into twenty-two panels, ranging from five to eleven feet in length. In each panel there are two main and one counter diagonal braces of the proper sizes, resting between two cast-iron brace-bearing blocks, which blocks are fastened one to the upper side of the lower chord, and one fastened to the under side of the upper chord, and of the proper angles, so that the ends of the braces come squarely upon the face of the cast-iron block. Two truss rods run perpendicularly through the truss, dividing each panel, with heavy wrought-iron plates under the lower chords, and on the upper side of the upper chords, to serve as washers to receive the nuts of truss rods or bolts. The lower chords are fourteen inches by twenty-eight inches, and are composed of four pieces. The upper chords at the ends are twelve inches by twenty-eight inches, and at the center thirty-six inches by twenty-eight inches, being thus increased at the center to give sufficient material to sustain the weight of the bridge when open. Both upper and lower chords are thoroughly framed together with iron clamps, keys, and bolts.

The bridge is turned upon its pivot by means of a cast-iron rack, or gear-circle, securely fastened to the center pier, into which runs a pinion, fastened to a three-inch wrought-iron shaft, secured to the turn-table, and running perpendicularly up through the center of the roadway of the bridge, upon the upper end of which is fitted a wrench, by means of which one or two men can open and close the bridge with ease.

SWING BRIDGE OF BREST.

The great swing bridge of Brest was represented by a model on a scale of one-fiftieth for the whole, and of one-tenth for one of the piers. The distance between the walls of the Penfield inlet, which the bridge is to span, is 571 feet. Two wrought-iron lattice frames revolve upon turn-tables upon the top of two circular towers, thirty-four feet nine inches in diameter, and 347 feet apart.

These frames are each formed of two girders twenty-five feet four inches deep over the piers, and four feet seven inches at the center. They are strongly braced together and support the roadway. The shore ends of these frames are loaded with counterweights. The weight upon each pier is 590 tons. Each part of this bridge can be opened by two men in fifteen minutes. The cost was 2,118,835 francs.

MINING.

In mine engineering the novelties, aside from the many interesting maps, sections, and models of mining ground, were confined chiefly to the very remarkable exhibits of the tools and methods of boring large shafts in watery strata. Messrs. Kind and Chaudron, Messrs Dru, and also Dégousée and Laurent incurred the expense of installation of the enormous tools (*trépans*) for this work, and sections of the iron tubbing employed by them. By these tools, weighing many tons, shafts from ten to fifteen feet in diameter are successfully and cheaply pierced to the depth of more than five hundred feet without pumping out the water. The great expedition and economy of this method, in all places where the nature of the strata will permit the tools to be used, are sufficiently evident. It is claimed that shafts can be sunk in this way for less than one-quarter of the expense required to execute the work in the usual manner.

As the methods and the tools have been described in detail in the report upon mining, in this series, this short reference will suffice to direct attention to an exhibition which was full of interest and instruction to American mining engineers.

GEOLOGICAL MAPS.

The geological surveys of the principal countries were represented at the Exposition by the results in the form of maps, sections, and printed volumes. Russia, Australia, Egypt, Chili, and other remote countries were included in the representation, but the surveys in the United States were scarcely represented, the State of Illinois being the only one which sent a geological report.

This department of the Exposition is the subject of two very interesting memoirs; one by M. Edmond Fuchs, mining engineer, and the other by M. Daubrée, inspector general of mines, &c. Both memoirs were published in Paris, in the reports of the international jury, Volume II.

WILLIAM P. BLAKE.

NOVEMBER, 1869.

PARIS UNIVERSAL EXPOSITION, 1867.

REPORTS OF THE UNITED STATES COMMISSIONERS.

REPORT

ON

BÉTON-COIGNET,

ITS FABRICATION AND USES:

CONSTRUCTION OF SEWERS, WATER-PIPES, TANKS, FOUNDATIONS, WALLS, ARCHES, BUILDINGS, FLOORS, TERRACES, MARINE EXPERIMENTS, ETC.,

BY

LEONARD F. BECKWITH,

CIVIL ENGINEER.

WASHINGTON:
GOVERNMENT PRINTING OFFICE.
1868.

PREFACE.

The following remarks on béton-coignet are drawn from numerous partial reports which have appeared from time to time during the last fifteen years, and from personal observations on the methods in actual use, which are somewhat in advance of the publications on the subject.

LEONARD F. BECKWITH, *C. E.*

PARIS, *December*, 1867.

CONTENTS.

NATURE AND VARIETIES OF BÉTON.

DEFINITIONS.

THEORY.

COMPOSITION.

VARIETIES.

FABRICATION AND PROPERTIES OF BÉTON.

MIXING.

PACKING AND MOULDING.

PROPERTIES.

APPLICATIONS OF BÉTON—CONCLUSION.

APPLICATIONS.

CONCLUSION.

ILLUSTRATIONS.

BÉTON-COIGNET.

NATURE AND VARIETIES OF BÉTON.

DEFINITIONS.

Common béton is a conglomeration of sand, pebbles, broken stones, common lime, and water.

Common béton for marine uses is a conglomerate of similar stones, hydraulic lime and water.

Béton-coignet, to which this memoir chiefly relates, is an artificial stone formed of sand, lime and water, and is used in blocks or in continuous masses for foundations, walls above and below ground, sewers, water-pipes, floors, pillars, arches, embankments, aqueducts, reservoirs, cisterns, and the entire walls of buildings.

The elements are the same as those of common mortar for masonry, but the relative proportions of each, the method of making, and the results are different.

THEORY OF CONCRETION.

Common mortar being composed of sand, lime, and water, the theory of its concretion may be briefly stated as follows:

1. The chemical changes which occur from the contact of quicklime (oxide of calcium) and water produce hydrate of lime, and the subsequent absorption of carbonic acid from the air, displacing the water, produces carbonate of lime.

2. The strength and hardness of mortar result from the cohesion of sand and carbonate of lime, and from the crystallization of the carbonate which grasps and binds the grains of sand.

3. Homogeneity depends upon the equal and uniform diffusion of the lime among the sand.

4. An excess of lime in proportion to sand produces great shrinkage and imperfect crystallization, and leaves the mass brittle and weak.

5. An excess of water in proportion to lime cannot combine with it, but lodges between the particles of sand and lime, and by slow evaporation leaves the mass porous and friable.

6. The practical difficulties are, first, to find the proportions in which the elements will best combine; and, second, to produce the conditions most favorable to their combination.

Observation: Common sandstone is usually composed of large quantities of silicious sand and small quantities of some cementing substance, oxide of iron, clay, carbonate of lime, &c., &c.; therefore,

7. The right elements being properly mixed and in due proportions, each grain of sand enveloped in a coating of moistened lime, and all the grains brought into contact, the conditions in short being right, crystallization should be simultaneous and uniform throughout the mass.

This line of thought, pursued through a long series of experiments, has produced the béton-coignet, a kind of calcareous sandstone, of great durability, admirably adapted to numerous and common wants and of small comparative cost, its elements being found in abundance in all countries.

COMPOSITION.

A large quantity of sand, a smaller quantity of lime and a little water; only water enough for quick assimilation with the lime to prepare it for crystallization, and lime enough, when uniformly diffused, to form a thin coating to the grains of sand.

These ingredients when properly manipulated are barely moist, but the preparation is complete and ready for use.

The mixture is handled with shovels and transported in carts and wheelbarrows, the same as dry sand. It may be spread on the ground for foundations or floors, placed in moulds for blocks of different models and sizes, and shovelled into cribs of planks to give shape to walls, or dumped into trenches provided with wooden forms for the sides and arches of sewers.

The béton when placed should be slightly compacted by the use of light hand-pestles, to perfect the contact of particles and hasten the processes of solidification. In a short time the spontaneous action which follows will be complete, and the forms may be removed.

VARIETIES.

Bétons cemented with different sorts of lime attain the same final solidity and strength, but require various periods of time for consolidation.

Common lime sets slower than hydraulic lime, and the latter sets slower than cement; in other words, crystallization is quicker in each of the varieties named, reversing the order.

Hydraulic lime, in addition to quicklime, contains alumina oxide of iron, silica, magnesia, &c., &c., and cement consists of similar elements with the alumina, silica, &c., augmented; the latter hardens quicker than the preceding and gives a finer and smoother surface.

Consequently, when time is of importance and structures are required for immediate use, hydraulic lime is substituted for common lime; and to quicken the result, a portion of cement is usually added.

Lime for common mortar should be slacked at least 24 hours before it is mixed. For béton-coignet the lime should be slacked but two or three hours before it is mixed; barely enough water should be applied to reduce it to powder, and the supplementary water applied in mixing should be only sufficient to render the lime damp and adhesive, leaving still in the lime a capacity for the absorption of water. The natural affinity of the lime for moisture being thus incompletely satisfied, renders the taking or crystallization more vigorous and rapid, and promotes the subsequent carbonation by the readier absorption of carbonic acid.

Coarse sand makes a harder béton than fine sand, and the taking is stronger. Clean river sand, one-twentieth to three-twentieths of an inch in diameter, is best; all kinds, however, are used, and if it contains earthy particles, more lime is required; fine sand requires greater care and more packing for consolidation.

Béton-coignet may be described generally as composed of: *Sand*, 4 to 5 parts in volume; *lime*, common or hydraulic, 1 part in volume; *cement*, $\frac{1}{4}$ to $\frac{3}{4}$ of 1 part in volume; *water*, variable. But the exact proportions vary in conformity with the variations in the properties inherent in the elements, which will be subsequently noticed.

FABRICATION AND PROPERTIES OF BÉTON.

MIXING.

The machinery most in use for mixing consists of a vertical cylinder, an oblique elevator, and a locomobile for working the machine.

Mixing cylinder.—The drawing (Plate I, Fig. 1) represents the cylinder and elevator in place, drawn to scale. *a*, section of the vertical cylinder showing the interior. It is constructed of boiler-plate, and rests on a cylinder or base of cast iron *b*, with projecting arms for supports and for sustaining the bottom plate P, which is suspended. *c*, a vertical shaft passing through the centre of the cylinder, to which shaft curved arms *d*, are attached, which revolve horizontally, for mixing the sand and lime. Q, a distributor, which revolves horizontally, receiving the lime and sand as they enter the cylinder from the conducting trough I, and distributing them equally around for mixing.

Fig. 2. *d c* Q represents an inverted curved arm, distributing arm, and cross-section of vertical shaft. *dd*, cross-section of the curved arm.

E E, short stationary horizontal arms, which are attached to the sides of the cylinder, forming with the movable arms breaks for dashing and mixing the sand and lime. *e e*, three warped or helicoidal blades attached to the lower part of the shaft for forcing the mixture downwards and outwards. *f f*, cycloidal arms revolving horizontally near the floor of the cylinder, to expel the mixture at the side opening around the bottom.

Fig. 3. Horizontal section of the cylinder, presenting a vertical view of the helicoidal blades *eee*, and of the cycloidal arms *fff*, below them. *g*, a horizontal opening at the base of the cylinder for the expulsion of the mixture. GG, a movable ring or band of iron, passing around the cylinder, for enlarging or diminishing the opening for the expulsion of the béton by moving the band up or down. *hh*, vertical guiding shafts and pegs for the movable band. HH, the handles for lifting it up and letting it down. P, immovable bottom plate. N, a plate which is attached to the vertical shaft *c*, and revolves horizontally. L, a curved plate of iron fixed to the plate P, remaining stationary, and scraping off the mixture from N as it revolves. S, the support of the vertical shaft *c*; it is of cast-iron, and bolted to a ring on the upper edge of the cylinder *a*.

Fig. 4. Cross-section of the support S of the vertical shaft *c*.

Driving gear.—The driving gear consists of: *j*, a bevel wheel fixed to the vertical shaft *c*; receives its motion from *k*, a bevel wheel on the horizontal shaft *m*. *i*, fly-wheel. *l*, fast pulley on the shaft *m*, run by the crossed belt *nn*, which connects it with the fast pulley *o*, of equal diameter, on the shaft *q*. *p*, a spur wheel fixed to shaft *q*, and engaging with *t*, a pinion on the shaft *r*, to which is fixed a driving pulley run directly by a belt from a locomobile (portable steam-engine) stationed near by.

Elevator.—The elevator is supported on a double frame M, and consists of small sheet-iron buckets *v*, attached to an endless chain *u*. Each frame is composed of two pieces MM, united by a joint *x*, and strengthened at intervals with iron plates in which are set rollers *w*. The upper ends of the frames are bolted to the support R of the shaft *r*, and the lower ends to the support T. The endless chain revolves round two drums *s z*. The drum *s* at the upper end transmits the power from the shaft *r* to the chain *u*. The drum *z* supports the chain at the lower end, and keeps it in position.

The mixing apparatus produces daily about 100 cubic yards of béton, and is run by a locomobile, or portable steam-engine, of about eight horse power.

Locomobile.—The annexed drawing (Plate I, Fig. 5) presents a side view of the locomobile, which is non-condensing and double-acting. It is provided with a cylinder for warming the water by the escaped steam, and the whole is placed on springs. The number of revolutions per minute is about 100; length of stroke 16 inches; diameter of steam cylinder 8 inches. The pressure of steam is 5 atmospheres, corresponding to 73 pounds on the square inch.

Description of engine.—A, fire-box. B, tubular boiler. C, water-gauge. D, steam-reservoir. E, safety-valve. F, pipe supplying steam to cylinder. G, centrifugal governor. H, steam-cylinder. I, eduction pipe. J, steam-pipe for cleaning. K, warming cylinder. L, smoke-box. M, movable sections of chimney. N, connecting-rod. O, fly-wheel and driving-pulley combined. P, bearing wheels of engine. Q, fore-wheels.

General view.—Fig. 6 presents a general view of the arrangement of the apparatus for work. A, barrels of lime. B, sifting the sand. S, mixing the lime and sand and passing it into the buckets of the elevator E. T, shoot. C, mixing cylinder. L, locomobile.

Details of fabrication.—Alternate layers of sand and lime thrown into a heap, about a cubic yard in quantity, are mixed with shovels on the ground, and then passed into the buckets of the elevator. The latter discharges into the inclined shoot T, which conducts to the mixing cylinder. When cement is added, it should be previously well mixed with a little water in a trough, through which revolves a small shaft with arms, and then added in small quantities to the materials in the cylinder. The mixing apparatus being in operation, small quantities of water, a glass or pint at regular intervals of time, are thrown in at the top of the cylinder by a boy stationed for that purpose. To insure regularity in the distribution, a circular pipe round the upper end of the cylinder *a* is sometimes used. It is pierced at regular intervals with a series of small holes, through which the water, supplied from a reservoir above, trickles into the cylinder. The quantity of water to be added varies with the materials, and must be regulated by observation. The béton issuing from the cylinder should be moist, and when made into a ball and slightly compressed in the hands, should retain its form and harden rapidly. The mixture in the lower part of the cylinder *b* is forced downwards by the helicoidal arms *e*, and outwards by the cycloidal arms *f*, through the opening *g*, extending round the cylinder. The expulsion through the opening *g* pushes it off the bottom plate P, at every point of its circumference, and falling on the revolving plate N, it is carried round till arrested by the fixed scraper L, which collects and shoots it off on to the ground or into boxes.

For ordinary masonry, one mixing is sufficient; for finer work, a second mixing in the same apparatus is advisable.

When a rapid taking is necessary, as in winter work, &c., the mixture may be artificially heated up to about 212° Fahr. (100° C.) during the operation of mixing. For this purpose heated air or steam is introduced into the mixing cylinder through a pipe bored with small openings, or else the cylinder itself may be heated by a spiral tube in which steam or hot water circulates. Heating quickens the drying and hastens the taking and hardening of the materials; it also darkens the color.

PACKING.

The béton taken directly from the mixing cylinder is shovelled into moulds or forms in successive layers and compressed moderately by hand-pestles weighing from 15 to 30 pounds. (Plate II, Fig. 7.) Generally $1\frac{6}{10}$ cubic yards of loose material from the mixing apparatus will thus compact into a cubic yard of wall.

MOULDING.

There are two methods of moulding: 1st. *Moulding in place.*—Walls for buildings are constructed in sections of about 3 feet in height, and 10 to 15 feet in length. For this purpose a crib or framework and boards, forming two sides of a box, is constructed with an interior space equal to the thickness of the intended wall; the sides of the crib are kept in place by small iron rods which connect them, passing through the wall, and to be subsequently withdrawn. The loose béton is shovelled into the crib and compacted with the pestle; subsequently the connecting rods are withdrawn, the sides of the crib or mould are lifted up, a second section is formed in like manner on the top of the first, and the work continues in this way till the wall reaches the required height.

Plate II, Fig. 8, presents a side view of the crib or mould. Fig. 9, a cross-section of crib and wall. Fig. 10, horizontal section of crib and wall, with splayed opening for window, door, &c.

2d. *Moulding in blocks.*—Building blocks of various sizes, hardness and forms, with or without ornaments, are made of béton in moulds, in the same manner as sections of wall above described, and the blocks are laid with joints of mortar like other stone. Blocks and slabs for balconies, steps, fountains, columns, cornices, pilasters, &c., are formed in like manner.

PROPERTIES.

Different varieties of béton-coignet tested at the *Conservatoire des Arts et Métiers* give the following results, indicated in the annexed table.

Experiments on the crushing strength of béton made at the Conservatoire Impérial des Arts et Métiers, by Mr. P. Michelot, chief engineer in the Ponts et Chaussées, Paris, July, 1864.

Date of fabrication of the samples.	Composition of the samples experimented on.	Dimensions in centimetres.			Weight in kilograms of a cubic metre.	Crushing strength—			Observations.
		Length.	Breadth.	Height.		In kilograms.	In kilograms per square centimetre of section.	In pounds pr. square inch of section.	
						Total.			
February, 1864*	River sand, half size 4 Lime of Argenteuil 1 Cement of Paris ½	7. 60 5. 20	5. 80 2. 40	8. 10	2, 085	12, 809. 678 16, 213. 541	226. 48 286. 66	3, 269. 56 4, 130. 77	Fissured.
February, 1863*	Common sand 5 Lime of Argenteuil 1 Cement of Paris 1	7. 60 5. 00	5. 70 2. 40	8. 10	2, 196	17, 452. 641	315. 49	4, 546. 21	
February, 1862	Coarse sand 4 Lime of Theil (hydraulic) 1 Boulogne cement ½	10. 10	8. 30	10. 00	2, 277	32, 866. 798	392. 06	5, 649. 58	
November, 1862	Mixed sand 4 Lime of Theil (hydraulic) 1 Boulogne cement ¾	7. 60	5. 75	8. 10	2, 348	21, 761. 241 22, 729. 641	497. 98 520. 13	7, 175. 89 7, 495. 07	Fissured.
May, 1863*	Sand of Vésinet 4 Lime of Argenteuil 1 Paris cement ¼	7. 80 5. 20	5. 60 2, 60	8. 05	2, 146	10, 456. 141	182. 80	2, 634. 14	

* OBSERVATION.—The samples marked with an asterisk have the form of a T; the double numbers in the columns of length and breadth indicate the size of the two rectangles composing the total surface.

An examination of the preceding table will show that the strength or bearing power of each variety of béton is sufficient for ordinary uses, but that the differences are great; and a more careful study will trace these differences to the properties of various sands, to the proportions of sand, lime, cement and water, and to the peculiar ingredients inherent in the various limes, derived from different localities.

But an elaborate explanation of the table would have no particular value, as similar substances derived from different localities are never exactly alike, and the best mixture in each particular case must be ascertained by actual experiments, which are easily made, the results being simple and obvious.

Most of the bétons in the preceding table are stronger than is necessary for ordinary uses, and if used, the thickness of the structures as compared with common masonry may be diminished. For the more common purposes bétons of more sand and less lime are used.

The tensile and bearing strength of bétons is variable, as is that of every kind of stone. The following table shows the range of strength in the particular kinds, and the relative strength of the different kinds of building materials named:

	Mortar.	Béton.	Brick.	Limestone.	Sandstone.	Granite.
Crushing strength in pounds	280	2, 634	550	4, 000	4, 000	5, 500
	to	to	to	to	to	to
Per square inch of section	2, 100	7, 495	1, 700	5, 000	5, 000	11, 000
Tensile strength in pounds............	50	288	115	120	180	....
	to	to	to	to	to	
Per square inch of section	290	426	280	864	900	....

A cubic yard of béton weighs about 3,700 pounds.

APPLICATION OF BÉTON—CONCLUSION.

WAREHOUSES, CHURCHES, GRANARIES, CELLARS, FOUNDATIONS.

Structures and buildings of solid masses of béton suffer less than ordinary materials from unequal settling of the ground, and underground rooms and cellars built of it are particularly free from damp.

The railway station at Suresnes, several houses at St. Denis, the church at Vésinet, &c., are examples of this kind, and from the absence of joints are the same as if made of one block of stone.

Cheap dwellings for workmen are now in course of construction in several localities in France.

A small house of béton-coignet was exhibited at the Champ de Mars, with specimens of arches, piers, slabs, statues, fountains, &c., finely moulded and well made by Mr. Coignet.

The materials for common work of the above kind are five parts of sand, one of lime, and the ordinary quantity of water.

ARCHES AND VAULTS.

Various experiments have been made with good results to test the strength of béton for arches, and it is now much used for that purpose; in the structures of the Northern railway, at Paris, in the new prison of the Madelonnettes, and in the new barracks of Notre Dame. In the latter, an arched vault was built, of 18 feet span, 1½ foot versed sine, 8½ inches thick at the crown, with surface of 14 square yards, on which experimental weights of 47 tons were placed for a fortnight without damage. Béton was afterwards used for all the similar arched vaults in the building, giving a surface of 3,588 square yards.

An experimental arch on the quay de Billy, has a span of 55½ feet, versed sine 4 feet, thickness of crown 14 inches, with good results.

At Aubervilliers the machinery of a considerable saw mill is placed on an arch of 33 feet span, versed sine 6½ feet.

The ventilation of the Exhibition building, at the Champ de Mars, is effected by underground works, consisting of a series of circular and radial galleries, arched with béton, span about 10 feet, for the circulation and supply from below of cool air through openings in the floor.

The outer gallery is 33 feet in width, and 1,443 yards in length; the groined arches of béton are supported on two rows of béton pillars, 864 in number, carrying a roof, the upper surface of which forms a floor of 15,873 square yards of surface.

The quantity of béton consumed in these galleries was 353,166 cubic feet. Plate II, Fig. 11, is a cross section of the outer gallery.

The materials of this structure were: Four parts of sand, one of lime, and one-half part of Portland cement.

WALLS.

The embankment on which runs the avenue de l' Empereur, at the Trocadero, for a quarter of a mile is supported by a wall of béton about 40 feet high; the outer side is strengthened by pilasters; the inner side consists of a series of arches at right angles to the wall, built one upon the other, and extending into the embankment, forming a bearing for the mass of earth, and diminishing its lateral pressure against the wall. The walls and arches are a solid mass of béton. Plate I, Fig. 6.

The steeple of the church of Vésinet is constructed of béton, 130 feet high, and shows no sign of weakness.

FLOORS, TERRACES, ROOFS.

If the area does not exceed 13 or 16 feet in width, a slab of béton 10 or 12 inches thick will be strong enough to sustain itself; if the area be greater, double T-joists of iron should cross the space for ceilings, floors, &c., and the slabs of béton may be made thicker or thinner, depending on the distance of the joists one from another, the flanges of which form the holding of the slabs.

Joists being thus placed and a temporary scaffolding or floor of boards erected underneath, the béton is dumped upon it and packed, the edges hold upon the flanges, the béton hardens, the scaffolding is removed and the ceiling remains firm; if the upper side should serve for a floor also, the béton should be laid thicker and carried over the joists so as to form a smooth surface above them.

Béton for this work should be five parts of sand, one part of lime, and one-fourth part of cement.

FLAGGING, SIDEWALKS.

Béton being impervious to water and without joints, no moisture is absorbed beneath, if the ground be properly drained; therefore no heaving or disturbance results from frosts in the ground. Flagging and floors of béton for courts, stables, cellars, coach-houses, schools, railway stations, warehouses, &c., &c., are much used.

Sand five parts, lime one part, cement one part.

FOUNDATIONS FOR MACHINERY.

Foundations for machinery of béton are usually cheaper and as good as masonry of stone. For engines, a cubic yard of béton corresponds to a horse-power, and a 30 horse-power engine should have 30 cubic yards of foundation.

Foundations of béton for water-wheels and turbines may be seen at St. Maur, for steam engines at the percussion cap factory at Paris, the tobacco factory at Châteauroux, the glass works at St. Gobain, &c.; at Oyssel a steam-engine of 400 horse-power, which works admirably, rests on a block of béton 7 yards in thickness, and at the Exposition of 1867 a great portion of the machinery was placed on béton foundations laid in winter, and worked well.

Composition: sand five parts, lime one part, cement one-fourth part.

SEWERS, AQUEDUCTS, WATER-PIPES.

Twenty-five miles of main sewers in Paris have been made of béton, and its use for this purpose is rapidly increasing.

A trench is cut as usual, a floor of béton is laid on the bottom, a frame-work of timber and boards introduced as for masonry to give form to the sides and arch; the béton is dumped and packed by the commonest labor, the wood-work removed, and the sewer is finished.

The regulations for sewers requiring walls of 10 inches of stone masonry admit of walls of 8 inches in béton; their construction of béton requires less time; the economy in masonry is reckoned at 30 per cent., and the saving on the whole work at 20 per cent.

Dimensions and cost of the principal sewers in béton of Paris.

Type of sewer.	Dimensions of sewer. Greatest height in feet.	Greatest diameter in feet.	Area in square yards of cross-section of sewer.	Length in yards of inner circumference of cross-section of sewer.	Thickness of wall in inches.	Cubic feet of béton per linear foot of sewer.	Entire cost in Paris per linear foot of sewer, including cost of excavation, centring, and masonry.
	Feet.	*Feet.*	*Sq. yards.*	*Yards.*	*Inches.*	*Cub. feet.*	
Main sewer, No. 8	9, 186	7, 546	6, 045	8. 667	10. 63	26, 156	$5 92
9	9, 022	6, 562	5, 071	8, 503	9. 45	22, 075	5 00
10	7, 874	5, 641	3, 959	7, 170	7. 87	15, 608	3 53
11	4, 493	2, 296	0, 969	4, 044	10. 25	9, 257	2 35
12	7, 054	4, 265	2, 894	6, 492	7. 87	14, 639	3 31
Branch sewer No, 1	6, 562	3, 281	1, 794	5, 574	7. 87	12, 465	3 18
2	6, 234	2, 524	1, 419	5, 301	7. 87	11, 948	3 04
3	5, 577	2, 524	1, 292	4, 263	7. 87	11, 087	2 84

Plate II, Fig. 12, is a cross-section of a large sewer in béton, (type No. 8,) showing the mode of construction and the appearance when finished. Fig. 13, a water-pipe.

Water-pipes of béton are made at half the expense of iron and they cost little for repairs. The whole of the underground drainage of 40 acres roofed by the palace of the Exhibition was through béton pipes of 12 to 16 inches tube discharging into sewers of béton. The cubic contents of materials used in these pipes amounted to 264,825 cubic feet.

For the sewers of Paris, and for this service, the following proportions of materials were used:

175 cubic feet of sand.
35 cubic feet of hydraulic lime.
550 pounds heavy Paris cement, equivalent to Portland cement.

CISTERNS, RESERVOIRS, TANKS, CESS-POOLS.

These, when built of masonry and coated with cement, are impervious to water, but need constant repairs; of béton they are equally impervious, cost less and are more secure.

A cistern 39 feet in depth, 5 feet in diameter, with sides of 10 inches in thickness, after two days receives water, and remains sound an indefinite period.

The cess-pools of béton authorized by the prefect of the Seine in 1862 are without cement, hold good, and are water-tight; structures of this kind are adopted for the great opera-house now building, and for the great railroad stations, &c., &c.

Gasometer tanks of large dimensions, 130 feet diameter, 49 feet in depth, are built of common béton-coignet at Rueil and St. Denis. The difficulties of making structures of this size in masonry water-tight are said to be much less in béton.

Composition: five parts of sand, one of lime, and one-half part of cement.

MARINE STRUCTURES.

For the foundations of breakwaters and piers stones of irregular and various sizes are used, but small stones are preferred. Being cast into the sea without order and left to find their position as they sink, small stones pack closer and form beds more solid than large ones; they are also less liable to disturbance than large stones from the "hydraulic press action" of waves arrested in their horizontal movement and thrown downwards.

Banks or ridges with more or less sloping sides are thus raised from the bottom of the sea nearly to the surface at low tide, and upon these walls of masonry are built of sufficient height and thickness to resist the force of the sea.

The force of the waves against a vertical wall, as measured in different localities, shows the following results, in weather ranging from ordinary to tempest: At Cette, in the Mediterranean, from 14,000 to 24,000 pounds per square yard; Bell Rock, Scotland, as high as 30,675 pounds per square yard; island of Serryvor, Scotland, 5,000 to 19,000, and 55,760 pounds per square yard; Cherbourg, 36,000 to 55,000 pounds per square yard.

The horizontal movement arrested by a wall in deep water becomes vertical and produces a descending wave of great force, which tends to excavate and sweep away the bank and undermine the wall.

The banks or foundations are therefore protected by covering the slopes with large blocks of stone, of sufficient size and weight to resist displacement by the descending waves, and in very exposed situations the talus of blocks thus formed is raised above the surface to afford protection also to the wall.

The difficulties and expense of obtaining blocks of stone sufficient in size and abundance for this purpose have led to the use of artificial blocks of concrete. These blocks are also extensively used to form the interior of walls and piers, the facings being of stone. In solidity and strength they are equal to the purpose, but they suffer more from the action of sea-water than the best kinds of stone, which is attributable to the ingredients in the cementing substance.

Hydraulic limes.—Hydraulic limes are exceedingly variable in their elements, but may be divided into three general classes—silicious, aluminous, and cements.

Silicious limes.—Limestone composed of carbonate of lime intimately mixed with fine silicious sand, after burning leaves 70 to 80 per cent. of quicklime, and 30 to 20 per cent. of silicate of lime, forming a hydraulic lime usually called "silicious," and expressed by the formula:

$$CaO. + SiO^3. 3\ CaO.$$

Slaking of this produces hydrate of lime and hydrous-silicate of lime; formula:

$$n. CaO. HO. + SiO^3. 3 CaO. 6 HO.$$

Aluminous limestone.—Limestone containing 8 to 18 per cent. of clay, the principal elements of which are hydrous-silicates of alumina, after burning leaves 70 to 80 per cent. of quicklime, and 30 to 20 per cent. of mixed silicates and alumina, forming an hydraulic lime called "aluminous," which, after slaking, is expressed by the formula:

$$n. CaO. HO + SiO^3. 3 CaO. 6 HO + Al^2 O^3. 3 CaO. 6 HO.$$

Cement.—Limestone containing from 18 to 36 per cent. of clay, which leaves after burning quicklime, silicate of lime, alumina, silicate of alumina, produces "hydraulic cement," which, after slaking, contains hydrates of the preceding elements.

Hydraulic limes and cements usually contain, in addition to the substances above enumerated, small quantities of oxides of iron, silicates alumina and magnesia, sulphate of lime, &c.

Mortar properly made of either of these limes crystallizes simultaneously, and sets quickly and strongly, though the presence of magnesia and sulphate of lime is detrimental to good setting, as these bodies crystallize slower; oxide of iron does not impede the setting.

ACTION OF THE SEA.

The action of sea-water on hydraulic mortars is excessively complicated. The elements of lime, as above shown, are variable, and the salts of magnesia, carbonic acid, and sulphureted hydrogen in sea-water are variable, and differ in localities but little removed from each other.

I do not propose to follow in detail the results of the observations and experiments which have been made of various sea-waters on different sorts of hydraulic mortar.

The mortars are all exposed to the mechanical action of the sea, and to the chemical action of the salts and gases which it holds in solution; they are sharply attacked, and the effect is considerable before the hydrate of lime on the outer surface is converted into carbonate of lime by the absorption of carbonic acid from the water and air. The crust of carbonate of lime thus formed resists the chemical action of the sea, and the protection thus given to the interior is increased in some cases by the growth of sea-shells and of marine plants. The waste is thus diminished, but it is never extinguished; the destruction goes on, and the best hydraulic mortars are gradually eaten away.

Blocks of concrete contain more mortar than masonry of dressed stone; they are consequently more exposed to waste from the causes in question, and are sooner destroyed.

Many remedies have been proposed, and numerous trials of them made, but hitherto without important and permanent success. The method proposed by Mr. Coignet is to get rid of the hydraulic limes and their perishable ingredients by the substitution of common lime as the cementing substance.

EXPERIMENTS OF MR. COIGNET.

Time is evidently required to test experiments of this kind, and those of Mr. Coignet are too recent to prove conclusively success or failure. His method of experimenting is by continually diminishing the quantity of hydraulic lime and cement, and continually increasing the proportion of common lime in the composition of his blocks. The blocks are placed in exposed positions in different localities to the action of the sea-water, and followed by periodical examinations and records of the progressive results of the experiments.

His first experiments were begun, by order of the government, in November and December, 1858, and January, 1859, on the Socoa breakwater at St. Jean de Luz, in a very exposed situation. The blocks were of several kinds, as follows:

First series of blocks.—Blocks made several months before being placed in the sea:

1st. Blocks composed of seven parts of sand and one part of common or fat lime.

2d. Blocks composed of seven parts of sand and one part of lime, slightly hydraulic.

3d. Blocks composed of seven parts of sand and one part of fat lime, and one-fourth to one-half part of cement.

4th. Blocks composed of seven parts of sand, one part of lime, slightly hydraulic, and one-fourth to one-half part of cement.

These blocks are all alike in good condition at this date, (1867,) and have resisted the action of sea-water with satisfactory results. They are compact and hard, and the only effect noticed has been the wearing of the edges of the blocks and the rounding off of the angles, produced by the friction of pebbles and the general mechanical action of the sea. No difference has yet appeared in the durability of blocks made of common lime and those containing hydraulic cement.

Second series of blocks.—This series is composed of 12 small blocks, made on land, and allowed to harden for eight days before being placed in the sea.

Six blocks were composed as follows:

1st. Seven parts of sand, one part of fat lime.

2d. Seven parts of sand, one part of fat lime.

3d. Seven parts of sand, one part of artificial hydraulic lime, made of fat lime and clay.

4th. Seven parts of sand, one part of lime, slightly hydraulic.

5th. Seven parts of sand, one part of hydraulic lime.

6th. Seven parts of sand, one part of very hydraulic and siliceous lime.

The remaining six blocks were composed as follows: Each of seven parts of sand, one part of the same varieties of lime as the above blocks, with the addition to each of one-fourth to one-half part of cement.

This series of blocks has completely resisted until now (1867) the action of the sea, and show no trace of decomposition. The blocks of fat lime and hydraulic lime are in equally good condition. Some blocks are slightly worn by the mechanical action of the sea.

Third series of blocks.—Large blocks made on land at the same time as the blocks of the second series and allowed to dry for nine months before being placed in the sea.

These blocks were composed in a similar manner and of similar ingredients to those of the second series.

Under the influence of this long exposure to the air, these blocks at the end of nine months had attained great hardness and solidity. Their structure was compact, and chips could be struck off with a hammer, as if the blocks had been made of stone. Some of them showed small cracks on the upper surface, owing, it is supposed, to the unequal quality of the fat lime used in their fabrication.

When exposed to the sea they have all proved good, and are alike in good condition at this date, (1867,) the fat and hydraulic limes and cements giving a similar result.

Fourth series of blocks.—Blocks made in place at low tide, and immediately covered by the rising tide.

These blocks, seven in number, were composed as follows:

Blocks 1, 2, 3, of seven parts of sand, one part of a very hydraulic and siliceous lime, and one-half part of cement.

Block 4, of seven parts of sand, one part of artificial hydraulic lime, and one-half part of cement.

Block 5, of seven parts of sand, one part of hydraulic lime, and one-half part of cement.

Blocks 6 and 7, of seven parts of sand, one part of common lime and pozzuolana, and one-half part of cement.

The rocks on which these blocks were constructed are situated at the extremity of the breakwater; at low tide they are uncovered for an hour or two, and at high tide are covered with water several metres in depth.

The moulds were made of thin pine boards and established on the rock as a bottom. Their form was a truncated cone of four feet diameter of base and three feet in height.

At low tide the moulds were filled with béton and carefully packed. They were immediately covered by the rising tide and in less than 24 hours the béton was sufficiently hard and firm to allow the moulds to be taken apart and the blocks entirely exposed to the sea.

Examined at the end of nine months, the four blocks first mentioned were in perfect condition and showed no sign of decomposition. They were very hard and sonorous when struck with a hammer. The 5th block was at first partially decomposed, but immediately hardened. The 6th and 7th blocks were respectively reduced to one-half and three-fourths of their original size by the destructive action of the sea.

At this date (1867) the four first mentioned blocks are in perfect condition, having completely resisted the action of the sea; the fifth block is now as hard and solid as the preceding ones and shows no signs of decay; the sixth and seventh blocks perished in two and a half years, which is attributed to the presence of pozzuolana, which had been added to quicken the taking of the fat lime by rendering it hydraulic.

EXPERIMENTS AT MARSEILLES AND AT CHERBOURG.

Another series of experiments was commenced at Marseilles at a later period. A large number of blocks of béton-coignet, made with numerous varieties of lime and cement, were exposed to the sea on the outer breakwater of the Bassin Napoléon. When last examined in November, 1867, they were in good condition and had not suffered decay; fat and hydraulic limes giving equally good results.

Lately a number of blocks have been ordered by the navy department for further experiments at Cherbourg.

Evidently the experiments have not been continued long enough to test fully the relative resisting qualities against the chemical action of sea-water of blocks cemented with common fat lime and blocks cemented with hydraulic lime, since both show thus far equal enduring qualities.

But the results, on the whole, are interesting and suggest the following conclusions:

1. Common lime can be substituted for hydraulic lime in béton-coignet, with an equally durable result, provided the blocks are allowed to harden for a few days on land previous to immersion.

2. Blocks of béton-coignet (sand and hydraulic lime) can be made in direct contact with the sea, provided they be protected by a crib during the time necessary for the taking, say 24 hours. Blocks thus made have proved as durable as those made on shore, while under similar circumstances of immediate immersion in the sea, and 24 hours' protection by a crib, blocks of ordinary concrete (sand, hydraulic lime, and stones) made with the same hydraulic lime would disappear in a short time.

3. Blocks of béton-coignet made on land are quite ready for immersion after drying and hardening for three or four days, while blocks of hydraulic concrete usually require from three to six months for drying and hardening.

To supply the daily demand for these blocks of concrete in the construction of a breakwater large yards are necessary, which are usually at a distance from the breakwater. They must have space for 1,000 to 2,000 blocks in various stages of fabrication and drying; they require, also, a large establishment of machinery and railways; a large capital is thus invested and the expense is heavy.

In making béton-coignet less machinery and plant, less ground for drying, less preparation in advance are required, the time and capital involved are less, and the whole cost is consequently diminished.

Mr. Coignet now proposes the construction of piers and breakwaters in the following manner:

1. Blocks of béton to be made on land, in length equal to the breadth

of the pier and of corresponding size, weighing say 140 tons, to be lowered into the sea, and placed side by side, across the line of the pier, for foundation.

2. The wall to be constructed likewise of béton, in place, forming thus a single mass, binding the blocks below by the weight and solidity of the wall.

For this he would use from five to seven parts of sand, one of lime, fat or slightly hydraulic, and one-fourth to one-half part of cement.

But it is not probable that the government engineers consider the experience already gained sufficient to warrant them in recommending so great an outlay at present as this experiment involves.

CONCLUSION.

The materials of béton-coignet exist in abundance in all countries and in most localities, seldom requiring long and expensive transportation.

Sand is easily excavated, lime is a simple preparation, and both are materials of low cost; most of the labor in making is performed by machinery, and little of the manual labor required need be skilled labor.

Sand, lime, water, machinery, motive force, few tools and common labor, are the elements of structures made of béton, and the béton itself is well adapted to numerous daily wants, in which solidity, durability, and cheapness are preferable to beauty of materials, the evidence of which is shown in the ground and underground structures of the great palace of the Exposition, and in its increasing application to sewers, tanks, foundations, floors, walls, &c., enumerated in the preceding pages.

The cost of béton varies with that of the lime and cement employed. In Paris, works in béton cost, including fabrication and construction, from $5 to $8 per cubic yard. Flagging, two inches thick, costs 56 cents per square yard.

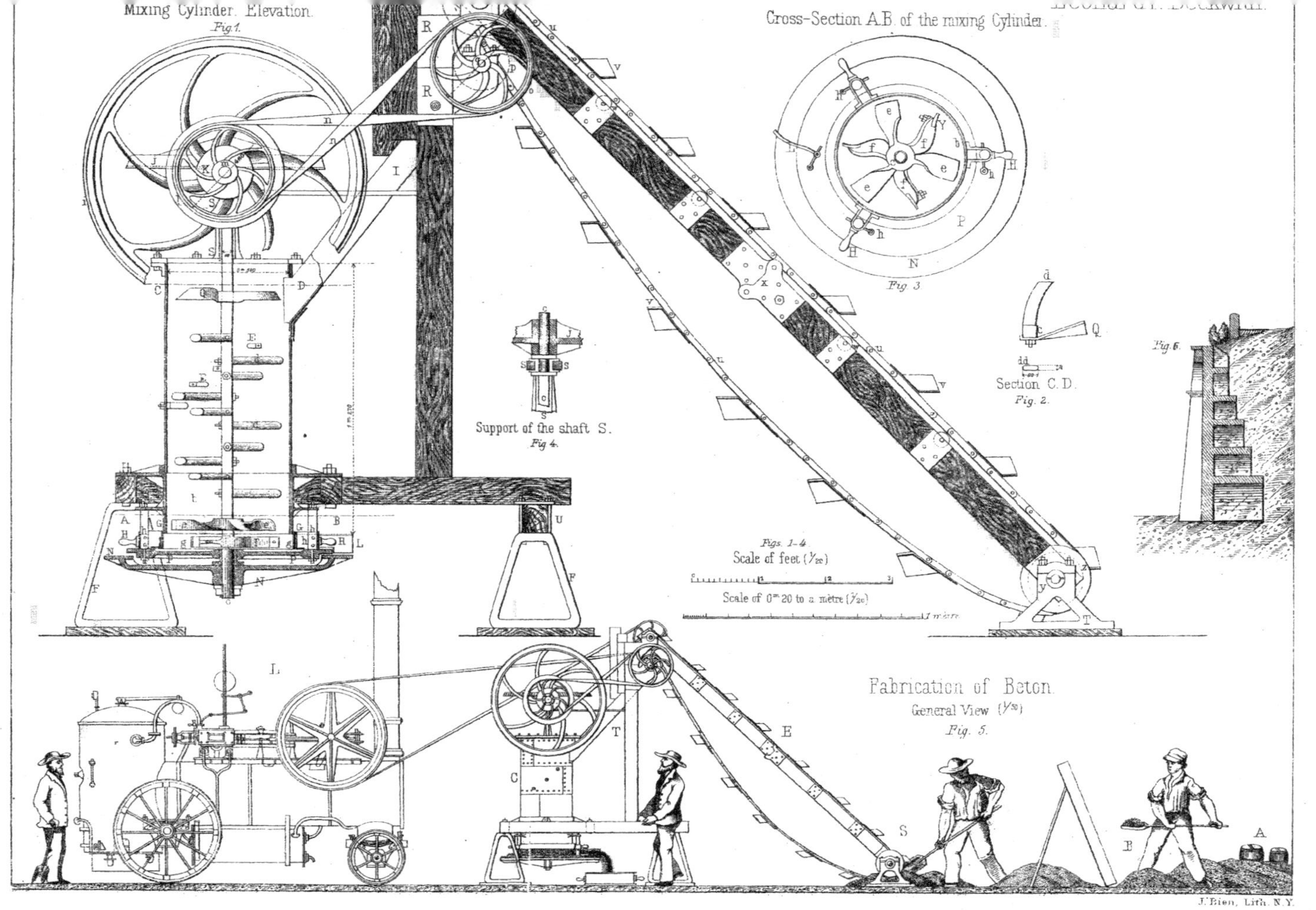
Mixing Cylinder. Elevation.
Fig. 1.
Cross-Section A.B. of the mixing Cylinder.
Fig. 3
Section C.D.
Fig. 2.
Fig. 6.
Support of the shaft S.
Fig. 4.
Figs. 1–4.
Scale of feet (1/20)
Scale of 0m 20 to a mètre (1/20)
Fabrication of Beton.
General View (1/50)
Fig. 5.
J. Bien, Lith. N.Y.

PARIS UNIVERSAL EXPOSITION, 1867.

REPORTS OF THE UNITED STATES COMMISSIONERS.

REPORT

ON

ASPHALT AND BITUMEN,

AS APPLIED TO THE CONSTRUCTION OF

STREETS AND SIDEWALKS IN PARIS;

ALSO TO

TERRACES, ROOFS, ETC., AND TO VARIOUS PRODUCTS IN THE EXHIBITION OF 1867;

WITH OBSERVATIONS UPON

MACADAMIZED STREETS AND ROADS,

BY

ARTHUR BECKWITH,

CIVIL ENGINEER.

WASHINGTON:
GOVERNMENT PRINTING OFFICE.
1868.

CONTENTS.

SECTION I.

ASPHALT AND BITUMEN AS APPLIED TO THE CONSTRUCTION OF STREETS AND SIDEWALKS IN PARIS.

SECTION II.

MACADAMIZED STREETS AND ROADS.

ILLUSTRATIONS.

SECTION I.

ASPHALT AND BITUMEN, AS APPLIED TO THE CONSTRUCTION OF STREETS AND SIDEWALKS IN PARIS.

INTRODUCTORY REMARKS.

Asphalt is used in Paris chiefly in two different forms: first, the natural rock, unalloyed, with which streets are made; second, a mixture of asphalt with bitumen and fine gravel for the construction of sidewalks.

The rock is found principally at Seyssel and Vale-de-Travers, where it can be procured at $7 90[1] per ton. It is transported to Paris by rail or canal, and is sold here for $14 or $16 per ton. A few hundred tons of rock have been transported to the United States from France at different times.

The mixture above spoken of is called mastic of asphalt, and is manufactured in many places in France. At Seyssel a manufactory is established, producing 40 to 50 tons of mastic of asphalt per day.

The term "asphalt" or "asphaltic rock" is applied only to a species of limestone impregnated with bitumen.

"Bitumen" is a dark, viscous substance of organic origin, which impregnates bituminous limestone, flows from various rocks, or is found in natural deposits.

"Mastic of asphalt" is a composition formed of bituminous limestone (asphalt) reduced to powder and mixed with a small quantity of bitumen.

This mastic, with a further addition of bitumen and fine gravel, is used for sidewalks.

DESCRIPTION AND COMPOSITION OF ASPHALT.

Asphalt, or asphaltic rock, is a limestone of natural formation, composed of pure carbonate of lime impregnated with bitumen, and found in numerous localities forming strata of various extent.

Color: dark chocolate, nearly black.

Fracture: fine-grained, irregular, without cleavage planes. In some formations the fracture in the direction of stratification is dark and mealy, but in the opposite direction it is drier and the color is lighter.

Asphalt is affected by changes of temperature. At a low temperature it is hard and sonorous, and under the hammer breaks like common limestone. At the temperature of high summer heat it yields to the blows of the hammer, becomes flattened, and is easily reduced by repeated blows to a paste; and at the temperature[2] of 140° or 160° it commences

[1] The prices given in this report are in gold.

[2] All temperatures mentioned are expressed in degrees of Fahrenheit.

to disintegrate and crumble. Above 212° the disintegration is complete. The average specific gravity is 2.235, (water being 1.000.)

VARIETIES OF ASPHALT.

The structure of asphaltic rock varies in different localities; the best localities are fine-grained, homogeneous, free from interposed particles of limestone not impregnated with bitumen. The fracture of this quality presents the same aspect whether broken parallel or perpendicular to the stratification. The aspect of all formations is not uniform; some rocks present darker and lighter spots like the skin of a tiger. Others contain numerous shells, of one-twentieth or one-tenth of an inch in diameter, filled with crystals of carbonate of lime impregnated with bitumen; the crystals are often large, rhomboidal, with cleavage planes of one-twenty-fifth or one-tenth of an inch. All those varieties constitute excellent asphalt, provided the whole mass be thoroughly penetrated with bitumen.

The rock may be uniformly impregnated, but if it contains less than six per cent. of bitumen it is too poor to be worked. The rock may be cracked in numberless directions, and disintegrated in a manner to admit of the absorption of bitumen, and the fracture may present the fine dark color of good qualities; but if this be crushed to powder or examined by the microscope, it will be discovered that the impregnation is only apparent and owing merely to infiltration and absorption, which gives color and coating only to the granules.

The conditions necessary to perfect impregnation have been the subject of fruitless speculations, the most plausible of which is the theory that reduces the bitumen to the condition of gas, and supposes a high temperature and great pressure, which results in the complete saturation of the rock without disintegrating it.

The rock may also appear rich in bitumen, but contain elements of clay, which not being impregnated like the carbonate of lime, destroy the homogeneity of the formation. The fissures seen in side-walks are often attributable to this cause, but the presence of clay is easily detected.

Some beds of asphalt contain an oily element, which renders them too fat and prevents the solidification of the mastic; but rock of this kind may be freed of this oil by distillation, and then becomes fit for use.

Formations of asphaltic rock exposed to air lose their bitumen to a certain depth, and then present on the surface the ordinary appearance of white chalk formations; but experience has shown that after 40 years of exposure the evaporation of bitumen does not extend below the $\frac{1}{100}$ of an inch from the surface.

COMPOSITION OF ASPHALT.

The chemical composition of asphalt varies in the proportion of limestone and bitumen, being generally from 7 to 8 per cent. of bitumen, and 93 to 92 per cent. of limestone. The qualitative analysis gives nearly identical results everywhere.

Very pure varieties, such as those of the Val-de-Travers in Switzerland and of Seyssel in France, contain absolutely nothing but carbonate of lime and bitumen.

Less pure varieties, such as those in Auvergne, (France,) which is a volcanic region, contain other elements, which are common to the neighboring rocks, such as clay, silica, magnesia, iron, &c. The asphalt of Auvergne contains, in addition, traces of arsenic.

A rigorous analysis applicable in general, therefore, cannot be given; each bed may present different results. As a rule, it may be stated that asphaltic rock is quite free from foreign matters.

Proportion of bitumen.—To ascertain the proportion of bitumen in asphalt, bituminous sands, asphaltic mastic or other bituminous bodies, the following method may be used:

Reduce a small proportion of the bituminous body, say 20 ounces, to powder; expel the water by exposing the powder to a current of air heated above 200°, but below 300°, to avoid the escape of essential oils from the bitumen; stir the powder freely and weigh a portion of it, say 10 ounces, upon which pour 10 ounces of pure sulphide of carbon. (Impure sulphide of carbon contains sulphuretted hydrogen, which may attack the limestone and sulphur, which would also falsify the weight.) Stir the mixture with a glass rod, let it settle, then pour off the sulphide of carbon, which will be charged with bitumen, upon a filter which has been weighed. Pour another equal quantity of pure sulphide of carbon upon the powder, drain it off again, and filter as before. Repeat this operation until the limestone powder left in the glass becomes white, and the liquid drained off retains no longer a brownish tinge. Dry the powder and weigh it together with the filter; deduct from the weight of both the weight of the filter; the remainder is the weight of limestone powder. And the difference between this weight of powder and its weight of 10 ounces will show the quantity of bitumen which has been extracted.

The operation may be verified by evaporating the sulphide of carbon in water at 160°; the sulphide of carbon being vaporized at 118°, the residue thus obtained will be the bitumen, which should equal in weight the loss sustained by the powder in the previous operation.

ASPHALT STREETS AND ROADS.

STREETS.

The remarkable properties of asphaltic rock permit of its being used unalloyed for streets. At the temperature of near 160° the bitumen which impregnates the molecules of carbonate of lime begins to yield, and the particles separate and crumble to a mass of brown powder at 212° to 280°. If this dust, while hot, be compressed in a mold and allowed to cool in its new form, the molecules will adhere, and the rock will recover the aspect, hardness, and all the qualities it originally possessed when extracted from the quarry. If the hot powder, instead of being placed in a mold, be spread about two inches thick on a hard foundation, and pressed or packed by a hot iron pestle used with the hands, or by a roller, and allowed to cool, the surface will immediately solidify, forming a monolithic crust, identical in all respects with the primitive rock, as if it had been taken in that form from the original bed. Such is the principle on which roads of compressed asphalt are made.

The first indication of this method was due to accident. Fragments of asphalt, dropping from the carts which transported it from the quarries along the road, became heated by the sun and were crushed to powder and compacted by the continued passage of carts, until they formed a hard, smooth track. The phenomenon thus presented led by many experiments to the perfect method of rock-road now in use, which suffers no material change from the influence of the sun.

In 1854, the first street of compressed asphalt that was established in Paris covered 960 square yards. Since then these roads have steadily increased and are laid in the most frequented thoroughfares.

	Square yards.
Up to 1866, the streets of compressed asphalt covered a surface of	96, 000
During 1867, there were laid in Paris	54, 000
And in the suburbs	30, 000
Total surface covered to to-day	180, 000

The contract of the Cie Générale des Asphaltes with the city of Paris covers at present at least 96,000 square yards of streets of compressed asphalt to be laid in 1868–1869.

CONSTRUCTION OF ROADS.

The construction of roads comprise the following operations: Formation of road-bed; crushing the asphalt; roasting the asphalt; transporting and laying the hot powder; packing the road.

Formation of road-bed.—As soon as the earth has been beaten down so as to become compact and solid, it is covered with a layer of concrete (made of 90 parts of gravel and 40 parts of mortar) 2½ inches thick, which is allowed to become hard and perfectly dry before receiving the asphalt.

The first elements of a road-bed are good surface drainage and good under drainage. The damage and disturbance of all roads by frost are diminished in proportion to the perfection of the surface and under drainage. The asphalt roof or covering being impervious to water, there is no vertical absorption from rains, and if the drainage is perfect there will be no lateral absorption. Consequently the road-bed will remain dry at all seasons, and the frosts of winter will produce no upheaval nor disturbance of the road-bed, as it contains no moisture.

Crushing the asphalt.—The asphalt is brought from the quarries in blocks and fragments of all sizes, like ordinary building stone. The blocks are crushed between rollers with steel points, to the size of an egg, and the fragments are then passed between smooth rollers, which reduce them still further. The debris is now ready for roasting. There are various methods of roasting adapted to large or small establishments.

Furnace for roasting asphalt.—The ordinary roasting furnace consists of a concave surface of sheet-iron open to the air, resting on walls of bricks, with a furnace underneath. (See Plate I, Figs. 1 and 2.) The sheet-iron pan measures 2 yards 7 inches by 3 yards 11½ inches. A charge of crushed asphalt of about 1,700 pounds is thrown upon the pan, and during the process of roasting it is shovelled and turned by two men, to render the roasting equal throughout, care being taken in the shovelling not to throw up and expose the powder too much to the air. After an exposure of an hour and a half to a gradually increasing temperature, which rises to 250° or 300°, the disintegration is complete and the powder ready for use. Particular care and some experience are required in roasting, that each portion may be exposed to a temperature as nearly equal as possible, and sufficient to produce a uniform and complete disintegration of particles throughout the mass. In cold weather allowance must be made for increased loss of heat in transporting the powder to the road-bed, that it may not become too cool for consolidation before it is laid and packed. Uniform and equal roasting are important; if any portion of the mass is not sufficiently heated to produce complete disintegration and softening of the oils, that portion will not concrete when laid; also, a portion of the moisture which should be dispelled will remain and prevent the oily substance from cementing the particles. If, on the other hand, any portion be overheated and burnt, the cementing substance will be expelled and leave a dry powder, destitute of the quality of cohesion. Defects which appear in asphaltic roads soon after they are laid often result from this cause.

Second method of roasting.—In this method of roasting an apparatus on the principle of a common coffee-roaster is used. (See Plate II, Figs. 3, 4, 5.) A horizontal cylinder revolves within a stationary cylindrical enclosure. The air in the intervening annular chamber is heated from a furnace beneath. The revolving cylinder, charged with about 4,400 pounds of crushed asphalt, in its rotary motion over the fire, roasts in succession every portion of asphalt regularly. Various gases escape at the orifice *a b c d*, which is partly closed by a thin iron safety lid *e*, which gives way in case of any sudden pressure. At the end of an hour and a half, when the vapor ceases to rise, the roasting is finished. The furnace beneath, which rests on wheels running on rails *f*, is then withdrawn, and a cart is brought in its place; the bolt *g* is drawn, and the powder discharged into the cart. The lid of the cart is closed to retain the heat, and the cart is moved off with the load; the furnace is brought back and the process of roasting asphalt recommences.

Transporting and laying the hot powder.—Formerly asphalt was roasted by the side of the road to be laid, producing smoke and vapor which disturbed the circulation and was inconvenient to the neighborhood. It is now roasted in large establishments in the suburbs and transported in carts lined with sheet-iron, and in a distance of three or four miles in summer will not lose over 10° or 12° of heat, and in winter 30° or 40°.

The asphalt must not be laid on a moist bed. If the surface is moist the heat of the powder vaporizes the moisture, and the steam escaping through the powder prevents the complete cohesion of the particles, and the road will be out of condition in a few months.

If it is impossible or inconvenient to wait for the drying of the concrete bed, it must be dried by artificial means, such as covering the surface with hot ashes or hydraulic lime for a few minutes.

The bed being in condition, the asphalt is spread upon it uniformly, giving it a coat of 2 or 2½ inches in thickness, to produce a final crust of 1⅗ to 2 inches thick.

Packing.—The packing then commences immediately by hand with *hot-irons* or *pestles*, with a smooth under-surface, which are applied lightly and uniformly to the surface.

The packing of the edges is done with rectangular irons, (see Plate III, Fig. 6,) and that of all other parts of the service is done with circular irons, (see Fig. 7.)

When the crust of asphalt has been compressed to its definitive thickness, a thin coat of dry sifted powder is spread over it to fill up inequalities, and the whole surface is then smoothed over with a flat iron, (see Plate III, Fig. 8,) which has been heated nearly to a red heat.

While the asphalt is still hot, smooth iron rollers are passed over it, the first weighing about 440 pounds, and the second 3,300 pounds, which completes the packing.

The process of rolling is sometimes omitted, and it is still doubtful whether it adds anything to the solidity of the coat resulting from the immediate concretion under the smoothing irons.

The packing thus completed, the road may be opened in a few hours to the circulation of vehicles of all kinds.

Resuming and continuing the work.—To resume the work of the previous day, the edge of the solid asphalt must be cleared of dust and loose particles and a layer of hot asphalt thrown upon it to heat it; when the edge is sufficiently heated the layer thus thrown down is removed and returned to the furnace for reheating; and as this removal takes place, a hot layer from the carts is thrown down and spread, and the packing immediately commenced as before described.

The edges of the old and new work thus unite perfectly, and no joint or seam remains visible.

It is unnecessary to interrupt the circulation of a wide street to cover it with asphalt. The process is carried on upon one side of the road; and when that is completed and delivered to circulation the other side is commenced. The joint or seam along the axis of the road being formed in the manner described for continuing the work from one day to another, no vestige of it remains if well done.

The use of compressed asphalt is not limited to the construction of roadways. Courtyards of railway stations, hotels, private houses, quays, and crossings for foot-passengers from one sidewalk to another, are often paved with compressed asphalt, and without even interrupting circulation during the process of construction.

ADVANTAGES OF ASPHALT ROADS.

Constant wear for a year does not reduce the surface more than $\frac{1}{25}$ of an inch; consequently these roads produce neither mud nor dust.

They diminish draught to a very low point. They are almost noiseless; carriage-wheels roll along without being heard, but foot-passengers are warned by the audible tramp of the horses' feet.

The jar and straining of carriages is almost annihilated, and their wear from these important causes becomes nearly imperceptible.

The roofing of the road-bed being impervious to water, the bed becomes harder and drier, and once made is imperishable. These roads, when completed, are absolutely free from bituminous odor.

Objection has been made that asphalt roads are slippery in wet weather; but this objection is ill-founded, if the surface be nearly horizontal, with just sufficient convexity to cause water to flow freely and wash the surface clean.

In proof of this, direct observation shows that on parallel streets, one paved and the other of asphalt, 1 horse in 1,308 falls on the paved street, and only 1 in 1,409 on the asphalt, thus giving the superiority to asphalt roads.

A noteworthy advantage is the facility with which repairs are made by simply cutting away the damaged portion and replacing it by new hot powder.

Cost.—Asphaltic streets in Paris cost, on an average, (concrete foundation included:)

Per square yard	$2 50
And for annual repairs	25

I add the cost of other streets at Paris for comparison: Pavement of hard stone, (Belgian porphyry:)

First cost, depending on the size of the stone, per square yard	$3 00	to	$3 67
Annual repairs, depending on the size of the joints between the stones, per square yard	08⅓	to	25
Macadamized streets:			
First cost, per square yard			1 17
Annual repairs	42	to	50

This does not include the great expense of watering and cleaning the surface and removing the mud from the sewers.

Thus the first cost of asphalt streets is greater than that of macadamızed streets, but the cost of repairs is much less, while the first cost is less than that of the Belgian pavement, and the expenses of repairs greater.

MASTIC OF ASPHALT.

The substance known by the name of mastic of asphalt, of which sidewalks are made, is composed of asphaltic rock reduced to powder and mixed with bitumen, to which may be added sand or gravel.

The asphaltic rock used for mastic is usually of inferior quality, containing less bitumen than that which is used for roads.

SOURCES AND COMPOSITION OF BITUMEN.

The bitumen employed in Paris is derived chiefly from the following sources: 1. From bituminous molasse (a species of sandstone, or a sand and limestone, impregnated with bitumen) by a process of boiling in water, which releases the bitumen. 2. From bituminous sands, found plentifully in the centre of France and elsewhere. 3. From natural deposits of bitumen, as in Trinidad, &c.

Tar obtained by distilling the bituminous schist or boghead from Scotland; also, coal-tar, produced in the manufacture of gas, have been used as a substitute for bitumen, but they are considered to give poor results.

Composition and properties.—Bitumen is composed of several carburetted hydrogens more or less oxygenated. These carbides can be separated by vaporization. The following represents the average composition of bitumen:

Carbon	85
Hydrogen	12
Oxygen	3
Total	100

From whatever source derived, superior bitumen exhibits the following properties: Its *color* is brilliant black with a reddish tinge. The reddish tinge augments when bitumen is softened and drawn into threads. The *fracture* is conchoidal, at a low temperature. Below 50° it is solid and brittle; from 50° to 70° it is elastic and begins to soften; from 70° to 90° it becomes soft and pasty; from 90° to 100° viscous; and at 110° or 120° it melts. Its specific gravity is 1,025, (water being 1,000.) The *odor* is empyreumatic and free from the noxious smell of coal-tar.

FABRICATION OF MASTIC OF ASPHALT.

1. Asphaltic rock is broken into fragments by hammer or grinding cylinders, and then pulverized If it is fat and rich in bitumen, it is pulverized by exposure to heat in an oven, or placed in an iron case and subjected to the action of steam at a pressure of four atmospheres. If the rock is dry and contain little bitumen, it costs less to reduce it to powder by crushing cylinders.

2. The powder is sifted through horizontal cylindrical bolters of wire-gauze of one-tenth inch meshes.

The following dimensions of a bolter are suitable:

Length of wire-gauze portion	5 feet.
Diameter at the entrance.........	1 foot 6 inches.
Diameter at the exit.............	2 feet.
Diameter at the axle.............	2 inches.
Size of iron for framework........	12 inches by 12 inches by 2½ inches.
Number of revolutions per minute.	25

3. A quantity of bitumen (about 330 pounds) is placed in an iron boiler, semi-cylindrical, with a fire under it. (See Plate I, Figs. 9, 10.) As the bitumen becomes heated and liquefied, the powder of asphalt, brought from the bolters, is thrown in from time to time, till the amount of asphalt employed reaches 4,400 pounds. A revolving shaft with spokes (E) passes horizontally through the semi-cylinder, which stirs up and mixes the compound, until the whole mass becomes homogeneous and of the consistency of paste. It is then drawn off into moulds (see Plate III, Fig. 11) holding about 55 pounds each, where it is left to cool and form solid blocks. The mastic thus formed is ready for sale and transport to all places. During this operation about seven per cent. of water and essential oils will be evaporated, leaving 4,400 pounds of mastic.

Good mastic should contain 18 per cent. of bitumen; consequently the quantity of bitumen added to the asphalt must be regulated by the quantity inherent in the rock.

Cost.—The cost of mastic in Paris is $1 09 per 100 pounds.

BITUMINOUS SIDEWALKS.

Bituminous sidewalks cover in Paris a surface of 1,430,896 square yards. They are made of mastic of asphalt, with an addition of bitumen and fine gravel, in the following proportions:

Mastic..	100 pounds.
Additional bitumen...............................	5 to 6 pounds.
Fine gravel	60 to 70 pounds.

Fabrication.—Place three per cent. of the bitumen in the mixing cylinder, (see Plate I, Figs. 9, 10,) and stir with an iron puddling bar, (see Plate III, Fig. 17,) and when this is hot and liquid add ⅓ of the mastic broken in lumps; this being melted and mixed add one per cent. more of bitumen, and another ⅓ of the mastic, and in due course the remaining one per cent. of bitumen and ⅓ of mastic.

When this mass is melted and well mixed add half the gravel, and after an interval of heating and mixing add the remaining half. Clean, dry, silicious river sand is best; the proportion to be added is not absolute; it is usually thrown in as long as the mass retains the proper mortar-like consistency, and no longer. A large proportion of sand or gravel is advantageous in a hot climate, as the sidewalk will be less affected by the rays of the sun.

The temperature in mixing should range from 300° to 400° for two or three hours, the mass being all the while agitated by the revolving spokes, when the mixture will be ready for use.

Transportation.—It is then drawn off into a portable sheet-iron boiler, on wheels, (see Plate III, Figs. 12, 13,) supplied with a small furnace, and revolving shaft and spokes; a moderate fire is required on the way to keep the mastic in a semi-liquid state, and the shaft is occasionally turned by hand to avoid the unequal heating of the mastic.

A portable boiler like the one represented will carry enough to cover 31 square yards of $\frac{3}{5}$ inch thick.

It weighs when empty 2,630 to 3,300 pounds; when full, 4,650 to 5,500 pounds. The cost in Paris is $475.

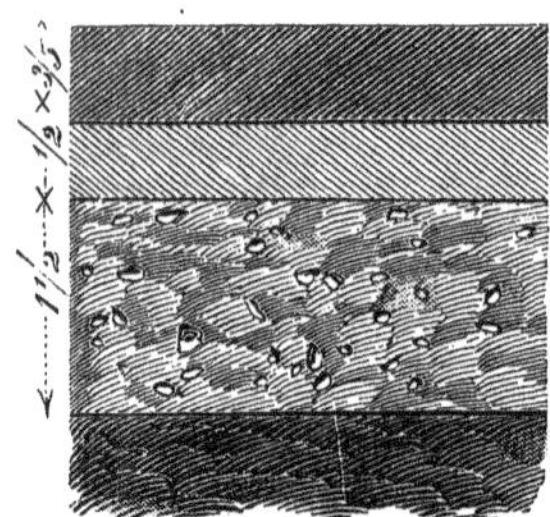

Sidewalk upon hard soil.

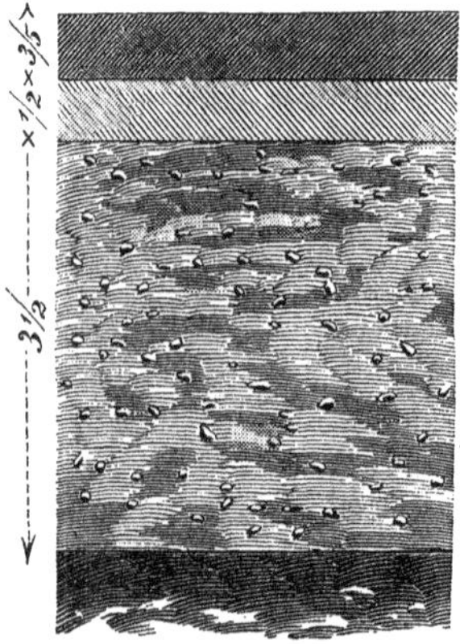

Sidewalk upon loose soil.

Foundations.—The ground should be thoroughly drained, and if it is hard a layer of concrete $1\frac{1}{2}$ inch thick is first spread upon it; and then a layer of mortar $\frac{1}{2}$ an inch in thickness is spread on the concrete. If the ground is loose it should be beaten till it is compact, and then covered with a layer of concrete $3\frac{1}{2}$ inches in thickness, and upon this a layer of mortar $\frac{1}{2}$ inch thick; this formation should be left to become completely dry before the mastic is applied.

Laying.—To secure uniformity and facility in spreading the mastic on the bed a couple of iron rods or rules are used, of the thickness of the intended coat, usually $\frac{3}{5}$ of an inch. These are laid across the sidewalk parallel to each other, with a convenient distance between them, thus forming a gauge for the workmen. The mastic being of the consistency of ordinary mortar and brought hot from the portable boiler in an iron ladle, (see Plate III, Fig 16,) is dumped on the ground in small charges between the rods, and is immediately spread over the surface with wooden trowels. (See Plate III, Figs. 14, 15.)

One belt being thus laid, another is commenced while the first is still hot; the edges of the first and second belt, if kept clean, will readily unite, and the work is then continued.

The surface of the coat being smoothed by wooden trowels, a light shower of dry fine sand is sprinkled on it while it is still soft, to produce a more stony surface, but the mastic being already saturated very little of the sand will be retained.

The cooling and hardening are rapid, and in a few minutes the sidewalk is ready for use.

To resume the work of a preceding day, a process similar to that described for roads of asphalt is necessary, in order to soften the edges of the previous belt, and produce a complete soldering of the edges of the successive belts.

The sketches represent the disposition of the mastic next to the wall and the curb-stone.

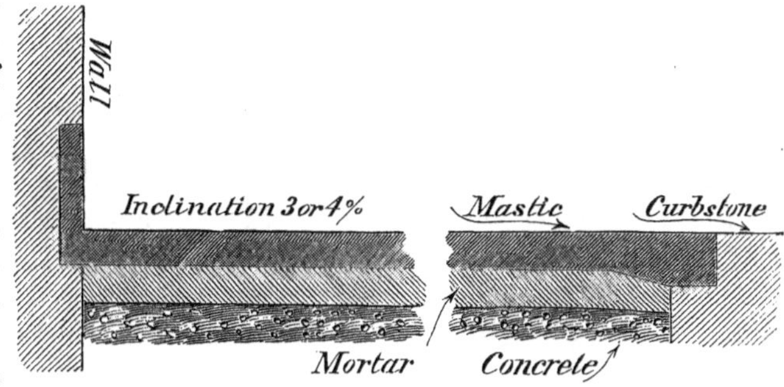

Cost.—The cost of the crust of mastic applied to a surface of at least 1,000 square yards, of $\frac{3}{5}$ inch thick, varies in different towns of France, per square yard, from 67 cents to $1 12, being in Paris 75 cents. If the foundation of concrete and mortar be included, the cost of the sidewalk varies in Paris, per square yard, from 92 cents to $1 12 according to the thickness of concrete. Annual repairs are estimated at, per square yard, five cents.

VARIOUS USES OF ASPHALT AND BITUMEN.

Asphalt and bitumen have been used in many ways from time immemorial; they are found in abundance in the Assyrian and Egyptian remains, and are still among the best materials for constructions of numerous kinds, some of which will be briefly noticed.

FOUNDATIONS IN DAMP GROUND.

The ascent of moisture in the walls of a building on wet ground can be cheaply and effectively prevented by a layer of asphalt between two courses at the base. (See Plate I, Fig. 11.)

A remedy may be applied to a building already erected by digging a trench round the foundations and lining the outer side with planks, leaving a space of three to four inches between the plank and the wall, and filling in the space with hot concrete of mastic and gravel, and the planks are then removed and their place filled with earth.

TERRACES.

If the terrace is roofed in, the mastic is laid as for sidewalks.

If the terrace is exposed to the weather the process presents several differences. Thus, suppose the terrace to be formed of a series of arches, the space between the veins are filled with gravel to a level with the keystones, forming an even surface over the whole. A coating of concrete is first laid on the surface; second, a thin coating of hydraulic morter, giving to the surface a gentle slope of 3 to 4 per cent. When the mortar is perfectly dry, a covering of fat mastic one-fifth of an inch in thickness is laid, of which the proportions are, to the square yard,

Mastic of asphalt	$13\frac{1}{2}$ pounds.
Bitumen	$\frac{1}{2}$ pound.
River sand	$\frac{1}{3}$ pound.

This coating is allowed to cool. Finally upon this is laid a covering one-half to three-fifths of an inch thick of mastic mixed with 80 per cent. of fine gravel, and while it is still warm a sprinkling of fine sand is thrown over it.

The two different coatings of mastic are intended for different purposes; the first, containing more bitumen, is more elastic and less liable to crack, and therefore resists water best; the last, with more gravel, resists better the heat of the sun.

FLOORS.

Floors covered with a coating of mastic are common in factories, hospitals, &c., on each story, and are a good preventive of dampness, especially on ground floors. The mastic is sometimes laid between boards, and in all cases the mastic is prepared as for sidewalks.

Great use is made of mastic for the floors of stables. It is elastic to the feet of animals; it is not deteriorated by the washings of the stable, and absorbs no moisture to produce exhalations. The floor should be grooved by an iron mould while the mastic is hot, to prevent animals from slipping.

SURFACE OF ARCHES.

The surface of arches of bridges, tunnels, and military works, are often protected from infiltrations by mastic.

The extrados of the arch having been coated with mortar and allowed to dry, a coating of mastic rich in bitumen is applied, and upon this a coating of two to two and one-half inches of clay, to protect the mastic from the pressure of angular and broken stones.

PITS FOR GRAIN, ROOTS, ETC.

Cellars in the ground for the preservation of grain, roots, &c., were extensively used by the ancient Egyptians.

Pits of this kind are constructed in France as follows: An excavation is made of the required dimensions and floored with concrete eight to sixteen inches in thickness; upon the concrete is laid a coating of mastic rich in bitumen; the sides of the pit are constructed of brick, cemented with liquid mastic, and a space outside, about two inches in thickness, between the wall and the earth around the wall is filled with mastic, charged with broken stones.

If the surrounding earth is loose and moveable it may be sustained by a rough stone wall, the space of one to one and one-half inches between the stone and brick wall being filled with mastic. A brick dome cemented with mastic is erected over the pit, the surface being covered with mastic; an opening is left in the top for introducing the dry grain, &c., and when filled closed with a stone to fit and sealed with mastic, and a final covering of earth and grass is then added. Pits of this description are almost imperishable, and will preserve grain for a long period.

MARINE CONSTRUCTIONS.

Mastic of asphalt has been used for making blocks for marine foundations, but experiments of this kind require long periods of time to test them, and the trials are all too recent to establish reliable conclusions.

Blocks of concrete cemented with mastic cast into the sea at Point-de-Grave, and greatly exposed, in 1859 and 1860, remain good at this time, and show no marks of decay, but the cost of mastic renders them expensive.

For this purpose the mastic is prepared with bitumen as for sidewalks, by placing in the semi-cylinder and melting; 50 per cent. of broken stone the size of an egg is then thrown in and mixed, subsequently an equal quantity of stone is added and finally a third.

The mixture will then contain the following proportions:

	Pounds.
Mastic of asphalt	95
Bitumen	5
Broken stone	150
Total	250

A wooden mould is prepared by washing the inner surface with lime water, the mixture poured into it and pounded heavily. At the end of ten days the mould is removed and the block is ready to be lowered into the sea. Blocks of this kind measure about 5 feet by 6 by 10 feet.

Experiments have been made to economize mastic as follows. The annexed sketch represents a block, the interior of which is formed of rough stones cemented with fat lime, the outer coating 4 inches thick, being of mastic as above described, and the block costs $7 90 the cubic yard.

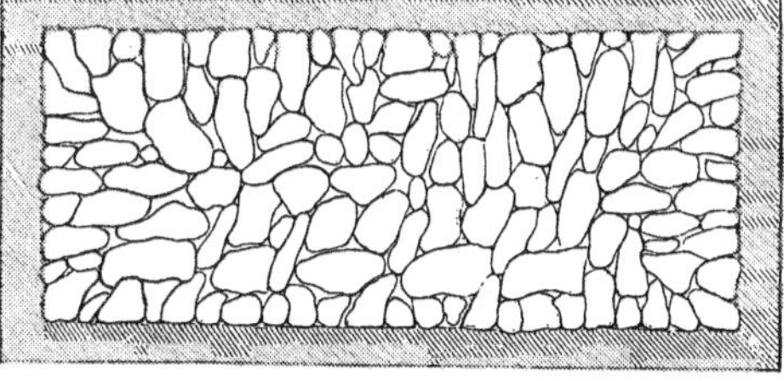

Blocks of concrete.

PIPES.

Bitumen mixed with clay and gravel is extensively used for coating gas pipes to protect them from corrosion.

Pipes of this kind (system Chameroy) were exhibited in class 65, French section. Great quantities of this pipe, made of sheet iron, were laid in Paris between 1856 and 1866. They are now furnished at the following prices:

Cost of Chameroy's gas pipe.

Diameter of pipe.	Thickness of iron.	Thickness of bitumen.	Cost per linear yard, including joints, bolts, &c.
Inches.	*Inches.*	*Inches.*	
3 1-5	0. 045	0. 50	$0 64
7½	0. 060	0. 60	1 79
12	0. 072	0. 70	3 27
24	0. 140	0. 84	10 20

REMARKS.

Those who have frequented the exhibition cannot have failed to observe that it abounds in the products of recent inventions and improvements, intended to supply the commonest and most numerous wants, at continually diminishing cost. Some of these products have already gone into general use; others will doubtless obtain equal success, and a mere description of the products themselves might be readily and easily made; but such a description would present no more interest than an advertisement.

An accurate account of the methods and processes by which such products are made is the only description of value to the public. This would enable many individuals to engage in similar industries, increasing the supply of the products and still further reducing their cost. But descriptions of this kind are often difficult and not unfrequently impossible, owing to the unwillingness of producers to disclose their methods.

This cannot be complained of however, since inventors are entitled to profit by their studies, and for this purpose to preserve their secrets, although this is a bar to inquiry and a considerable restriction upon the utility of international exhibitions. It may not be useless nevertheless to mention the following products which are analogous to those I have described in the preceding pages, premising that the notices will be found incomplete and limited to such information as may be gathered by observation and inquiry without intruding on the reserves of inventors.

Pipes of bituminized paper.—Pipes of this kind were exhibited in Class 65, by Jaloureau & Co., which resist a pressure of 15 atmospheres. The paper is dipped in melted bitumen, and rolled around a cylindrical mould until the thickness desired is produced. These pipes are light and durable, and are used with good results for water and gas.

Diameter of pipe, cost per linear yard, including joints, bolts, &c.: 2 inches, 37 cents; 4 inches, 81 cents; 7 inches, $2 14; 8½ inches, $2 73.

(Patent for the above sold to a house in Boston.)

Protection of walls from dampness.—A liquid bitumen prepared by Jaloureau & Co., exhibited in Class 65, is used for protecting walls from damp, iron from rust, and wood from decay. The liquid is applied with a brush. If the wall is to be painted in oil, a wash of white liquid glue is applied after the bitumen and before the paint. By heating the bitumen it will penetrate deeper into the wood, &c. Cost of liquid bitumen, per 100 pounds, $4 38.

Artificial bitumen for sidewalks.—(*Bitume factice*, or *lave fusible.*) Numerous attempts have been made to fabricate bitumen for sidewalks, but in general they have failed. The only exception is that of Jaloureau & Co., (Class 65.) This composition was used for the beds of the artificial lakes and streams, in the park of the Exhibition, also for the aquariums, floors of stables, and part of the sidewalks.

It is adopted to a considerable extent in and about Paris, and appears well adapted to many uses.

The record of the patent (expired) gives the following elements: coal tar, heated to a degree that renders it hard and brittle, 25 parts; slacked lime in fine powder, 50 parts; river gravel, 75 parts.

These ingredients are mixed in a cast-iron boiler, heated for two hours and drawn off into moulds.

The blocks thus obtained are treated subsequently the same as mastic of asphalt for sidewalks, except that the temperature is carried higher.

An improvement on this patent, also on record, gives the following elements: bituminous residue of tar of all kinds saturated with 25 to 50 per cent. of non-volatile bituminous oils, 25 to 50 per cent.; carbonate of ime in dry powder, 50 per cent.; silica and clay, 25 per cent. Stirred in a boiler over a slow fire for ten hours and run off into moulds.

Cost for sidewalks, four-fifths inch thick, 50 cents per square yard; courts, stable floors, &c., two inches thick, $1 16 per square yard; lake beds, streams, &c., $1 10 per square yard; layers in walls to prevent rise of moisture, 58 cents per square yard.

Bituminous roofing.—A covering called *carton-cuir* (leather-card) was exhibited by P. Desfeux, Class 65; a fabrication of bitumen, sand and thick paper, which was used in many of the roofs of buildings in the park and appeared to answer well. It is said to resist rain, frost, and heat, and being very light, slender timber work only is required to carry it.

It is put up in rolls of 13 yards by 27½ inches, sanded on one side, weighs 3 pounds 10 ounces per square yard, and costs 17 cents per square yard.

Asphaltic roofing.—Another covering, a species of felt impregnated with a proportion of asphalt, bitumen, and rosin, was exhibited by A. d'Azambuja, which appears to give good results. It is used with or without sand.

Weight of square yard, not sanded, 3 pounds; cost 17 cents; weight with sand, 7¼ pounds; cost 26 cents.

Varieties of this fabric are used as covering for walls, sheathing of vessels, coating for gas, water, and steam pipes, &c., and being elastic and tenacious has advantages over several other kinds.

SECTION II.

MACADAMIZED STREETS AND ROADS.

INTRODUCTORY REMARKS.

Few foreigners who travel in France, or visit the city and environs of Paris, fail to observe the excellence of the macadamized roads, and not unfrequently imagine that there must be something peculiarly favorable in the nature of the soil, or perhaps even something unique in the method of construeting roads.

Neither of these impressions is entitled to any weight; the soil and subsoil are variable, no better nor worse for roads than in other countries, the formations in general are rather unfavorable to drainage, and there is nothing secret nor peculiar in the methods.

The quality of the roads is attributable to good engineering, and to the great care and exactitude bestowed in all the successive operations in their construction and preservation.

HISTORY OF MACADAMIZED ROADS.

The earlier stone roads in France were formed of horizontal beds of flat stones covered with broken stones, large below and smaller above.

Roads and repairs were made at that period under the feudal system of *corvées*, and the necessity of great thickness of stone-crust arose from the infrequency of repairs, which occurred but twice a year.

In 1760, the corvées going out of use, Trésaguet introduced changes, diminished the thickness of the crust, discarded the flat stones, except on marshy and flat ground, where they are still used, and substituted for a bottom, blocks of the form of ancient paving stones, packed on a bed slightly arched to correspond with the form of the surface. (See Plate IV, Fig. 2.)

This method was followed until the early part of the present century, when, in the construction of the "Simplon," the large stones of Trésaguet were in turn discarded, and the crust of small broken stones was laid directly on the ground.

In 1816–'19 the success of Macadam, in England, resulted in attaching his name to the system of road-making already in use in France. Many of his precepts are proved by experience to be good, but his theory of roads contained errors: thus, it was the practice of Macadam to disregard the nature of the soil and to lay the road-crust directly upon the ground. Nevertheless, to the energy of Macadam, and the interest he awakened, are due great improvements in the roads of England.

Another English school soon arose, at the head of which was Telford, who advocated a return to the system of stone pavement at the bottom, (Fig. 9.) He brought forward many good ideas, and his method is well adapted to soft and wet ground, and is still much used, but it has the great objection that the surface is formed of rough broken stones, left to be worn and packed and the surface made smooth by use, which augments the resistance to movement and makes a rough, disagreeable road during half the period of its existence, as may be frequently seen in England.

The theory of Macadam, as gathered from his writings, implies that perfection of road consists in imperviousness to water and smoothness of surface.

Both these propositions are defective. The surface may be smooth, as very frequently occurs, but elastic, which requires an increase of tractive power, and renders the road heavy and bad. The necessity of imperviousness is disproved by experience. Many excellent roads are permeable in a high degree. When the subsoil is not readily softened by water, or when the crust of the road is provided with transverse passages for the quick discharge of water, permeability is not an object.

ESSENTIAL QUALITIES OF ROADS.

The characteristics of good roads are: foundations adapted to the nature of the soil; drainage neither too quick nor too slow; hardness and solidity of crust, and smoothness of surface.

The first two propositions are self-evident. The importance of the third and fourth is easily seen; for the external wear of roads produced by friction and pressure will be diminished by a smooth and hard surface, and the internal wear, which is greater still and arises from the friction of the stones against each other, will be small when the stones are packed so as to be solid and immovable.

Materials.—The crust of the road is constructed of two parts, a substratum of broken stones and a surface of detritus and broken stones mixed.

Detritus.—Detritus is spread on the broken stones as soon as laid, and rolled in to fill the interstices of the surface, making it compact and smooth. Coarse clean sand, or silicious mud, from the wear of neighboring roads, is used for detritus, but the debris of stone quarries is better, and when none of these can be obtained, soft stone may be used. Clay should be rejected; it adheres when wet to wheels, and tears up and carries off the surface; chalk is only good in summer, in winter it splits with frost and disintegrates the crust.

The proportion of detritus to be added to the broken stone varies with the nature of the stone, and should be determined by experience, but seldom exceeds 10 per cent.

Stone.—The stone most preferred is a question of first cost as well as of quality and durability, and is generally determined by locality of deposits and facility of obtaining a supply.

But there are differences in the expense of quarrying and breaking, and great differences in the wear. Hardness is an essential quality; also, stones which present a rounded form are not easily compacted together, and the addition of detritus becomes necessary to the solidity of the road-crust; whilst angular stones are much preferable, as they soon constitute of themselves a self-sustaining crust.

Around Paris and in the north of France a species of *millstone grit* is most used and is good when not porous or vitreous; it is chosen white, effervesces but little with chlorohydric acid, and weighs 1.6, water being 1.

Great use is also made of the nodules of *flint* which abound in chalk lands and are readily separated from the soil by sifting. But silex, however hard, is frequently brittle, and these flints crush easily and grind up rapidly, and are only used because they are at hand and cost less at first than better stones.

Granite and *granitic porphyry* have often a tendency to decompose by the action of the air, and then give poor results.

Basalt, *trap*, and *porphyry* are the best materials for wear. These rocks which appear to have once been subjected to a complete fusion, without any vitrification, are not brittle like silex or hyaline quartz, and do not crumble like quartzite.

Whatever the kind of stone, it should be broken into fragments that will pass in every direction through a ring of $2\frac{1}{2}$ inches internal diameter; indeed, for smooth roads adapted to light traffic like the boulevards and avenues of Paris, smaller stones are used not exceeding $1\frac{1}{4}$ to $1\frac{3}{4}$ inches in diameter.

Uniformity of size is very important, and smaller stones should be discarded; the stones should be clean and free from dirt, the intermixture of which below expands with frost and moisture and causes disaggregation of the crust.

The cost of macadamized roads may be greatly reduced by the use of Blake's rock-breaking machine, which was invented for the purpose of preparing hard trap-rock for road-metal. This machine will break 150 cubic yards of trap-rock in 24 hours. The fragments pack better and closer than those of stone broken by hand.

CONSTRUCTION.

The line of direction being settled, and the degree of acclivities determined, the grading begins and the side ditches are cut.

Profile.—Figs. 1, 2, 3, Plate IV, are types often met with in the roads of France constructed previous to the present century. They are open to objections arising from the formation of mud on the sideways which are made of the soil, and too great convexity of surface in Figs. 1 and 2, and the too great wash on the single slope of Fig. 3.

Figs. 4 and 5 present the profiles usually adopted in England. They are much better than the preceding; the whole width of surface is macadamized; the convexity is less, and a sidewalk or an embankment separates the roadway from the ditch.

The improvements above noticed have been adopted in France. Fig. 6 presents the profile generally used in the eastern section of the country. The profile in Fig. 7 is seen in the environs of Paris; these roads are modifications of the old paved roads, the pavement being preserved in place, and macadamized ways constructed on each side, thus giving three parallel lines, which is a method well adapted to heavy and light traffic and to greater or less speed.

But in making a new road there is no advantage in copying any of the old forms in preference to the modern profile, Fig. 8, which is highly approved by the engineers of the Ponts and Chaussées.

Admitting the width of 26 feet 3 inches to be sufficient for the circulation, the way should be macadamized over its whole width, receiving a crust 10 inches thick in the centre, and six inches at the sides, with a convexity of $\frac{1}{80}$, and bordered by slight embankments of earth four or five feet wide for sidewalks.

The preceding relates to country roads; for city roads an entirely different system of drainage is required. The side ditches are suppressed and substituted by subterranean sewers, into which the gutters discharge the surface wash by conduits descending at frequent intervals. The following table shows the measurements adopted for the boulevards and avenues of Paris, as regulated by the decree of June 5, 1856.

Dimensions of boulevards and avenues of Paris.

Width of the boulevards and avenues.	Width of road between sidewalks.	Size of each side alley.			Disposition of line of trees in side alleys.		
		Total width.	Width of sidewalk with uniform slant in front of houses.	Width of convex portion with double slant between sidewalk next the houses and the edge of road.	Number lines of trees.	Distance from edge of sidewalk for the line next the houses.	Distance from edge of sidewalk for the line next the road.
Feet.	*Feet.*	*Feet.*	*Feet.*	*Feet.*		*Feet.*	*Feet.*
86.5 to 91.8	39.4	23.0 to 26.2	....	....	1	18.0 to 22.5	4.9
104.4 to 117.5	34.1	26.2 to 32.8	....	....	1	22.5 to 27.9	4.9
125.3 to 130.6	39.4 to 33.8	39.4 to 41.1	12.1	26.2 to 27.9	2	16.4 to 18.0	4.9
131.2	34.1	33.8	12.1	32.2	2	22.5	4.9

Convexity.—The least convexity of surface compatible with the free flow of water is best; less wash and guttering result from it, and vehicles are less disposed to keep the central line, circulating more freely on all parts, and producing a more equal wear with less waste, requiring less repairs. Ancient roads have a convexity as high as $\frac{1}{20}$; subsequently $\frac{1}{50}$ was adopted, and at present $\frac{1}{70}$ to $\frac{1}{00}$ is considered ample.

Ditches.—The object of ditches is not to form reservoirs, but to effect drainage; many of the old ditches are too wide; they retain too much water, which soaks into the road-bed and softens it in summer, and exposes it unnecessarily to the action of frost in winter.

Five feet in width at the top is sufficient for ditches with walls of earth, and three feet with walls of stone; the grading should be accurate and in conformity with natural lines of flow and drainage.

Foundations.—Evidently foundations must be adapted to the nature of the soil, and their fitness must be determined by the judgment of the engineer. 1. In damp or loose soils, which are soft and yielding, the best foundations are of flat or quadrangular stones. These stones, as recommended by Telford, should be set on their broadest edge lengthwise across the road, the upper edge measuring, at most, four inches; they should be seven inches deep in the middle of the road, five inches deep at nine feet from the centre, and three inches at 15 feet. All the irregularities of the upper part of this pavement are to be broken off by hammers, and all the interstices to be filled with stone chips firmly wedged by hand with a light hammer. Upon this close pavement the macadamized road crust is laid.

2. In wet and marshy ground good foundations may be made of fascines crossed at 45° with intermediate layers of sand and gravel, as in the annexed woodcuts.

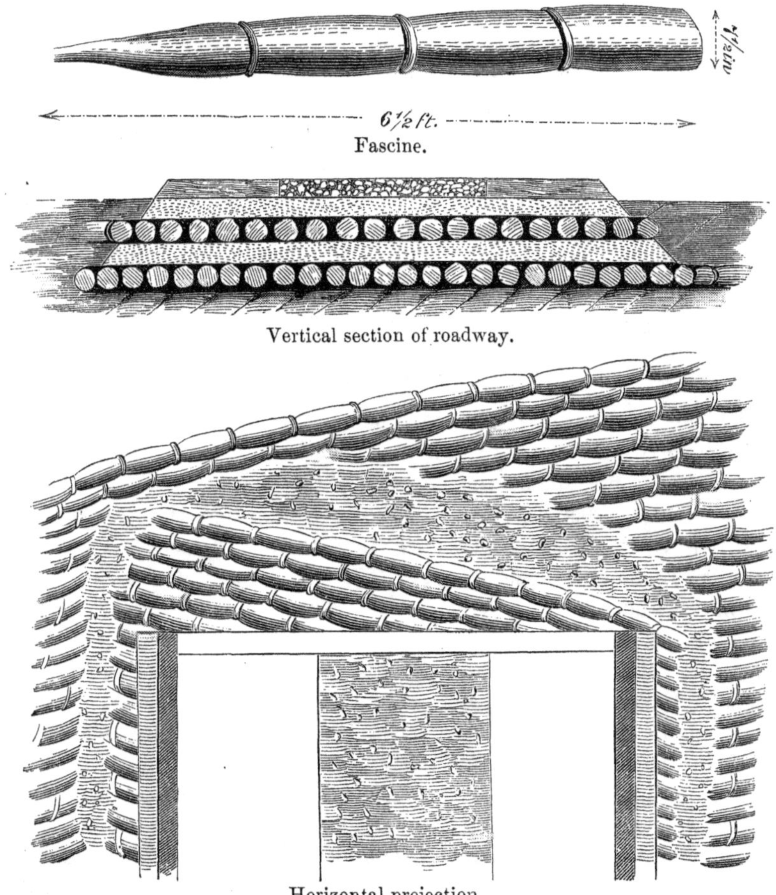

Fascine.

Vertical section of roadway.

Horizontal projection.

3. Chalky soil is liable to split and open by frost, and requires to be overlaid with silicious materials and dry earth to form a bed for the crust.

4. Clay soils dissolve readily at the surface and "slip," which displaces the whole crust; they require a first layer of chalk well beaten down and packed, or sand with a little lime and water, and if the situation is wet and bad, a coating of concrete may be necessary, or numerous transverse "dry" stone drains under the crust.

5. But an ordinary firm soil (neither marshy, clayey, nor chalky) requires none of these preparations, and may receive the crust directly without any intervening foundation, which is the system of Macadam, the system of the Simplon, and the method generally used.

Laying and packing.—The road-bed being completed and free from mud, the broken stone is spread with uniformity and care, thicker in the centre, thinner at the sides, in conformity with the profile adopted, the whole mass intended to form the crust being put on at once in a single layer.

Rolling then commences with an iron roller, five feet wide, weighing three to seven tons, and requiring from six to twelve horses for the draught.

The rolling commences at each side, fixing the edges first and finishing in the centre; when the roller has passed four or five times, the detritus is spread over the surface with the same uniformity, and watered, and the rolling is resumed until the packing is satisfactory, when the road is completed and ready for use.

Steam power in place of horses for rolling is now successfully adopted, and in the great thoroughfares of Paris the rolling is done chiefly in the night, to produce the least interruption possible to circulation. The steam roller now used is described more fully on page 29, and figures of it will be found on Plate IV, Figs. 10, 11, 12.

REPAIRS.

With the completion begins the destruction of roads; wear increases detritus, detritus increases wear, and both hasten decay. The secret of preservation is not in the making but in the keeping. Clean roads are always good roads. Experience shows that when the proportion of detritus in the road-crust becomes equal to 0.35 or 0.45 for 1 volume of stone, the road can bear no more; at 0.50 it is poor, and at 0.75 it is more than half ruined.

Macadamized roads must be watered and swept and scraped of mud and dust. With this they are the cheapest for country and town, the easiest and pleasantest for men and horses, and the best for carriages, houses, shops and populations; without it they are the dearest, dirtiest and unhealthiest of roads, for nothing is worse for eyes, stomach and lungs, than an atmosphere of powdered lime, flint, granite, quartz, &c.

Railways derive support from the macadams which are the perennial sources of the streams of internal commerce, and internal commerce is prosperity and civilization.

The administration of roads therefore is worth considering, but I need give no more than a glimpse of the apparatus that preserves the cleanliness and protracts the longevity of roads. The arrangements for this in France are very simple. Each road is divided into sections from two-thirds to two miles in length, called "cantons." Each canton has a cantonnier, and each third canton is short, and has consequently two long cantons on each side. The cantonnier of the short canton is called a "chef cantonnier," and his duties are to clean his own canton, and to see that the work of his two neighbors corresponds with the written register they are instructed to keep.

The cantons on a road or neighboring roads are grouped in districts, in charge of engineers who make the heavier repairs, and oversee the chefs, as they in turn overlook the cantonniers, the inferior being always exposed to the unannounced visits of inspection from the superior. This organization of surveillance and accountability is graduated up to the central administration at the head of all the roads in the empire, and is kept alive and quickened by the distribution of a limited power, diminishing at every stage downward, of applying summary justice, which consists in a restricted cutting down of wages for neglect of duty. Thus the engineering required to make good roads would come to little without the organization to preserve them.

Repairs are of two kinds, the constant and the periodical.

Constant repairs.—Slight depressions of limited area occur often, and if neglected soon become deep and spoil the road. The "stitch in time" maxim is the rule in this case, especially on roads and streets of great traffic. The depression is sprinkled and swept, and the surface dug off with pickaxes to the depth of 2½ or three inches, preserving the surrounding wall or edges uniform and vertical. The excavation is then filled with broken stones and 20 per cent. of detritus, which is watered and packed with hand pestles of 25 or 30 pounds weight.

Circulation is then allowed to begin. The ruts formed at first are smoothed down with the pestle, and the addition of sand and smaller stones.

Periodical repairs.—The periodical repairs consist of an entire renewal of the surface at intervals of time determined by the amount of traffic.

Renewal should be made before the crust is so far weakened as to begin to break. When the surface is reduced about four to five inches it is usual on well kept roads to restore it. This work is commenced by watering and sweeping clean, then digging and loosening the surface with pickaxes to the depth of two inches, after which the steps followed in succession are precisely the same as those described for the original formation of the crust.

The periodical repair of streets and roads of great traffic are made in sections of convenient length, limited to a margin on one side extending to the central line of the road, throwing the circulation to the other side, and when one side is restored to use, the other side is commenced.

Annual wear.—The annual wear on different roads may be compared by computing the wear per 100 horses in harness, passing over a given length of road.

In making the estimate it should be remembered that one cubic yard of broken stone will be reduced by packing to 0.71 cubic yard. The following table gives the average result found on various roads :.

Table showing the annual wear upon various macadamized roads in France.

Annual consumption of materials per mile and per 100 horses in harness.	Number of days' work per cubic yard.	Name of road.	Observer.
Cubic yards.			
	1.20 to 1.40—average, 1.30[1]		M. Bardonnaut.
	1.27 to 1.63—average, 1.45[2]		Do.
76.2[3]	2.51	Moselle	M. Lemasson.
52.5 to 78.7[4]	2.18		M. Berthand.
115.5[5]	1.96—3.23—4.54	Various	M. Dupuit.
82.95[6]		National road No. 19	M. Bardonnaut.
289.80[7]			Do.
109.22[8]		National road No. 33	M. Parnier.
122.75[9]		National road No. 34	Do.
68.73[10]		Departmental road No. 2	Do.
105 to 115.5[11]		Various	M. Muntz.
84[12]		All roads	
52.5[13]		Streets of Paris	

[1] Imperial road; fatigued; middling limestone.
[2] Departmental roads.
[3] The wear was not entirely replaced.
[4] Average result.
[5] Results obtained in various departments.
[6] Beyond Langres.
[7] Heavy traffic near Langres.
[8] Silicious materials.
[9] Silicious materials.
[10] Good limestone.
[11] Average.
[12] This is the number on which the public administration bases its estimates.
[13] This number is the average obtained in Paris, and is a safe basis for properly kept, and for light roads traffic.

Cost of repairs.—The average cost of repairs may be analyzed as follows:

		Per cent.
Cost of materials		47.13
Cost of wages:		
Cantonniers	30.24	
Assistants	8.49	
		38.73
Cost of accessory:		
Earthworks, bridges, &c.	6.80	
Superintendence	2.12	
Sundries	6.22	
		14.14
Total cost		100.00

The average number of days' work of cantonniers per linear mile of road and per year is 205, and of auxilliaries, 64. The average wages of cantonniers is 35 cents per day, and of assistants, 30 cents.

The total expense of annual repairs on macadamized roads per linear mile varies with traffic, &c., but averages as follows:

In the department of the Seine the average cost is	$1,003 20
In the department of the Seine and Marne the average cost is	510 40
In the department of du Nord and du Rhône the average cost is	457 60
In the department of the Ariège the average cost is........	158 40
In the department of the Ardèche the average cost is	123 20
In the department of the Finistere and Morbihan the average cost is	105 60

Every year a sum of 4½ to 5 million of dollars is set down in the budget for keeping in repair the macadamized roads of France.

STREETS OF PARIS.

The ancient streets of Paris were without sidewalks, paved with large square blocks, the grade sloping from the sides to the middle, forming a gutter, which formed the central line of the street. Sidewalks began to appear and the surface to be reversed, taking a convex form and throwing the gutters to each side, about the year 1825.

In 1852 the old Boulevards were macadamized; and in 1858 this method was improved for heavy traffic by introducing margins along the sides from 2 to 4 yards in width, formed of blocks of Belgian porphyry, of small size—say 4 inches by 6½ by 6½—which method is approved and extended.

Streets of asphalt have also taken considerable development in the last few years, and are greatly liked.

The entire surface of streets and sidewalks in Paris is now (1868) constituted as follows:

	Sq. metres.	Sq. metres.
Streets—Paved	4,883,643	
Macadamized	2,146,005	
Of asphalt	165,164	
		7,195,302
Sidewalks—Of granite	545,939	
Paved	14,024	
Bituminous	1,192,414	
		1,752,377
Total surface covered, (square metres)..............		8,947,679
Total surface covered equivalent to (square yards)...		10,701,416

STEAM ROLLER.

The steam roller, (Figs. 10, 11, 12,) invented by Ballaison and made by Gillerat & Co., has been adopted and is now in use in Paris.

The force is transmitted from a single engine to the roller by means of endless chains, which mesh with cog-wheels. The movement of the roller reverses with the reversion of the engine, moving forwards and back on the same line, and the roller is adjusted to admit of convergence adapted to a curve of 14 to 15 yards radius.

Principal dimensions, weight, and results.

	Type of machine.		
	No. 1.	No. 2.	No. 3.
Heating surface: Fire-box, 3.84 square yards; tubes, 30.96 square yards. Total .... square yards..	....	....	34. 80
Diameter of pistons .... feet..	....	....	0. 76
Stroke .... feet..	....	....	1. 18
Diameter of rollers .... feet..	4. 91	4. 76	4. 76
Width of rollers .... feet..	4. 76	6. 24	4. 91
Weight of machine when empty .... tons..	....	....	19. 393
Average weight when ready for work .... tons..	17. 393	27. 972	22. 300
Average speed per hour when at work .... mile..	1. 169	1. 409	2. 093
Number of mile-tons per hour, or product of weight of machine in tons by number of miles gone over per hour .... mile-tons..	20. 3	39. 2	40. 2
Pressure exercised by each roller per foot of width .... tons..	1. 820	2. 240	2. 270

It has been determined by numerous experiments that the number of mile-tons necessary for packing is directly proportionate to the volume of material to be packed, whether laid thicker or thinner, within the range of $3\frac{1}{4}$ to 10 inches; and when rightly conducted, $1\frac{4}{5}$ to $2\frac{1}{2}$ mile-tons are sufficient for the packing of one cubic yard of stone.

Consequently, in a day of twelve hours, corresponding to 10 hours of effective work, the steam rollers of Gellerat & Co. will pack:

	Cubic yards of stone.
Type No. 1	85 to 111
Type No. 2	170 to 215
Type No. 3	196 to 258

The advantages of steam rollers over rollers drawn by horses consist in economy, rapidity of execution, excellence of work.

The cost of these machines averages $6,500; the work done is paid in proportion to the weight of machine and distance overrun. The mile-ton is paid at the rate of 15 cents by day, and 16 cents by night.

HORSE-BROOM.

This broom, lately introduced by Mr. Tailfer, is of very simple construction.

The broom is 5 feet 8 inches wide, and is placed obliquely to the axis of the cart, so that one end is $1\frac{4}{5}$ feet out of line with the other, and sweeps the mud or dust to the sides of the street, (Plate IV, Fig. 13.)

A handle placed near the driver allows him to raise the broom from the ground.

A conical toothed wheel, fixed on the axle of the cart, engages with a smaller toothed wheel attached to an intermediate axis. An endless chain communicates the motion of this axis to the axis of the broom, and as the cart moves the broom revolves.

The toothed wheels can be readily disengaged, enabling the cart to move without setting the broom in motion.

The weight of the machine is thus distributed:

	Pounds.
Two wheels	568
The broom	110
The endless chains, ironwork, &c	244
Ordinary cart and shafts	1,212
Total weight	2,134

Although the width of the broom is 5 feet 8 inches, the band effectively swept is only 5 feet at each passage, as each bands laps the preceding.

By the passage of these carts over the whole width of the street, the mud or dust is finally accumulated in one narrow line along the gutter, and is then carried off in carts.

Eight of these horse-brooms have swept in 1 hour and 10 minutes a surface of road covering 48,720 yards; which would have required 100 men to do the same work in the same time.

In general, one of these brooms will sweep 600 square yards per hour, working at a cost of $0.30 per hour, while the work by hand would employ 13 men at 6 cents or $0.78 per hour.

The above cost of $0.30 may be thus divided:

Interest of horse-broom, costing $400, at 6 per cent. per day	$0.066
Sinking fund, per day	0.133
Man and horse	2.000
Annual repairs of horse-broom $60, gives per day	0.166
Repairs of broom	0.600
Total expense per day of 10 hours	2.965
Or per hour	0.30

PARIS UNIVERSAL EXPOSITION, 1867.

REPORTS OF THE UNITED STATES COMMISSIONERS.

REPORT

UPON

BUILDINGS, BUILDING MATERIALS,

AND

METHODS OF BUILDING.

BY

JAMES H. BOWEN,

UNITED STATES COMMISSIONER

WASHINGTON:

GOVERNMENT PRINTING OFFICE.

1869.

CONTENTS.

CHAPTER I.

ARCHITECTURAL DESIGNS AND MODELS, AND BUILDINGS IN THE PARK.

CHAPTER II.

MATERIALS, AND METHODS OF CONSTRUCTION.

CHAPTER III.

DWELLINGS CHARACTERIZED BY THEIR CHEAPNESS COMBINED WITH THE CONDITIONS NECESSARY FOR HEALTH AND COMFORT.

LIST OF EXHIBITORS AND OF AWARDS IN CLASS NINETY-THREE.

BUILDING MATERIALS AND METHODS OF BUILDING.

CHAPTER I.

ARCHITECTURAL DESIGNS AND MODELS—BUILDINGS IN THE PARK.

COMPETITIVE ARCHITECTURAL DISPLAY CONFINED ENTIRELY TO DESIGNS AND MODELS—NUMBER OF EXHIBITORS IN CLASS FOUR—CHARACTER OF THE FRENCH EXHIBITION—INSTRUCTION OF ARCHITECTS—AUSTRIAN EXHIBITION—ENGLISH EXHIBITION—AWARDS IN CLASS FOUR—PRESENT STATE OF ARCHITECTURE IN EUROPEAN COUNTRIES—BUILDINGS IN THE PARK—INTERESTING CHARACTER OF THE EXHIBITION—THE EMPEROR'S PAVILION—PAVILION OF THE EMPRESS—CHALET OF THE COMMISSIONER GENERAL—THE TURKISH MOSQUE—THE SULTAN'S KIOSQUE—THE EGYPTIAN SALEMLIK—THE PALACE OF THE BEY OF TUNIS—THE RUSSIAN IZBA—THE RUSSIAN STABLES—THE MOVABLE COTTAGE—THE BUILDINGS OF SWEDEN AND NORWAY—THE ENGLISH COTTAGE—THE SWISS CHALET—THE TEMPLE OF XOCHICALCO—THE ROUMANIAN CHURCH—JAPANESE AND CHINESE BUILDINGS.

INTRODUCTORY.

The duty of reporting upon buildings and building materials having devolved upon the undersigned, his attention has been directed chiefly to Class 93, "Buildings characterized by their cheapness combined with the conditions necessary for health and comfort," and to those materials and methods of construction which by their beauty, novelty, or cheapness appeared worthy of special mention. Considerable attention was given to the efforts which have been made abroad to provide the working classes with cheap and comfortable homes, particularly as, through the writer's connection with the building known as the Illinois cottage or American farmer's home, he was much interested in examining and comparing the relative merits of the various buildings exhibited by the societies organized for the above-named purpose.

It has also been deemed proper to notice many of the most interesting buildings in the park, especially as they were to a certain extent types of different national styles of architecture, or of modes of construction, and as they derive additional interest and value by association. Building is so inseparably connected with architecture that it seemed hardly fitting to complete the report without some reference to Class 4 Group I, "Architectural Designs and Models," which by the classification was placed among the fine arts, with painting, sculpture, drawing, and engraving. But as it was beyond the scope of the reporter's expectations to discuss architecture as an art, or to describe the very interesting and instructive exhibits in that class, he presents only a brief notice, compiled chiefly from the reports by able masters of the subject, which have recently appeared in the reports of the international jury and the current publications upon the subject at the time of the exhibition. Throughout the report, also, free use has been made of all accessible sources of valuable information upon this department of the exhibition.

ARCHITECTURAL DESIGNS AND MODELS.

The exhibition in this class was confined entirely to designs and small models of buildings, and details of building, and although in many respects very full and complete, it furnished to the public but an inadequate idea of the present state of architecture or of the genius of the architects whose designs and models were displayed. It is very justly observed by Chesneau substantially as follows: "The public is more interested in the realization of the designs than in the designs themselves. The public square or the street is the true place of exhibition for the architect, where the finished work can be seen and its merits or defects exposed to criticism. To the critic, however, designs afford the readiest and easiest method of determining artistic merit, and of judging equitably in a competitive exhibition. The possession of a cultivated taste, the ability to produce grand effects, to design in good architectural proportions, and to show originality in details and ornament, are not now all that is required of the architect. He must be able to guarantee the strength and stability of his work when finished, and to construct in such a manner that his buildings may be most effectively ventilated, warmed, and lighted, and be perfectly adapted to the purposes for which they are intended. Under these circumstances plans and designs alone can show, and only to competent judges, the amount of knowledge which the architect possesses, the readiness with which he makes use of it, and the value of the resources which science has given him to accomplish the tasks which he undertakes."

The number of exhibitors in Class 4 was very large. France alone had fifty exhibitors, each one displaying a great number of designs; England, including photographs of designs, had seventy-seven; Austria, eighteen; Russia, Belgium, and Switzerland, each twelve; Spain six; Italy seven; Greece and Portugal, each two. There were no entries in the catalogue of exhibitors in this class from the United States. The buildings displayed were included in Class 93.

The exhibition of French designs may be divided into three groups or classes, according to the subjects represented: 1. Drawings representing restorations of classic monuments and buildings of antiquity. 2. Illustrations of French medieval art as it exists to-day. 3. Designs and plans by living architects.

The exhibition in the first division is due entirely to the direction exercised by the government in the education of architects. The study of the monuments of antiquity forms an important and necessary part of their education, and a certain number of pupils are yearly sent to Greece, Italy, and other places to make drawings of the ruins themselves. The success with which this plan of instruction has been attended is shown by the beautiful drawings and restorations of the ruins at Rome, Tivoli, Pompeii, Ancyra, Heliopolis, and Athens, by MM. Ancelet, Baudray, Therry, and others, which are executed with accuracy and precision and show a thorough understanding and knowledge of the subjects treated.

The importance of such studies cannot be too highly estimated. It is necessary for the young architect to devote many months, sometimes alone, among the ruins which are to assume their ancient form and grandeur under his pencil. A longer time must then be given to the completion of the drawings, and to achieve success the subject, whatever it may be, must be carefully selected and elaborated with perseverance and diligence. The study, too, of the ancient forms of construction, and their uses, cannot fail to render the architect more competent and efficient in his art.

The second division, consisting of illustrations of medieval architecture, had its origin in the recent endeavors which have been made, under the direction of the secretary of state, to preserve the ancient monuments and buildings in different portions of France which are connected with the history of that country, and which are rapidly falling into decay. A large number of designs and drawings was exhibited; the subjects were classified under the head of religious monuments, and military and civil architecture. The illustrations and drawings were, as a whole, of a high order, and were faithfully and carefully executed. The third division consisted of plans by living architects of works proposed or erected by them. Among those are to be especially noticed the designs by M. Chauvin, of the Concert Hall of the Imperial Conservatory, the decoration of which, in the Pompeian style, was finely conceived and executed. The works of M. Questel deserve high commendation, as do those of MM. Huot, Lamécre, and Normand. The Pompeian house, erected by the last-named gentleman for Prince Napoleon, is a most perfect reproduction, and adhered to the original type in every particular.

The countries of Austria, England, Italy, Holland, Switzerland, Prussia, Russia, Norway, Belgium, and Spain were represented. Among these Austria deserves especial notice; the display of designs being very rich, and some of them possessing very great merit.

Mr. Ferstel exhibited a model and plans of a Gothic church recently erected at Vienna. The academy at Pesth, erected by the same architect, is also a fine design, while the palace of the grand duke in Vienna shows with what admirable success he can handle Italian architecture.

The English display consisted of designs by the best English architects, and included specimens of ecclesiastical architecture, municipal institutions, commercial architecture, and of buildings erected both in England and her colonies.

There was nothing very remarkable in the exhibitions from other countries, although many of them were very creditable to the architects by whom they were designed.

AWARDS IN CLASS FOUR.

The awards of Class 4 consisted of four grades: grand prizes, first prizes, second prizes, and third prizes, corresponding to those given to painters and sculptors. The architectural displays in the park were *hors concours*, but the exhibitions of buildings characterized by cheapness and other advantages (class 93) received medals of gold, silver, and bronze, the Emperor himself receiving a grand prize for workmen's houses.

Only three grand prizes were given in class 4: One to Ancelet of France, one to Ferstel of Austria, and one to Waterhouse of Great Britain. The first prize conferred on M. Ancelet was for his restoration of the *via appia*, a remarkable work, and a true creation, since nothing remains to suggest the ancient form to the artist but huge and almost shapeless masses of masonry. The prize to Mr. Ferstel was for the designs of the church, academy, and palace, which have been referred to.

Of the twenty-three prizes awarded by the jury, France received twelve; Great Britain four, one of which was the grand prize to Waterhouse; Austria three, one of which was a grand prize; Prussia one; and Belgium and Switzerland, each one. Among the twelve French prizes, nine were for plans for restoring ancient monuments, and four only (one of the exhibitors having sent at the same time an original plan and a plan for a restoration) for original designs. The eleven prizes contributed to exhibitors other than French were all for original plans. This want of originality in French designs displayed at the Exposition cannot be taken as an evidence of the inferiority of French architects, while such buildings as the market-house, the new opera-house, and the church of the Trinity and other new buildings, attest the high order of their architectural ability. It is explained rather by the fact that the most eminent architects have not the time to prepare designs, and that those exhibited were for the most part by young men, and are the natural results of the study of the ancient models which forms so large a part of their education.

The English reviewers of the architectural displays of the Exposition admit the great superiority of the French drawings over the English. The methods adopted by the two countries are very different. The English designs, after those of the French, seem like miniatures, and are filled up with water color drawings, with bright foliage, clear skies, and figures in the foreground, to bring forward the perspective and render the picture more complete. The French, on the other hand, make use of geometric drawings on a large scale, to convey to the observer the idea of the actual architecture and composition of the building. The love for color and the enrichment obtained by introducing human figures is expressed in the elaboration of the design instead of being thrown away, architecturally speaking, on the landscape of the picture.

The drawings of the interiors of buildings, exhibited by some of the French architects, are apt illustrations of this point, which, though as pictures they could not be compared to many of the drawings in the English department, as architectural compositions, containing elaborate decoration and coloring, were vastly superior.

It is interesting also to note the difference in the styles of the drawings exhibited by the two nations. There was scarcely a design in the English department worthy of attention where the author had attempted Italian or renaissance treatment, and the same may be said of the French department in regard to gothic architecture. While the English have settled upon the gothic style as the one adapted for large buildings, (as the Parliament house and the design for the new law courts show,) the French appear to have discarded it as a style which has reached its full development, and in the study of which no further advance can be made.

The designs sent by Great Britain, though they were rather water-color drawings than architectural plans, nevertheless possessed great merit and evinced great talent in their authors. They were all remarkable, and the poorest possessed great beauty. M. Charles Garnier, the architect of the new opera house in Paris, after referring to the more striking features of this display sums up by saying that, though the absence of plans and geometrical drawings is to be regretted, and though the architecture of Great Britain is represented by water-color sketches and perspectives, one is forced to acknowledge that this collection does the greatest honor to the artists who have contributed to it.

The present state of architecture and the architectural taste of different nations of Europe is concisely epitomized by Professor Donaldson in his report on the architectural designs and models of the Exposition, and as generalizations in matters of art, perhaps more than on any other subject, are valuable, only when made by one who has pursued it as a profession or as a recreation it has been thought advisable to present in this report his conclusions.[1]

"It is a remarkable circumstance that in France, and most of the continental schools except the Austrian, gothic architecture seems to be ignored for modern buildings, unless for some churches; and (with the same reservation of Austria) the principles of that style are not thoroughly understood, and, consequently, the treatment of the parts evinces an absence of knowledge of the principles which directed the medieval artist. Very frequently, in northern Germany and in France, there is in the *modern* architecture a vagueness of idea, and an attempt

[1] British reports on the Paris Universal Exposition, vol. ii, p. 67.

to produce novelty; but, then, in the former it is an adoption of the Lombard or Byzantine as a basis; in France the classic leading features, as cornices, strings, and dressings, are pared down, and there is introduced a profusion of florid decoration, and a coqueting with the past times of the country, still with gracefulness of composition. In England gothic architecture has assumed, under clerical influences, possession of the churches and of the ecclesiastical buildings connected therewith, such as the parsonage house and the schools; and in provincial towns, from a certain reverence for tradition, frequently with the town halls. The commercial architecture of Paris and London is generally Italian, modified according to the tastes of the people; rarely, if ever, gothic. Still, it will be observed that there are noble conceptions of noble-minded men in this collection, whose ideas cannot be fully appreciated by drawings alone; for it is only in the building itself, when carried out, that all the capacity of the architect for his work can be thoroughly realized. Hence the reluctance of many able men to imperil their hard-earned reputations by mere drawings, in which so much depends upon the technical skill of the draughtsman.

"All these circumstances in modern architecture are evidenced in the French International Exhibition; and the result shows an unsettled state of thought and intent throughout Europe; a transition, but to what end or purpose it is impossible to say. Whole nations and states have recently had their political transitions, and apparently must continue to have them. These may be ruled and decided by some determined self-will and resolute mind of a sovereign or his minister. But there is no such dominant physical power to direct the intellect of art, and unfortunately, under capricious influences, the pure seems to yield to the fantastic, and the sound, well informed, and well directed frame of mind is thrown upon the wild waves of the rage for novelty."

BUILDINGS IN THE PARK.

As a feature of the architectural display of the Exposition, although not entering into competition for prizes, the buildings in the park deserve no small part of our attention. To the mere observer the exhibition could not fail to be attractive and interesting, while to the architect a rare opportunity was afforded of studying and comparing the existing types of national architecture by buildings which were the exact models and representations of the most perfect specimens of their kind. Here, within the same inclosure, in many instances standing side by side, were to be seen the graceful and brilliant buildings of the east, the rough log dwellings of northern Europe, the gothic church, the architecture of modern Europe, and the monuments and temples of antiquity.

Some of the most striking and remarkable of these buildings will be briefly noticed. Owing to the peculiar conditions under which they were erected, and their ephemeral character, in most cases the full details of construction, cost of materials, and of the completed building, though not uninteresting, are perhaps without much practical value. They are instructive chiefly in the direction of design, decoration, and the use of materials, and it is hoped that our architects and constructors may derive some advantage from the descriptions.

THE EMPEROR'S PAVILION.

The imperial pavilion, on the left hand side of the grand avenue leading to the main entrance of the Exposition building, was one of the most original and attractive of the ornamented structures in the park. It was a palace in miniature, exquisite in its details, and luxurious in its interior furnishing, and was designed as an imperial resting place. In its external aspect it was decidedly oriental; yet one could find in it, on examination, something to recall the structures of imperial Rome, of Moscow, of the period of Louis the XIV and XVI, of the first Napoleon, and of the Moors of Spain.

It consisted of a central building surmounted by a dome and flanked by four wings or projections, with rounded ends, and the whole surrounded by a broad veranda, above a marble terrace, approached on four sides by flights of marble steps. The supports of the broad and highly ornamented veranda consisted of bronze lances set in pairs on each side of the steps, and inclined at an angle so as to appear like poles supporting a tent or awning. Each lance supported an imperial eagle, in bronze, and brazen shields. Eagles, in bronze, guarded the steps of the chief entrance, and an enameled terra cotta balustrade, surrounding the terrace, was ornamented with vases of the same material in various colors. The white marble steps, and the floor of the terrace, in the balcony, were curiously inlaid in colors. Designs were first deeply engraved in the stone, and were then filled in with colored stones or a composition, and then ground down so as to give the effect of elaborate mosaic work. This had a very pleasing appearance, and the work appeared to be durable, for the constant, though limited, use for three months did not produce any appreciable effect upon it.

The quadrangular portion of the main building, which rose above the balcony and supported the dome, was decorated with majolica plates, and the dome, in Russian style, was constructed of metal and highly decorated.

The frames of the four glass doors giving access to the interior were made of wrought iron, and the principal one was a very beautiful specimen of workmanship and design. It was finely chiseled and is said to have cost sixteen thousand francs.

This building was about twenty-six yards (twenty-four meters) in its longest diameter, and sixteen meters in its shortest diameter, without, in either case, counting the steps. The central saloon was seven meters square, but with the corners cut off, so that it was octagonal in form. Four magnificent windows of plate glass gave views of the principal portions of the park, including the great number of the most important buildings, and with the crowd of visitors of every nation passing and repassing formed a most pleasing panorama.

The walls were covered with the most magnificent specimens of tapestry of Nieully, representing various subjects. The curtains were from the manufactories of Lyons, worked in tapestry, in patterns harmonizing with the other decorations, and costing twenty-five dollars a square meter.

The cupola, forty-five feet high in the interior, was also decorated with allegorical designs worked at Nieully, and sustained a superb chandelier pendant from the center.

The furniture, of the most elegant design and materials, was supplied by Messrs. Duval of Paris, and was intended by them as a display of their skill and taste as decorators. The various pieces were modeled after the most luxurious articles of furniture which existed at the time of Louis XIV.

Immediately adjoining the central apartment was a chamber called the Empress's saloon, also fitted up in the most luxurious and tasteful manner. The walls were covered with the finest figured satin, adorned with allegorical groups of figures, and the chairs and sofas were covered with the same rich material.

A piano from one of the best makers of France was provided, and indeed nothing was omitted that could conduce to the comfort and ease of their Imperial Majesties during their visits to the Exposition. The style preserved in the saloon of the Empress was that of Louis XVI, and was derived principally from the palace of Versailles and from the Trianons. The ceiling was painted by Voillemot.

The saloon of the prince imperial, or the "smoking room," was also fitted up in the most superb style, and in a manner which, with all the other decorations and fittings of this building, reflected the greatest credit upon the skill and taste of Messrs. Duval of Paris, who are the proprietors of the whole.

It was not possible to ascertain the cost of this building. It was erected in a few weeks, although it must have been for a much longer time in preparation. At the close of the Exposition it was offered for sale, with the furniture, for seventy thousand dollars.

PAVILION OF THE EMPRESS.

This modest little pavilion was certainly one of the most beautiful specimens of architecture at the Exposition.

The idea of this building originated as follows: Mr. Henry Penon, a manufacturer, being desirous of exhibiting a very elegant and artistic carpet of some two hundred and sixty-five square feet of surface, and being unable to obtain the necessary space within the Exposition building, obtained permission to construct this pavilion in the park.

The designs were furnished by M. Demimuid, a young architect of great talent, and numerous contractors and manufacturers contributed to its erection.

The design of the architect was to construct a building of polychromatic style, which by the brilliancy and variety of its colors, would enliven the somber aspect of the park, but would still be solid enough to resist the weather, and remain unchanged in a climate as variable as that of Paris. These two objects governed the choice of materials.

The result of this work was extremely happy, and the details were irreproachable.

The pavilion, which was situated on the borders of the lake in the reserve garden, was octagonal in plan, and was elevated three steps above the walk. Taking advantage of the descent of the ground on the opposite side from the entrance, a balcony was thrown out which overlooked the lake.

The four large windows from within had the appearance of four large frames containing the most beautiful landscapes of the garden.

The construction lines of the pavilion were of cut stone. The plain surfaces were of brick of three colors—blue, green, and yellow.

The frieze was made of terra-cotta panels, in stone frames; the ornamentation was upon a yellow groundwork.

On each opening there was a medallion containing the letter E upon an azure ground, and these medallions were surmounted by an imperial crown.

The carpentry of the dome was of oak, covered with lead and slate.

The dome was surmounted by a cornice placed about one-quarter of the distance above the base, and ornamented at each angle by an eagle, and the summit was surmounted by a conical ornament, like a pine cone, resting on a sculptured pedestal.

The slates were cut circular at the ends, laid so as to look like the scales of serpents.

The balconies were in wrought iron; that overlooking the lake was particularly graceful in its design and execution.

The decorations of the interior were designed and executed by M. Henry Penon, who employed all the artistic ability that the manufactory he directs could command. The form of the building, the character of the decoration, and the ingenious combination of light and shade secured for the Empress what the artist intended—a quiet retreat and resting place which should be in harmony with the rural and quiet scenery of the reserved garden.

The carpet was of velvet tapestry, the general tone light, and the colors blended with exquisite taste.

The hangings, which were of satin, were ornamented with figures of birds, animals, and flowers.

The wood-work, the curtains, the furniture, and the chandeliers were all ornamented with designs of fruit, foliage, and flowers.

The cost of the pavilion and its decorations is said to have exceeded two hundred thousand francs, (forty thousand dollars.)

CHALET OF THE COMMISSIONER GENERAL.

An elegant and commodious building was erected in the park for M. Le Play, the president of the imperial commission. It was designed and executed by Huret & Son, architects and constructors. It was one of the most imposing of all the structures in the park, and is a design which seems adapted for villas in the United States. The wood engraving below gives a very good idea of the appearance of the exterior.

Chalet of the Commissioner General.

The frame of this building was made of wood diagonally braced in an ornamental manner, with the spaces between the timbers filled in with plaster, thus leaving the timbers exposed to view, and producing a very picturesque effect.

The roof was broad and overhanging, and highly ornamented at the eaves and at the ridge by open and carved wood-work.

The tower at one corner served as a main entrance. This tower was surmounted by a broadly projecting roof shading a balcony which surrounded the tower.

The chimney, constructed of brick, was placed on the outside, and rose in the center of the gable end of the main building. Graceful verandas, in the Swiss style, extended on the sides of the main building.

The appearance of the interior was as effective as the exterior; the lower story, which was about three feet above the ground, was divided into offices for the members of the committee, but the second floor, designed for the council chamber of the commission, was in one room extending to the roof, and impressed the visitor by its great size, so unlooked for in a building which, from the outside, seemed to be divided into numerous sleeping apartments. The omission of an attic floor, and the rich carving of the tie-beams of the roof, added greatly to the comfort and beauty of this chamber.

The architects during the Exposition received several orders for modifications of this building for country residences, for which it is well adapted.

THE TURKISH MOSQUE.

The mosque at Broussa, built by Mohammed I, in 1412, furnished the plan and model of this building. It was, moreover, in its dimensions about the size of the mosques seen in Turkish villages, and may be considered a very truthful type of them. The interior was divided into four rooms. The one first entered was the hall, where the worshipers take off and leave their shoes; to the right of this vestibule was a very small circular room, where the *Zebil* or sacred fountain is placed. On the left a similar chamber contained several clocks, which indicate the fives times of prayer observed each day by Mohammedans. These rooms were closed in by a lattice-work of plaster only, being with that exception open to the exterior.

This building had also the minaret from which the worshipers are called to prayer. From the vestibule the visitor entered into the mosque proper. Immediately in front of the entrance was the *mirhab*, made of and covered with enameled tiles, and decorated on each side by large wax candles. This *mirhab* marks the point of the compass which directs to Mecca, and before it the faithful kneels and adores. To the right of the *mirhab* or altar the *mimber* or pulpit was placed, from which the Iman reads portions of the Koran.

There was also a very curious luster, formed of two equilateral triangles which crossed each other, and from which innumerable little lamps hung. This luster or chandelier was suspended from the interior of the cupola. The floor was covered by a rich Turkey carpet, and the walls were decorated with Turkish inscriptions.

The exterior decoration was neither handsome nor striking, but the form of the building itself was perfect, being a model of one of the most beautiful mosques in Turkey, and following the proportions exactly, though on a reduced scale.

The work was executed by M. Flandrin. The edifice itself was square, surmounted by a dome, and adorned by the towers before referred to, and by the minaret. The whole building is well worthy of attention.

The Moorish or Hispano-Arabian type of architecture furnished the most striking buildings in the park. The Ottoman Empire displayed the Sultan's kiosque, erected by M. de Parville. Egypt, a *selemlik*, or summer palace; Tunis, a reproduction of the Bardo; and Prussia, a pavilion erected by M. de Diebistch.

The Sultan's kiosque will first occupy our attention.

THE SULTAN'S KIOSQUE.

If the mosque represented the severe and somber architecture which characterizes the buildings of the first Ottoman dynasties, this kiosque, on the other hand, was of a different type, and furnished a natural and easy transition to the highly ornamented architecture of the Moors and of the Spanish Arabs.

The exterior of this building was severe in form and generally devoid of ornamentation, but the interior revealed all the luxury of color and play of light of which the Persians are so fond. The edifice was copied from one of the many summer resorts of the Sultan which are to be found on the Asiatic side of the Bosphorus. It consisted of two portions, the first or front part containing a vestibule and servants' apartments, and the second or principal part containing a large square reception room. The front is wider than, but not so deep as, the principal portion.

The approach to the building is by a flight of steps, and a covered gallery supported by plain octagonal wooden columns resting on square bases. The center arch of the gallery is elliptical in shape, while those on either side are ogival, terminating in a point.

The windows in the lower range were rectangular, while those in the range above were ogival-shaped, with colored glass panes.

The exterior of the square portion conforms in its decoration to that of the rest of the building. The distribution and shape of the windows was, however, different. The exterior presented no features worthy of imitation; but on entering the pavilion the visitor was surprised and delighted by the splendor and richness of the ornamentation, due almost entirely to painting. It is in decoration rather than in architecture that Persian taste has reached its highest development.

The ceiling and walls were divided into panels, decorated in blue and gold and other colors, with arabesque patterns, leaves, and flowers.

The light penetrated through a double row of windows with colored glass panes, while the rich carpets and divans gave to the apartment the richest and most luxurious appearance.

The Sultan, during his visit to the Exposition, ordered some changes in decoration of the interior of this building. The carpets were replaced by ordinary mattings, and the divans, which were covered with rich silk, extended only on the side of the wall facing the entrance. Sofas and chairs of the beautiful inlaid work of Constantinople, covered with Bagdad tapestry, were substituted for the divans with which the room was formerly furnished. An elegantly carved table was placed in the center of the room, which was formerly occupied by a fountain.

This building was designed and executed by M. Parvillé, and is the result of his careful and accurate study of Persian buildings—a study which he has entered upon with enthusiasm, and conscientiously pursued.

THE EGYPTIAN SALEMLIK.

The salemlik of the Viceroy of Egypt was prepared by the Egyptian commission in the hope that his highness would visit Paris during the Exposition, and in order that he might have a palace where he could receive those who could claim the privilege of paying their respects.

The salemliks are summer palaces, separated from the ordinary dwellings, and used as apartments for visitors. The building in the Champ de Mars is divided into two parts, a large exposition hall, which is entirely independent from the salemlik proper, and the pavilion of the Viceroy.

The style of architecture is Moorish, intermediate between the kiosque of the Sultan and the palace of the Bey. It is an edifice of elegant proportions and brilliant decorations. A fine cupola surmounts it, while the capitals, arches, windows, doors, and ceilings are excellent specimens of the prevailing architecture of the building. Over the entrance gate is seen an inscription in the Arabic character, borrowed from the Koran. It is an invocation to God, to be seen quite frequently on the dwellings of Mohammedans, and signifies—"O Thou who openest the gates, open to us the gates of goodness."

In the decoration of their buildings the Moorish and Arabian architects have always shown a wonderful fondness for geometrical combinations. The whole ornamentation of the Moors is constructed geometrically, as the decoration of the Alhambra and their fondness for mosaics testify, in the geometrical forms of which the imagination had full play.

Their method of ornamentation was, however, without symbolism. This the religion of the Moors forbade; but the want was more than supplied by inscriptions from the poets and from the Koran, which, addressing themselves to the eye by their outward beauty, at once excited the intellect by the difficulties of deciphering their curious and complex involutions, and the imagination, when read, by the beauty of the sentiments they expressed, and the music of their composition.

This building afforded excellent examples of this peculiar and distinctive method of decoration. The ornamentations of the salemlik of the viceroy were executed by French artists. They were beautiful specimens of arabesques, and were reproduced in the most creditable manner.

The principal room in the palace is an exact copy of the room in which the viceroy was born. The furniture, the hangings, the decoration of the walls, the fountain in the center, the two graceful terraces which communicate with the garden, and the rich accessories, give a very faithful idea of Oriental life as it exists to-day.

Surrounding the principal room, which is lighted by a dome and by large windows, are four other rooms, used as retiring or sleeping rooms.

The metal work of the gates and doors was executed in Cairo by Arabian artists, the wood-work in Paris, from Egyptian designs.

The exterior walls were painted in blue and white bands.

Among the other constructions erected by the Egyptian commission was an *okel* or caravansary, stables, and other buildings. These *okels* serve as inns, storehouses, bazars, and work-shops. There are some features of the present building which are not to be seen in the ordinary *okels;* in other respects, such as in the doors, windows, and galleries, it is a reproduction of buildings actually in existence.

Edifices of this class are to be seen in Cairo, and particularly in Assouan, in Upper Egypt, where the excessive heat is more supportable in the interior courts of these buildings than in the streets of the city.

In addition to the stables, which were erected by the commission of Morocco, a tent of camels' hair-cloth of large dimensions was exhibited. Its arrangements show that the art of constructing and furnishing movable dwellings of this kind is remarkably well understood.

THE PALACE OF THE BEY OF TUNIS.

The object that the Tunisian commissioners seem to have had in view in the construction of this graceful edifice, situated at the right angle of the park, was the truthful representation of the arts, manners, customs, and manufactures of Tunis.

The façade was an exact reproduction of the bardo, a summer palace erected near Tunis.

The dimensions were, however, much smaller than in the original building, though the exact style of decoration and internal arrangements were preserved. The building was elevated on a platform or basement, which was occupied by the Tunisian café, shops, stables, &c. The approach was by a grand staircase guarded by six lions in a sitting posture, three on a side. The veranda projects in front of the main building, and is supported by six columns surmounted by cissoid-shaped arches. The center arch is larger and higher than those on the sides. The tympanums of the three arches and the angles of the central arch are ornamented in open work. The architraves are decorated with inscriptions in golden letters on a blue ground.

The main entrance to the building at the back of the portico is surmounted by a richly ornamented arch, corresponding to the central arch of the portico.

The floor of the portico is surrounded by a richly carved railing. The wall at the back has a base of red marble supporting two large panels of polychromatic faïence. The decoration at the upper part consists of open work panels in plaster.

On either side of the entrance is a square pavilion surmounted by a dome. The lower stories of these pavilions, which are used in the original building as dens for wild animals, are furnished with large barred windows.

This entrance to this palace is very imposing. Ascending the steps between two Tunisian soldiers, who stand here as sentinels, you enter a fine wide hall, on the left of which is the guardhouse, which contains a small armory, while adjoining is the chamber of *Sidi Mustapha Khazmadar*, who filled the office of prime minister during three successive reigns. This room opens into that of the Bey, thus affording the minister continual access. The chamber of the Bey is styled *beit-el-bacha*, and is lighted by peculiar windows called *moucharabi*, a sort of grating, by which light is admitted through a trellis work of plaster. These openings afford a full view of all that passes outside, but do not allow those outside to see what is within.

There is a deep bay window in this hall, where the Bey sits on a splendid ottoman surrounded by his court, who at a given sign disappear and reappear according to his pleasure. Nothing can exceed the rich decoration of this room. The most costly ornamentation of the East has been used, and the light, admitted through an arabesque open work supporting colored glass panes, lends richness to the scene. The walls of this building are of panels of plaster, richly ornamented at the upper part; on a level with the peristyle is a frieze, which has inscriptions of gold on a blue ground.

The upper part of each pavilion is pierced on each side with four ornamented windows with arched tops. The whole is surmounted by a dome.

The main entrance opens into a vestibule, on the right of which is the hall of justice. This apartment is decorated with panels of polychromatic marble, and has a large window at the back. Above are a number of small square panels in arabesque open work, ornamented with colored glass. The frieze is covered with inscriptions representing the ninety-nine epithets of God, and that of *Sidi Sadeck*, (the just ruler.)

The cornice supports a quadrangular drum pierced with four arched windows on each side, decorated with open work and colored glass. The cupola is cylindrical, and ornamented in the same manner.

Opposite the hall of justice, at the left of the entrance, is the museum or armory, in which are exposed the arms worn by all the Beys of Tunis since the crusades.

From the vestibule the visitor also enters the *patio*, or central open court-yard. This is surrounded by a covered gallery, the roof of which is supported on each side by four columns and three arches, the larger one being in the center. The floor of the gallery is covered with bright colored tiles; the columns and capitals are of marble, and were brought from Tunis.

In the center of the court was a fountain. The walls of the rooms were ornamented with bright colors, while the furniture consisted of divans and rich carpets—the whole forming a most delightful summer retreat.

Beyond the summer saloon are the sleeping apartments of the Bey, furnished in the most luxurious manner. The rest of the space is occupied by apartments for women and servants.

In the rear of the building, parallel with the façade of the front, is the grand saloon of the Bey, with the hall of honor and the banqueting hall on either side. The saloon of the Bey was by far the richest in the building, both in ornamentation and design.

The prevailing colors employed in the decoration of this building were blue, yellow, green, and red.

It may be said that the interior of this charming edifice offered exact specimens of the architectural art of Tunis in its most elevated type, and that on the outside, also, there were equally good exhibitions of some of the industries, trades, and arts of the country.

In the basement of the building there was an Arabian café. This was a faithful copy of Tunisian establishments, where the visitor could take a cup of coffee in true Oriental style, the powdered coffee and the liquid being served together; a drink which has a flavor that amateurs well know how to appreciate. A barber's shop was fitted up near the café; the rear of the shop containing divans where the customers could lounge.

In the East, the barber shops are the rendezvous of loungers and gossips, and correspond to the European club-rooms. To complete this faithful picture of life in Tunis, there was a long row of graceful and attractive shops filled with rare eastern productions. The merchant stood in the center of his shop surrounded by his goods, smoking calmly, and in a dignified manner, his long *schibouk*, condescending now and then to wait on a customer.

In concluding, a just tribute should be paid to the talents of the architect of this building, M. Alfred Chapon, by simply repeating the high compliment paid him by the artisans sent from Tunis at the request of M. De Lesseps, to assist in the ornamentation of this work. When told that the object of their visit was to assist in arranging an exact representation of Tunisian art and industry, they replied, "What can we do? Everything is done."

One of the most interesting features in the erection of this building was the bold and skillful manner in which the artists worked and molded plaster. Their only tools were two chisels of different sizes.

No drawing was made in advance. The artists seemed to be inspired, and executed figures and sculptures of the most complicated patterns with a precision and regularity that surprised every beholder. In the openings, pierced through the plaster, panes of colored glass were inserted which produced the most fantastic and beautiful effects.

The four structures which have been successively noticed: the Turkish mosque, the Sultan's kiosque, the Egyptian salemlik, and the palace of the Bey of Tunis, were all well defined types, and characteristic of the different systems of Mussulman architecture—that of the Ottoman seldjoucides, that of the Persians, of the Moors, and of the Spanish Arabs.

THE GOTHIC CHAPEL.

On entering the park from the gate of the bridge of Jena, one of the first buildings which attracted the visitor was the Gothic chapel. This building was erected at the instance of M. Charles Léveque, glass painter of Beauvais, and originated in the desire to bring together in a prominent position a collection of all the art materials which are used in ecclesiastical architecture. In this respect it was similar to the architectural court in the English section. No fewer than seventy-one individuals and firms contributed toward the erection and furnishing of this building. Although externally the building was open to adverse criticism, yet internally it was very costly; though perhaps there was wanting in it a unity of design which would necessarily be the result of the manner in which the collection was made. The floor displayed tiles of different colors and patterns; the windows were filled with stained glass; the arches and capitals were painted. Each chapel had an altar of elegant design and workmanship. The sanctuary was inclosed by metal grilles, while specimens of carved wood-work, enamelled shrines, stalls, candelabra, and other articles which are used in the furnishing of a church, were to be seen in their appropriate places. The object of this exhibition was to elevate the character of the arts employed in the service of the church; and the cost of the building and objects displayed is said to have exceeded two hundred thousand francs (forty thousand dollars.)

The materials of which the building was constructed were brick, stone, and plaster; the roof was of slates of different colors, and was furnished with an ornamented metal crest; the edges of the arches were of brick-work covered with plaster moldings; the columns were formed of pieces of wood surrounded with brick-work and coated with plaster; the capitals of the columns and the mullions were of the same material. Very pleasing effects were produced by the use of this material at very moderate cost, and its use is to be particularly recommended where polychromatic decoration is to be used.

THE RUSSIAN IZBA.

The buildings seen in Russia represent many different styles of architecture. The older edifices, with their cupolas and domes, bear the impress of the Byzantine school. The public buildings and palaces are specimens of *rennaissance*, and are similar to those seen in other countries. The truly national architecture of the country is to be seen only in the wooden cottages and homes of the peasantry and middle classes. In no other country is wood, when used as a building material, worked and ornamented to such a high degree.

All the buildings and structures representing Russian architecture in the Champ de Mars were of wood. These were the izba, the stables, and the fittings and decoration of the Russian section in the interior of the main Exposition building.

The izba was an exact specimen of the peasants' cottages of Russia, such as are seen at Moscow and other places. Its details of ornamentation, however, were not so carefully executed as they often are in that country. The izba is formed of two houses united by a kind of shed. They are built of logs, hewed or sawed, and in this respect are like the log-houses of Sweden, Norway, and some parts of Austria. The roofs are steep and overhanging, and are highly ornamented by cut woodwork.

One of the houses is entered by four steps under a veranda supported by four columns as posts. The other house is without a veranda, but has an artistically cut balcony extending along the entire front just above the eaves of the roof.

The first story, or ground floor, the ceiling of which is very low, is lighted by three small windows, and is used for housing the cattle. The second story serves as the habitation of the family. The stairway is outside of the building, protected by the shed which covers the entrance to the courtyard. The upper story is divided into two rooms, a large and small one, the interior of which is lined with dressed boards, in many cases smoothed and polished with sand.

In these buildings the wood-work was not painted, though in Russia, especially in the interiors, the carved wood-work, as well as the casings of the windows, and the shutters, are usually painted, and often in strong colors—red, yellow, and blue.

One of the houses is called the *letnik*, and is used by the family as the summer home, but at other times as the storehouse. It contains only a single room, raised a little above the ground.

The ornamentation of the izba is generally done by the proprietor himself, and is sometimes of the most elaborate character. The ridge of the roof is always ornamented; the casings of the gables project above and below, and are carved at the top in the form of horses' heads turned inwards toward each other. This style of decoration is very ancient, and has been explained by the fact that the horse was held sacred by the ancient Scythians. The lower ends or extremities of the casings, which extend some distance beyond the roof, are also highly ornamented. Carved pendants also extended from the ridgepole at the gable end of the house.

In the Russian section models of the existing architecture of Russia, adapted to its various climates, were also displayed. In the northern provinces the izbas have the foundation made of brick, with the first story of logs cut in the usual manner. The *letnik* serves only as a storehouse. The roof is made of dressed planks. In the central provinces of Russia, the buildings are made entirely of wood; the ornamentation is much more abundant, and the sheds and balconies are usually covered with thatch. In the southern portions of the country the izbas are built of masonry, and very little carved wood is used. The roofs are always thatched, and the ground floor is generally surrounded by a veranda covered by the projection of the roof, and supported by rustic woodwork instead of posts as at the north.

According to a writer in the Engineer, "The building of a peasant's house of the plainest kind does not cost, in the neighborhood of Moscow, Toula, and other great towns, more than eighty to one hundred and forty roubles; that is to say, from twelve to twenty pounds sterling—materials, labor, furniture, and stove, all included. The furniture, it should be explained, consists simply of one large table and benches which stand round the room in the daytime, and form—two put together with a hard matress on the top—the beds of the family at night, except in the coldest season, when father, mother, and children find a warm corner on the top of the stove, which is nothing more than an oven composed of bricks and faced with ornamental tiles. To explain this extraordinary cheapness the price of wood must be stated. A plank of best fir wood, twenty-one feet long, eight and three-fourth inches wide, and nearly two inches thick, costs fifty copecks, or seventeen pence, and oak is only worth from two shillings threepence to three shillings fourpence the cubic foot. The wood is very carefully seasoned, being built up in stacks with interstices, and submitted to the action of steam, and is full of turpentine and resinous matters."

The walls of the house are calked like the deck of ships, either with the large moss of Russia or, where that is not to be obtained, with oakum, and the calking is dressed with turpentine. The angles are filled with a cement composed of lime, cow dung, and coarse flour or meal, and the building is made as tight as possible.

RUSSIAN STABLES.

The Russian stables at the Exposition represented the style of architecture which dates back to the seventeenth century, anterior to the time of Peter the Great. The ridge of the roof is very high, and is ornamented with a lattice work of wood, forming a very prominent and picturesque crest. The covering of the roof consists of planks laid in three courses and overlapping like shingles. The main portion of the stable building projects so as to form a porch, which is supported upon wooden pillars. The doors and windows are rectangular and almost square. The pediment of the main part of the building is in unpainted wood, very much carved, and ornamented with pendants. The casing of the pediment at the upper end terminates in the customary carved horses heads, while the lower end projects two or three feet and is curved upwards and cut into some fanciful shape. The windows are divided into two parts by carved supports. The roof has a row of dormer windows much more highly ornamented than those of the lower story, and furnished with carved casings and ornaments similar to those on the gables. The gables of the wings are covered with ornamental carving. The casings are not only carved but further enriched by decorated brackets and cross-ties.

Another very interesting specimen of purely national architecture was the entrance to the Russian section in the interior of the Exposition building. It was a type of the interior ornamentation of the Muscovite palaces, and consisted of a colonnade crowned with a highly carved border ornamented with polychromatic decorations. The ornamentation and carving of wood could not reach greater perfection than it has done in this instance, nor respond better to the requirements of fancy.

All these structures were the work of Russian artizans sent to Paris for the purpose. The stable is said to have cost one thousand pounds sterling in Russia.

To the citizen of the United States the display of Russian buildings and methods of ornamenting wood could not fail to be interesting. The two countries have many features in common. Our prairies correspond to the steppes, our forests to hers, and our climate in many respects is similar. Constructions adapted to the necessities of life in Russia, and built of the same kind of material that we have at command, and possessing a peculiar beauty and elegance in form and decoration, and withal cheap, offer many useful hints to our architects and builders.

THE MOVABLE COTTAGE.

Messrs. Waaser & Madin, 70 Avenue St. Ouen, Paris, exhibited a very picturesque "chalet," the general style and appearance of which may be understood by reference to the annexed outline drawing from a photograph. Page 25.

This is built of wood and so framed and rabbeted together that it can be taken down at any time without injury and be erected in some other locality. It is a portable house which can be moved from place to place as the owner desires. Even the slates of the roof are movable, being hung in their places upon hooks.

THE BUILDINGS OF SWEDEN AND NORWAY.

These buildings, like those of Russia, were entirely built of wood. The walls were squared logs, a method of construction which it seems has prevailed in these countriès since the twelfth century.

The Swedish exhibit was made by the royal commission, and consisted of a Dalecarlian house, the exterior, the mode of construction, and the interior arrangements of which were copied from a house built in Dalecarlia in 1309, and called the house of Gustavus Wasa, who took refuge in it when flying from his enemies in the year 1520.

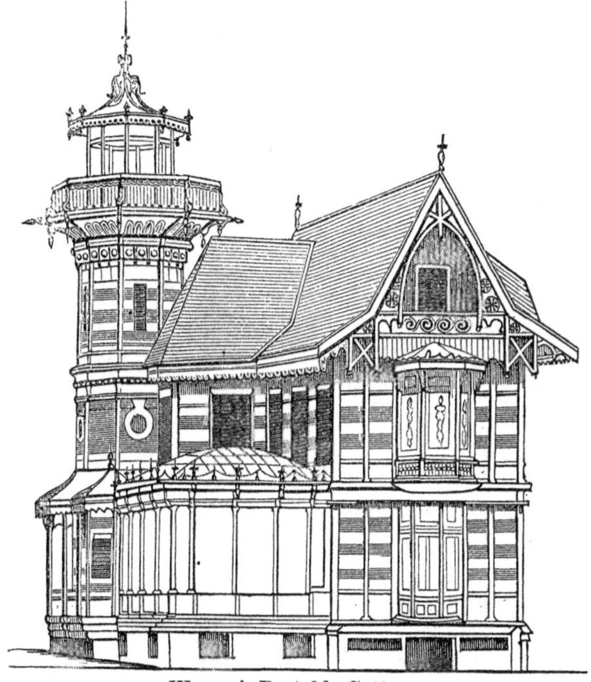

Waaser's Portable Cottage.

This building rests on a foundation of masonry. The gallery, which is only on the principal front, is supported at the two ends by the projecting beams which form the outer walls, and between these beams by wooden brackets. A winding stairway on the outside of the building leads to this gallery, and is inclosed in a semi-cylindrical casing covered with large shingles cut in the form of fish scales. The second story of the house is covered in the same manner. On the ground floor, the ceiling of which is quite low, are three rooms, one of them fitted up as a primary school-room, while the others form the *annex* of the Swedish section. The windows are formed of small square panes of glass set in lead.

The roof was of boards and birch bark covered with earth, in which lichens and mosses were planted. The whole building was noticeable for the absence of ornamentation. The style was simple, primitive, and characteristic.

The Norwegian house is similar in many respects to that from Sweden. This building, which rests upon blocks of wood six inches in height, is built of squared logs notched at the ends and projecting at the corners in the usual manner. A gallery supported by the projecting ends of the beams and by brackets surrounds the second story of the house. This and the staircase leading to it are covered by the projecting roof, and are richly ornamented by wood carvings.

THE ENGLISH COTTAGE.

The English cottage, with its many gables and ornamented roof, was one of the first buildings that arrested the attention of visitors who entered from the bridge of Jena. It stood nearly opposite the imperial pavilion, and was erected by the British commission as an example of the English cottages that are found in the suburbs of London and other great cities of the kingdom. It was only one story in height and was modified considerably in its plan and construction from that of a dwelling, in order to give a good opportunity for the display of various methods of ornamenting and finishing the walls, both of the exterior and interior. A part of the walls were of brick, another portion of béton, and other portions were covered with incised plaster with slates and tiles, or with ornamental plaster work. The roof, also showed a great variety of styles of slating and of ornamenting with iron work.

The interior was not divided into rooms or chambers, but was devoted to the display of various forms of apparatus for heating and lighting and for cooking. The walls also were adorned with many brilliant and beautiful specimens of ornamental encaustic and enamelled tile work from the principal British establishments. The floor was also laid with tiles in a great variety of styles.

THE SWISS CHALET.

This building was erected by Messrs. Kaffer & Co. as a specimen of their work, and possessed all the picturesque features of a Swiss chalet modified to meet the necessities of a modern country house.

It was thirty-four feet six inches long and sixteen feet four inches in breadth. It was built of wood with double walls, and would be warm in winter and cool in summer. The building on exhibition had no fire-places, but they might be easily added. The height of the building was such that the architect was enabled to cover it with a wide overhanging roof without interfering with the light, an inconvenience often found in Swiss edifices of this description. On the ground floor there were covered passages; on the second story beautiful verandas; all protected

The Swiss Chalet.

by the roof, which was covered with tiles. A double staircase with highly ornamented balustrade led to the front entrance. The center window opened into a large dining or billiard room. The walls and ceilings were covered with carved wood. There was also a side entrance for servants, and a back entrance leading to the garden. In addition to the dining-room there were two other excellent rooms, one of which might serve as a kitchen, and one as a breakfast-room. The passages were wide, lofty and airy. On ascending to the second story the visitor found two moderate sized drawing-rooms with folding doors, a good bed-room and dressing-room in front, and two excellent bed chambers in the rear. All these opened on verandas. On the second floor, or third story, there were four good rooms for servants, thus affording ample room for a moderate sized family. All the windows were provided with Venetian shutters, painted green or red according to the taste of the occupant. Nothing could exceed the pretty appearance of this chalet, which was constructed in such a manner as to be a pleasant residence throughout the year. It was free from damp, being elevated three feet from the ground, and was strongly built and air-tight. The price asked for this building by the architect was thirty thousand francs, or six thousand dollars.

THE TEMPLE OF XOCHICALCO.

As a type of the architecture of one of the most interesting, and at the same time one of the least known, of extinct races, a model of this temple was erected in the Champ de Mars.

It was claimed for this structure that it was a faithful restoration of a monument found about twenty-three leagues southeast of the city of Mexico, and described by Alzate, Humboldt, and others. This restoration was made under the direction of M. Léon Méthédin. A broad quadrangular terrace, with a pyramidal base, supported in the center a pyramidal building with a truncated summit and an ornamented cornice. The entablature, or vertical border of the terrace, was decorated by boldly-cut hieroglyphics in relief. A broad flight of steps on one side led to the front of the building, where a copy of the colossal statue found at Teolihuacan was placed, and copies of other objects of interest to archæologists.

The upper story in the original was in a state of utter ruin; but it is claimed that the fallen stones were found in sufficient numbers to enable M. Méthédin to make a reliable restoration. It is admitted, however, that four notable modifications were made in this reproduction:

First. The grand staircase has been made easier of ascent, for the convenience of visitors.

Second. The terrace upon which the temple stands, and which was of masonry in the original, is here constructed of carpentry, and used to exhibit numerous objects brought from the Criméa, Egypt, Italy, and Mexico by M. Méthédin.

Third. Glass panes, painted with designs drawn from ancient manuscripts, fill the openings which, in the original, allowed the air to enter unobstructed.

Fourth. The interior walls were hung with Egyptian tapestry brought from Thebes.

This curious collection bore the inscription "*Missions scientifiques et artistiques de Léon Méthédin dans les deux mondes.*"

The most ancient monuments of the Toltecs were pyramidal in form, and were usually surrounded by an inclosure. The top of the pyramid, on which the temple or teocallis was placed, was reached by a broad and imposing flight of steps, furnished sometimes with a balustrade. The interior of the temples was adorned with hieroglyphics in relief, and not cut into the stone, as in Egyptian monuments.

The temple, or teocallis, frequently covered a subterranean apartment. The temples of Cholula and Xochicalco are the most celebrated and best preserved specimens of this ancient mode of building.

The latter is an immense conical-shaped rock, cut into five steps or courses, the sides of which are revetted with masonry. On the summit is the teocallis, the exterior walls of which are covered with sculptures of life-size, representing men and animals. The gates are rectangular or trapezoidal, similar to those of Egyptian temples. The interior hall has a flat roof. There were no windows, light and air being admitted only through the door. In some temples of this kind there were columns, entirely devoid, however, of ornamentation. If pillars were necessary for the purpose of support, they were cylindrical, and without capitals, the weight of the roof resting on the plinth.

The plan in the Champ de Mars differed in many important particulars from the original monument, the details of its construction being made subservient to the purposes for which it was used, as already noted.

Among the objects displayed were authentic casts of the statue of the sun, of the divinity of death, and of the great zodiac of Dendérah. Copies of the troughs of stone, which, in the Aztec temples, were used to receive the blood and heart of the victims of the sacrifices, and other objects of interest to the antiquary and archæologist, were also exhibited.

THE ROUMANIAN CHURCH.

The building in the park was only a partial reproduction of the chapel of the Greek monastery of *Kurtea d'Argis*, in Wallachia, following the original in internal decoration but not in plan. A model, however, of the original in the gallery of the History of Labor, gave the visitor an excellent idea of the peculiar features of this interesting monument. As this building is one of the most remarkable specimens of Byzantine architecture in existence, a brief description of it is presented.

The Byzantine style of architecture reached its culminating point in the brilliant reign of the Greek Emperor Justinian, and since that time it has not undergone any important modifications either in construction or decoration. In fact, it fell rapidly into conventional stiffness, empty formalism, or simple mechanism, stripped of all its creative energy, and became so scrupulously attached to early traditions that all the vigor and strength which predominated under Justinian was lost. There have been, nevertheless, many attempts to break from the narrow lines of traditional art, and to open a new road in the construction and decoration of church edifices, though it must be said that, in the Greek church at least, there is little to be hoped for in this direction. Among these attempts the chapel of the monastery of *Kurtea d'Argis* must be considered as the most successful.

The recent occupation of the provinces on the Danube by the Austrian troops has brought this edifice to light. Its existence up to that time was unknown to architects, and, on account of the many new features it presents, cannot fail to be considered of importance.

The credit of first calling the attention of the public to this building is due to Count Coronini, and a full description of it was published in the fourth volume of the Annuaire de la Commission Centrale Autrichienne des Monuments Historiques. We are indebted to the brochure, published by M. Louis Reissenberger, for most of the facts and details here given.

This edifice is supposed to have been built about the commencement of the sixteenth century, but it has been adorned and beautified since that time by many of the rulers of the province in which it is situated.

The architect, instead of following the usual form of Byzantine churches—that of a rectangle or square, in which a Greek cross is inscribed—has given to a portion only of the exterior of the church the shape of a cross, while in another portion he has preserved the traditional square. This square portion is surmounted by a cupola, supported in the interior by twelve pillars, and is joined to the cross-shaped portion of the building, which is also surmounted by a cupola, so as to cut off one of the arms of the cross. The polygonal termination of the arms of the cross is also a peculiar feature.

This arrangement, by means of which the architect seems to have intended to unite the architectural forms of the East with those of the West, is considered to be faulty. It is said to lack the idea of unity, which should always prevail in architecture, and that the grand effects which characterize the Byzantine churches of an earlier period are lost.

The front of the building is further ornamented by two small cupolas resting on cylindrical drums, pierced with light narrow windows, winding obliquely around the drums at an angle of 70° with the horizon, which gives them a spiral form.

The interior is constructed of brick, and the exterior of ordinary limestone. Brick was preferred for the interior, inasmuch as it gives the best surface for the reception of mortar upon which in all Greek churches frescoes are painted.

The limestone gives to the building a soft and agreeable tint, and is a material which could be readily carved into rich and effective ornaments.

The external decoration seems to have been borrowed from Arabian and Moorish architecture, and is characterized by its lightness and variety. There are two rows of windows, the lower ones being rectangular and very narrow, while those above are circular openings, partly closed by arabesque tracery in open work cut in stone. A rich cornice supports the roof, and the upper and lower panels into which the exterior elevation is divided are separated by a carved *torus*, which, in buildings of this character, is generally painted.

Although the exterior of the church is distinguished by a richness and abundance of decoration of the most varied character, the interior does not display any great novelty or attractive feature either in architecture or ornament.

The walls are almost perfectly plain, and their tone is scarcely heightened by the paint frescoes which cover them. Even the twelve columns in the principal part of the church which support the cupola are but slightly ornamented. The external beauty and rich decoration of the church leads the visitor to expect more costly and hidden beauties within; this expectation is not realized, but the severity of the interior and the dim light which pervades it, the absence of all beautiful forms which might attract the eye and divert the attention are accepted as fitting accompaniments to contemplation and religious thought. The building as a whole is a most interesting monument, and is well worthy of attention and careful study.

JAPANESE AND CHINESE BUILDINGS.

There were several striking examples of the peculiar architecture of the Japanese and of the Chinese. Of the former, the most notable was a complete Japanese cottage in the park, surrounded by a garden in the appropriate style. A very good example of the curved and highly ornamented tile-covered roof of the temples of that country was placed in the outer gallery of the building, near a model of a temple from Siam, and the model of the Roumanian church. This roof was supported upon light, simple columns of wood placed in pairs at the corners.

The Japanese Temple.

CHAPTER II.

MATERIALS AND METHODS OF CONSTRUCTION.

GREAT VARIETY OF BUILDING MATERIALS DISPLAYED AT THE EXPOSITION—IRON BEAMS AND GIRDERS—ARTIFICIAL STONES AND CONCRETES—BUILDINGS IN PARIS—CHARACTER OF THE STONE USED—METHODS OF CONSTRUCTION IN PARIS—BÉTON COIGNET AND CONCRETE—METHODS OF BUILDING WALLS WITH CONCRETE—ARTIFICIAL STONE—RANSOME'S ARTIFICIAL STONE—NICOLL'S NEW WALL SLABS—THE MAREZZO MARBLE—TILES FOR FLOORS AND WALLS—ENGLISH TILES—TILES OF FRANCE, SPAIN, AND OTHER COUNTRIES—TERRA COTTA, ITS ADVANTAGES—ORNAMENTAL WROUGHT-IRON WORK—ROOFING MATERIALS—ROOFING FELT—USE OF PAPER AND PASTEBOARD IN BUILDING—CARPENTERS' AND JOINERS' WORK—AMERICAN CARPENTRY AND JOINERS' WORK—FRENCH JOINERS' WORK—INLAID FLOORS—PARQUETRY.

I.—EXTENT OF THE EXHIBITION OF BUILDING MATERIALS.

The descriptions of the buildings in the park serve in a measure to indicate the nature of the materials used and the methods of construction in various parts of Europe, but fail to show what they are in the great cities.

It cannot be claimed, perhaps, that any very important novelty in the nature of materials used for building was shown at the Exposition, but the variety of materials was very great, and in those dependent upon the arts or improved methods of manufacture a very notable advance was evident.

In iron beams and girders, for example, the great size which can now be given to them by improved machinery and methods of rolling, permits the rivetted girder to be replaced by those in one solid piece. Messrs. Petin Gaudet & Co. exhibited a beam over thirty-two feet long and thirty-nine inches wide, and another twelve inches wide and over one hundred and six feet long. Another establishment showed beams over forty-three inches wide.

In building stones and ornamental stones of all kinds the exhibition was remarkably rich. There were masses of cut and polished granites from Scotland and Cornwall, and porphyries, syenites, serpentines, and ornamental marbles from nearly all parts of Europe.

There were numerous displays of artificial stones, concretes, béton coignet, cements, bricks, solid and hollow and molded in various forms; terra cotta, for construction and for ornaments; tiles of all kinds for roofs, drains, floors, and walls; slates of various colors and forms, cut with remarkable precision; felt and other materials for roofing; timber, boards, moldings, and shingles, and, indeed, almost every material, raw or manufactured, that is used in construction.

It is impossible to describe all these materials within the limits of this report, and some of the more important and least known only will be noticed.

In general, the buildings in Paris and the cities of Europe are more substantially and solidly built than those in the United States. Comparatively little wood is used. Iron replaces wood to a great extent for floor beams, girders, and for roofs. In connection with bricks and concrete, and with the remarkable monolithic pieces obtained by béton coignet, it forms solid and fire-proof floors and roofs as durable and indestructible as stone itself.

Stairways are constructed of stone or brick, and the balustrades are made of iron. A great result of this substantial method of construction is the comparative freedom from destructive fires, such as in the United States annually destroy vast amounts of property. The fire risk is so much lessened abroad by this superior construction that insurance is remarkably cheap.

II.—BUILDING IN PARIS.

MATERIALS.

The city of Paris is fortunate in having at command inexhaustible supplies of excellent building materials, particularly a calcareous stone, which has a pleasing color, a fine grain, and uniform texture, comparatively light yet sufficiently strong, and which can be easily worked into any desired shape. It is so tractable under the chisel that it invites decoration, and has led to the existence of a class of decorative artisans or finishers, who sculpture the cornices and fronts of buildings after the masons have finished their work. But since the construction of railways leading to all parts of the empire, and the increase of wealth and a desire to employ more showy and durable materials, the architects of Paris have introduced other and firmer stones, and Paris is now supplied not only from the ancient quarries in its vicinity, but partly from Champagne, Lorraine, Bourgogne, Poitou, and Dauphiné. Marbles, granites, and ornamental stones are drawn from various sources: from the Vosges, the Alps, the Pyrenees, and other countries.

In the new and splendid edifice, the Grand Opera House, no less than twenty-four different varieties of stone are employed, including granites, syenites, porphyries, marbles, jaspers, sandstone, and soft calcareous stones.

France has also vast supplies of lime, cement, plaster, asphalt, and bitumen, all of which enter largely into construction in many ways, and are generally used instead of wood, as already mentioned. It is in this country also that the important improvements in *béton*, known as *béton aggloméré, système Coignet,* has been made and has been applied with great success in various important constructions.

The stranger in Paris cannot fail to be impressed with the beauty and regularity of the new streets, and the fine appearance of the buildings.

The houses are generally erected of a uniform height and size, and in the same general style of architecture. Full scope, however, is left to the taste of the builder, as the variety of designs and ornaments will testify; each building may thus have individuality and beauty without conflicting with the general appearance of the street. In this way those disagreeable contrasts so frequently seen in the finest streets of English and American cities are effectually prevented. The houses are all built of stone, in a sort of renascence of Louis Quatorze style, and are generally four or five stories in height.

The stone principally used is the *calcaire grossier* of the Paris basin, and has a light drab or cream color, very similar to the limestones used for buildings in Chicago.

When taken from the quarry it is quite soft, and admits of being easily cut with a saw or hewed into form. It hardens, however, on exposure to the air, and in a climate like that of Paris resists the effects of the weather for a long time. This stone is only used for the superstructure of the buildings, for, by municipal regulations, the foundations and the basements on all principal streets must be built of hard stone. The price of this soft limestone of Paris varies from thirty-seven to sixty-eight francs per cubic meter, according to the size of the blocks.

Of the harder stones there are some thirteen varieties, some of them found in the immediate vicinity of Paris. The price varies according to the size and quality of the blocks. First-class stone delivered at the works in blocks two and a half meters long and one and a half meters thick costs one hundred and ninety-three francs per cubic meter.

Blocks five and a quarter meters long by two and a half meters thick, four hundred and eighteen francs the cubic meter; blocks six meters long by two and a half meters thick, five hundred and eighteen francs the cubic meter.

This stone is used principally for the parapets, balconies, copings of bridges, and ornamental work much exposed to the influence of the weather, and for floors, staircases, steps, &c., where a durable material is required.

Marbles are extensively used in Paris for fountains, statues, &c., and for the internal and external decoration of buildings. In many of the shops beautiful specimens of inlaid marbles of different colors are to be seen in the counters, walls, and floors.

There are in Paris, alone, about twelve thousand persons employed in working marble, who receive from four to six francs per day. Of the sixty kinds of marble used, forty-one are found in France. The price varies from three hundred and forty francs to one thousand one hundred and twenty francs per square meter. Colored marbles, of which there are ten kinds, cost from nine hundred and fifty to one thousand four hundred and thirty francs per square metre; Spanish marbles, yellow and violet, one thousand and seventy francs per square meter; while the five Belgian varieties vary from four hundred and twenty to seven hundred and twenty francs per square meter.

METHODS OF CONSTRUCTION IN PARIS.

The following extract from the Artisans' Reports[1] is interesting as embodying the observations and opinions of a practical mason on the modes of construction adopted for houses in Paris:

"In the science of construction, and the judicious use of the materials, stone, wood and iron, the French architects display great skill. The right material is generally used in the right place. Their buildings being constructed as much as possible fire-proof, we seldom read of a great fire in Paris. They are generally well built, for the builder and the architect have to insure their stability for ten years, and are held accountable during that period for the expense of any repairs arising from imperfect workmanship, or from defective material. The fronts are all built of large stones, bedded and jointed, which run the full thickness of the wall. They are laid dry on each other, and afterwards run with plaster. There are openings left for the doors and windows, and projections for the cornices, moldings and carving. When the walls are carried to their full height, the masons work the front of the building, commencing at the top; they finish and take down their scaffolding as they descend. The back and end walls are built with small squared stones on the outside, and with unsquared or rubble on the inside. They are bedded in plaster; very little care is used in the bedding of this rubble, as the plaster sets soon after the stone is laid. The flues to carry off the smoke are constructed with earthenware pipes built into the walls; and as those walls settle unequally on the foundations, you observe on every gable-end exposed to view that open joints are left close to the quoins, so that each wall may settle of itself, without drawing the other with it, and causing rents in the building. Those open joints may be filled up when the work is seasoned. The floors are constructed with light wrought-iron girders of an I-section, laid about two feet apart, and arched from one to the other with hollow bricks bedded in plaster. The arches are very slightly curved, and their springers rest on the bottom flanges of the girders. The soffit is dubbed up and made level for the plaster of the ceiling, and a slight piece of wood is laid on the top of each girder, to which the floor boards are screwed. The staircases are all built of hard stone, with iron balusters and hand rails.

"The halls and corridors are generally floored with marble squares of various colors, or a composition of cement and marble chips, which is often a good imitation of mosaic. Very little wood is used, except for the flooring-boards, doors, windows and roof. In all the houses which I have seen, the sanitary arrangements seem to be of a very defective character. Water is used very sparingly; in fact they never think of

[1] Pages 258 and 260.

letting it run through their closets, although, judging from the liberality with which it is used in flushing the kennels of the public streets, Paris must be abundantly supplied.

"When the ground has been excavated for the basement of a building the stone work of that portion is usually bedded in mortar composed of lime and sand, or in cement mixed with sand, but all above the surface is bedded in pure plaster, the extensive use of which enables them to erect their buildings in a very short space of time, and to use any small pieces of stone in the cross-walls. The gypsum of which this plaster is made is raised at the hill of Montmartre, in the suburbs of Paris, the supply of which I learn is almost exhausted. It is prepared close to the quarries, and brought to the works in sacks, where it is sold for seventeen francs the cubic meter. It is a good, strong, coarse material; the ashes of the fuel used in the burning being allowed to intermix with the gypsum, but when required for exportation, or for finishing and ornamental work, it is passed through a very fine hair sieve.

"As in London, the building erected in Paris is chiefly done by contract, but with the important difference that each description of work is let to a contractor of that trade alone; whereas in London the entire works are let to one person. The contractors in Paris are usually men who have been brought up to the trade in connection with the works. They contract for and will necessarily have the skill to direct it themselves. The London contractor, in most cases, is not brought up to any of the building trades; he merely finds the capital, and some other persons supply the brains. It is clear that a better description of work is the result of the French system, where it is executed under the personal superintendence of a man who understands it, and who has a personal interest in its proper execution; and that there are greater facilities for a steady industrious workman to advance himself, and become a contractor some day. This method of contracting existed in London before the concentration of capital in the hands of a few; and it is still practiced in many of our provincial towns, with the same beneficial result as at Paris.

"The mason's contract, in addition to the stone work, includes the plastering and the brick work. Of the latter there is very little done in Paris. I have only observed an odd house built of brick. I presume the cost, which is sixty francs per thousand for middling brick, is some impediment to its more extensive use.

"The bricklayer and the plasterer are not distinct trades, as in London, but are included in the mason's trade, the operatives of which are classified into *limousins*, *poseurs*, and *ravaleurs*. The *limousins*, or wallers, build the sewers, drains, and basement story of the building, with rubble-stone, and as this description of work requires very little skill to execute it, the men employed being nothing more than handy laborers, they are paid from four and a quarter to four and three-quarter francs per day. The masons who fix the stones of which the fronts are built are called *poseurs;* they generally confine themselves to this branch of the trade. Their method of fixing, as before stated, is to lay the stones dry into their places, and when the course is completed to run the joints with plaster. In large buildings, where the walls are raised to a great height and the stones press heavily on each other, to preserve them from flushing, the plaster is prevented from running to the front by placing thin pieces of wood about two and a half inches broad in the joints, which are slipped out when the plaster sets; and when the walls settle these open joints are pointed up. Owing to this precaution of directing the weight on the center of the stones, you will very rarely see the moldings or other ornamental work on the face of a building flushed through pressure.

"Except in marble or polished work, the French masons use very little care with the beds and joints of the stone work; they are often three-eighths of an inch apart, but as the plaster with which they are filled is almost as durable as the stone, and like it in color, it does not affect the general appearance of the building. The skill of the *poseur* does not seem to be highly estimated, as his wages are only five and a half francs a day, or one and a half franc less than the *ravaleur*, which comprises two classes, viz: *ravaleurs* in plaster and *ravaleurs* in stone.

"The *ravaleurs* in plaster erect all the walls of the building above the basement, in which small squared or rubble stone is used. They build all the fireplaces and flues, and turn the brick arches for the floors. When the house is covered in with slates or tiles they coat all the walls with plaster, and form the ceiling and cornices.

"The plaster used for building the walls is mixed with water in a wooden trough, the sides of which slope outward towards the top. It is brought to the scaffold by the laborer on his head, and when it sets a little, the *ravaleur* spreads it on the walls with his trowel or hands—he is not particular which—and beds the stone; the stones are placed dry in the center of the wall, and afterwards grouted with thin plaster. The ceilings and walls are all finished with one coat of whatever thickness may be required by the unevenness of the walls, which he ascertains by plumbing screeds or narrow strips of plaster at each angle of the room, and at convenient distances from each other. Between the screeds he puts on wet plaster with a broom, his hands, or the trowel, and forms the surface of it level with the edge of a long, straight trowel, having fine teeth like a saw; a little thin plaster laid on and rubbed with the flat of a trowel makes it a fine, smooth surface. The cornices are made of pure plaster and run with a mold; but when very large and ornamental, they are done by molders, who make them of a composition of plaster, whitening, and glue, in which flax fibers are intermixed to add strength. It is hollowed at the back, and made so light, and yet so strong, that it may be attached with plaster, or nailed to the walls and ceiling. The *ravaleurs* in plaster are a very useful and skilled class of workmen, and are paid six francs a day. The trowels and other tools used by them are very awkward and clumsily made, and although those men execute some excellent work, they do it in a very unworkmanlike manner. You seldom see an English operative use plaster or mortar with his hand while he has a tool to do it with.

"The *ravaleur* in stone corresponds to the trade of a mason in London; but as the principal part of the work in Paris is executed in soft stone, and after the walls are built, while in London it is done with hard stone, worked on the banker before it is fixed, the method of working in the two places is entirely different, and one would have some difficulty in using the tools of the other without considerable experience.

"The *ravaleurs* in stone are divided into two classes, viz: those who finish the fronts of the building and those who work the beds and joints of the stone before they are fixed. This latter class are called *tailleurs de pierre.* The blocks of stone for a building are generally deposited near its site if there is room, and, if not, on the next convenient open space; and when cut into the required sizes these men work the beds and joints, and if the stone is required for a molding or cornice, they scribe on the mold and chamfer off the surplus. They seldom use a mallet and chisel, except to run a draught around the arris, but work the stone with a pick, a tooth-axe, and a diamond hammer. The mallet and chisel they use very imperfectly, but the pick and axe they use with great dexterity, and turn out a great quantity of that kind of work. They never banker a stone to work it, but merely lift it on a slant, and seldom turn it more than once before it is finished. They have no sheds to protect them from the weather, and are paid at the rate of six francs per day.

"The *ravaleurs* who work the fronts of the buildings are the most skillful men in the trade, and are paid seven francs a day when employed at day work; but as a gang of men generally do the work of a front by contract, they often earn more than day wages; but when an architect requires to have his work well done he will not allow it to be done by contract. M. Duc, the architect of the palace of justice, would have the front of that building done by day work; and it is plainly observable how superior the work is to that of the tribunal of commerce, which was executed by contract. For the *ravaleurs* to do their work, a scaffold is erected to the front, as the walls of most edifices are built overhand; then, commencing at the top cornice, they cut in the mold at each end, and with a piece of twine rubbed with red chalk, strained from end to end, they strike the horizontal lines, pitching off the waste from the front with a hammer and chisel; they then work it very close with a tooth-axe, and finish it off with a diamond hammer, or a plane, when the surface requires to be made smooth. These planes are about nine or ten inches long, having two irons, one in the middle and one in the front, to enable it to cut into an angle. The irons are merely thin pieces of steel or saw-plate, slightly beveled on the cutting edge. The *ravaleurs* have a number of these planes, of all shapes and sizes, with which they work the moldings on stone, just as a joiner would make them on wood. They seldom use a mallet and chisel, and when they do it is very awkwardly, but execute their work chiefly with the pick, axe, diamond hammer, and plane. It is astonishing with what celerity they finish off the front of a building, but everything is in their favor; the stone, being of a nice, fine quality, is not flushed at the joints or ends by the working of the plane or axe, and the stones being the full thickness of the wall, are not disturbed on their beds by the working. There is certainly something to say in favor of this system of working stone after the wall is built. In the first place, no time is wasted on the parts that are not exposed to view; and in the next place the lines will be more accurate, as they are struck the full length or full height of the building; and although much of their stone-work is not so perfectly masoned, and will not bear so minute an examination as the stone-work in London, their buildings will look better, owing to that circumstance.

"However perfectly the stones may be worked on the banker, unless they are carefully fixed, you will not have the lines straight, and you cannot make them so without disfiguring the moldings."

III.—COIGNET BÉTON AND CONCRETE.

Much attention is now given in France to the construction of monolithic buildings, bridges, piers, and walls, by the use of a mixture of sand, lime, and water, as proposed and perfected by M. Coignet, and now known as Coignet béton.

This mixture, when properly made, soon solidifies and acquires the properties of stone. While soft it may be molded and shaped into any desired form.

Common béton is a mixture of broken stones, lime, or hydraulic lime, and water, and is generally known in the United States as concrete. This also is used to a considerable extent in the construction of dwellings.

A small house constructed of Coignet béton was exhibited, and cheap dwellings for workmen are now constructing in several localities in France. This material was also used in the construction of the foundations and arches of the exposition building.

The adaptation of this material to various constructions and the method of preparing and using it has been fully shown by Mr. Leonard Beckwith, in one of the reports in the Exposition series, and to which reference is made.

The use of ordinary or Portland cement concrete for cottage walls is urged on the score of economy and ease of construction. It is asserted that with a proportion of from one-fifth to one-eighth of cement to sand, gravel, or small stones, a wall may be made one-third stronger than common brick-work; or that a concrete wall one-third of the thickness of common brick wall will be equally strong, and that it will cost only about half as much as a brick wall. It is stated also that common brick absorbs about twenty per cent. of water, and that a concrete wall does not absorb one-quarter of that quantity, and that it takes about one-quarter as long to dry, and that when set, and if made with hard stones, it is impermeable to wet.

The Emperor adopted a concrete construction for the forty dwellings which he had erected for the French artisans. The mixture consisted of the sand, gravel, and stones dug out of the foundations, mixed with one-eight-part of Portland cement. By the use of Tall's movable case, or a similar contrivance described below, walls of concrete can be raised with accuracy and without the aid of regular masons and bricklayers, an advantage which those who wish to secure a cheaply constructed dwelling, in these days of enormous prices, will not be apt to lose sight of.

METHOD OF CONSTRUCTING WALLS OF BÉTON OR CONCRETE.

Mr. Clarke, of New Haven, Connecticut, has made use of a contrivance for concrete building which consists of a movable frame sustaining planks on the inner and outer sides of the wall, thus forming a sort of trough or case, in which the concrete is laid or filled in by an ordinary laborer. When the space between the planks is filled the case of planks is loosened by turning a screw, and is then raised and readjusted and filled as before. It differs from the ordinary contrivances chiefly in this: that it is supported by a frame from above, and not by posts set in the ground or clamped to the wall below. Its construction is shown in the annexed figure, which also shows the manner in which a hollow wall W may be formed by using a wedge-shaped plank or "core" C C as long as the case. This core is set up edgewise in the space between the planks of the case, and when the concrete is filled in around it to the top the core is drawn out, and thus an air space from two to three inches wide is left in the wall. The outer and inner walls are bound together by tie-bricks set at regular intervals corresponding to notches cut in the lower or thin edge of the plank. The plank rests upon these bricks, and the notches allow it to drop down even with the top of the opening from which it has just been taken, and thus, as the wall is carried up, a continuous air space is left from the foundation to the top.[1] The

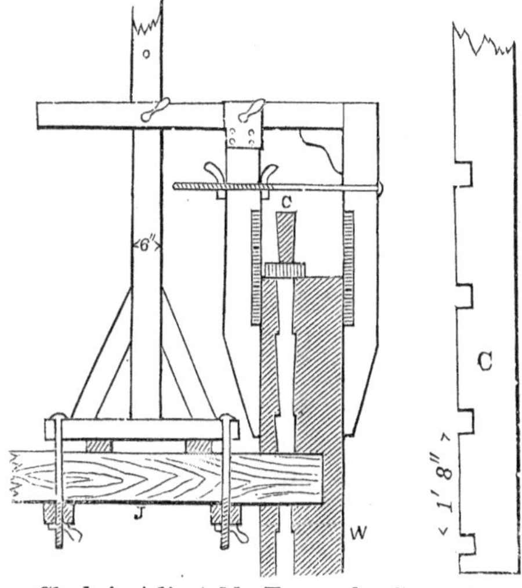

Clarke's Adjustable Frame for Concrete building.

[1] The following are the dimensions of the frame designed and used by Mr. Clarke: Joist, 12 inches; standard, 6 inches by 4 inches; arm, 4 inches by 3 inches; clamps, 6 inches by 3 inches; core, 2½ inches and 2 inches; wall 1 foot 4 inches; spaces between tie-bricks, 20 inches.

other method of forming concrete walls between a frame supported from below is shown by a figure in the report of Mr. Leonard Beckwith. The apparatus used by Mr. Tall is shown by a figure beyond, accompanying the account of work done by his method.

Another great advantage of concrete construction is the facility with which flues and air passages may be formed in the wall by simply molding the concrete around cylindrical forms of metal, which can be raised or drawn up as the work progresses, so as to leave a continuous pipe or flue of uniform size and smooth interior.

It is of the greatest importance that the materials for concrete should be most thoroughly mixed together. Success depends mainly upon this part of the work. Only a small quantity of water should be used, sufficient only to give the requisite plasticity to the mass. Five to six parts of gravel, or broken stone, with some sand added, and one part of cement, are regarded as the proper proportions. They should be mixed when dry, and the water is to be added slowly and thoroughly incorporated. It is best to use a sprinkler in order to insure a uniform and gradual wetting of the mass.

BÉTON AND CONCRETE BUILDING IN ENGLAND AND FRANCE.

Considering the great attention which has been given of late to this method of building, and its importance to the people of the United States, it is deemed advisable, though involving some repetition, to present the following extracts from the Builder which contain many valuable details of methods, advantages, and cost of concrete building:

[1] "The advantages which concrete, under some circumstances, possesses as a building material have already been so fully demonstrated that it seems superfluous to reiterate them. It is, perhaps, a matter of surprise, these advantages considered, that this material is not more often adopted, particularly in the construction of dwellings for the working classes. One reason for this, we think, is, that although such use of concrete is by no means new, as the concrete walls of the old Romans testify, its economical and other qualities are not known or appreciated by the general public. Moreover, until recently mechanical difficulties stood in the way. These, however, have been lessened by the apparatus and scaffolding lately patented by Mr. Joseph Tall, by which the walls of buildings in concrete may be carried up to any required height. Excepting some houses erected by Mr. Tall at Bexley Heath, and others, including a church and a farm-house, neither of them very favorable examples, however, by Lord Salisbury, at Hatfield, at the instance of the late Captain Fowke, very little has been lately done in concrete construction in England.

"In Paris the use of concrete is rapidly extending. The well-known invention of M. François Coignet, called béton aggloméré́s, described on more than one occasion in our pages, is being largely used for buildings

[1] The Builder, April 13, 1867.

and public works in the French capital, in every instance with the most satisfactory results. This artificial stone is produced simply by a mixture of any kind of sand with a small quantity of hydraulic lime, to which occasionally is added a trifling quantity of cement. No new material, we believe, is employed in the production, and notwithstanding the great proportion of the sand used, an artificial stone is obtained which is harder, more lasting, and better able to withstand the change of climates, to resist frost, heat, drought, and moisture, than many natural stones. By employing superior materials a stone is obtained equal to granite or jura-stone. It can be molded into the most delicate forms of art, and has the advantage of hardening instead of softening in the air, according to the well known law of mortars and concretes. Among the more recent constructions with béton agglomérés may be named the supporting wall of the Boulevard de l'Empereur, measuring thirteen thousand cubic meters, with ornamental staircase seven meters wide; the vaults twelve thousand cubic meters; the underground drains, twelve thousand cubic meters, and the water and river works, twenty thousand meters, at the new Exhibition building—about thirty-one English miles of sewers, barracks, and numerous other works for the city of Paris. Indeed, Parisian engineers and architects hold that this material cannot be surpassed in applications for underground and foundation works. It is equally well adapted for buildings of great height, as may be seen by the church at Vesinet. The bell tower of this church is forty meters high, and we are assured that it has not suffered in the least from vibration or sinking. At his manufactory at St. Denis, M. Coignet has succeeded in producing stones that surpass natural stones in homogeneous formation, and in the power of resistance against breaking, frost, drought, or moisture, at a cost of fifty per cent. less than the ordinary material.

"Some time ago specimens of the cheaper concrete were submitted to the Emperor of the French, and his Majesty, recognizing the importance of economy in this class of construction, ordered forty houses for workmen to be built with it. A piece of ground was obtained in the Avenue Dusmenil, and the dwellings are now being executed from the Emperor's own designs, by Mr. W. E. Newton, civil engineer, of Chancery Lane. About half the number, we believe, are already finished. They are double houses of three stories in height, each furnishing accommodation for six families, each family being provided with three apartments, namely, a sitting-room, 4.50 meters by 3.47; bed-room, 3.70 meters by 3.47 meters; kitchen, 3.47 meters by 2.02, with cellar, water-closet, &c. A small inner court affords light to the back rooms. The doors, windows, and stairs have been made by machinery outside of Paris, the wood-work, consisting of deal, sycamore, and oak sills. The bed and sitting rooms will be furnished with marble chimney pieces, which can be made at a cost of twenty-three francs a pair, and with stoves, the kitchen with a cooking apparatus. Water and gas will be laid on, and the water-closets are to be fitted up in the English fashion, in compliance with the orders of the Emperor. The floors are of concrete and iron; the chimney flues round and smooth internally; and in short the entire tenements are built on the ordinary concrete principle. The design shows no architectural ornamentation, but is plain, neat, and substantial. Besides Mr. H. E. Newton, the resident architect, and an English foreman, no skilled labor has been employed in the building, the entire work having been done by ordinary French laborers, at two francs (fifty cents) a day. The cost of each double house, accommodating six families, will be about five hundred pounds sterling, exclusive of the land, which was obtained after considerable difficulty, and on rather high terms. The whole outlay is borne by the Emperor, but in what way it is intended to dispose of the dwellings is not known. We are also unable to say at what rent the dwellings will be let. Sufficient ground has been marked off for a block of sixteen additional tenements. The concrete used by Mr. Newton consists of four measures of large gravel stone, four measures of sharp sand, and one measure of Portland cement, mixed in the usual way. The walls contain about forty per cent. of conglomerate. We may mention that Mr. Newton has also in course of construction a number of two-story houses in concrete, intended for dwellings for the workmen of the *Société Anonyme des Forges et Fondries*, at Montmartre, a few miles from Paris, and likewise one or two private villa residences.

"The Emperor of the French has here set us a good example. It is agreed on every side that one of the most pressing questions of the day is how to provide suitable homes for the poor. To some extent the question has been practically met, but only partially, and not so well as it might have been. Concrete constructions, it can be shown, are cheaper, healthier, and safer, and therefore better than ordinary houses. The objection in a sanitary point of view, to all the common brick and lath-and-plaster constructions, is their absorbency of moisture, and in closely crowded habitations their absorbency of miasma. Concrete is not by one-quarter so absorbent of moisture and damp as brick, while it gives a washable interior surface. Its great economical quality is that concrete costs about one-half the price of brick-work. The Waterlow model dwellings, which have turned out the most remunerative of their kind, pay about five and a half per cent.; but had concrete been used as a building material instead of brick, we believe these houses would have yielded seven and a half per cent. Laboring-class tenements, built of brick on the most economical plan, will cost one hundred pounds sterling for living-room, bed-room, and scullery; the same thing can be done in concrete at a cost of seventy-five pounds sterling for each separate dwelling. We say better, for the walls and roof, besides being stronger, will be nearly impervious to wet and damp; the interior walls will be washable, the dividing walls less pervious to sound, which in close tenements is a great comfort, and the whole will be fire-proof, for there will be nothing but doors and windows to burn. We hear that a number of gentlemen, including several well-known sanitary reformers and architects, convinced of the great advantages which this material offers in the construction of improved dwellings for the poorer population, at lower rents than has hitherto been possible, are endeavoring to form a company with the object of erecting houses of this class in the metropolis, and generally of making capitalists and others better acquainted with the merits of concrete for building purposes of every kind."[1]

TALL'S METHOD OF CONSTRUCTION WITH CONCRETE.

Some valuable details regarding Mr. Tall's method of concrete construction are given by him in a communication to the Builder, (August 3, 1867,) in which he maintains that his system of building is far superior to the use of concrete in blocks or "lumps," as proposed by Mr. May. He says: "His blocks are made one day and laid the next, necessitating a larger proportion of cement than one in eight, as in my concrete, and thereby sacrificing both strength and economy. I am at a loss to understand how he can call it concrete building, as it is built with cement blocks as bricks, and with a large proportion of bricks in chimney-jambs, &c.

"He thinks hollow walls far beyond solid ones. I differ in opinion, and, at the same time, think he must be totally ignorant of my system of building, or he must know, in the way my houses are cast, in one solid block, I have only to insert cores, say two feet long, two inches thick, and nine inches, ten inches, eleven inches, or twelve inches wide, in the center of my mold, and four inches or six inches apart, in the same way that I form the recesses for my joists, &c., and I get the hollow wall he thinks so much of. A six-inch wall may be made hollow by one and a half inch cores or prints."

The accompanying figures show the construction of Mr. Tall's bracket scaffolding. It will be seen that the brackets or platforms P are sustained by clamping them to the walls W as they are built up, holes or cores *c* being left for the insertion of the tie-bolts *b*. The case is also shown in section above the scaffolding and in plan on the right. The latter indicates the method of forming the angles of walls, fire-places, and joints with window-frames. The figure *f* on the left shows the form of the short cylinder, provided with a handle at the top, used for making flues or air-passages in the walls.

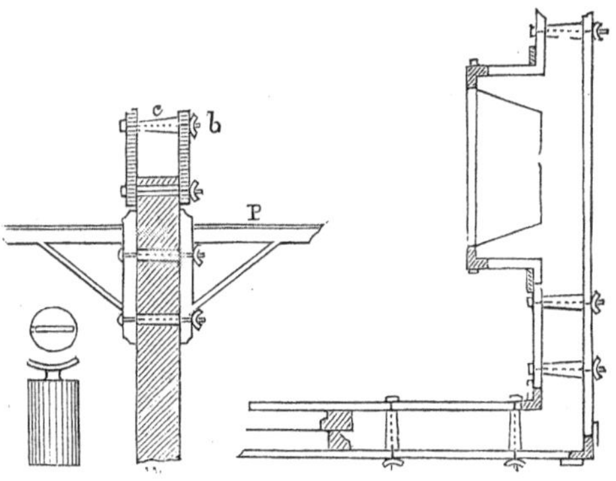

Tall's Bracket Scaffolding.

[1] Mr. Newton gives the following description of the nature and composition of the concrete which has been successfully used in constructing the Emperor's "*maisons ouvrières*" in the Avenue Dusmenil, Paris, and also that used by him in the works carried out in England: "In Paris we used one part of Portland cement (C. Francis &

In regard to the cost of Mr. Tall's building, and the character of the labor employed, he says:

"I commenced two houses on Monday, the 22d of July, and on Saturday, the 27th, my houses were up nine feet six inches in height, the work done being equal to laying fourteen thousand five hundred and eighty bricks. The whole of this was done in forty-three hours, by two laborers and one strong boy. They fill the apparatus every day in seven hours, (excepting on Saturday, when, owing to so many gentlemen visiting the building, they took one hour longer.) I have no hesitation in saying my two houses will be up and covered in by August 10.

"My men being laborers do not understand work by the rod, and take it by the superficial yard of nine-inch work. Fourteen thousand five hundred and eighty bricks will do one hundred and forty-five and three-quarters superficial yards, which, at sixpence per yard, equals £3 12*s.* 10½*d.*—the amount earned by two men and one boy in four days and three hours, which I paid on Saturday last. When the houses are ready for the roof, the labor for the walls will have cost me £7 5*s.* 9*d.*, the amount of work being equal to laying twenty-nine thousand one hundred and sixty bricks, including molded reveals to windows and doors."

PISÉ WALLS.

Cottages, the walls of which are constructed of clay and gravel, and known as *pisé*, are common in some parts of Europe and Great Britain. The mixture is pressed or rammed into a frame like that used for concrete, and it answers very well for dry climates, but when exposed to rain or wet must be protected with a coating of plaster or cement.

IV.—ARTIFICIAL STONES—CERAMIC MATERIALS.

NICOLL'S NEW WALL-SLABS.

Mr. B. Nicoll, of England, exhibited in the English section a new kind of wall, for which he claims great advantages in non-absorsency of moisture, non-conduction of heat, economy of space, a washable surface, and, withal, cheapness. It is described by Mr. Chadwick, as follows:[1] "Over

---

Sons) to five parts of large gravel stones, varying in size from the size of pearl barley to that of peas. The fine sand is sifted or screened out, put on one side, and used for making stucco for facing the work. At this place I find it more economical to use burnt brick earth or 'brick ballast,' as it is called, from which I sift out the very fine, and add one of Portland cement to eight of ballast. This makes a very hard wall. I have even reduced the cement to one in ten with perfect success. I burn the ballast myself, and it costs me under two shillings per cubic yard. Therefore, if we take one yard of ballast at two shillings, and two and a half bushels of cement at one shilling tenpence, we shall have a cubic yard of concrete for six shillings sevenpence, to which add two shillings threepence per yard for labor, and we shall find that we can put up a superficial yard of nine-inch work for less than three shillings. One gentleman ventured to question the possibility of building a wall thirty feet high in nine-inch work. I only say that this has been done by Mr. Tall, and the houses so constructed have been sold by him at a very large profit."

[1] British Reports of the Paris Exposition, vol. iii, p. 282.

a framework of strong cross-wires, of about one-eighth of an inch thick, there is woven, by a powerful pressure, fibrous matter, which is saturated with a solution that renders it fire-proof. It is then subjected to a very powerful pressure. A coating of light Scott's cement, mixed with parian cement, is then put upon it for inside facing, and of Portland cement for the outside facing. The surfaces are impermeable to moisture, smooth, and washable with water, so as to save the expense of repeated lime washings. It is formed into slabs in iron frames, which are put together and closely and securely fastened with bolts. The slabs are from one and a half inch to four inches thick. These slabs serve as superior paneling for dividing walls and partitions. Where space is of importance it has the advantage, perhaps, over concrete walling, in enabling a wall to be made of not more than one and a half inch or two inches in thickness, and yet its quality greatly deadens sound. It has also great advantages for weather-proof roofing, superior to slate or tile, though not, as I conceive, superior to well-made hollow brick (when it can be got) tied together with iron ties and covered with layers of asphalt and cement. In the Prince Consort's model the principle of the flat roof was adopted, but none of the model dwellings in the Exhibition have attained to that principle."

RANSOME ARTIFICIAL STONE.

This is a remarkable and important compound for building purposes. It was exhibited by Mr. Frederick Ransome, of London, the inventor. He takes clean sand and binds the grains together with a cement of silicate of lime, producing a hard and enduring mass, fully equal to sandstone from the quarry. It is said that the strength of this compound even exceeds that of most of the rocks commonly used in building. It can be molded into any desired form, either into solid or hollow rectangular blocks or into elaborately carved and ornamented moldings or capitals for columns. It is in extensive use, and is largely manufactured by the Patent Concrete Stone Company.

THE MAREZZO MARBLE.

This is an artificial compound, which is formed into slabs of any required size, or into molded work, or cornices, as may be required. It is claimed for it that it is the most perfect imitation and substitute for various marbles that has yet been produced. It is solid and durable, and its hardness allows it to take a high polish. It has the great advantage over stucco or scagliola, that it can be made at the works and be at once and rapidly put into place in buildings without the delay which necessarily attends the execution of stucco-work. It is applicable especially to the decoration of interiors, halls, stairways, walls of churches, hotels, and private houses. It was exhibited by R. R. Cox, Old Kent Road, S. E. London, England.

TILES FOR FLOORS AND WALLS.

There was a profuse and brilliant display of plain and ornamental tiles for floors and walls in the English, French, and other sections. They are freely used abroad not only for floors but for wainscoting and the exterior as well as interior decoration of walls. The English cottage in the park was almost lined with samples of tiles of all kinds, upon the floor and on the walls, showing the manner in which they are used, particularly in kitchens, around the ranges, fireplaces, and sinks, and wherever it is necessary to wash and scrub frequently. The chief consumption is for floors of public and private buildings, churches, banks, and warehouses, in vestibules, halls, libraries, dining-rooms, hearths, and conservatories.

Tiles may be grouped in three classes—plain, of various colors, encaustic or inlaid, and enameled. The usual colors are buff, red, black, drab, chocolate, blue, and white, and the shapes are squares, octagons, hexagons, and their divisions, so that almost infinite changes may be made in the patterns by combinations in laying.

The encaustic tiles are made by cutting out the designs or engraving them to a considerable depth in the unburnt tile, and after filling the indentations so formed with pastes of different colors the whole is burned together. The tile thus made is nearly homogeneous in its composition, and the design does not wear off. The enameled tiles, which are made and used upon the continent chiefly, are very different from the encaustic or inlaid just described. The designs upon the enameled tiles are painted on with the brush and then burned. The figures form a superficial coating, which is soon obliterated if the tile is exposed to wear. Tiles of this description are suitable for wall decoration only. They are used for the fronts of buildings, for borders to grates and fireplaces, and for insertion in wainscots, mantels, and furniture.

The principal exhibitors were the Messrs. Minton, of Stoke upon Trent, England; Messrs. Maw & Son, of Benthall works; Broseley, Shropshire, and Mulkin & Co., Newport works, Burslem.

It is now about thirty years since Messrs. Minton & Co. began the manufacture as at present conducted, and for the past eighteen years they have been represented in the United States by the firm of Miller & Coates, of New York. The taste and perseverance of the late Herbert Minton, for a long time the head of the firm, brought the manufacture to its present state of excellence in colors, hardness, and accuracy of shape. The tiles from this establishment are extensively used in the British houses of Parliament, and have been sent to every part of the continent of Europe, and there is scarcely a city or well-known town in the United States in which they have not been laid. The floors of the extension of the Capitol at Washington, executed under the direction of General M. C. Meigs, then captain of engineers, form the largest piece of work yet done, and they contain some of the finest original designs.

The tiles made by this firm are of the two kinds—encaustic or inlaid, and the plain. The latter are of various sizes, the largest being squares of six by six inches, and octagons of nearly six and a quarter inches. They are of two thicknesses, half an inch and one inch. The inlaid tiles are one inch thick, and, excepting some border pieces, are nearly all six by six inches. In the plain tiles the colors extend entirely through. Those half an inch thick are sufficiently strong for ordinary floors. Some of the most pleasing effective floors are made at moderate cost by combining plain and inlaid tiles, as shown in the beautiful pattern sheets. The cost of these floors varies from sixty cents to $3 50 per square foot, according to the patterns.

The circular of the firm contains the following directions for laying the tiles in floors:

In buildings of the usual kind the best way to prepare a foundation for tiles is to set or cut the beams or joists low enough to admit of a course of bricks being laid, in mortar or cement, on a strong board floor. When this cannot be done, nail strips, about three by one inch, firmly on the sides of the beams, at a proper distance below the upper edges. Then cut one-inch boards to the proper length to fit between the beams, and nail them down at each corner to the strips. The boards should not exceed six inches in width, and should be laid slightly apart at the edges. Lay a course of bricks, brickbats, or flat stones, in mortar or cement, on the boards, taking care to fill the joints thoroughly. The bricks may be about a half to three-quarters of an inch below the bottom of the tiles; and it is better to cut the beams down an inch below the top of the bricks that there may be more cement above the beam. The tiles are laid in common hydraulic cement, such as is used for cisterns. Good lime mortar is the best substitute. There should be thin joints of cement between the edges of the tiles. The tiles are cut by chasing them with a sharp chisel and snapping them at the line. The edges are rubbed on a stone with sand and water if required to be smooth.

The collection of Maw & Son, in a special alcove or court in the Exposition building, contained, among a great variety of rich designs for pavements and walls, a specimen of a frieze which the firm had just made for the quadrangle of the new India office, partly in mosaic and partly in encaustic tiles from designs by Mr. Digby Wyatt. In the pictorial mosaic pavement from a design by Westlake, representing the four seasons, there were no less than ten thousand pieces to the square yard.

TILES OF FRANCE, SPAIN, AND OTHER COUNTRIES.

Nolla, of Spain, sent many specimens of terra cotta tiles excellent for pavements, and at a low price. Carpentier, of France, exhibited a great variety of designs. He claims for his products that they are harder than stone, and that they give a pavement which is extremely solid and rich, and particularly well adapted for halls, chapels, and churches.

They are sold at fifteen francs (about three dollars) the square meter for the ornamental tiles, and twelve francs for the white. The tiles are twenty-one centimeters square.

Of the French display Mr. Digby Wyatt observes:[1] "In France, however, the progress made has been most rapid, and the tiles made in imitation of the old Persian examples are first-rate in quality and effect. Some of the large *faience plâques* painted by artists of the first distinction, such as Hamon, Auker, Ranvier, Lessore, and Bouquêt, are both of large dimension and admirable design, realized in the liveliest coloring, and with a happy freedom of handling which betrays the dexterity of the highly educated and accomplished artist. The little landscapes, by the last named, are extraordinarily full and brilliant. Such plâques are veritable pictures, and for insertion in architectural frames, as for over doors, in chimney-pieces, or simply as panels inclosed in a modest framework of moldings, formed upon the surface of internal or external walls; nothing could be more suitable for our climate, or more likely to produce agreeable and permanent effect in decoration. Similar plâques, with more or less brilliancy of coloring and excellence of drawing, are shown by Wedgwood and Minton of England, and by Dutch and Belgian manufacturers."

TERRA COTTA.

This material is now largely used in constructions abroad. It is of great value for architectural purposes, and was highly appreciated by the ancients, as the collections in the British Museum and in the Louvre will show, where there are specimens which date back for more than two thousand years.

The material is well adapted for window trimmings and ornaments, trusses, panels, columns, capitals, cornices, and for all those parts of a building where a hard finish, lightness, and durability are required.

Among the buildings in England and on the continent constructed of terra cotta, are the Kensington Museum, the Hall of Arts and Sciences, the chemical college at Berlin, which is nearly completed, the new cathedral at the same place, which is built of terra cotta and brick, and several buildings in Munich. At the Exposition the columns of the English boiler-house, an imposing structure in the park, were made of this material. There were nearly thirty exhibitors, but the principal displays were from England, France, Prussia, Wurtemburg, Austria, Spain, and Italy. Some of these exhibitions were extremely interesting, consisting of architectural ornaments of elaborate designs, vases, busts, and statues.

In regard to the character of the work displayed by different nations, England may be said to stand first in rank. The specimens displayed were remarkable for their high finish, good color, straightness of molding, when made in long pieces, and hardness, rendering them capable of enduring any climate. Prussia ranked next. The collection at the

[1] British Reports, vol. ii, p. 326.

Exposition was very large, and in general the specimens were hard and well finished. The color was also good and the surface close.

France exhibited some very well executed figures and vases, and also a few specimens of architectural work. The color was, however, in general too light, rendering paint necessary where color is desired.

The specimens of red terra cotta from Italy, though excellent in workmanship, were not sufficiently hard to stand the weather.

The clays used in the manufacture of terra cotta are intermediate between those used for ordinary bricks and those employed for porcelain. They should be more finely ground and be freer from impurities than brick clays, but they need not be worked with so much care as porcelain clays. The red color is due to the presence of oxyd of iron in the clay, and varies from a light drab to a dark red in proportion to the amount of iron. When the materials are well chosen and well baked, terra cotta is more enduring than even marble or granite.

The revival of terra cotta must be regarded, however, as still in its infancy. The price is very variable. In France glazed slabs two feet long and eighteen inches wide cost five francs. In England the same cost eighteen shillings, while in France columns, such as are made by Messrs. Minton, cost four times as much as they do in England. The London price of ordinary terra cotta, such as is used for facing buildings, varies from three shillings and fourpence to three shillings and sixpence per superficial foot. The price is determined also by the character of the ornamentation and the size of the blocks. The cost of laying terra cotta on house fronts in England, including hoisting, materials, &c., is from one shilling to one shilling and twopence per superficial foot.

The number and extent of the exhibitions of terra cotta from various countries show that this manufacture is increasing in importance. It formed one of the novelties of the Exposition and gratified the eyes of all lovers of decorative art. Mr. Digby Wyatt, in his report upon decoration, says: "Among the germs of 'fresh starts' shown in the Exhibition, none are more important, as affecting the arts of decoration in the future, than the new life which in all countries appears to have been infused into the revivals of the manufacture of terra cotta, of the application of enamel and vitrified colors upon earthenware, or metallic bases to the general purpose of the decorator, and of the art of mosaic working in every form. These revivals have as yet most largely affected furniture, ornaments, and decorations, for the service of the church, but there are many indications that they will be rapidly extended in every direction into civil structures from national museums to ladies' boudoirs."[1]

The same authority states that to no one is the art of terra cotta making more indebted than to Mr. J. M. Blashfield, of Stamford, England. He has made a careful study of the English clays, and has ascertained

[1] Vol. ii, of the British Reports, p. 321.

how to mix them with foreign substances so as to permit them to be perfectly vitrified without being distorted. He has also experimented on the best forms of kilns, fuel, and cooling; and in the selection of designs and models has been guided by a natural taste for the purest forms. He exhibited a large mediæval window, designed for Dulwich new college, a chimney-piece for the new India office, and several other specimens of his skill. This manufacturer has recently executed some garden decorations for the Marquis of Northampton, from designs supplied by Mr. Wyatt, and also some exterior works for the buildings of the horticultural society, the great central Royal Albert Hall of Arts and Sciences, and the buildings of the Department of Science and Art.

V.—IRON-WORK, ROOFING MATERIALS, CARPENTRY.

ORNAMENTAL WROUGHT IRON WORK.

The number of exhibitors of ornamental wrought iron work in the Exposition of 1867 was very limited—France and England being the only nations exhibiting anything worthy of particular notice. The English department indicates that there has been but little improvement since the Exhibition of 1862, and many of the objects displayed were made for that Exhibition. The progress, however, which has been made in France within the last few years is quite remarkable, and the objects exhibited form an interesting and instructive display. Wrought iron has to a great extent taken the place of cast iron, formerly used so largely for gratings, balustrades, and balconies. The revival of this beautiful art in France is to be attributed to the present perfection of machinery for working iron, and to the attention which has been given to this art by skillful workmen and artists. In England and in Germany this art has never entirely fallen into disuse. In France, however, for twenty-five years little or no work of this kind was done; but by the aid of intelligent and enthusiastic workmen she has been able in a few years to surpass all other nations in this difficult branch of industry. The difficulties to be overcome are great. The substance is capricious and not easily handled, and to become a good forger requires not only long experience but great natural aptitude. The French workmen in the most essential part of their work—the repoussé—have reached such a degree of excellence as to leave almost nothing to be desired. Their skill is explained by the fact that they are kept constantly employed on this class of work, and are in almost every case excellent draughtsmen and modelers. Another cause is the demand for and appreciation of good work, and the artistic education which enables the workman to meet the requirements of a cultivated public taste.

The specimen of iron-work exhibited by the Skidmore Art Manufacturers Company consisted of one of the gable frontals of Prince Consort's memorial. This is one of four frontals forming the principal features of the canopy which is to be placed at a height of seventy-five feet from the base. As the design and combination of materials was somewhat novel, it has been thought well to make a brief notice of this piece of workmanship. The angle pieces of the framework are of iron, coated over with lead about one-quarter of an inch thick in the thinnest part, in order to prevent the iron from rusting. Into this lead ornaments of stone consisting of pieces of marble, polished granite, crystal, onyx, agate, and jasper, are inserted, and held in place by the lead being hammered up over the edges. This setting is sufficiently firm, and is unaffected by the weather. Masses of enamel of different tints are added at certain points, at others the natural color of the lead forms the background. The ridge decoration is in repoussé copper, highly ornamented. In this piece of workmanship an attempt has been made to revive the jewelled work of the thirteenth century, specimens of which may be seen in shrines of the cathedrals at Aix-la-Chapelle, Cologne, and at other places. Although this piece of work is of large size, and designed to be placed in the open air, yet, when in position, it will have the same effect as the best specimens of medieval jeweled work.

Among the exhibitors in the English section were Messrs. Barnard, Bishop and Barnard, who displayed some finely wrought iron gates; Messrs. Hart, who exhibited a candelabrum—an excellent specimen of smiths' work; Messrs. Skidmore, Benham, and a few others.

The two principal exhibitors in the French section were Messrs. Baudrit and Roy. The repoussé work of the former and the forging of the latter were beautifully executed. Among those whose names deserve to be noticed is M. Boulanger, to whose efforts are mainly due the revival of this art. His iron-work on the central gate of the church of Notre Dame, at Paris, is not inferior in style to the celebrated iron-work of the latter part of the twelfth century attached to the two side gates. These are considered the most beautiful specimens of medieval forging in existence.

The application of machinery to this class of work has contributed greatly to its cheapness. The results obtained in France have been very satisfactory, and many firms are able to furnish wrought-iron balconies and gratings at a price not greater than that paid for the same in cast iron, so largely used within the last ten years.

ROOFING MATERIALS.

The principal materials displayed at the Exposition for roofing purposes were slates, tiles, zinc, copper, and tarred or bituminous felt and paper. Shingles do not seem to be used in Europe to any extent; the only specimens seen being on the wooden buildings in the park erected by those countries where wood is plenty and enters largely into the materials used for the construction of buildings. In general, roofing materials such as are used in England, France, Prussia, and Austria, for public and private buildings, are cheaper, better made, and more durable, than they have been at any time within twenty years.

The manufacture of roofing tiles has attained a great degree of perfection. Slates, which are now quarried and cut by machinery, are remarkable for their excellence and the regularity of their dimensions.

Since the introduction of iron beams for roofs, the substitution of some other material for wood as a surface upon which slates or tiles can be laid, has, among architects, attracted considerable attention. The difficulty of attaching boards or strips to iron rafters without considerable expense, is apparent to all. This has been obviated by M. Lachambre, who uses laths of iron, to which the slates are attached by means of hooks. This is a marked improvement over the sheet-iron strips formerly employed, and permits the tiles to be placed directly on the iron without the intervention of any combustible material.

The prevention of the destruction of zinc roofing when placed in contact with iron has also attracted considerable attention. Many plans have been proposed to obviate this difficulty, such as placing wood, plaster, tarred paper, or other materials between the iron and zinc. All of these methods, however, are expensive.

The Exposition contained many specimens of wrought and corrugated zinc, but the extreme sensibility of this material to variations of temperature diminish its value, especially when there are many soldered joints. France, Prussia, Austria, and Holland, made a fine display of this metal, showing remarkable results in stamping it, when cold, into various forms intended for the exterior decoration of buildings. It must, however, be admitted that such ornaments are of limited durability when exposed to the weather.

Attempts have been made to substitute zinc tiles for a continuous roofing of sheet zinc, which is not only disagreeable in appearance but is liable to warp and twist at high temperatures. These efforts have not been generally successful, as the tiles are liable to be blown off or displaced by high winds, and have not been found to be sufficiently water tight. It, however, appears probable that since zinc is so easily stamped by machinery at the present day, and has such a degree of ductility given to it that it does not tear when stamped, its use for roofing purposes might be extended by its being manufactured into tiles of graceful shapes and sufficient size to allow them to be attached to the roof without solder or nails, in the same way that ordinary slates are fastened. The discovery of some cheap material to prevent their contact with the iron beams would largely increase their use.

ROOFING FELT.

The display of tarred or bituminous felt at the Exposition was very large. Besides the applications for roofing, it is also used in sheathing ships, in the foundations of houses, and for lining moist walls. As a building material, it is to be particularly recommended on account of its cheapness, ease with which it can be attached to a roof or walls, impermeability to water, and lightness. The manufacturers claim that as now made it is uninflammable. Russia, Austria, Prussia, Belgium, Denmark, Sweden, England, and France, sent large quantities of this product. Its want of durability is its great defect, and though an excellent material for covering temporary constructions, it can never take the place of slate or tiles as a permanent roofing material. It answers admirably as an interior lining for walls to prevent the effects of moisture, in which place it is not exposed to the heat of the sun nor to the sudden variations of temperature. The best specimens of this article were from Russia, Denmark, and Prussia, where it is largely used. It is also used to a great extent in northern Germany, where the climate is better suited to it than the more southern portions of Europe.

Various expedients have been adopted to diminish the action of the sun upon the bituminous matter with which this material is soaked. Among these may be noticed the felt displayed by a French exhibitor covered with a thin coating of powdered schist. An article somewhat like this is made in the United States by the Mica Roofing Company of New York.

Some of the advantages claimed for the Belfast (Ireland) roofing felt. were its lightness, durability and cheapness, and its fire-proof qualities, It is put up in rolls twenty-five meters in length, and 0.80 millimeter in breadth, sufficient to cover twenty square meters of surface. The price given in Paris is one franc ten centimes the running meter, when taken in quantities of one hundred meters in one package.

The following directions are given for placing the felt upon roofs:

The roofing boards should be laid with the slope of the roof, and the inclination should be from 0.15 to 0.20 centimeter per meter. The felt should be of good quality, and may be laid either up and down with the slope or horizontally. In either case it must be well stretched and the edges should overlap about 0.05 centimeter. It must be nailed with suitable nails placed at a distance of from three to four centimeters. On the edge of the roof the felt is to be turned in and nailed in the same way. After it is thus secured upon the roof it is covered with a coating composed of equal parts of coal tar or melted pitch or asphaltum, and of powdered lime. This mixture should be laid on with a brush while hot, and when a few square yards have been covered, and while the coating is still soft, it is to be sprinkled over with dry sand and gravel.

The coating should never be applied to moist felt; it should be perfectly dry. After a roof has been coated four or five times in this way at intervals of four or five years, a very superior and permanent roof is obtained.

USE OF PASTEBOARD AND PAPER IN CONSTRUCTION.

The Exposition abounded with specimens of pasteboard prepared for roofing and for lining rooms. It is usually prepared with bitumen so as to be more or less water-proof. The examples were most numerous in the Prussian and Austrian sections. In the Prussian, B. Dahse exhibited bituminous "carton-pierre" and bituminous pasteboard; Engell & Co., bituminous pasteboard for roofing; E. A. Lindenberg, Dantzic, asphaltic paper for roofing; J. C. Leye, pipes of bituminous paper and roofing pasteboard. In the Austrian section, C. Haller exhibited incombustible and impermeable roofing paper, and F. Sterba, bituminous and roofing paper.

This description of material is now coming into extensive use in the United States, particularly at the west, where it is so often required to erect dwellings with expedition and economy. The Rock River Paper Company, of Chicago, manufacture an article which they call "sheathing and roofing board." It is a coarse, yellow pasteboard, made in rolls of various lengths, and thirty-two and forty-eight inches wide. It is made very compact and firm—the fibers being closely pressed together at first, and then subjected to an enormous pressure and calendered down until the whole is made stiff and hard almost like a piece of board. It has a straight, smooth edge, and weighs about one and a quarter pounds to the square yard.

It is used advantageously in various ways; either on the studs outside as a substitute for sheathing, or over the sheathing before siding; or on the inside of the studs before lathing, so as to form an extra dead air space. It is laid under floors and on roofs below the slates or shingles for the purpose of keeping out air and cold, and it may also be used as a substitute for inside plastering. It is found to make a very smooth, nice finish for a wall or ceiling, and to save four-fifths of the expense of ordinary plastering. It can be tacked on over the laths and then be whitewashed or papered in the usual manner. In this way a wall warmer than plastering may be secured, and it will be equally as good, if used with care, for all purposes. It will not crack or fall off, and it commends itself to those who build in earthquake countries. It can be put on by almost any one, it being merely tacked on with ordinary tacks.

The cost of this sheathing-board is slight. It is sold by the pound at five cents for the bituminized, and six cents for the plain. Thus one square yard of the bituminized costs eight cents, and the plain seven cents and a half. A house twenty-two by thirty-six feet and twenty feet high can be covered with this saturated board for less than twenty dollars. The annexed figure shows the method of applying the board on the roof of a house before covering with cement or shingles, on the studs before siding, and on the sheathing-boards before siding.

Some of the principal advantages of this sheathing-board are: First, its cheapness compared with boards or plastering. Second, the rapidity with which it can be put on, and thus render in a few hours a bare frame habitable. A house lined with this board can be safely occupied immediately, while a plastered house requires months to become dry. Third, it is warmer than boarding or plastering, for it does not conduct heat so rapidly, and a room so lined can be warmed in a few minutes by a moderate fire, while in a plastered room it takes a long time to heat up the walls.

CARPENTERS' AND JOINERS' WORK.

The opinion seems to prevail among those who have devoted attention to the subject, that in France and many parts of Europe carpentry is falling more and more into disuse, being confined mostly to the construction of scaffoldings and temporary buildings. Iron is now almost universally substituted in Europe for wood in the erection of permanent edifices. Nearly all the houses now in course of construction in Paris are being built with iron lintels and girders, the floors being constructed with iron joists filled in with brick-work, while the roofs are made flat and of the same materials. It is the great superiority of these materials for construction that has led to their substitution for wood. Iron is stronger, more durable, and is fire-proof. Its cheapness at the present day permits its use, while, at the same time, timber is increasing in cost, and is becoming more and more scarce. Timber is also often badly seasoned. The oak ordinarily used in Paris is transported from the forests directly by rail, and is often full of sap. If put into a building in this condition it decays in a short time, especially when exposed to the air.

As a general thing the Exposition was very poor in models of carpentry as applied in buildings. The specimens to be seen in the French section were generally of a very rude description. The partitions were mostly of rough scantling; the joists were at irregular distances, and appeared to be placed rather by unskilled laborers than by mechanics. The floors were generally badly laid and joined; indeed, none of the carpentry work presented features worthy of imitation.

The specimens of American carpentry shown in the United States section were in strong contrast, especially in the farmer's cottage, which was a remarkable specimen of what may be done where wood is plenty and other materials scarce.

The cottage from Louisiana also displayed excellent workmanship. The entrance doors, of different kinds of wood, were well made and carefully finished.

Specimens of carpentry and joiner's work manufactured by machinery occupied an important place in the Exposition. Prussia, England, Austria, Bavaria, Russia, France, and Belgium, sent specimens of this kind of work, and were rivals in excellence and cheapness of execution.

There, as in this country, the number and size of the planing and sawing mills have largely increased of late.

A short extract from the report of one of the British artisans, Mr. Alexander Kay, will give an excellent idea of the estimate formed of the condition of the carpenter's and joiner's art in the United States:[1]

"America will always maintain an elevated position among the nations of the earth for good joinery; and it need not be wondered at when we look at the vast resources and inexhaustible supply of materials which form the materials of the joinery trade.

"The construction of a driver's shed on the locomotive engine is a good representation of what the American joiner can do. It is constructed of maple, beech, ash, hickory, and black walnut, well selected, and strongly and neatly put together. It is my opinion that British joiners have received some very useful and ready methods from the Americans; and from their superior wood-cutting machines they must derive great advantages over all other nations. Considering her plentiful supply of easily worked and beautiful timber, of first-rate quality, I feel thoroughly satisfied that no other nation can compete with America in the production of good joinery, at the same cost, with equal profit.

"The American joiner has several advantages over those of other nations. His tools are second to none, being superior in many instances to British, but the British are not slow to adopt the advantages brought forward by Americans. We, however, are supplied with Norway white deal, not so easily worked as the American pine. The Americans have the advantage in possessing this easily worked timber."

The Austrian section contained some good specimens of joinery. The workmanship was generally good, the various parts were strongly and neatly fitted together, and the wood was well selected. In hinges and fastenings there is room for improvement, both in quality and style of manufacture. The supply of material for the joinery trade in Austria is excellent, and many samples of wood were exhibited in planks and in moldings, such as beech, fir, oak, maple, Hungarian ash, and veined walnut.

Belgium also displayed some excellent specimens of joiners' work and carving.

The forest products of Bavaria show that the country is well supplied with materials.

The work exhibited from Russia was made principally of pine, of which there is an unlimited supply of the best quality. There were also many specimens of other wood used in carpentry and joinery, all of excellent quality.

The Russian workman is peculiarly fortunate in possessing such a wood as the Finland pine, which, when well selected and free from knots, is easy to work, and is admirably adapted for building purposes.

Buildings made of this wood are more durable and last longer than those of oak, the rosin in the pine protecting it from decay.

The French joiners' work, of which not only the Exhibition afforded an

[1] Artisans' Reports, page 219.

ample display, but the public buildings recently erected in Paris many excellent specimens, lacks the precision and accuracy of execution to be seen in the work of many other countries, and is in many instances defective in construction. There seems to have been but little, if any, advance made in this art of late, if we except the work done by machinery. Their methods of construction are old, and the work is always roughly finished. This is to be seen particularly in the doors, frames, windows, and in the internal wood-work generally of their buildings.

The opinion expressed on this subject by an intelligent English writer, himself a practical mechanic, may be of interest:

[1] "On the whole we consider Parisian joiners' work to be far inferior to that done in this country. Their moldings, as a general rule, are very well designed, and their carving is remarkably well executed. We can easily understand how an art student may be attracted by the tasteful and artistic appearance of a piece of joiner's work, and may fancy that he sees in it an evidence of the superiority of French work; but the practical workman will arrive at a very different conclusion. He will at once understand that, for the portions of the work which are so attractive to the eye the joiner is in no way responsible, since he is neither the designer nor the carver, while the framing itself will be found to be very defective both in strength and finish.

"French workmen will require better tools, and an entire revolution of their system of working, to enable them to execute a class of work fit for the English market."

An interesting feature connected with this portion of the Exposition was the carpentry and joiner's work displayed in the Egyptian section, and in the oriental constructions. It consisted of a wooden background on which were nailed moldings, mitered together and forming certain geometrical designs and patterns. This form of decoration is applied to doors, wainscotings, ceilings, &c., and has a most pleasing effect, being at the same time very cheap. The pieces of wood nailed to the background prevent it also from warping or swelling to any great extent.

With the mechanical means at present in use this method of decoration, so excellent in principle and construction, and which permits of such infinite variations, could be revived at small cost, and would replace that style of decoration which by cheap expedients strives to imitate the elaborate ornamentation of former times.

In Spain and in Africa many wainscotings and ceilings of the fifteenth and sixteenth centuries executed in this style, and of wonderful beauty, are yet to be seen, and in good preservation. This style of work is also well adapted for painting in bright colors, or for other styles of internal decoration.

---

[1] Artisans' Reports, p. 211.

INLAID FLOORS—PARQUETRY.

The displays of ornamental inlaid flooring were numerous and attractive. The use of machinery for cutting the pieces of wood has greatly improved the product and lessened the cost. All the pieces are now cut with precision, and are joined together upon panels, so that they can be easily laid and fitted upon floors. Woods of different colors are selected, and in fitting them together they are so placed upon the panel that the grain of the wood above and below shall run in opposite directions. This obviates the defect of undue shrinking, and of the creaking which is often so annoying in inlaid floors.

There are large establishments for the manufacture of these parquetry panels in Marseilles, in Austria, and Savoy. Interesting exhibitions were made by Oliver & Co., 55 Rue de Flandre, Paris, and Arrowsmith & Co., London; by Babitz, of Berlin, of parquetry in strips; Morand & Co., Bernay, France, of floors inlaid in various ways; and by Ignatius Silva, France, specimens of marquetry and parquetry panels.

BALLOON FRAMES.

The Illinois cottage, or American farmer's house, sent from Chicago, and the school-house, were almost the only examples of what is known in the United States as "balloon framing," or "balloon construction," and it is but little known or used in Europe.

The Chicago balloon-framed houses are constructed as follows: When no foundation of brick or stone has been laid, the sills are placed upon cedar posts the same size as the sills, and from four to six feet in length, and they are set below the reach of frost, and are based upon two thicknesses of planks, laid cross-wise, about two feet square and four inches thick. The sills are framed into the posts and are framed together and well pinned. Both the studding and the joists are framed into the sills; the joists are laid double around all of the openings. At the corners of the building two or three studs are placed together, and are well spiked, so as to make solid, strong corner posts. For one-story houses, wall plates are laid upon the top of the studding; they are laid double, and are well spiked together and to the studs. The rafters are framed so as to bear laterally upon the wall plates, and are well spiked to them.

The entire outside of the studding and rafters is covered with common boards, well nailed down to the sides; these are then covered with siding, and the roof is covered with shingles, laid so as to lap three times.

The floors are laid upon the joists and are nailed down through the face; after the floor is laid the inside partitions are set upon the floor. The lathing and plastering follows, and when dry the casings are put up and the work is painted.

When there is to be more than one story, the studding is set to the full height of the walls, and a "ribbon," one inch thick and four wide, is framed into the studding on the inside at the height of each story, and the joists of the upper floors rest upon this ribbon and are spiked to the studding.

SUGGESTION FOR CHEAP FIRE-PROOF WALLS AND FLOORS.

One important subject to the interest of the citizens of the United States is, that some plan shall be adopted in the mode and manner of constructing buildings to prevent, in a measure, the burning of such an immense value of property as is annually consumed in America. No country suffers so severely, and we cannot afford it.

The reporter would respectfully suggest that all buildings shall be constructed with a view to prevent such vast destruction of property. The use of iron beams, with brick arches turned, undoubtedly are the most safe; but, as they are somewhat expensive, the following mode of building is commended to the special attention of all Americans. It is one of trifling expense compared to its advantages. It is a system that has been thoroughly tested. Lay a floor of seasoned hemlock boards upon the timbers, or floor-joists, and then lay a coat of cement, a large proportion of which may be sand, entirely over this floor, from wall to wall, of one inch thick; then let the cement become thoroughly dried, over which lay a floor of matched boards, nailed with forty-penny nails. If there are wood partitions, there should be laid two courses of bricks between the studs, and plastered to the base-board, to prevent all circulation of air. A floor laid as above will resist an immense volume of flame in the room for one hour before breaking through the cemented floor above; and the expense of cement is only ten to twelve cents per square yard—a trifling matter compared with its value.

This has been tested by actual experiment, and found to require one hour before the fire ignites with the next story; and also has been tested when the combustible material of a large druggist's shop was wholly on fire, creating an immense volume of flame, (the floor timbers above burning nearly through,) and the carpets above were not even smoked or caused to be taken up. Therefore, any system adopted whereby the fire is confined to one room for an hour, gives abundant time for an engine to be present, or to apply all other means at command; which certainly is of great advantage toward extinguishing a fire.

The above plan of construction has many advantages. It deafens the floor, prevents all insects and odors from passing from story to story, and water in small quantities from above to the ceiling below; it makes the house warmer, and, above all, is considered the cheapest and one of the best modes of construction to diminish the annual loss by fire in the United States.

In addition to the above, every family should have twelve or twenty-four pails always filled with water, at a moment's command, in some convenient locality, in case of fire; for one pail of water at an early moment is of more avail than twenty at a later time.

Many builders deafen floors between the timbers, which plan is not as beneficial or as safe, because all timbers season, and thus leave a space between the cement and beam for circulation of air; and when the timber burns off, the fire ignites at once with the story above. Attention has been called more particularly to this subject from the fact that insurance on property in France is of minor consideration. For instance, in an insurance upon one hundred and fifty thousand francs for six months, upon a house and furniture, the charge was only fifty francs. The very modest price of insurance in France is because they have comparatively no buildings burned. Their buildings are vastly more safely constructed than those in the United States, and they have more floors of brick, tile, and cement. Even their stairs are often covered with tile and bricks, and in the better class of buildings their stairs are of stone or marble; their walls are mostly of stone and much thicker, and they have less wood-finish in the interior.

CHAPTER III.

DWELLINGS CHARACTERIZED BY THEIR CHEAPNESS COMBINED WITH THE CONDITIONS NECESSARY FOR HEALTH AND COMFORT.

Early efforts to improve the condition of the homes of the working classes—Degraded condition of the working classes in Europe—Causes of this condition—Principles to be observed in the establishment of homes for the working classes—Societies in France for improving the condition of the working classes—Buildings erected by the Emperor—The Mulhouse Society of cités ouvrières—Real estate co-operative association—Beaucourt real estate association—French artisans' houses—French miner's cottage at Blanzy—English societies for improving the condition of the working classes—Metropolitan association—Society for improving the condition of the laboring classes—Improved industrial dwellings company—Columbia square—Miss Burdett Coutts's lodging-house.—Western farmer's house.

Group X of the Exposition included articles exhibited with the special object of improving the physical and moral condition of the people, and in class 93 were placed the examples of dwellings characterized by cheapness combined with the conditions neccessary for health and comfort. It is greatly to the credit of the Imperial Commission that it thus recognized the importance which the movement for improving the condition of the homes of the working classes of Europe has attained. This movement commenced more than twenty-five years ago, but it first became manifest in the great exhibition in 1851, at London, where, under the auspices of the late Prince Albert, a model of a house suited to the wants of agricultural laborers was shown. As early as 1844 the society for improving the condition of the laboring classes was formed in London, and a set of model dwellings was erected.

In Prussia, in 1848, an association was organized with the object of improving the homes of the working people. It was under the patronage of the King, and included Prince Albert and the Emperor of Russia among its members.

Louis Napoleon, in 1849, when President of the republic, turned his attention to this subject and erected in Paris a *cité ouvrière* in the Rue Rochechouart, and his efforts in this direction were prominent at the Exposition of 1867.

The attempt will not here be made to extend and complete these historical notices of the great efforts for the amelioration of the condition of the working classes. The special notices which follow will in part supply this information. The British reports of the Exposition upon the new order of rewards contain the names of more than thirty commercial undertakings which made returns of the means employed by them to improve the condition of the laboring classes. It contains, also, information in detail concerning ten building societies which have achieved great results. The munificence of Mr. George Peabody in this direction is well known. The original gift of £150,000 has been increased to £350,000, and dwellings for nearly two thousand persons have been completed.

The Industrial Dwellings Company (Sir John Waterlow's) provides homes for four thousand persons.

A list of the principal exhibitors in this class at the Exposition will be found at the end of this chapter. There were over thirty. France numbered seventeen; Great Britain five; Belgium three; and, if we enumerate the Illinois cottage, the United States had one.

But, although so much attention was given to this class in the Exposition, it cannot be said that the displays were commensurate with the importance of the subject or the attention which it has lately received, not only in France and Great Britain but in other countries.

Many of the important societies and organizations were not represented. But it may be justly observed that the benevolent operations of these companies do not permit of objective representation; they can be described with greater success and utility. The exhibition was comparatively meager, but the publications upon the group are by no means so; they are voluminous and comprehensive, and reference may be advantageously made to them by those who are especially interested in this subject. To this end, the titles of some of the most important that have come under the writer's notice are subjoined.[1]

It is difficult for those persons in the United States who have not investigated the subject to understand the distressing condition of the mass of the working population in Europe as compared with the condition of our own people who are similarly occupied. The rapid industrial expansion of the last thirty years, the increase of large manufacturing establishments, and the consequent crowding together of operatives, have converted quiet villages into busy and populous cities.

In this manner a city built for a few thousand inhabitants, suddenly,

---

[1] L'enquête du dixième groupe. Catalogue analytique des documents, mémoires et rapports exposés hors classe dans le dixième groupe et relatifs aux institutions publiques et privées créées par l'état, les départements, les communes et les particuliers pour améliorer la condition physique et morale de la population. Paris, E. Dentu, 1867, 8vo., p. 284.

Rapports du Jury International, vol. xiii, (particularly the report upon Class.93, by Messrs. Degrand and Faucher.)

Returns relative to the new order of awards, vol. vi, of the British reports upon the Paris Universal Exhibition, London, 1868. (This report contains plans and elevations of many of the buildings.)

Les institutions ouvrières de la Suisse, par Gustave Moynier, Génève, 1867, 8vo., pp. 190.

Les cités ouvrières de Mulhouse et du Haut-Rhin, par A. Perrot.

by the erection of factories, became the home of treble or quadruple that number, in almost every case destitute of means, and attracted by the hope of employment. The lodgment of this class seems not to have entered into the minds of the founders of the factories, or if it did, the uncertain and precarious condition of a manufacture then in its infancy forbade the outlay necessary for this purpose; while in many cases the limits of the town or city walls prevented the erection of more buildings.

Every house was filled, a single room in many cases containing several families, while even the cellars were crowded with people huddled together in the most revolting manner. Nor was any relief to be obtained by removing to a distance from the factory. Besides the fatigue of the day's work, that of reaching a home situated not unfrequently at a distance of several miles, was to be added. This journey was to be taken before light in the morning, and after dark in the evening, through mud, rain, and snow, by men, women, and children, always wretchedly clad, and as badly fed.

The condition of the workmen, as shown by the boards of inquiry established during the commencement of the present century, is painful and distressing in the extreme. It was little, if any, better than that of wild beasts, and referred to by Bruyère when, describing the agricultural population of France, he says: "which one sees in the fields everywhere, black, earth-stained, burned by the sun, but having the voices of men, and displaying, when they raise themselves on their feet, human faces."

The manufacturing population are described in no less distressing terms: "Covered with rags, begrimed by the oil of the factory, pale, weak, decimated by disease, brutalized by all the vices which physical and moral misery engender, they lived a few years, capable of little work, and died in almost all cases before maturity." Mulhouse may be taken as no more than a fair illustration of the misery of the operatives in the manufacturing towns and villages. Here the average length of the life of the workmen was not more than thirty-three years, while that of certain classes of them, spinners, for instance, was not more than eighteen years. Manchester, Leeds, and other towns of England and France, could show no better record. And when to this is added the fact that a war, a commercial crisis, or a political disturbance might throw the workman out of employment or reduce his wages, it is difficult to imagine a more wretched existence. It is needless to multiply instances to show the degree of wretchedness which the laboring classes abroad had reached. A single instance, cited by Jules Simon, will suffice.[1] "At Thann, in the suburb Kattenbach, a lodging of two small rooms, which was the home of a father, a mother, a daughter, a son-in-law, and four children, had no other entrance than through a piggery, where the landlord raised hogs side by side with his tenants. Near at hand two brothers, having each a wife and three children, ten persons in all, lived in a room three meters by five, and lighted by a single window. Not far off, a room of

[1] In *L'Ouvrière.*

fair size, and well lighted, served as the lodgings for nine persons in 1855 when the cholera broke out. The epidemic carried off seven victims in two days."

This state of things could not fail to attract the attention of the leading minds in Europe. Commissions were established and inquiries made almost simultaneously in England, France, and Prussia.

The late Dr. Villermé, of the Institute, visited and examined into the condition of the working classes in the manufacturing towns, and drew a frightful picture of the misery, drunkenness, and moral disorder in which he found them. M. Reyband, of the academy, was also deputed to continue these studies among the woolen and silk manufactories. Mr. Chadwick, in England, and Mr. Huber, in Prussia, pursued similar investigations. M. Jules Simon also devoted himself to examining the condition of the working class, and published the remarkable books entitled "L'Ouvrière" and "Le Travail."

Perhaps not more useful, but at least more practical, were the efforts made by M. Dolfus. This gentleman, an eminent manufacturer, and at present the mayor of Mulhouse, deemed the great point of attack on the mass of evil so constantly increasing to be in the improvement of the habitations. The success of the institution he has founded at Mulhouse seems to establish the truth of these conclusions, and shows how far inferior are the results of cure and alleviation by charities to well-directed exertions in the way of prevention. It is not therefore the mere bodily comfort of the working people that is promoted by these efforts, but their moral elevation and well-being is involved. For it may be laid down as a law, that the moral amelioration of the working classes follows their physical amelioration as an effect does a cause; the moral welfare of the individual being to a great degree dependent upon his physical condition.

In the establishment of workmen's houses there are considerations beyond those of cheapness and healthfulness which it is necessary to carefully study and understand. It must be remembered that the workman is not a mere animal to be housed and sheltered, but that his opinions and wishes in the arrangement and location of his home are to be consulted and respected.

Though that type of dwelling which will give the workman an entire house for himself and family, surrounded by a garden, undoubtedly possesses the greatest advantages, yet in many localities such a house is impossible on account of the dearness of land, as is the case in large cities. It is necessary to leave the populous centers, where land is dear, and go into the suburbs to find a suitable location. The workmen, and particularly those of Paris, refuse to do this. The city offers too many attractions, with its gay streets and public gardens, while the erection of grand public works, and the objects displayed in the shops, constitute a species of permanent and instructive exhibition.

In France, also, it is only in the cities that the free schools for children are to be found, and the night schools for workmen, the lectures, and many other advantages of instruction from which the workman living in the country is debarred. The women also find it inconvenient to be distant from the shops, and the men complain that riding in the railway cars to their homes, after a hard day's work, is uncomfortable and exhausting.

It is impossible not to be struck with the truthfulness and force of these arguments; nor is it surprising that the *cités ouvrières* at a distance from the city in which the workmen are employed have not in France generally proved successful. It is necessary also that the workmen's lodgings, wherever built, should vary slightly one from the other in the arrangement and number of their rooms, in order the better to comply with the needs of different families. If, on the other hand, they are all alike, as it has been proposed in some instances, they will be rented by only a certain class of families, while it is well known that in all poor populations there are families whose condition and wants are very different, and yet that they are equally worthy of consideration.

It is necessary also to render the home, wherever it may be, pleasant not only for the wife and children, but also for the father; there is nothing so trivial as to be considered unworthy of attention if it contributes to this result. The workman, fatigued by his day's work, needs both diversion and repose in order to maintain his effective working powers in their highest condition. Anything which, without adding sensibly to the cost of construction, will render a house more convenient and agreeable, which will beautify and give it even an appearance of luxury, so that the legitimate tastes of the occupant can be gratified, will be the most effective means of attaching the laborer to his home, and encouraging in him habits of order and economy.

The moral of the whole matter has been forcibly stated by the late Dr. Southwood:

"A clean, fresh, and well-ordered house exercises over its inmates a moral no less than a physical influence, and has a direct tendency to make the members of the family sober, peaceable, and considerate of the feelings and happiness of each other; nor is it difficult to trace a connection between habitual feelings of this sort and the formation of habits of respect for property, for the laws in general, and even for those higher duties and obligations the observance of which no laws can enforce. Whereas a filthy, squalid, unwholesome dwelling, in which none of the decencies common to society, even in the lowest stage of civilization, are or can be observed, tends to make every dweller in such a hovel regardless of the feelings and happiness of each other, selfish, and sensual. And the connection is obvious between the constant indulgence of appetites and passions of this class, and the formation of habits of idleness, dishonesty, debauchery, and violence."

Apart from these general considerations it will be obvious to all that there are special necessities which must be regarded in the erection of buildings of this class, such as proper heating, lighting, and ventilation.

In respect to materials and methods of construction, it is to be observed that they vary so much with the requirements of the people of different countries, the climate, the cost of materials, and the rate of wages, that no general plan or rules can be laid down which will be of universal application. The house which would afford a high degree of comfort in France would be uninhabitable in Northern Germany, and the English laborer's home would not meet the requirements of our Western American life.

But the general principles which have been stated have universal application, and the day has already arrived when in our great cities we in the United States are beginning to experience the same evils which abound in Europe, and for the amelioration of which efforts are now so generally and nobly made.[1] It has therefore been deemed important to devote considerable space to the subject, and to describe briefly what was presented at the Exposition in this field, and to notice also several of the prominent associations which have been organized and have already achieved important results for the working classes.

BUILDING SOCIETIES IN FRANCE.

THE EMPEROR'S WORKMEN'S COTTAGES.

In the movements made in France for improving the dwellings of the working classes, no one has taken a more important part than the Emperor Napoleon. As early as 1849, on his accession to the presidency of the republic, he founded a *cité ouvrière*, or set of workmen's dwellings, in the Rue Rochechouart, designed especially for unmarried men.

This building did not meet with the success which was anticipated. A prejudice, wholly unfounded, was excited against it, and the name of

---

[1] A recent editorial in the New York Tribune states: "The British metropolis, under the transforming influences of railways and skilled labor, has changed so much within the last quarter of a century as to furnish a fair parallel to the growth and expansion of this city. In both cities like causes have destroyed street after street of workingmen's lodgings and given them up to large manufactories and immense commercial houses. In London, as in New York, dwelling-houses of a higher class have multiplied indefinitely, while small tenements, so far from increasing, too often fall before the march of improvement. Everybody is aware of the effect of this policy in this city, where, year after year, increased rents are demanded for poorer lodgings. A workingman whose weekly earnings are from $18 to $30 per week cannot find a comfortable dwelling anywhere upon the island at a rent at all within his means, and the consequence is that he is driven from the city altogether, or compelled to submit to all the inconveniences and annoyances of lower class tenements. Where a man can place his family in a snug little home in one of the surrounding villages, he will find himself better off than in contending against the exactions of landlords in the city; but many persons are so situated that they cannot get out of town, though it is degradation and death to stay in it. To this latter class Mr. Stewart's dwellings, and others which would be sure to follow from his example, would prove a benefaction without being a charity, and stimulate toil by offering a reward to manly independence."

casernes or "barracks" was applied to the lodgings which it contained; and although the rent was very reasonable and the accommodations much better than could be obtained in houses in the quarter in which it was situated, the workmen refused to occupy it.

In November, 1849, a commission was sent to England, under the direction of the minister of commerce, for the purpose of studying the results obtained in the construction of improved dwellings for the working class by the Metropolitan Association, and in 1850 and 1851 the reports of the commission were published. They contained many important and valuable facts and suggestions, and among them was a translation into French of the memoir of Mr. Robert Scott Burns on "Dwellings for the Working Classes." In 1852, by a special decree, a loan of ten millions of francs was effected for the improvement of workingmen's houses in large cities, and during the same year the first amount, five hundred thousand francs, was placed at the disposal of the minister of interior. The object of this loan was not to construct buildings at the expense of the state, but to aid in the formation of societies by guaranteeing to them, by means of subsidies, one-third of the cost of the buildings erected by them.

As an immediate result of this legislation, seven sets of buildings were erected in Paris in the course of two years, namely, the *cité* Napoleon, the buildings in the Rue Rochechouart, those of the Chapele St. Denis, those of the Boulevard Mazas, those of the Boulevard Batignolles, those of the Rue de Montreuil; in the provinces, the *cité* of Marseilles and the three hundred houses which the model village of Mulhouse contained.

Four new villages were also authorized to be built at Marseilles, at Lille, and at Paris. In addition also to the subsidies furnished by the minister of interior, the Emperor gave large sums from his civil list for the purpose of aiding and assuring the success of these new enterprises.

Special measures were taken to call the attention of architects to this subject. In 1852 a competitive exhibition was opened for plans for workmen's houses; a prize of $1,000 was awarded to M. Puteaux, of Paris, and subsidies were granted to him in addition, for the purpose of building thirty houses similar to his plans.

In addition to those enterprises subsidized by the government, a large number of others were undertaken by companies, or by the heads of manufacturing establishments, and in some cases by private individuals.

The most satisfactory results have been obtained, and the movement which was set on foot by the measures taken by the Emperor has spread to every part of France. It is no more than justice to say that the success of this movement and the important results which have been obtained in France are mainly due to the initiative, the encouragement, and to the earnest and incessant efforts of Napoleon, both as President of the republic and as Emperor. In addition to the establishments before mentioned, measures have been taken in France to associate the workmen themselves in efforts to improve the condition of their dwellings. The success of the workmen's village at Mulhouse, which will be referred to hereafter, shows that by economy and saving a workman can in a few years become the owner of the house in which he lives. It is true that up to this time societies like those of Mulhouse have been initiated and supported by wealthy capitalists, but there is no reason why workmen may not combine among themselves for attaining the same result, and the success of the co-operative societies generally in England and other countries would seem to indicate that the plan is neither chimerical nor impracticable.

In the International Exhibition the Emperor appeared as an exhibitor, and his services were recognized by the award of a grand prize. The buildings exhibited by him being of large size, could not, save at great expense, be reproduced in the park, nor would models furnish an adequate idea of them. They were to be seen in the places in which they were permanently built, in the Avenue La Bourdonnaye, in the vicinity of the Champ de Mars, and in the Avenue Dausmenil, in the neighborhood of the forest of Vincennes.

The first range of buildings was composed of four contiguous houses five stories in height, with shops on the ground floor, containing each eight sets of lodgings on the four upper stories, and containing in all apartments for one hundred and sixty families. The second group of buildings consisted of fifty houses, containing in all more lodgings than the group of the Champ de Mars. The peculiarity of these buildings is that each set of apartments has a separate landing and staircase, so that they are rendered independent of each other. The cost of these two groups of buildings exceeded one million francs, which was contributed by the Emperor from his private funds. The group of the Avenue La Bourdonnaye is to be sold, and the money devoted to the erection of another group of similar buildings in some other part of Paris.

The fifty houses of the Avenue Dausmenil have been given by the Emperor to an association of workmen, who have formed a co-operative society, the object of which is to place it within the power of every family to purchase the house it lives in.

This society is the same which, under the name of the "Associated Workmen of Paris," has constructed the house for six families exhibited in the Champ de Mars.

The award to the Emperor by the imperial commission of a grand prize was a most proper recognition of his services.

It was given to him not as the head of a powerful nation, but for his individual services, for his constant attention, for his advice and encouragement, and for all those acts which have contributed to so large an extent to the advancement of the important work of improving the condition of workingmen's houses in general, and particularly those of manufacturing cities.

In Class 93 there were from France seventeen exhibitors, six of whom displayed full-sized models of the buildings erected by them, while the remainder exhibited only plans, designs, and small models of their buildings. This number does not include all the societies in France for improving the condition of the workingmen, though it does include the most important ones. It is proposed to mention briefly a few of these, and show the results which they have accomplished.

THE MULHOUSE SOCIETY OF CITÉS OUVRIÈRES.

The condition of the workingmen and their families in the manufacturing city of Mulhouse had, for a long time prior to the formation of the society of *cités ouvrières*, attracted the attention of the most enlightened and intelligent manufacturers of that city. The price of lodgings was exceptionably high; fifteen and frequently eighteen francs being paid per month for rooms which admitted of none of the comforts and very few of the decencies of life. This society was established in 1853. Its object was two-fold—to furnish the workmen with suitable dwellings, and, at the same time, to afford a permanent and safe investment for capital. The location chosen for the *cité* or workmen's village was near Mulhouse, on a broad plain which stretches between that place and Domach, where the drainage was good, the air pure, and untainted by the smoke and odors of a city. We must pass over without mentioning the many difficulties which beset this new undertaking. It was fortunate in having for its members men of a high degree of ability, who were impressed with the necessity of rendering this new project successful, and who gave to it their most earnest co-operation.

The practical difficulties of construction were overcome by their architect, Mr. Muller, to whom is largely due the success of this institution. The first houses were constructed in 1853, four hundred and twenty-eight in number; of these three hundred and eighty-four were sold during the first year. The number of houses in 1866 was eight hundred, and material and financial condition of the society was eminently prosperous.

The following extract, translated from the Jury Reports of the Exposition, gives an excellent idea of the present condition of this society, and the difficulties which have been overcome:[1]

"The Society of Mulhouse has tried various plans for the arrangement of the houses which they have constructed, but the houses grouped by fours, like the specimen on exhibition, appear to be almost exclusively preferred. Each building contains four sets of lodgings, and is placed in the center of a rectangular garden, divided into four portions of equal size and similar shape, so that each family has one of these portions attached to their dwelling. The lodgings are absolutely distinct from each other, having nothing in common but the party walls which divide them. The amount of living-room in each set of lodgings, deducting the space occupied by the partition walls, is five meters by $5^{m}.50$ on the

[1] Rapports du Jury International, Tome XIII, p. 916. Report on Class 93, by M. E. Degrand, of Paris, and Dr. J. Faucher, of Berlin.

ground floor, and $5^m.05$ by $5^m.55$ on the second story—being in all $55^m.53$ square meters, which permits of a kitchen and living-room on the ground floor and two bed-rooms above. This, of course, is independent of the cellar and garret, which is the full size of the building divided into four equal parts.

"There are also other houses of different sizes, and arranged on different plans, so as to comply with the different wants of the inhabitants. Some have one story only, others have two, and the grouping is sometimes in rows and sometimes by fours as before described. The last arrangement is the favorite one, both on account of the economy of constuction and on account of its admitting of windows on two sides of each lodging. Houses built in this way are less exposed to the variations of the temperature than those standing by themselves.

"Whatever the arrangements, however, each house occupies, with the garden about it, one hundred and sixty square meters of land, of which the garden occupies about one hundred and twenty square meters.

"By the last returns of the society, there existed at Mulhouse twelve groups of contiguous houses, in rows of ten, eighteen, and twenty, in all one hundred and ninety-six houses; four groups of houses standing by themselves, in rows of ten and of four, in all twenty-eight houses; one hundred and forty-four groups of houses in fours, in all five hundred and seventy-five houses; making a total of eight hundred houses.

"There are, in addition, bath-houses, a laundry, a baker's shop, a restaurant, and a nursery, which contributed largely to the well-being of the inhabitants, and toward the construction of which the government made a donation of three hundred thousand francs. Broad streets bordered with sidewalks, and planted with trees, and lighted with gas by night, separate the groups of houses from each other. Some of these houses may be rather more desirably located than others. The houses are provided with water and gas, and the supply of both for private and public uses is abundant. The price of the houses making one of a group of four is two thousand six hundred and fifty francs for those of one story only, and three thousand four hundred francs for those of two stories.

"The object of the society is to sell these houses to the workmen, and not to rent them, and for this purpose they have had recourse to long terms of credit and annual payments. The purchaser pays, according to the value of the property, from two hundred and fifty to three hundred francs, cash down, which goes to pay the charges incident to the transfer of the property and the expenses of the sale, which is not concluded till after a certain time, when the society is convinced that the purchaser is in earnest, pays his money regularly, and is in a fair way to buy the house within the specified time. In addition to the first payment, the purchaser of a house worth three thousand francs has only to pay twenty-five francs a month, or three hundred francs a year, which is but very little greater than the price ordinarily paid for the rent of a house of the same kind in the city. At this rate the workman will, in the course of thirteen years, have entirely paid for his house, which he will then hold in fee and unincumbered.

"Such a result as this, one can easily see, could not have been attained except through the disinterested efforts of the founders of the *cité*, with whom the primary motive was a philanthropic one. Their labors have been entirely gratuitous, and they have been contented with a profit of four per cent. on the capital invested. The assistance from the government has largely aided the operations of the society, by relieving them from a large part of the expense necessary for public works, such as the construction of the streets, the baths, and other buildings.

"Without further remark on our part it will be sufficient, in order to appreciate the nature and importance of the results obtained, to cite the following passage from a report presented to the Industrial Society of Mulhouse, by Dr. A. Pénot, in August, 1865, the figures in which have been changed so as to show the condition of the society on the 31st of December, 1866."

"After stating the fact that of the eight hundred houses of which the town is composed, six hundred and eighty-four have been bought by the workmen, the author adds: 'Of this number of six hundred and eighty-four houses, sold up to December 31, one hundred and twelve have been paid for in full, and the larger part of those which were constructed in 1853 and 1854, during the first two years after the establishment of the village, have only small amounts still due on them. In this way the workmen have become proprietors, fortunately, by a system of economy wisely practiced, a result which till within a few years they could not have dared to hope for.'

"On the 31st of December, 1866, the society had placed to the debit of the purchasers the sum of 2,491,119 francs, divided as follows:

Sale of six hundred and seventy-six workmen's houses	1,937,625 francs.
Sale of eight overseer's houses	63,600 francs.
Expenses for transfer of property	117,368 francs.
Interest since 1853	337,284 francs.
Taxes and insurance	35,242 francs.
Total	2,491,119 francs.

"On the other hand, the books of the society show that there is still to be paid by the purchasers the sum of one million one hundred and nine thousand four hundred and sixty-eight francs, by which it is seen that the society has already received the difference, which amounted to one million three hundred and eighty-one thousand six hundred and fifty-one francs; if we deduct from this last number the sum of thirty-three thousand five hundred francs due by the purchasers to the *Crédit Foncier* of France, which has advanced this sum to them, it will be seen that the entire value of the property acquired by the workmen is one million three hundred and fifty thousand francs, and this is, as we have already had occasion to say, the sum total of savings, for thirteen years, of a population whose number during that period certainly has not averaged two thousand souls.

"Such facts as these show what an effect the desire of property has in promoting among the poorer classes habits of order and frugality, and are themselves the best arguments against those attacks which have been leveled against such institutions as that of Mulhouse.

"It has been observed that if the acquisition of property by annual payments on long time has some advantages in its normal condition, that is to say, when the workman can meet his engagements promptly, it is not the same when long stoppages in the work occur, when the character of the industry is changed, or, as it must frequently happen, the workman falls sick or dies.

"When the workman, from whatever cause, cannot find sufficiently lucrative occupation in the place in which he lives, nothing can be easier for him, if his money is in the savings bank or in public securities, to move to some place where he can get better pay. If, on the other hand, he is engaged in purchasing a piece of property, by annual payments on long time, he will be bound to the place where his property is by a tie almost impossible to break, which will be a source of discomfort and misery to him, instead of ease and happiness which he had looked forward to. If he dies, his widow and children, whether the house is wholly or only in part paid for, may find it extremely difficult to dispose of the capital saved by him during his life, and on the failure of his pay, especially if the family, as is often the case, earn nothing for themselves, their condition cannot fail to be deplorable. When to this is added the difficulties of guardianship, division and sale of the property, and the incidental expenses, it would seem that the improvement which societies of this kind have had in view have not been fully realized.

"These objections would have weight if in addition to institutions like that of Mulhouse there were those which by other means than the desire of property had succeeded to the same extent in causing the workmen to contribute to their own physical and moral improvement, while at the same time they were enabled to lay by a portion of their earnings. It is necessary not to lose sight of the fact that by discarding a means which is so effective—that of constructing improved dwellings—and which consists in associating the workmen for an object in which they themselves are directly interested, the only way would be irrevocably closed which leads not only to local and partial results, like those obtained up to the present time, but to general results which are closely related to the important objects in view. By inviting the workman, by the desire of acquiring property, which is one of the most powerful motives to action, to gain, at the price of savings amassed with difficulty, a healthy and convenient house, is not only to elevate his moral condition by teaching him habits of order, but his social condition by making him a proprietor. In this way also the money so saved can be devoted to the construction of a second house, by means of which the same benefits can be placed at the disposal of still another family."

"To obtain this result is in our opinion all important. The plan adopted by the society of Mulhouse has been eminently successful, and has been imitated by a great number of societies in other localities. Moreover, experience has shown that even if the habit of saving, which in itself has no attractions, is practiced by certain families, as the regular deposits made in the savings banks and other institutions prove to be the case, the sums saved in this way cannot be compared with those which the desire to hold property has caused to be accumulated within the last thirteen years at Mulhouse out of a population averaging not more than three hundred and forty-two families, who, besides this saving, have also participated in the benefits of co-operative societies and made deposits in the banks. If also the difficulties inherent to the transmission of real property are insisted upon, it can be said in most cases that if the workman did not have this kind of property to leave to his children he would leave them nothing at all.

"Finally, whatever opinion is expressed on this subject, there is one point upon which there can be no doubt, that as regards the moral and physical elevation of the workmen, the practice of economical habits in order that they may be able to purchase healthy and comfortable houses, the occupation of which commences thirteen years before they are paid for, is very different from the development in the workman of miserly and avaricious habits."

INTERNAL ARRANGEMENT OF MULHOUSE DWELLINGS.

"The bed-rooms are airy and well lighted. One is apportioned to the husband and wife, one to the sons and one to the daughters. The methods of heating and ventilation have been carefully studied. The cast-iron stove which heats the living-room has warm air pipes, furnished with registers so arranged that the upper chambers can be sufficiently warmed, and the air, by being constantly renewed, kept pure and fresh. Great care has been taken in the economy of space, and in the arrangement of the rooms, and the house is as healthy and comfortable as can be desired.

"The work accomplished by the Mulhouse society of *cités ouvrières* is an example of what can be done in a large manufacturing city by a private association, animated by sentiments of elevated philanthropy, and at the same time by a high appreciation of the true interests of the place. By the formation of a company of twelve manufacturers only, with a capital stock at first of three hundred thousand francs, which was afterwards increased to three hundred and fifty-five thousand francs, by the admission of nine new stockholders, a town of six thousand inhabitants has been created; six hundred and forty-eight families of workmen have already become, or are in the way to become, the owners of the houses in which they live, and for a large portion of the entire population the most radical and desirable changes as regards lodgings have been effected.

"The relations of the society with the workmen render it possible for them to see that the children are first sent to the nursery, and later to the schools, so that in addition to the physical amelioration the moral amelioration has been equally rapid. Not only is a change to be seen in the families brought directly under the influence of these reforms, but a marked improvement in the tone of society may be noticed throughout the place."

These facts are substantiated by Jules Simon, the most eminent writer in France on the condition and future of the working classes. In referring to this society, he says:[1]

"On visiting the *cité ouvrière* of Mulhouse, a strong desire is felt to see this institution, so excellent in its results, established everywhere throughout France, and the observer cannot fail to be surprised that the example set by this city six years ago has not borne fruit in other places; but while in other places there are merely projects and trials, this society has realized what others have only dreamed of.

"It can be said without hesitation that there is not an academy in Europe which has shown so much intelligent activity, and rendered such eminent services to the cause of industry and humanity as this society. It is an association between the first manufacturers of the district for studying all industrial questions, for rewarding and propagating useful discoveries, and for inaugurating all possible improvements in the habits of the workmen. A watchful care and interest for the workman is its peculiar characteristic, and it is by this means that it performs such incalculable services."

"It was the first to perceive, and has demonstrated to all, that a good workman is the great agent in the increase of national wealth, and that by caring for his well being, both physical and moral, an act is done not only good in itself, but the results of which are most beneficial to the nation."

It should be stated that, since the publication of *L'Ouvrière*, from which the above extract is translated, the example set by Mulhouse has been followed in the majority of the manufacturing cities where the conditions of life are analogous. Workingmen's villages have been founded at Guebviller, Beaucourt, Colmar, and Marcq-en-Bareuil, all of which are in a flourishing condition.

REAL ESTATE CO-OPERATIVE ASSOCIATION.

"The following is a translation of an article published by Stanislas Ferrand in the Journal des Propriétaires,[2] describing the objects and operations of the Société Co-opérative Immobilière of Paris:

---

[1] L'Ouvrière, p. 337, published in 1861.

[2] De Journal des Propriétaires, Revue de la Science Économique de la Propriété Immobilière urbaine et rurale, 30 Avril, 1867, p. 54.

The problem proposed for solution by the real estate co-operative association is this:

To build distinct or contiguous houses, uniting cheapness, comfort, and health, on cheap lands purchased in quantity, by the company in Paris, and out of ordinary materials.

There is a material as well as a moral question involved in this problem. Laborers want a cheap house, and a home they can love. It is the design of the association to furnish such homes. Its intention is not merely to build small houses; it proposes tenement houses, as well as separate dwellings, on account of the high price of land in Paris. For economy, four and eight houses will be constructed under one roof.

The houses may be built not only in Paris, but in the suburbs near the railway stations, and wherever the land is cheap, the locality healthy and convenient.

Arrangements of the House.—The house exhibited is a private dwelling, suitable for a clerk or laborer. It can be joined by other houses at each end, and the gable walls are constructed with reference to this.

It has a cellar with a stone stairway. The four walls, as well as the partition wall, are of common stone, rough cast, and with the seams pointed.

The arches, resting on the walls and T joists, are of brick, plastered with cement. The privy box is movable, and leans against the back wall; it has the dimensions required by law.

The three walls and the arch are of the same masonry as the cellar. The hole for extracting the box has a stone frame and movable plug. For health and economy the sink is outside of the building, but it may be under the cellar, with a pipe leading into the back yard. To prevent dampness, it is placed a little above the level of the cellar, on beds of stone, bitumen, and gravel.

The height of the cellar should be two meters. The cellar is ventilated by two air-holes in the front wall.

The Ground Floor.—The house is entered by a hall, in which there is a stairway to the first story, steps under it to the cellar, a privy, and door to the kitchen.

This hall is lighted by the glazed entry door and the stairway transom, which must be on a level with the stair beam, so as to light every part. The walls and ceiling are painted with silicate of potash.

The privy is inclosed by walls of hollow bricks plastered with lime. It is separated from the kitchen by two brick walls and not in contact. The hollow bricks and the air between the two walls deaden any sounds in the privy. Three or four hollow bricks are inserted in the outward wall, over the crevice between the two inward partitions. Their tubes will lead to the open air, so as to lead all sound outward. The privy is lighted by a glazed window that opens. The seat is of oak, with hole covers of the same wood. The vessel is enameled, and has a vertical pressure. The walls are painted with silicate of potash.

The Kitchen-Dining Hall.—The co-operative association has united the kitchen and dining-room. This combination is preferable, because it saves ground, building materials and fuel. The moral advantages of this arrangement are also of importance, as it answers the modest requirements of a frugal household. The housekeeper wants to overlook the stove, the cradle, and the table, all at once. Each one of these objects is of great interest to the mother, and she wants to see them all together, as she is often obliged to give her attention to each, alternately, and this arrangement is very convenient for her. In winter, coal or coke is used for cooking, and to warm the family room at the same time. This is a great economy for poor families. In summer, cooking may be done with wood or gas. If the funnel is properly arranged, all the noxious vapors will be carried off by it. The street window, door transom and the drawing of the chimney flue will afford sufficient ventilation, and constant renewal of fresh air. In winter the ventilator and chimney will suffice for ventilation without letting in the cold air by the door.

The kitchen stove is of cast iron; next to it comes the stone trough leading the slops off to the sink; and above it a hydrant cock.

If tenants prefer to have the dining-room separate from the kitchen, it can easily be partitioned off; or the hall may be made into a kitchen by moving the stairway.

This floor may be composed of a solid mosaic cement, more durable than tiles, costing only four francs a square meter, the bitumen included.

The stair leading to the first story is of oak, on a framework of iron, after Remery and Gauthier's patent. The baluster is of cast iron, ending in a swan's head, and faced with walnut. In the first story are two sleeping rooms, with ventilators in each, like those on the ground floor. Above this is a long garret 1.80 meter in height, reached by a ladder. A second story might be made at small expense by putting a few panels under the roof.

The whole is covered with lapping tiles, made by Laforest on Royaux's style. There is a pipe in front and a gutter in the rear.

System of Construction.—The system of construction rests on the following principles: The suppression of huge buttresses of masonry; of partition walls; of iron and stone floors. The use of hollow cast iron columns for all vertical props, with joints and screws, so they can be examined; of light hollow brick arches, resting on iron joists, for floors; the separation of the iron from the stone; the use of thin hollow bricks for front walls; complete ventilation; and cheap decorations, owing to the mode of construction and nature of the material used. This system has the following advantages:

First. Economy of ground. The suppression of partition walls and the use of thin front walls make great economy of ground.

Second. Economy of construction.

The use of cast iron saves large stone or brick walls, and of course saves material and labor. The cast iron pillars are hollow, and the air that passes through them keeps them from melting in case of fire.

In large houses these hollow pillars may be used for ventilation, chimneys, water pipes, &c., to save the expense of special tubes for such purposes. This use would only be resorted to when convenient to health and comfort.

Floors on hollow brick arches, resting on iron pillars, are cheaper and less sonorous than other kinds of floors. Wrought iron is very useful everywhere in these buildings.

The floors in the houses exhibited are made on two iron beams that rest on cast-iron pillars, and are fastened to them by screws, so as to be easily removed.

A girder is placed over the upper wing, on a level with the joists, and fastened by anchors at the ends; so the floor has no braces, ties, or girders. The space between the joists is filled with hollow bricks, covered with cement. The pressure of the arches on the joists is neutralized by counter pressure. The partition walls form an abutment for the ends of the arches.

If a counter wall be required by law the ends of the arches might rest on iron beams let into the medium wall, over the first front pillar. Arches thus constructed would serve as supports to all the others.

The beams of the floors are out from the wall, so that the iron may be preserved from moisture and last the longer.

Outside Walls.—Ventilation.—In this system of construction all the weight is on the cast-iron pillars, and the outer walls only serve to protect the rooms from the external temperature.

We must attend to sound and to health in construction; moisture must not penetrate nor sound molest through walls. To effect this, the association rejects stone walls, for these reasons: Stone walls are not strong unless they are thick; and as they support no weight, they are not needed in our system; all carbonates of lime are porous, and absorb humidity; they have to be plastered; they are more costly; they decompose rapidly; the stone is decomposed by heat, and the walls tumble down; and stone walls require expensive plastering.

The front walls are of brick, thicker for the first story than above. The walls of the first story are made of hollow brick, and are double, with a space between. In practice, a double brick might be used instead of two bricks.

The advantages of this mode of construction are these: The use of solid and durable materials; economy of ground; saving of expense of construction.

There are tubes of molded bricks in the solid base walls communicating with the cellar, and passing up through the double wall to the garret. One of the great causes of sickness in houses is sudden change or temperature. In common houses the miasmatic gases readily permeate the plastering and walls at every change of temperature outside, and thus make the house unhealthy. In our system, this danger is not feared; the silicate of alumina is less hygrometric than lime, and of course more healthy, and moisture has less influence on brick than on stone.

Hollow bricks admit the external air as far as the median cavity, where it is driven to the roof by the air that comes from the cellar below. By this simple and cheap process of ventilation the interior of the house is kept at an equable temperature, to the great benefit of health.

Air holes might be made in the walls and floor to ventilate the rooms in summer.

This current of air between the bricks in the walls also deadens the sound. If a noise from without strikes the outer wall, it will only disturb the air between the bricks, and will not pass inside of the house. Thus the street noises, so annoying in Paris, will not be heard in our houses.

Special ventilation of the rooms may be effected in a simple way; let bricks, with holes through them, be inserted into the walls so as to admit the external atmosphere. A register may be fixed over the internal opening to regulate the ventilation. These ventilating bricks should be inserted in the wall, opposite to the fireplace or window, so as to have a proper draught. In this way rooms may be perfectly ventilated without being made too cool.

Cast-iron Pillars.—The pillars rest on stone bases. The second pillar rests on the top of the first, and is fastened to it by a screw bolt.

The ends of the joists rest on the top of the second pillar, and are fastened with screw bands. The pillars are fastened together by chains and anchors.

The timber is all pine. The gutters are supported by the rafters of the roof. The outer doors are of oak; the inner ones of oak and pine. The window sash is of oak; the upper story has a plank floor. All the rooms are corniced.

The outer doors have a strong iron lock; the inside ones have a latch and bolt.

The paint used is silicate of potash—a good and cheap color. The bed-rooms are hung with common paper bordered.

Outside Decoration.—The style of the house on exhibition is the realization of an idea effected by peculiar materials and style of architecture.

The patent brick, colored by metallic oxides, can be ornamented infinitely.

The casings are formed by the arches of the floors, which project in front; they may be made of the brick used in the arches, or fancy white brick; under these casings are projecting bricks of different colors.

The arches of the openings are constructed on the same principles.

The girder of the two arches of the double window that lights the dining-room rests on a small hollow iron pillar. The joints are cemented.

We avoid the vulgar uniformity of windows in this plan; no two windows are alike, because the size of the rooms is different; a small room has a small window, and a large room has a large window. This arrangement is true to art, because it is the positive expression of a necessity.

In a word, the style is the *consequence* and not the principle of the programme.

Large Buildings.—The larger the scale of this system, the more economical it is; in houses intended for several families the economy is really important.

When the possibility of constructing small houses at little cost is demonstrated, it is evident that larger houses may be built in the same way at less cost.

The Co-operative Association calls the attention of the jury to this last advantage as meriting serious consideration.

The by-laws of the Real Estate Co-operative Association show how property may be acquired.

BY-LAWS OF THE BEAUCOURT REAL ESTATE ASSOCIATION.

ARTICLE 1. The undersigned enter into a partnership for the construction of dwellings, separate from each other, surrounded by a small garden, at a cost of two or three thousand francs each. They will share the costs and expenses with those who purchase shares, in proportion to the stock they hold in the company. These dwellings are intended to be rented or sold to the operatives in the house of Japy Brothers, or to any other resident of Beaucourt who wants one; they can pay the whole sum at once; or rent, and pay a sum annually sufficient to pay for the house in five or eleven years.

ART. 2. Persons renting the dwellings cannot become owners of them in fee simple till they have paid the whole price; till then, they will be considered as tenants. In case they do not continue, from any cause whatever, to pay the promised yearly instalments, only the money they have paid above their rent will be returned to them.

ART. 3. This civil and private association shall be regulated by the provisions of articles 1841, and following, of the Code Napoleon.

ART. 4. The partnership shall last eleven years, reckoning from the 1st of April, 1864, to finish on the 30th of April, 1875.

ART. 5. Its title shall be The Beaucourt Real Estate Company, and its location and domicil shall be at Beaucourt.

ART. 6. The partnership capital is fixed at thirty-four thousand francs, divided into three hundred and forty shares of one hundred francs each. The house of Japy Brothers and Company subscribes for one hundred shares, and the founders take the balance of two hundred and forty. The ground is given by Pierre Japy. An additional number of shares, amounting to six hundred and sixty, may be issued, of one hundred francs each. The citizens of Beaucourt and employés in the branches of the house of Japy Brothers and Company, may subscribe for these shares. To give clerks and laborers in the house of Japy Brothers a chance to purchase shares and invest their savings, they may pay for them by deductions or investments of ten francs a month, or multiples of ten francs. Temporary receipts will be given for these instalments, to be converted into certificates of stock when a whole share is paid up.

Other stockholders than clerks and laborers in the house of Japy and Brothers shall pay their dues by calls from the company.

ART. 7. The certificate of shares are taken from a stock register, stamped with a dry seal of the company, and signed by one of the managers; these certificates shall be numbered from one to one thousand.

ART. 8. The shares are transferable when paid for; the certificate thereof is entered in a book kept for that purpose by the company; it is to be be signed by both parties or their attorneys, and attested by the manager. The act of transfer is indorsed on the certificate.

ART. 9. Shares are indivisible. The company recognizes but one owner for each share; hence the owners of one share must be represented to the society by a single person.

ART. 10. The rights and obligations of a share follow its transfer; the holding of a share implies acceptance of the charter of the company.

The heirs and creditors of a shareholder cannot seize or sequestrate the property of the company, or interfere in any way with its management; to enforce their rights they must appeal to the company.

ART. 11. Stockholders are only responsible for the shares they hold; no call beyond the amount so invested shall be made upon them.

ART. 12. Japy Brothers & Co., as directors of the company, together with the supervising board, shall have the sole management of the business; decide upon the plans, estimates, localities, and size of the dwellings; conclude all bargains with the contractors, clerks, and others, and cancel or remove them; and fix upon the terms of lease or sale of the dwellings.

ART. 13. The stockholders in general assembly shall name a supervising board, composed of four members who hold at least ten shares of the stock, to hold office for five years; after which time a new board shall be appointed in the same manner.

ART. 14. The directors and supervising board shall appoint a treasurer and an actuary to receive investments, pay dividends, and make all other disbursements; and to have charge of all the funds of the society, and to take care of the archives.

ART. The sale of the dwellings shall constitute a fund to be used in redemption of the shares by lottery as far as they are paid up.

ART. 16. As the dwellings are to be sold at cost price, there will be no dividends, but the stockholders shall be entitled to a yearly interest of five per cent. on their shares, payable every six months, in March and September, the first payment to be made next September. The house of Japy Brothers insures the payment of this interest, in case the proceeds of the sales of the dwellings and the rents of the same are not sufficient.

ART. 17. When the company's charter expires, or the partnership is dissolved, the house of Japy Brothers promise to pay the cost price of the remaining dwellings, so that all the shares will be redeemed at par.

ART. 18. The building contractors shall receive in payment for their work fifteen per cent. in shares of the stock, at par value, and the balance in cash when the work is completed.

Cost-price of a house.

Specifications.	Size.	Cubic meters.	Each.	Total.
EXCAVATION.	*Meters.*	*M. c.*	*Fr. c.*	*Fr. c.*
Digging foundations, in earth	27. 90 × 0. 55 × 0. 40	6 150		
Digging for cellar door, in earth	0. 80 × 0. 40 × 1	0 320		
Cubic meters		6 470	0 60	3 88
Digging foundations, in rock	1. 40 × 0. 50 × 2. 50	1 750		
Digging cellar, in rock	1. 80 × 2. 25 × 4. 70	19 350		
Cubic meters		21 100	2 50	52 75
STONE-WORK AND PLASTERING.				
Stone-work, plastered with lime	1. 40 × 2. 50	3 50		
Stone-work, plastered with lime	27. 90 × 3. 54	98 39		
Stone-work, plastered with lime	6. 50 × 2. 70	17 55		
Square meters		119 44	5 30	633 03
Stone-work of chimney, (cubic meters)		0 684	13 00	8 89
Brick partitions and chimney, (cubic meters)		11 66	4 25	49 55
Same, five centimeters thick, (cubic meters)		23 30	2 40	55 92
Chimney cover of brick and tiles				4 00
One mantel-piece, wood and brick				7 00
One fireplace of brick, eleven centimeters high				6 00
One sink and fixture				12 00
Cut stone for doors and windows		38 10	3 15	120 00
Ceiling, (gray and white gypsum)		40 90	1 75	71 57
Wainscot, laths and tiles		75 00	3 70	278 24
CARPENTERS' WORK.				
Nine joists of pine, ground floor	6. 45 × 20-14	1 625		
Nine joists of pine for garret	6. 90 × 20-14	1 737		
Two pine sills	7. 00 × 18-12	0 302		
Thirty-two pine rafters	4. 65 × 8-7	0 834		
Sixteen pine girders	2. 80 × 8-7	0 230		
One pine partition sill	6. 20 × 8-5	0 025		
Twelve pieces wood, for door hinges	0. 22 × 8-5	0 010		
Three pine shelters for doors	1. 30 × 8-5	0 015		
Six pine shelters for windows	1. 30 × 12-10	0 140		
Six pine garret windows	1. 10 × 18-10	0 120		
One frame stair-landing, (pine)	2m × 14-14	0 039		
Two pine door shelters for kitchen	2. 25 × 18-10.	0 081		
One support for cellar stair, of pine	1. 90 × 14-14	0 037		
Two hearth frames, of pine	0. 90 × 14-14	0 017		
Total		5 212	47 00	244 96
JOINERS' WORK.				
Tongue and groove floors, in square meters		41 29	2 00	82 58
Unplaned floors for garret		41 80	1 60	66 88
Rough flooring for cellar stairs		0 80	1 60	1 28
One front pine door, without lock			22 00	22 00
Three inside panel doors			18 00	54 00
Two leaf doors, for cellar and garret			1 50	3 00
Three oak windows, complete			18 00	54 00

Cost-price of a house—Continued.

Specifiĥations.	Size.	Cubic meters.	Each.	Total.
		M. c.	*Fr. c.*	*Fr. c.*
Two oak windows, for garret			6 00	12 00
One kitchen window, of oak				14 00
One cellar wicket, complete				2 50
Twenty-five stair steps, three francs each				75 00
Pine socles and plinth, &c		43 40	0 75	32 55
Five wooden window sills		1 50	2 00	3 00
Casing of the stair frame in the garret		0 40	1 50	0 60
LOCKS AND TIN-WORK.				
Four locks for doors, complete				22
One bolt for chimney piece		*	1 00	1 00
Six bolts for stairways		†	1 00	6 00
Gutters and pipes		21 40	1 95	41 73
Four kilograms lead pipe, for drains, &c				3 79
Total				2, 045 70

* 1 kilogram. † 6 kilograms.

Many workingmen of capital wanting more comfortable houses propose to make sleeping-rooms in the garret, and add privies, &c. The increased cost of these modifications is expressed below.

Specifications.	Quantity.	Unity.	Total.
	M. c.	*Fr. c.*	*Fr. c.*
Total of preceding estimates			2, 045. 70
Deduction of roof fixing, &c	75. 00	1. 10	82. 50
Remainder			1, 963. 20
Stone-work for the mansards	13. 95	5. 30	73. 94
Brick partitions, five centimeters thick	13. 82	2. 40	33. 16
Ceiling of the mansards	50. 40	1. 75	88. 20
Three panel doors		18. 00	54. 00
Three locks		3. 50	10. 50
Water-closets			40. 00
Plaster cornice	17. 60	2. 00	35. 20
Total			2, 298. 20

FRENCH ARTISANS' HOUSES.

By far the most elegant and attractive of the models of cheap houses in the park was that erected by the "Associated Workmen of Paris." The cost of this building was twenty thousand francs, which was contributed by the Emperor from his private means for the purpose of calling the attention of the public to this society, and to the houses similar to the model which they propose to erect in Paris.

The model in the park was designed and erected by the workmen themselves without the assistance of architect or builder. It is, therefore, the embodiment of the workman's own wishes in regard to the arrangement and appearance of his house, and as a whole may be considered as a decided success. The appearance of the front is cheerful and tasteful; the materials are carefully selected, and the internal decoration is excellent. The houses are three stories in height and are built in pairs, with an entrance and winding staircase in the center, which gives access to the various apartments. Each building of two houses contains lodgings for six families. The basement or ground floor is designed to be used as a shop for small tradesmen, and is arranged with a kitchen and sleeping-room, so that it is complete for a small family.

The building is $13^{m}.83$ front by $8^{m}.90$ depth, (about forty-five feet by twenty-nine feet.) The hall is about six feet three inches wide, and the principal rooms up stairs ten feet five inches by eleven feet six inches; the dining-room seven feet six inches by eleven feet six inches; and the kitchen, which is back of the dining-room, is four feet by seven feet. The height of the ceilings is eight feet eleven inches. The exterior walls are thirteen inches in thickness. A courtyard seventeen feet six inches wide divides the two houses at the back.

The second and third stories are divided into chambers or apartments for a family, there being two sets on each floor. They contain a dining-room, a kitchen, and two bed-rooms, so arranged that the dining-room may be used during the day as a parlor if the wife is engaged in any trade, such as a dressmaker, seamstress, or milliner, which will bring her in contact with customers. All these rooms are of good size, are well lighted and ventilated, and are well planned for the convenient arrangement of furniture.

These buildings are constructed of brick, stone, and iron. The window jambs and caps are of stone, and the panels between of red brick. The mansard roof is decorated by slating in lozenge-shaped patterns, with slates of different colors, and the upper portion of the roof is of metal. Each shop front has two large and well-glazed windows, one on each side of the door.

The arrangement of the lower floor for shop purposes is the most noticeable feature in the whole building. The Parisian workmen do not wish to become a distinct society or class in the community, living in quarters and among themselves. It is both their desire and policy to associate themselves with the shopkeepers or tradesmen, and by renting out the lower portion of their houses to derive a small revenue from the rent, and thus to participate, somewhat, in the shopkeeper's profits. The cost of this structure was twenty thousand francs, (four thousand dollars,) not including the price of the land. At this price the society estimates that each suite of rooms could be let from three hundred to four hundred francs (sixty to eighty dollars) per year. The rent of the shops would necessarily vary with the price of the land, being higher in populous quarters than in those in which the buildings are more scattered.

FRENCH MINERS' COTTAGE AT BLANZY.

The coal mining company of Blanzy exhibited in the park a specimen of the houses of their workmen. It was quite a large and well-shaped building, divided into two tenements, each designed for a single family. The walls are of brick or rough stone ornamented with plaster, and the floors as well as the roof are covered with flat, red tiles. The building is raised about two feet from the ground, and each tenement contains a sitting or living-room, sixteen feet three inches square, a sleeping-room thirteen feet by eleven feet six inches, and a smaller bed-room on the upper floor. There are also cellars and *greniers*, or garrets, which may be used as storerooms, besides six hundred square meters (seven hundred and seventeen square yards) of land for a garden for each house. The whole cost of one of these cottages, including the land, is only two thousand two hundred francs, (four hundred and forty dollars.) This, of course, is much cheaper than the same kind of building would be in or near a city where labor, and particularly land, cost so much more. These houses rent at the works at Blanzy for fifty-four francs (ten dollars and eighty cents) per year; and this includes fuel. There are six hundred and seventy-nine cottages of this kind constructed at the works, ninety-nine being built by the workmen themselves.

GREAT BRITAIN.

There were five principal exhibitors from Great Britain in Class 93:

1. Digby, Lord, 39 Belgrave square, London.
2. Improved Industrial Dwellings Company, 2d West street, Finsbury circus, London—models and plans of improved dwellings for the industrial classes.
3. Metropolitan Association for Improving the Dwellings of the Industrial Classes, 19 Coleman street, London—models of dwellings.
4. Galt, Titus & Co., Saltaire, Bradford, Yorkshire—drawings of their manufactory and of the town of Saltaire.
5. Society for Improving the Condition of the Laboring Classes, 21 Exeter Hall, London—drawings of model lodging-houses and renovated dwellings.

In the British reports upon the Exposition, in volume vi, containing the returns relative to the new order of award, ten building societies are enumerated, and much information in detail is given regarding their organization, objects, and results. It is impossible to here notice all these associations at length, or to give even a brief and intelligible statement of the great good they have accomplished. A few only of the more prominent that were represented at the Exposition will now be described.

METROPOLITAN ASSOCIATION.

The "Metropolitan Association for Improving the Dwellings of the Industrial Classes" was organized in 1841, and commenced active operations in 1845, when it was incorporated by royal charter. In 1867, after continuing in operation for twenty-three years, it possessed, in London, one hundred and twenty-three buildings, six of which were of large size, capable of containing, together, five hundred and seven lodgings; two buildings divided into three hundred and sixty-two single chambers for unmarried men, and one hundred and fifteen cottages for an equal number of families. The entire population in the buildings of this association averaged, for the year 1866, two thousand five hundred and seventy-two persons.

This society is essentially a commercial enterprise, a joint stock company of limited liability, differing only perhaps from an ordinary company by the spirit with which it is conducted, and the object which it has in view.

The amount of dividends is limited to five per cent. of the capital invested. It has never received any assistance from the government, and in all cases where individuals have pressed donations on the association they have been declined and returned, the object of the association being not to solicit charitable contributions, but to show that a fair profit can be made by renting healthful lodgings at moderate rates, so as to induce capitalists to invest their money in such buildings as a commercial enterprise.

The buildings of the association have been so arranged as to provide dwellings on three different plans, viz: Dwellings in flats and in chambers; dwellings in cottages both in town and in country, and dwellings for single men in large buildings, where they are supplied with cooking utensils, beds, bedding, and other necessaries.

During the last twenty-five years £119,429 have been expended. For the year 1866 the income of the association exceeded £8,000.

The returns from the society show that the capital invested in dwellings for families yields an interest of more than five per cent., but that owing to the expenses incident to the formation of this society, and the fact that the chambers for single men have proved a bad investment, the dividend payable on the entire capital stock has been less than three per cent.

The health of the occupants of the buildings of this association has generally been excellent. While the average rate of mortality of the city of London generally has been twenty-three and two-thirds per thousand, in the dwellings of this association it has not been more, on an average of six years, than seventeen per thousand. The association claims that it has combined the commercial or self-supporting principle without losing sight of the more important and philanthropic object it had in its foundation.

Since the establishment of this association in London, two branch associations have been founded, one at Bristol, with a capital of £6,000, and the second at Ramsgate, with a capital of £2,000.

SOCIETY FOR IMPROVING THE CONDITION OF THE LABORING CLASSES.

The Society for Improving the Condition of the Laboring Classes has, as its name indicates, a broader field of action than the improvement of dwellings and lodgings alone. It is nevertheless to the construction of convenient and healthy houses that it has directed its main efforts, and from this point of view its labors present the same degree of interest as those of the Metropolitan Association. Its method of action and system of organization is however entirely different from that society. The members, instead of being shareholders, are subscribers, and pay an annual assessment, to which donations, legacies and other gifts are sometimes added, so that the society is stripped of any commercial character or tendency, and is, in fact, merely a benevolent institution. Its object, according to the terms of its statutes, is to build model houses, to improve old habitations known to be unhealthy, and to render wholesome, by every means in its power, the courts and alleys of the poor quarters of large cities; to publish designs and plans for the construction of houses suited to the needs of workmen in London, in the manufacturing cities, and in the agricultural districts; and further to communicate with clergymen, proprietors, and other persons who are disposed to assist them in their respective localities, either individually or as members of local institutions.

Among the donors and annual subscribers to this society is the Queen of England, the corporation of the city of London, the Earl of Shaftsbury, president of the society, and many members of the aristocracy.

In 1866 the revenue of this society, from the rents of its houses, the annual subscriptions of its members, and from donations, amounted to more than £6,000. As there was no dividend to be paid from this amount the whole sum could be devoted to maintaining and continuing the usefulness of the society.

In the same year the houses, or groups of houses belonging to this society, were nine in number; four of them were arranged for lodgings for families; the fifth for lodgings for twenty families, and for the use of one hundred and twenty-eight unmarried women, and four buildings, containing in all two hundred and sixty-seven single rooms, for unmarried men. The rent received from these buildings shows that the society is in a prosperous condition. The four houses for single men paid five per cent. on the capital invested. Those for families four and two-tenths per cent., while that for families and unmarried women three per cent. These results may be considered as highly satisfactory, especially those in regard to single men's lodgings, since it proves that this class of dwellings can be successfully rented. The success in this instance may be attributed to the excellent situation of the buildings, the very moderate rent of the lodgings, and the high degree of comfort afforded, as compared with the ordinary disagreeable and dirty lodging houses.

This society has provided accommodations for three hundred and fifty-three families, one hundred and twenty-eight single women, and two hundred and eighty single men, a population which, during the last four years, has averaged one thousand six hundred and seven persons. The death rate in the company's houses has been reduced one-third, as compared with that of London generally.

When we consider the great wealth and resources which these societies have had at their command, it must be admitted that neither of them have effected so much toward the improvement of the working classes as the French societies, and particularly that of Mulhouse, where six hundred and eighty-four families have already become, or are in the way of becoming, proprietors, and six thousand persons have been furnished with comfortable homes; yet great credit is due to them for the care which they have shown in all that concerns the interior arrangement of their buildings. All that regards drainage, heating, lighting, ventilation, or any other matter which would be of importance in the construction of lodgings for poor families, have been made the object of repeated and patient researches. In this way great progress has been made in the construction of workmen's houses, not only in London but all over England, with a corresponding advancement in the comfort of the occupants and decrease in the rate of mortality.

IMPROVED INDUSTRIAL DWELLINGS COMPANY.

As an example of a successful company, organized for the purpose of improving the dwellings of the working classes, the "Improved Industrial Dwellings Company" may be cited. It was founded in 1863 by Sir Sydney Waterlow, and was afterwards incorporated as a limited joint-stock company. This company now houses about four thousand persons, and has extended its buildings with great rapidity. In 1867 it owned nine buildings, built upon what is called the open stair-case plan, containing, in all, five hundred and seventy-one separate tenements, with one thousand eight hundred and eighty-five rooms. The capital invested amounts to £250,000, and a dividend of six and one-half per cent. is paid upon it—five per cent. being paid to the stockholders, and one and a half per cent. being retained as a reserved fund for contingencies. The following extract, from a printed statement made by the secretary of this association, gives the best account of what it has accomplished:[1]

"The object of the Improved Industrial Dwellings Company is to prove that an effective solution of the most difficult social problem of the age—the proper housing of the working classes—is within the com-

[1] Returns relative to the New Order of Reward.—British Reports Paris Exposition, vol. vi.

pass of ordinary commercial enterprise; and that the physical suffering, as well as the moral degradation and antagonism of feeling, which now often exist between the lower and other classes, may be gradually, but surely and safely, removed by the free and spontaneous application of means always at the disposal of the people, and without the aid of special legislation.

"The rapid spread of manufacturing industry, the development of vast natural resources, the great increase of wealth which has characterized the present century, have not been productive of unmixed good to the operative and poorer classes of society; for upon masses of workmen whose occupations oblige them to reside within the limits of great cities the march of progress has imposed conditions of social existence of the most baneful kind. Foremost among these deleterious influences is the overcrowding of dwellings, which, from the frightful proportions it has attained during the last few years, has attracted the special attention of all social reformers. Its physical and moral effects need not be depicted here; they are universally admitted. Indeed, no one at all acquainted with the subject can impugn the declaration of a noble philanthropist, that 'the improvement of the dwellings of the people is a condition precedent to all other reforms.' Nor is it necessary to describe here the various unsuccessful attempts which have been made toward the abatement of this great social disease either by philanthropists, benevolent societies, or by politicians. It is enough to say that, however well intentioned they may have been, the results of either benevolent or legislative interference have hitherto fallen altogether short of the enormous demands of the case. It is now clearly understood by all who have carefully studied the subject that the only plan which is capable of dealing comprehensively with so gigantic an evil is one which, while feasible and capable of unlimited extension, will not only invite the active imitation of those whose ordinary commercial avocations give them a personal interest in the question, but will also commend itself to the notice of capitalists and professional builders in such a way as to provoke healthy competition on the part of those seeking fair interest and investments of unquestionable security.

"The comparative failure of all previous attempts in this direction is in the main attributable to a neglect or misappreciation of the one indispensable condition of success—that the scheme should be commercially profitable.

"The Improved Industrial Dwellings Company claim that by the exercise of a 'free and spontaneous initiative,' and unassisted by any special legislative enactments, they have succeeded in putting this question practically before the public by exhibiting in itself the practical working of a joint-stock company having a comparatively large capital, raised and invested in such a manner as to place the fact of its business being profitable beyond all doubt.

"At the present date about £63,000 have been raised by the subscriptions of its shareholders, and of that amount some £40,000 have been invested in the purchase of land in densely overcrowded districts, the removal of dilapidated and unhealthy dwellings from the sites, and the erection in their places of several blocks of lofty, commodious, and substantial residences. Altogether about twenty-seven separate and distinct tenements have been thus provided. Each tenement is totally self-contained, and distinct from its fellow in every essential respect. It consists of two or three light, commodious, and cheerful apartments, together with a separate wash-house or scullery, and a water-closet, all inclosed within its own front door. Every tenement is well supplied with fixtures and fittings, so as to make it, so far as the house itself is concerned, a comfortable and attractive home for a working man—a benefit of which he is not slow to avail himself, for all the buildings yet erected have been filled with eager tenants from the moment of their completion, and the representatives of the company are constantly beset by applicants for possible vacancies.

"The improvement of the *morale* of the inhabitants of these buildings is unquestionable. It arises, doubtless, from the families occupying these houses being removed from the bad associations and influences to which they were before unavoidably exposed, as well as to the pure air and the ample supply of water to which most of them find access for the first time; but above all other proofs of the suitability and salubrity of the dwellings is the unimpeachable testimony of a diminished rate of disease and death. This most unmistakably shows that the new conditions under which the occupants of these houses are placed strike at once at the heart of those deadly influences, acting equally on the mind and body, which have been the growth of years in the fetid, unwholesome, and filthy dwellings incidental to the old state of things.

This society is referred to in the "Report of the Council of Hygiene and Public Health of the Citizens' Association of New York upon the Sanitary Condition of the City," as having most successfully met and overcome the difficulties inherent to an undertaking of this kind; and they recommend that houses similar to that erected by Sir Sydney Waterlow in Finsbury Square, London, for twenty families, be built in New York. There is no doubt, if this were done, and the plans modified and Americanized so as to suit American tastes and preferences, that such domiciles would become sufficiently popular to make them pay a rental which would be remunerative to the builders.

COLUMBIA SQUARE, MISS BURDETT COUTTS'S LODGING-HOUSE.

The first of the four structures which compose the lodging-house of Columbia Square was opened in 1859, the last in 1862. The object which the founder, Miss Burdett Coutts, had in the erection of this building was to afford decent domestic accommodation for the poorest members of the industrious classes, whose weekly wages would not allow them to live in dwellings with a higher rental.

Miss Coutts was the first to erect dwellings solely for this class of tenants. Her success has been very complete, and several other buildings similar to these have been built, all of which have fulfilled their requirements and made a good pecuniary return on the cost.

The following description of the buildings in Columbia Square is furnished by the architect, Mr. Henry Astley Darbishire:

[1] "The general arrangement of the building closely resembles that of the Victoria lodging-house; and, as it has been highly approved by all the leading sanitary authorities who have visited it, no material departure from this arrangement has been made in any of the buildings of the same class which I have since erected. There are four stories of dwellings, and a fifth or attic story, which is occupied by wash-houses, club or reading rooms, and large areas for drying clothes and for the exercise of children in wet weather. The dwellings are situated on each side of a corridor, which is lighted and ventilated by windows at each end, and by a wide stone staircase in the center of its length. This staircase has one of its sides uninclosed, except by iron railing, so that the corridor is constantly supplied with fresh air—an advantage of considerable importance, as the poorer classes endeavor to exclude, with jealous care, every breath of fresh air surrounding their habitations; and were not their dwellings supplied with a fresh current from the corridor whenever their doors were opened, the sanitary condition in large blocks of associated homes would not be so highly satisfactory as the registrar's returns prove it to be. The dwellings generally consist of two rooms, a living-room twelve feet by ten feet, and a bed-room twelve feet by eight feet six inches. Of these two-roomed dwellings there are twenty-eight. There are nineteen dwellings with two bed-rooms of the same dimensions, and there are five dwellings of one room twelve feet by ten feet six inches, intended for adult members of families occupying the first specified dwellings. Each living-room is provided with two cupboards, the upper one arranged with shelves, the lower one adapted to receive coal and fuel. The fire-place is furnished with stove for cooking, oven, boiler, hot plate, and trivet. There are four water-closets, two lavatories, and two baths on each floor. In the center of each corridor, and adjoining the staircase, is a dust hopper or flap, connected with a shaft communicating with a vault in the lowermost part of the building, which is the only portion basemented. Access to this vault for the removal of dust is provided from the exterior, so that no effluvia or annoyance arising therefrom may enter the building. The dust-shaft is carried up over the roof for the purpose of ventilation.

"The staircase and corridors are of stone. The external walls are faced with picked stock-bricks of the ordinary description, and are fourteen inches thick; those of the internal walls which have fireplaces are nine inches thick; the partition walls between the living-rooms and bed-rooms

[1] British Reports on the Paris Universal Exhibition—Returns relative to the New Order of Reward.—Vol. VI, p. 216.

are four and a half inches thick. All the internal walls are worked with as fair a face as common brickwork will allow, and are colored with two coats of well-sized distemper color of a warm cream tint, which gives them a clean and comfortable appearance. The ceilings of the dwellings are the only portions of the building which are plastered.

"The foregoing brief outline may serve to explain the description of building which it is considered desirable to provide for a class of tenants hitherto unaccustomed to the ordinary decencies of domestic life; a class which required to be tempted to try something rather better, but not too much better than anything which habit had rendered acceptable and pleasant, and which they would reluctantly forsake. As Miss Burdett Coutts felt that she was the first to try the experiment of providing homes for the very poor, and possessed no previous data to guide her, it became necessary to fix the rents of the dwellings at a rate which would not exceed that hitherto chargeable for very inferior accommodation. For this reason twenty-four of the two-roomed dwellings were offered at three shillings sixpence weekly rental; four two-roomed dwellings, which were rather smaller, were offered at three shillings weekly rental; nineteen three-roomed dwellings were offered at four shillings weekly rental, being an increase of only sixpence; and the five single-roomed dwellings were offered at two shillings weekly rental. These rents include all charges to the tenant. By degrees the building became occupied. More applicants applied for residence than could be accommodated; and as Miss Coutts was entirely satisfied with her success, the whole square was ultimately completed in May, 1862. The buildings are always full, and the tenants regard it a privilege to be admitted; and although there are between seven hundred and eight hundred residents since the completion of the first building, there has not been a single case of a tenant becoming amenable to the law. The management of the building is conducted as follows: A resident superintendent inquires into the character and antecedents of all persons applying for residence. He collects the rents, disburses all small payments not paid by check, and pays the balance into the bank every week. He keeps account of the sums received and paid by him, and submits the books to the secretary for periodical examination. He refers all questions of importance to the secretary, and is in all respects under his direction. Under him are two porters, who attend to the general cleanliness and order of the building, who light and put out the lamps, and attend to other minor duties."

The pecuniary return on the cost of this building is only two and one-half per cent. This is to be attributed to the fact that the external character of the building, though simple, is more elaborate than need be; to the low rates of rent demanded from the tenants, and the high rates of the parish in which it is situated; and to the loss of revenue entailed by the use of the whole upper story for wash-rooms, reading-rooms, play-rooms, &c.

Had the object of this undertaking been to render it remunerative in a financial point of view, a much larger rent could have been obtained for the lodgings; in so doing, however, the object of this institution, which is mainly a benevolent one, would have been defeated. In the erection of this building Miss Coutts has not only supplied one hundred and eighty-nine families with lodgings, but by her example has induced the proprietors of cottages in the neighborhood to improve their own wretched property. This result is almost always sure to take place when a better class of dwellings for laborers is erected in a poor community or quarter.

UNITED STATES.

WESTERN FARMERS' HOUSE.

In the section of the park assigned to the United States the State of Illinois presented, for the examination and consideration of the visitors to the exhibition, the Western Farmers' Home, or American cottage. It was constructed by Colonel Lyman Bridges, of Chicago, from plans furnished by Mr. O. L. Wheelock, architect of that city, and was forwarded in sections by railway from Chicago to New York, and was installed among other types of residences and palaces that were exhibited in the Champ de Mars. The object of this exhibition was to illustrate the kind of dwellings much in use in the agricultural regions of the United States.[1]

The building was regarded with much favor. It combined beauty and comfort at an outlay within the reach of all prudent and industrious persons. It did not conform to any special order of architecture, and was constructed of pine lumber, so abundant in Wisconsin and Michigan, generously contributed by Hon. William B. Ogden, of the Peshtigo Company, and Wood & Lawrence, of the Newago Company.

The capacity of the dwelling was sufficient for a family of six or eight persons, and contained three large rooms on the first, and five chambers on the second floor. The plan was such that one of the rooms of the ground floor could be first constructed and occupied as a temporary home for a new beginner in a new settlement, at an expense of only three hundred dollars, and the other rooms and wide hall added at the pleasure of the owner. It also represented the fact that the farming population of the United States may, and do very generally, own the homes in which they live, and that they have liberal protection in the ownership by the laws of the different States.

This dwelling was made the center of attraction by the distribution of documents and information relating to the extent and resources of the United States, which information was eagerly sought for by the numerous European nations. The walls were lined with maps and photographs, and the library supplied with valuable works giving information upon

[1] This valuable exhibition was secured through the exertions of Commissioner Bowen.—EDITOR.

the extent and resources of the United States, and this information was freely imparted to thousands of visitors.

In connection with this notice some facts in detail concerning the cost of buildings supplied to actual settlers upon the western prairies will be interesting. They have been obtained from Colonel Bridges, at whose establishment in Chicago the Illinois farmer's cottage was made, and who has had great experience in supplying cheap homes to settlers in the west.

The majority of settlers do not order more room than they at first actually require, or from two to four rooms, costing from two hundred to six hundred dollars each. Many only wish shelter, and do not have their rooms finished inside. About one family in seven desire a building costing from six hundred to one thousand dollars, and it is rare that a more expensive house is ordered.

The school-houses usually ordered are twenty-four by thirty-six feet in size, and cost one thousand dollars. Portable stores are sold at from five hundred to two thousand dollars. The size usually ordered is twenty by forty feet. Some details upon the construction of these buildings will be found on page 58.

LIST OF EXHIBITORS IN CLASS 93.

FRANCE.

1. THE EMPEROR OF FRANCE.—Cheap dwelling-house for many families; Avenue de La Bourdonnaye.

2. JAPY BROTHERS & CO.—Beaucourt, (Haut-Rhin.)—Single lodging-house, used by a single family of clock-makers.

3. THE SOCIETY OF WORKMEN'S VILLAGES OF MULHOUSE.—Group of four houses similar to those built at Mulhouse.

4. MINING COMPANY OF BLANZY, Blanzy.—Miner's house, with two sets of lodgings.

5. ASSOCIATION OF THE WOKMEN OF PARIS.—Cheap house for many families.

6. CO-OPERATIVE REAL ESTATE ASSOCIATION OF PARIS.—Cheap dwelling-house for a single family.

The following exhibitors displayed models only of the buildings erected by them.

7. GOLDENBERG, ZORNHOF.—Models and plans of houses of different types, for a single family.

8. COAL MINING COMPANY OF ANZIN, Anzin.—Miner's house.

9. RICHEBÉ, mayor of Lille, Lille.—Models and plans of workman's houses to be erected by a company.

FRANCIS DE WENDEL, SONS & CO., Hayange, (Moselle.)—Model of the village of Styring, Wendel.

11. SCRIVE, Marcq-en-Bareuil.—House for the working class.

12. DUPONT PAUL, Paris.—Models and plans of workmen's houses at Clichy; model of a projected lodging-house for women.

13. TRONCHON, Paris.—Model of a cheap house in iron and plaster.

14. JOUFFROY-RENDAULT, Mone, Paris.—Models and plans of the single houses of the cité Jouffroy-Rendault, Rue des Cailloux.

14. JANIN BROTHERS, Montluçon.—Model and plan of a group of six houses for agricultural and industrial workmen.

16. TABIEN, Paris.—Model and plans of a cheap house.

17. SCHNEIDER & CO.—Houses for the working population of Creuzot.

FRENCH COLONIES.

1. THE ALGERINE SOCIETY OF CLIMATOLOGY, Algiers.—Plan of a projected colonial village; model in plaster of a farmer's house.

PRUSSIA.

1. BEHR, (FRIDERIC-FELIX DE) Vargatz, near Griefswald.—Model of the house of an agricultural laborer of Pomerania; model of a stable.

2. SOCIETY OF BERLIN FOR THE ERECTION OF WORKMEN'S HOUSES, (Patron, the Prince Royal of Prussia.)—Designs of houses constructed by the Hoffmann Society, Neustadt.

BELGIUM.

1. Houget & Teston, Verviers.—Houses for factory operatives.

2. Jacquemyns, Minderhout, Antwerp.—Type of an agricultural workman's house.

3. Rypens-Peters, Neil, Antwerp.—Materials for the construction of the workmen's houses exhibited by Houget & Teston.

WURTEMBERG.

1. Staut & Co., Kuchen.—Plans and descriptions of workmen's houses.

SWITZERLAND.

1. Schaeck, Jacquet, Geneva.—Houses constructed for benevolent purposes.

ITALY.

1. Neapolitan Philanthropic Association, Naples.—Plan of a group of houses in course of construction at Naples.

GREAT BRITAIN.

1. Lord Digby, London.—Models of rural dwellings.

2. Improved Industrial Dwellings Company, London.—Models and plans of improved dwellings suited to different classes of workmen.

3. Metropolitan Association for Improving the Dwellings of the Industrial Classes.—Models of dwellings.

4. Salt, Titus & Co., Saltaire, Bradford.—Designs of their factory, and of the village of Saltaire.

5. Society for Improving the Condition of the Laboring Classes, London.—Designs of model dwelling-houses for workmen, and of houses which have been rebuilt.

UNITED STATES.

Illinois Cottage, or Western Farmer's Home.
Portable Cottage, Louisiana.
Country District School-house.

PRIZES AWARDED TO EXHIBITORS IN CLASS 93.

GRAND PRIZE.

THE EMPEROR OF FRANCE.—Workmen's houses, France.

GOLD MEDALS.

MADAME LOUISE JOUFFROY-RENAULT, Paris.—Cité Jouffroy-Renault, at Clichy la Garonne, France.

SOCIÉTÉ DES CITÉS OUVRIÈRES DE MULHOUSE.—Houses arranged for the lodging of four families.—France.

METROPOLITAN ASSOCIATION FOR IMPROVING THE CONDITION OF WORKMEN'S HOUSES, London.—Great Britain.

SOCIETY FOR IMPROVING THE CONDITION OF THE WORKING CLASSES, London.—Great Britain.

SILVER MEDALS.

ASSOCIATION OF THE WORKMEN OF PARIS.—House with six lodgings, for six families.—France.

CO-OPERATIVE REAL ESTATE ASSOCIATION OF PARIS.—Cheap house for a single family.—France.

JAPY BROTHERS & CO.—Beaucourt.—House.—France.

HOUGET & TESTON, Verviers.—House for a workman's family.—Belgium.

THE COMPANY OF ANZIN.—Workmen's quarters.—France.

SCRIVE BROTHERS, Marcq-en-Bareuil-près-Lille.—Workmen's houses.—France.

BARON DE BEHR, Vargatz.—Houses for two families of agricultural laborers.—Prussia.

GOVERNMENT OF THE UNITED STATES.—Wooden house for a farmer.—United States.

BRONZE MEDALS.

SCHNEIDER & CO., Creuzot.—Workmen's houses.—France.

LORD DIGBY, Ireland.—House for the families of agricultural laborers.—Great Britain.

STAUB & CO., Kuchen.—Workmen's houses.—Wurtemberg.

HONORABLE MENTIONS.

TABIEN, Paris.—Plans, models, and workmen's houses for Paris.—France.

SOCIETY OF THE MINES OF BLANZY.—Houses for two families of miners.—France.

JANIN BROTHERS, Montluçon.—Workmen's houses.—France.

HENRY DRASCHE, Vienna.—Workmen's houses.—Austria.

JEAN LIEBIG & CO., Reichenberg.—Workmen's houses.—Austria.

PARIS UNIVERSAL EXPOSITION, 1867.

REPORTS OF THE UNITED STATES COMMISSIONERS.

REPORT ON MINING

AND THE

MECHANICAL PREPARATION OF ORES,

BY

HENRY F. Q. D'ALIGNY,
UNITED STATES COMMISSIONER,

AND

ALFRED HUET, F. GEYLER, AND C. LEPAINTEUR,
CIVIL AND MINING ENGINEERS, PARIS, FRANCE.

WASHINGTON:
GOVERNMENT PRINTING OFFICE.
1870.

PREFACE.

The matter of this report was submitted to the Department of State by the Commission, in three distinct portions, with the following titles:

First. "Report on the Exploitation of Mines, by Alfred Huet, Civil Engineer, Paris, France, and Henry F. Q. D'Aligny, United States Commissioner."

Second. "Report on Boring Machines, by Alfred Geyler, Civil Engineer, Paris, France, and Henry F. Q. D'Aligny, United States Commissioner."

Third. "Report on the Mechanical Preparation of Minerals, by C. Lepainteur, Engineer to the Syndicat of Class 47, Paris, France, and Henry F. Q. D'Aligny, United States Commissioner."

These reports were originally prepared in the French language, and having been imperfectly translated, the translation required revision. This has been done by the Editor, and considerable additions and changes have been made. In general, however, the original arrangement and presentation of the various subjects treated of has been followed as closely as possible, and in some portions with perhaps not as many changes in the diction of the first translation as a due regard to style would require.

As the three reports were upon different branches of the art of mining, the three have been combined, under one general title, into one report in three parts, corresponding to the three reports originally submitted. Their distinct character is thus, to a certain extent, preserved.

WILLIAM P. BLAKE,

Editor of the Reports of the United States Commissioners.

CONTENTS.

BORING, DRILLING, AND EXCAVATING.

CHAPTER I.

BORING SHAFTS OF LARGE SECTION, AND ARTESIAN-WELL BORING.

CHAPTER II.

DRILLING ENGINES AND COAL-CUTTING MACHINES.

TRANSPORTATION, HOISTING, AND PUMPING.

CHAPTER III.

UNDERGROUND TRAMMING; HOISTING AND PUMPING ENGINES.

CHAPTER IV.

MAN-ENGINES AND PARACHUTES.

MECHANICAL PREPARATION OF ORES.

CHAPTER V.

ORE-CRUSHING, AND ORE-DRESSING MACHINERY AND PROCESSES.

LIST OF PLATES.

I.—BORING, DRILLING, AND EXCAVATING.

CHAPTER I.

BORING SHAFTS OF LARGE SECTION, AND ARTESIAN-WELL BORING.

INTRODUCTION—BORING LARGE MINING SHAFTS IN THE DEPARTMENT OF MOSELLE—SURFACE PREPARATIONS—TOOLS AND METHODS OF BORING—TUBBING—CONCRETING—TOOLS USED AT THE SECOND SHAFT—LINING THE SHAFTS—OPERATION OF LOWERING THE SECTIONS OF TUBBING—THE MOSS-BOX—GENERAL OBSERVATIONS ON BORING APPARATUS—KIND'S NEW TREPAN—SINKING AND BORING ARTESIAN WELLS—TOOLS OF DEGOUSÉE AND LAURENT—TREPAN WITH DROP—TREPAN OF MESSRS. DRU BROTHERS.

INTRODUCTION.

Until within a few years tools and apparatus for boring into the earth to great depths were used almost exclusively for obtaining water, or to explore for beds of coal or for mineral deposits. Fifty years ago the art of boring was in a primitive condition, as practiced by the well-borers of Artois and Italy; but now, thanks to the French societies of art, agriculture, and industry, it has received a new impulse, and scientific engineers have been called to project and direct extensive operations of this nature. Under their influence the art which was so long neglected has been rapidly developed, and the boring rod has passed from the hands of workmen simply into those of skillful engineers. The humble boring rod of Bernard Palissy has now been converted into an engine which is applied in many ways, and which accomplishes results at the depth of several hundreds of metres as complicated and difficult as any which may be attained at or near the surface.

The diameters of artesian wells formerly did not exceed $0^{m}.30$, (11.81 inches,) but they have been increased regularly, until at Passy, near Paris, an artesian well was commenced at more than one metre in diameter, and was completed with a diameter of $0^{m}.70$ at the bottom. It is now known to be possible to sink shafts, either for wells or for mining purposes, with diameters as great as $4^{m}.10$, or over thirteen feet, and through strata of great hardness.

Apparatus for these purposes, shown in the Exposition by Messrs. Kind and Chaudron, Degousée. Charles Laurent, and by Dru Brothers, mark the new era in the art of sinking shafts and wells, and make it evident that the new methods and engines are destined to have a great influence upon the development of coal-fields, especially such as underlie permeable strata heavily charged with water, and alternating with impermeable beds of solid rock, as in the coal basins of Mons and La Moselle, in France.

I.—BORING LARGE MINING SHAFTS.

These new methods of boring shafts avoid the necessity of pumping out the water during the operations of sinking, as must always be done when the work is performed by hand labor. This method of working in a shaft full of water is called in France *à niveau plein*, in distinction to the other and old methods of working with the shaft drained, called *à niveau plat*.

The importance of this mode of sinking will be evident from the following brief notice of the coal basin of Saarbruck. This basin extends beyond the limits of the Rhine provinces, in the department of La Moselle. The coal occurs under barren strata, composed of the (*grès des Vosges*) sandstone formation of the Vosges, and the new red sandstone formation, (*grès rouge.*) The formations are at first very silicious and full of fissures, giving free passage to water. They then become argillaceous, and finally, near the junction with the coal measures, are impermeable to water.

Eleven mining concessions have been made in this department since 1820, and in 1858 it was estimated that twenty-one millions of francs had been expended, and chiefly in prospecting.

Boring and tubbing (lining the shaft) from the surface was completely successful for the first time, from 1854 to 1856, at St. Vaast, and later at Bessaix, in Belgium, in 1862 and 1863; but in these two first attempts the water-bearing strata were scarcely $0^{m}.70$ thick, and the pits were of small dimensions.

In order to explain the apparatus and these methods of sinking in detail, we give a description of the work of sinking shafts of large dimensions in the department of the Moselle.

SHAFTS IN THE DEPARTMENT OF MOSELLE.

The works about to be described were executed at L'Hôpital (Moselle) for the St. Avold company, represented by Messrs. Pereire and Morny, upon the method called the *niveau plein* of Messrs. Kind and Chaudron, under the direction of Mr. Levy, the company's engineer. The work was under the superintendence of Mr. Chatelain, engineer, formerly a pupil of the *École Centrale des Arts et Manufactures* of Paris. Two pits were sunk; one for an air-shaft (No. 1) with a diameter of $1^{m}.80$ within the tubbing, and $2^{m}.56$ in its greatest diameter; the other (or No. 2) for a winding or hoisting shaft was bored with a diameter of $4^{m}.10$, and was $3^{m}.40$ when finished. The operations, according to this method, succeed in the following order:

1. Construction upon the surface—buildings and derricks.
2. Boring the pits.

3. Lowering the tubbing.
4. Puddling or packing.
5. Packing at the base of the tubbing.

BORING SHAFT No. 1.

SURFACE PREPARATIONS.—The preliminary operations consisted in the construction of the necessary buildings for the engines and tools, and the erection of a derrick over the site of the pit. All these were of temporary construction, intended to be used merely during the progress of the work.

The derrick was made of four supports strongly framed together, and sustaining a platform about thirty feet above the surface of the ground. Upon this a railway or tramroad was laid for the trucks, which carried the boring tools and rods.

The engines for sinking comprised the *capstan*, the *jumper*, and the *donkey-engine*. The capstan was used for lowering and hoisting the boring tools in the pits, and for lowering the tubbing or lining of the shaft. The engines used at L'Hôpital had a nominal force of 25 horse-power. The diameter of the cylinder was $0^m.56$, and the length of stroke $0^m.70$. The respective diameters of the gearing were $1^m.70$ and $0^m.35$. Admitting an effective pressure of three atmospheres, the initial force upon the driving shaft was 48,513 kilogrammes. These machines worked regularly; nevertheless we think it would be well to increase the size of the engine, inasmuch as the tendency is constantly to an increase of the size and weight of tools in use.

The first rope used at the air-shaft had a section of 54 square centimetres, capable of sustaining a strain of 5,400 kilogrammes. It was made of good hemp; but after working for one year, it broke in lifting a trepan weighing 3,858 kilogrammes. The tool fell from a height of 86 metres, taking with it 17 metres of the rope. This accident occasioned a stoppage of nine days. The cable was replaced by another having a section of 85 square centimetres, and after using it for fourteen months the work was suspended for three days in order to make a new splice.

The second machine—the jumper—was made of an engine cylinder, open at the bottom and closed at the top. The piston-rod was connected directly with the wooden beam, carrying the tool for cutting and boring at its other end. By the alternate lifting and falling of this tool with the attached beam, the rock was cut away. The diameter of the piston of the jumper was $0^m.60$, and the greatest length of stroke was one metre. The jumper did not require any repairs during the whole operation of sinking the shaft.

The third machine—the donkey-engine—was used to work a pump for hot and for cold water. It is indispensable for the supply of the boiler, as the capstan and the jumper work irregularly. Experience has shown that the feed-pumps should be in duplicate, so as to avoid the necessity of stopping for repairs.

The preparations for sinking the air-shaft were commenced in October, 1862, and were finished in the following month of April. The expense was as follows:

	Francs.
Buildings	28,302.65
Machines and tools	37,326.91
Total	65,629.56

Boring the pits.—Before commencing the sinking with the special tools, a preparatory pit was sunk to a depth of $21^m.40$, and was lined with masonry to a diameter of $2^m.80$ up to within five metres of the surface, where the diameter was increased to four metres. This shoulder in the stone lining afforded a foundation for a platform.

The sinking was accomplished by two different operations. First, a central pit of $1^m.37$ was sunk and then enlarged to $2^m.26$. The debris of this enlargement fell into the first pit. The tubbing was inserted in the enlarged pit.

The boring tools employed in these operations will now be described; the scraper, the scrape-hook, and the different apparatus used indiscriminately in the two pits will be afterward noticed.

The little trepan first employed is represented by Fig. 1, Plate I. It weighs 2,085 kilogrammes, and is formed of two principal parts—the fork and the blade. The blade is $1^m.26$ long, and is provided with teeth of cast-steel, or of iron faced with steel, intended to cut the rock. These teeth increase the diameter of the trepan to $1^m.37$. The blade is joined by means of keys to two strong iron arms, which are united above with a central shaft, which was connected by a slide with the suspension apparatus.

This trepan worked easily through the sandstone of the Vosges—*grès des Vosges*. The fall given was $0^m.30$. The progress per day was at first $0^m.79$, and it diminished to $0^m.52$, and then to $0^m.28$ at a depth of 121 metres; but at 135 metres in depth, in a stratum of strongly aggregated silicious red sandstone, the progress was only $0^m.15$ and $0^m.11$. It was soon found that this trepan was too light to stand the shocks of the blows, and three successive ruptures of the stem made it necessary to procure a stronger trepan, shown by Fig. 2, Plate I, weighing 3,858 kilogrammes, divided among the various parts as follows:

	Kilos.
Body of trepan	2,700
Guide	340
Blade	230
Four teeth of the head	148
Four intermediate teeth	88
Plates and keys	352
Total weight	3,858

The teeth are fixed upon this mass of iron by means of keys. The sockets for the reception of the tenons are conical, and are $0^m.10$ in diameter at the base and $0^m.09$ at the top. The progress in the work made by this trepan, from the commencement, was from $0^m.28$ to $0^m.32$, and even as high as $0^m.83$, giving a mean of $0^m.39$, being three times as much as made by the first trepan. This shows clearly that the heavy trepans are best for the hard strata.

The trepan which was first used for the enlargement of the pit to the diameter of $2^m.56$ had a blade $2^m.46$ in length; it was formed like the little trepan first used, and had a blade fixed upon a fork, and weighed in all 3,980 kilogrammes, divided as follows:

	Kilos.
Fork	2,500
Blade	906
Six teeth of the head	102
Three intermediate teeth	48
Two plates	430
Total weight	3,980

In order to avoid the frequent breaking out of the teeth, this trepan was lifted only $0^m.20$. The progress made with it daily was from $1^m.10$ to $0^m.18$ at the last, when a stratum of hard sandstone was encountered and the weight of the trepan was found to be insufficient. Two blades, one above the other, were then united to the fork by rings and bolts, as shown in Fig. 3, Plate I. Each of these blades carried the teeth so as to cut the strata in two steps. This new tool weighed about 5,000 kilogrammes. It worked four months, and required frequent repairs. The rate of progress per day was only $0^m.11$. It was then decided to replace this trepan by a more massive one, weighing 8,000 kilogrammes, and $2^m.50$ in diameter, constructed as shown in Fig. 4, Plate I. With this the progress was increased to $0^m.34$ a day, thus showing a second time that in hard rock heavy trepans are required.

The diameter of the pit at the beginning was $2^m.56$; at 134^m depth it was reduced to $2^m.45$; at 155^m depth it was reduced to $2^m.40$; from $155^m.00$ to $155^m.50$ depth it was reduced to $2^m.33$; from $155^m.50$ to $158^m.00$ depth it was reduced to $2^m.25$. At this depth the little pit was continued for a depth of seven metres, and a circular curb of $0^m.40$ was fixed to receive the base of the tubbing.

The work of sinking this air-shaft lasted about twenty-eight months and a half. The central pit required 392 days, including 46 days during which work was stopped, so that only 346 of actual work were necessary. The enlarging operations to a diameter of $2^m.56$ occupied 469 days, including 148½ days of no work. The depth of the central pit being $143^m.70$, (equal to 471.46 feet,) the mean progress for each working day was $4^m.15$, (13 feet,) and the enlarging to $2^m.40$ gave a daily mean of $4^m.25$ for a depth of $136^m.60$.

The expenses of boring were as follows:

	Francs.
Salaries and wages	55,039.81
Fuel	12,513.11
Oil and grease	2,381.71
Ropes	2,987.20
Iron, steel, and repairs to tools	12,530.90
Cartage and sundries	7,560.66
Total	93,013.39

TUBBING.—Before entering upon a description of the operation of tubbing the air-shaft, it will be best to explain the system adopted by Messrs. Kind and Chaudron.

The tubbing of the pits is accomplished by lowering into them a metallic cylinder, which finally rests upon a proper seat or foundation, carefully cut for it at the bottom. This cylinder is made smaller than the bore of the pits, and the space between the cylinder and the walls is afterward puddled or filled in with concrete, so as to make a solid continuous lining. The metallic cylinder or tubbing is formed in sections of a cylinder, made of cast iron, and provided with flanges projecting inward, by which they are securely bolted together. (See Figs. 5, 6, 7, and 8, Plate I.) One section or length is added after another to the top as the whole descends in the pit, so that at the completion of the work the whole pit is lined with iron from the top to the bottom. The outer surface of all these sections of the cylinder is quite smooth; but in the inside, besides the flanges for the bolts, there are horizontal ribs or webs cast with each segment, and intended to strengthen them.

The thickness of the tubbing will evidently vary with the diameter of the pits and that of the different segments, according to their position in the pit. Messrs. Kind and Chaudron determine the thickness by the following formula:

$$E = 0^{m}.02 \times \frac{R \times P}{500}.$$

E represents the thickness of the tub, R the radius, and P the pressure expressed in kilogrammes upon the square. The flanges for bolting the rings together should be carefully faced in a lathe, and exactly at right angles with the perpendicular of the shaft. The joints are made tight by a packing of lead, in the form of a ring, $0^{m}.003$ thick, covering all the surface of the flange, so that after the bolts are tightened there will be a surplus of lead along the points suitable for calking. The first attempts to secure a tight packing for the joint at the bottom of the shaft to prevent the entrance of water at the lower part of the tubbing were unsuccessful, but the difficulty was finally overcome by the use of what is now known as the "moss-box." This consists of an attachment to the lower end of the tubbing of an inner tub, or cylinder, provided with a flange at the bottom projecting outward. The bottom of the tubbing is also provided with a flange projecting outward toward the sides of the pit. The space between these two flanges is filled with a packing or wrapping of moss.—(See Fig. 5, Plate I.) This moss is securely held in its place by a web or net drawn tightly around it. The whole, including the inner cylinder, is suspended by iron tie-rods, which prevent its falling out from the bottom of the tubbing, but which do not interfere with the descent of the tubbing upon the moss when the lower flange reaches and rests in the seat or shoulder cut in the rock at the bottom of the pit. At this time the whole weight of the tubbing being allowed to press upon the moss by means of the upper flange, it is compressed and extended outward forcibly against the side of the pit, and thus forms a complete and perfectly water-tight joint. Its office and operation is similar to that of the "seed-bag" used by the borers of petroleum wells in Pennsylvania. The outward movement of the moss is facilitated by thin segments of sheet iron, $0^{m}.005$ thick, so placed at the upper and lower parts of the moss-box, at an angle of fifty or fifty-five degrees, that they present a sloping surface, upon which the moss slides outward when the pressure commences.

The operation of lowering the tubbing into its place in the pit is easily performed by means of the arrangements about to be described. Upon the lower edge of the last section but one of the cylinder a hemispherical-shaped bottom is attached, which closes the lower end of the column. The attachment to the tubbing is securely made by means of a flange bolted to an annular plate.—(See Fig. 6, Plate I.) This hemispherical bottom plate has a central opening into a cast-iron column rising within the tubbing. This column is called the equilibrium column, and at distances of from seven to eight metres it is pierced with holes $0^{m}.01$ in diameter, for the purpose of admitting water to the inside of the tubbing as fast as the latter is sunk in the pit. These holes are closed by screws, and as the tubbing is lowered into the pit the water rises around it and within the open column in the center, until the weight of the water displaced is equal to the weight of the tubbing, thus causing the whole to float in the pit. By removing some of the screws closing the holes, water is admitted to the interior, and the cylinder is made to sink. It is found in practice that it is best to allow sufficient water to enter to give a weight of from twenty-five to thirty tons to the tubbing, or, in other words, to permit so much of its weight to be suspended from the surface as to secure its vertical position and its descent in a proper manner.

The apparatus for suspension consists of four upright posts, sustaining a platform through which the six suspending iron rods pass, and are terminated in long screws. This platform must be strong enough to sustain a weight of thirty tons. Its height above the ground must be equal to that of the four lowest sections of the cylinder, including the moss-box. All these, together with the first sections of the equilibrium column, are first united before being lowered into the pit. Each suspension rod is made in three parts: First, the lower rod, the lower end of which is cut with a screw-thread, for the reception of a stop-nut after it has been passed through the eye of a flange; second, an adjusting screw, (the minimum length of which is four metres,) placed at the upper part of the rod, upon which a nut works by means of gearing and a crank on the platform, as shown in Fig. 7, Plate I. The third part of the rods consists of the intermediate lengths, each four metres long, and coupled together like the boring rods. These are added as the tubbing descends.

The connecting flange at the bottom of the tubbing, through which these suspending rods pass, is composed of six segments, bolted together and to the collar of the third section of the tubbing. Its form is shown by Fig. 8. It has six eyes to receive the suspending rods.

After this connecting flange has been bolted to the tubbing and the moss-box, the hemispherical bottom and the four lowest sections are placed under the platform, and directly over the mouth of the pit; the adjusting screws are united to the connecting flange by intermediate rods, and the whole apparatus is brought into suspension by means of the nuts on the top of the scaffolding. Two workmen are placed at each screw, and by turning the nuts this first portion of the tubbing descends into the pit. After it has been lowered four metres, (the length of the screw on the rods,) the tubbing is suspended to beams resting across the mouth of the pit by means of holding-hooks catching upon the shoulders of the suspending rods, as in the case of boring apparatus. The screws are then detached and are raised by means of the nuts, so as to leave a distance of four metres between their lower ends and the rods below. A new set of intermediate rods is then added, the suspending hooks are removed, the tubbing again rests upon the screws above, and the lowering is proceeded with as before. This operation is repeated until the tubbing floats in the water of the pit. It is then made fast as before, by the suspension rods, to the beams at the mouth of the pit. The screws are raised to a height of four metres, and then the next section to be added is brought forward and placed on beams over the pit. Fresh intermediate rods are then added through this new section to the rods below, and the suspending hooks are removed. The new section is then raised a little by means of the capstan, so as to permit the removal of the beams upon which it rested. It is then lowered by means of the capstan into the pit, until it rests upon the top of the tubbing below. The joint is then made, and the adjusting screws are worked to effect a further descent of the whole tubbing.

When in this manner all the sections have been united, and the metallic lining is upon the point of reaching the bottom of the pit, the rim of rock or seat upon which the flange of the moss-box is to rest requires to be cleaned. This operation is effected by lowering through the equilibrium column a tool represented by Fig. 9, which scrapes the bottom of the pit and throws into the central pit any fragments of rock or accumulations of earth which rest upon the foundation. The lowering is then continued until the lower flange of the moss-box rests gently upon the rim of rock. The weight of the tubbing increases slowly as the water enters through the holes of the equilibrium column; the moss-box is shortened, the moss is expanded and compressed against the sides of the pit and becomes perfectly tight when the weight of the tubbing rests upon it. At this moment the tubbing must not be abandoned to itself, or it may incline to one side. It is therefore secured carefully at the top by three or four beams fixed upon the last section. The puddling or concreting can then be proceeded with, and the suspension rods can be removed.

TUBBING PIT No. 1.—The following are the details of the operation of lining the air-shaft, or No. 1: The tubbing was composed of seventy sections, each two metres high, and $1^{m}.80$ in diameter inside of the flanges. The thickness of the cylindrical part was as follows: $0^{m}.046$ ($1\frac{3}{4}$ inch) for the sections of the lower part; $0^{m}.043$ for the ten succeeding, and then successively $0^{m}.040$, $0^{m}.037$, $0^{m}.034$, $0^{m}.031$, and $0^{m}.028$.

Each of the sections was provided with two internal flanges $0^{m}.07$ broad and $0^{m}.03$ thick. There were in addition two little ribs $0^{m}.04$ thick and $0^{m}.025$ deep. These were cast at equal distances between the flanges. The flanges had twenty-eight holes for bolts, each $0^{m}.03$ in diameter and $0^{m}.21$ apart. The entire tubbing weighed 258 tons, including the bolts. It was furnished by the Fourchambault works.

The moss-box cylinder was cast without any flange at its lower part, and an oak ring was fitted to it to form the base. The width of this box was $0^{m}.175$, its height $1^{m}.60$, representing a capacity of 1,824 cubic centimetres. The pressure of the tubbing upon the moss reduced it to one-sixth of its former volume.

The lowering of the tubbing was effected without the least difficulty the twelve first sections took about fifteen days, but the operation was afterward accelerated and two sections were added daily. Before the addition of the thirtieth section the tubbing was heavier than the water displaced; it was afterward necessary to introduce water to the interior by the equilibrium column. When the moss-box reached the rocky foundation the compression of the moss commenced, and the equilibrium column maintained its upright position. The tubbing was then allowed to fill with water for two days, in order to gradually obtain the maximum compression of the moss.

The descent of this tubbing lasted forty days, and the expense attending the operation was as follows:

	Francs.
Cost of sections	66, 426. 94
Lead for joints	1, 665. 60
Bolts, &c.	1, 340. 98
Red lead, &c	95. 20
Netting	21. 10
Moss	34. 80
Wood	345. 00

	Francs.
Salary and wages	3,447.82
Fuel burned	1,375.25
Oil and grease	258.03
Sundries	3,566.80
Total	78,577.53

CONCRETING PIT No. 1.—It has been shown that the metallic column which forms the tubbing can be maintained perfectly tight throughout its entire height, provided the joints are carefully made. At the bottom the moss-box, resting on impermeable soil, is intended to cut off all communication between the upper water-level and the pit to be sunk below. Notwithstanding all these precautions, it is indispensable, in order to insure a permanent impermeability of all the joints, to make a complete concreting around the entire height of the tubbing, within the annular space left between the soil and the tubbing itself. The expense of concreting pit No. 1 was relatively of small amount. The work lasted twenty-five days. Three sets of workmen were employed, working three spoons of a mean capacity of three hectolitres. Each set was composed of six men—two for working the windlass, to which the spoon was attached by a rope; two for working the windlass for the piston-rope; and, lastly, two on the working stage to fill the three spoons as they were raised from the pit. The mortar was brought, in a case, upon the working stage by the capstan.

The spoon for concreting (Fig. 10) was made of two sheets of iron united on two wooden uprights. It is provided at its upper part with a piston, which forms part of a movable bottom placed at its lower part. By pushing the piston the bottom is expelled and the mortar filling the case falls out. The concrete used had the following composition: Vassy or Rappe cement, (Haute Saône,) one-fourth; hydraulic lime, one-fourth; sand, one-fourth; and powdered trass, one-fourth.

The space to be filled around the tubbing was about 236 cubic metres, neglecting the fissures of the soil; 284 cubic metres of materials were employed. The concrete was allowed to harden for one month. Lastly, the water was pumped out, and the false bottom of the tubbing and the equilibrium column were taken apart and removed. The moss-box was found to be in good order and perfectly water-tight.

The expense for the concreting was as follows:

	Francs.
Salary and wages	4,440.43
Cement	1,396.33
Trass	1,329.50
Lime	1,586.00
Fuel burned	599.11
Oil and grease	178.05
Sundries	2,281.78
Total	11,811.20

A coffer-dam is sometimes inserted at the base of the tubbing. This operation is not indispensable, but increases the solidity of the base of the tubbing. It consisted in placing at two metres below the moss-box two coffer-dams of cast-iron, $0^{m}.25$ high each, and bolted together; then a cylinder $1^{m}.60$ high. It was formed of six pieces, bolted vertically, which were united on the one part to the coffer-dams and on the other part to the bottom of the moss-box, where a little horizontal packing was necessary for the adjustment.

The expenses of packing can be estimated as follows:

	Francs.
Cost of false tubbing	2,347.20
Salary and wages	2,179.23
Fuel burned	897.20
Oil and grease	146.75
Sundries	439.10
Total	6,009.49

Fig. 11 represents the two coffer-dams and the adjusting cylinder.

To sum up, the entire cost of sinking through watered strata to a depth of 140 metres, the internal diameter of the pit being $1^{m}.80$, amounted to 256,041.16 francs, divided thus:

	Francs.
Preliminary works	65,629.56
Sinking the pit	93,013.39
Tubbing	78,577.53
Concreting	11,811.20
Packing	6,009.59
Total	255,041.27

Which gives an expense of 1,600 francs per running metre.

MAIN SHAFT No. 2.

The information which we have furnished upon the construction of the air-shaft applies to the pit No. 2. It will suffice to mention the modifications in this second piece of work.

The tower for sinking the winze of the main shaft was built in masonry, and was intended to serve subsequently as the building for extraction.

The capstan was of the same size as the one employed for shaft No. 1; yet it became evident that, notwithstanding the exaggerated dimensions of the large gearing in this machine, it was still too weak; it broke at the boss, and the repairs occasioned a loss of two days.

The rope was $0^{m}.30$ broad by $0^{m}.06$ in thickness, corresponding with a practical resistance of eighteen tons. Notwithstanding these dimensions, it was necessary to replace it after working eleven months. One year later a stoppage of two days was necessary for repairs to the new rope; and toward the end of the work its rupture appeared so threatening that another stoppage of sixteen days was required to put it in good working order. The jumper piston was $0^m.70$ in diameter. Several accidents occurred with the machine. In the first place, it became necessary to change a segment and two springs broken in the piston, which caused a stoppage of six days; at a later period the piston-rod broke, and one month later one of the piston-rod guides also gave way; these different accidents necessitated a stoppage of eight days.

The donkey-engine was common to the two engines of shafts Nos. 1 and 2. We have already mentioned that a duplicate engine was necessary to insure regularity in the sinking.

The preliminary works were commenced in September, 1863; they lasted nine months, and the expenses attending them may be thus distributed:

	Francs.
Building	46, 702. 47
Machines and tools	57, 869. 30
Total	104, 571. 77

TOOLS FOR BORING.—The boring tools (Fig. 1) and the first enlarging tool of the shaft No. 1, which we have previously described, were again employed for boring the main shaft; but to reach the diameter of $4^m.10$ a third tool was used, the blade of which was $3^m.95$ wide, and with the teeth $4^m.10$. On account of these dimensions, they were obliged to make it of five pieces, united by bolts and keys. That part which contains the teeth was attached to the three arms united to a central rod adapted to the apparatus to which the boring tool is suspended. It was soon proved that the apparatus weighing eight tons was too light, and two additional blades had to be attached to it in order to augment its weight. One only of these blades was provided with teeth. The weight of the tool with these two additional blades reached about ten tons, but it proved still too light, and the one represented by Fig. 12, weighing fourteen tons, was used; and this weight was considered necessary in order to produce the best effect on hard rocks.

The work of sinking with the boring tools was preceded by the construction of a preliminary shaft 21 metres deep, lined with masonry, having a diameter of $5^m.50$ up to the working stage, at five metres from the ground, and for $4^m.50$ at the lower part.

The boring operations were divided into two periods. The first commenced on the 9th of June, 1864; and on the 18th of September, 1865, the central shaft had attained a depth of $148^m.03$ with the small forked trepan, (Fig. 1.) The daily progress varied from $0^m.89$ to $0^m.26$.

The enlargement was immediately made to $4^m.10$ with the large two-bladed trepan, and at that period (September 18, 1865) it reached a depth of $121^m.08$.

This first period lasted 448½ days. The working of the small trepan was only stopped one day, and that of the larger 22½ days; and it must be remembered that the small trepan had already traversed hard strata.

The second part of the operation was more difficult, on account of the hardness of the rocks. The large trepan was too light, while it could not be reasonably augmented on account of the weakness of the machines that worked it.

It was decided to bore the large shaft by three successive operations. A central hole, $1^{m}.37$, was first bored with the small trepan, (Fig. 2;) it was then enlarged to $2^{m}.50$ with the massive trepan, (Fig. 4;) so that there only remained for removal by the large tool an annular surface of about $0^{m}.75$.

The central shaft reached in this second period of 42 days, without stoppage, a depth of $170^{m}.85$; the mean daily progress was $0^{m}.54$. The enlargement to $2^{m}.50$ required 103½ days, including 13½ days' stoppage, to reach a depth of $164^{m}.08$; the daily progress averaged $0^{m}.38$. With the large trepan, in order to increase the depth from $121^{m}.08$ to $159^{m}.28$—that is to say, to enlarge to $4^{m}.10$ for a total height of $38^{m}.20$—216 days were required, including 43 days of stoppage; the daily progress, therefore, was only $0^{m}.22$.

Notwithstanding the small amount of labor to be performed by the large trepan, the accidents which occurred proved that the strength of the blade, of the arms of the holding bolts, as well as the teeth, was insufficient to act with effect against the red sandstone.

The bottom of the shaft on which the moss-box was placed was 159 metres below the surface, and the labor lasted twenty-nine months and a half. The expenses attending this operation were divided as follows:

	Francs.
Salary and wages	72, 738. 51
Fuel burned	27, 524. 60
Oil and grease	4, 720. 49
Ropes	3, 602. 55
Iron, steel, and repairing tools	16, 469. 83
Sundries	16, 603. 50
Total	141, 659. 31

TUBBING SHAFT No. 2.—The tubbing of this shaft was formed of 94 cylindrical sections, $3^{m}.40$ minimum diameter at the flanges. The height of the first section was $1^{m}.75$, and that of the others $1^{m}.50$. The flanges were $0^{m}.04$ thick and $0^{m}.08$ wide on the inside of the cylinder. Between the flanges there are two little horizontal collars $0^{m}.04$ high and $0^{m}.04$ deep, which were placed at equal distances apart. The general thickness of the cylindrical part was $0^{m}.060$ for the 14 lower sections, $0^{m}.055$ for the following, and successively $0^{m}.052$, $0^{m}.048$, $0^{m}.044$, $0^{m}.040$, $0^{m}.036$, $0^{m}.032$, $0^{m}.028$.

The shoulders or joints were faced perpendicularly with the axis, so as to make perfectly parallel surfaces. These sections, adjusted and placed one on the other, make a cylinder 141 metres high. Each flange has 50 equidistant holes $0^{m}.03$ in diameter, drilled in the center of the flange.

In order to do away with the use of the wooden shoe which had been fixed to the bottom of the moss-box in shaft No. 1, an outer flange was cast with the piece, which is much stronger. The moss-box is $1^{m}.75$ high; consequently the packing during the descent of the column was $1^{m}.54$ high by $0^{m}.17$ wide, representing a capacity of three cubic metres.

The cast-iron equilibrium bottom was made of one piece, the maximum diameter of which at the flange is $3^{m}.36$, which admitted of its passing inside the tubbing. This false bottom was bolted on an adjustment ring, as shown in Fig. 6. The same equilibrium column was employed as for shaft No. 1.

The castings for this shaft were made of refined iron manufactured at Hayanges, in the works of Mr. De Wendel. The cylinders were tried at a pressure of 28 atmospheres for the largest, of 24 for the second series, and successively 21, 18, 15, 12, 9, 6, 3 atmospheres for the parts composing the following series. The entire metallic column weighed about 635 tons, including the bolts and other accessories.

The lowering of the column was conducted in a similar manner to the one mentioned for the shaft No. 1. The moss-box having touched the bottom, the column descended regularly, compressing the moss, which was reduced to $0^{m}.15$ thickness—about one-tenth of its primitive volume. The weight of the tubbing exerted a pressure of 32 kilogrammes on the square centimetre. On the 29th of December, 1866, all the parts of the tubbing were ready for lowering, and on the 16th of February, 1867, the moss-box came in contact with the sole of the pit.

Thus, this work was effected in fifty days. The expense was:

	Francs.
Price of sections	138, 494. 34
Lead for joints	3, 601. 10
Bolts, &c	4, 915. 20
Red lead	126. 40
Tar for painting	443. 80
Netting	25. 00
Moss	40. 00
Wood	1, 461. 05
Salary and wages	8, 456. 44
Fuel burned	3, 357. 45
Oil and grease	754. 40
Various expenditures	7, 544. 79
Total	169, 220. 07

CONCRETING AND PACKING SHAFT No. 2.—The operation of laying the concrete in this shaft was exactly the same as for shaft No. 1, except that four spoons were used. The concrete was composed of the same materials. The operation commenced on the 1st of March, 1867, was finished on the 6th of April following, and cost 15,000 francs.

The operation of packing was effected in the same manner as for the shaft No. 1, with this difference, that the adjusting cylinder placed between the coffer-dams and the moss-box was two metres high. The cost of this labor was estimated at 10,000 francs.

From what has been described, the cost of the shaft No. 2 can be estimated as follows:

	Francs.
Preliminary works	104, 571. 77
Boring the shaft	141, 659. 31
Piping	169, 220. 07
Concreting	15, 000. 00
Packing	10, 000. 00
Total	440, 451. 15

or at the rate of 3,100 francs per running metre.

The preliminary works commenced in September, 1863, and on the 6th of April the concreting was finished; the work lasted three years and a half.

BORING APPARATUS.

The slide or jar represented by Figs. 21 and 22, Plate I, is one of the important parts of the boring apparatus, since without it it would be scarcely possible to strike a blow with the trepan without breaking the rods.

The boring rods in the operations described were eighteen metres long and eighteen square centimetres in section. Their dimensions were increased in order to sustain the great shocks to which they were exposed.

The dredging spoon which was used for the removal of the debris is represented by Fig. 15. It was formed of a sheet-iron cylinder one metre in diameter and two metres high, with two valves at the bottom to facilitate emptying the mud when raised to the mouth of the pit. Its construction, it will be seen, is similar to the sand-pump used in boring petroleum wells, but it was much broader and shorter. Its capacity was about $1^{m}.50$; consequently it would contain from three to four tons of debris, and this amount would be extracted at each elevation. It was so suspended, a little above the center of gravity, that it could be overturned by a slight effort after removing a key which secured it in its vertical position while in the shaft. The hoisting was done by means of the capstan, a rope being used.

BORING TOOLS USED AT HÔPITAL.—The hook represented by Fig. 16 was used most when the boring rods were broken. Its epicycloidal form permits it to hook the rods which may be standing obliquely against the sides of the pit after a fracture. By turning the hook they are made to assume a vertical position, and are caught below the shoulder, and are brought into the narrow part of the hook, so that they can be raised. The pincers, *la fauchère*, (Fig. 17,) are for a similar purpose, and are adapted to seizing and raising rods that may have been broken immediately below the shoulder. The lower part is an annular shoe, or disk-shaped ring, which limits the separation of two blades or jaws pitted with sharp teeth on their inner surfaces. When this tool is used these jaws are kept open by a block of wood; but when it is brought over the rod or object to be seized the block is displaced by the end of the latter, and the jaws then close tightly upon the rod and hold it while it is raised out of the pit.

The grasping hook (Fig. 18) was used with advantage to raise masses of iron or steel and the teeth of the trepan which became detached or broken during the work. It has two arms jointed like a parallelogram, on the ends of which the grasping hooks are placed. The rods which form the slide are loaded with a weight, placed as required on the cross-bar *a a*, and it is this load which produces the friction on the bottom. The rods are raised by means of a rope, the extremity of which is held at the surface. This tool is closed while it is suspended to the boring rod and while the load bears on the cross-bar *a a;* when it is lowered the load is raised by means of the rope, the boring rods are pushed down, and this causes the grasping irons to open. If at this moment the load is again placed on the cross-bar *a a*, and if, on the other hand, the boring rods are gently drawn up, the grasping hooks close and scrape the bottom, retaining tightly between them any hard object that they encounter.

The stoppages and accidents which arose from the trepans employed at the works of L'Hôpital, as well as those which occurred from the use of instruments too weak to resist the shocks, and the frequent repairs of the slide, led Mr. Kind to modify the construction of his trepans. He exhibited a model of a new description of tool, with which the fall is unimpeded, and which we will now briefly describe.

The figure of the trepan (Fig. 19) shows that the teeth-holder, instead of having a smooth surface at its base, is graduated in steps, so as to cut the earth and rock in steps inclining toward the center of the pit. A guide fixed by four bolts to the teeth-holder enters the central shaft and causes the enlarging tool to remain perfectly vertical.

Three vertical arms or standards connect the teeth-holder with a double cross-bar placed at the upper part of the tool. Two oak bars are fixed to the arms and the cross-bar, and serve as guides for the tool at its upper part. The middle standard, or central shaft, is made long enough to be connected by keys and plates to the apparatus above, designed to give the unimpeded fall to the trepan.

This apparatus for unimpeded or free fall is operated in the following manner: When the entire apparatus is raised the water of the shaft bears on the disk *d*, and the carriers *e e* are tightened under the blocks *b b*, which allows of the trepan being removed. During the descent the water opposes resistance to the disk, the carriers *e e* separate themselves by the action of the rods, and the trepan falls freely. When the trepan has to be raised, the wedges *g g*, which rise in contact with the blocks, allow of the entire apparatus being raised.

This new description of trepan led Mr. Kind to believe that he might make use of the dredging tool represented at Fig. 20. This is a cylindrical tub or vessel, intended to receive the debris while the central shaft is being enlarged. It is slightly conical and provided with four arms which expand like a parachute and sweep around the top and sides of the smaller pit. The rock, crushed by the larger trepan sliding on the inclined bottom, falls into this vessel, and the broken teeth follow the same direction and no longer form an impediment to the work. This device is a very ingenious one, but experience must, however, decide whether this kind of spoon will meet Mr. Kind's expectations.

CONCLUSION.

The successful boring of the Hôpital shafts leaves no room to doubt the advantages of the system of boring *à niveau plein;* and we recapitulate these advantages as follows:

1. *Complete insulation of the watered strata*, by means of the water-tight tubbing.

2. *Great strength of the lining of the shaft.*—It is evident that the annular circular tubbings are stronger than the segmental. The following experiment made at Fourchambault will give an idea of the resistance which this cylindrical tubbing offers: A section $1^{m}.80$ in diameter inside the flanges and $0^{m}.025$ thick was submitted to an external pressure of 37 atmospheres; it resisted perfectly, while the pipe enveloping it, which was $0^{m}.065$ thick besides the rims inside, broke from the internal pressure. On the other hand, the pumping of the water which arises in the method called *à niveau plat*, produces excavations varying in size. The slides and broken strata which follow, besides being dangerous in future working, often produce disastrous effects on the sides of the shafts.

3. *Considerable reduction of expense.*—In every case where water-bearing strata have to be traversed, the economy cannot be contested; thus, the two shafts at the Hôpital have not cost 700,000 francs, while those of Carling, Merleback, and Stiring, in the same department, each cost several millions.

4. *Economy of time.*—We have shown that, notwithstanding stoppages in the main shaft, the boring was effected in twenty-nine and a half months, and the lowering of the tubbing in four and a half months. It is to be expected that future works will be executed more rapidly than the first.

5. *Possibility of traversing all kinds of strata, of whatever thickness or description.*—Boring operations at great depths are very limited. Drawing off the water and making water-tight tubbing offer nearly insurmountable difficulties, particularly so in traversing the sands of shifting soils. The extraction of the water itself becomes an insurmountable obstacle, irrespective of the means at the disposal of the miner. Undoubtedly the boring *à niveau plein* at large diameters will necessitate great precaution, but the results obtained at Bessaix in 1862 and 1863, in traversing, with a diameter of $3^{m}.65$, a stratum of shifting soil eight metres thick, tend to show that the difficulties of this kind of work are not as great as they appear.

II.—SINKING AND BORING ARTESIAN WELLS.

The apparatus exhibited by the houses of Degousée and Ch. Laurent and by Messrs. Dru Brothers is designed chiefly for sinking artesian wells of large diameter, but is equally applicable to sinking shafts of large section.

The apparatus, doubtless, does not present, for the most part, the interest of a new invention; but in examining the details of its construction, it is easy to see that the novel and diversified condition in which the sinkings have been executed, and the unforeseen accidents which these have produced, have been studied with great care and intelligence by these able engineers, and that all the teachings of practice have been profited by and have led to many important modifications and simplification of the forms of the tools.

We have already stated, in describing the method of sinking *à niveau plein*, (sinking a shaft kept full of water,) that the boring rods applicable to artesian wells, before the wells of Passy were sunk, did not exceed $0^{m}.30$ in diameter. To-day the two wells undertaken by the city of Paris—one at La Chapelle, by Messrs. Degousée and Ch. Laurent, the other at La Butte-aux-Cailles, near the Ivry station, by Messrs. Dru Brothers—have been commenced at a diameter of $1^{m}.80$.

We will now give some explanations of the tools and methods employed in boring these wells. It is evident that these tools and methods can be applied to sink mining shafts of three or four metres in diameter.

The boring apparatus comprises two essential parts—the tools which serve to excavate the earth, and the appliances at the surface for working or handling the tools, which become much more important as the diameter of the wells or shafts is increased.

CONSTRUCTIONS AT THE SURFACE.

The preparations for sinking made at the surface by the house of Degousée and Ch. Laurent, at the wells of La Chapelle, are completely different from those we have described as made at the wells of the Hôpital. Their preliminary work appears to be much better designed and executed, and the results obtained up to this day confirm the opinion. In order to show more distinctly the differences that exist between the mode of preparation which Mr. Kind still follows and that followed by Messrs. Degousée and Ch. Laurent, we will describe, in a few words, the appliances for working the boring tools of the artesian wells of La Chapelle.

The machine is worked by a horizontal steam-engine of 15 horse-power. The fly-wheel shaft makes 50 revolutions per minute. It carries, first, a pinion of $0^{m}.30$ diameter; secondly, two brakes; thirdly, two clutches; fourthly and lastly, a pulley of $1^{m}.50$ diameter.

The pinion of $0^{m}.30$ diameter drives a toothed wheel fixed on the axle of the drum of the capstan, upon which the chains for lifting the shafts of the borers are wound, and also the percussion and cleansing apparatus. The diameter of the drum of the capstan is $0^{m}.55$; its length is $1^{m}.60$. It has a spiral groove which guides the chains and causes them to wind regularly upon it. The pulley of $1^{m}.50$ diameter is belted to another pulley of $1^{m}.00$ diameter, fixed at the extremity of an axle which carries at the other end a pinion of $0^{m}.40$ diameter. This pinion is geared with a wheel of $2^{m}.00$ diameter, fixed on a second axle, where is also fixed the crank-plate which, by means of a connecting rod, gives a reciprocating motion to the striking beam. This beam is supported at a point about two-thirds of its whole length distant from the connecting-rod end.

The two clutches mentioned serve, on one part, to throw into gear the pinion of $0^{m}.30$ with the driving wheel of the drum of the capstan, and, on the other part, to drive the pulley of $1^{m}.50$ diameter, keyed on the fly-wheel shaft, by which motion is given to the striking beam, at the end of which the boring tools are attached.

The two brakes placed upon the fly-wheel shaft are for the purpose of regulating the speed of the descent of the tools, the weight of which might cause a great acceleration of speed, and, consequently, a fracture, which is always to be dreaded.

The timber framing which forms the derrick or tower for the sinking of the wells is more simply arranged than that adopted by Mr. Kind. The tools, in place of being received upon a platform about ten metres above the surface, are upon the surface itself, and it is, consequently, much more easy to work them. The linked chain for lifting the tools has stood the wear of ten years without any accident; while the breaking of the cables employed in the system of Messrs. Kind and Chaudron have occasioned, as we have seen, serious accidents and delays.

To finish the comparison of the two different methods of surface preparations which we are considering, we will state that at the boring of the wells of Passy, undertaken by Mr. Kind, there were two machines of 25 horse-power, one of 10 horse-power working the striking beam, and one of 15 horse-power working the capstan drum. The trepan, at the shank, did not weigh more than about two tons. Messrs. Degousée and Ch. Laurent used an engine of only 15 horse-power to work their trepan, which weighed about four tons, and to bring the broken or bored earth to the surface. This engine did not require any repairs, except such as are ordinarily necessary during a service of two years.

BORING TOOLS OF DEGOUSÉE AND LAURENT.

We will now consider the boring tools devised by Messrs. Degousée and Ch. Laurent.

The construction of the trepan employed at the artesian well of La Chapelle differs completely from that of Mr. Kind. It is represented by Figs. 21 and 22, Plate I. It is composed of six branches, so arranged as to break up the earth in an annular belt or zone, leaving a central core. The six teeth which are keyed into the blade-holder are $0^{m}.35$ wide, and the mode of fixing them into the six branches is so secure and solid that, up to this date, no accident has happened. Even when a tooth becomes unkeyed it cannot get out of the blade-holder, while at the shaft of the Hôpital there have been twenty-three teeth out of their sockets, all of which fell into the shaft. One of these accidents caused a stoppage of a month.

The percussion of the trepan with the regular rotating movement cuts out an annular channel of $0^{m}.45$ to $0^{m}.50$ large, leaving in the center of the shaft an unworked piece of earth, or core, of $0^{m}.80$ or $0^{m}.90$ diameter. This mass, when in slightly coherent earth, crumbles down and forms an irregular cone. In this case they bolt on one diameter a transverse blade, which triturates the core.

This trepan weighs about four tons. Its first cost is greater than that of Mr. Kind's, but it proves in practice to be much more solid and durable, and it works better.

Messrs. Degousée and Ch. Laurent have been very successful in giving a free fall or drop to their trepan. With more than ten thousand blows, the trepan has not once failed to be caught again upon the descent of the rods, and its fall has always worked with the greatest regularity, while at the shaft of the Hôpital eighteen fractures of pieces of the slide have occasioned a stoppage of more than a month. The contrivance for the free fall of the trepan is constructed as follows: A movable piece surrounds the shaft above the hooks and terminates in a fork, of which the two branches extend below the cutters and touch the bottom of the bore. This piece is not lifted, unless the borer is raised more than the stroke allowed by the collar which attaches around the hooks. The upper part of the hooks lifted by the boring rod slides, therefore, in the collar, and, meeting a striker which makes them open, the tool immediately falls with all its weight on the bottom of the bore. The boring rod, being lowered, catches the tool again by the hooks, and this action is repeated so as to obtain a succession of blows. The figures show the arrangement of the fixed shaft and the hooks for the drop.

The suspension rods employed by Messrs. Degousée and Ch. Laurent are of iron. They have a section of $0^m.045$ square, and are $12^m.00$ long. These rods have worked for two years without accident, and we prefer them to those made of wood, for the following reasons: It is evident that wood at a great depth will take from the pressure of the water a density at least equal to that of the water; and, moreover, the iron fittings add to the weight in a certain proportion; and if we compare the sections of the shafts or wooden rods of the wells at the Hôpital to those of iron at the wells of La Chapelle, it is seen that the metre in length of the first weighs at least 35 kilogrammes, (70 pounds,) while that of the second does not exceed 16 kilogrammes, (32 pounds.) It is true that as the wooden rods displace a greater quantity of water their weight is diminished, but this small advantage is largely over-balanced by their rapid deterioration, whether in store or at work. The wood in drying heats and loses its qualities. Well made, their construction appears to us sufficiently costly to make the matter of renewing them at each sinking rather an important item; they augment sensibly the cost of work to be done. On the other hand, the iron shafts that can be balanced as practiced by Messrs. Degousée and Laurent require for their descent and elevation but a little more force, and with steam-engines this increase of expense is so little that it may be disregarded.

The draining and cleaning tools of the wells at La Chapelle differ equally from those of Mr. Kind; and we think them also superior. The modification of the trepan intended to work out the annular groove or zone led to a modification of the auger, which is annular and composed of nine augers joined together, of $0^m.35$ diameter.

The spoon or bucket which lifts the detritus in the middle of the wells is a cylinder $1^m.00$ in diameter and $2^m.50$ in height. The bottom, in place of carrying two valves, is pierced with seven round holes, which are closed by hemispherical hollow valves carrying in their axis a shaft which traverses the whole length of the spoon. This shaft is terminated by a handle which permits the workmen to lift up the valve in order to empty out the mud when the bucket is withdrawn from the well. This arrangement is intended to obviate the inconvenience of the hinged valves, which often, by not completely closing, let the matter in the bucket escape during the ascent of the dredge.

The bucket at La Chapelle is emptied with great ease, it being lifted one metre above the surface and placed on a little truck, which carries it immediately under a crane placed at the side where the contents are to be emptied.

The recovering tools are composed simply of the ordinary screw bell, (*cloche à vis*,) a grapnel, and a new form of pincers, with four branches. These four branches are arranged in a parallelogram, and one of their ends is fixed to a single piece bored and tapped in its center. It is easy to understand the part this plays: in raising or lowering the nut in the screw which is attached to the boring rods, the four branches expand or contract at will, which, resting on the bottom of the well, gather the objects which may be there. The working of this apparatus is very simple. It is sufficient, when the pincers have arrived at their destination, to turn the boring rods, and when the piece they wish to catch is taken and caught, it produces a resistance which indicates that there is nothing more to do than to lift the whole apparatus to the surface. Every time this apparatus has been tried it has given the results expected.

TUBBING.

The artesian well of La Chapelle traverses the Tertiary strata of the Paris basin, and penetrates the chalks and marls of the Secondary.

According to the agreement between the contractors and the city, the boring is expected to be 600 metres deep before it reaches the water-bearing bed of the greensand formation. After working two years, the well has already (1867) reached a depth of 337 metres, but it has been found necessary to tub or line the shaft to avoid the caving which would inevitably happen without it.

A first column of sheet-iron lining, $1^{m}.80$ diameter, $34^{m}.50$ high, and weighing about thirty-six tons, was put in immediately below the preparatory pit, which last was lined with masonry to a distance of about six metres below the surface, where the working platform was placed.

A second column, $1^{m}.70$ diameter, 135 metres high, and weighing 11 tons, was next put in; and lastly, a third column was put down just to the chalk. This column has a height of 139 metres, its diameter $1^{m}.37$, and its weight about 110 tons.

The tubes are made of sheet iron of a mean thickness of $0^{m}.02$; the height of each section being determined by the breadth of the iron plates. These plates were fastened together by rivets with countersunk heads, so that the interior and exterior surface of the lining were quite smooth.

To form one of these cylinders, *two* sheets of iron of the thickness of $0^{m}.01$ are taken and riveted together in such manner that one of them, the inner one for example, projects slightly beyond the other, and thus forms a shoulder to which the next section above can be riveted. By this arrangement it will be seen that each column of tubbing presented the same diameter throughout its length. When the sections of the column are thus prepared, they are lowered and put together as they descend into the well.

This operation is performed in the following manner:

A wooden frame is made and supported upon a wheeled truck. This frame is composed of two strong vertical walls of a height of four or five metres, connected at their upper part by a cap or top, to which four nuts are fixed to receive four screws intended to sustain the pipe in its descent. Each of these screws is worked by two men by means of a crank and conical pinion conveniently arranged. Plate I, Fig. 7.

The lower part of these four screws is fixed to a strong circular wooden plate, about $0^{m}.50$ thick, and equal in diameter to the inner diameter of the column that is to be lowered.

Upon the working platform a species of tubbing in wood is placed, the interior diameter of which is equal to the exterior of the iron tubbing or pipe. The height of this tubbing is two metres; the segments of which it is composed are united together, and can be drawn together or expanded by means of screws, so as to squeeze the column and act as a clamp or support during its descent. When this kind of tubbing is put in place, and the frame which carries the screws is put in the axis of the well, the first section of pipe is brought forward and placed over the well. Previously several iron ears are bolted upon the interior face of the tub, and about a metre below its upper edge, the use of which will be presently explained. Other projecting ears are fixed in the inside of the tub, and on these ears the lower part of the wooden plate is allowed to rest, and is then bolted to them. When the work is thus prepared, this first tub is lowered until the outer ears rest upon the upper edge of the wooden tubbing which surrounds the column on the outside. The inside ears are then removed and the pipe is supported upon the outer tub. The inner plate of wood is then lifted up by the aid of the screws, and the rivet holes of the ears are closed up by hot rivets with countersunk heads. The second cylinder is then placed in the axis of the well. This second cylinder has inside and outside ears like the first, and the circular plate is introduced and bolted to the ears. These hold it at its upper part, and it is then lowered regularly, with the aid of the screws, until the lower part fits into the first cylinder. The two sections are then riveted together by hot rivets. The tub is then lifted a little in order to remove the outside ears of the first section of the cylinder, and the whole is allowed to descend by its own weight till the outer ears of the top cylinder rest in their turn upon the upper part of the wooden tubbing. They proceed in the same way for all the other sections of the column or tubbing of the well until it is finished.

The lowering screws are each calculated to withstand a strain of fifty tons; but to prevent a too rapid descent of the lining when it has attained a considerable weight, Messrs. Degousée and Ch. Laurent make use of the species of tubbing upon the surface of the working pits already noticed. This tubbing not only serves to guide the column and to make it descend vertically, but also, and above all, to act as a powerful break, and thus enable the workmen to control the velocity of the descent at will.

Tightening the segment screws gives a strong compression and friction over a height of two metres, sufficient to control the descent of the tubbing.

The three columns of sheet-iron lining which have been mentioned were put in place by this system of operating with the greatest ease, at the rate of four metres a day, including the time spent in riveting the sections of the tubbing.

When the artesian well of La Chapelle is sunk to the depth of 600 metres, a tub in one column will be lowered to the same depth. Messrs. Degousée and Ch. Laurent propose to employ the same method of lowering, and there is no doubt that these able engineers will succeed completely in this magnificent work.

The false bottom for the tubbing, which is used by Messrs. Kind and Chaudron, would not answer in this case, because it would prevent the water from rising in the well. The work carried forward at La Chapelle proves that by the system *à niveau plein*, of sinking from the surface, large shafts for mines can be executed by the tools and method of Messrs. Degousée and Ch. Laurent with great success in similar formations.

TREPAN WITH FREE FALL.

There remains little to be said of the ordinary boring tools shown by this house, all are known; we will give only some details of the tool with free fall and on the bayonet principle, and of those tools for verifying the nature and the inclination of the strata.

The trepan with slides working the free fall is provided internally with two bulges, which force the palls to open and to abandon the head which forms the upper part of the slide screwed to the great shaft which carries the trepan. The height of the fall depends on the distance which exists between the pincers and the head of the disengager at the time when the trepans of the little additional shaft are both upon the bottom. Every time that it is wished to alter this fall, it is sufficient to divide the lower part of the additional shaft, and to replace it by a longer or shorter one.

The first instrument for taking a sample of the strata is called the *decoupeur*. It is made with a head terminated by four vertical branches carrying at their ends four chisels. The four branches are strengthened together between two concentric pieces of sheet-iron, and riveted. Any length can be given to these branches. This tool is used by percussion, like the trepan.

The core once formed, they lower a punch. It is composed of a pipe fastened throughout its entire height to a fork, one of the branches of which receives a flat band of iron the same length as itself.

A wedge is intended to work between the band of iron and the band of the fork; the first is furnished with three pins riveted to the pipe; the iron band is pierced with three holes intended to receive, without being fixed thereto, the ends of these pins.

The punch is lowered into the well, the wedge being placed as low as the slide will admit of. At the moment that the instrument is about $0^m.10$ or $0^m.15$ from the bottom, the rod is left to fall; the shock makes the wedge enter between the two branches, which open, and presenting a thickness greater than that of the annular space produced by *le decoupeur*. A horizontal thrust is thus created which throws the iron pipes on one side, and consequently the cylinder of earth which it envelopes is detached from the bottom of the shaft and remains caught in the instrument by the springs.

Messrs. Dru Brothers, successors to Messrs. Mulot, also exhibited a complete series of boring tools, among them a model of a trepan which they employ for the boring at the *Butte-aux-Cailles*.

This trepan, (Fig. 23, Plate I,) is a *lame pleine*, (full blade.) The teeth are let into the blade their full size, and are maintained in their sockets by bolts. This arrangement holds them more solidly than keys, and allows of their being tightened when they get loose.

To obtain a free drop of the trepan, these engineers usually employ a mechanism which opens the hooks by the shock of the working beam striking against a fixed point.

For the large shaft they have replaced this apparatus by another. When in boring the rod has arrived at its greatest height by the upward movement of the working beam, the tool does not fall, but is unhooked when the rod descends. This is effected by the action of a cleat which bears against the side of the hook and opens it; the tool then falls to the bottom of the shaft and is followed slowly by the boring rod, which almost immediately re-seizes the tool. Mr. Dru thinks that he has obtained by this arrangement for the simultaneous descent of the tool and the boring rod the most favorable condition for the preservation of the working parts, and for the regularity of the sinking.

CHAPTER II.

DRILLING ENGINES, AND COAL-CUTTING MACHINES.

MACHINES FOR BORING OR DRILLING BY PERCUSSION—TROUILLET'S EXCAVATOR—DRILLING MACHINES ACTUATED BY STEAM OR COMPRESSED AIR—SOMMEILIER'S DRILLING ENGINE—DÖRING'S DRILL—BERGSTROEM'S DRILL—HAUPT'S DRILL—BEAUMONT AND LOCOCK'S DRILLING ENGINE—DRILLING BY ROTATION OF THE TOOLS—LISBET AND JACQUET'S BORER—LESCHOT'S DRILL—DE LA ROCHE-TOLLAY AND PERRETT'S BORING APPARATUS—MACHINES FOR CUTTING OUT COAL.

The application of machinery, worked by steam or other power, to the drilling or perforation of rocks originated in the United States. Before the year 1853 several such machines were at work in North America. Some served to perforate the rock by means of drills worked by percussion, and were employed simultaneously with powder; others, applied to the driving of underground galleries, acted directly to cut and break down the whole of the rock of the size of the gallery, and were not intended to prepare the rock for subsequent use of powder. Messrs. Talbot and Wilson had invented one of these machines, which drove a gallery of $5^{m}.20$ diameter by the aid of cutting disks fixed to the arms of a kind of wheel turning on a central axis. These disks, in turning on their axes, scooped like a plane at the same time that they were carried around by the rotary motion of the central axis. They formed an annular groove or channel, leaving in the center of the gallery a core of solid ground. This machine had a certain amount of success in the talcose schists, where the core could be easily broken off. The speed of working was $1^{m}.23$ (4.04 feet) for twelve hours of work. The expense was estimated at 100 francs per running metre, but it is evident that in hard rocks this machine could not compete with those which only drilled the holes or chambers for the reception of powder, by which the rocks could be blown out much cheaper than they could be cut away.

Other machines were constructed so as to cut away only a small part of the rock, isolating it by deep grooves or channels into large blocks, which were then broken up either with levers or by powder.

All these machines were worked by steam, and their mode of action was sometimes that of the common drill of the miner, sometimes that of a cutting tool, but in neither of these machines had the idea of boring like an auger into wood, or a drill into iron, been applied.

For some years this last-mentioned mode of boring had been employed in France with better results than those of other machines which had preceded them.

Perforators, or rock-drilling machines, can be divided, according to their mode of working, into two principal systems—percussion and rotary.

The different machines of the two systems which were shown at the Exposition, or which have been employed in driving large tunnels, will now be noticed.

I.—MACHINES FOR BORING BY PERCUSSION.

The apparatus for boring by percussion can be divided into two classes—the first, those that are worked by manual labor; the second, those which use compressed air or steam as the motive power. Only one apparatus, the *cavateur Trouillet*, is comprised in the first class.

TROUILLET'S EXCAVATOR.

This apparatus, invented by Mr. Trouillet, is intended to scoop out the rock at the bottom of the drill holes in mines, so as to give a chamber for the reception of a larger quantity of powder than the drill hole would contain. It can also be used to enlarge a round hole throughout its whole length, beginning the work at the bottom.[1]

The principal parts of this apparatus are—

1. An iron bar or stem *d*, projecting $0^{m}.80$ beyond the tube *k*. This stem is provided with a pair of cutters *e e*, (Fig. 1, Plate II,) fixed together by hinges, which allow each to describe a quarter of a circle. The pin *g*, upon which they are hinged, is kept in place by the side of the tube *k*. There is, however, but a small amount of pressure on this pin, for the tools are so arranged as to receive the shock due to the percussion directly. The lower part of the stem is made of steel.

2. A pair of tools or cutters *e e*, (Fig. 1,) in steel, destined to attack the rock by the movement they receive from the stem, worked like the ordinary mining bar. For convenience of working, Mr. Trouillet has made a series of tools, composed of four pairs of different sizes.

3. A tightening piece composed of two pieces, united by nuts, and intended to fix the tube at the required height. This piece rests by its lower extremity on the top of a long hollow screw which, by working in a nut in the top of a standard, enables the operator to change the height of the tool. The hollow screw is made of bronze, or brass, and the nut is of cast iron.

4. A tube *k*, (Fig. 1,) for guiding the stem. This is a little longer than the depth at which it is required to enlarge the hole. The lower part of this tube is closed by a piece of iron solidly riveted. Two steel anvils rest upon this piece, (see Fig. 2,) and the width of each anvil is equal to that of the steel tools, which, by striking the anvils, are suddenly thrown apart. These anvils are only fixed by a rivet, which can be drawn out when the anvils ought to be renewed. They are arranged so that the tools or cutters striking them can be extracted from the inside of the tube by an opening left for that purpose.

[1] An apparatus similar to this was made in San Francisco, California, a few years since. The cutters were adapted to hand-drills alone.—W. P. R.

In working with this machine two workmen give to the stem *d* a vertical movement, like an ordinary jumper, causing the cutters *e e* to strike against the sides of the rock. Another workman turns the whole machine by means of handles. In this manner the cutters are made to strike successively all the parts of the cavity to be hollowed out, and follow a series of heliacal lines. When the screw has arrived at the end of its stroke the operation commences again in the contrary direction, and so on until the cutters have arrived at their maximum of expansion. This will be known by the collar of the stem coming in contact with the tube. The tools are then changed for larger ones, until the cavity has been sufficiently enlarged; the largest tools can produce a chamber with a diameter of $0^{m}.30$.

Mr. Trouillet states that, beginning with the little tool, the jumper ought to strike twenty blows for one turn of the screw, while in using the largest it ought to make seventy blows. He also says that a chamber of $0^{m}.30$ by $0^{m}.50$ in height, holding 35 kilogrammes of powder, requires fifty hours' work in rock of ordinary hardness.

The price of this percussion apparatus complete, to work up to three metres of height, is 650 francs, delivered in Paris. Inspection alone of the machine shows that it is only applicable to rocks of a certain hardness. It has been employed with success in some sea-ports, where a series of holes in line have been fired with the electric wire. The lifting of the debris is made by a scoop, shaped like an Archimedian screw.

BORING BY STEAM OR COMPRESSED AIR.

The boring machines of the second class, actuated by steam or compressed air, are divided into two systems, according to their mode of working.

The first includes the apparatus which serve to make the holes to be blasted with powder. The second comprises the machines intended to cut out the rock the size of the gallery by direct action, unaided by powder.

The best known power machines for boring blasting holes are—

1. Those of Mr. Sommeilier, employed at Mont Cenis.
2. The apparatus of Mr. Döring, of Prussia, employed for the last three years at the Vieille Montagne mine.
3. The borer of Mr. Bergstroem, of Sweden.
4. And lastly, the steam-borer of Mr. Herman Haupt, C. E., of Philadelphia, United States.

BORER OF MR. SOMMEILIER.

Before undertaking the description of this machine, which has produced such a sensation among engineers, we will give a few words upon the machines which give motion to the striker. These machines are composed of air-compressors and iron pipes to carry the compressed air to the boring apparatus.

On the Italian side of the Alps, at Bardonnèche, (the Piedmont entrance,) the air-compressors are a kind of hydraulic ram, the valves of which are arranged in such a way that at each lift of the valve admitting water a certain quantity of air, at a pressure of five atmospheres, is forced into a reservoir ten metres long and seventeen cubic metres capacity.

The air-compressors at Modena (north side) are composed of a horizontal cylinder full of water, in which a piston works, and of two vertical cylinders receiving the air and provided with valves in their upper part. By the motion of the piston a quantity of air, equal to that of the water displaced by the movement, is introduced and expelled at each stroke. The air is conducted to the boring machine by cast-iron pipes of $0^{m}.20$. It has been ascertained that the loss due to friction is about one-tenth of an atmosphere.

The boring machines of Mr. Sommeilier (Figs. 6, 7, 8, Plate II) are essentially composed of a cylinder H, in which the compressed air works. The piston-rod traverses the heads of this cylinder, and carries on one side a screw which commands the distributor. A machine I, similar to a steam-engine, commands the slide-valve of this distributor. This arrangement was adopted inasmuch as the stroke of the piston which carries the drill varies with the hardness of the rock and the position of the drill in the hole, and no reliance could be placed upon the introduction of the compressed air by means of the percussion alone.

The whole apparatus weighs 200 kilogrammes. It rests upon two beds $0^{m}.03$ wide by $0^{m}.05$ high, and $0^{m}.09$ apart. Their length is $2^{m}.70$. They are cut upon their inside faces in the form of a nut, in which the screw V moves, (Figs. 6, 7,) and the edge of their lower faces is formed like a rack.

The cylinder of the distributing machine is $0^{m}.06$ in diameter. The stroke of the piston is $0^{m}.10$; it is furnished with a connecting rod and a crank, and by means of gearing gives a rotary movement to a square stem T, (Fig. 7,) upon which is fixed, first, a pall D, which advances tooth by tooth the ratchet-wheel R, provided with sixteen teeth, and fixed invariably on the prolongation of the piston-rod in such manner that after sixteen blows of the drill, the ratchet, the piston, and the drill have made a complete revolution; second, a plate furnished with a cam C, which moves the slide-rod *t*, and if we suppose that the slide-valve pushed by this cam advances and stops the aperture for admission, the air which acts escapes through the opening which communicates with the atmosphere by the hollow passage in the slide-valve, and the piston is carried to its original position by the constant pressure which is exerted on its front face. At this instant the valve abandoned by the cam C is pushed back suddenly to its initial position by the difference of pressure which is exerted upon the two faces, and thus opens the inlet port.

The diameter of the piston of the boring machine is $0^{m}.06$, its stroke $0^{m}.20$, and it gives 200 blows per minute. This machine is single-acting. The compressed air enters by the opening in constant communication by the conduit with the front part of the cylinder; when the piston is at the end of its stroke the slide opens the inlet port, and the piston only advances in consequence of the difference of the pressure of air on its back face fitted with a slender rod, and on its internal face, of which the section is reduced by the large shaft of the tool-carrier. The impulsive force upon the piston is for some of these machines 95 kilogrammes, and for others 150 kilogrammes.

We have before explained how the drill is made to rotate; it remains to show how it is made to advance, and how it can be rapidly taken out in case of need. If the screw V, constantly geared into its nut formed by the internal filleted faces of the beds, were fixed permanently upon the shaft T′, it would follow that in each rotation of the drill it would advance the cylinder by a length equal to its pitch; but it should, on the contrary, only advance at the same speed that the drill enters the rock, therefore the screw V works loosely upon the shaft, and only turns when the clutch-box M catches it, this clutch being continually pushed by the action of a spiral spring N, which is retained by the rod F, the use of which will be explained, (Fig. 7.)

The rod F connected with the clutch carries at its front extremity—

1. A fork, the teeth of which rest against those of a rack on the lower part of the bed plate.

2. A prolongation Q, terminated by a semicircular appendage.

If we now suppose that the piston is reaching the end of its stroke, with the drill scarcely touching the bottom of the hole, the tappet P fixed upon the shaft of the tool-carrier (Fig. 6) strikes the appendage Q, forces it to drop, and detaches the tooth S from the rack. Then the clutch-box M, impelled by the spring N, catches and turns the screw V. The striking cylinder advances till the fork S is caught by the following tooth of the rack, and thus disengages the clutch.

It may be granted that Mr. Sommeilier has constructed an ingenious machine, which fulfills the following conditions:

1. It strikes hard and rapid blows upon the rock.

2. It transmits a self-acting rotary motion to the drill, required to prevent it from becoming fixed in the hole.

3. It imparts also a progressive, self-acting, and regular advance to the drill as the hole deepens in working.

4. And lastly, it can be rapidly drawn back to change the tools.

The tool is a drill, with the cutting edge in the form of a Z; it makes a hole of $0^m.09$ and $0^m.04$, but in the first case it is furnished for $0^m.20$ behind its head with a bulge which trims or reams the holes to full size. The stroke of the machine is but $0^m.80$, but it can make a hole to a depth of $0^m.90$ by reason of the length of the drills, which vary from $0^m.50$ to $2^m.00$.

Let us now inquire if this apparatus has answered the expectations of its author, and if this system of percussion will really render the service expected from it. We do not hesitate to express the opinion that it has not, and the following data will, we think, prove beyond a doubt that a percussion machine is not the one that should be employed in this kind of work.

The apparatus placed before the breast of the gallery to be attacked carries 8 drills, which cover a section 4 metres wide by 3 metres high, equal to an area of 12 square metres. Eighty holes are bored, 6 of $0^{m}.09$ and 74 of $0^{m}.04$ diameter, and $0^{m}.90$ deep. The daily work has varied evidently according to the hardness of the rock; in March, 1863, it was $1^{m}.10$ in twenty-four hours, in April $1^{m}.40$, and in some parts of the strata even $2^{m}.50$; but when the bank of quartz was met, (which was 308 metres thick,) the advance was hardly $0^{m}.50$ per day.

During the month of March, 1863, it was shown that each explosion of $0^{m}.70$ to $0^{m}.80$ required six hours for boring the holes, and four hours for the miners carrying away the rubbish.

The staff employed for the boring of the holes during twenty-four hours was as follows:

	Men.
Two shifts	16
Miners	2
Laborers for taking away the debris	8
Superintendents	2
Total	28
Although we have not to take into account the motive engines, we ought to add that the compressors required	9
Total	37

If we examine the staff employed in repairing the tools, we remark that in 1863, for 8 machines working, there were 60 in the shop. At this time, when the work is carried on both from the French and the Italian sides, the number of engines working is 16, and of those in the workshops repairing 200.

In 1863, as we have stated, for repairing 8 perforators working in a coarse sandstone, (*grès à gros grains*,) the staff attached to the workshops was composed of—

	Men.
Blacksmiths repairing tools and parts of machines	14
Fitters, turners, firemen, and boiler-makers	10
Total	24

Thus 24 men were occupied daily in repairing 8 machines. At this time the number is much larger; unfortunately it is almost impossible to obtain exact accounts of the cost of repairing. All that we know to be exact is that at this time the work has been offered to a company at 6,000 francs per running metre, giving them all the apparatus; they to repair the tools and clear away the dirt. This was refused, although the price was equal to 500 francs per cubic metre.

The enormous shocks which the machine was subjected to obliged them to change the iron beds for Krupp steel ones; the springs often broke, and the drills cannot advance $0^{m}.20$ or $0^{m}.30$ without requiring repairs.

Even admitting the possibility of constructing these machines strong enough to resist these causes of destruction, we still say the percussion system presents such disadvantages that renders its adoption impossible; for when, by the blows of the drill, pieces of rock are broken off, and instead of being thrown out they are still subjected to the blows and reduced to powder, this causes a loss of work. It is true that, to aid in clearing the holes at Mont Cenis, they injected water under a pressure of five atmospheres, but this was abandoned because the tool became clogged. At this time a jet of air at five atmospheres is forced in and drives the dust from the bottom of the hole. This dusty atmosphere must be injurious to the health of the workmen.

Besides, when the drill has penetrated the rock a short distance, it is no longer guided and supported, and its vibrations are so considerable that they can only be compared to those of the axles of railway wheels. These vibrations evidently prevent the making of a uniformly circular hole, and leave ridges in the hole, which prevents the use of cartridges, which are much better than to ram in powder.

We ought, lastly, to add that the boring of the holes is but a part of the work to be done; there still remains the work of clearing out and removing the dirt and debris. It is necessary that the boring machine should be solid enough to require little repair, so that the cost for tools shall not be altogether out of proportion to the work done.

DÖRING'S BORER.

This apparatus is worked by compressed air, and is composed of a cylinder $0^{m}.400$ in diameter, and $0^{m}.300$ long, (Fig. 10, Plate II.) In this cylinder a piston moves, to which is fixed the stem of the drill. The compressed air is distributed by means of a slide-valve, and, after acting freely, escapes into the air. Two ratchet-wheels, furnished with dogs, are placed at the back of the cylinder, and are put in action by the prolonged rod of the piston by means of a fork which commands the dogs. One of the ratchet-wheels serves to give to the drill a rotary movement on its axis; the other ratchet, which is nearest to the cylinder, is equally commanded by the forks joined to the prolongation of the stem of this latter. This ratchet, by means of a toothed wheel with which it is connected, drives a gearing which advances the tool upon the screwed stem, which forms one of the supports. The arrangement of the tool is such that the drill only advances when the piston has run its stroke, a plan which we think is very defective. It is evident that the advance of the tool ought not to depend upon the stroke of the piston, but upon the hardness of the rock, as in Mr. Sommeilier's machine.

This apparatus of Döring weighs forty-five kilogrammes, and constitutes the borer, properly so called. It is erected upon a special carriage, which allows any direction to be given to the drill that is desired. The pressure of the air varies from $\frac{3}{4}$ of an atmosphere to $1\frac{1}{2}$. This machine has been employed for some few years at Moresnet, at La Vieille Montagne. The following information has been given to us by the chief engineer of this company.

The rock is a quartzose and porous dolomite. A six horse-power engine is required to work two machines; the air is compressed to $1\frac{1}{2}$ atmospheres. For one working machine it requires two in reserve. The speed per minute is $0^{m}.03$, including replacing the drills. Each drill will not bore more than $0^{m}.20$ to $0^{m}.30$ without being replaced. Its speed of advance at Vieille Montagne over ordinary borers has been treble in hard rock, but only double in soft rock.

With such results one may ask what is the real advantage of such an instrument which, with a force of three horse-power, does only three times or twice the work of a man?

We ought to add to these explanations that we assisted at experiments made at the Universal Exposition. The granite rock chosen for the trials was of ordinary density, and perfectly homogeneous. Nevertheless the tool underwent heavy shocks, although the pressure of the air did not exceed $1\frac{1}{2}$ atmospheres. The rate of speed was from $0^{m}.03$ to $0^{m}.055$ per minute; we ought also to add that the machine, valued at about 350 francs, required several days' repairing, valued at nearly 500 francs.

We are convinced that this apparatus would not stand one instant the shock produced by attacking quartz and flint under a pressure of five atmospheres. The cutting edge of the drills employed is about the same as those at Mont Cenis. The diameters of the holes are of $0^{m}.025$ and $0^{m}.030$.

BERGSTROEM'S PERFORATOR.

This borer, of which we can only give a very brief notice, because we did not see it at work at the Exposition, although efforts were made for that purpose, is operated by compressed air, but has the disadvantage over the preceding ones of not having a self-acting advance movement. The workman gives this movement by hand as required. It is represented by Figs. 11 and 12, Plate II. A A is a slide in two cylindrical parts, united with the rod *a*, moved by means of the fly-wheel V by the connecting rods S S. B, wedge, driven by the screw D, furnished with a fly C, allows of closing more or less the escape-valve E, so as to offer a varying resistance to the motion which it receives from the tappets *f f*. The escape takes place freely into the air by the opening in the upper part of the slide-valve chest. G, cylinder, in which moves the piston H, $0^{m}.014$ diameter, with a stroke of $0^{m}.208$. I, iron rod, forged with the piston, and provided with a socket K to receive the drill. This rod is hollowed, and in its interior there is another cylindrical rod L, attached to the body of the piston by the keys M. Upon this rod is fixed a worm-wheel N, gearing into an endless screw P, fixed upon the fly-wheel shaft *r*. It follows from this arrangement that in giving motion to the fly-wheel, motion is imparted on the one hand to the piston *a a*, in order that the air admitted on one face of the piston H may cause it to advance, and on the other hand the endless screw imparts its movement to the gearing N—that is, to the piston itself, and, consequently, to the drill; and in continuing the movement of rotation, the admission of air takes place at the opposite face of the piston, and the air on the other side escapes into the gallery, and so on.

The forward movement is effected in the following manner: The whole arrangement is borne upon a piece T, fixed to the roof, or the walls, of the gallery, which carries a rack on one side in which a wheel, attached to the borer, works so that the apparatus may be raised or lowered.

This apparatus weighs 65 kilogrammes; the price is 550 francs.

It works with air compressed to one atmosphere. It gives 300 to 400 blows per minute. The diameter of the drills varies from $0^{m}.018$ to $0^{m}.025$.

This apparatus requires power to compress the air, and a regulating reservoir. The force of the engine required varies from four to five horse-power.

We think that this apparatus has imperfections similar to those that we have previously pointed out; nevertheless its construction appears to be such that it can resist the blows in working.

HAUPT'S DRILL.

This percussion borer differs essentially in its construction from those described. It works by means of steam. The drill passes down a hollow piston rod, to which it is fixed by the extremity which is before the workman.—(See Figs. 2, 3, 4 and 5, Plate II.) The reciprocating movement is communicated directly to the drill, and by a special arrangement of the slide-valve the introduction of the steam into the cylinder is avoided until the piston has arrived at the end of its forward stroke.

The force of the blow of the drill upon the rock evidently depends on the pressure of the steam upon the piston. It will be observed, besides, that the useful effect of the drill depends much more upon the section of the piston and the pressure of the steam, than on the length of the stroke of the piston, and that the consumption is proportioned to this last dimension. The length of the stroke of the piston is $0^{m}.102$, and the number of blows per minute is 375.

The movement of rotation is given to the drill in the following way: The box in which the shaft of the drill is held, and which turns with it, carries a ratchet-wheel on one part of its circumference, and around this wheel is a ring furnished with a pall, which catches in the teeth of the ratchet-wheel. This ring also carries a projecting tappet, which passes in an inclined groove left in the outer envelope of sheet-iron which surrounds the steam-cylinder. The tappet participates in the movement of the piston and drill, and by sliding in the inclined groove turns a screw with which it is combined, and by means of the pall gives the ratchet-wheel and the drill a rotary motion.

This arrangement would be insufficient alone, since the tappet moving in both directions in the groove destroys, to a certain extent, during the forward stroke, the useful effect produced during the back stroke. To obviate this imperfection, and to maintain the rotation transmitted to the drill, there is a second ratchet-wheel placed at the front end of the box that carries the drill. A steel spindle placed in a recess formed by the cylinder jacket locks into the teeth of this second ratchet-wheel, so that the movement of rotation only takes place one way. The first ratchet-wheel allows the transmission of the rotating movement to the tool; the second forces this movement to be always effected one way.

Mr. Haupt has contrived a special arrangement which causes the drill to always strike upon the rock with the same force, and to vary its advance according to the hardness of the rock. If the drill is put into the drill-carrier in such manner that at any given time the motion of this latter can be suddenly arrested while the tool itself continues to move, it is clear that each stoppage of the tool-carrier will be followed by an advance of the tool; but as this stoppage would diminish the force of the blow upon the bottom of the hole, it is only allowed to take place at intervals.

Mr. Haupt estimates that three-horse power is required for each borer, and that the rate of progress in rocks of ordinary hardness is $0^{m}.05$ per minute.

BEAUMONT AND LOCOCK'S DRILLING ENGINE.

This machine is worked by compressed air; its object is to pierce a gallery of two metres diameter entirely by the machine, aided by powder for disengaging the core of rock which is left in the middle of the annular trench cut by the drills.

This machine is composed of a cast-iron plate A, (Figs. 1, 2, 3, Plate III,) which carries on its circumference fifty drills made of cast-steel, *a a*, and in its center a similar drill *b*. The diameter of the plate is about two metres, and is the same as that of the gallery to be driven. It is fixed on a hollow iron shaft B, about two-thirds of its length being a piston, which moves in a cylinder C.

The stroke of the piston is about $0^{m}.30$. D is the slide-valve which introduces the air (compressed to two atmospheres) to each face of the piston, and gives it an alternate movement of 250 blows per minute. A worm worked by a special mechanism turns the axle B, with the drills by means of the screw wheel R, combined with the axle. The carriage on which the piston shaft is mounted receives a forward motion by a special arrangement. The water which is thrown into the groove formed by the drills enters the interior of the shaft B, and by pipes branched upon this axle is conducted to the circumference of the plate A.

We will not dwell longer on the description of this machine, which has seen daylight, but which, we think, will never see the end of a gallery in a mine or tunnel. The fifty-one working drills augment not only in a considerable proportion the causes of breaking that we have previously pointed out; but even admitting that this machine will not destroy itself, the regular work that it is capable of doing would cause its rejection. It is evident that, in a rock of ordinary hardness, the drills could not do more than $0^{m}.90$ without being replaced once or twice; the machine would therefore have to be unscotched and driven back at least the length of the work to replace the army of drills of which it is composed, (this last work does not appear easy to do,) and again advance, scotch it, and set it at work. We have not calculated the time necessary for all these operations; but this we do know, that when the boring is finished and it is necessary to draw back the machine for the last time out of the gallery to have space to take away the debris, the volume of this latter, broken up by the powder, would not exceed $2^{m}.82$ cubic. It is evident that under such conditions the work performed would be comparatively nothing. But it is evident that the work of the drills will be very irregular on account of the nature of the rock itself, and the unequal wear of the drills; consequently a few only of the drills would work at a time, and these would receive all the blow of the machine; under these circumstances they would frequently break, necessitating, as we have stated, the frequent withdrawal of the machine, which weighs more than ten tons.

II.—BORING BY ROTATION.

We have before pointed out the imperfections inherent and inevitable in the system of boring by percussion, and however ingenious the combination given to the apparatus, we are convinced they are destined to disappear and to give way to the system of rotating borers, which will now be described.

The borers by rotation are divided, like those by percussion, into two classes; the first comprises those worked by hand, the second those which require water, steam, or compressed air as the motive power.

Among the first we remark the borer of Lisbet and Jacquet, Mr. Leschot's borer, constructed by Mr. Pitet, and lastly Mr. Trouillet's rotating excavator.

BORER OF LISBET AND JACQUET.

The tool of this borer is formed of a blade of corrugated steel $0^{m}.007$ thick and $0^{m}.035$ wide, twisted like an auger bit, so that it draws from the hole the debris of the rock detached by the cutting end, which has two edges, making a very obtuse angle, like a drill for perforating metals. This tool offers a certain peculiarity; the drill, instead of advancing according to the hardness of the rock, works in the manner of a screw turning in a fixed nut, and is expected to penetrate at a certain rate, irrespective of the hardness of the material being bored. By this arrangement, if the rock is too hard to be overcome by the motive power used, the drill either stops or breaks. The screw of the drill-carrier has four threads per centimetre, so that the rate of progression is $0^{m}.01$ for four turns.

The frame of the drill-carrier is ingeniously arranged, to enable it to be moved rapidly and to make holes in all directions.

The support or frame for this drill consists of an upright, or standard, to be sustained in the drift, or gallery, by steel points at each end, one of which can be forced against the roof by a screw, while the other rests upon the floor. The body of this standard is double, and so made that a sliding-drill support can be raised or lowered in it, and be sustained at any desired height by means of pins. Motion is given to the drill by means of a winch and ratchet working in the usual way.

RESULT OF THE EXPERIMENTS. On the 11th May, 1861, a commission of engineers made some experiments with this borer, and obtained the following results:

First experiment—soft schist; rate of advance, $0^{m}.10$ per minute, including fixing the tool.

Second experiment—a little harder schist, about the same rate.

Third experiment—sandstone, coarse grains, ordinary hardness; rate per minute, $0^{m}.023$.

Fourth experiment—same stone, $0^{m}.086$ per minute.

Fifth experiment—very hard sandstone, $0^{m}.018$ per minute.

These experiments only lasted 6 hours and 8½ minutes for the two first, 15 hours for the third, 5 hours and 5 minutes for the fourth, and 11 hours for the fifth, and the workman turning the handle exerted double the force of regular labor.

Further experiments were made in October, 1861, at the pits at Carling, (Moselle,) giving the following results:

First. Soft coal schist; rate, $0^{m}.046$ per minute.

Second. *Grès houillier*, compact; rate, $0^{m}.05$ per minute.

Third. Coarse grained, hard sandstone; rate, $0^{m}.035$ per minute.

These experiments showed that the advantages resulting from the employment of Lisbet and Jacquet's borer were for the second experiment in the proportion of 3.64 to 1, and in the third experiment 7 to 1.

The difference of the results obtained in the third and fourth experiments of the 11th May, 1861, was, that in the third experiment the sandstone was wet, and the chips and dust worked up by the tool formed a paste which required the tool to be often removed for cleaning, from which it may be concluded that the arrangement of the bit is bad for boring holes in wet strata.

At Montigny-sur-Sambre, in an experiment in ironstone, the following results were obtained:

A hole in compact schist of $0^{m}.65$ was bored in 7 hours. A hole in compact schist of $0^{m}.61$ was bored in 7.30 hours; in moderately hard sandstone of $0^m.31$, in 10.30 hours; in less hard sandstone of $0^m.67$, in 10 hours.

During these trials the workmen made greater efforts than would have been made for a work of eight or ten hours.

In the carboniferous sandstone the trials were not decisive. In the hard calcareous rock of Soignes the advance was only $0^m.013$ per minute. In the hardest coal grit the trials failed completely; the drill only worked out a small quantity, and became heated and blunted in a few moments.

In 1864, at La Fosse de Villare at Anzin, the borer was experimented with for two days; two men worked it; the rate of advance was $0^m.045$ per minute, in a pretty hard pyritous rock.

In 1864, at Séraing, in a block of sandstone of medium hardness, a rate of $0^m.017$ per minute was obtained; the diameter of the hole was $0^m.04$, and two men worked the machine.

From what has preceded it may be observed—

1. That the erection and working of the apparatus require considerable skill and judgment.
2. That in granular and homogeneous stone the borer acts well.
3. That in hard sandstone and quartz it has no action on the rock, and the tool wears up quickly; also that it works irregularly in rocks that contain masses of quartz.
4. And lastly, that in wet rocks the work is difficult, and the rate scarcely appreciable.

LESCHOT'S DRILL.

The imperfections that Mr. Leschot, civil engineer and pupil of the Central School, had recognized in the employ of iron or steel in the boring of hard rocks or of metals, the drills softening rapidly, and often producing only an advance of $0^m.07$ to $0^m.10$ per hour, gave him the happy idea of applying a rotating tool acting in the manner of an annular cutter, and in which steel teeth should be replaced by diamonds. To accomplish this, he sets into a tubular washer or ring, about $0^m.005$ or $0^m.006$ thick, black diamonds projecting $0^m.0005$ at the most, some from within, some from without, and some in front.

The opposite end carries an adjustment like a bayonet joint, which admits of this crown being adjusted upon a tube as a bayonet is placed upon a gun-barrel. He imparts to this ring so arranged a rotary movement, and at the same time presses it with considerable force against the stone to be bored.

The first experiments that were made with this apparatus, which was mounted on a frame something like that of the Lisbet borer, led to the belief that this new system of boring the rock would be a complete success. In a granite of medium hardness, two men could bore $0^m.025$ per hour; the cylindrical core left in the center was $0^m.031$ in diameter, and the annular groove $0^m.043$ in diameter; consequently the part pulverized was equal to a cylinder $0^m.012$ thick.

Unfortunately experience has not since confirmed the happy debut of this apparatus; not because the employment of the ring was bad, but solely on account of the mode of advancing the drill, which depends on the velocity of the rotation of the cutting ring. The principle of this arrangement for advancement is evidently defective, for it is impossible to have a constant regular rate of advance in rocks which, by their nature, are constantly varying in hardness. In the soft parts of the rock, the advance of the tool not having been quick enough, it did not produce its maximum amount of work; while in the hard rocks, quartz for instance, the advance was too rapid, and the diamonds either were displaced or reduced into powder.

TROUILLET'S ROTATING EXCAVATOR.

This, like the percussion apparatus by the same inventor, is intended to enlarge the lower portions of ordinary drill holes so as to make chambers for the reception of powder. It is similarly constructed, except that the work is performed by the rotation of steel cutters, attached to a central stem or shaft, to which motion is given by two cranks and gearing. The weight of the apparatus is 60 kilogrammes, and its price is 450 francs.

DE LA ROCHE-TOLLAY AND PERRET'S BORING APPARATUS.

The complete apparatus of Messrs. De La Roche-Tollay and Perret is composed of four distinct parts:

1. The carriage which bears the borer.
2. The motive power.
3. The borer.
4. The tool.

Carriage or support.—This borer is intended to be arranged differently, according to the conditions under which it is to work. When it is intended to bore but one hole a single tool is used; when the front of a gallery or a tunnel is to be pierced in several points simultaneously, several boring machines will be indispensable. Consequently, in each particular case, the carriage or tool-bearer should be modified according to the local requirements. We do not, therefore, enter into the relative details of this part of the machine; we will merely state that Messrs. Huet and Geyler, engineers, have studied the different arrangements of the tool-carrier, and they have succeeded in rendering the working of the borer or borers easy and quick, in permitting them to assume any required direction on the carriage which bears them, and in giving an arrangement by which the carriage or support can be attached easily to the roof or wall of the gallery as well as upon the sides, and removed away rapidly to allow the powder to be fired and to carry away the debris. This arrangement is shown by Fig. 4, Plate III.

Motive power.—This hydraulic motor has been contrived by Mr. Perret, civil engineer at Bordeaux; it is composed of a horizontal cylinder bolted on the frame of the borer.

This cylinder carries at its upper part a nozzle, to which is adapted a pipe in india-rubber, intended to conduct the water to the engine.

In this cylinder a bronze tube is fitted, which we call the regulator. This is bored and turned with the greatest nicety, and is pierced with port-holes at the end. It receives a reciprocating motion from an eccentric, made of one piece, upon the axle of the engine.

Two boxes furnished with segments in bronze, pressed by steel springs, maintain the regulator rigorously in the axis of the inner cylinder, which serves to envelop it. These segments have the effect of stopping the passage of the water round the regulator during its longitudinal movement.

In the interior of the regulator there is a movable piston $0^m.055$ in diameter, furnished with capped leathers, upon the two faces of which the water alternately exerts its pressure. The length of stroke is $0^m.120$. A connecting rod changes it into a continuous rotary motion in connection with a cranked shaft provided with two fly-wheels acting as regulators.

In order to ascertain the power of this new motive engine, we took 300 litres of water, the pressure of which varied from 3 to 9½ atmospheres, and we proved, by means of Prony's break, in seven experiments that we made, that the practical result of the engine was 47 to 57 per cent. of the theoretical effect. This machine represented, under the maximum pressure of 9½ atmospheres, theoretically 3.82 horse-power, and practically 2.11 horse-power.

We shall presently show that the regular speed of this little machine ought to be from 200 to 250 revolutions per minute. This is represented by 140 litres of water per minute, and a practical effect of 1.70 horse-power, the water being at a pressure of 8 atmospheres.

It will at once be seen what an important service this motive power will render when there is a sufficient supply of water. For example, at Mont Cenis (Bardonnèche) the torrent of Melzet has a fall of 45 metres; admitting that it is 35 metres only, to give allowance for loss, it follows that each machine on Mr. Perret's principle would expend 320 litres per minute for one boring tool; thus, for the eight machines which are at work on the face of the rock, 2,560 litres, or 44 litres per second, would be required. The quantity of water at present used for working the compressors is 600 litres. It will be claimed as an advantage that the compressed air serves to aerate the gallery; this is true, but we find in the official returns that it requires for working the eight borers 6,250 cubic metres of air for 24 hours, while 2,160 cubic metres is sufficient to renew the air vitiated by the fifteen men at work in the head of the gallery; it is also true, that they have sought to establish the fact that the balance, 4,000 cubic metres, were necessary to expel the noxious gases produced by the explosion of the powder; but practice has proved that much more powerful and altogether artificial means were required for this purpose. It would appear to us more rational to employ a part of the 566 litres remaining to work a Perret machine to drive an air ventilator. We ought also to add that the erection of the compressors and their buildings at Bardonnèche has cost 1,250,000 francs, and three-fourths of this expense would have been saved by the employment of Mr. Perret's machine.

The boring machine of Mr. Perret is composed of a six-sided cast-steel shaft, $1^{m}.45$ long, bored throughout its entire length with a hole $0^{m}.016$ diameter. This axle receives the boring tools at one of its extremities.

The other extremity of the axle carries a bronze piston $0^{m}.11$ diameter, upon which the requisite pressure is exerted for maintaining and pressing the drill against the face of the rock. This pressure is varied according to the hardness or the nature of the rock. A pressure of eight atmospheres is abundantly sufficient for boring hard rocks, such as the quartz of Mont Cenis and the granite of the Pyrenees. The pressure should be diminished for calcareous rocks to five or six atmospheres at most. Thus, with a pressure of eight atmospheres, the effort on the drill is equal to 784 kilogrammes.

The water employed to act against the piston of the propeller is conveyed by an india-rubber hose, the extremity of which is provided with a cock to regulate the pressure as may be required.

To remove the perforating tube after a hole has been cut, the passage of the water to the cylinder is intercepted by a cock, and the flow is directed against the front face of the piston, admitting, at the same time, of the cylinder being emptied. In this manner the tube can be replaced with the greatest facility.

The perforating shaft is fitted on the inside with a bronze frame, accurately bored to a depth of $1^{m}.14$, for the propelling piston to work in. Holes from $0^{m}.90$ to $1^{m}.00$ deep, and from $0^{m}.035$ to $0^{m}.06$, can be bored by this machine.

The tool-bearing shaft traverses an iron socket held between two bearings arranged in front of the framing. The socket is provided with a bevel pinion, to which motion is imparted through the medium of an inclined shaft by a brass wheel keyed on the main shaft.

From the foregoing it will be seen that in order to apply this borer to the Mont Cenis works, it should have a piston $0^{m}.16$ diameter, since the pressure of the water there is only $3\frac{1}{2}$ atmospheres.

The perforating tool made use of until recently by Messrs. De La Roche-Tollay and Perret is the Leschot ring previously described, but there are still some points to be explained to complete the information relating to this kind of drill.

It is understood that after the ring has been attached to the six-sided perforating shaft, if it is rotated at a speed of about two hundred revolutions per minute, by the effect of pressure exerted on the propeller piston, the black diamonds brought in contact with a softer substance will cut and wear it to an extent which will depend on the pressure on the piston and the hardness of the rock. By continuing this labor the groove can be made to a great depth, and the cylindrical core which remains attached to the rock enters the hole through the axis of the tool-carrier. When the operation is terminated the core is taken out in the shape of quite a regular cylinder, which only breaks when the rock is of a brittle nature, or has been previously cracked. It is evident that the use of this cutting ring saves considerable power, since a part of the rock is not pulverized. In the example which we have given in describing the Leschot perforator, the effort was only 61.441 tons per hour, while it would have been 204.5 tons if the entire matter had been pulverized. The ring employed by Messrs. De La Roche-Tollay and Perret is only 0m.035 outside diameter, and the core worked was 0m.014 in diameter.

COST OF THE TOOLS.—We will now reply to an objection which has been raised as to the price of the tool. It is true that when the ring was first used a difficulty existed in the selection of the diamonds, which, from the nature of their cleavage, would be the most serviceable. The setting was not always performed as solidly as could be desired; but these difficulties have disappeared. We have examined two rings which were worked for seven months at the Exposition, and which have perfectly resisted. We believe that we can affirm that in a hard stone like granite, a ring properly worked will cut holes to an aggregate depth of 150 metres. A ring for boring holes, 0m.036 diameter, costs about 150 francs, but as the black and opaque diamonds used in its construction are ordinarily employed in the shape of dust for polishing transparent diamonds, and as their wear during the act of perforation is very slight, they can be extracted from the socket in which they are set, and be returned to the trade with a depreciation proportionate only to the diminution of weight. The diamonds extracted from a worn-out ring generally fetch from seventy to eighty francs—that is to say, about one-half of their first cost.

The following are the results of the experiments made during the Exposition. The pressure on the propelling piston was eight atmospheres, and the speed varied from two hundred and fifty to two hundred and eighty revolutions per minute.

Advance per minute: In the pure Mont Cenis quartz, 0m.054; in the Morvan porphyries, 0m.042; in granite, 0m.050; in ———, 0m.018; in very hard calcareous dolomite, 0m.080.

The holes were perfectly regular, and being so, were well adapted to the use of powder cartridges, which are much less dangerous than the ordinary use of powder.

As the pressure of the water injected into the hole through the hollow is the same as that acting on the piston, the powdered debris are washed away with the greatest facility.

The hydraulic engine and the perforator have worked every day, during four hours, in a period of seven months, without necessitating any serious repairs. The most important were repairing the piston-head bearings of the water engine and verifying the state of the segments belonging to the engine.

The weight of the entire apparatus is equal to that of those used at Mont Cenis, viz: about two hundred kilogrammes; its price, including the engine, but without the support, is 2,500 francs.

We cannot refrain from making a comparison between this perforator and the one employed at Mont Cenis. Its solidity, proved by seven months' work, gives the assurance that twenty to twenty-two of these perforators would be sufficient for the heads of both galleries, including duplicates, instead of at least two hundred and twenty actually existing. Mr. Sommeilier's perforators cost the same as those of Messrs. De La Roche-Tollay and Perret. The staff would be four times less, for one man can easily attend four perforators; thus four men instead of sixteen would suffice for twenty-four hours at the two galleries.

The repairs to the rings require neither forges, lathes, or workshops; and we are convinced that a workman to each gallery would be sufficient for the repairs of all the perforators. We have stated that the rate of advance in the Mont Cenis quartz was $0^{m}.054$ per minute, under a pressure of 874 kilogrammes on the propelling piston; therefore a hole $0^{m}.90$ could have been driven in 16 minutes, say 20, and as each perforator should make 10 holes, say $3\frac{1}{2}$ hours, even doubling this time for preparing the work, it will be seen that five stopes can be done in two days, including the time for blasting and clearing away the debris, which is equivalent to an advance of $2^{m}.25$ per diem, instead of barely $0^{m}.50$, the actual rate of advance.

The apparatus of Messrs. De La Roche-Tollay and Perret is not subjected to any shock; the pressure is exerted on the rock irrespective of the speed of the tool, and such pressure can be regulated as may be desired; and when water power is obtainable, which is generally the case in mines and tunnels, the motive power actually costs nothing.

Mr. Perret's machine can also be worked by compressed air, and for this it would be sufficient to add a hydraulic accumulator to the perforator carriage Such an accumulator would be but small since the volume of water required for advancing the piston one metre is $9\frac{1}{2}$ litres, it would be sufficient to add two or three litres per hole, one metre deep, for washing out the holes.

III.—COAL-CUTTING MACHINES.

The two machines about to be described are intended for use in coal-mines, for under-cutting or blocking out coal. One is the invention of Messrs. Jones and Levick; the other, of Messrs. Carrett, Marshall & Co., of England.

JONES AND LEVICK'S MACHINE.

This machine is composed of two distinct parts—the first for cutting or striking the coal; the second, the motive power which supplies the compressed air.

This coal-getting machine may be said to be a miner's pick, actuated by compressed air. It is represented in section by Fig. 5, Plate III. A is a cylinder in which the piston B works, and the hollow stem of which carries at its extremity a connecting rod C, driving, by means of an arm D, the shaft E, to which the pick *a* is affixed. This shaft E is held between two species of lugs F attached to the cylinder G.

In order to give to the pick *a* any requisite position, the workman has only to turn the hand-wheel *m;* the pinion *n* keyed on the same shaft as the hand-wheel and gearing, into a wheel *h* cast with or attached to the cylinder G, carries with it this cylinder, which rotates freely in two collars I I fixed to the carriage on which the cylinder A is fixed, thus the pick *a* fixed on the shaft E will assume any position which may be required, and will be maintained in such a position by a bolt traversing one of the holes in the wheel *m*. A very ingenious arrangement, which we describe below, admits at the same time of the pick being brought back automatically in case it experiences any resistance before having come to the end of its stroke.

We have mentioned above that the piston rod is hollow. A small rod M, bearing a tappet at each extremity, enters the said hollow part, and an ellipsoidal piece P, of cast-iron or brass, slides without friction on the rod between these two tappets.

The rod M, at its free end, is connected to one of the arms of a lever, the fulcrum of which is at *o*, and the other arm actuates the rod N of the slide H.

A hand-lever S is arranged so as to work the slide by hand.

Supposing that the piston is in the position represented by the figure, the compressed air enters at K and drives the piston in the direction of the arrow, and the pick strikes the coal to be broken up. If now we suppose that the pick is arrested before the piston has finished its stroke, the cylinder P, moving forward by the impulse imparted by the piston B, will continue to advance, and will strike the tappet and the rod M, moving in the direction of the arrow, which will alter the position of the lever *o*, so that the introduction of the compressed air will take place at L, and the pick *a* will be brought back out of the groove. When the machine is at work a sharp knock is distinctly heard at each stroke of the piston, caused by the motion of the piece P.

This machine is mounted on a carriage or truck with four wheels, and has an extended cast-iron platform T in the rear, for the man that works the machine. A crank-pin on a fly-wheel R actuates two bevel-wheels W, for moving the machine back or forward on the rails of the gallery.

The handling of this machine is very simple. The workman on the platform turns the wheel *m* so as to bring the pick into the proper direction; he then opens the cock admitting the compressed air, and admits the air into the cylinder A, by working the slide with the lever S. The machine being thus set in motion, it is merely requisite to move it forward by means of the wheel R to follow up the work done by the pick. The air, on leaving the cylinder, escapes freely into the gallery.

We subjoin the results of two experiments made by this machine in two mines in England.

In the High Royd colliery, in a hard coal, and in a gallery in which the rails were in a bad state, with an air pressure of from 2 to 2½ atmospheres and 70 to 80 blows per minute, the average hour's work of the machine was a channel from $8^m.20$ to $9^m.15$ long and from $0^m.90$ to $1^m.00$ deep, including stoppages. The width at the bottom was $0^m.037$, and on the face $0^m.08$. During 10 hours' consecutive work the work produced by this machine was equal to that of 20 miners during the same time; and it appears that the consumption of air is equal to about 3 horse-power.

CARRETT, MARSHALL & CO.'S COAL-CUTTING MACHINE.

Messrs. Carrett, Marshall & Co.'s machine works like a hand-plane, and is actuated by water at a pressure of twenty atmospheres. It is composed of a horizontal cylinder A, (Fig. 6, Plate III,) in which the propelling piston works. To the rod of this piston is attached a bar M M, furnished with steel knives *c c c* placed about sixteen inches apart. A vertical cylinder B is connected with the preceding one, and its piston is provided with a rod, on the extremity of which is fixed a tappet or wedge C in such a manner as to turn around the point on which it is suspended. By means of a special combination of the distributing slide and a four-ways cock, the water is let on alternately and simultaneously on the faces of the two cylinder pistons in such a manner that, while the knives *c c c* are working, the wedge C bears solidly against the roof of the gallery and scotches the machine on the rails. On the contrary, when the knives are retreating the piston of the vertical cylinder descends, the wedge abandons its first position, and the machine is unscotched and moves forward. The horizontal cylinder can turn between the wheels of the carriage so as to work either to the right or to the left.

These two cylinders and pistons, with their accompanying parts, rest on an iron framing, which can be raised or lowered on slides fixed to the axles of the carriage by means of screws.

The angle at which the instrument works in the gallery can be varied by means of the pinion G and the semicircular rack H. The nuts I I afford the means of regulating the inclination of the knife-carrier M with respect to the breast of the cut.

The machine works in the following manner: The water comes up to the distributing valve, acts on the piston of the press B, and drives the tappet or wedge against the roof. During this time the water also arrives at the back of the piston of the cylinder A, and the cutters move forward $0^m.40$ each, which gives a total depth of $1^m.20$ of cutting in the coal at each stroke of the piston.

When the tools have reached the end of their stroke the water penetrates above the piston of the press B and unscotches the wedge C, while the piston of the cylinder A and the tools return. During this time a special mechanism turns the ratchet H; the machine draws on the chain K, and advances the requisite distance to take a new cut.

According to the statement of Mr. Louis Perret, engineer at Paris, Messrs. Carrett, Marshall & Co.'s agent, this machine, working at the rate of fifteen strokes of the piston per minute, requires three horse-power. One hour's work produces a cut $1^{m}.20$ deep and $13^{m}.50$ to $15^{m}.00$ advance. The consumption of water is 135 litres per minute at a pressure of twenty atmospheres. The weight of the machine is about one ton.

This machine does not make vertical cuts. When the cuts have been run successively at the roof and at the foot wall of the gallery, the coal is hewed down between these two parallel faces. According to Mr. Perret, the economy of waste is estimated at one-fifth, and the coal got is worth twenty-five per cent. more per ton.

This machine is working regularly at the Rippax colliery, near Leeds, in several Scotch mines, as well as in the counties of Northumberland, York, and Stafford. It can be worked by a man and a boy.

The use of this kirving machine is not exclusively limited to coal-getting; it can also be employed in iron and copper mines, freestone quarries, and generally in all rocks which can be easily cut—provided, however, such places have a good solid roof to which the machine can be attached by means of the wedge or tappet at the top.

II.—TRANSPORTATION, HOISTING, AND PUMPING.

CHAPTER III.

UNDERGROUND TRAMMING—HOISTING AND PUMPING ENGINES.

INTRODUCTORY—TRANSPORTATION UNDERGROUND; TRAMMING—EVRAR'S LUBRICATING BOXES—EXAMPLES OF UNDERGROUND TRANSPORTATION—HOISTING ENGINES—STEAM-BRAKES—DIAMETER OF WINDING DRUM—IRON DERRICKS—PUMPING AND DRAINING MACHINERY—CORNISH ENGINES—ORDINARY PUMPING ENGINES—RAISING WATER BY GUIDED KIBBLES—CHAIN PUMP—RUSSIAN PUMP.

INTRODUCTORY.

Although few of the machines in this class at the Exposition of 1867 could be regarded as new inventions, most of them having been known and used in one form or another for a long time, great improvements were shown in their construction and adaptation to the increased duty required of them in the present advanced state of mining industry.

The rapidly-increasing production of the coal mines of Great Britain and the Continent has necessitated great improvements in the methods of transportation underground. The wagons used for the purpose and their running gear are no longer roughly and rudely constructed, but are made with great care. The wheels are accurately made, well bored, and fitted with carefully-turned axles, and these are kept well lubricated with grease-boxes, so as to prevent loss of power, wear, and friction. In some of the coal mines in England men and horses for drawing the loaded cars have been replaced by steam-engines, which, by means of cables, give motion to twenty or thirty wagons at one time.

In hoisting coal or ores from mines very great improvements have been made in the engines and in the cages or platforms for the wagons. By means of properly-guided cages over four times as much material can be raised now in a given time as was formerly possible. This is accomplished, not only by increasing the quantity or weight hoisted at one time, but by increasing the *velocity* of movement, which is rendered possible by the improvements in the hoisting engines, and by the appliances to prevent accidents, such, for example, as powerful steam-brakes, parachutes, and other contrivances.

Machines have been made, as is well known, to convey miners from the surface to the bottom of the mines, or the reverse, with safety and expedition, and without exertion or fatigue on their part. Great changes have been made in the methods of sinking shafts, and in the tools for the purpose, and in machines for pumping, ventilating, and for drilling and cutting rocks and excavating coal.

I.—TRANSPORTATION UNDERGROUND—TRAMMING.

EVRAR'S LUBRICATING BOXES.

This is a contrivance for supplying oil in moderate and regular quantities to the journals or bearings of the wheels of wagons for underground tramming, and for excluding all grit and dirt from the bearing surfaces. The wheels are supported by journals J J, (Fig. 1,) working in a hollow cylinder or box *a* extending across the bottom of the car. This cylinder is calibered at each end, for one-third of its length, for the reception of the journal. The middle third of the cylinder is left rough, and receives an oil-box, which may be filled through a hole in the cylinder, closed by a screw *s*, with a conical point which enters the oil-box and nearly closes the hole in it, leaving only a small opening, through which oil can exude in small quantities whenever a bubble of air enters. The journals are retained in their places by caps *c c*, fixed to the truck and fitting over the ends of the cylinder and catching upon a shoulder left upon the journal.

Fig. 1.

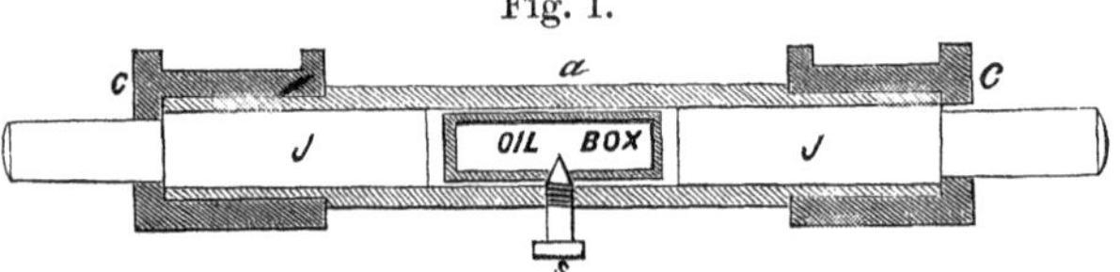

Evrar's Self-lubricating Axle.

Axles of this kind used upon wagons at the mines of the Vicargne Company consume a decilitre of oil in running an aggregate distance of 150 kilometres—about 62 miles. Oil is renewed every fortnight.

EXAMPLES OF UNDERGROUND TRANSPORTATION.—In most of the coal mines of England the regularity of the strata is such that a shaft may be used for a long time for the extraction of an enormous amount of coal brought to the shaft from great horizontal distances below. It is not unusual to see in Great Britain shafts from which 600, 1,000, 1,200, and even 1,500 or 1,600 tons are extracted in twenty-four hours. Such an amount of work, extending over great periods of time, requires all the parts of the shaft to be constructed in a solid and permanent manner. In France the formations are generally more broken and dislocated.

For the conveyance of such immense quantities of coal to the shafts it is necessary to use power greater than is afforded by men trundling the wagons in the usual way. The coal is loaded into wagons containing from 350 to 450 kilogrammes each, and five or six of these wagons are then formed into trains, which are drawn by horses to the main tram-ways, which vary in length from a few hundred yards to even a mile.

Tram-ways may be divided into three classes: first, those in which the slope towards the shaft is sufficient for trains to descend by their own gravity, and, in descending, to draw up the empty trains; second, those in which the grade is reversed, and sufficient to permit the empty trains to descend from the shaft to the end of the road by their own gravity; third, those in which the bed or grade is horizontal, or nearly so, necessitating power for the movement of the trains either way.

In the second class the loaded trains are usually drawn up toward the shaft by means of a cable wound upon a drum by a steam-engine, while the empty cars are lowered by a cable unwinding from the same drum. In the third class an endless rope or cable, which traverses the gallery along the track between the rails, is moved by an engine, and the trains are coupled to this moving rope and so carried to their destination. A few details upon this third class of tram-roads may be desirable. It is understood that a double track is laid on the levels where this method of moving the trains is used. The general arrangement of the cables, the engine, &c., are shown by Fig. 2.

Fig. 2.

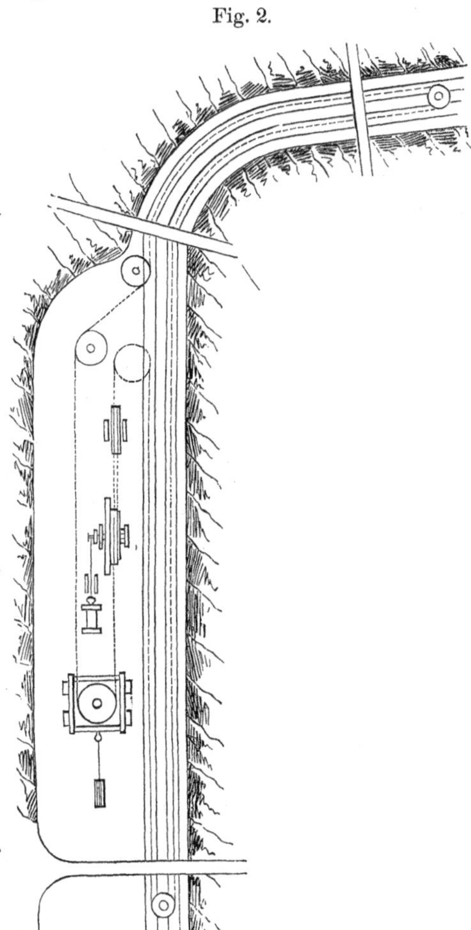

Tramming by steam power underground.

The driving engine is generally placed in a recess cut at one side of the gallery, and near an air-shaft, by which the smoke from the furnaces can escape. The cable is wound upon a drum, and is supported throughout its course by horizontal rollers, and in the curves is guided by vertical rollers. At the ends of the route the cable turns upon drums placed between the tracks, the diameter of which is equal to the distance from the center of the roads. In some cases the cables run for a part of the distance underground. In order to secure a proper tension of the cable, it is passed over a pulley upon a movable frame, counterpoised in such a way as to take up the slack of the cable and give a constant tension. The cable travels constantly in one direction, and thus moves opposite ways upon the two tracks. Trains of twenty or thirty wagons are moved by this arrangement.

In some mines the engine was established on the surface,

and the cable was guided to the bottom by pulleys and sheaves; this was the first plan adopted, but it occasions too much friction and wear of the rope, and now the engine is always placed underground.

To start or stop the trains it is not necessary to stop the cables. There is a conductor in the first wagon of each train. When he wants to put the train in motion he lifts up the cable with a hook, makes it pass along a wooden block fixed under the wagon, and by means of a lever he brings forward a wooden wedge which squeezes the cable against the wooden block. Cable and wagon, being then connected, move together. By maneuvering his lever the other way, the conductor disconnects the rope and stops the train. When the train arrives opposite the machine, or where the cable runs underground, the conductor loosens the rope and the train runs alone. The momentum carries the train up to the point where the cable reappears; the conductor then again connects the rope to the train as before.

In the coal mines of Pelton the principal road is 1,500 metres in length It is partly horizontal and partly on a slope of five degrees. The driving cable is $0^{m}.022$ in diameter, its running speed is $6^{m}.00$ per second, and it carries a train of 30 wagons; the width of the rail is $0^{m}.60$; the strength of the motive power is 40 horse-power; and the cable transports 52 trains in 12 hours, representing a duty of 560 tons of coal.

	Francs.
The labor costs	13. 50
Coal (refuse) for fuel, 6 tons at 3 francs	18. 00
Repairs, interest, &c	76. 50
Total	108. 00

Which represents a cost of 0.137 franc per ton per kilometre. Under the most favorable conditions transportation by horses costs 0.21 franc per ton, and by trammers, 0.67 franc.

II.—HOISTING ENGINES.

The hoisting engines exhibited in the palace of the Champ de Mars were all double-cylinder engines, acting directly on the drum or reel. This style now predominates throughout the mining regions of England, France, and Belgium.

Hoisting was formerly done at a very low speed, and consequently the drums turned very slowly. To run them directly by the engine would have required very heavy machinery, and considerable expense to put them up. Practice gradually proved that engines of comparatively small power could be conveniently run at high speed. Such small hoisting engines were from thirty to thirty-five horse-power. They were quite light—had only one cylinder—but could be run three or four times as fast as the drum, which was geared by a cog-wheel.

But as the weight of stuff to be hoisted was constantly increasing, as well as the number of the revolutions of the drum, the motive power was also increased to reduce the number of revolutions of the engine, until the number of revolutions of both engine and drum was about equal. At that time it was thought more simple to get rid of the cog-wheel and gearing in general, and to connect the drum directly with the connecting rod of the steam-cylinder.

In order to facilitate the reversing of the motion in these engines, the power was divided between two coupled cylinders instead of one. The two connecting rods acted on the drum by cranks at right angles.

This method has both advantages and inconveniences. The steam can be reversed immediately, and the drum may be turned at will, and in an instant, either one way or the other. With the fly-wheel and gearing construction, it was quite dangerous to reverse the steam. On the other hand, the exhaust of the steam must be very perfect, or the action of the cylinders would be irregular. The larger the cylinders are the greater the slide-valve must be—more strength must be exerted by the engineer when they have to be moved.

Considerable improvements have been made in the slide-valves. In France and in England they have been replaced by distributing valves, which require very little exertion to operate, and can be maneuvered as as well by Mr. Stevenson's reversing motion.

The double-cylinder direct-acting engines are made either with vertical or horizontal cylinders. In England they generally prefer the former, inasmuch as they have the advantage of permitting the main drum to be placed above at a considerable height, and thus to diminish the slope of the cable. This is, doubtless, an important point; but when the drums are set up so high it requires very strong and expensive frameworks to sustain them, and such frames are more or less liable to vibrations, whereas with the horizontal-cylinder engines the drum and engine are placed on the same foundation and are much more stable and solid.

The Creuzot company exhibited in the French section an engine with two coupled horizontal cylinders, with very long strokes, and acting directly on the drum.

In the Belgian section Messrs. Dorzee and Oudry exhibited a double-cylinder hoisting engine, some features of which are new. The cylinders are vertical, and are supported on two substantial and firm cast-iron frames or towers, above the drum-shaft, placed level with the floor. The cylinders act downward on the drum instead of upward, as in the English vertical engines. This style does not diminish the obliquity of the cable, and although it may secure a firm foundation for the drum, yet we believe that horizontal cylinders would act better, be firmer, and cost less to put up.

STEAM-BRAKES.

Powerful steam-brakes are now quite extensively used to avoid accidents when hoisting at high speed. Collisions will frequently occur between the two cages or buckets, and sometimes the cages or buckets will be drawn up too high and be in danger of passing over the sheaves at the head of the shaft. It is, therefore, necessary to have the means of quickly arresting the motion of the drum. A great deal has been said against steam-brakes; it is claimed that they never are in good working order, and that when the accident happens they do not act in a satisfactory manner. These objections may be avoided if the steam-brake is constantly used by the engineer for all the maneuvering.

DIAMETER OF WINDING DRUMS.

Notwithstanding the great increase in the velocity of the drum and the rate of hoisting, it was long before the diameter of the drum was altered. It used to vary from two and a half to four metres, but it was found, as the mines grew deeper, that the wear and tear of the ropes and cables (wire ropes especially) when coiled around a small drum were very great. To avoid the short bend around small drums, their diameter was greatly increased, and was finally carried to seven metres, (from twenty-one to twenty-two feet.) Of course, in this case, the number of revolutions of the drum for the same hoisting speed has been reduced, but, as it requires very expensive engines to run them directly, there is a tendency to return to the old style of gearing the drum by a cog-wheel, and to run it with lighter but higher-speed engines.

These large drums are particularly desirable for wire ropes, which are destroyed very fast by a short bend. On these large circumferences the turns are fewer, and the cable need not be coiled several times over itself, which causes great wear and destruction of the strands. Each turn of a drum 22 feet in diameter represents 66 feet of length of cable, and 25 rounds will reach 1,650 feet deep. With a rope one and a half inch thick the drum would have to be a little over three feet in length. In such a case the radius of the drum in winding would remain the same when wire rope is used; but this is not the case with hemp rope, which has a much greater diameter, and when winding up around the drum it must coil upon itself several times, and thus increase considerably the radius of the drum, and, on the other hand, in unwinding or lowering into the shaft, the radius of the drum is rapidly reduced.

The difference of radius is insufficient to compensate for the weight of the unwound cable, and such an arrangement requires powerful engines to lift up the dead weight of cable at the start. From that moment less and less power is required until the two buckets or cages meet in the shaft; then the descending cable gradually takes the advantage of the ascending one, and the steam-engine, instead of driving, is soon driven with an increased velocity by the increasing weight of the descending cable. To avoid these inconveniences a system of counterpoises is used. Ropes carrying a counterpoise are wound around sheaves placed on the shaft of the drum; these counterpoises play up and down the shaft for about fifty or sixty metres; the cable unrolls as it goes down, and the radius of the sheaves diminishes. It is so arranged that when the entire cable is paid out and the counterpoise is down, the two buckets or cages pass each other in the shaft. At that time the strain upon the hoisting drum changes, as also the action of the counterpoise. The rotary motion of the hoisting drum continues in the same direction, as also that of the sheave, which now winds up the rope of the counterpoise in the opposite direction. The force required to raise up this counterpoise counterbalances thé weight of the descending cable.

Another way, which gives better results, consists in using a very heavy cast-iron chain as a counterpoise.

Some attempts have lately been made to suppress the sheave entirely, and to hoist directly with the drums, by placing them over the shaft.

Drums seven metres in diameter are placed on the top of the shaft, instead of the sheaves, and are driven directly by a double-cylinder engine. This system, which is fully described in "*Le materiel des houillères*," by Professor A. Burat, has not been entirely successful so far; but it has shown, however, that an economy of fifty per cent. can be realized on the wear and tear of cables.

If it is difficult to do away entirely with the sheaves, yet it is quite easy to increase their diameter so as to avoid giving a short bend to the cables, which quickly ruins them, and particularly wire ropes.

A series of rollers placed on a curve of a very large radius might be advantageously used instead of large sheaves.

IRON DERRICKS.

One of the most recent improvements is the substitution of iron for wood in the construction of poppet heads or derricks over shafts. Such constructions, made of wood, soon decay, and are insecure, but when made of iron they are at once more durable, stronger, and lighter. The collective exhibition from St. Etienne contained a fine example from the mines of St. Louis. This structure rises about thirty-five feet from the mouth of the shaft to the axis of the pulleys. The pillars and girders are hollow, and are formed of segments of cast iron bolted together by means of suitable flanges. The principal supports are oval, the longest diameter being placed in the direction of the greatest strain. The total weight of the iron is 22,000 kilogrammes, and the cost, at 55 francs per 100 kilogrammes, is about 12,000 francs. This does not include the pulleys or the guides for the cages, or the painting.[1]

III.—PUMPING AND DRAINING MACHINERY.

The Universal Exposition of 1867 contained no full-size model of pumps or draining machines. Most of these machines are only made to order, and, besides, their tremendous weight would have occasioned too great an expense for transportation. They were represented only by

---

[1] *Vide Revue de l'Exposition de* 1867, 1 and 2, with an excellent plate showing the details of construction.—Ed.

drawings and small models, most of which were inventions of a mere theoretical kind and which had not been put in practice.

Another reason which explains the slight importance given to these machines at the Exposition is that for many years past no very novel features have been introduced in their construction. Doubtless, their construction has been improved as well as that of all other kinds of machines, but no radical change has been effected in their principle.

Although the most costly of all kinds of machines, as far as the erection is concerned, the Cornish engine continues to be exclusively used for elevating large quantities of water from very great depths.

CORNISH ENGINES.

The Cornish engine has been for some time past constructed on two different plans, viz, the beam engine and the direct-acting engine.

When this last form was first introduced it was thought to be a great improvement, on account of the suppression of the beam; but it was soon discovered that the working of these machines was far from being perfect, and the beam was quickly re-established, as much for the sake of carrying the weights employed for counterbalancing the rods as for imparting motion to the condenser, without which the Cornish engine loses its most precious advantage, viz, the economy of fuel.

Brought back to this new form, the direct-acting engine has all the organs of the old Cornish type, and costs nearly as much. If it has the advantage of taking less room, and consequently necessitating less extent of building, on the other hand it blocks up the mouth of the shaft, and very often its foundations cost as much as those of the first kind.

There is, therefore, no reason for giving the preference, at first sight, to either of these two systems; local circumstances will cause a decision either in favor of one or the other.

Those who would like to become acquainted with all the newest models of this sort of machine will find full descriptions in the "*Le materiel des houillères*," by Professor Burat, of Paris, and in the "*Portfeuille Cockerill*," of Belgium.

With regard to novelty of details, we have none to call attention to, unless it be the increasing tendency of placing the main rod in the axis of the pumps. When the rod is of wood it is separated into two parts where it passes a pump in the shaft, and the pump is placed between the two parts of the rod. When the rods are made of iron two separate ones are placed one on each side of the pumps, and they are united together at certain distances so as to keep them equidistant.

For distributing the steam the cataract and Hornblower's well-known equilibrium valve are employed.

ORDINARY PUMPING ENGINES.

Pumping engines of a smaller description show considerable variety in their construction; none, however, possess any striking novelty.

Among them we would mention the double-action engine, placed at the bottom of the works, and working directly one or two pumps equally double-acting, and forcing the water at one stroke up to the surface. This system is simple and cheap as regards first cost, but consumes too much fuel, as it is generally constructed without condensing apparatus. It can hardly be used except when the machine can be established over some large excavations deep enough to gather the water for ten or fifteen days; otherwise it would be impossible to make any repairs either to the pumps or the engine without danger of being overflowed. This has tended to prevent the system from being adopted, notwithstanding its simplicity.

In depths not exceeding one hundred metres (three hundred feet) suction and lifting pumps are used, and worked directly from rods at the orifice of the shaft. These rods, which are either of wood or iron, work in the pipes of the pumps. The pipes are united directly to the body of the pumps, and have a slightly-increased diameter, so as to permit the easy removal of the pistons.

In many cases, when the driving engine has more power than is absolutely necessary for hoisting, the surplus of power can be made available for working a couple of lifting pumps of the kind above mentioned. In this case the pumps work under the same conditions as the hoisting itself, stopping when necessary to fasten or unfasten the kibbles, and turning in one or the other direction according to the change of the working.

A temporary and inexpensive system of pumping is thus obtained, and is very serviceable until the increasing amount of water requires a special pumping engine.

RAISING WATER BY GUIDED KIBBLES.

In some cases one of the most ancient systems of pumping is still in use; we allude to the extraction of the water by means of kibbles suspended on cables.

As at first established, this system only permitted the elevation of small quantities of water; but owing to the perfection of the engines now employed, this class of machines can be employed with great advantage. Since the perfection of the guides employed in the shafts is such that ponderous loads of water can be raised very rapidly, the ancient wooden kibbles, which brought up 500 to 600 quarts at a time, have been replaced by iron tanks of horizontal rectangular or circular form, which will hold from 2,500 to 3,000 quarts, and travel from 9 to 36 feet (3 .00 to 12^{m}.00) per second.

Under these circumstances large quantities of water can be brought to the surface, if care be taken to render as easy as possible the filling and emptying, which can be readly accomplished by making use of large valves.

HUET AND GEYLER'S CHAIN PUMP.

Lastly, we mention a trial made by Messrs. Huet & Geyler of their well-known system, but which to our knowledge had not been employed before for the drainage of mines.

The chain pump, which has been much used for domestic purposes, is composed of a pipe open at both ends and in which an endless chain passes, carrying at equal distances disks of iron, which nearly fill the pipe and act as buckets.

Messrs. Huet & Geyler construct these buckets with an india-rubber ring, which acts as a stuffing and fits the tube closely.

Two twin pumps were mounted and had to lift the water to a height of twenty-five metres (about seventy-five feet) only. One pump alone was intended for working, the other being simply placed there for use in case of accident.

The internal diameter of the pipes was $0^{m}.07$. These pipes were of copper drawn without being soldered, and only $0^{m}.002$ thick.

They were made in lengths of six metres, (eighteen feet,) and were united together by means of flanges and bolts. The endless chain was of ordinary construction; its links were of iron, $0^{m}.01$ in diameter.

Fig. 3.

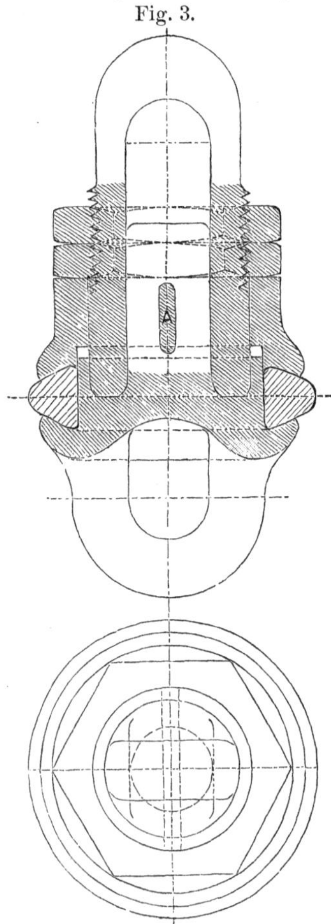

Huet & Geyler's Chain Pump.

The pistons or buckets were made in five pieces; (see sketch.) The stuffing was composed of a single india-rubber ring. Experience has taught that in order to obtain the maximum amount of work it was necessary that this caoutchouc ring should come in contact with the sides of the pipe, but without pressing on them. As the india-rubber wears, it is screwed up by a nut and a set nut. When it becomes necessary to renew the ring, it is easily accomplished by unscrewing the two nuts and removing the key A.

These pistons were placed at distances of three metres (nine feet) apart. The chain passes over a grooved pulley or sprocket-wheel, the groove of which is $0^{m}.01$ larger than the buckets. Studs introduced in this groove prevent the chain from slipping; they are adapted to the pulley and can be easily changed as may be desired. The speed of the chain is ninety metres (270 feet) per minute.

Thus constructed, this pump, which has now been at work for ten months without any other stoppage or repair than that of changing three times the india-rubber stuffing, has constantly raised quantities of water varying from 150 to 200 cubic metres per day of nine to ten hours.

On account of its simplicity and its small amount of wear and tear, this pump might be well adapted to larger diameters and to operate at much greater depths, taking care to divide the column at every twenty or twenty-five metres by means of reservoirs.

RUSSIAN PUMP.

A model of an apparatus for raising water was exhibited in the Russian section. It is very ingenious, but has not been yet practically used. This apparatus is composed of a tube running from the reservoir to the surface outlet. (Fig. 4.) This tube is divided by equidistant partitions, with a valve in the centre of each.

Pipes fixed in the partitions and under each valve, descend into each compartment and stop quite near the bottom. Two tubes follow the length of the central pipes, and by means of elbow pipes establish communication between two alternate sections of the central pipe. The pipe which communicates with the compartments of even numbers 2, 4, and 6 connects directly with the outside air.

Fig. 4.

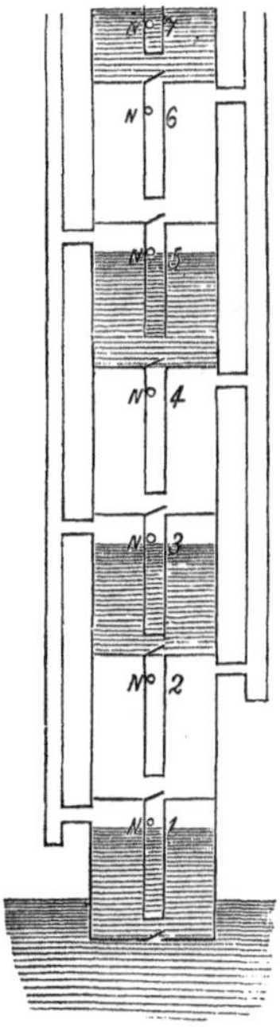

No 7
No 6
No 5
No 4
No 3
No 2
No 1

Russian Pump.

The other pipe in communication with the compartments of odd numbers 1, 3, and 5 is connected with a large pump which alternately rarifies or compresses the air.

A vacuum being made by the pump, the water rises from the reservoir and runs in the section No. 1. Then the pump compresses air and the water passes from section No. 1 to section No. 2 by the connecting tube, and the excess of compressed air escapes through the open tube.

When the pump makes the vacuum again in all sections of odd numbers, the compartment one fills as before, and, at the same time, the atmospheric pressure forces the water from section No. 2 into section No. 3, which is empty. When the apparatus is put in motion the pumps create the vacuum, the compartments 1, 3, 5, &c., fill under the influence of the atmospheric pressure, and when the pump compresses the air in the odd sections the water runs in the compartments of even numbers, and so on.

It is possible that air contained in the water, when escaping under the influence of the vacuum, might prevent the action of this pump. It is probable, however, that the greatest amount of air escapes through the open pipe at the time the water is forced from the odd to the even numbered sections.

Practice only will prove whether this ingenious contrivance can be made available for mining purposes.

CHAPTER IV.

MAN-ENGINES AND PARACHUTES.

Descent of miners by means of fixed ladders—Lowering men by means of cables—Construction of the man-engine—The rods—Landing-places or stages—Support of the rods—Hydraulic regulators—Movement of the man engine—Parachutes for the prevention of accidents to cages—Cages.

I.—THE DESCENT OF MINERS.

Fahrkunst, or man-engines, are not of recent invention; one or two early examples are known in Germany, and were established there toward the middle of the last century. These first machines were abandoned, perhaps, from not acting properly or from not being a real necessity at the time, and seventy or eighty years passed away before they again came into use.

As by degrees the mines of Germany, Belgium, and England became deeper, various plans were devised to procure cheap and easy means of descent for the workmen; and the man-engine was again brought into notice. From the most remote antiquity three methods have been in common use for the descent into mines, viz: inclined planes, ladders, and ropes.

Inclined planes have been used only in shallow mines; in deep mines the length and cost becomes so great that they cannot be used.

DESCENT BY FIXED LADDERS.

The descent by fixed ladders is the most common, and is certainly the safest and the most economical of all the ways yet tried to get to the bottom of mines of moderate depth and in all preparatory workings. When ladder-ways are well made, they are isolated from the rest of the shaft by partitions or brettices. The serious fall of a man in these cases is very rare, and can only happen through imprudence or carelessness. The workman has his safety in his own hands, and the accidents are few and slight.

Statistics show that of one hundred accidents occurring upon ladders, there are only about twelve fatal. But this mode of descent is inadmissible in deep workings and is then subject to three great inconveniences—first, it ruins the health of the miners who are compelled for a certain time every day to go up and down; second, the fatigue imposed upon the miners deprives them of some of their energy at their daily work; third, it takes a considerable time to change the shifts of mên or relays.

To go down 100 metres of ladder requires about 15 minutes, (900 seconds,) equal to 9 seconds per metre. If we suppose that the men follow each other at 2 metres distance, after the first man has arrived at the bottom of the shaft, it will be 18 seconds before the second man gets to the bottom, and so on; so that if the shift is composed of 200 men, it will require 900 seconds + 200 × 18 seconds = 900 + 3600 seconds = 4500 seconds, or 1 hour 15 minutes, for them all to descend to the bottom.

If the shaft is 400 metres deep, 15 minutes per 100 metres must be added for the descent of the first man, which makes altogether 2 hours for 200 men; with this basis for calculation it is easy to find the time required for the descent of any number of men to any given depth.

The ascent of 100 metres of ladder requires about twice as much time as the descent; then if we take the depth of 400 metres, and the number of men 200, we have for the descent by ladders 2 hours, and for the ascent 4 hours, in all 6 hours, which, added to 8 hours work per shift, makes 14 hours, during 6 hours of which the work in ascending and descending is much harder than the actual mining.

It is impossible for men to continue to perform such labor, so that in most mines over 250 metres deep the hours of real work are shortened and the balance of the time is set apart for the work of ascending and descending.

The Polytechnic Society of Cornwall, in comparing the rate of mortality amongst men working at different depths, (accidents deducted,) estimates that in works of 400 to 500 metres in depth, where ladders are used, the lives of the men are shortened by twenty years. However this may be, it is certain that the prolonged use of ladders gives rise to serious derangements of the organs of respiration and renders a certain number of men unfit for work before they are thirty years old.

LOWERING BY ROPES AND CAGES.

The time required for lowering and raising a shift of men by cables, is not as easy to estimate as that required where ladders alone are used. It depends, in fact, on two variable elements—the rate of speed, and the number of men that can be lifted at each time.

The rate of speed varies according to the importance of the workings; in shafts without guides it is often from one to two metres per second; in shafts provided with guides and cages, it is from three to twelve metres per second; but when the men are taken up and down in the cages, the speed is often slackened, keeping it about three to six metres per second. The number of men carried at once is from two to three in the small workings, and sixteen to twenty, or more, in mines of greater extent.

A comparison of the time required for the descent by ladders and by lowering in cages may be made as follows: Assuming that there are 200 men in a shift and that the depth is 400 metres, the rate of speed, averaging, say five metres, and that eight men are carried at once—at five metres per second, to ascend or descend 400 metres requires $\frac{400}{5} = 80$

seconds. To this must be added about two minutes (120 seconds) for the stepping in and out of the men, and the starting and stopping of the engine, which makes altogether $120 + 80 = 200$ seconds. Lowering 8 men at once, we have $\frac{200}{8} = 25$ journeys in all for the shift; the time will therefore be 25×200 seconds $= 5000$ seconds $= 1$ hour 24 minutes. Doubling this for the entire time in going into and out of the mine, will be 2 hours 48 minutes, which is half the time taken for the ascent and descent of the same number of men by ladders.

But these figures are not absolute; they may vary widely, either more or less, according to the extent of the workings.

The advantages and disadvantages of the rope are inversely to those of the ladders; the health of the men does not suffer, but there is less security, and accidents are much more serious.

Accidents by ropes and by ladders are as 3 to 2; but this ratio is still increased by the fact that of 100 accidents to men, 94 are killed and 6 injured.

These deplorable consequences from this method of transportation of miners caused the Prussian government to prohibit the lowering or raising of men by the cages in the mines of Prussia.

In other countries they are still used together with the ladders up to this time, but the man-engine has again come into use, and will now be described.

CONSTRUCTION OF THE MAN-ENGINE.

The movable ladders *(echelles mobiles)* called in Germany *Fahrkunst*, and in England *man-engine*, present, when well constructed all the desirable conditions for security, rapidity of motion, and for health.

They are all alike in principle, and consist essentially of two strong beams or rods hung side by side in the shaft of a mine. Each beam has platforms or landings large enough for a man to stand upon placed at equal distances from the top to the bottom. Handles to be grasped by the hands of the men are attached at a convenient height above each platform.

One of these beams, or both of them, is connected with an alternating movement, combined in such a manner that, at the moment the movement changes, the stages of both beams or rods are level with each other.

The difference between one man-engine and another consists only in the particulars of construction, and in the manner in which the motion is given to the rods.

There was nothing especially new in the Exposition, either in the small models or in the drawings, and we will therefore abstain from describing them, but will point out the improvements in the details while reviewing successively all the separate parts forming the whole of the man-engine.

Before noticing these details, we will give a description of the principle of the man-engine for those persons who may not be familiar with its action.

Let us suppose that the rods E and D range all the depth of the mine shaft, and that at equal distances stages A, B, C, &c., are fixed to the rods opposite to each other.

Fig. 5.

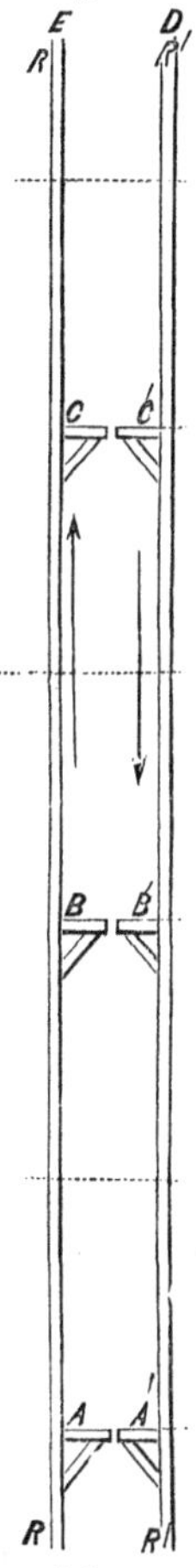

Fig. 5 shows a portion of the rods R R′, with their stages or platforms A A′, B B′, C C′, placed at equal distances. An alternate upward and downward movement is given to each of these rods; while the rod R, with its stages, is ascending, the opposite rod R′ is descending. This movement brings the platform A on the rod R opposite to the platform B′ on rod R′, and the platform B opposite the platform C′. The motion is then arrested for a moment, and is immediately afterward reversed, and the platforms return to their original position. If now miners are standing upon the platforms of R, they will all be raised by the upward movement a distance equal to half the distance between the platforms. At this point, the motion ceasing, the miners step from the platforms of the rod R to those upon the rod R′, and by the next movement are again lifted, when they step across as before, and so on until the top of the shaft is reached. The descent is similarly accomplished.

In a few cases only one of the rods moves, and the other remains stationary, or rather the second rod is omitted and stages are fixed to the side of the shaft in the rock itself; in such cases the single rod has to move the whole distance between two stages instead of half that distance, as when two rods are used.

When a single rod is used in connection with fixed stages, the miners pass alternately from the stage on the rod to the stage fixed in the rock. They then wait until the half-stroke brings a fresh stage opposite to them, on which they place themselves, and so on.

The distance between two stages on the same shaft generally varies from $4^m.50$ to $8^m.00$. The stroke of the apparatus with two movable shafts is always half the distance between the stages, consequently it varies from $2^m.25$ to $4^m.00$. There are from four to eight double strokes per minute.

In order to estimate the time required for the ascent and descent of miners by this engine, let us take our standard example, 400 metres of depth and 200 men to send down or lift up for each shift.

Allowing the stages to be 6 metres distant from each other, and the man-engine to make 6 double strokes per minute—in one minute a man will then have passed upon and from 6 stages, he will then have been lifted $6^m.00 \times 6 = 36^m.00$, and consequently will rise the 400 metres;

in $\frac{400}{36}$ = 12 minutes, in round numbers. Each double stroke thereafter will deliver another man at the surface, or, which is the same thing, the machine will lift 6 men per minute; the 200 men will therefore arrive at the surface in $\frac{200}{6}$ = 34 minutes in round numbers, which, added to the 12 minutes required for the whole ascent of the first man on the stages, gives in all 46 minutes; doubling this for the lowering and lifting of one shift of men, and we have 92 minutes (1 hour and 32 minutes) for the whole, and that without either danger or fatigue.

So that for 200 men and 400 metres of depth, the ascent by ladders requires 6 hours; by hoisting, varying from 1 to 4 hours; by the man-engine, only 1½ hour.

The fitting up of a man-engine is doubtless, a considerable expense, but it is soon repaid by the time saved, and the prevention of muscular fatigue of the miner.

DETAILS OF CONSTRUCTION.

THE RODS.—The rods are either made of wood or of iron, according to the local convenience. Iron is lighter with the same power of resistance, and requires less room.

Fig. 6.

Whether the rods are made of wood or of iron, they are all made with a decreasing section from the top to the bottom of the apparatus. The wooden rods are made in two ways—either of beams adjusted end to end, like the rods of lifting pumps, or they are made with planks, the ends of which are stepped together, as indicated in the annexed figure. (Fig. 6.) Gradually, as the load to be carried allows of it, a plank is left out so as to reduce the weight as much as possible and yet retain all the necessary solidity.

Iron rods have been made in various forms, but generally in the shape of angle iron. The round or flat iron has the inconvenience of allowing too much vibration, especially at the bottom.

The number of rods for each side of the man-engine may be one, two, three, or four. The single rod is generally used in the inclined shafts. It is composed of a piece of wood running on rollers at about six or eight metres apart. These rollers of wood or cast-iron are laid on sills of wood fixed in the rock.

The stages or platforms are made of planks large enough to receive both feet, and are firmly supported by iron brackets below; iron handles are securely fixed by bolts to the rods, at a height of about $1^m.00$ to $1^m.30$ above each stage, to enable the miner to keep his balance.

Where the rods are separated by fixed ladders, as in some instances, the distance required to pass over from one stage to the other varies from $0^m.65$ to $0^m.75$, which renders the apparatus incommodious and even dangerous.

Man-engines in vertical shafts always have at least two rods, balancing each other.

Mr. Havrez, manufacturer in Belgium, and exhibitor, constructs man-engines with three rods in each of the lifts.

Rods are sometimes made with the landing-stages large enough to carry two men at once, which permits the miners to pass each other with ease in going up and down, some ascending while others are descending.

THE LANDING PLACES OR STAGES.—The stages are made of the lightest wood possible, and their dimensions vary according to the space at command; they should not be less than $0^m.50$ to 0 .60 square; but some are made which are only $0^m.40$.

But with these small dimensions they are dangerous. These stages are generally put in iron frames, which serve at the same time to bind the rods. When two stages, one on the ascending, the other on the descending rod, are level with each other, the distance which separates them varies from $0^m.03$ to $0^m.250$, and even to $0^m.30$.

When the space is wide, there is danger in crossing from one stage to the other, for the miner may step into the empty space and be precipitated to the bottom. But if, on the contrary, the space is very narrow, the passage is very easy, but there is danger that the miner may imprudently let his head or his shoulder project beyond the stage on which he is, so as to be struck or caught by the stage of the opposite rod during the movement.

This difficulty is avoided in two ways—either by making the stage in two pieces, one fixed and the other hinged, so that it rises when it meets with an obstacle, or in fixing under each stage inclined planks, well dressed and smoothed, which push against an obstacle and force it back within the limits of the opposite stage. This last plan can only be used where the movement of the man-engine is not too rapid; if the motion is rapid, the first is preferable.

The hinges of the stages are made either of copper or of very strong leather to avoid oxidation. In the mines of Freiberg, Saxony, the stages are not placed opposite each other, but side by side.

BALANCE WEIGHTS AND PULLEYS.—The rods and stages work in guides at distances which vary from twenty to fifty metres from each other. But this is not sufficient. It would not be prudent to leave such a mass, 200 to 500 metres long, suspended without any other support.

The whole weight is therefore balanced by what are called balance pulleys. They are placed two and two alongside the rods. The opposite rods are then connected by chains, which pass over these pulleys and thus sustain a part of the weight of the rods. The weight of one rod also counterbalances the weight of the other. Adjusting screw rods at the ends of the chains give the means of changing the length of the chain so as to secure the proper strain on each support or pulley. The arrangement of the rods, the central ladder-way, and the balance pulleys and chains, are shown in the annexed figure.

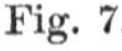
Fig. 7.

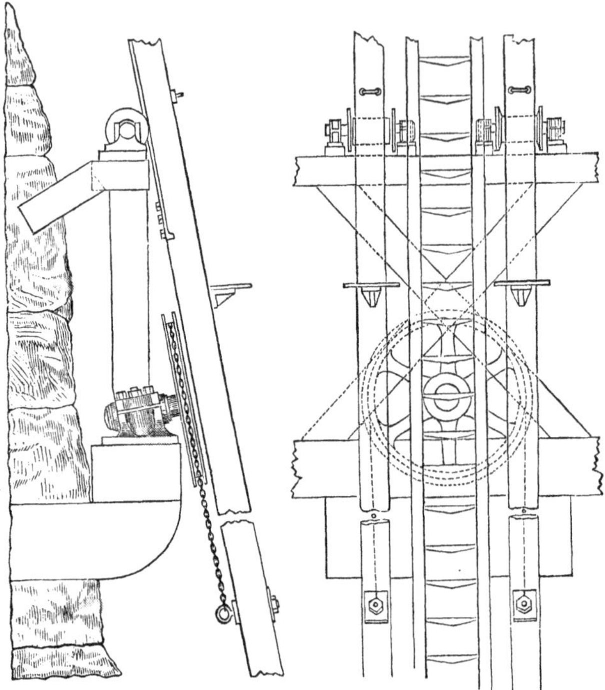

Support of the rods of the Man-engine in an inclined shaft.

The hydraulic balance has been tried for the same purpose. It is composed of two pistons: one is placed on the first set of lifts, the other on the second. To these pistons two pump-barrels correspond, connected with each other by a pipe giving free communication. The descending set of lifts taking the piston with it, forces the water into the other pump-barrel, and as the water has no outlet, it forces up the other piston, lifting the other set of lifts with it.

The hydraulic balance would be very good if the packing of the pistons could be kept tight; unfortunately it cannot, water is lost, and then the descending piston does not transmit its pressure to the rising piston before some part of the stroke is lost, so that the balance is disturbed. It has been abandoned for this reason. When the man-engine is single-acting, (that is to say, where there is not more than one set of lifts and the other set replaced by a line of fixed stages,) the movable lift must be balanced to prevent the shock it would receive at the bottom by the impetus gained during its descent. This balance can be obtained by chains attached to different heights of the lift, passing them over pulleys attached to the rock, and attaching to their ends counterpoises of sufficient weight. Such an arrangement is very dangerous from the liability of the chains to breakage.

In England such pulleys are replaced by beams carrying balance weights; but although this arrangement is safer, it is much more expensive. The stroke, always a long one with a man-engine, requires beams of large dimensions, and they cannot be lodged in the shaft without making very large excavations in the rock, which are very expensive.

HYDRAULIC REGULATORS.—To regulate the descent, a hydraulic regulator or brake is also used. It is a pump furnished with a suction-valve, and the outlet of the pump is furnished with a tap. The piston of this pump is fixed to the shaft of the lift; when this latter rises the pump fills with water; when the piston falls the water can only escape by the small opening, and the issue can be regulated by the tap. The rapidity of descent may thus be varied at will. The different contrivances we have just described constitute, properly speaking, the whole of a man-engine. It only remains to mention the different methods of putting the apparatus in motion.

THE MOVEMENT OF THE MAN-ENGINE.

Up to this time two methods have been employed—the direct-action engines and the ordinary steam-engine, giving rotation and the communication of motion by a crank. The first idea of the man-engine consisted in employing the pump-rod for carrying the men. Stages were fixed on the rod, and in connection with them fixed landing-stages. It is therefore natural that with this origin the first man-engines should have simple motive machines and cataracts. Since that time motion has been given to the man-engines by ordinary engines, with connecting rods and cranks; but as the man-engines work very slowly, several contrivances have been used as intermediates between the rods and the motive power.

When direct-acting engines are used, there is a stoppage after each stroke to give the miners time to pass from one stand to the other. This stop varies from two to eight seconds, which is ample, as the passage from one stand to the other does not take more than one second. This would be a very good system if the stop were always rigorously the same. But all who have worked the machine with direct single action and cataract know that it is impossible to obtain this regularity. The irregularity may indeed cause accidents. The miner relying on the normal time of the stoppage may be surprised in the midst of the movement he is making, and as the single-action engine starts suddenly and very quickly acquires a great velocity, he may have one leg roughly taken up while the other remains on the stage which rapidly goes down.

When the man-engines receive their reciprocal motion from a crank on a revolving shaft, there is, so to speak, no stoppage. The stages which approach each other are hardly on the same level when they separate again; but by taking care to have the machines provided with regulators and heavy fly-wheels, the movement is regular and there is no change to surprise the miner at the moment of his passage from one stage to the other.

It must not be forgotten that the movement of the machine being uniform, that of the connecting rod which commands the man-engine is variable. It is very slow at the commencement of its stroke, is accelerated at the middle of the stroke, and becomes slow at the end. The miner, thanks to the regularity of the movement and the slowness of speed, when the stages approach the same level and separate from each other, can begin his passage from one rod to the other a little before the stroke, and continue it a little after.

Experience proves that this second method is the safest. The persons who go down for the first time on these machines do not experience any disagreeable sensation. It is not so with the single acting machines; when, after the stoppage, the stage lifts or lowers a person suddenly who is not accustomed to them, he experiences a disagreeable sensation, (a sinking at the stomach,) which is increased by the sudden stop at the end of the stroke.

Man-engines worked by direct-acting engines, in order to raise the same number of men in a given time, must move more rapidly than when the motion is communicated by a crank.

Let us suppose two man-engines, worked by these different engines, having a stroke of $3^m.00$ and making 6 double strokes per minute. The speed per minute is equal to $3^m \times 12$ strokes single $= 36^m$. Therefore, while the crank machine will take 60 seconds to go over these $36^m.00$, or a mean velocity of $0^m.60$, the single-acting engine will take 60 seconds diminished by 12 stoppages, which are generally of $2\frac{1}{2}$ seconds $= 30$ seconds; its speed must then be double—$1^m.20$. The diagrams annexed clearly indicate the difference that exists between the working of these two methods. (Figs. 8 and 9.)

Fig. 8.

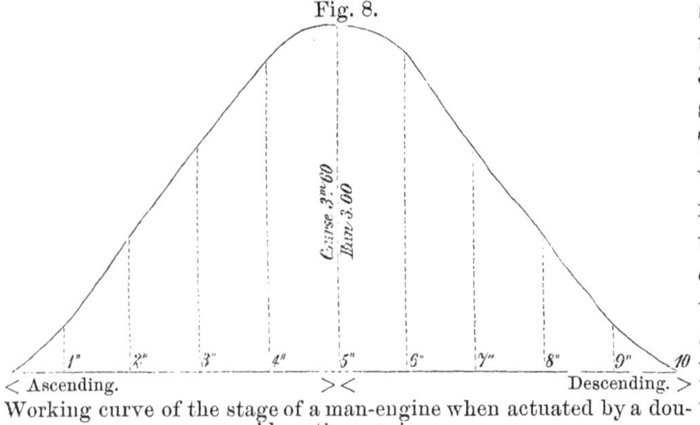

Course 3m.00
Run 3.00
1"
2"
3"
4"
5"
6"
7"
8"
9"
10
< Ascending.
><
Descending. >

Working curve of the stage of a man-engine when actuated by a double acting engine.

Fig. 9.

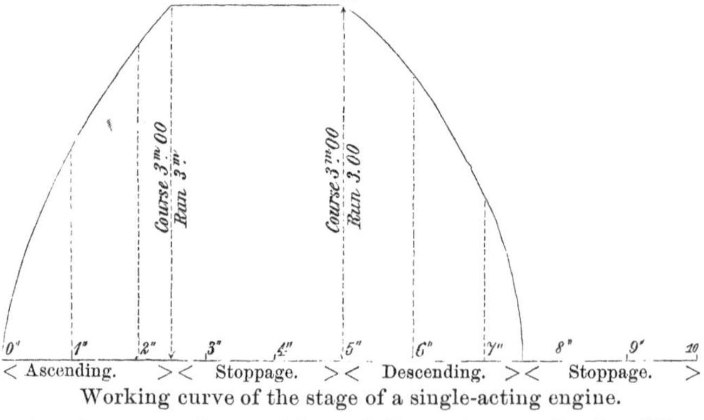

Course 3m.00
Run 3m.
Course 3m.00
Run 3.00
0"
1"
2"
3"
4"
5"
6"
7"
8"
9"
10
< Ascending.
>< Stoppage.
>< Descending.
>< Stoppage.
>

Working curve of the stage of a single-acting engine.

In these curves the abscisses represent the number of seconds from the beginning of an oscillation, and the ordinates the corresponding spaces passed over by a stage.

The machine with single action predominates in Belgium, while the crank machine is more used in Germany and England. The single-acting machines are generally placed directly over the shaft.

These engines are composed of two steam-cylinders joined together; the piston-rods are attached directly to the man-engine. The steam acts directly and alternately underneath or above one or the other of the pistons.

But there is an important condition to be observed, which complicates this arrangement a little. The platforms of the man-engines must have exactly the same velocity, and the strokes must terminate at exactly the same moment, so that both sets of platforms will be connected. This problem has been solved in two principal ways.

The first consists in extending the piston-rods through the upper cover of the cylinders, so that these two rods may be connected by a chain working over a pulley. They then necessarily move simultaneously. As a pulley working between the cylinders would have too small a diameter, two leading pulleys are placed over the cylinders, surmounted by a larger one.

The second method has been used at several places in Belgium by Mr. Havrez, already mentioned. The construction is shown by Fig. 10.

A strong rack is placed on each rod, and these work into opposite sides of the same pinion, steadied by an intermediate guide-rod. Uniformity of motion has thus been secured, for it is evident that when one rod descends, the other must move simultaneously and equally. Every precaution has been taken by the constructor to prevent breakage. The teeth are strong and carefully cut and flanged, and up to this time very few accidents have occurred.

Fig. 10.

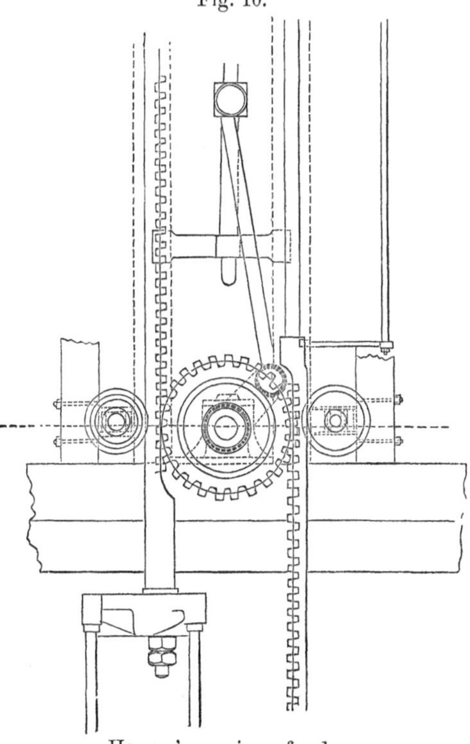

Havrez's gearing of rods.

When a man-engine receives the motion from the rotation of a crank, the two rods must also be connected together to secure their equal motion, and this is the more necessary where there is only one engine.

The methods of lifting are varied, and we will only mention some of the principal ones.

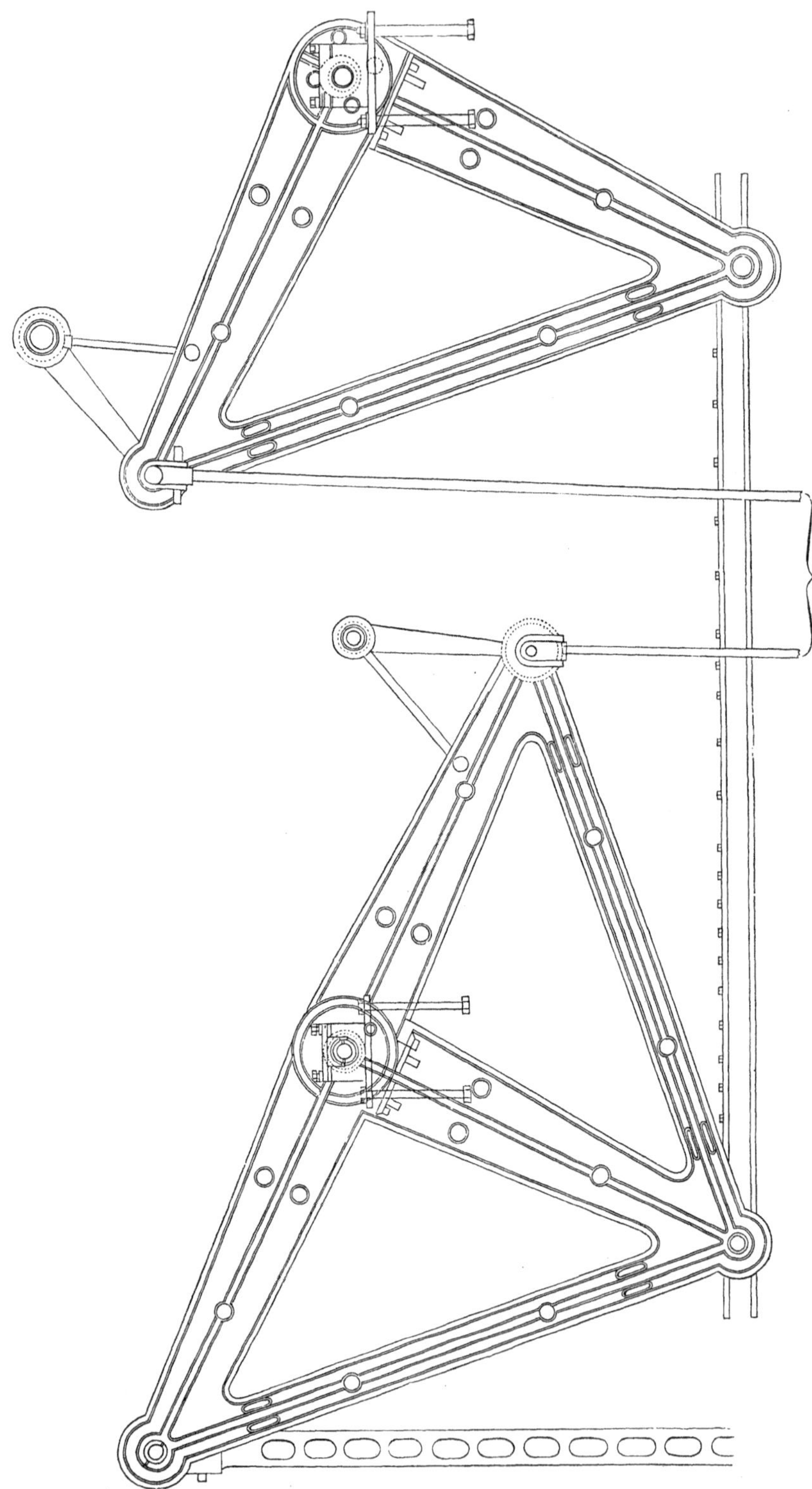

Fig. 11.—Arrangement for communicating motion to the rods of a Man-engine.

Balance beams and varlets are worked together by a connecting rod, moved by another connecting rod, taking its motion from a gearing, the pinion of which is placed on the main shaft of the steam-engine.[1]

Fig. 11 will give an idea of this arrangement. To avoid the great expense incurred by these balances, Mr. Graffin suspends the rods to flat cables which pass over leading pulleys and are attached to the two extremities of a wagon rolling on rails and worked by a connecting rod moved by the engine.

An ingenious arrangement by Messrs. Vaux and Guibal has been tried, but its utility has not yet been established by practice; but it is nevertheless worthy of being noticed.

Two cylinders are placed above the rods, as in the direct-acting engines. The engine gives motion to a strong pump without valves, which alternately forces and draws water from the cylinders over the shaft of the mine, thus alternately raising and lowering the pistons attached to the rods of the man-engine. The result is an alternate and opposed action of the rods. This plan would be excellent if the loss of water could be prevented.

The force required for the action of the man-engine varies from ten to fourteen horse-power for 100 metres of height. So far as our knowledge extends, the strokes have never exceeded four metres, except in an apparatus which was designed for extraction as well as for a man-engine, but which was abandoned, and in another very ingenious apparatus by Mr. Colson, of which a brief notice will be added.

Instead of making the rods of a continuous piece for the whole depth of the mine shaft, which requires them to be strong enough at the top to carry the whole weight of the apparatus, Mr. Colson divides them into a certain number of small shafts, suspended by chains to pulleys, balancing themselves two and two. These isolated rods are much lighter than in the other construction. The principal rod, extending down the whole depth of the mine, binds the small shafts together, without supporting them; therefore its strength must be proportioned only to the strain it has to overcome, which is very little, compared with the strain in the man-engines with continuous rods. Mr. Colson gives a stroke of ten metres, which he obtains by the alternate winding and unwinding of two cables.

The velocity of movement until now, except in the Colson machine, has never exceeded fifty metres per minute. The cost of construction varies considerably, according to the construction, and above all, according to the price of materials and labor in different countries. It varies between seventy-five to two hundred francs a metre for a depth of 200 to 500 metres. The engines made recently are nearer the lesser price, and hardly exceed the sum of 100 francs per metre.

Special and detailed descriptions of this apparatus will be found in the following named works, from which a part of the information herein given has been taken:

---

[1] In Freiberg the Fahrkunst is operated by water-power.

Portefeuille de Cockerill; Zeitschrift des œsterreichischen Ingenieur-Vereins, 10ter Jahrgang; Annales des Travaux Publics de Belgique, vols. 4 and 6; Annales des Mines de France, 5me, vol. xv; Revue Universelle, vols. iv, v, vi, xiv, xvi.

PARACHUTES.

The great depths to which mining operations are now carried; the increased rapidity of movement of the cages, (often as great as thirty and forty feet in a second,) and the paramount obligation to protect the lives of the miners who often ascend and descend by the cages, has led to the adoption of a variety of contrivances for arresting the fall of cages in the event of the breakage of the cables by which they are suspended. Such contrivances are known as *parachutes*.

The great velocity of hoisting requires the cages to be guided in the shafts by vertical tracks, which are commonly constructed of wood, though of late they are being replaced by iron and steel; these tracks, called *guides*, being continuous and equidistant along the path of the cage, furnish a foundation upon which the various parachutes can act to sustain the cage in the event of breakage.

A large number of patents relating to this important and indispensable apparatus have been taken out, but it may be said that there are only three plans, and that these originate from the same principle—levers drawn up and inward by the traction of the cable, and in an opposite direction by the tension of a spring which tends to throw the levers outward upon the guides, so as to press upon or into them with a force capable of stopping the fall of the cage in case of the rupture of the cable.

All parachutes combined and constructed on this principle have given satisfactory results, and it may be said that, if the security obtained is not complete and absolute, they have, nevertheless, rendered such great services that their application has become a question of humanity, which cannot be ignored. The following figures will speak in a stronger and more peremptory manner than any description can to persuade miners and engineers to adopt parachutes in their mines. At the mines of Anzin, from 1851 to 1859,[1] in fourteen shafts supplied with parachutes, twenty-nine cable ruptures occurred, after which parachutes were adopted and saved the lives of one hundred and fifty men. What can be more eloquent and more persuasive than this fact?

At the mines of Blanzy the experience has been similar, and it is probable that if an account had been taken of all the accidents by the rupture of cables in Europe since parachutes came into use, it would show that the men who have been thus saved from certain death can be numbered by thousands.

In order that a parachute should act well, it is necessary that the strength of the spring should be equal to 150 kilogrammes, (300 pounds,)

[1] Burat, Matériel des houillères.

and then the weight of the cage makes the rest; and the heavier that weight the more energetic is the grasp on the guides.

As we have said before, there are three types, viz:

1. *The parachute with claws*, which acts by a pressure exerted upon the guides and tending to penetrate them longitudinally.

2. *The parachute with eccentrics*, which acts by a pressure exerted laterally on the faces of the guides, and perpendicularly to the plane which passes through both their axes.

3. *The wedge parachute*, which acts by means of a set of metallic jaws taking hold of the guide, which is made wedge-shaped. This parachute gives a lateral pressure exercised upon the faces of each guide, and perpendicularly to the plane of the parachute.

These several types will be considered one after the other.

FONTAINE'S CLAW PARACHUTE.

The Fig. 12 represents Fontaine's parachute with claws. It is the oldest, and was constructed and put in use at the mines of Anzin, and may be said to have originated with this company. At first this parachute was supplied with only one spring, but two are now used, as shown by the drawing. It was the type exhibited in Class 47, upon the two-story cage sent by the company of Anzin.

Fig. 12.

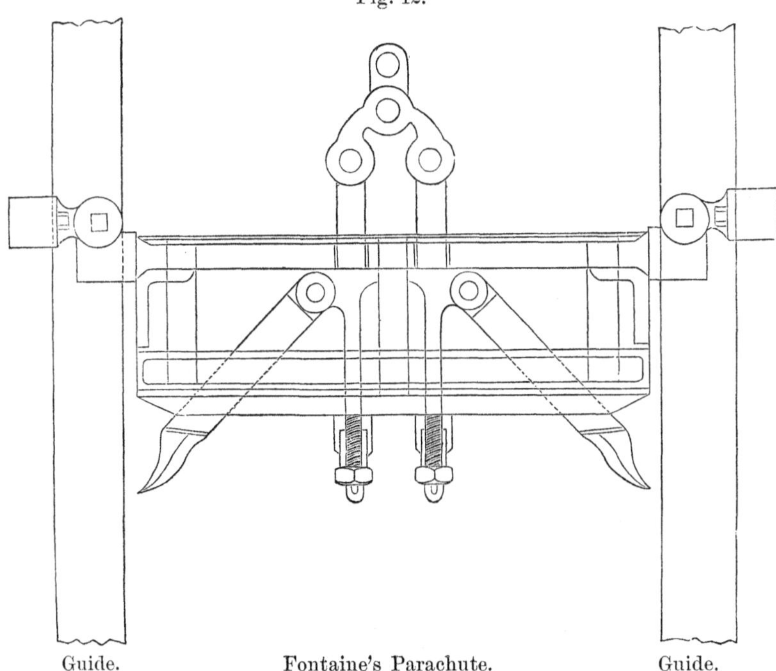

Guide. Fontaine's Parachute. Guide.

The two stout levers or claws are armed with sharp steel points, and are so placed in the frame that when the cage is suspended in the shaft by the cable, these claws are drawn up so as not to touch the guides. Two strong spiral springs, replaced in some parachutes by steel elliptic springs, are placed below, and in the event of the breaking of the cable they draw down the upper ends of the claws, and the lower and steel-armed ends are forced outward into contact with the wooden guides, penetrating and sometimes splitting them. The cage is thus arrested in its fall, and is sustained entirely by the wedging of these claws against the guides and timbers of the shaft. This construction has given satisfactory results in saving the lives of men, but the claws injure or destroy the guides. It also necessitates the use of very heavy timbers for the guides and their supports, inasmuch as pressure from the claws is exerted in one direction, and if the guides should yield or bend outward the effect would be lost. The first cost of such heavy guides and timbering is very great, and any accident by destroying a portion of the guides requires a great expenditure for repairs.

AUDEMAR'S PARACHUTE.

In order to avoid these difficulties other constructions have been devised; one by Mr. Audemar, engineer in the service of the mining company at Blanzy, is shown by Figs. 13 and 14. It consists of four eccen-

Fig. 13.

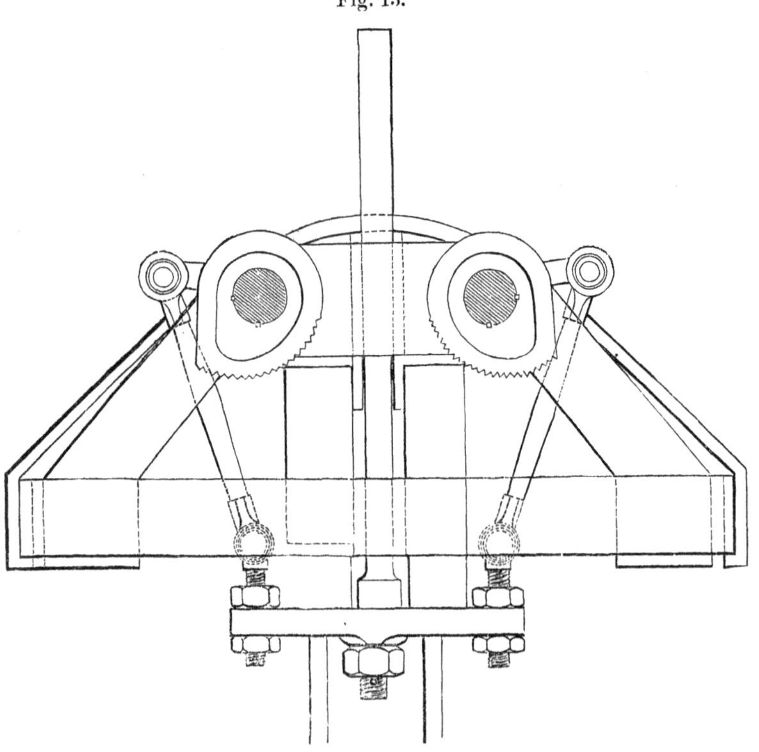

Audemar's Parachute.

Fig. 14.

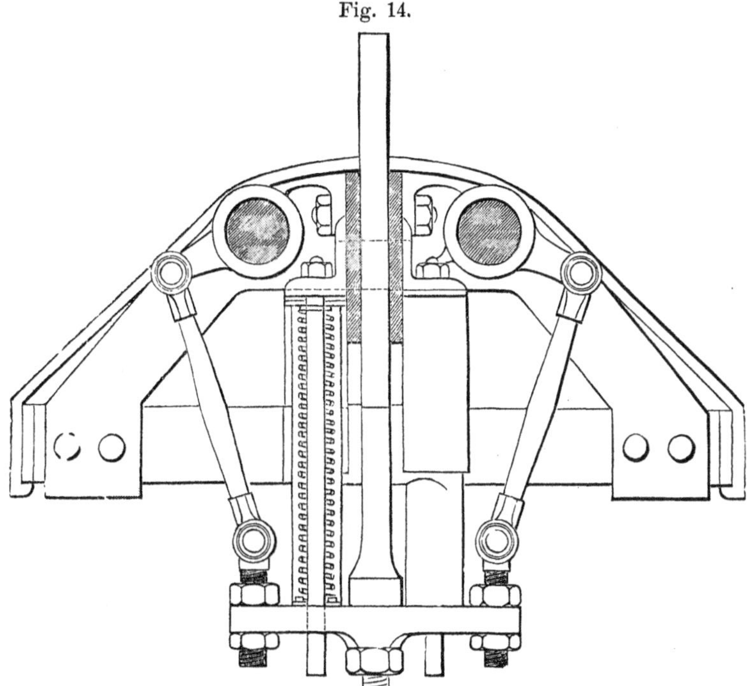

Audemar's Parachute—section showing one of the springs.

tric wedges, two on each side, and placed on opposite sides of the guides; the release of the springs by the breaking of the cable causes these eccentrics to turn and to powerfully squeeze the guides, and thus stop the descent of the cage. This parachute is as certain in its action as that of Fontaine, and does not split the guides. The guides and the framework may also be made much lighter, for there is no outward thrust or pressure tending to bend or break the timber.

The spiral springs used by Mr. Audemar are made of steel wire $0^{m}.01$ in diameter. When fully expanded they are $0^{m}.39$ long, (nearly 10 inches,) and they may be condensed to a length of $0^{m}.25$; but in order to preserve their full elasticity, the springs are condensed from $0^{m}.09$ to $0^{m}.11$ only. A compression of $0^{m}.09$ is sufficient, and this gives a resistance of 180 kilogrammes, (about 360 pounds.) Motion is communicated from the springs to the eccentrics by means of arms and levers, as shown in the figures. Fig. 13 shows the position of these arms and the eccentrics when the cage is suspended by the cable; and Fig. 14 shows their position when the strain from the cable is released and the springs are expanded. The spiral springs are contained in cylindrical boxes, one part sliding over the other. One of these boxes and the spring are shown in section in Fig. 14.

MICHAT'S PARACHUTE.

A variety of the same type as the Blanzy construction was exhibited by a model in the French section, designed by Mr. Michat. The construction is shown with sufficient clearness by Fig. 15, appended, and a description is unnecessary. It is evident that it does not differ essentially from the parachute just described.

Fig. 15. Fig. 16.

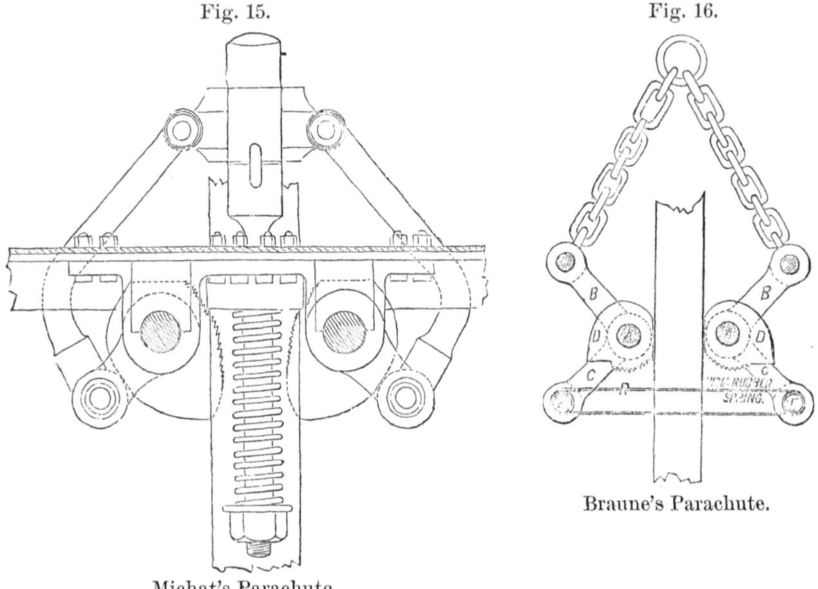

Michat's Parachute.

Braune's Parachute.

BRAUNE'S PARACHUTE.

Fig. 16 indicates a third variety of the same type, but it differs from the others by its extreme simplicity and the nature of the spring. This apparatus was exhibited in Class 47 of the Prussian section, and originated with Mr. Braune, the chief engineer of the mines of the Vieille Montagne Company. Instead of steel springs he uses an india-rubber band spring. It has been in use for the last three years with satisfactory results, but we regard it as designed for the protection of the material of the shaft, rather than for the safety of the men, and we should hesitate to apply it to cages used for the ascent and descent of miners. It has been used chiefly in mines where the loads to be lifted are not so heavy as those raised from collieries.

PARACHUTE WITH WEDGES.

The third type of parachute is constructed with wedges. It may be called a parachute with claws, in which the latter are replaced by a metallic jaw, in the form of a hollow wedge, fitting to the form of the guide, which is made wedge-shaped. When the parachute with the cage is sustained by the cable, the jaw moves along the guide without touching it; but if a rupture occurs, it then presses upon the guide in such a manner that the jaws wedge powerfully, and arrest the descent of the cage within a distance of only $0^m.25$ or $0^m.30$. The action is thus very prompt, but it is so gradual that there is no perceptible shock.

This construction does not injure the guides, and it has the advantage over the parachutes of the second type that iron guides may be used, the reduced size of which is much less cumbersome in shafts than heavy timbers. It, however, requires the guides to be made with great accuracy, and uniform in size and angle of the wedge, and the difficulty of obtaining them has prevented this construction of parachute from coming into general use.

In conclusion, it may be observed that although parachutes cannot be said to have reached perfection, (there certainly being great room for improvement,) they have rendered the greatest service in mining operations, have prevented great losses of life and property, and should be attached to every mining cage in use.

III.—MECHANICAL PREPARATION OF ORES.

CHAPTER V.

ORE-CRUSHING AND ORE-DRESSING MACHINERY AND PROCESSES.

INTRODUCTORY NOTICE OF THE CONDITION OF THE ART—SUBSTITUTION OF IRON FOR WOOD IN ORE-DRESSING MACHINES—ORE-BREAKING AND CRUSHING MACHINES—BLAKE'S ROCK-BREAKER, ITS CONSTRUCTION AND OPERATION—CRUSHING BY ROLLERS—STAMP-MILLS—RITTINGER'S IMPROVED STAMP-MILL—IRON-STEM STAMPS—ORE-DRESSING MACHINERY AND PROCESSES—MACHINES FOR CLASSIFYING OR SIZING CRUSHED ORES—TREATMENT OF STAMP STUFF—WASHING BY SIEVES AND JIGS—SEPARATION OF ORES BY FALLING THROUGH A COLUMN OF WATER—SLIME SEPARATORS—SHAKING TABLES AND CIRCULAR BUDDLES—CHAIN ELEVATORS—CONCLUSION.

INTRODUCTION.

The art of ore-dressing, or the separation, cleansing, and concentration of minerals and ores by mechanical means, has made great progress within the last twenty years. It is an art which has occupied the attention of government mining engineers and practical men in all mining countries, but particularly in Austria, France, Prussia, Saxony, and in Great Britain and the United States. Not only have great improvements and modifications been made in machines and processes long in use, and many new and important machines been invented, but the construction of all machinery for these purposes has been carried to a great degree of accuracy and perfection. This was shown in a striking manner by the exhibits in this class at the Exposition. These exhibits comprised some of the most important and interesting of the modern machines, of full size and in operation, together with models and drawings of others. It was evident that with these improved machines it is possible to obtain economical results of great importance, and to a great extent to supersede hand labor in ore-dressing, and at the same time to perform the work better and with greater rapidity, so that rough ores which were formerly too poor to be worked can now be concentrated with profit.

The two most prominent exhibitors were Mr. P. de Rittinger, of Austria, and Messrs. Huet and Geyler, of France. The machinery now in use in the United States and in Australia was not represented. To each of the above-mentioned exhibitors gold medals were awarded for their respective machines. The materials used by these exhibitors in the construction of their apparatus are quite different. Rittinger's machines were made of wood and iron; those of Huet and Geyler, of metal alone. The choice of materials for the construction of such machines depends upon the relative cost of the materials at the place of manufacture, and upon the conditions under which the machines are to be used. At the Austrian and Hungarian mines wood is abundant and cheap, and is used in construction almost to the exclusion of iron. In Paris, however, the reverse is the case, and Messrs. Huet and Geyler have excluded wood from all the machines which they manufacture. It is claimed by these constructors, also, that iron is much better than wood for all ore-dressing machinery for several reasons, which are enumerated at considerable length by them in a memoir upon the mechanical preparation of ores.[1] They urge that although wooden machines may be made with the greatest accuracy and care, they are no sooner put into place for work than they begin to swell and warp, and in the case of a circular buddle, for example, the whole surface must be made anew. Then, if for any cause the operation of such machines is suspended for a time, the wood dries and shrinks, and when they are again set in operation they are always found to be out of order, and to require extensive repairs. Another important objection to wood is the great bulk of the machines made of it as compared with those made of iron of equal strength. Again, wooden machines do not bear transportation to distant regions, neither are they so durable or so exact and regular in their operation as machines made of iron.

With cast iron the most favorable forms can be given to those parts with which the stuff to be worked comes in contact. All unfavorable angles and joints can be avoided. The constructors say that with iron and cast iron the forms of machines, and of their various parts, recognized in practice as the most favorable to the end in view can be adopted. The joints being perfectly tight, the loss of earth, water, or ore is prevented. No change of form in the machines, or any injury to them, need be feared by their exposure to either dryness or moisture. If they are required to remain unused for a greater or less time, or if they have to be transported to a great distance, they are not injured. Changes of season or climate do not affect such machines. During the severity of winter, the taps being opened and the tubs and pipes being drained of water, the hardest frosts will not injuriously affect them.

These advantages, and the necessity for machines that can be transported to distant regions unchanged, has already been recognized in the United States. Iron has for several years past been extensively substituted for wood in the construction of stamps, batteries, and concentrating machines in California and Nevada. Most of the concentrating machines and batteries now in use in California, Nevada, Idaho, and Northern and Western Mexico are made of cast iron. When such machines (made in San Francisco) arrive at their destination, they can be set up and put in operation at once, without requiring alteration or repairs.

Without attempting in this report to consider the whole subject of the mechanical preparation of ores, or the principles involved, we shall briefly

[1] Mémoire sur l'outillage nouveau et les modifications apportées dans les procédés d'enrichissement des minerais; par Messrs. Huet et Geyler, Ingénieurs, anciens élèves de l'École Centrale, Paris, 1866.

describe some of the most important of the machines brought to the notice of the public at the Exposition, and note incidentally some others, in order to give, as far as possible within the limits of this report, a connected view of the art of ore-dressing. We shall thus successively consider—

1. Machines for breaking and pulverizing ores;
2. Sorting or classification of the fragments and fine materials.

I.—MACHINES FOR BREAKING AND PULVERIZING ORES.

BLAKE'S ROCK-BREAKER.

The preliminary breaking or crushing of large masses of ore is now effected, to a great extent, in Europe and the United States by means of the machine known as Blake's rock-breaker, the invention of Eli Whitney Blake, of New Haven, Connecticut. Two machines of this kind were exhibited in the French section by Messrs. Huet and Geyler, who manufacture under the patent in France. The general construction of this machine has been rendered familiar by numerous figures and publications in the United States and in Europe. It consists, essentially, of a strong iron frame, supporting upright convergent iron jaws, actuated by a revolving shaft. The stones or masses of ore to be broken are dropped between these jaws, and a short reciprocating or vibratory motion being given to one or both of them, the stones are crushed, and drop lower and lower in the converging or wedge-shaped space, until they are sufficiently broken to drop out at the bottom. The size of the broken fragments may be regulated by increasing or diminishing the size of this opening between the jaws.

The type of the machine made in France is the same as that generally used in England, and differs from the common construction in this respect: that the lever is dispensed with, and the pitman from the eccentric shaft or crank operates directly upon the toggles. A few machines of this pattern have been made in California. The arrangement of the parts is shown by the section, Fig. 17. The mouth of this machine, as constructed by Huet & Geyler, is expanded, hopper-like, so as to be more convenient for the reception of the masses to be broken. This may be a desirable addition in some cases, where comparatively small stuff is to be broken and is to be shoveled in from a floor lower than the mouth of the machine; but when the mouth is placed, as it should be, on a level with the floor of the dump pile, the hopper is not required.

The rock-breaker may be successfully used instead of stamps to obtain either coarse or fine fragments suited to concentration. Messrs. Huet and Geyler seek to increase the fineness of the product of the machine by placing an "obturator" or obstruction, such as a triangular bar of iron, under the outlet between the jaws, arranging it so that it can be raised or lowered by means of screws, so as to diminish or increase the size of the outlet for the delivery of the crushed stuff. The effect of this obstruction is to retain the stuff between the jaws until it is so much broken and comminuted that it will sift through the narrow slits left on

Fig. 17.

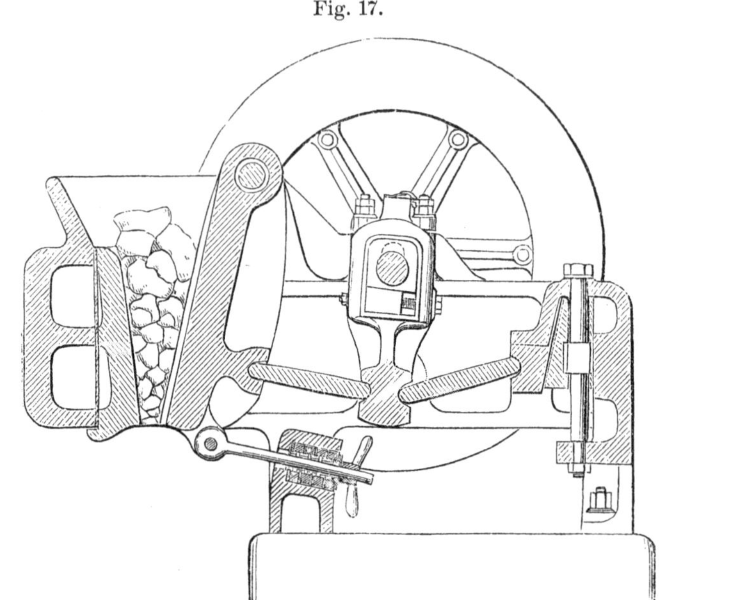

Blake's Rock-breaker.

each side of the bar. This method of operating is successful with some materials, but involves a considerable expenditure of power, and it is attended with some danger to the machine.

The fragments of ores produced by rock-breakers are better adapted, in size and shape, to washing and concentration by jigging than those from rollers and stamps. With hard and silicious rocks the breakers work dry, but when the ores are argillaceous, and are inclined to pack, it is necessary to employ a large quantity of water in order to obtain the best results.

CRUSHING BY ROLLERS.—A modification of the well-known Cornish crusher was exhibited by Messrs. Huet and Geyler. They substitute springs of vulcanized rubber for the lever counterpoise usually employed to keep the surface of the rolls in contact. With springs, the resistance increases as the rolls become more and more widely separated by the stuff to be crushed. These rollers were beautifully made, and worked very well. They were geared together, but were driven by a belt.

STAMPS.—There were two exhibitors of stamp-mills—one from Sweden, a wooden model showing the ordinary construction; the other by Mr. de Rittinger, of Austria, also a model. This last showed some interesting modifications of ordinary stamp-batteries, intended to increase the delivery of crushed stuff through the grates in wet crushing.

RITTINGER'S BATTERY.—The general construction of the battery is the same as in common use in Europe, with this difference, that a water-box is adapted to the front of the grates so that they are

are wholly or partly immersed in water, as shown in the accompanying drawing, Fig. 18. The swash and strong currents produced by the fall of the stamps wash both faces of the grates and keep the openings clean and free, so that the stuff passes more rapidly, while, at the same time, a delivery or escape-pipe, leading from the bottom of the water-box considerably below the level of the water in the mortar, determines a strong and constant current through the meshes of the grates outward. An increase of the product, with a diminution in the amount of slime, is claimed to be the result of this construction. The crushed stuff passes off with the water through the escape-pipe, and the amount of water required is less than in the ordinary construction.

Fig. 18.

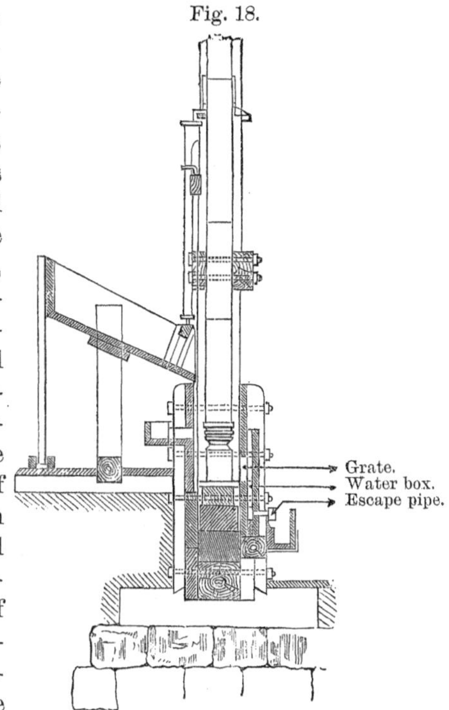

Rittinger's improved Stamps.

Iron-stem stamps.—Some iron-stem stamps, with cast-iron frames and mortars, have been made by Messrs. Huet and Geyler for the mill at the mines of Serena, in Estramadura, Spain. The stamps do not revolve, and the cams work through the center of the stem, and not upon a cylindrical tappet surrounding a revolving stem, as in the California batteries.

II.—ORE-DRESSING MACHINERY AND PROCESSES.

MACHINES FOR CLASSIFYING OR SIZING CRUSHED ORES.

In the mechanical concentration of ores a proper classification or sizing of the particles is one of the principal elements of success. It must not be carried to a great extreme, or be performed too roughly. A great variety of forms and combinations of sieves, screens, and trommels are used for the separation of the coarse from the fine particles.

Trommels.—Messrs. Huet and Geyler exhibited a classifying trommel which is in some respects novel in its arrangement. It is not supported upon a shaft passing through from end to end, but it is sustained by, and revolves on, trunnions at each end, as shown by Fig. 19, which is a sectional representation of a distributing trommel constructed so as to supply a system of four twin sieves. This trommel was in operation in the *annexe* of Class 47.

The crushed stuff is introduced by the hollow trunnion A, and falls upon a grate or iron plate B, perforated with large holes. The stuff which passes this plate falls upon a second plate C, with finer holes, where it is again divided, and the finer parts pass through to the outer plate of all. Each compartment has suitable openings at intervals in the annular crown at the end for the delivery of the different grades of stuff. With this apparatus four grades are usually obtained.

Fig. 19.

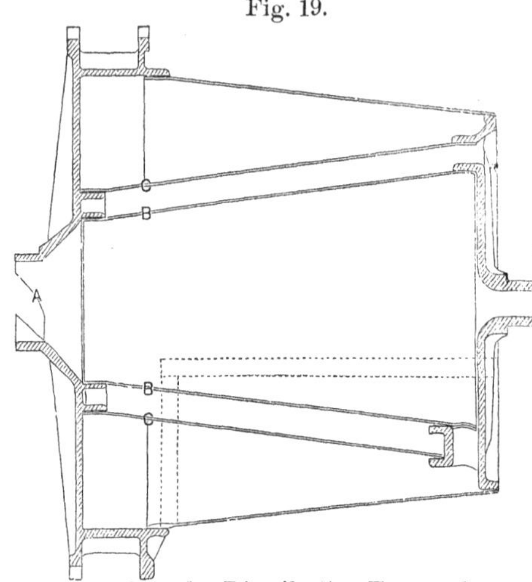

Section of a Distributing Trommel.

PERFORATED IRON PLATES.—Perforated iron plates are now generally used instead of wire screens, which wear out too quickly. It is essential to the best working effect that the thickness of perforated plates should always be less than the diameter of the holes punched in them. The space, also, between the holes in the finer plates should not be greater than the diameter of the holes, and in the medium plates half a diameter, and in the coarser plates one-third of the diameter of the holes. In France, perforations less than $0^{m}.002$ in diameter are considered as fine; those between $0^{m}.002$ and $0^{m}.005$ are medium. The fine numbers begin at $0^{m}.0005$. The finely-perforated plates for trommels are generally made of copper, and the other sizes of steel.

Some of the best exhibits of metal plates that we observed were made by Mr. Deny and by Mr. Callard, of Paris, and by Henry Foulon, of Liege, Belgium. In the United States section samples of perforated iron plates of different grades, such as are used for battery screens in stamp-mills in crushing gold-bearing quartz, were shown by the Union Iron Works of San Francisco, through J. S. Detrick.

TREATMENT OF STAMP STUFF—WASHING BY SIEVES AND JIGS.

The simple hand-sieve is the most ancient form of apparatus for sorting and concentrating ores in water, and it is still in use. Numerous modifications have been made from time to time, with the object of increasing the product by increasing the size of the sieve and supporting it in a frame, as in the hand-jig or brake-sieve, the construction of which is familiar, and by substituting machine power for that of the hand. Much attention has also been directed to the construction of automatic, or continuously working, jigs, by which the stuff to be washed enters in a constant stream, and, after being washed and concentrated, is delivered in two separate portions, without stopping or requiring manipulation.

In such machines the sieves, instead of being alternately plunged into and raised out of a vessel of water, are made stationary—are fixed firmly in a tub—and the water is made to alternately rise and fall, so as to pass in a strong current through the meshes of the sieve and the layer of ore above it. This motion of the water is produced by means of plungers or pistons acting below the sieve, either vertically or horizontally, or by elastic diaphragms, (as in Petherick's separator at Fowey Consols, 1831,)[1] which are alternately pushed out and in, as, for example, also in Edwards and Beacher's patent mineral and coal-washing machine.

In France some of the earliest automatic sieve washing machines were designed for washing coal, as in that of Berard and of Menier, the general arrangement of which is seen by Fig. 20.

Fig. 20.

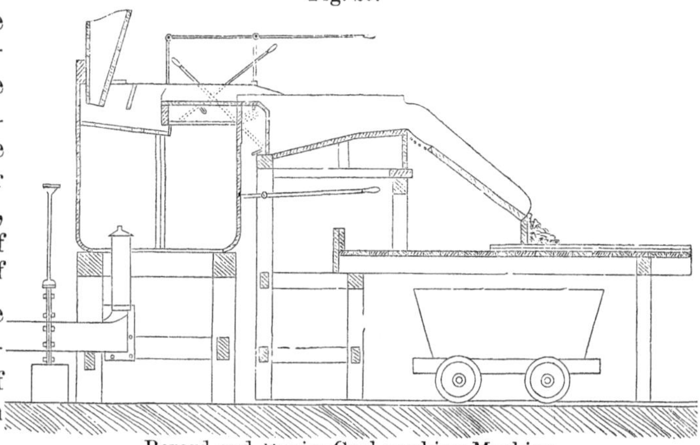

Berard and Menier Coal-washing Machine.

In 1855 Messrs. Huet and Geyler constructed an automatic machine with a valve in the center of the sieve, through which the concentrated stuff could be delivered. Although the first trials were not successful, the results were sufficient to encourage further efforts. The great difficulty was that, after the concentration had been effected upon the grate, opening the valve caused such a current that the waste stuff was carried down with the rich material. To prevent this difficulty the engineers of the Harz—Mr. Vogel, of Joachimsthal, and Mr. Wimmer, of Clausthal—invented an arrangement shown by Fig. 21.

Fig. 21.

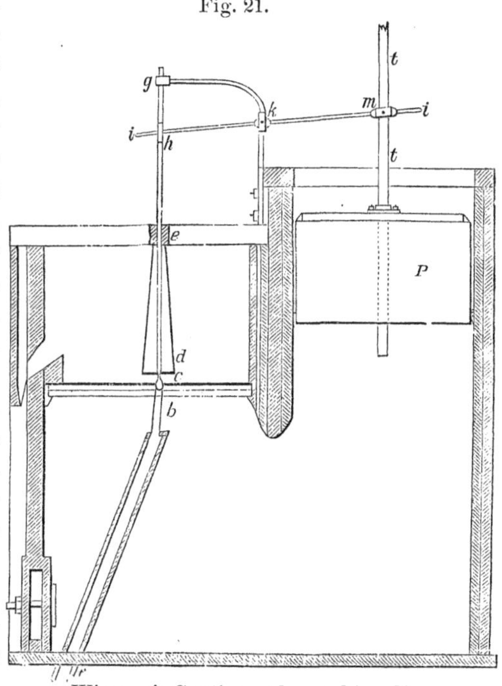

Wimmer's Continuously-working Jig.

The central outlet for the rich stuff is covered by a tube *d*, supported

[1] Ure's Dictionary, supplement, p. 852.

from a bar of wood above and reaching down through the layer of poor stuff so low that only the heavy and richer portions resting directly upon or near the sieve can pass downward into the discharge pipe *b f*. This pipe is alternately opened and closed at the top by an iron stopper placed at the end of a vertical rod the upper part of which slides through a supporting ring *g*. By means of an arm *i*, supported on a pivot at *k*, the stopper is alternately raised and lowered as the piston P rises and falls. The opening in the discharge pipe is thus opened when the piston descends, and is closed when it ascends.[1] It has been found in practice, however, that this arrangement for opening and closing the discharge pipe does not give satisfactory results, and it has been abandoned. A similar machine, in use in the Harz, has a perforated cylinder *d* surrounding the outlet in the sieve, and the bottom of the hutch is inclined toward a central orifice, so that it becomes self-discharging. The general construction is shown by Figs. 22 and 23. From five to six

Fig. 22. Fig. 23.

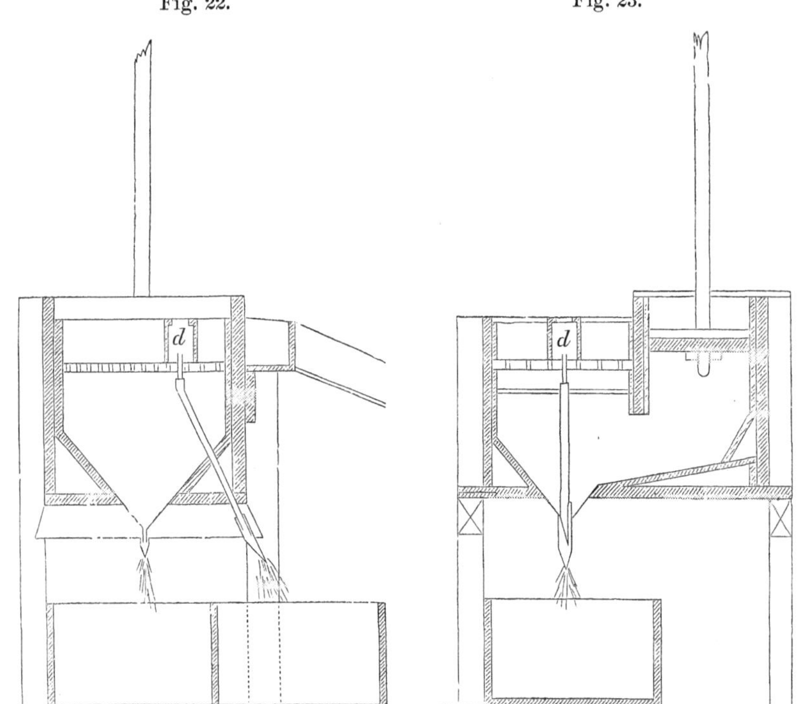

Self-discharging Jig—Harz.

cubic metres of stamp stuff can be passed through this apparatus in twelve hours.

[1] *Vide* La Préparation Mécanique des Minerais au Harz en 1857. Rapport par M. Aug. Gillon; Paris, 1858.

CONTINUOUSLY-WORKING JIG, HARZ.—In 1863 Mr. Geyer, an engineer from Baden, introduced continuously-working jigs into the great ore-dressing establishment erected by him on the banks of the Lahn. In the construction of these machines both wood and metal were employed. The arrangement of the parts is represented by Figs. 24 and 25. It is a double machine, composed of two grates and two pistons, acting simultaneously. The grates are inclined forward, and are provided with a chink or gutter at the lower edge, through which the concentrated ore falls into inclined troughs *c*. The stuff passes from one grate to another, and thus two different grades of fineness may be secured. Iron plates or partitions are placed so as to govern the discharge, and these may be raised or lowered at pleasure by the thumb-screws *e e*. These machines, worked at seventy strokes per minute, will wash about nine cubic metres of stamp stuff, diameter of 0m.005, in a day, and they require about 300 litres of water.

Fig. 24.

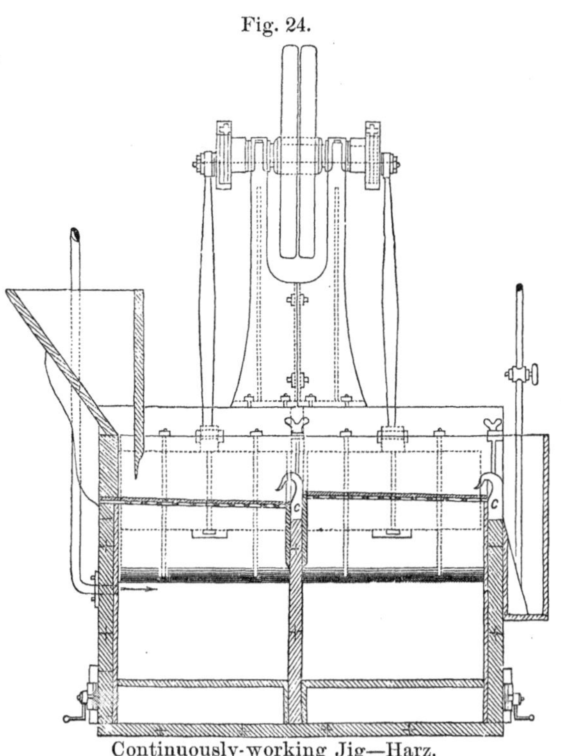

Continuously-working Jig—Harz.

Fig. 25.

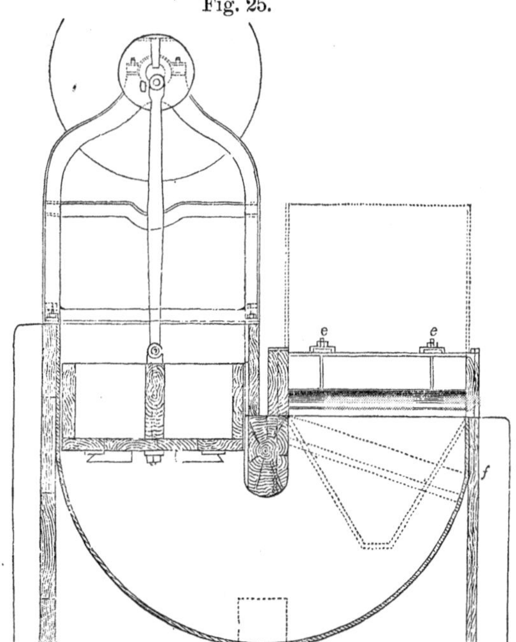

Continuously-working Jig—section through piston.

RITTINGER'S SELF-ACTING JIG.—One of the most interesting machines of this class was exhibited in the Austrian section, and is the invention of Rittinger. It is represented by Fig. 26, and is characterized by the inclination of the grates and the lowness of the front partition, over which the poor and lighter stuff falls continuously, and with very little water, while the heavier and richer portions fall through the opening or slit *o*, at the base of the partition. This partition is the segment of a cylinder, and is supported upon the lever or arm *d*, so as to be movable back and forth in such a manner that the opening or slit *o* may be increased or diminished at pleasure. The heavy stuff passing through the opening falls into the box K, from which it is removed as required. The inclination of the grate in this machine is from five to eight degrees. It is fed through the hopper B, which plunges below the surface of the stuff accumulated on the grate. The loss of water which occurs at each stroke of the piston is replaced from a reservoir W, at the back of the apparatus. According to Rittinger, experience has shown that the duty of self acting machines of this kind is generally three times as great as that from the ordinary intermittent working apparatus.

Fig. 26.

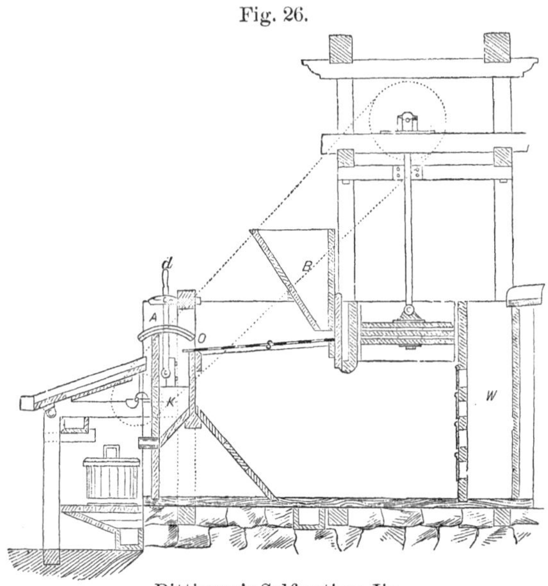

Rittinger's Self-acting Jig.

HUET AND GEYLER'S SELF-ACTING JIG.—Most self-acting jigs require a large quantity of water, and this in many localities is a great objection to their use. Messrs. Huet and Geyler exhibited several jigs designed to work with but little loss of water, and, at the same time, by the aid of an automatic scraper, to increase the product of the machine. These jigs are constructed entirely of iron, and have the form shown in Fig. 27.

The tub is shaped like the letter U, and is divided into two compartments, one for the piston and the other for the working grate. Water is supplied through the valve A, at the side, and the fine stuff or slime which falls through the sieve settles upon the bottom, and is discharged through an opening B, controlled by a lever reaching out to the front of the apparatus. The piston is operated by means of a shaft and crank, which works in an inclined slide C, connected with a lever carrying the piston, so as to give a rapid descending stroke with a period of rest at

Fig. 27.

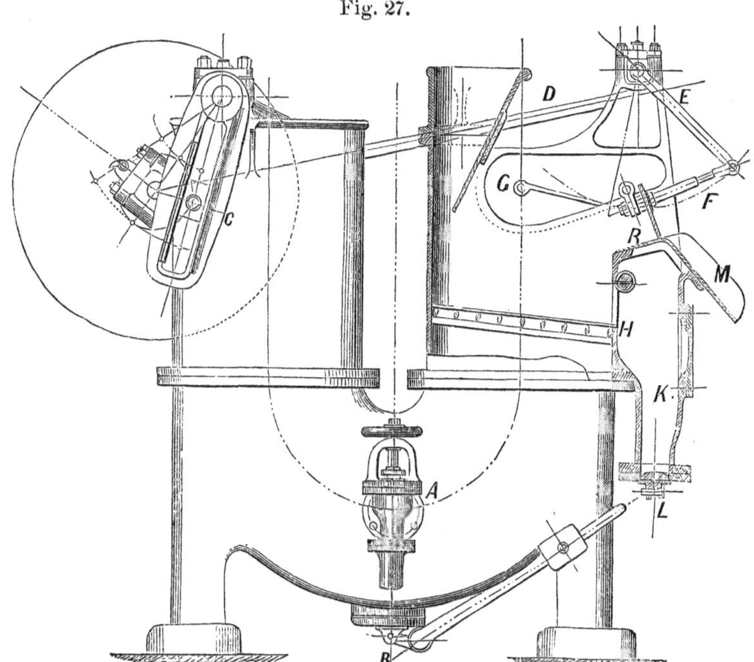

Automatic Jig of Huet & Geyler.

the bottom, and then a slow upward movement; thus giving the most favorable conditions for the rapid and perfect separation of the stuff upon the grate.

The motion of the piston may be varied at will, in order to secure the best flow or motion of the water for different grades of ore. This adjustment is effected by shifting the position of the head of the piston along the lever or arm, and by this means increasing or diminishing the amplitude of its motion. The construction of this slide is shown in the figure. By turning the fixed screw *s s*, Fig. 28, the head of the piston may be moved forward or backward.

Fig. 28.

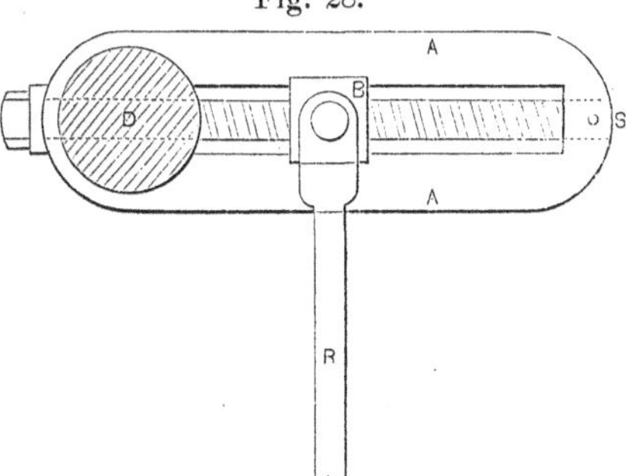

The machine is provided with a scraper R, Fig. 28, actuated by the long rod D, which is attached to an eccentric on the main shaft and moves the levers E and F, giving to the scraper a forward and backward motion over the top of the stuff upon the grate, and throwing out a portion of it at each movement. The path of the scraper is determined by the guides G, attached to each side of the tub. It can be varied by means of screws upon the lever or arm F. In passing backward, the roller or projection on the scraper, which follows the guides, rises upon the movable inclined plane G, and on its return passes below this plane, following the double-dotted line in the figure. The poor stuff from the top, which is constantly thrown forward and off by this scraper, falls over the front of the tub at R, along the shute M. The grate is inclined as in the machine of Rittinger, and the opening for the escape of the heavier and rich portion is similarly placed at the foot of the incline and just below the bridge over which the poor stuff is scraped. The opening is shown at H. It is closed by a valve which extends along the whole front edge of the sieve, and can be opened and closed at pleasure by a lever. The stuff passing through this valve falls into a receptacle K, from which it may be removed at pleasure through the opening L. The scraper is so made of perforated sheet-iron that it does not throw the water out together with the waste. These jigs are made with great care and accuracy, and work in a satisfactory manner.

SEPARATION OF ORES BY FALLING THROUGH A COLUMN OF WATER.

Various forms of apparatus have been devised to effect the separation of the grains of either coarse or fine stamp stuff having nearly the same volume, but differing in density, by allowing them to fall through a column of water either at rest or in motion. Such machines may be regarded as modifications of the jig; a greater length of fall of the materials in water being substituted for a succession of short falls, the result of the repeated shocks or jerks given to the sieve. Apparatus of this kind forms a connecting link between jigs and the slime separators. Three different forms of this apparatus were shown at the Exposition, viz:

1. The apparatus of Mr. Hundt, engineer from Baden. 2. The apparatus of Mr. de Rittinger. 3. The apparatus of Huet and Geyler.

HUNDT'S APPARATUS.—This was exhibited in the Prussian section, Class 47. Mr. Hundt, who has had large experience in the separation

Fig. 29.

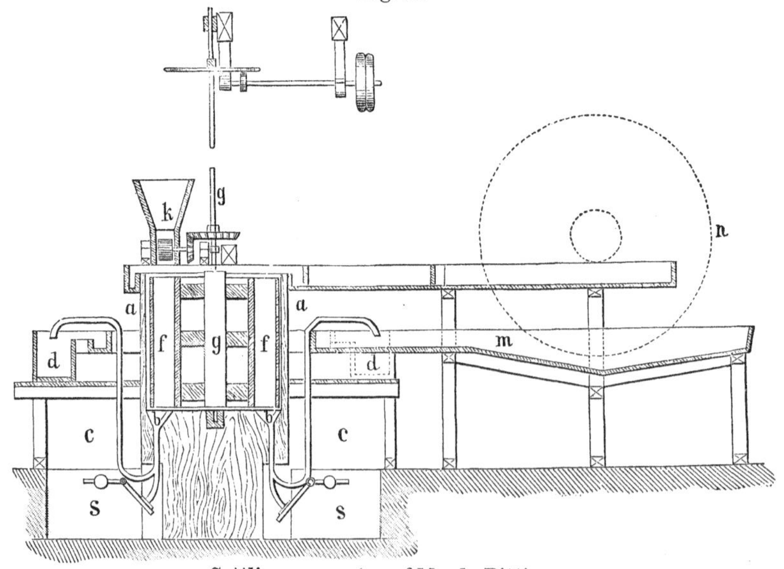

Settling apparatus of Mr. de Rittinger.

of coal, states that he has obtained excellent results with this machine. It was first put into operation at the mills of the Landerkrone mines, near Wilnsdorf, in July, 1864.

RITTINGER'S APPARATUS.—The construction is shown by Fig. 29. It consists of a stationary wooden tub *a a*, the bottom of which is divided into eight conical compartments connecting with pipes *c*, which, after descending for a short distance into the foundation, turn upward and outward, and are curved at the end so as to deliver the water from the tub into an annular trough *d*. A double cylinder *f f*, supported by a shaft *g*, is made to turn in the tub *a*. The stuff to be separated is delivered in a constant stream through the hopper and distributor *k* into the revolving cylinder, and falling through the water in this space is sorted and collected in the conical reservoirs and tubes *b*. A branch tube, closed by valves *s s*, permits the removal of this concentrated stuff from time to time. The waste stuff delivered through the tubes *b* into the annular trough *d*, flows into another trough or conduit *m*, whence it is lifted by the wheel *n*, and returned to the tub *a*.

APPARATUS OF HUET & GEYLER.—This was shown in the French section, and consists of two stationary concentric cylinders, about three feet long—(Fig. 30, E and I.) The outer cylinder is terminated at the bottom by a movable cone C, with an outlet in the center. A rotating tub B is divided into compartments, and is so placed under the aperture of the cylinders, that it receives the stuff that falls from them. The stuff for separation is dropped at intervals into the hopper-shaped top of the cylinder I, and, in falling through the column of water, is separated according to the difference of the specific gravities. The revolution of the receiving tub B must correspond in time to the time required for the descent of the different grades of the stuff. The level of the water in the apparatus is maintained by a supply pipe T, and any excess of water overflows by the gutter G around the top of the outer cylinder. The same water may be used over and over by pumping it from the bottom

Fig. 30.

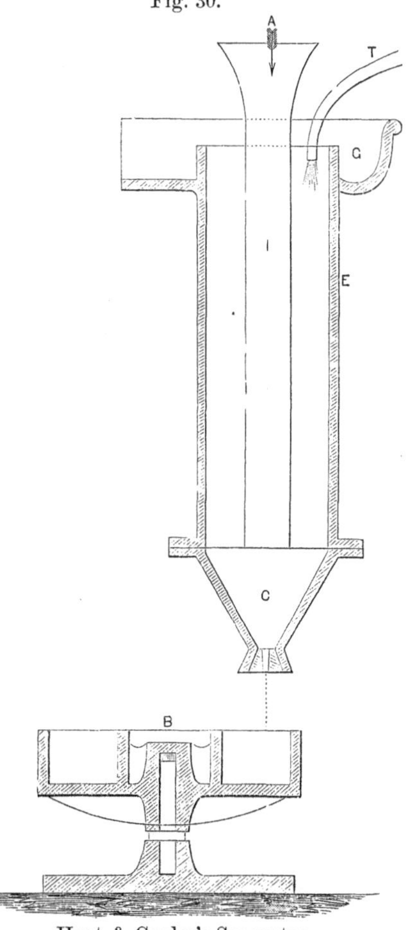

Huet & Geyler's Separator.

of the apparatus. It is essential that the stuff should be well sized before it enters the apparatus.

The following tabular statement shows the time required for the fall of stamp stuff of different minerals, and of different diameters:

Size of the gravel in millimetres. From	to	Galena, gravity 7.56.	Pyrites, gravity 4.60 to 5.00.	Barytes, gravity 4.50.	Blende, gravity 4.15.	Quartz, gravity 2.70.	Carbonate of lime, gravity 2.60.
		Seconds.	*Seconds.*	*Seconds.*	*Seconds.*	*Seconds.*	*Seconds.*
30.00	18.00	0.90	....	....	....	2.36	....
13.00	7.00	1.11	....	....	....	3.67	....
7.00	5.50	1.50	....	....	....	4.61	....
5.50	4.44	1.84	....	....	....	6.10	....
4.44	4.17	2.03	2.54	2.81	2.88	7.27	3.86
3.94	3.67	2.48	3.43	3.73	4.61	7.61	5.56
2.77	2.50	3.11	4.41	5.55	6.53	....	6.83
1.77	1.50	4.14	6.21	8.30	9.78	....	10.17
	1.00	5.27	10.36	11.33	11.67	14.64	17.21

This table shows that the velocity of the receiving tub must be proportioned to the size of the particles of the stuff to be separated and to the height of the fall. For a height of $1^m.00$, the number of revolutions of the tub per minute must be, for particles of $0^m.016$ in diameter 21 revolutions; $0^m.004$, 11 revolutions; $0^m.001$, 6 revolutions; $0^m.00025$, 2.7 revolutions.

This apparatus has not yet been long enough in practical operation to prove its value, and it requires to be studied and experimented with further before the results will be satisfactory, yet it has already been found that a thorough classification of the stuff is essential; that the feeding and the motion of the rotating tub must be regular; that the grains which separate best are those between $0^m.004$ and $0^m.01$ in diameter; and that with fine stuff the results are incomplete. When the particles are $0^m.014$ in diameter and have a density of 3.15, they will precipitate from compartment to compartment in the following order:

First compartment - - - - - density, 4.2; 7 per cent.
Second compartment - - - - density, 3.2; 52 per cent.
Third compartment - - - - - density, 2.9; 24 per cent.
Fourth compartment - - - - density, 2.9; 12 per cent.
Fifth compartment - - - - - density, 2.9; 3 per cent.
Sixth compartment - - - - - density, 2.8; 2 per cent.

For the particles of $0^m.014$ in diameter, the proper number of turns is three and a half, and for particles of $0^m.004$, five turns. One of these contrivances will deliver about 750 quarts of gravel per hour.

In conclusion, it may be said that although the different forms of apparatus described have not yet given results in all respect satisfactory, several mills have found it advantageous to use them. There is no doubt that great improvements may yet be made in this direction.

In concluding these observations upon apparatus for separating stamp stuff, where the particles are more than 0ᵐ.00025 in diameter, it may be mentioned that Messrs. Huet and Geyler are still engaged in constructing an apparatus for the purpose. It consists of a series of inclined fixed sieves connected with a piston, which will make from 150 to 200 strokes per minute, so as to keep the stuff suspended as long as possible in its passage across the sieves. Some preliminary trials with the apparatus promise good results.

CLASSIFICATION OF SANDY STUFF.

In classifying gravelly or comparatively coarse materials in jigs, it is sought to obtain by means of the trommels particles of equal volume, but for the classification of sands it is the reverse; for it is necessary to obtain a combination between the weight and the volume, or, in other words, to unite smaller grains or particles of great density with larger or coarser particles of less density, thus obtaining a mixture which is very favorable for enrichment by concentration on tables or buddles.

In general, the apparatus for classifying or separating the sandy and fine stuff consists of vessels or cisterns into which the mixtures are delivered in currents of water, so that the lighter portions flow off at the top, while the sand and heavy particles fall to the bottom and are drawn off through a small aperture. The sizing cisterns and separating boxes with sloping sides, in use at Schemnitz, are of this character.

Fig. 31.

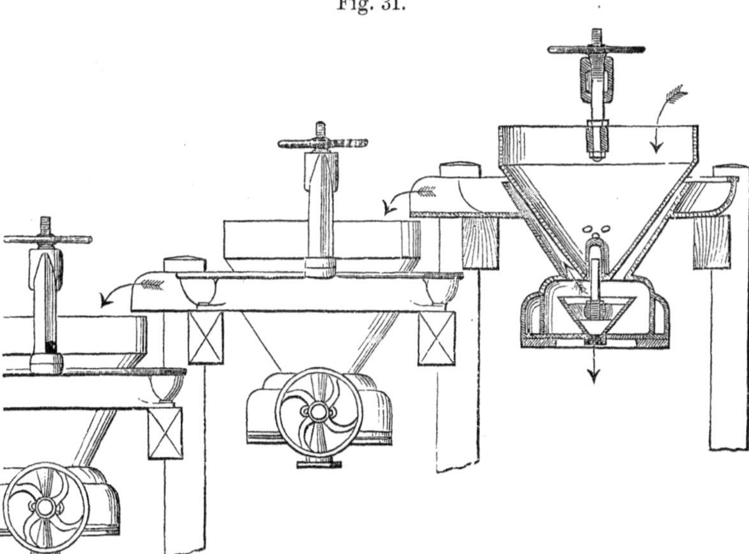

Conical Separators.

The conical separators shown by Fig. 31, make one of the most complete and effective forms of apparatus, but they require a large quantity of water. The construction may be readily understood from the drawing. It consists of two concentric fixed cones, so placed that the space between them may be increased or diminished at pleasure by means of an adjusting screw which raises or lowers the inner cone. The mixed stuff enters by the middle cone and falls through holes into the annular space between the cones, where it encounters an ascending current of water. In the upward flow of this water the lighter stuff is removed and the heavier particles fall to the bottom and are discharged in a constant stream through a conical valve. A series of such separating cones placed one below another, so that the second may receive the overflow of the first, and so on in succession, is one of the best forms of apparatus for the separation of slime from sand.

Fig. 32.

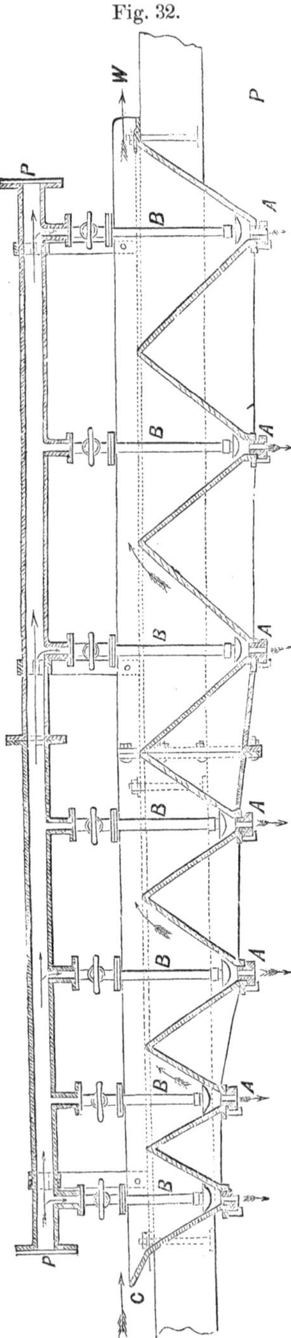

Rittinger's Separating Tubs with ascending currents.

RITTINGER'S SEPARATING TUBS WITH ASCENDING CURRENTS.—In this apparatus, shown in section by Fig. 32, tubs or compartments increasing in size are placed one below another so as to form a continuous series, and they are supported upon an inclined frame so as to give free access to the bottoms of the tubs. The sides of these tubs slope toward a central opening at the bottom, thus forming hopper-shaped vessels, or inverted hollow pyramids. The opening at the bottom is closed by a valve or plug A, through which the heavy stuff which collects may be drawn off. The tubs are joined together by the edges, and the outer edges of the series are the highest, so that when filled with water the edges between one tub and the next are below the surface, and thus permit a continuous flow of water from one end of the series to the other. A long supply-water pipe extends over the top of the tubs, and by means of branches B B delivers a current of water near the bottom of each tub. The stuff enters by a launder at C, and the heaviest particles fall gradually toward the bottom of the vessel, and in their descent meet with an ascending current from the pipe B. The lighter portions are thus carried upward and flow over into the next tub, and so on to the third, and finally are delivered at the outlet into the waste pipe at W. As the size of the tub increases the ascending currents from the pipes have less and less force and only the finest and poorest portions are carried away.

This arrangement gives very satisfactory results. It will wash and separate about a ton of sand each hour, and it requires from 120 to 150 quarts of water per minute. The apparatus is usually constructed of wood, but the figure represents it as made of iron, the advantages of which for such apparatus have already been noted.

SLIME SEPARATORS, SHAKING TABLES, AND CIRCULAR BUDDLES.

Several forms of apparatus for concentrating fine stuff and the separation of slime from sands by washing upon inclined surfaces were shown in the different sections of the Exposition, but none of the various contrivances for this purpose which have originated and are in use in the United States were shown. The principal exhibits were a shaking table with an endless belt, or cloth, constructed by Messrs. Huet and Geyler, shaking or percussion tables with lateral motion, (the stossheerd of Rittinger,) and rotary tables, or circular buddles, constructed entirely of metal.

SHAKING TABLE WITH ENDLESS CLOTH.—A machine of this description was exhibited by Messrs. Huet and Geyler, in connection with their other apparatus for ore-dressing. It consists of a strong iron frame, with rollers at each end, over which an endless band of cloth as wide as the table is stretched. This cloth, which forms the surface of the inclined table upon which the stuff is to be washed, is made to revolve by means of motion communicated to the upper roller by a pulley. The whole table with the frame is so suspended in an outer frame that a shaking motion or shock can be given to it by cams acting on each side of the frame. With the exception of this shaking or percussion, it is similar in construction to Brunton's machine, used at Devon Great Consols, in Cornwall, and described in the supplement to Ure's dictionary.

The slope of the surface of the cloth, and its speed of rotation, may be changed at will, and the number of jerks and their strength can be varied by means of the adjusting screw provided for the purpose.

RITTINGER'S CONTINUOUSLY WORKING STOSSHEERD.—This is one of the most interesting and important concentrating machines which has yet been invented. It was shown by models in the Austrian section, and was examined by one of the writers at the Kronprinz Concentration Works, near Freiberg, Saxony. A very full description of this stossheerd, with large drawings made to scale, has been published by Mr. Rittinger; but as that information is inaccessible to the majority of the persons interested in the mechanical concentration of ores in the United States, a brief description is desirable.

Fig. 33.

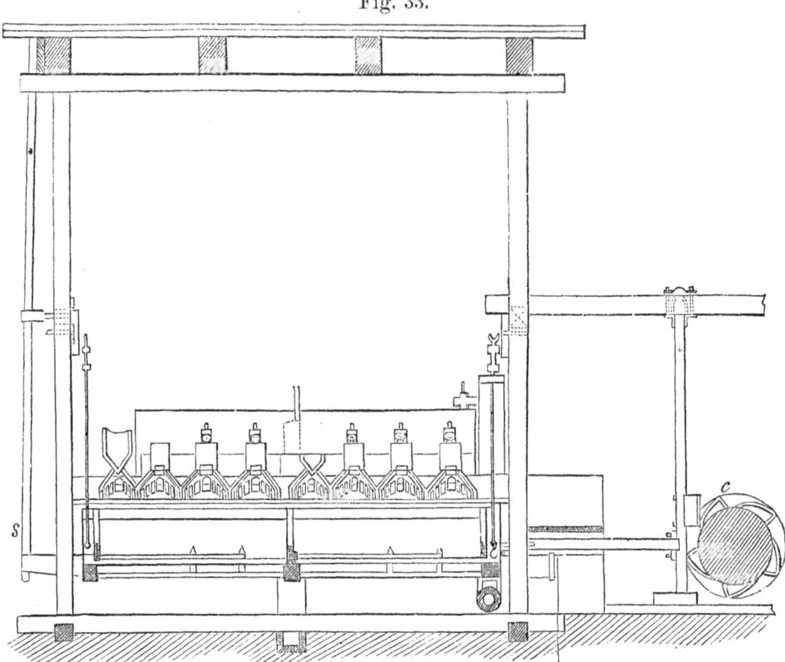

Rittinger's Continuously-working Stossheerd—s: de view.

Fig. 34.

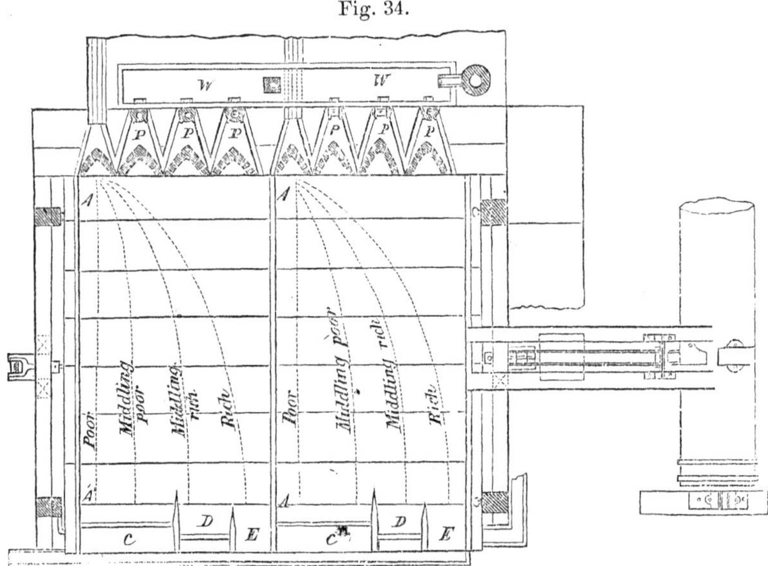

Rittinger's Continuously-working Stossheerd—vertical view.

A side view of this apparatus is given in Fig. 33, and a vertical view in Fig. 34. It consists of a wooden table or platform, about eight feet long and four wide, suspended at the four corners, and inclined forward so that water and fine stuff poured upon the upper part will flow evenly down to the front edge. A lateral throw and percussion is given to the whole table by means of cams *c* upon a shaft at the side, and the reacting wooden spring S upon the opposite side of the table. Two tables are usually combined in one, and they are separated by a narrow strip of wood extending the whole length; similar strips are placed on each side of the table, and serve to keep the water and stuff from flowing off. The stuff to be washed is delivered upon the tables at the upper left-hand corner, at A, in Fig. 34. The distributors P P P furnish clear water. While the table is at rest, the tendency of the stuff is to flow down the slope in a direct line from A to A′. By means of the lateral percussion, however, the path of the heavier particles is changed, and they are gradually thrown from left to right, along the surface of the table, at right angles to the direction of the current of clear water. This current tends at the same time to sweep the particles downward, and it acts upon the light sterile matters more rapidly than upon the heavy ore. The result is, that the heavier and richer particles are gradually separated from the poor stuff and describe the path upon the table indicated by the dotted lines. By the time the particles have reached the foot of the table, the richest portions have been transferred to the corner of the table diagonally opposite to that upon which the stuff entered, and they flow off into the compartment E. The "middlings" are dropped into the next compartment D, and the poor falls into C.

In order that good results may be obtained with this apparatus, the following conditions must be observed:

1 The surface of the table must be very smooth.

2 The length must be about $2^{m}.50$, and the width from $1^{m}.25$ to $1^{m}.50$. The width of space over which the stuff is delivered must be from $0^{m}.20$ to $0^{m}.30$.

3. The inclination of the table must be in direct ratio to the size of the stuff to be washed. For sand, it requires to be about six degrees, and for fine powders about three degrees.

4. The amount of clear water to be admitted at the top of the table, and to be spread over a width of from $0^{m}.30$ to $0^{m}.35$, will be nearly constant. For sand, about six quarts a minute is necessary; and for dust, or fine stuff, from three to three and a half quarts. If the slope of the table is diminished, and the size of the stuff remains the same, the quantity of water should be increased. It is necessary to distribute this supply of water quite near to the stuff to be washed, so as to facilitate the separation of the light and poor stuff from the rich.

5. The number of shocks per minute should be, for sand, from 70 to 80; for dust, 90 to 100; for poor and fine slime and dust it is sometimes advantageous to carry the number of shocks or jerks as high as 120, and sometimes 140 per minute.

6. The tension of the spring is equal to 100 or 112 kilogrammes. The amount of movement necessary to produce the requisite vibrations is, for sand, $0^{m}.065$; and for dust, $0^{m}.020$ to $0^{m}.013$.

7. The velocity of the current upon the table should be from $0^m.25$ to $0^m.15$ per second, according to the nature of the stuff.

8. The greatest regularity must be observed in the number of jerks or shocks; in the quantity of stuff admitted upon the table, including water; in the nature of the stuff to be treated; in the slope of the table, which must be diminished as the stuff to be washed grows poorer and lighter. Careful attention to all these points is essential to success.

The apparatus gives three products. The mixed or middlings can be passed over the table a second time. Stuff of which the particles are $0^m.004$ in diameter can be treated as successfully as the finest slime. It saves much labor. One man can attend two twin-tables. The power required for ten twin-tables is about one-quarter of one horse-power.

ROTATING BUDDLES.—Two forms of rotating buddles were shown in the French section by Messrs. Huet and Geyler, one being concave and the other convex, and both made entirely of iron and accurately finished. The construction of the concave buddle is shown by Fig. 35. The stuff to be crushed is supplied at the circumference of the circular or annular table, and is discharged into different compartments at the center.

Fig. 35.

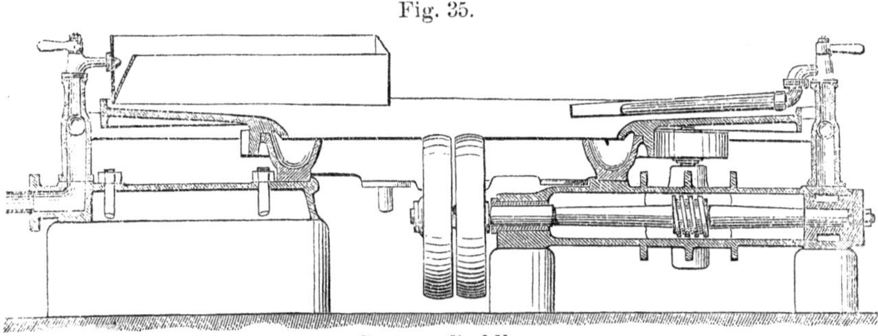

Concave Buddle.

The foundation plate sustains the distributing pipe, the water pipe, the waste gutter, and the driving shaft. An endless screw upon this shaft gives motion to the concave table. Experience in using this buddle has shown that it is desirable to have a greater number of sprinkling pipes than are generally used in the Harz. It is said that the washing of the stuff is completed in one operation, while with the German construction it sometimes happens that the stuff must be passed twice over the machine to obtain an equal result.

The convex buddle is also an annular table, but instead of sloping inward toward the center, it slopes from the center outward, being the reverse of the concave buddle. The stuff is supplied on the inner margin and flows outward to the lower edge, and is delivered into a sucession of annular troughs.

The construction is similar to that of the concave buddle. A cast-iron frame supports the table, the driving shaft, the water pipes, and all the fixtures. The tangent screw and the driving shaft work in a hollow case of cast iron.

These buddles are intended to wash only the fine slimes, and should be fed from the conical separators or trunking apparatus. Satisfactory results depend upon regularity in the motion and the even and proper supply of stuff and of clear water. It is well to work these buddles in pairs and even to use three, the second taking the middlings from the first, and the third the middlings from the second. It is claimed for this apparatus that the duty is equal to that of Rittinger's continual working stossheerd. The quantity of water required varies from 60 to 70 quarts, or more, for the concave buddles, and from 90 to 120 quarts a minute for the convex buddles. They require about one-fourth of a horse-power to run them. One man can attend to six machines. For feeding them with regularity, Messrs. Huet and Geyler use a hopper with a distributing helix, so arranged as to give a regular supply of the material to be washed, from the commencement to the end of the operation.

CHAIN ELEVATORS.

In the apparatus for ore-dressing shown by the firm of Messrs. Huet and Geyler, much use is made of a very ingeniously constructed chain elevator, which drags, scrapes, and hoists the materials from one piece of apparatus to another, thus saving a great amount of hand labor. It consists of a succession of buckets, made of cast iron, united so as to form a chain, as shown in Figs. 36 and 37. The wheels D, which sup-

Fig. 36. Fig. 37.

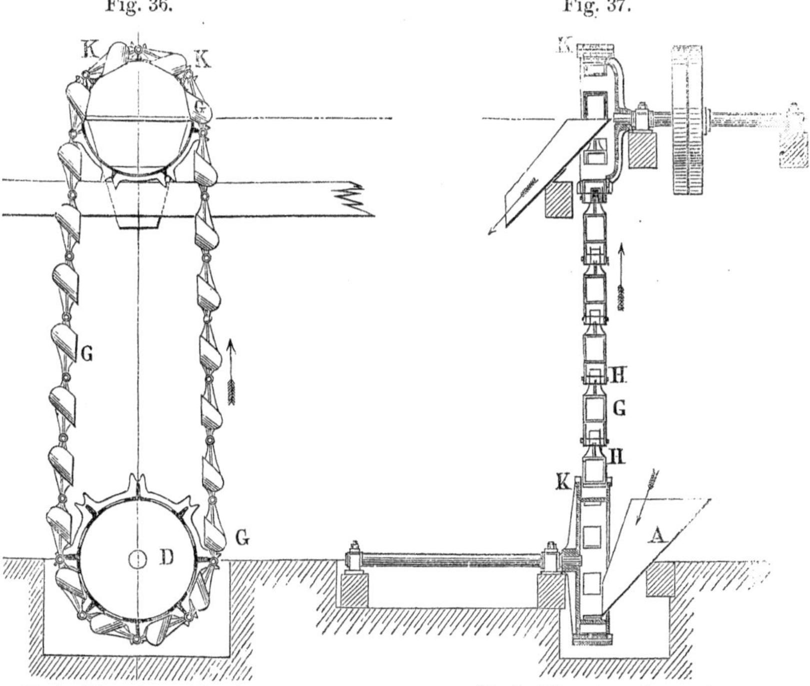

Chain Elevator—side view. Chain Elevator—front view.

port and give motion to this elevator, are cast with arms K K, which catch regularly upon the joints H H, between the buckets G.

CONCLUSION.

In concluding this resumé of the machines and apparatus for ore-dressing shown at the Exposition of 1867, reference should be made to the great advances made in the United States during the past ten years. The discovery of the wonderful silver-bearing veins of Washoe, and the rapid increase of both silver and gold mining, gave an impetus to the manufacture of machinery for the rapid crushing, stamping, sorting, grinding, and concentration of ores of all kinds which has never been equaled. The nature and extent of the improvements made in stamping and grinding machinery upon the Pacific coast is as yet hardly known in Europe, or even in the Atlantic States.

At Lake Superior, Ball's stamps have been used with great success. The duty of these stamps has been increased so that they now crush nearly 100 tons of rock each per day. Blake's rock-breaker is in almost universal use in the United States and Europe and Australia, and is one of the most useful and labor-saving machines which has been added to the list of machines for the mechanical preparation of ores.

Of the apparatus which has been described, it is probable that the sorting or sizing boxes, the improved stossheerd of Rittinger, and perhaps the automatic jigs of Huet and Geyler, can be adopted with advantage by most of the concentrating works in the United States.

www.ingramcontent.com/pod-product-compliance
Lightning Source LLC
LaVergne TN
LVHW021257110826
845150LV00003B/412
9781425561024